TOLSTOY

A Life of My Father

TOLSTOY

A Life of My Father

by

ALEXANDRA TOLSTOY

Translated from the Russian
by Elizabeth Reynolds Hapgood

OCTAGON BOOKS

A DIVISION OF FARRAR, STRAUS AND GIROUX

New York 1973

Reprinted 1973
by special arrangement with Alexandra L. Tolstoy

OCTAGON BOOKS

A DIVISION OF FARRAR, STRAUS & GIROUX, INC.

19 Union Square West

New York, N. Y. 10003

This book has been reproduced from an original
copy in the Harvard College Library.

Library of Congress Cataloging in Publication Data

Tolstaia, Aleksandra L'vovna, grafinia, 1884-
  Tolstoy: a life of my father.

  Reprint of the 1953 ed.
  Translation of Otets.
  1. Tolstoi, Lev Nikolaevich, graf, 1828-1910.   I. Title.
PG3385.T53   1973   891.7'3'3 [B]   73-3185
ISBN 0-374-97956-1

Printed in USA by
Thomson-Shore, Inc.
Dexter, Michigan

To the young people of America

ILLUSTRATIONS

The illustrations, grouped in a separate section, will be found following page 180.

Tolstoy driving with Tokutomi and his daughter Alexandra
A late portrait of Tolstoy smiling
Tolstoy with Dr. Makovitsky
Countess Tolstoy denied admission to the house where Tolstoy lay dying
Tolstoy's grave

The following three pictures are reprinted by permission of Dodd, Mead & Company from *The Life of Tolstoy* by Aylmer Maude: Tolstoy in 1848 after he had left the University; Tolstoy in 1856, the year he left the army; and Tolstoy in 1862, the year of his marriage. Acknowledgments are also gratefully made to Appleton-Century-Crofts, Inc., for permission to reprint the photograph of Countess S. A. Tolstoy denied admission to the deathbed of her husband, which appeared in Ilya Tolstoy's *Reminiscences*; and to Yale University Press for permission to reprint the photograph of Vanichka with Alexandra which appeared in Alexandra Tolstoy's *The Tragedy of Tolstoy*.

PREFACE

I am well aware that this book on my father suffers from many defects—I could have done a better job if I had had all the necessary material available; authentic manuscripts and books which could not be obtained because they are now in Moscow.

Furthermore, I could not spare all the time I wanted and had to work mainly during my so-called free days, that is to say, Saturdays and Sundays, as I had to devote the rest of my time to my work for the Tolstoy Foundation.

Yet I am happy to have written this book, be it good or bad, thus fulfilling my duty to my father to whom I owe everything.

In this book I have tried to describe a man who, all his life, worked for moral improvement. In all his failures, errors and mistakes, he never sank in the quagmire of life—he struggled out and went on, rising still higher and higher. . . .

I should like to share with all the readers my love for this extraordinarily kind, sensitive, gay and inspiring man, who yet was great in his simplicity and humility as a human being—my father—and I would like to bring him nearer to you. If I achieve this even partially, I shall have succeeded in my purpose.

I would never have been able to complete this book without the help of my oldest friend, a prominent and cultured woman from our "Last of the Mohicans," Countess Sophie Vladimirovna Panina, who sought and sorted out the material for me and gave me the most valuable advice, and also patiently recopied my manuscripts over and over again. To her I wish to express my deep and heartfelt gratitude.

Alexandra Tolstoy

TOLSTOY

A Life of My Father

❧ 1 ❧

IT IS difficult for us to carry ourselves back to the days of the early nineteenth century, to picture the life of the Russian land-owning nobility that produced Pushkin, Lermontov, Gogol, Turgenyev and Tolstoy. There can be no doubt that the life of men of that class disposed them to creativeness. They spent unhurried days, traveled by carriage, had time to think, to read; they produced children and trained them in accepted traditions of chivalry, courage, love of their country; they studied languages, believed in the stability of the state, in their own incontrovertible right of dominion over the peasants; they observed holidays, attended church services; when they were ill they rarely had doctors to attend them, they died quietly, resigned to God's will.

They had everything for their needs on their estates. There were cows, sheep, hogs, chickens, turkeys, ducks, heavy sweet cream, fresh butter, rich breads—a full measure of good things. Dogs and horses played a large part in the lives of these landed proprietors. They took pride in their high-spirited mounts and hounds, made a show of smart turnouts and expert coachmen. No one fussed because of the slowness of getting about, because of snowdrifts, blizzards, lack of bathrooms, remoteness from civilization. They knew no other life.

Generations of serfs were born and died on the estates where they served generations of masters. The occupation of chef or coachman was often handed down from father to son. Though sometimes they were severely flogged out in the stable yard, many of the household serfs grew to be so much a part of the family they forgot their conditions; they grumbled at their masters, watched over their children, gave orders—in a word, the interests of their masters were so interwoven with their own that they were even more upset than their owners by ailments of the horses and cows, failure of crops or any derangement of house or farm economy.

[1]

The landowners' estates swarmed with simple-minded vagrant beggars, itinerant pilgrims, various hangers-on; on the eves of holidays the oil lamps glimmered in the ikon corners; and children respected their parents. All in all people lived serenely and well.

It was into such surroundings that Lev Tolstoy was born.

The house no longer exists, and the spot where it stood has long since been overgrown with tall spreading trees.

"Do you see that larch?" Tolstoy used to say. "Well, up there about where that branch is was the room where I was born. . . ."

He was born on a leather couch, which stood in his study to the end of his life. On this couch all of his own children were born.

His birth took place on the 28th of August, 1828, at Yasnaya Polyana, formerly the property of his grandfather Nikolai Sergeyevich Volkonski. "He was a strict man," said Tolstoy of him, "but I never heard that he was unjust toward the peasants; they thought highly of him and loved him for his uprightness, his fairness." He was one of those proud, independent landowning aristocrats who never bowed to the powerful people of the world. He was intelligent, austere, and kept a tight rein on his emotions.

Tolstoy rather enjoyed telling of various incidents which illustrated the old prince's pride and incorruptible honesty. It so happened that the government found it necessary to survey certain forest lands contiguous to Yasnaya Polyana. The surveyor to whom this job was entrusted offered to leave a large slice of the forest on Prince Volkonski's side of the boundary if, in return, he would give him a troika of horses. Volkonski was infuriated and drove the surveyor out of his house.

Another favorite story was about the fat redheaded lady with bangs whose portrait hung on the landing outside the dining room, then was moved from place to place until it finally wound up in the attic. She was Varenka Engelhard, former mistress of the all-powerful Potëmkin, eventually the wife of Prince Golitsyn. What pleased Tolstoy was his grandfather Volkonski's rage when Potëmkin suggested that he marry Varenka: "What does he take me for that I would marry his strumpet!" said he.

It is beyond all doubt that Tolstoy reproduced his own grandfather in the character of old Prince Bolkonski in *War and Peace*.

In accordance with the custom of the time Nikolai Volkonski was enrolled for a military career when he was still a child. In 1780 he was appointed a member of Catherine the Great's suite and was present at her meeting with Joseph II. Later he accompanied the Empress on her famous journey to the Crimea. On his return he was named ambassador in Berlin.

When Emperor Paul came to the throne he began with a show of meticulous attention to the military establishment. He demanded that Volkonski appear to give him a special report on his regiments. Volkonski took this order as an expression of lack of confidence. How could he, a combat general, a former member of the great Catherine's suite, be the object of suspicion and investigation!

Volkonski sent word he was ill and did not appear for inspection. Paul, who could not tolerate any insubordination, dismissed him from his service. Volkonski's whole career seemed wrecked by his absence on that one occasion. But inside of six months he was recalled, promoted to lieutenant general, and then named military governor of Archangel with the rank of full general. When he retired as an old man, Volkonski withdrew to his estate of Yasnaya Polyana. He was a good manager; he loved to build, to set out trees, to improve his property in every way.

He gave the same careful attention to the education of his only daughter, Maria, the mother of Lev. She was the object of his deep and tender affection, and although he took her lack of beauty much to heart, he never for a moment admitted that she was just the ordinary empty-headed "young lady" of the aristocratic circles of her time. His daughter must be cultivated, and he himself undertook her instruction. Princess Maria knew four languages; in addition, her father made her study agriculture, to have "some kind of grasp of grain raising in the hamlet of Yasnaya Polyana"; furthermore he gave her a grounding in "mathematical and political geography and astronomy," and instructed her in various forms of state administration.

It is not very likely that Princess Maria was happy in her early youth. She was always shy with her father; she was not popular in society and had no knack of attracting the attention of brilliant young men. Even the journey she took with her father to St. Petersburg, where he with pedagogical zeal took her through all the picture galleries and museums, did not give her the wide sense of the enjoyment of life so much a part of youth.

What traits did Lev Tolstoy inherit from his grandfather Volkonski and his mother, the Princess Mary?

From the one he obviously inherited a spirit of genuine aristocracy, a healthy pride which took the form of scorn for the powers that be. From his mother Tolstoy had his artistic talent, the gift of vivid story-telling, the power of poetic allusion, extreme modesty, a disregard for public opinion, and a certain shyness. From her too came his chief trait, the gold thread that runs through the pattern of his whole life, his "love of love"—the love that swallows up all else, a grateful love, a love of nature, people, animals, a love engendering gentleness and goodness.

Yet it may be that he also had one strong trait handed down to him from his paternal grandfather, Count Ilya Andreyevich Tolstoy. They say the old Count was incapable of refusing anything to any-body. His grandson inherited that trait in full measure. Tolstoy found it difficult indeed to refuse a request. He always spoke affec-tionately of this grandfather, and the Tolstoy family in general was particularly attached to Count Ilya Andreyevich.

There was something most engaging and genial about his roly-poly moon face with its reflection of the uncomplicated nature be-hind it. Tolstoy used to regale the family with accounts of the amaz-ing feasts his grandfather used to give, ordering sturgeon all the way from Astrakhan when there was a funeral. Or tell how he sent his serfs with his laundry, after the first snowfall, off to Holland, famous for the doing up of starched materials, and how they barely reached Moscow on the return trip before the last snows melted.

Good-hearted, hospitable Count Ilya knew nothing of order, or the reckoning of money. He loved to give parties, invite guests to the house. In 1816 he was named Governor of Kazan. There he demoralized the whole administration through his inability to ex-ercise any restraint. Advantage was taken of his softness and kind-ness, and abuses ensued. Tales were carried to St. Petersburg about the state of affairs in Kazan and the Senate named a special com-mission of investigation. Count Ilya was relieved of his post but was obliged to remain in Kazan until the investigation was finished. The kindly, irresponsible old gentleman did not survive the disgrace. He died, but whether his death was due to the severe shock or to suicide, no one ever knew.

At the time his son Nikolai, Lev Tolstoy's father, was twenty-five years old, and already a lieutenant colonel on the retired list, having served in the war with France. Thick as snowflakes in a blizzard, troubles now clustered about the head of this vivacious, handsome young man. The old count's estate was insolvent. It fell to Nikolai to support his mother, the former Princess Gorchakov, spoiled from her childhood and always accustomed to surroundings of great luxury, and also to care for her sister Aline Osten-Sacken. Her younger sister, Pelagea, had married one of the Yushkovs and lived in Kazan.

Aunt Aline had married early. It seemed at first that she had made a brilliant match, but not long after the wedding Count Osten-Sacken showed signs of abnormality; evidently he was obsessed with a persecution mania.

After several murderous attacks on his wife, he was placed in an institution for the mentally ill and Aline went to live with her mother.

Nikolai was in a difficult position. At home, in the Nikolskoye-Vyazemskoye estate, a definite style of living had been established with a whole train of old servants, relatives, hangers-on to be supported. Yet he could not assume his father's property because his debts exceeded the assets. So the young Count had to let it all go. He kept only the family home, which he gradually cleared of indebtedness.

His relatives, anxious to be of service, looked around for a rich wife for him. Their choice fell on Princess Maria Volkonskaya.

The princess was five years his senior. She was wealthy, lonely since the death of her severe father, she had no suitors and, by the standards of her times, at thirty-two she was definitely classed as an old maid.

The marriage between Count Nikolai Tolstoy and Princess Maria Volkonskaya was one of reason. Lev Tolstoy as an old man used to remark that such marriages, as they were arranged in the old days, especially in peasant families when the bridegroom took no part in the decisions, were often happier than marriages based on infatuation. The storm of passion and infatuation go by. It is important that mutual respect remain, the principal bond being children, who give to conjugal life its meaning and its interest. And the Tolstoys were happy for the short span of years they lived together. Maria was deeply devoted to her husband as the father of her children, and he felt respect for, as well as sincere devotion to her.

They moved to the Volkonski estate, to Yasnaya Polyana. Nikolai added on to the main house, which the old prince had begun and where Lev Tolstoy was born.

All the buildings of Yasnaya Polyana reflect the epoch of Alexander I. Those were the days when famous architects were brought from Italy, to create their own peculiar style of buildings with Italian-ate semicircular windows, walls five feet thick, and pillared porticos.

The masters lived in the large wooden structure and the servants in the two stone wings. In a long one and a half story building off to one side old Prince Volkonski had set up a spinning room where women serfs worked. This is the most beautiful of all the buildings at Yasnaya Polyana. With the years it grew into the soil, became shabby and was converted into stables. Nevertheless, passengers looking out of the windows of the trains on the Moscow-Kursk line often mistake these stables for the main buildings of the Tol-stoy home; they have such distinction of beauty, such architectural balance and are set off so well by the thick surrounding greenery. All one can actually see of the main house from the railroad is its roof. The rest is screened by the age-old trees of the park. The heavily-leaved, stout linden trees, silent observers of many gener-ations, of great historic events, form a perfect square in the upper section of the park.

Nikolai now devoted himself to the management of the estate, and kept a pack of hunting dogs. He was frequently called away to carry on litigation connected with his father's affairs, which he gradually put in order, but when he was at home the whole atmos-phere of the place was enlivened. He joked with the household, his witty sallies had them all laughing; he poked good-natured fun at the various pensioners and old retainers, spent much time with the children and was duly affectionate with his elderly mother who adored him.

"My father was of medium height, well-proportioned, had a sanguine disposition and an agreeable countenance with eyes which were always sad," wrote Lev Tolstoy in his memoirs. "I remember him especially in connection with his hounds. I can recall his riding out with the pack. Later on I was always convinced that he was Pushkin's model for his description of the hunt in his *Count Nulin*."

Surely it was from his father that Lev Tolstoy inherited his hos-pitable, friendly manners, his gay wit, his love of nature and the hunt, physical prowess which verged on recklessness.

Count Nikolai was often away from home and in his absence Countess Maria quietly built her family nest in Yasnaya Polyana. Surrounded by faithful servants, absorbed in the care of her children, her household, she still retained her romantic, artistic and somewhat sentimental disposition. She kept up her music, read a great deal, even wrote verses, and devoted herself with all the passion of a mother to the education of her children. There were five of them: Nikolai, Sergei, Dmitri, Lev, and Maria.

Mother! What tremendous significance Tolstoy gave to that word. He saw in it the principal, the sacred destiny of a woman. He embodied in it all the tenderness, the concern, the affection he so yearned for as a child and never knew. It is hard to believe that he did not remember his mother; for he carried in his heart a wonderful image of her which he not only honored and loved during all his life but which he also reproduced in his writings.

"For me she was such a high, pure spirit that often in the middle part of my life, when I was struggling to overcome certain temptations, I used to pray to her, imploring help, and this prayer always helped me. . . ."

He was only a year and a half old when she died. Although he did not remember her, he had a vivid picture of her: "From her large eyes there came a kind and shy light. Those eyes illumined her painfully thin face and made it beautiful" (*War and Peace*).

From remarks in her diary concerning the behavior of her oldest boy, Nikolai, it is easy to see how much thought and strength Countess Maria put into the education of her children:

"May 14, 1828: Little Nikolai was very bright and obedient all day. It is only too bad that he showed signs of cowardice when walking with me, and took fright at a beetle. . . . Little Nikolai was bright all day, read well. But when he read about a bird that was shot and died, he was so sorry for it he burst out crying. . . ."

A year later she wrote in the same diary: "If he [young Nikolai] can overcome his fears he will in time be a brave boy as befits the son of a father who has served his country well."

These and other comments show that Countess Maria was carefully analyzing the characteristics of her eldest even at this early age! She was already correcting his shortcomings, instilling in him courage, a strong religious faith, a sense of duty, perseverance, kindness— all the qualities she herself possessed.

A private apartment was occupied by Countess Pelagea, Lev's paternal grandmother, together with her own servants, a retinue of pensioners and even her own blind storyteller, a serf bought for her in his day by Count Ilya, because he had such a gift for narration.

No wandering pilgrims, simple-minded vagrants, or "seekers after

God" were ever refused shelter. Countess Maria loved to listen to their spontaneous tales. She received them kindly, gave them food and drink, and even provided them with money to help them along their way.

When one boy after another was born to the Tolstoys and they were anxious to have a little daughter, Countess Maria made a vow that if her next child was a girl she would ask the first woman she met on the highroad to be her godmother, no matter who she was. When a little girl actually was born to her Countess Maria kept her vow. She sent a servant out on the highroad with instructions to bring back the first woman he met. This proved to be a half-witted vagrant pilgrim, Maria Gerasimovna, who went around in male dress. She christened the little Tolstoy child, who was named for her godmother—Maria.

"Her best trait," wrote Lev Tolstoy in his memoirs, "was, according to what the servants said, that although she was hot-tempered she was restrained in manner. Her face would flush, she might even weep, but she would never utter a harsh word."

Countess Maria's death was the first sorrow to strike the Tolstoy family. The children lost a wise, tender, thoughtful mother. They were all still very small for the oldest, little Nikolai, was only six.

The cause of her death was not exactly known. It occurred some months after the birth of her only daughter. Some said that it was caused by fever and others claimed it was inflammation of the brain. Her aged maid said that it was the result of a blow. She loved to swing and one day the servant girls were pushing her as high as they could. Suddenly a board sprang loose and struck her in the head with such force that for a long time she was unable to form a single word. She just stood still and held her head in her hands. The peasant maids were alarmed; they thought they would be punished for their carelessness, until Countess Maria was able to reassure them:

"It isn't anything," she said at last. "Don't be afraid, I shan't tell anyone."

After her death her five children were left in the care of their father and aunts.

How would Lev have developed had he received his early training from his mother, had she lavished on her little "Benjamin," as she called him, all the tenderness and affection he so yearned for? Their mother might have restrained the Tolstoy children from much that was evil; in Lev's life there might not have been the abysmal lapses which so tormented him afterwards . . . and, too, there might not have been the anguish of remorse and the powerful surging to greater heights which we see throughout the course of his whole life.

The children came under the influence of their aged grandmother and also of their kind and deeply religious Aunt Alexandra, but the main burden of their education was shouldered by "Auntie" Tatiana Yergolskaya. Tolstoy put her third, after his father and mother, as a main influence in his life. "She was a distant relative of Grandmother's on the Gorchakov side. She and her sister Lisa were left as penniless orphans at an early age. They had several brothers who were taken in by relatives, but it was Tatiana Semyonovna Skuratova, a lady of imperious and imposing ways and a great name in her own circle who, together with Countess Pelagea Tolstoy, decided to adopt the girls. They put the names on two slips of paper, shuffled them and laid them in front of the ikons. After saying a prayer they each picked up one of the slips: Lisa was drawn by Madame Skuratov and brunette Tanya by our grandmother.

"Tanya was the same age as Nikolai Ilyich Tolstoy, and she was brought up on an equal footing with Pelagea and Alexandra. She was tenderly loved by them all and who could have failed to love her for her firm, decisive, vigorous character! She was very attractive with her long braid of coarse dark curly hair and her black agate eyes with their snapping, lively expression.

"My memory of her begins when she was over forty," writes Tolstoy in his memoirs. "It never entered my mind whether she was beautiful or not. I simply loved her, loved her eyes, smile, little broad hands with their pulsing veins."

Aunt Tanya was one of those whole, forceful, self-abnegating natures who know how to love, to sacrifice themselves, who have a great sense of duty and unselfishness—qualities in which she saw the purpose and meaning and perhaps, too, the joy of her own existence.

"It is most likely that she was in love with my father, as he was with her," Tolstoy wrote in *Childhood*, "but she did not marry him when she was young because she did not want to stand in the way of his marrying my wealthy mother; nor did she marry him later on because she did not want to spoil her pure, poetic relationship to him and to us. . . ."

No one suspected her real relations with Nikolai. Until her death no one knew of the note she wrote on August 16, 1836: "On this

[9]

day Nikolai made me a strange proposal—to marry him, be a mother to his children and never leave them. I refused the former, but promised to do the latter as long as I live."

"Her main trait was her love," continues Tolstoy, "and, no matter how much I could have wished it otherwise, that love was for one person: my father. It was only from this center that it radiated and embraced all others. One felt that she loved us for his sake, that through him she loved everyone, for her whole life was love."

In another place he wrote: "Aunt Tanya had the greatest influence on my life. Above all this was because from my childhood she taught me the spiritual satisfaction of love. She did not teach me this in so many words, her whole being was infectious with love.

"I could see, I could feel how much good it did her to love, and I sensed the happiness it brings. The second thing I learned from her was the charm of an unhurried, solitary life."

2

THESE are my first memories. . . . I am tied; I want to pull my arms loose but I cannot. I scream, I weep and my cries are unpleasant to me; yet I cannot stop. . . . Someone is standing there, bending over me, but I do not remember who it is. All this is in the half darkness. But I recall that there were two people. My cries affect them, they are upset by them, but they do not unbind me, which is what I want, so I scream louder and louder. To them it seems necessary that I should be tied, whereas I know it is not necessary; I want to prove this to them, I pour out screams that are horrible to me yet which I cannot restrain. I sense all the injustice and cruelty, not of these people who pity me, but of destiny, and I feel self-pity too. I do not know and I shall never know what this is all about: was I put in swaddling clothes when I was still an infant and I tried to pull my arm loose, or was I swaddled when I was over a year old so that I would not scratch some prickly heat rash? Whether or not I gathered into this one memory various impressions, as one does in dreams, it is nevertheless true that this was my first and strongest recollection in my life. And what I remember is not my screams, my sufferings, but the complexity, the contradiction of my impressions. I want my freedom, it does not bother anyone else, yet I, who need the strength, I am weak, but they are strong.

"Another impression I have is a happy one. I am sitting in a wooden tub. All around is the unpleasant odor of some stuff with which my little body is being rubbed. Probably it was bran and no doubt it was in the water in the tub, but the novelty of the impression made by the bran aroused me and for the first time I noticed and was pleased by my little body, with the ribs I could see on my chest, also the smooth dark tub, my nurse's arms in rolled-up sleeves, the warm, steaming water mixed with bran, the sound it made and especially the feel of the slippery edges of the tub as I passed my little hands along them.

"It is strange and terrible that from my birth to the age of three, in all the time I was nursing, when I was weaned, began to crawl, walk, talk—no matter how I rack my memory I cannot recall anything but these two impressions. When did I begin—begin to live? Why do I enjoy thinking of myself in that state, even if it was alarming, as alarming as to many when they think of themselves, as I shall do when I again enter the deathlike state of being without memories recordable in words. Was I not alive when I was learning to look, to listen, understand, talk, when I was sleeping, nursing, kissing my mother's breast, laughing and causing her joy? I was alive and blissfully so! Was it not then that I acquired everything by which I now live, and acquired so much, so quickly that in all the rest of my life I never acquired even a hundredth part as much?"

Consciousness was awakened very early in Tolstoy. Certain traits of character, which were to remain with him all his life, were already in evidence in his early childhood.

"Oh happy, happy childhood days beyond recall!" he wrote in *Childhood*. "How can one keep from loving and cherishing memories of that time. They are fresh, exalt the soul and serve as the source of the best satisfactions in life. . . .

"The persons who surrounded me in my childhood, from my father to our coachman, seemed to me to be exceptionally good people. Probably it was my pure, affectionate feelings which like a bright ray brought out the best in people—it is always there; and the fact that everyone appeared to be exceptionally good was far nearer the truth than when I saw some of their shortcomings."

To little Lev the world was beautiful; he loved it and everyone in it. Human cruelty and injustice, annoyances, he neither understood nor accepted.

Why had a servant been flogged out in the stables? He was in despair when he heard about it, and his despair was increased when he realized it had been done without his father's knowledge and that had he spoken to him in time, or to his Aunt Tanya, he might have averted this unnecessary cruelty. Why did his kindliest of tutors, Fyodor Ivanovich, hang his dog when his paw had been run over? Why did Praskovya Isayevna, the old housekeeper, of whom he was so fond, give him an enema supposed to be for his brother and not believe little Lev when he assured her he did not need it?

"What man alive has not had that blissful feeling at least once, and most often in early childhood, when one's soul is not spotted with the lies which clutter up all our lives—that blissful feeling of tenderness when one wants to love everybody and everything: one's intimates, father, mother, brothers, and wicked people, and enemies, dogs, horses and grass; when one's only desire is to have everything right in the world for everybody."

So the happy-go-lucky, broad-faced, lively, chubby little Lev, who was so full of trust and readiness to love all and sundry, was amazed and taken aback when he did not meet the same attitude in others. He was affectionate with everyone, but of his brothers and sisters he loved the eldest, Nikolai, most deeply and steadfastly. Of them all this brother with his modesty, self-depreciation, scorn of public opinion, his intelligence and seriousness, most resembled their mother.

"I was chummy with Mitenka [Dmitri]," wrote Tolstoy. "I respected Nikolenka, but I was thrilled by Serezha, I aped him, adored him and wanted to be like him. I was thrilled by his handsome exterior, his voice—he was always singing—his ability to draw, his gaiety and especially, strange as it may seem, by his frank egotism. I always remembered, always felt, rightly or wrongly, what the thought and feelings of others were toward me and that took the joy out of life. That is probably why I like the opposite quality in others—a frank egotism. That was why I loved Serezha especially—the word love is not the right one. I loved Nikolenka, but I was thrilled by Serezha, as by something strange, incomprehensible."

Until he was five Lev lived in the nursery with the girls—his sister Maria (Mashenka) and an adopted child Dunechka, who

was the charge of Aunt Tanya. About her Tolstoy wrote: "Dunechka
. . . was a sweet, simple, quiet girl, but not intelligent, and a great
crybaby. I remember when I, who already knew how to read French,
was obliged to teach her the alphabet. At first all went smoothly
(she and I were both five), but then, probably because she was tired,
she stopped giving the right answer when I pointed to a letter. I
insisted. She cried. So did I. When others arrived on the scene we
were unable to bring out a word because we were crying so hard."

Being moved downstairs to live with his older brothers and under the care of their tutor Fyodor Ivanovich Ressel was a source of
real sorrow to him.

"When I was moved downstairs to Fyodor Ivanovich and the boys
I was struck for the first time, and therefore with a stronger impact
than later on, with a sense of something we call duty, carrying one's
cross, a feeling which each human being is called upon to bear. I
was sorry to leave the familiar surroundings (familiar because it
was all I had ever known). I was sad, sentimentally sad, to leave
not so much the people—my sister and nurse, my aunt—as my crib,
with its canopy, my little pillow, and I was frightened by the new
life into which I was entering. I did my best to look for the bright
side of the life opening before me, I made an effort to believe in
the affectionate expressions with which Fyodor Ivanovich tried to
win me; I did my best to overlook the scorn with which the boys
received me, the youngest, in their midst; I did my best to believe
that a big boy like me should be ashamed to live with little girls
and there was nothing nice at all upstairs with them and nurse. But
inside I was awfully unhappy. . . ."

The German tutor, Fyodor Ivanovich Ressel, to whose hands little
Lev was now entrusted, was a poorly educated, sentimental but
thoroughly goodhearted person. The children loved him, but as
often happens in childhood, Lev did not realize how much he was
attached to Fyodor Ivanovich until he lost him.

Now and then their father would come downstairs to see them,
draw pictures or play games. In the evening Lev liked to sit in the
drawing room and watch his imposing grandmother, "with her long
chin, dressed in a cap with ruching and ribbons, laying out a game
of patience, and from time to time raising her gold snuff box to her
nose." Near the round mahogany table sat Aunt Alexandra and Aunt
Tatiana and one of them would read aloud. Once, in the middle of
a game of patience and a story, his father stopped the aunt who was

reading, pointed to the mirror and whispered something. . . . It was the old butler Tikhon who, knowing that the master was in the living room, was on his way to his study to take some tobacco from the large, round-topped leather humidor. Lev's father saw him in the mirror and watched him tiptoeing cautiously along. The aunts laughed. The grandmother could not make out for a long time what was going on, but when she understood a smile came over her face too. Little Lev was delighted with his father, his good nature, and when he said good night to him he kissed his white, veined hand with special tenderness.

The grandmother was imposing—everyone respected and feared her. Yet even she took part at times in the general merriment. Two of his father's footmen carried her in a light carriage "to a small grove to gather nuts, of which there were an especially large quantity that year," wrote Tolstoy in his memoirs. "I remember a heavy thicket into the depth of which the footmen (Petruchka and Matyuska) forced the yellow cabriolet with Grandmother, and how they pulled down the laden branches to her, with a showering of ripe nuts, and how she herself picked them, putting them in a bag. . . . I remember how hot it was in the glades, how pleasant and cool in the shade, how it smelled of the tart fragrance of leaves. . . ."

There is nothing more varied than nature in central Russia. In the winter, with its severe blizzards, snowdrifts, narrow sledding roads, there is only an occasional signpost to guide a lonely traveler muffled in his sheepskin coat, jogging along on his sleigh behind a shaggy old jade. When the snowfall is heavy the peasants' houses are so submerged that they have to be dug out and the highroad is almost on a level with the roofs. Winter is replaced by violent thaws, rivers flood their banks and for weeks people are cut off from other settlements and from towns. The wooden bridges disappear beneath the raging streams or are entirely carried away by the foaming floods. But the sun is already hot. Heavy sheepskin coats are no longer needed and felt boots are exchanged for heavily oiled, waterproof boots. Near the sheds and along the fences the tender reddish brown shoots of nettles and chicory show their heads. The deep deposits of muddy snow gradually shrink and disappear from ravines and ditches, the soft country roads dry out and grow smooth, and in the villages one hears the mooing of cows, the bleating of sheep released from the long winter confinement. Upland meadows blossom with pale blue forget-me-nots, the woods are alive with fragrant lilies of the valley, the buds on the great oaks swell and burst. . . .

One cannot say that Tolstoy loved nature in Yasnaya Polyana; he was a part of it, he lived in and with it. He loved the small grove where during all his life trees were being cut down and young trees were growing up, its deep-cut ravine at the bottom of which a tiny rivulet gurgled past bits of strangely formed iron ore. Near here was where he asked to be buried. He loved the hills, the meadows through which the narrow but deep stream Voronka picked its erratic way. It was swarming with fish and crayfish. The youngsters, pasturing the horses, could pull them out with their bare hands from the pools under the steep banks and broil them over open fires. Tolstoy loved the sleeping woods of the State Preserve, running all the way to the border of Kaluga province, with its broad cuts, washed roads that never dried out even in the hottest summer weather, mysterious little paths, with ferns and mushrooms. He loved the western part of Yasnaya Polyana with its rolling fields, wide vista, where the peasants toiled from early morning until nightfall, plowing, sowing or harvesting their share of the crops. One of his favorite haunts from the time he was a child was the village of Grumont some two miles from Yasnaya Polyana. Nearby in a ravine at the foot of a hill was a famous spring, whose water was so excellent that at one time the Tolstoys used to send every day for a cask of it to drink. In his memoirs Tolstoy described one of these trips to Grumont.

"Up would come a surrey with a canopy and dashboard, and Nikolai Filipovich in the driver's seat. In the center was the bay, on the left the light bay, a broad horse, and on the left the dark raw-boned one, 'the tough one' as Nikolai Filipovich used to call it. After this carriage came the big bay with the yellow gig.

"Auntie Tanya and the girls got in and sat where they pleased. Our places were rigidly assigned. Fyodor Ivanovich always sat on the right side and drove. Beside him were Serezha and Nikolenka; the gig was so deep that we could sit behind them, Dmitri and I, with our backs to the sides and our feet together in the middle. All the way, past the threshing floor and through the grove, was sheer fun. . . . After crossing the bridge the road led along the river up a hill to the village. We drove through a gateway, into a garden and up to a little house. The horses were tied up. They trampled down the grass and smelled of sweat more strongly than they ever did again. . . . Matryona, the herdswoman, came running out in a threadbare dress. She said she had been expecting us this long time, that she was glad we had come. I not only believed this, I could not keep from believing that everything in the world was doing nothing but be glad. Auntie Tanya was glad to see Matryona, she made interested inquiries about her daughters . . . the dogs who had run after our carriage were glad . . . the hens were glad, so were the roosters, the peasant children, the horses, calves, the fish in the pond, the birds in the woods. Matryona and one of her daughters brought out a large, thick chunk of black bread, they unexpectedly produced a marvelous, extraordinary table, and laid on it soft, succulent cottage cheese still marked with the cloth it had hung in, cream, almost clotted, and jugs with fresh, whole milk. We drank and ate, and ran down to the spring, chased around the pond, while Fydor Ivanovich threw out his fishline. Then after spending a half hour or more in Grumont, we drove back the way we had come, still filled with gladness."

On weekdays everyone worked and on holidays they went to church and had a good time. Best was the Christmas celebration. The immemorial custom in Old Russia was that at Christmas one put on a fancy dress and at New Year's one told fortunes. "All the household servants, there were many of them, some thirty in all, dressed themselves in their best and came into the house, they joined in all sorts of games and danced to the fiddling of old Grigori. . . . It was very jolly. There were mummers—always a bear with his master, a goat, Turkish men and women, peasants—men and women and girls dressed up as Turks—and old crones. I remember," wrote Tolstoy in his memoirs, "how beautiful some of the mummers seemed to me, how especially pretty Masha, the Turkish girl, looked . . . and how handsome I felt myself to be with my burnt cork mustache. . . ."

"Lev was always full of high spirits," his sister Maria said. "He seemed to expect only good in life and when he met with evil he was upset, but he did not weep. He wept more when he was touched by something. And if anyone was affectionate with him the tears would come. He used to run into the room all radiant, his face beaming, as though he had just made some important discovery about which he must tell everyone. He loved to say unusual things, to startle people."

Once, when the family was living in Moscow, young Lev conceived the idea that he could fly. If only he could hold his knees together tight enough with his fists and throw himself down from a height he would fly off like a bird. When everyone had gone to dinner he made up his mind to put his plan into execution. "He climbed to the open window on the mezzanine floor and jumped into the courtyard. . . . They found him out there unconscious. Fortunately he did not break any bones and received no worse injury than a slight concussion: from unconsciousness he slipped into unbroken sleep and woke up eighteen hours later perfectly well" (Biryukov).

It is easy to picture with what enthusiasm five-year old Lev fell in with an invention of his elder brother Nikolenka, who was also gifted with a great imagination and a facility for storytelling evidently inherited from their mother, about Braggarts Mountain and the Muravian brothers.

"Yes, Braggarts Mountain," Tolstoy used to say, "was one of my earliest, sweetest and most important memories. My brother Nikolenka was six years my senior. He was perhaps ten or eleven and I was four or five, when he took us up Braggarts Mountain. . . . He was an astonishing boy and later an astonishing man. Turgenyev made a very true remark about him when he said that all he lacked were the defects necessary to make a writer. He did not have the main shortcoming for that purpose: conceit was not in him, and he was utterly uninterested in what other people thought of him. The qualities of a writer which he did possess were first of all a delicate, artistic sensitiveness, a keen feeling for proportion; he was good-natured, humorous, was gifted with an extraordinary, inexhaustible imagination, a true, highly moral outlook on life—and all this without a grain of smugness. . . .

"So it happened that when I was five, Dmitri six and Serezha seven, he announced to us that he had a secret by means of which, when he would reveal it, all people on earth would be made happy; there would be no sickness, no unpleasantness, no one would be angry at anyone else, and everybody would love one another—they would all become *Muravian* Brethren (I imagine they were supposed to be Moravian Brethren about whom we had read or heard tell, but we called them Muravian Brethren). I remember that we were particularly fascinated by the word because it suggested ants [*Muravi*] in a hill to us. And indeed when we played the game of being Muravian Brethren it consisted of crowding in under chairs, and barricading ourselves with baskets draped with shawls, and sitting in the dark pressed close together. It gave me, as I remember, a special sense of love and tenderness, and I was very fond of this game.

"We knew about the Muravian Brethren but their principal secret of what to do so that nobody would have any more unhappiness, nor ever quarrel, and always be happy—that was inscribed on a green stick, and this stick was buried near the rim of the ravine in the old Zakaz Forest, in the very place where, since my body must be buried somewhere, I have asked in memory of Nikolenka that I be laid to rest.

"Besides the stick, there was also some kind of a Braggarts Mountain, up which we should be allowed to go if we fulfilled all of certain conditions. These were: first, stand in the corner and not think about a white bear. I remember how I stood in the corner and tried and tried, but could not possibly keep from thinking of a white bear. The second condition was: walk, without losing one's balance, along the crack between two floor boards, and the third—an easy one— was not to see a rabbit for a whole year, not a live, dead or cooked one. Then one had to swear not to give away the secrets to anyone. . . .

"The ideal of the Muravian Brethren, bound to each other by love, not crouching under two chairs draped with shawls but including all human beings under the wide vault of heaven, has always remained with me. And just as I believed then that there is a little green stick with the words on it to destroy all evil in men and bring them great blessings, so I believe today that that truth exists, that it will be disclosed to men and give them what it promises."

In the autumn of 1836 the whole Tolstoy household—including Lev's father, grandmother, aunts, Aunt Aline, Pasha, the children, servants—moved to Moscow.

In the excitement and fuss of departure, obliging servants ran hither and thither, getting in each other's way; the last things were carried out, shoved into the carriages; the horses snorted and stamped before the main entrance, the dogs whimpered. Milka, the hound with the brown eyes, looked on sadly; she was to be left in Yasnaya Polyana. At last a quiet fell and according to custom everyone, including the servants, sat in silence in the living room, said a prayer, crossed themselves before they set off on their journey. In the lead, in the coach pulled by six horses, drove the grandmother, the aunts and the little girls. The coach was a whole house on heavy wheels, roomy, with wide seats, under which the luggage was stowed. Everything was there, a hamper with food for the journey, a mirror, soft pillows for the grandmother, and even a toilet seat for the children. Count Nikolai drove in the barouche and the boys took turns riding beside him. In those days the two-hundred-verst drive from Yasnaya Polyana to Moscow was a big journey. Horses were changed several times at stations to which relays had been sent the day before.

Immediately on leaving the avenue the carriages rolled past the round brick towers onto the "big" willow-lined Moscow road, a broad, well-beaten highway which stretched across all Russia from the days of Catherine the Great. Here it ran along the little river Yasenka, past a square, squat brick landmark, also dating back to Catherine the Great, with an iron eagle perched on top, to mark the dividing line between the districts of Krapivna and Tula.*

"Did you ever, dear reader, at a certain moment in your life notice that your point of view was completely changing, that the things you had been looking at up to that time suddenly showed a different and as yet unfamiliar side to you?" wrote Tolstoy, in his story called *Childhood*, which tells what the trip meant to him. "That kind of a moral metamorphosis took place in me for the first time in the course of our journey, and from it I date the beginning of my boyhood. For the first time the thought came to me that we, my family, were not living alone in the world, that not everything of interest revolved just around us, that there were other lives of other people who had nothing in common with us, cared nothing about us and were not even aware of our existence. No doubt I knew all this before, but I was not aware of it as I now became, I had not felt it. . . . As I looked out at the villages and towns we drove through, where in every house there was a family at least as large as ours, at the women, the children, who gazed at us curiously for a moment and then vanished from our sight, at the storekeepers, the peasants, who not only did not bow to us, as I was accustomed to see done . . . but who did not even favor us with a glance, for the first time the question came to my mind: what can they possibly be occupied with since they are not concerned with us? And from that question came others: How and on what do they live? How do they train their children; are they taught anything? Do they allow them to play? Do they punish them?"

Indeed, it was a whole new world that the young Tolstoy was discovering.

* During the revolution of 1917-1919 this landmark was destroyed—the peasants used the bricks for building.

[19]

3

IN MOSCOW the Tolstoys settled down in a large, handsome private house. Their living habits were little altered. They kept their own horses; the same household serfs waited on them. The boys had lessons and their tutors came to the house. Nikolenka was already fourteen and being prepared for the university. Young Lev was a poor scholar but he continued to harbor a lively interest in everything that went on around him as he took walks through Moscow streets with Fyodor Ivanovich. Their father came and went; Auntie Tanya as ever surrounded the children with affection and love.

No one really knew how it happened or who broke the terrible news to the grandmother and all the family. Word came from Tula where Count Nikolai had gone on business. Suddenly, on the street, he had been taken ill, collapsed and died without regaining consciousness. Rumor had it that his two footmen, the brothers Petrusha and Matyusha, who were always with him, had poisoned him. The papers and money on him disappeared. The money never was recovered, but the papers were later returned to the family by some mysterious beggarwoman who claimed to have found them on the steps of a church.

This sorrow was shattering to all the family.

At first Lev could not believe in his father's death. That his lively, energetic, handsome, high-spirited father was no longer in existence, that he would no longer laugh, make jokes, that he would never see him again, was something he could not conceive of. There must be some mistake, some misunderstanding. As he walked through the streets, he searched for him among the people he met.

In the beginning the grandmother did not believe in her son's death either. Her grief was violent and she was unable to reconcile herself to it or to be comforted. She took to her bed and died in less than a year.

The children's nearest relative was Aunt Aline—Alexandra Ilyinichna Osten-Sacken—who was named their guardian.

The Tolstoy fortune was put in the hands of a council of guardians. It became necessary to cut down expenses, so the Tolstoys moved to a more modest house. No one suffered from the external change in their lives; in fact they were delighted with the little five-room house which Lev accidentally found for them on one of his walks around Moscow with Fyodor Ivanovich. His grandmother's death did not upset him much aside from the terror he felt at seeing a dead person for the first time in his life. He had another grief—the removal of his German tutor Fyodor Ivanovich. Even before his grandmother's death, Lev had been put under the guidance of another tutor, St. Thomas, a narrow-minded, conceited, swaggering Frenchman, whose whole appearance, unnatural pomposity and almost theatrical affectation were repelling to the sensitive boy. St. Thomas had his own theory of education and discipline; he despised the stupid, sentimental, psychological reasoning of the kind-hearted German. Yet Fyodor Ivanovich, who did not hold any educational theory, possessed little knowledge or real discipline, simply loved his charges, understood them, always could gauge their characters with great perceptiveness. So young Lev did not take to St. Thomas.

"It was a real feeling of hatred I had for him," wrote Tolstoy, "the kind of hatred that inspires you with a boundless aversion to a person who yet commands your respect; it makes you dislike his hair, neck, gait, the sound of his voice, all his members, all his movements, yet at the same time you are drawn to him by some inexplicable force which obliges your uneasy attention to follow every little thing he does."

It is terrifying to think of the suffering of this child, who was always ready to return a hundredfold any sign of affection, any little kindness. "I shall never forget," Tolstoy recalled in *Youth*, "how St. Jerome [St. Thomas] pointed to a place on the floor and ordered me to get down on my knees, but I stood in front of him, pale with anger and saying to myself that I would rather die on the spot than kneel to him; and how he took hold of me by the shoulders with all his strength and twisting my back forced me to kneel. . . ."

Whether or not this scene was imagined by Tolstoy no one knows, but in his memoirs he said: "I cannot recall why but for some utterly undeserved reason St. Thomas first of all locked me up in a room and then threatened to whip me. I experienced the most dreadful emotions of resentment, indignation and disgust not only for St. Thomas but also toward the violence he proposed to visit on me."

It was fortunate that with time their relations became somewhat smoother and Lev's outbursts of hatred for his tutor grew more and more rare. It may have been that the Frenchman, despite his insensitivity, sensed that there was something out of the ordinary in his little charge. *"Ce petit a une tête! C'est un petit Molière!"* he used to say.

Years went by. Young Lev continued to yearn for affection and love. His yearning took the form of idolizing a handsome, self-confident boy called Sasha Mussin-Pushkin, who looked down on the shy child with the bristling hair and small gray eyes, and of worshiping a pretty girl, Sonechka Koloshina. He loved them with no thought of return. In *Childhood* he wrote: "I could not understand how one could demand any greater happiness than this emotion of love which filled my soul with solace, or wish for anything except that this emotion would never cease. I was satisfied as it was."

He was the smallest boy in the family; he was ugly and felt lonely. He sought attachments but did not find them; he sought to assert himself, in any way that would bring him out of the background, but could not do it; he sought encouragement, but people laughed at him; and no one understood him. A university student who was giving lessons to the three younger boys described them as follows: "Sergei can and will study, Dmitri will but cannot, and Lev neither will nor can."

Little Lev felt that he could; he felt that he was not a nonentity, but no matter how he tried he could not extricate himself from his impasse.

"Often there were moments of despair that swept over me: I imagined that there was no happiness on earth for a person with the broad nose, thick lips and tiny gray eyes I had. I begged God to perform a miracle—to turn me into a beautiful creature, and I was prepared to give up everything I had in the present and anything I might have in the future for the sake of a handsome face."

If his parents had been alive they would have helped him. They, perhaps, might have discerned in him the artistic flame which his father had sensed when Lev, still a tiny boy, recited with such verve some verses of Pushkin he had learned by heart: "Farewell, free element!" and "The splendid destiny has been fulfilled, a great man has passed on." But as it was the boy was lonely and restless.

At one point he was caught up in a surge of patriotism. This was after a visit by Emperor Nicholas I to Moscow, when Lev began to dream about how he would distinguish himself in a war.

"I will join the hussars and go to war" was how he described his thoughts in the story called *Youth*, when his tutor had locked him up alone in a dark closet. "The enemy swoops down on me from all sides, I brandish my saber and kill one of them, another blow—I kill a second, a third. Finally, faint with exhaustion and wounds, I fall to earth, crying out: Victory! The general rides up and asks: Where is he? Where is our savior? They point to me, he throws himself on my neck and through tears of joy exclaims: Victory! I recover and with my arm in a black sling I saunter down the Tverskoy Boulevard. I am a general! Along comes the Emperor toward me and asks: Who is that young wounded man? They tell him it is the famous General Nikolai. So the Emperor approaches me and says: I thank you. I am prepared to grant your every wish."

These childish dreams were replaced by more serious ones. Young Lev became more and more absorbed in a variety of philosophic questions. "One could scarcely believe what my favorite and most constant subjects of consideration were in my boyhood; they were so incongruous to my age and situation," wrote Tolstoy in *Youth*.

"For a whole year, during which I was leading an isolated, self-concentrated life, I was absorbed in questions of the destiny of man, life hereafter, immortality of the soul; and my weak childish mind struggled fervently in an attempt to clarify questions, to propound which required the highest caliber to which the human mind can aspire. . . ."

In the diaries he kept in his old age, when the entries were sometimes made late at night, Tolstoy had the habit of inserting the date, month and year of the following day, frequently adding the initials of the words meaning: "If I am alive." The idea that tomorrow might not come never left him, and every hour he was preparing himself for death. In *Youth* he recalls this reasoning: ". . . suddenly realizing that death was awaiting me any hour, any minute, I decided, without understanding why, as others up to now have not understood, that man cannot be happy except in making the most of the present and not thinking about the future."

The boy's reasoning about life eternal, about happiness, stirred him deeply. "Once the thought came to me that happiness does not depend on external causes, but on our attitude toward them, that a

[23]

man who is accustomed to stand suffering cannot be unhappy—and in order to train myself to hardship I forced myself to hold a big dictionary for five minutes in my outstretched hands . . . or I went into a closet and lashed my bare back so hard with a piece of rope that tears came to my eyes."

At twenty-four, when Tolstoy wrote *Childhood, Boyhood* and *Youth*, he said that out of all the moral hardships he put himself through "I got nothing except mental agility, which undermined my will power, and the habit of incessant moral analysis, which destroyed all spontaneity of feeling and clarity of judgment." Nevertheless those childish experiments did give him at the time a kind of self-confidence of which he was sorely in need.

". . . The philosophic discoveries I made were vastly flattering to my self-esteem: I often imagined I was a great man, discovering new truths for the benefit of all mankind, and I looked down on all other mere mortals with a proud consciousness of my own worth. Yet strangely enough, when I came into actual contact with those mortals I was shy with every one of them, and the higher I raised myself in my own esteem, the less capable I became not only of manifesting my consciousness of my own worth, but even of accustoming myself not to be ashamed of every simple word and gesture."

Young Lev followed his own heart, feeling his way, but he had no one with whom to share his thoughts or to take counsel. . . .

※ 4 ※

THE Autumn of 1841 brought the death at the convent of Optina Desert of the Tolstoy children's guardian, Alexandra Osten-Sacken—Aunt Aline.

"*Ne nous abandonnez pas, chère tante, il ne nous reste que vous au monde,*" wrote Nikolai to Pelagea Yushkova—Aunt Paulina.

At that time Nikolai was in his first year at the university and the youngest children, Lev and Maria, were thirteen and eleven.

Their kindhearted aunt was touched, she wept, and decided to make the necessary sacrifices, to take all five children home with her to Kazan.

As usual, the Tolstoy family had spent the summer in Yasnaya Polyana. From there a cortege of carriages moved them to the Volga and thence they continued their journey on two barges specially chartered for that purpose by their aunt. They moved their serfs: chefs, footmen, tailors, cabinetmakers, four valets—one assigned to each of the Tolstoy brothers—and they moved their belongings. The ride in the carriages was long and gay. They stopped often, rested, went in swimming and gathered mushrooms.

Kazan, thanks to its university, was already a cultural center for the whole Volga region. The gentry from the surrounding country came to town for the winter. They put their children in schools, the young men studied at the university, the young ladies were brought out in society and acquired beaux. Elaborate banquets were followed by balls, plays, suppers, after which they danced again or played cards. The gilded youth led a dissipated life. Lev was as lonely at Kazan as before—perhaps even more so. He did not have even his beloved Auntie Tanya near him, as she had not followed the children to Kazan. Aunt Paulina was not fond of Auntie Tanya. In her early youth her good-natured husband, V. A. Yushkov, a former officer in the hussars, had been in love with charming "Toinette" and this was something Aunt Paulina could neither forget nor forgive.

The Tolstoy family spread out easily over the roomy, large house of the Yushkovs. Kazan society then was divided into two groups. The more numerous was made up of the intellectuals grouped around the university, and the professors who were seriously absorbed in work on abstract social and scientific questions. Then there was the second group, the local "high society" which included the aristocracy, the landed gentry and the upper ranks of the bureaucracy. This latter group was smaller in number and clustered around the governor, keeping quite distinct from the intellectuals.

The Yushkov household belonged to the aristocratic circle. Aunt Paulina carried herself with dignity, she was looked up to as a very religious and at the same time a worldly figure. Her husband was an agreeable and gay member of society, a wit, an amusing and hospitable host.

Soon the three eldest boys were students at the university. Nikolai did well, moving easily from one class to the next. Sergei plunged head first into society distractions, was popular with the ladies, had a jolly time and enjoyed an easy and simple outlook on life. Dmitri led a life apart, frequented church, fasted; his classmates despised him and gave him the nickname of Noah. Maria went to a private school for girls.

It was only to be expected that neither Aunt Paulina, with her restricted outlook, nor her ordinary, sociable husband, nor St. Thomas could provide any moral guidance for fourteen-year-old Lev. He went stumbling along his own way. "With all my heart I wanted to be good," he wrote in his *Confessions*, "but I was young, I was filled with passions, and I was alone, utterly alone, in my search for good. Each time I tried to express my most intimate yearning—to be morally good—I met with contempt and derision; and whenever I gave in to disgusting passions, I was praised and encouraged. Ambition, love of power, self-interest, lust, pride, anger, vindictiveness—all these were respected. When I yielded to these emotions I was like a grownup and I felt that they were pleased with me."

Sexual inclinations developed early in him, first stirred by a simple easygoing affair his brother Sergei was carrying on with a chambermaid. Lev was envious and at the same time vaguely disgusted. Yet could his passions have governed him so powerfully as to lead him to go with his brothers to a house of prostitution? That is not likely. He went because he feared ridicule, and because there was no one to check him; he wanted to be a real man. And standing by the bed of the woman with whom he had known his first sin, he wept bitterly, overwhelmed with remorse.

"No moral principles had been instilled in me—not any at all—and all around me were self-confident grownups, smoking, drinking, leading wanton lives (especially this last), they beat human beings and exacted work from them. I did much that was evil, not because I wished to do it, but merely in imitation of the grownups."

Tortures of remorse, the pangs of his conscience—these Lev kept to himself. Was there no one to understand him? Sergei would probably have looked down on him (he was taller than Lev), his black eyes would have snapped with ridicule, and his handsome mouth with the incipient mustache would have curled ever so slightly in a sarcastic smile; Lev's brothers and schoolmates would have had fresh confirmation of what they already knew, that Lev was a strange boy, not like the others—a crybaby and milksop.

The sciences did not attract Lev but his Aunt Paulina insisted on his preparing to enter the university. His whole desire was as soon as possible to get into a uniform with gold buttons, a cocked hat, hang a sword on his belt and at last be "quite grown up."

"I remember how, when I was fifteen, I suddenly awakened from my subservience to the views of others, in which I had lived until then, and I realized for the first time that I had to do my own living, choose my own path, be responsible for my life and the principle from which it derived.

"I remember, I felt deeply, albeit confusedly, that the main purpose of my life was to be good—good in the evangelical sense of the word with its meaning of self-denial and love. I remember that I then attempted to live in that sense, but it did not last long. I did not have faith in myself but in the insistent, self-confident triumphant commonplace sense to which I was consciously and unconsciously subjected by everything that surrounded me. So my first impulse was supplanted by another very definite yet many-faceted one, the desire to be successful in the eyes of others: to be famous, a scholar, orthodox, rich, powerful and so on—not what I was but what others thought it was good to be."

This period of inner isolation was brightened by one great happiness: his friendship with Dmitri Diakov. Probably Dmitri, who was as sensitive and shy as Tolstoy, sensed something unusual in the timid boy who was at the same time so daring in his speculations.

This is how Tolstoy describes the beginning of the friendship in the story *Youth*, when Dmitri (Nekhlyudov) remarked with astonishment that he had not thought Tolstoy to be so intelligent: "This praise acted so powerfully not only on my emotions but also on my mind that under its pleasant impact I felt that I had become ever so much more intelligent, that one thought after another was crowding my mind with unusual speed. . . . Despite the fact that our discussions might have seemed completely senseless to an outsider because they were confused and one-sided, still to us they were of highest significance. Our souls were so attuned to one another that the slightest touch on one string brought forth a resonance in the other. . . . It seemed to us that we did not have enough time or words to tell each other all the thoughts that were pressing for expression."

"I have said that my friendship with Dmitri opened up to me a new angle of vision on life, its purpose and relationships. The essence of this point of view was the conviction that man's appointed destiny was to strive for moral perfection, and that its fulfillment was easy, possible, and everlasting."

As time passed, it was only natural that the first fervor and zeal of this new love should cool: "In early youth we love only passionately and therefore only perfect beings," and "I had been studying him for too long not to find some flaws in him," wrote Tolstoy. Yet a feeling of devotion to Diakov and a warm sense of gratitude for what he did for him in his early youth remained with Tolstoy all his life.

In those days Kazan University's fame was centered on its brilliant faculty in the province of Oriental languages—Chinese, Persian, Armenian, Sanskrit, teaching which included Arabic, Mongolian, Turkish, Manchurian and other dialects. Lev Tolstoy decided on a diplomatic career and took his entrance examinations on June 5, 1844, but failed. He made another attempt on August 4 of that same year, and was examined in Arabic and Turco-Tatar, this time with success. He was delighted. At last he had grown up. He had his own carriage, the policemen would now salute him, he would be entertained everywhere, St. Thomas was now superfluous and no one could forbid him to smoke. At first he did well in his studies, but then he was caught up in the gay social life of Kazan and his attendance at lectures became less and less regular.

Despite the fact that Kazan society received Lev with open arms he could not move about in it with the easy freedom of his brother Sergei. He always envied Sergei his ability to approach beautiful women, to entertain them easily and freely, to pay court to them, his knack of wearing a uniform and greatcoat with a beaver collar, his capacity to lead a gay and dissolute life without being tortured by remorse—in a word, to be conventional and *comme il faut* to the marrow of his bones.

"The winter season of 1844-45, when Tolstoy began to go out into society, was very lively. Balls at the residence of the Governor, the Marshal of the Nobility, at the Rodionov Institute for girls, dances in private houses, masquerades at the Assembly of Nobles, theatrical benefits, tableaux vivants, concerts—they followed one another in unbroken succession," wrote Zagoskin. "The old inhabitants of Kazan remember seeing him [Tolstoy] at all the balls, parties and social gatherings, invited everywhere, dancing everywhere, yet far from being as popular with the society belles as his rivals, fellow student aristocrats; they were always aware of a strange angularity, shyness in him. . . . The bear Lev, whom we all dubbed the philosopher, was awkward and always shy."

Yet he was incredibly persistent in pursuing a society life, devot-

[28]

ing himself to the ideal set up by his brother Sergei. He persisted in being with people with whom he instinctively felt ill at ease.

"My favorite and principal method of classifying people in the days about which I am writing was—people who were *comme il faut* or *comme il ne faut pas*. These latter were further subdivided into people who were essentially not *comme il faut* and plain people. Those who were *comme il faut* I respected and I considered them worthy of equal relations with me; the second I pretended to look down on but actually I hated them; the third group did not even exist for me, I completely despised them.

". . . To be *comme il faut* was not only an important accomplishment, a magnificent quality, perfection, to which I aspired, but it was also an indispensable condition of life, for lacking that there was no happiness, no fame, no good thing to be had in the world."

Such were the exaggerated expressions which Tolstoy reproduced in *Youth* in describing his fascination by a life of external form, something to which, in reality, he never attributed the slightest significance. It is possible that if the life which surrounded him had not so obviously run counter to his reason, his simple, natural, unaffected aspirations, he might have felt as much at home in it as did the people close to him.

It is difficult to conceive of the flood of thoughts and emotions that surged through the youth at this period. There were so many of them, of such variety and contradiction. He read a great deal. Among his favorite books we find *Eugene Onegin* of Pushkin, Schiller's *Robbers*, Lermontov's *A Hero of Our Times* and *Taman*, Sterne's *Sentimental Journey*, all of Rousseau, and the Sermon on the Mount, the Gospel according to St. Matthew.

Of this period, which he considered the transition from boyhood to youth, he wrote in his story entitled *Youth*: ". . . At the base of my speculations were four emotions: the first . . . love for her, an imaginary woman . . . the second . . . love of love. I longed to have everyone know and love me . . . the third was the hope of extraordinary, vainglorious happiness, a hope so powerful and firm that it verged on madness. . . . Finally, the fourth and main emotion was a disgust for myself and remorse, a remorse so intimately bound up with my hope of happiness that there was no sadness in it. . . . I even reveled in my disgust for my past and tried to make it even darker than it was. . . . This voice of repentance and passionate aspiration toward perfection was the main new sensation in this period of

[29]

my development, it laid a new basis for my attitude toward myself, toward others and God's world."

It was in Kazan that Tolstoy fell in love for the first time.

Zinaïda Molostvova was a schoolmate of Mashenka Tolstoy. Probably it was not her exterior, although she was attractive and very graceful, that enthralled Tolstoy, but her powers of observation, her keen mind, her humor and, above all, her kindness, fine feelings and tendency to poetic speculation. This love always remained a wonderful and bright memory. At the time his thoughts of "her," the imaginary woman, were often uppermost in Tolstoy's mind.

"When the moon was full I often spent whole nights through sitting up in bed, watching the effects of light and shade, listening to the silence and the sounds, dreaming about various things, in the main about poetic, voluptuous happiness. . . ." he wrote in *Youth*. ". . . And *she* was there with her long, black braid of hair, her high breast, she was always sad and beautiful, with bare arms and voluptuous embrace. She loved me and for one moment of love she sacrificed her whole life. But the moon rose higher, brighter and brighter in the heavens, the gorgeous sheen, spreading in an ever-widening sea, swelled like a sound, grew brighter and brighter, the shadows blacker and blacker, the light more and more transparent until, as I looked and listened, something told me that *she* of the bare arms and ardent embraces was far, far from being all of happiness, that love for her was far, far from meaning bliss; and the longer I looked up at the high full moon, the more it seemed to me that true beauty and bliss were higher and higher, purer and purer, nearer and nearer to Him, the source of all that is beauty and bliss, and tears of unslaked but moving joy started from my eyes.

"And although I was alone, I kept feeling that all this mysteriously magnificent nature, this mysteriously magnetic bright disc of a moon hanging for some reason on the unbounded heights of a pale blue sky, while at the same time it flooded all space—that all this and I, a miserable worm sullied by petty, mean, human passions, yet possessed of limitless powers of imagination and love—for these minutes, so it seemed to me, were one—nature, the moon and I."

Nothing could give a clearer conception of Tolstoy than those words, an expression of his whole spiritual content. No matter how deep he sank, these glimpses of the power of love and light, given him from on high, kept raising him to ever-renewed searchings.

❧ 5 ❧

TOLSTOY did not reach the second year of his courses at the university: he failed in history and German. The professor who examined him had just quarreled with Lev's relatives and refused to pass him, although he knew both subjects well. Tolstoy was deeply indignant over such injustice and decided to switch to the law course. In direct contrast to the brilliant faculty in Oriental languages, the professors of jurisprudence were weak, while the student body was made up of the poorest scholars, mostly the gilded youth of the time.

The winter season of 1845-1846 was especially lively in Kazan. Tolstoy took part in all social distractions, was desultory in his studies and cut lectures. He had not the slightest respect for his professors, most of whom were Germans, and often he joined with his college mates in barbed and telling ridicule at their expense.

Beginning with the autumn of 1846 the brothers occupied a separate apartment. They were on a friendly footing with each other although they were all quite different. Evidently the one who kept most to himself was Dmitri. "It was in Kazan that he began to act strangely," wrote Tolstoy in his memoirs. "He studied well, regularly, wrote verse easily. . . . He talked little with us, was always quiet, serious and thoughtful. . . . We, especially Sergei, cultivated acquaintance with our aristocratic school fellows and young people in general; Dmitri, on the contrary, picked out all the needy, poor, ragged students he could find." He made friends with an unhappy, downtrodden girl, who lived at the Yushkovs'. She had a strange affection on her face; it was so swollen, she looked as though some bees had stung her. There was an unpleasant odor about her, she spoke with difficulty and obviously had some kind of swelling inside her mouth. She was physically so repulsive that it was hard for the others to tolerate her. But Dmitri would take her for walks, listen to her stories, converse with and read to her. These kindhearted feelings for the humiliated, the hapless, were the result of the Christian orthodox spirit by which Dmitri was carried away—the expression in acts of the teachings of Christ.

As early as his sixteenth year Lev began to have doubts about the truth of the orthodox faith.

"The religious teachings inculcated in me from childhood disappeared after I was fifteen and when I began to read philosophical writings . . . my renunciation of those teachings became conscious. From the time I was sixteen I ceased to pray and no longer went to church or fasted of my own volition. I no longer believed what had been taught me as a child, yet I believed in something. What this was I could not say. I believed in God, or rather I did not deny the existence of God—what God I could not tell. Nor did I refuse to accept the teachings of Christ—yet what those teachings were I also would not say.

"Now, as I look back on that time, I see clearly that my faith—that which in addition to animal instincts affected my life—my one and only true faith was in a striving for perfection. Of what did that perfection consist and what was its purpose? I could not tell that either. I tried to perfect my will, to set up rules I tried to follow; to perfect myself physically, by all kinds of exercises to develop strength and agility, and, by means of all kinds of deprivations, to teach myself endurance and patience. All this I considered striving for perfection. The origin of it was, of course, a striving for mental perfection, but this was soon converted to a general perfection, that is to say, the desire to be better not in my own eyes or those of God but a desire to be better in the eyes of other men. And soon that striving to be better in the eyes of others was changed to a desire to be stronger than others, that is to say more famous, more important, richer."

It is possible that this pitiless self-analysis, self-castigation was due to the strong influence of Rousseau, whose works Tolstoy kept mulling over, especially his *Confessions*. Yet all through his life, as he pursued the path of self-perfection, he was merciless in lashing out at himself. He did not like to recall his youth, and when anyone close to him would question him about that period of his life, he would knit his brows from inner pain and answer only with reluctance. The trait which is common to nearly every human being, especially to a child or youth early deprived, as Lev was, of parents and all moral guidance, the desire to advance oneself, to make a show of one's exceptional mind or talents—this he considered a great shortcoming.

Yet this ambition is innate in almost everyone; it is encouraged and looked upon as a valuable asset. Tolstoy called it vanity and wrestled all his life with this his sin, as he considered it.

His worst torments, however, derived from the storms of passions he was subject to and his lapses caused by them. He was healthy, strong, unusually passionate and sinned accordingly. It was as though he were trying to protect himself against women and the temptation they offered to him when he wrote in his diary:

"Look upon the society of women as a disagreeable part of social life and keep away from them as much as possible. From whom indeed do we derive sensuality, effeminacy, frivolity and many other vices, if not from women? Who but they are responsible for our loss of our inherent qualities of audacity, firmness, sobriety of mind, justice? Woman is more perceptive than man, and for that reason in the days of her virtue she was better than man: but in this dissolute wicked age women are worse than we are."

Among the few gifted teachers in the school of jurisprudence was a young Professor Meyer, who lectured on Russian law. At the time of the midyear examinations in January, 1847, Meyer, though obliged to give Tolstoy a low mark, felt his attention drawn to him; he asked one of his students if he knew him, remarking: "I was examining him today, and I noticed that he has no serious desire to study, which is too bad: he has such an expressive face, such intelligent eyes, I am convinced that with a little good will and self-reliance he might become a remarkable person."

Evidently Professor Meyer made up his mind to interest Tolstoy, to make him work, and thus keep him at the university. He gave his student a subject for comparison—the *Decree* (*Nakaz*) of Catherine the Great and *The Spirit of Laws* of Montesquieu. Tolstoy for the first time became seriously wrapped up in a piece of scholarly work. But something the professor could not foresee occurred: Tolstoy's personal research on the comparison between the *Decree* and *The Spirit of Laws* convinced him that outside the university he could study much more freely along lines that interested him and would not be tied down to subjects prescribed by dull-witted professors. "I remember how in my second year I became interested in the theory of law, I began to study it, not just for the examination, but because it seemed to me that in it I should find the key to much that was strange and unclear in the setup of people's lives. Yet I recall that the deeper I delved into the underlying thought in the theory of

[33]

law, the more I became convinced that either there was something wrong with the whole science of the matter or else I was incapable of understanding it."

On one occasion Tolstoy and one of his fellow students, Nazariev, were put into the college lockup. Tolstoy was evidently in a mood to talk, and he spent the whole night holding forth on the futility of sciences as taught in the university.

"History," he rashly concluded, "is nothing but a collection of fairy tales, sprinkled over with useless figures, worthless details, and proper names. . . . And how is history written? Everything is molded to a certain pattern invented by a historian. A terrible Tsar, about whom the professor is lecturing at present . . . suddenly is changed from a beneficent, wise ruler into an insensate, violent tyrant. Why and how did this happen? There is no use asking. . . .

". . . Yet we have the right to assume," Tolstoy summed up his thoughts, "that we are to go forth from this temple as useful persons in possession of some knowledge. Actually what are we carrying away from this university? Think and then answer according to your conscience. What are we taking from this sanctuary back home with us? What are we fitted for? . . ."

He was so keyed up with his reflections concerning the "temple" of science that he did not even notice how wearing they were on his obviously dissenting companion: "Tolstoy pulled his cap down over his eyes and wrapped himself up in his overcoat with the beaver collar," Nazariev concluded his account, "and, with a slight nod to me, heaped a few more abuses on the temple of learning, then disappeared in company with the sergeant. I, too, hurried out and heaved a deep breath to be rid of my companion and to find myself in the frosty air, out in the quiet of an empty street just coming to life. My head was swimming, as if I had been drinking, and it was crammed with doubts and questions never raised before, but put there now by my strange, definitely incomprehensible to me, fellow prisoner."

The thought of leaving the university was maturing in Tolstoy's mind. "There were two reasons for my leaving the university," he wrote later. "The first was that my brother Sergei had finished his course and was going away, and the second, strange as it may seem, was because my theme on the *Decree* and *The Spirit of Laws* had opened up to me a whole new field of independent work, which the university with its requirements not only did not promote but interfered with."

Concurrently jurisprudence was losing its interest for him as he became more and more absorbed in philosophy. "Philosophy always drew me. I loved to trace the intense, orderly development of thoughts by means of which all the complex phenomena of the world in all their variety are summed up into one whole." Tolstoy read Hegel and Voltaire, but the main influence on the course of his own thinking was undoubtedly exercised by Rousseau. In 1905 he wrote to the Rousseau Society: "Rousseau was my teacher from the time I was fifteen. There were two great and beneficent influences in my life: Rousseau and the Gospels. Rousseau does not age. Quite recently I chanced to reread some of his writings, and I had the same sensation of exaltation and astonishment I felt on reading him in my early youth."

Philosophy so carried him away now that he even attempted to put his own thoughts on paper in the form of a commentary on the *Discours* of Rousseau. He called it "On the Aim of Philosophy." He was eighteen at the time.

His sister Maria wrote an entertaining account, with touches of her own peculiar humor, of the time Lev came down to Yasnaya Polyana, with his mind full of philosophy, to spend the summer holidays.

"Lyovochka probably considered himself a sort of Diogenes or else, under the influence of Rousseau, he was obsessed with the idea of leading a simple, primitive life. He adopted complete simplicity: whatever became of his aspirations to be *comme il faut*! He fashioned himself a kind of long, loose, horrible garment, which he wore day and night, and so that the long tails of it did not get in the way he sewed on some buttons to which he fastened them when he walked. For days on end he roamed the woods, and when tired he would lie down resting his head on fat philosophical tomes: Voltaire, Rousseau, Hegel. On one occasion Auntie Tanya sent for him when some guests arrived. He appeared in the drawing room in his sailcloth garment, his bare feet thrust into bedroom slippers. Auntie was horrified but Lyovochka quietly expounded the empty vanity of all conventions and the necessity of leading a simple, natural life."

Whether it was distaste for the empty society life of Kazan or fear of the loneliness he expected after his brothers left, whether it was dissatisfaction with what he was getting from the university, an urge to lead a simple natural life in Yasnaya Polyana, or perhaps a combination of all these reasons, Tolstoy decided not to wait for his own examination but left for Yasnaya Polyana with his brothers as soon as their finals were over.

"Change must take place in life," he wrote in his diary on April 15, 1847, "but it should be brought about as the result of inner decisions, not outward circumstances.

"The purpose of life is a conscious striving toward the all-around development of everything that exists."

However, Tolstoy had not the slightest intention of remaining an uneducated person. On the contrary he drew up, with all the daring and enterprise of youth, a grandiose program he intended to carry out while living in Yasnaya Polyana:

"(1) Study the whole course of jurisprudence as required to pass the final examinations in that subject in the university, (2) Study practical and in part theoretical medicine, (3) Study languages: French, Russian, German, English, Italian and Latin, (4) Study both theoretical and practical agriculture, (5) Study history, geography and statistics, (6) Study pre-university mathematics, (7) Write a dissertation, (8) Achieve the highest degree of accomplishment in music and painting, (9) Draw up a set of rules, and (10) Acquire some knowledge of the natural sciences, (11) Write compositions in all the subjects I shall study."

This program would seen impossible of execution. Yet with the exception of jurisprudence, painting and medicine he did acquire a serious amount of knowledge in all the other fields, and to the very end of his days he never ceased his self-education in the most varied subjects.

🦢 6 🦢

ON APRIL 11, 1847, the four Tolstoy brothers and their sister Maria came together to divide among themselves the inheritance left them by their parents. As was usually the custom in Russian families, the property inherited from the mother—Yasnaya

Polyana—fell to the youngest son, Lev. His eldest brother inherited the patrimonial estate of Nikolskoye-Vyazemskoye.

Tolstoy was undoubtedly describing himself when he wrote, in his story entitled "The Morning of a Landed Proprietor," ". . . I made a decision on which the fate of my whole life was to depend. I was leaving the university to devote myself to country life because I felt that I was born for that. . . . Was I not directly bound by sacred duty to care for the happiness of the seven hundred souls for whom I was to account one day before God? Would it not be a sin to abandon them to the arbitrary will of bailiffs and stewards for reasons of my own pleasure and ambition? And why should I seek a sphere in which to be useful and do good, when I can discover such excellent opportunities near at hand?"

One wonders what the source of this idea may have been.

Until now Tolstoy had given scarcely any thought to the condition of the peasants among whom he had grown up. One incident from his early childhood which contributed not a little to his respect and affection for the simple people he describes himself:

"My father had in his stables a pair of very high-spirited black horses. His coachman was Mitka Kopylov. He had been father's groom, was a skillful rider, horseman, magnificent driver and, above all, an invaluable postilion. He was invaluable as a postilion because a boy could not handle high-spirited horses, an older man would be too heavy and have the wrong figure, so Mitka had all the qualities necessary for that particular job: he was small of stature, light in weight, but strong and agile. I recall that the phaeton was brought around once for father, the horses bolted and galloped out of the gateway. Someone cried: 'The Count's horses have bolted!' Pashenka fainted, the aunts ran to pacify grandmother, but it turned out that father had not yet stepped into the carriage and Mitka was skillful enough to get control of the horses and drive them back into the courtyard.

"This same Mitka, when expenses had to be cut down, was released to be hired out. Various wealthy merchants vied with each other to get hold of him and they would have paid him a good salary for he made a fine showing in his silk shirts and velvet uniforms. But it so happened that his brother drew the lot of being drafted into the army and their father, being an old man, sent for Mitka to come home and help him with the work he had to do for his master. Mitka, the dandy, in a few months turned into a nondescript peasant in bast sandals, doing menial work, farming his two allotments of communal land, haying, plowing and in general carrying the heavy load of taxes of those days. All this he did without the slightest murmur of resentment; that was how things had to be and they could not be otherwise."

At the time this incident made an impression on the boy, then probably it slipped from his mind. He wrote that in his early youth the plain people did not exist for him.

In 1847 two stories were published: Grigorovich's *Anton Goremyka* and the first of Turgenyev's *A Sportsman's Sketches*. They both touched the youth deeply. Later on Tolstoy used to say that *A Sportsman's Sketches* were the best things Turgenyev ever wrote.

"I recall the emotion and enthusiasm," he wrote to Grigorovich in the autumn of 1897 when the golden jubilee of that writer was being celebrated, "stirred in my self-distrustful being by your *Anton Goremyka*. It was for me a happy discovery of the fact that we could and should describe the Russian peasant—our provider of food and, I should like to say, our teacher—not as an object of mockery or an item to enliven the landscape, but describe him in his full stature, not only with affection but with warmth and even excitement."

As an accidental spark sometimes smolders for a long time before it breaks, under the impact of some wind, into a sudden, bright flame, so the spark dropped in Tolstoy's soul by these stories suddenly flared up and he felt that all the seven hundred peasants on the estate of Yasnaya Polyana were not only serfs fulfilling their obligations to their masters, but were also living, thinking, feeling, human beings. As soon as this emotion reached his consciousness he felt compelled to act.

It was in that exalted mood that the youth came to his estate. It was spring, and springtime always inspired Tolstoy, raised him up above the world, aroused his energy and whetted both his emotions and his brain. He was happy; he believed that in self-sacrifice, in doing good to others he would find his own happiness.

The first time Tolstoy came face to face with the poverty of peasant life it upset him. One peasant's cottage had collapsed, another man had no grain, there were illness, ignorance, complete lack of confidence in the young master, who, from the peasants' point of view was either a crank or bent on squeezing a bit more profit out of them. Several did not hide their feeling of superiority over him, his inexperience, his youth; he sensed the same attitude on the part of his steward and Auntie Tanya.

For his aunt, as for everyone in her walk of life, serfs were of an inferior order and created to serve the people of the upper class, the landowners. And Tolstoy was too young to realize that only a change in the fundamental laws—the emancipation of the serfs—could uproot the evils he felt so keenly. The idea of freeing the serfs came to him only later.

Now there was only bitter disillusion: "My God, my God, can it be that all my dreams of the purpose and obligations of my life are empty nothings? Why am I depressed, sad, as if dissatisfied with myself, when I always imagined that once I found the path I should constantly enjoy the full measure of a greater satisfaction. . . . I am dissatisfied because I am not finding happiness. I have not felt any satisfaction and I have already cut myself off from everything that can provide it. Why? For what? Who has been relieved by this? Have my peasants grown richer, more educated, grown in moral stature? Not one whit. They are no better off, and with every day I am less happy. If I could see success in my enterprise, if I could see gratitude, but no, I see erroneous habits, vice, suspicion, helplessness. I am wasting the best years of my life for nothing." Tolstoy concluded his story "The Morning of a Landed Proprietor."

Thirst for personal happiness, gaiety, swept over him. He dropped his work in Yasnaya Polyana, his unfulfilled good intentions, and drove off to Moscow.

"I lived a very disordered life, with no job, no occupation, no purpose. . . . I lived that way . . . for the simple reason that I enjoyed it," he wrote. He kept no diary then, he had no time for it, he plunged head first, as he said later on, into "the aimless city life of carousing, the drunken, corrupt life of society."

The winter 1849 Tolstoy spent in St. Petersburg. "An undefined hunger for knowledge again led me far afield," he said. He decided to abandon his philosophic speculations which were without issue and to take an examination for a university degree, in order to get a government job like all the decent young men of his circle.

"I know you won't believe at all that I have changed. You'll say: This is the twentieth time and you still haven't found the right solution, you're the most good-for-nothing youngster. No, I have changed this time in an entirely different way. I used to say to myself: Watch me, I am going to change, but now I see that I have changed and I say: I have already changed." This he wrote to his brother Sergei.

Yet he was unable to change. He could not master the science of jurisprudence; he was even less able to make himself over into a well-regulated official who received his pay on the 20th of the month and went regularly to his office. Instead of that he drank, gambled and finally failed his examinations. Thereupon, in the depths of despair, he wrote a remorseful letter to his brother Sergei in which he implored him to send 3,500 rubles as soon as possible, because otherwise "in addition to the money I shall also lose my reputation. I know you will make a fuss, but what else can I do? Once in a lifetime a man does stupid things. I had to pay for my freedom (there was no one to whip me, that's my main trouble) and for my philosophy of life and, well, I have paid for it. . . . God grant I shall reform and some day grow to be a decent human being."

What should he do? Join the cadets and take part in the Hungarian campaign? Take a job in a government office? Go back to Yasnaya Polyana? Tolstoy chose this last. He gathered up a drunkard musician called Rudolf, with whose talent he had been greatly impressed, and off they went to the country. He registered for service in nearby Tula in the chancellery of the Provincial Assembly of the Nobles, but the tenor of his life was unchanged. He spent his time in riotous living, among the gypsies, or playing cards. The only rest he found was in Yasnaya Polyana.

"I think of the long autumn and winter evenings," he wrote in his *Memoirs*, "and they have always remained for me wonderful memories. . . . After my evil life in Tula or among my neighbors, playing cards, spending time with the gypsies, hunting, and all the empty, vain pastimes, I used to come home, and go to her [Auntie Tanya]. In our old custom we kissed each other's hands, I—her dear firm one, and she—my soiled, evil one . . . and then I slipped into an armchair. She knew everything I was doing, she regretted it, but never reproached me, always treated me with the same affection, with love."

In this period of his life, which he described as evil, he found some appeasement in music. Perhaps his talented German friend Rudolf inspired him. He was in a state of languor. The artist in him was searching for some form of expression. He made up his mind he could become a great musician and composer. He played the piano for hours, carried away by combinations of sounds, even attempting to formulate his own theory of harmony under the title of: "The Fundamentals of Music and Rules for Its Study."

Music always exercised a powerful influence over Tolstoy. Mozart, Haydn, Schubert, Chopin were his favorite composers. Yet his love for classical music did not in any way interfere with his fondness for folk and gypsy music.

At this time there was a magnificent gypsy chorus in Tula, and Lev, together with his brother Sergei, was a constant listener. The majority of young Russian aristocrats shared this craze for the gypsies. They were fascinated by their restless, wandering way of life, their gift for music, the kindness and sweet gentle ways of their women, despite the patriarchal structure of their lives and the severity and purity of their morals. It was rare that a gypsy girl or woman would agree to live with a man outside of wedlock.

The gypsies used to gather at the home of some person living in the outskirts of Tula. The members of the chorus took up their places: the women—in their bright-colored dresses, vivid kerchiefs, with gay shawls draped over one shoulder—in a semicircle in front. Behind them were ranged the slim, swarthy men with their guitars, in silk shirts of various colors and velvet sleeveless coats. The leader stood facing them. He would run his fingers over the strings of his guitar and faintly, barely audibly, in harmonious unison, the song began; louder and louder, faster, more piercing rang out the rich powerful chords of the guitarists. The tempo increased, the guests stamped the rhythm; faster, faster, louder, never losing the rhythm; now the guitarists were striking the strings full with their whole fists. Suddenly in floated the gypsy women dancers, serenely, one after another. In they came stretching their arms out as if to someone, first throwing themselves forward, then withdrawing, their heads proudly tossed back, and all the while tapping the rapid rhythm with their feet. Their teeth flashed, the golden coins on chains around their necks jingled. The men of the chorus yelled and whooped, the women dancers urged themselves on with guttural, staccato exclamations, the guests shouted. . . . Suddenly from the back row bounced a male dancer. He slapped his knees, the floor, and like some demon whirled around two of the women, flitting in and out at a frantic rhythm. The tempo went still faster, the whooping grew louder, the guests yelled, the excitement reached a peak. . . . The music stopped, the dance was over.

Wiping the perspiration from his brow the leader of the chorus then went over to a tiny, dark-skinned beautiful gypsy girl called Masha, with a gentle sweet face. A dead silence fell. Masha sang. . . . She sang of the wide rolling steppes, of a fading dawn, of swift prairie horses, of love. Her deep voice sank into one's very soul; through minds clouded with wine and champagne there flitted vague dreams of some beautiful unobtainable goal.

Masha had many admirers but she loved only one man—the handsome Sergei Tolstoy. She fell in love with him ardently, deeply, for the first and last time in her life. And the brilliant young society man gave up his worldly career for her. He became so attached to her that eventually he married her.

Lev's other pastime at that period was hunting. In the autumn he walked with his hounds to outlying fields, where he spent whole days, or he took his dog and gun, put on high boots and splashed around in marshes searching for wild ducks, woodcocks, double snipe. In the spring he stood on the boundary of the State Forest Preserve and watched the timid sun of the early season through the bare branches of the trees, listening for the familiar hoarse call of the woodcock.

He was making practically no entries in his diary now. On the 8th of December, 1850, he made this note: "This quiet life in the country has brought about a great upheaval inside me: my former stupidity and the necessity of attending to my own affairs have borne their fruit. I have stopped building castles in Spain and making plans beyond human power. My main and most favorable conviction is that I do not hope ever to accomplish anything on the basis of mere reason, and I no longer despise forms accepted by most people."

Whereupon he deliberately forced his broad, artistic and creative nature into the "forms accepted by most people," a decision immediately reflected in the notes he made in his diary: ". . . not to let any slightest disagreeable or stinging remark go by without paying it back with double interest. . . ." "(1) . . . get in with gamblers and, when in funds, gamble; (2) get into high society and, given certain conditions, take a wife; (3) find an advantageous government job."

He wrote down these rules for himself only to break them at once.

"I came to Moscow with my three purposes in mind," he wrote in his diary: "to gamble, to get married, to get a job."

"The first is a bad and low ambition and, thank God, after looking over my affairs and brushing aside certain prejudices, I decided to change my ways, mend my affairs by selling part of my estates. The second plan I put aside on the intelligent advice of my brother Nikolai, until such time as love, or reason, or even fate, will impel me to act on it in an irresistible way. The last project proved impossible until I had served two years in the provincial government—and, to tell the truth, I don't want a lot more things to attend to. . . . Therefore I shall wait until destiny forces the issue. I was guilty of many weaknesses at this time. The main one was that I paid little attention to moral rules, I was more interested in rules necessary to success."

In a biography of Benjamin Franklin, Tolstoy read that he kept a special notebook in which he entered all the shortcomings he must conquer, so Tolstoy immediately started a similar journal for himself. Unfortunately this was not preserved.

All his waverings, lapses and surges put him into a new mood of religion and remorse, which he described in the fragment "The History of Yesterday." "In my own Benjamin Franklin journal I have entered all my weaknesses under these headings: laziness, lying, greediness, indecision, desire to show off, sensuality, lack of self-respect and so on. . . . All such minor shortcomings. From these groups I extract my crimes and put crosses under the various headings."

While in Moscow Tolstoy visited the Chapel of the Iberian Madonna, had prayers said, and performed a fast. "My remorse was terrifying. I never felt it so deeply before. . . . I grew devout and became even more so when in the country."

Filled as he was with the impulse to turn over a new leaf in his life, Lev was naturally delighted when his brother Nikolai, who had gone into the army, proposed that he join him on a trip to the Caucasus. Perhaps Nikolai, with his perceptive nature, sensed how much Lev needed a change.

❧ 7 ❧

THE Caucasus—fit subject of many verses and stories from the pens of the great Russian poets Pushkin and Lermontov. Now Tolstoy saw it with their eyes:

> The Caucasus lies at my feet;
> I stand alone above the snows
> On edge of sheer abyss:
> From far-off towering peak
> An eagle takes its flight,
> Planing with wide-stretched wings
> On equal height with me.
> From here I view the fountainheads

Of torrent streams, an avalanche
In first portentous downward flux.
Beneath me clouds wind lazily,
Yet pierced by thundering cataracts
Which hurtle headlong over barren cliffs.
Below, the moss and meager bushes grow,
And farther down in leafy groves
The trilling birds and springing deer abound.
There too I see huts perched like nests
And sheep a-scramble along grassy bluffs,
A shepherd wandering down to smiling dales
Where the Aragva glides through shady banks;
While in the gorges of the foaming Terek,
That plunges down with savage sport,
The outcast rider finds a dark retreat. . . .

That was Pushkin's vision. To him the Caucasus spelled a stately, many-faceted magnificence. And then the gentle green slopes of the mountains, the quiet orchards, the peaceful *auls* or villages, inhabited by half-savage tribes—brutal, independent and revengeful:

To thee, O Caucasus, stern monarch of this earth,
Once more I offer these my random lines;
As on a son thy blessing spend on them,
And shelter them beneath thy snowy crown.
Since early youth the storms by thee instilled,
Rebellious, fiery passions, still have coursed
Through all my veins. . . .

That was Lermontov's vision. It was in the Caucasus that his poetic gift blossomed and grew strong.

It is not surprising that in Tolstoy's imagination the Caucasus was a land of heroic feats and that life there was filled with fantastic happenings and beauty.

Nor is it surprising that for him, too, the Caucasus was to prove the fountainhead of his first living "torrents" of inspiration, his first portentous avalanche of thoughts and emotions. Pushkin's words applied to him are prophetic.

In the nineteenth century, Georgia, the southern part of the Caucasus, which until then had been governed by an independent monarch, passed under Russian rule. Other independent mountain tribes, which lived between Russia and Georgia, still maintained their freedom and for half a century put up a desperate resistance to the Russians. There was incessant fighting between the mountaineers and the Russians (for the most part Cossacks) who held a line of defense along the left bank of the Terek and the right bank of the Kuban rivers.

The powerful and agile mountain tribesmen knew every path, they clambered like cats up the face of steep cliffs. They would appear suddenly on their tough small horses, attack an encampment, rob, kill and sometimes carry off prisoners, both men and women, into the mountains.

Tolstoy was thrilled to be going there. He was happy to be with Nikolai, happy because it was spring, he was young, and above all this was the beginning of something new, absorbingly interesting, something to change the whole course of his life, free him from his vices and help him find himself.

When he was describing the hero in his story *The Cossacks* was he not writing about himself?

"He recognized no bonds—either physical or moral: he could do anything, nothing was necessary to him, nothing bound him. He had no family, no fatherland, no faith, no needs. He believed in nothing, accepted nothing. Yet despite the fact that he held no faith he was far from being a gloomy, bored, or dryly intellectual youth. On the contrary, he enjoyed himself to the full. He decided that there was no such thing as love, yet the presence of a young and beautiful woman made his heart stop beating. . . . He kept turning over in his mind where to place the whole weight of his youthful powers, the powers that one possesses only once in a lifetime—into art, into science, into love, or into practical business? This was not the power of a mind, a heart, of education, this was the never-to-be-repeated power which man has over himself to choose what he will make of himself, to decide what above all else in the world he desires. . . .

"When he left Moscow he was in the gay young spirits of one who is conscious of his former errors and suddenly says to himself: all that was not the real thing, the past was merely accidental and unimportant, that he never really had made an effort to live *right* but that now, on leaving Moscow, he was making a fresh start in life, he would not make the same mistakes over again, there would be no fits of remorse, and he would surely find happiness."

Everything was marvelous: the fact that he was traveling with his beloved brother, whom he respected for his profound sense of decency, his scorn of the opinion of others. The journey, too, was marvelous as arranged by Nikolai: by carriage to Saratov, thence, after loading their carriage onto a primitive river boat, down the Volga. The river was marvelous, in the full tide of its springtime floods. Along the way they stopped off at Kazan. In the mood Tolstoy was in at the time it was not surprising that the urgency of love was like a freshet in his veins and that his passion for Zinaïda Molostvova, whom he had courted in his student days in Kazan, flared up again.

"Love and religion, those are the two pure and high emotions," he wrote in his diary on July 8, 1851. "I do not know what people call love. If love is what I have heard and read about then I have never experienced it. I had known Zinaïda when she was at school. . . . I liked her but I did not really know her. I spent a week in Kazan. Should anyone ask why I stayed there, why I was enjoying myself, why I was so happy, I should not have said that it was because I had fallen in love. I was not aware of it. And it seems to me that not knowing is one of the chief features of being in love, its greatest charm. How much at ease I felt at this time! There were none of the burdens of trivial passions, which ruin all enjoyment of life. I never mentioned love to her. Yet I am so sure she sensed my feelings that if she loves me I should attribute it just to this, that she understood me."

But his love for Zinaïda was merely a passing sensation. Under the impact of new impressions he soon forgot her: "Zinaïda is getting married," he wrote within a year. "I am chagrined, but especially because this should have upset me" (his diary for June 22, 1852).

Later on Lev said that he would never forget this journey down the Volga. The brothers floated downstream in a primitive skiff, admiring the beautiful banks of the great river with the green copses and meadows, the yellow sandy slopes of the Zhiguli Hills, the long flat shores but dimly seen through the vapors of an early morning fog. In Astrakhan they unloaded their boat and drove on to the Cossack village of Starogladkovskaya. When Tolstoy saw mountains for the first time in his life he was overwhelmed:

"The morning was crystal clear," he wrote in *The Cossacks*, "when suddenly he saw, as he at first thought, some twenty feet away—pure white massive cliffs with their crests delicately drawn in a fantastic but clear and airy outline against a far sky. When he realized what the distance must be between him and the mountains as well as between the mountains and the heavens, the hugeness of the mountains, and when he sensed the infinity of such beauty, he was frightened. . . ."

The officers into whose society the Tolstoy brothers now fell were distinctly inferior to them in social station and education. "I confess," he wrote to his Auntie Tanya in Yasnaya Polyana, "that at first there was much in their society that jarred on me, but now I am accustomed to it, although I have not made friends with these gentlemen. I have found a happy mean of social intercourse which smacks neither of cold pride nor backslapping familiarity. As a matter of fact all I had to do was follow Nikolai's example."

He was attracted by primitive, healthy, simple people. They did not jar him with their banalities and artificiality. "These people live," he wrote in *The Cossacks*, "as nature does: they die, are born, intermingle, give birth to children, fight, drink, eat, are happy and die again, and their lives are not conditioned except as nature herself inexorably rules the sun, the grass, the animals, the trees and them. They have no other laws."

Where now were Tolstoy's convictions about the necessity of being *comme il faut*, that a man who does not wear kid gloves is a "nonentity"? He was now veering to an opposite extreme.

"For once one must experience life in all its unaffected beauty. One must see and perceive what I do every day—the eternal, the inaccessible snows of the mountains and a sublime woman of primordial beauty, such as the first woman must have been who came from the hands of her Creator."

Women, as always, drew him, disturbed his peace of mind and interfered with his life and his work. No one knows how deeply he became attached to the beautiful Cossack girl in whose home he lived. But vague ideas of breaking with conventions, to live the simple life, to marry the Cossack girl, certainly passed through his mind. Here in the Caucasus the women, his old Cossack friend Epishka, the dashing Circassian horseman Sado, horses, wild boars, pheasants, the invigorating mountain air, the swiftly turbulent rivers—all fitted into one whole: "I had faith in my ability to love this woman. I admired her as I did the beauty of the mountains and the sky. I could not but admire her since she was as magnificent as they were. Then I began to feel that to gaze on this beauty had become a necessity in my life and I asked myself: do I love her. . . ."

For the two and a half years Tolstoy was to spend in the Caucasus his main friend was Epishka, an aged Cossack—"a grand fellow,

horse thief, scoundrel, robber, a trafficker in human beings, who led
Chechen prisoners on lariats. He never worked. He served either as
an interpreter or went on missions which, of course, only he could
execute, to bring in some mountaineer desperado dead or alive from
his village, set fire to a house . . . seize the famous heads of the high-
land tribesmen, or the Ataman chieftains of the Chechen and bring
them to the Russian camp. . . . Hunting and carousing—those were
the old fellow's chief passions: they were and they remain his only
occupation, all other adventures were merely incidental."

As an old man Tolstoy still remembered Epishka as the "most
amiable, simple, gay person." In this man of powerful and towering
build were combined agility and daring, incredible brutality toward
his enemies and tenderness for a moth fluttering near a flame, the
condoning of sin and a fear of it.

In *The Cossacks*, Tolstoy describes how the old man was angered
when a young officer asked him: "But have you killed people?"

The old man suddenly raised himself on his elbows and pushing
his face close to the officer's he exploded: "Blast you!" he yelled at
him, "What do you suppose? Why should I tell you? It's a grand
trick to wring the soul out of a person, a grand trick. . . . And now
be off. . . ."

When he grew old Epishka went into a hermitage to pray his sins
away and die.

Another companion Tolstoy had was Sado, the young son of a
wealthy and peaceable Chechen. He did not give his son money but
preferred to bury it in the ground to keep it from falling into the
hands of his enemies. Sado often came into camp to play cards with
the officers; but he was poor at counting and some of the officers
cheated him. Tolstoy noticed this and offered to play in Sado's stead.
After that Sado looked upon Tolstoy as his friend—his *kunak* as the
Caucasians say. They exchanged presents on various occasions. Sado
was a skilled horseman, a thief who risked his life to steal horses and
cattle from his enemies to sell for his own living. When Tolstoy's
horse fell sick and he wanted to buy another, Sado brought him his
own mount and insisted on his accepting it.

Soon after his arrival in the Caucasus Tolstoy had gambled away
a lot of money for which he had had to give promissory notes, as he
was not able to pay all his debt in cash. This debt worried him and
he even considered selling part of Yasnaya Polyana. Sado knew about
this. The time to make the payment on the note was drawing nearer

and Tolstoy had no cash with which to meet his obligation. Once, when in Tiflis briefly, as he was going to bed Tolstoy made a prayer begging God to extricate him from his difficulties. Suddenly, the next day, he received an unexpected letter from his brother Nikolai: "Sado was here recently," he wrote. "He won some money . . . enough to cover your note, and gave it to me. He was so pleased with his winnings, so happy, and repeatedly asked me: Do you think your brother will be glad that I did it?—that I really grew quite fond of him. He is truly devoted to you."

In June of 1851 Tolstoy took part as a volunteer in a raid on the mountain tribesmen. His valor was noted and the commanding officer, to whom he was presented, advised him to enter the army, advice which Tolstoy followed.

At the same time that he was accustoming himself to the colorful life, full of danger and adventure, of an army man in the Caucasus, an intense process was going on inside him. He was still casting around, trying to choose the field in which to "invest all his power . . . of youth."

Perhaps he himself did not realize that he was already on the right path. He was tortured with doubts, he lost his way, but again and again he returned in the direction to which he was inevitably drawn. Tolstoy was already a writer.

The people with whom he had spent his childhood and youth, his family, serfs and vagrants at Yasnaya Polyana, his German tutor Fyodor Ivanovich, the old Cossack Epishka, Sado, army officers, and everything seen or heard, psychological observations, personal experiences—all were preserved as material from which he drew as needed when he was building some artistic creation. Some of this material was used at once; some of it lay stored away for many years.

"If you want to show off your knowledge of what is happening in the Caucasus," he wrote his brother Sergei, "Hadji Murat, the second most important figure after Shamil, surrendered a few days ago to the Russian Government. He was the most daring horseman among all the Chechens and he has committed a low act."

The story of Hadji Murat, the comrade in arms of Shamil, leader of the warlike Chechens, made a deep impression on Tolstoy but it was fifty years before he used it as material for his own writings.

When out walking one day in Yasnaya Polyana he saw a clump of thistles—"Tatar grass"—and he was struck by the tenacity with which it kept alive. "It was evident that the whole clump had been crushed by wagon wheels, but had raised itself up sideways and was still standing—it was just as though a man with a part of his body, his vitals torn away, his hands lopped off, his eyes gouged out, still stood and would not give up . . . and it brought back to my mind a story of the Caucasus of long ago. . . ."

While in the Caucasus he wrote *The Story of My Childhood.* He did not know what would become of his writings; he wrote because he could not keep from writing, because it satisfied a craving. Meantime, while his thoughts were absorbed in the past he was receiving new impressions—events, fresh images and thoughts were being culled and formulated, ready sooner or later to be poured out in letters, lines, pages.

The attack in which he took part did not go unrecorded; his description and impression of war were written a year later (in 1852).

As early as this Tolstoy, then twenty-four, gave indications of the point of view he was to adopt after 1880; a stand against killing in any form.

"At the time, the only question I asked myself was: what emotion leads a man to decide, without any evidence of gain, to risk his own life or, what is more astounding, to kill others of his own kind?

"Can it be that people feel too crowded to live together in this beautiful world, under this boundless starry sky? Is it impossible for them, in the bosom of nature with all its fascination, to restrain themselves from feelings of revenge, from the passion to destroy others of their own kind? All that is evil in the heart of man should, one might suppose, disappear when it comes in contact with nature, the direct expression of beauty and goodness.

"Last night I could scarcely sleep at all. After writing in my diary, I turned to prayer. The sweetness of the emotions that I felt while praying is something I am unable to describe. . . . I had the impulse to fuse myself with the All-Embracing Being. . . . I thanked Him, but neither with words nor thoughts. I was wrapped in one emotion which contained everything—prayer and gratitude. All feeling of awe disappeared. I could not distinguish one single feeling—of faith, hope or love from my one general feeling.

"No—there was one feeling I did have last night—it was love toward God, an exalted emotion which included all that was good and excluded all that was evil.

"How strange it felt to contemplate all the trivial, sinful side of life. I could not grasp how it was that it could ever attract me. With

[50]

all my heart I implored God to take me into His bosom. I no longer felt my bodily being, I was only alive. . . ."

Nevertheless, his passionate, uncontrollable flesh, his human weaknesses still held their sway: "Scarcely an hour had passed and I was almost consciously listening for the voice of sin, of ambition, the empty vanities of life. I knew where that voice came from, I knew it would destroy my happiness. I wrestled with it, and I succumbed. I dropped off to sleep, my thoughts full of glory, of women. But I am not to blame, I could not do otherwise.

"Eternal bliss *on this earth*—is impossible. Suffering—is inevitable. Why? I cannot tell. How dare I speak? I do not know. How dared I think that one can know the ways of Providence! It is the fountainhead of reason, and reason searches for Him."

He was "not to blame." Tolstoy's spiritual power, even when he was immersed in sin, lay in the fact that he never *defended sin*, never accepted it as legitimate: he chastised himself for it and the only solace he gave himself was the explanation that perhaps it was dung, which can either be filth or else enrich the soil and give life to weeds or useful plants.

These spiritual flights were so all-embracing, so overwhelming in their magnificence that he was unable to express his emotions. "Why did I write that?" he says bitterly, after he has made an attempt in his diary to describe his inner state. "How flat, limp, even pointless my feelings appear. And yet they were really so exalted! . . ."

The desire to find some artistic outlet for the reproduction of his thoughts and emotions now became more and more evident. Gradually his efforts at shaping his material became a habit.

"Just now I was lying on the ground behind the camp. It was a marvelous night. The moon was moving out from behind a hilltop and casting its rays on two tiny, thin, filmy clouds. Behind me a cricket droned his monotonous, never-ending song. At a distance one could hear a frog, while up near the Tatar *aul* there were shrill voices, the bark of a dog, then silence and again only the cricket's chirrup, while a fluffy, transparent cloud floated past stars nearby and far away. I thought to myself: I'll go write down a description of what I see. But how shall I do it? I must go sit myself down at a messy table, get out a scratch pad, ink, daub my fingers, and scrawl some letters on the sheet before me. The letters will make words, words phrases; yet can that reproduce feelings? Is it not impossible to pour into anyone else one's own reactions at the sight of nature? To de-

[51]

scribe is not enough. Why is poetry so closely tied to prose, happiness to unhappiness? How must one live? Should one try suddenly to unite with prose, or enjoy the one and then give oneself up to the satisfactions of the other?

"There is one side to contemplation that is better than reality: in reality there is a side which is better than contemplation. Complete happiness would be the union of the two."

In his diary for July 4, 1852, Tolstoy returns to these thoughts: "It seems to me that it is really impossible to *describe* a man: but I can describe the effect that he has made on me. They say of a man: he is original, kindly, intelligent, stupid, consistent, etc.—words which give no conception of a human being but which make the pretense of drawing a person whereas in reality they only mislead the reader."

He was obviously searching for an artistic medium of expression in prose, something he always admired in his favorite writers Gogol and Pushkin, who were, as he always said, his teachers: "I shall never find out where the dividing line lies between prose and poetry. . . . There is question of its existence in literature but the answer is incomprehensible. Poetry means verse. Prose is not verse, or else poetry is everything except business papers and textbooks. To be good all composition should, according to Gogol in his last novel, be a song from the soul of him who composes it. . . ."

In September of this same year he wrote home to Auntie Tanya in Yasnaya Polyana: "You have often told me that you were not in the habit of making a rough draft of your letters before writing them; I am following your example, but I am not as successful as you are because I find I often have to tear up my letters when I read them over. I do not do this out of any sense of false modesty. I am not embarrassed by mistakes in spelling, inkspots, awkward expressions; but the point is that I have not succeeded in governing my pen and my thoughts."

Two months later, on November 12, he wrote her from Tiflis, where he had gone with his brother Nikolai to take his examination for an officer's commission and assignment of post: "Do you remember, dear Auntie, the advice you once gave me, to write novels? Well, I am following it and the occupation I write you about is literary. I do not know whether what I write will ever be printed but it is a piece of work which absorbs me and in which I have progressed too far now to stop."

※ 8 ※

TOLSTOY was still a lonely man. To those around him he seemed either strange or proud and he was unable to draw close to them.

"Why is it," he wrote in his diary for May 5, 1852, "that everyone without exception, not just people I do not care for, or respect or agree with, finds himself ill at ease with me? I must be an intolerable, depressing person."

On another occasion he wrote: "Once and for all I must get used to the idea that I am an exception, that either I am ahead of my times or one of those incongruous, intransigent natures who are never content." Yet his yearning for love, for affection, sympathy, was as strong as ever and his Auntie Tanya was still the only one close to him. Perhaps it was for the very reason that he had no one else to whom he could pour out his feelings that he wrote her in somewhat exaggerated terms: "I cannot express the feeling I have for you. I am afraid you will think that I am exaggerating. Yet I am weeping bitter tears as I write you. This separation is so painful because I realize what a friend you are to me and I love you."

Dreams of a happy family were still constantly in his mind. As he was writing of his childhood and reliving it, he recalled the time when he had had a family, a home, and he dreamed of a time when there would be one at Yasnaya Polyana again, *his* family.

"I thought of the happiness awaiting me. This was how I imagined it: after a certain number of years, when I shall be neither young nor old, I shall be in Yasnaya Polyana. All my affairs will be in order, I shall have nothing to disturb or annoy me. You will be living at Yasnaya too. . . . It is a wonderful dream. . . . I shall be married; my wife will be quiet, kindly, loving, she will love you as much as I do. We shall have children, who will call you Grandmother and you will live upstairs in the big house in the same room that was my grandmother's. The whole house will be kept as it was in my father's time and we shall begin that life over again, except that we shall change roles. You will take the place of my grandmother, but you

[53]

will be a better one than she was. I shall take my father's place, although I cannot ever hope to deserve that honor. My wife will take the place of my mother, her children replace us. Masha will take over the part of the two aunts but without their sorrows. . . . There will be three new faces, who will occasionally be seen among us, they will be my brothers, especially one who will be with us often— Nikolai, an old bachelor, baldheaded, a retired officer, but always the same kind and noble person."

These were Tolstoy's daydreams at a time when he had joined the Junker Corps and was taking part in a series of military actions against the Chechen mountain tribesmen.

From his diary it is evident that Tolstoy prepared himself for danger, and even for death, on the eve of battles:

"I am indifferent to a life," he wrote before he left to join his company, "in which I have experienced too little happiness to care much about it, therefore I do not fear death. Nor do I fear suffering, yet I do fear that I shall not be able to bear suffering and death well. I am not absolutely serene and I notice this especially because I change from one frame of mind . . . to another. Strangely enough my childhood attitude toward war—one of recklessness—is still for me the most quieting. . . ."

The question not only of his conduct but also of his inner state constantly worried him: "I make an effort to imagine that I was quite cold-blooded and calm," he wrote on February 8 after a battle, "but during the battles of the 17th and 18th I was not that at all. . . . It was a unique chance to show all the power of my spirit, but I was weak and therefore dissatisfied with myself."

The pressures he put on himself, the inevitable terror that every man feels when he takes part in a battle, these he forgot. All that remained in his memory were his actions and his conduct.

Thanks to his courage, which bordered on foolhardiness, Tolstoy narrowly escaped being captured by the Chechens. This incident, with a changed ending, was described, many years later, in "A Prisoner in the Caucasus"—the story of two Russian army men captured by the Tatars.

Campaigns, card playing, hunting, women—none of them interfered with the complicated process going on inside Tolstoy, dividing and merging but always following two main courses: the perfecting of himself and creative work.

"Insofar as I can analyze myself, it seems to me that three evil passions govern me: gambling, sex and vanity. . . . The passion for gambling derives from a passion for money but mainly (and this is true especially of people who lose more than they win) what occurs is that having begun to play out of idleness, or imitation of others, or a desire to win, one does not care so much about the winning as one does for the game itself and the excitement of the sensations it causes. The source of the passion then is only habit, and the way to destroy it is to break the habit. This I have done. . . .

"Sexual passions have an entirely different basis: the more one restrains oneself the greater one's desires. There are two sources for this passion: the body and the imagination. It is easy enough to control the body but very difficult to check the imagination which acts on the body. The means to combat the one as well as the other are identical: work, occupation, both physical, such as gymnastics, and intellectual, such as writing. And yet, that is not really so. Since this craving is a natural one and I look upon it as wrong only because of my unnatural condition (being twenty-three and unmarried), there is no help except in will power and prayer to be delivered from temptation. . . . Vanity is a kind of immature love of fame, a kind of self-esteem transferred to the opinion of others—you love yourself not for what you are but for what you seem to others to be. . . . I have suffered a great deal from this passion, it has tainted the best years of my life and robbed me forever of the freshness, the boldness, the gaiety and initiative of youth. I do not know how I did it but I crushed this passion and have even fallen into its extreme opposite: I am guarded in all my expressions, I think out every move in advance for fear of lapsing back into my previous weakness. . . ."

The training of his will power, the bettering of his inner being, now went on simultaneously with his physical exercises, gymnastics and fencing. Deep thoughts alternated with trivial, almost naïve, ones in his mind; he regrets having to give his companion Sado the music box Auntie Tanya sent him, he is carried away by the good looks of a Cossack girl, he is upset because he saw the new moon over his left shoulder. . . . In working on the story of his childhood he is in the depths of despair because he thinks it is no good. Then again his mood soars and he makes a note in his diary to the effect that: "*Childhood* is an honest piece of work," or "it has some fine places in it although there are weak ones too."

He was tired by the physical work of copying his manuscript so, after doing it three times in his own hand, he turned over the final draft to a copyist. On July 3, 1852, he sent the first part of his novel *The Story of My Childhood* to Nekrasov, the editor of *The Contemporary*. The manuscript bore as signature the two letters "L. N."

"I am awaiting your verdict with impatience," he wrote Nekrasov. "It will either encourage me to go on with the work I prefer or it will cause me to burn everything I have written."

The time he had to wait for the editor's reply no doubt seemed an eternity to Tolstoy. Perhaps he tried not to think about it. His teeth ached and went bad, he had pains in his legs, his digestion was upset, he was ill. He reread Rousseau's *Confessions*, and found in it as usual many echoes to his own thoughts, and also read the *Confessions of a Savoy Vicar*. Meantime he continued writing the "Story of a Landowner" (which he afterward changed to "The Morning of a Landowner"), *Youth*, "Letter from the Caucasus" (later entitled "The Raid"), "Notes of a Billiard Marker." As always, when all his forces were concentrated on the search for truth and the inevitable transmutation of this search into artistic form, he was satisfied with himself. "I know that womenfolk are better off for not having any conception of this kind of work. But God set my feet in this path. I must follow it," he wrote in his diary for August 25, 1852.

Nekrasov, evidently, was quick to appreciate the talent of the young writer. His reply, given the slowness of postal communications by mail coach, was very prompt. On August 29 Tolstoy received the letter telling him that the story *Childhood* had been accepted: "I do not know what the continuation will be so that I cannot," wrote Nekrasov, "express myself conclusively, but it seems to me that the author has talent. . . . I beg you to send me the continuation. Both your story and your talent have aroused my interest."

"This letter from an editor . . . threw me into a daze of happiness," Tolstoy put in his diary. Thereupon, when he, as was his custom, set down his plans for the following day, he finished with the one word "write."

No one except Auntie Tanya and his brother Nikolai knew who the author of *Childhood* was when it appeared in the September issue of *The Contemporary*. But it caused a stir.

At this time Tolstoy's sister Maria was living on her estate, Pokrovskoye, in the Province of Tula and their neighbor, on the estate of Spasskoye, was Turgenyev. He was a frequent visitor at Pokrovskoye. On one occasion he brought over the September *The Con-*

temporary and proposed reading aloud the story entitled *Childhood*, written by a very talented author unknown except by the initials "L.N."

"What was our astonishment when we recognized ourselves in the principals in the story, the description of all our relatives, and those close to our home. . . . Who could have written it? Who could know all the little intimate details of our life? We were far from suspecting Lev as the author," said Maria; "we decided Nikolai must have written the story."

Nekrasov evidently not only took a detailed interest in *The Story of My Childhood* himself but he also canvassed the opinions of others in literary circles concerning the writing of "L. N."

Tolstoy then received another letter from the editor of *The Contemporary*: "I sent it [the manuscript] to be printed in the ninth issue of *The Contemporary* and when I went over it carefully in proof, and not in obscure handwriting, I found that the story is far better than it appeared on first reading. I can state firmly that the author has talent. This conviction of mine will be, for an incipient author like you, I imagine, of more importance than anything else at the present time." Then Nekrasov asked him to tell the name of the author.

Thanks to his disorganized life, losing money at cards, Tolstoy was always in need of cash and was much disappointed not to be paid for *The Story of My Childhood*: "Praise, but no money," he jotted down in his diary. In a letter dated October 30 Nekrasov told Tolstoy that the rule of the magazine was not to pay for the first contribution but that all subsequent writings they published would be paid for at their highest rate, which was fifty silver rubles for each printed page.

The literary circles of St. Petersburg were in an uproar. Panayev, one of the contributors to *The Contemporary*, went from house to house to read bits from *The Story of My Childhood* to his friends. "All his friends are dodging Panayev, even on the Nevski Prospect," said Turgenyev, "for fear that even on the street he will stop them to listen to him read from *The Story of My Childhood*."

"His is a definite talent," wrote Turgenyev to Nekrasov. "Drop him a line and urge him to go on writing. Tell him, if it would interest him, that I salute him, send him my greetings and applause."

There were laudatory reviews in many magazines. "If this is the first piece of writing of Mr. L. N.," ran an article in *Fatherland Notes,* "we have to congratulate Russian literature on the emergence of a new and remarkable talent."

Dostoyevski was in exile at the time. *The Story of My Childhood* made a strong impression on him and he begged one of his friends to find out without fail who "the mysterious L. N." was.

While these two modest initials were exciting Russian literary lights and causing discussion and speculation as to the identity of the mysterious new talent that had so unexpectedly appeared in their midst, the lonely, unsociable Junker Corps cadet "L. N." continued his isolated, primitive existence, taking part in military activities, carousing, gambling with his fellow officers and finding some respite in hunting. Outwardly nothing seemed to be altered in the life of the young Junker, but actually something had occurred which was to change not only the whole course of his life but which was to give to Russia, and indeed to world literature, one of the greatest geniuses of human thought and creative accomplishment. One finds it difficult to speculate on what Tolstoy, diffident and unsure of his own gifts, would have made of his life had the editor of *The Contemporary* not judged him according to his merits.

From the very instant that he was recognized as a writer Tolstoy threw himself into "composing." He felt himself already a full-fledged writer. He peremptorily demanded that Nekrasov should not cut or revise his text. New subjects for stories flooded his brain, new and vivid images took shape, thoughts took on sequence and definition. . . . His restless soul acquired a new form. From this time forward he was to chafe under his military obligations. He wanted to be free, to write, and moreover he was yearning for his beloved Yasnaya Polyana.

On July 20, 1853, he wrote to his brother Sergei: "I think I have already written you that I handed in my resignation. But God only knows whether it will be accepted because of the war with Turkey. This disturbs me very much because I have already accustomed myself to the happy thought of moving soon to the country. If I have to go back now to Starogladkovskaya and wait around for an eternity—the way I had to wait for everything in my present position—it would be highly unpleasant."

It was "unpleasant" too that Tolstoy still did not have the officer's commission which should have been his. The obstacle lay in the fact that when he set off so suddenly for the Caucasus with his brother

Nikolai, he had left all his papers in Yasnaya Polyana. He was galled too because he had not received the St. George's Cross: "I always miss out on whatever I undertake," he wrote to his Auntie Tanya as early as June, 1852. "During the campaign I might have been recommended on two occasions for the St. George's Cross, but I was kept from getting it because that confounded document was several days late. . . ."

There were two other occasions when Tolstoy might have been given the St. George's Cross. But once he stepped aside in favor of an old soldier and the second time he was under arrest for failure to be on guard duty and the commanding officer refused to give the cross to such an incorrigible young man.

But in addition to lack of success in his military career Tolstoy had more serious worries: his gambling debts tormented him and he decided to pay them by selling off part of his inheritance. On his order a village, contiguous with Yasnaya Polyana and containing "twenty-six male souls," was disposed of.

From time to time he was troubled by bad health and used to take the waters at Kislovodsk, Zheleznovodsk, Piatigorsk. At this last watering place he joined his sister Maria and her husband Valerian.

His external worries and disappointments did not suffice, however, to keep him from writing. He worked hard on *Youth*. At times he would be in despair because the story was "not good for anything" and then he would get a fresh start. He wrote and sent "The Raid" to Nekrasov, he worked on "Christmas Night," making a tentative outline for it. The theme was the undoing of an innocent, confused youth and his unhappy end, and it turned up in another story—"The Notes of a Billiard Marker." He invented a whole series of stories on soldiering in the Caucasus: "The Felling of the Forest," "A Meeting While on Duty," and others.

"How much social intercourse and books can mean," Tolstoy wrote in his diary for August 4. "According to whether they are good or bad you are an entirely different person."

He was reading a great deal: his favorite Rousseau, Pushkin, Lermontov, Turgenyev. But the Caucasus weighed down his spirits; he was "unbearably bored," so he wrote his brother Sergei. In June, 1853, Russia declared war on Turkey. Tolstoy was not permitted to resign but he was able to arrange his transfer to the Army of the Danube. Nevertheless he felt that the two and a half years spent in the Caucasus had been of great significance to him. Despite what he called his "downfalls," which distracted him from his prime purpose in life—to progress on his way to self-improvement—he recognized, as he later wrote to his friend and cousin Alexandra A. Tolstoy, that "never either before or afterward, did I reach such heights of thought, without looking *beyond*, as I did during that span of two years. And everything that I discovered at that time has remained firmly rooted in my convictions."

$$ \text{ꝏ } 9 \text{ ꝏ} $$

SHORTLY after the declaration of war on Turkey, Admiral Nakhimov, a famous Russian hero, destroyed the Turkish fleet.

England and France could not countenance Russian domination over Turkey and the Black Sea, so they launched the famous Crimean campaign and Sevastopol was besieged by French and English troops. The heroic defense of the city lasted for eleven months.

In the artillery forces defending Sevastopol was Lev Tolstoy, newly commissioned as second lieutenant.

Before proceeding to the Danube, however, he went first to Yasnaya Polyana to see his sister, his brothers and Auntie Tatiana Alexandrovna.

The journey of some fifteen hundred miles from the south of Russia to the central provinces toward the end of January was not an easy undertaking. The beaten road, marked only by posts a verst apart amid the snowdrifts, was often quite obliterated. Many travelers, overtaken by blizzards, lost their bearings, missed the highway, and wandered off. Some, when their strength failed, were frozen to death out in the open fields.

It took Tolstoy two weeks to reach Yasnaya Polyana.

"I floundered around for a whole night," he wrote in his diary at one of the post stations, "and that was how the idea came to me for writing 'The Blizzard' (January 27, 1854).

"The snow whirled around in front of me and on the sides, burying the runners; the horses' legs were up to and over their knees in snow. . . ." he wrote. "It grew frightfully cold and if I so much as stuck my face out of my collar the icy snow would whirl into my eyelashes, my nose, my mouth, slipping down into my neck. Everything was white, bright and all snow; there was nothing to be seen but a lowering light and snow. I was seriously alarmed." Tolstoy wandered around all night and it was only toward morning that his post troika by a sort of miracle beat its way to the station.

In the two and a half years that Tolstoy had been "outside of Russia," as they used to say in speaking of the Caucasus, he had grown up both outwardly and inwardly. He said of himself in his diary for February 4: "The main deficiency of my character and its peculiarity consists of the fact that I have been morally too young for too long. It is only now, at the age of twenty-five, that I am beginning to acquire an independent viewpoint toward things—that of a man—which others acquire at a much earlier age, at twenty."

For his Aunt Tatiana Alexandrovna the arrival of her favorite member of the family was a source of long-awaited joy. Great changes had taken place in him since they had seen each other. Yet some of his strange fancies, such as his attitude toward the peasants and his desire to free them, frightened her. Her love made her feel instinctively that he had something out of the ordinary in him. But what? Try as she would she could not fathom his depths. And he, on his return, seemed somehow disappointed in her.

During the short period of his leave Tolstoy wished to see everyone and to put his affairs in order. He went over to see his sister Maria Nikolayevna at her estate Pokrovskoye, where she lived with her husband and children. He saw his brothers, who had gathered in Yasnaya Polyana, and he went up to Moscow with them. Before he went away he finally cleared up all his affairs, made his will and early in March, 1854, he left for the front.

Tolstoy remained in the army of the Danube until November. But in the interim they moved him around from one point to another, from Bucharest to a small town called Oltenitza, then back to Bucharest, where he was assigned to the commander of the artillery forces. Finally, toward the end of June, he was to take part in the storming of the fortress Silistria under the command of Prince Gorchakov.

The turbulent life in the army was not conducive to literary accomplishment. It was only in April that he was able to finish *Boyhood* and send it off to Nekrasov.

For nearly three months Tolstoy made no entries in his diary. This was in itself always a sign of a depressed mood. His surroundings, cards, his unsatisfied sex passions, his yearning for family life tormented him, pushed him to do things for which he despised himself and for which he atoned. He was ill, restless, and at times reduced to despair.

In addition to his own worries he was concerned over the state of the Russian army. With his characteristically keen powers of observation he could not fail to note the mistakes of the command, the black ignorance of the soldiers, the dissipation of the officers. Yet he had had scarcely time to look around when these same surroundings, with all the coarseness and laxity which he despised, began to suck him in.

The bravery and self-sacrifice of the Russian troops excited his admiration, but their lack of organization and discipline undermined and nullified all their efforts. Why was the storming of the fortress of Silistria ordered and then suddenly countermanded? In letters to his Auntie Tatiana and to his brother Nikolai he wrote:

"Some five hundred pieces opened fire against the fort to be captured and the shooting continued all through the night. It was a spectacle and a sensation one could never forget. Toward evening the Prince and his suite arrived to enter the trenches and take personal charge of the storming, which was set for three in the morning.

"We were all there and, as usual on the eve of a battle, we pretended that we thought no more of the coming day than of any ordinary day. Yet I am sure that all of us felt a little, perhaps even a great, tightening at the bottom of our hearts when we thought of the attack. As you know, Nikolai, the lull before action is always the hardest to bear, it is the only time when there is room to be afraid and fear is one of the most unpleasant emotions. Toward morning, as the hour of decision neared, the sense of fear faded and at almost three o'clock, when we were waiting to catch sight of the rockets sent up as signal for the attack, I was in such an excellent mood that if someone had told me the attack would not take place I should have been sorry. And then, just an hour before the time set to storm the fort, an adjutant arrived from the Field Marshal with the order to raise the siege of Silistria.

"I can state without fear of contradiction that this decision was looked upon by everyone—soldiers, officers, generals—as a genuine misfortune, especially as we knew from numerous scouts arriving from inside Silistria, people I myself talked to often, that we could take the fort and that no one doubted that Silistria was bound to fall at the latest in two or three days."

Having begun again to make entries in his diary Tolstoy renewed his pitiless self-flagellation, exposing from every angle what seemed to him his own shortcomings:

"July 7. There is no modesty in me! That is my great failing. After all, who am I? One of four sons of a retired colonel, left an orphan at the age of seven in the care of women and strangers, possessing neither a scientific nor social training, having been turned loose in the world at the age of seventeen without any great fortune, without any social position and, above all, without any rules of conduct. I am a man who has completely muddled his affairs, has squandered the best years of his life without aim or satisfaction, who finally exiled himself to the Caucasus to escape his debts and especially his habits. . . . Yes, that sums up my position in life. Now let's see what my personal qualifications are.

"I am ugly, sloppy and socially inept. I am irritable, a bore to others, immodest, intolerant and as bashful as a child—I am practically an ignoramus. What knowledge I possess I acquired somehow or other by myself, in snatches, without coherence or reason, and there is so little of it.—I lack restraint, decisiveness, constancy, I am foolishly vain and impetuous, like all who have no character. I am not brave. I lack order in my life and am so lazy that loafing has become for me a habit I can scarcely shake off.—I am intelligent but my brain has never been thoroughly tried out. I have no intelligence for practical, worldly or business matters. I am honest, by which I mean I love goodness, have made it my custom to love it and whenever I veer away from it I am dissatisfied with myself, I return to it with joy, yet there are things I value above goodness—fame, for one instance. I am so ambitious, and this sense in me has received so little satisfaction that often I fear, should I have to make a choice between fame and goodness, I would choose the former.

"Yes, I am not modest; for that reason I am proud inside myself and bashful and shy in society."

So, in quest of surcease, he turned to God with this fervent prayer:

"I believe in one all-powerful and good God, in the immortality of the soul and in the eternal retribution for our acts on earth; I long to believe in the religion of my forefathers and to respect it. Grant me a firm faith and hope in Thee, loving others and beloved of them, with a serene conscience and with benefit to my neighbor let me live and die" (diary for July 13, 1854).

But there was no surcease. He wrote little, without zest, he felt stale, his spirit was clouded by trivial everyday interests, his passions overwhelmed him. Dully and senselessly he repeated over and over this one phrase in his diary: "The most important thing for me is to rid myself of laziness, irritability and lack of character."

On the eve of Sevastopol, when military events and the fate of the city drew his thoughts away from himself, he once more felt a surge of patriotism and uneasiness over the outcome of the war, and the lot of the Russian forces. On September 21 he wrote in his diary: "In Sevastopol the decision hangs by a hair. . . . I lost all my money at cards. *Above all in life I must cure myself of laziness, lack of character and irritability.*"

Try as we may we cannot fathom all of Tolstoy's inner experiences. It would be all too easy to draw false conclusions from the apparently muddle-headed contradictions, clashes, convictions that overwhelm each other. One thing we can do and that is to follow attentively the steps of his long hard struggle.

The surroundings made his life difficult: any man who has been in the army knows the torture of having to pass time in inaction, in anticipation of battle, and how demoralizing this is to human beings. In such circumstances Tolstoy's writing proved his salvation.

Toward the end of August he had received a letter from Nekrasov which again offered encouragement to him as a writer. Nekrasov wrote that he "could not find adequate expressions with which to praise *Boyhood*." This praise heartened Tolstoy, although he continued to be a harsh, ruthless critic of his own work. As was always his custom, he rewrote the "Notes of a Noncommissioned Officer" many times, and later changed the title to "The Felling of the Forest." On re-reading *Childhood* he was dissatisfied with it. He made a note in his diary that it had "many weak spots," and if it had not already been printed he would undoubtedly have rewritten it from beginning to end. He never could write anything straightway in final form. His first draft was a hurried jotting down of just the fundamental theme. The working out of it, the polishing of the language, the pointing up—these were all subsequent stages in his work.

"One must always reject the idea of writing without correction. Three or four drafts are not enough," he wrote in his diary on October 8, 1852, and the longer he wrote the more severely painstaking became his attitude toward his work. In the manuscripts of this early period there are already signs of assiduous, detailed work—inserts in the margins, between lines, changes of title, ruthless cutting of parts which for any reason did not fit in with the course of the storytelling: "No brilliant inserts can improve a composition as much as cutting" (diary for October 16, 1853).

Tolstoy's contact with simple soldiers, his study of their psychology, their capacity for heroic self-sacrifice, turned his thoughts to their development. This was interwoven in his imagination with the idea of arousing the patriotic spirit of the army. In co-operation with a group of educated officers, Tolstoy organized a society for the extension of education among the troops. Their first decision was to publish a magazine to contain articles "descriptive of battles, but not dry false acounts as in other publications, stories of heroic feats, obituaries of worth-while men, mostly of the common people, army tales and soldiers' songs."

They resolved to apply to the Tsar for permission to print such a magazine.

Whenever Tolstoy had an idea he was impelled to put it into effect at once, no matter what the obstacles in the way. As for the question of where to get money for the magazine, this was not long a stumbling block. One wing of the house at Yasnaya Polyana was quite sufficient for Auntie Tatiana's and his needs. He must have money for his gambling debts, of which he was most anxious to rid himself, so why not sell the large, wooden house with columns, in which he was born? He wrote to his brother-in-law, Vaḷ̣rian, requesting him to arrange the sale. Later on he often regretted this act but at the time the publication of this army magazine seemed imperative. . . .

To idle away his time in the army of the Danube, when the main military action was centered in the Crimea, grew intolerable to Tolstoy. He burned to get into the fight and made every effort to be transferred to Sevastopol.

Early in November his wishes finally met with fulfillment. He was transferred to the second battery of a light artillery brigade in Sevastopol.

❧ 10 ❧

I T WAS November 7 when Tolstoy reached Sevastopol.
"The sun was shining and stood high over the bay, with its
warm, bright rays playing over the ships at anchor and the moving
sails and small craft. A light breeze softly stirred the sere leaves on
the branches of the oaks near the Post Office, swelled the sails and
ruffled the waves. Sevastopol was still the same, with its unfinished
church, the column, the quay, with its little deep blue coves crammed
with masts, the picturesque arches of the aqueduct." This was
Tolstoy's description in his *Sevastopol in August, 1855,* of that
unique city, the best Russian port on the Black Sea, with its great
natural harbor. This fortress, the pride and support of Russia, was
now faltering under the assault of the French and British fleet.

Arrived in the Crimea, Tolstoy was carried away more strongly
than ever by an emotion of patriotism.

"The city is besieged on the one side, the south, on which we had
no fortifications of any kind when the enemy approached," he wrote
his brother Sergei on November 20. . . . "The spirit in the ranks
beggars all description. Not even in ancient Greece was there ever
such heroism. When Kornilov rode through the troops, instead of
the usual salute he said: 'You will have to die, boys, die!' And the
troops yelled back: 'We will die, Your Excellency, hooray!!' And
this was not said for effect. On the face of every one of the men
you could see he was not joking but in real earnest, and 22,000 have
already kept their word."

Here as in the army of the Danube Tolstoy was witness to the
incomparable capacity for self-sacrifice of the Russian soldiers; he
saw officers, at another time drunk, dissipated and profligate, ready to
perform deeds of heroism, to do their duty in critical moments
without reflection; he found that "in the soul of each one there is
that noble spark which makes a hero of him. . . ." (*Sevastopol in
August*). By contrast he was horrified by the sloth and ignorance of
those who relied not on themselves but on St. Nicholas the Wonder-

worker. Thousands died because of poorly laid plans, carelessness, and negligence of their commanders.

"On the 16th I rode out of Sevastopol to my post," he wrote in his diary for November 23 from Simferopol, Eski-Orda. "On this ride I became more than ever convinced that Russia must either collapse or else be completely transformed. Everything is topsy-turvy, nothing is done to keep the enemy from reinforcing his camp, although it would be extraordinarily easy to do so. Yet we, with a smaller force and no expectation of help, with generals like Gorchakov who have lost their senses, their feelings and their enterprise, we do nothing to strengthen ourselves, we face the enemy and wait for the storms and bad weather which Nicholas the Wonderworker is to send to rout the foe. The Cossacks prefer looting to fighting, the Hussars and Uhlans fancy that military dignity is compatible with drunkenness and dissipation, and the ranks with thieving and moneymaking. It is a sad situation—in both the army and the state. I spent two hours chatting with wounded French and Englishmen. Each man had pride in his position and self-respect because he felt that he was an actual spring in the machinery of the army. Good weapons, skill in their handling, youth, a general notion of politics and the arts give him a consciousness of his own dignity. With us our senseless training in holding and carrying arms, our useless weapons, oppression, age, lack of education, poor maintenance and food, tend to destroy all respect, every last spark of pride, and even give our troops too high an opinion of the enemy."

Once Tolstoy realized what the situation was, his concern for the Russian soldiery made him want to contribute to raising their cultural level, but it was not so easy to introduce changes. The magazine he had proposed was banned by the Tsar. "The idea of a magazine did not meet with the views of the government—and the Emperor rejected it," wrote Tolstoy with bitterness to his Auntie Tatiana on January 6, 1855. "This failure, I confess to you, has been a source of great grief to me and has changed my plans. If, God willing, the Crimean campaign is crowned with success, and if I do not get a satisfactory position, and if there is no war inside Russia, I shall leave the army and go to St. Petersburg to the Military Academy. This plan occurred to me . . . because I do not want to give up writing, which I cannot pursue in this camp life of mine."

Cards, reading, attempts to translate a ballad by Heine, the composition in snatches of an outline for a novel, *The Russian Landowner*

—these occupied his time. But in addition Tolstoy undertook something entirely unsuited to him: a project for the reorganization of the army.

The death of Nicholas I on February 18, the oath to the new Tsar Alexander II, stirred all Russia, causing great excitement in the army.

"Great changes are in the making for Russia," Tolstoy wrote on March 1 in his diary. "We must take heart and make an effort to participate in these important hours in the life of Russia." Nor was he mistaken in his prophecy; Russia did enter a new era with the accession of the young Tsar to the throne. The question of the serfdom of the peasants had been maturing in the minds of the educated classes and now was pressed forward for solution. The repressive policy of Nicholas I after he put down the revolutionary rising of the Decembrists still agitated the minds of Russians. The literary circles of Russia enjoyed an ever-growing influence on society, writers were listened to, their works eagerly read.

Tolstoy found his military project hard sledding, his gambling debts tormented him and so he turned again for salvation to abstract religious questions. "I have just been to communion," was the entry in his diary for March 4. "Yesterday a conversation on the subject of divinity and faith put me on the track of a great, a tremendous idea to the realization of which I felt I could dedicate my whole life. This idea is the founding of a new religion, corresponding to man's development, the religion of Christ, but cleansed of faith and mystery, a practical religion making no promises of future bliss but producing it on earth. To bring such an idea into execution would, I realize, necessarily be the work of generations toiling consciously toward that goal. One generation would pass the idea on to the next and someday fanaticism or reason will fulfill the task. To work *consciously* for the union of men with religion, that is the fundamental idea which, so I hope, will absorb me."

It was as if this thought of God, together with bitter repentance, purified him; with a spurt of energy he began once more to write. He wrote *Youth* and almost simultaneously he conceived the stories about Sevastopol.

"An army career is not for me, and the sooner I extricate myself from it so that I can devote myself entirely to literature, the better it will be." Flattering comments on his "Notes of a Billiard Marker" gave him further encouragement to write.

On April 7, 1855, Tolstoy was transferred to the Fourth Bastion.

[68]

All around him shells were bursting, cannon were thundering, men were dying—but Tolstoy went on writing. From his pen, one after the other, came terrifying pictures of the wounded, the dead, of self-sacrificing heroism, of understanding and spiritual magnificence on the part of the soldiers, and, side by side with this, of their impenetrable ignorance. The Fourth Bastion! Could anyone who had not been there give such living descriptions of that dreadful spot?

"If to your question of where he is stationed a young officer answers: the Fourth Bastion, you will inevitably look more closely and even with a certain respect at this fair-haired young man when he pronounces those words 'the Fourth Bastion.' . . . It makes you want to go to the Bastion . . . and particularly the Fourth Bastion, about which you have had so many and varied reports. . . ."

Tolstoy lived for six weeks in the Fourth Bastion.

"You hear the crash of a shell and it seems not far from you, and all around you seem to hear a variety of noises of bullets, some humming like bees, others whistling, fast ones or droning ones like a string on an instrument—you hear the terrifying boom of cannon, it makes you shudder and seems somehow especially terrible.

"So this is it, this is the Fourth Bastion, that dreadful, truly terrifying place! You think of yourself, and a little feeling of pride as well as a great sense of suppressed fear runs through you. But I must disillusion you: this is not the Fourth Bastion yet. This is the Yazonovski Redoubt, a relatively safe and not at all terrifying spot."

It is impossible to believe that men do not experience fear during a battle. But despite fear some can summon within themselves a hidden strength. Tolstoy was not only an active artillery officer but also a psychologist and observer. By describing everyone he saw and everything he heard he distracted his thoughts from the danger around him. "I am writing a lot about that same Fourth Bastion, which I begin to like. I have now finished *Sevastopol by Day and by Night* and have written some on *Youth.* The constant fascination of danger and the observations I can make of the soldiers with whom I live, and the sailors, and even the whole war way of life is so agreeable that I do not want to leave here, especially as I should like to be at the storming if it comes off" (diary).

His exalted spirits, the power of his inspiration, his love for and delight in the Russian soldiers—all this was poured out.

"The principal and consoling conviction which we took away," says Tolstoy in winding up his story, *Sevastopol in December, 1854,* "is the conviction that it is quite impossible to shake the strength of the Russian people. . . . You see this clearly when you realize that these people you have just had before your eyes are those very heroes whose spirits in times of stress did not fall but rose, who prepared themselves with delight to die not for a city but for their country. For a long time Russia will feel the magnificent impact of this epic of Sevastopol, the heroes of which were the Russian people. . . ."

It is possible to understand that Tolstoy could write military stories while he was in the Fourth Bastion, but that he could carry his thoughts back to the peaceful life of his early youth and write *Youth* is more difficult to grasp.

"This is the same bastion," he noted in his diary for April 14, "where I am in such capital form. Yesterday I finished a chapter of *Youth* and it is not at all bad. Generally speaking my work on *Youth* is now going to engross me by the delightful fact of its being a piece of work already begun and almost half finished. Right now I am preparing a chapter on haying. I shall work over *Sevastopol,* and begin a story about a soldier and how he was killed.—Oh Lord, I am grateful, I am grateful to Thee for Thy never-failing protection. How surely Thou leadest me toward the good. And what a worthless creature I should be if Thou shouldst forsake me. Do not forsake me, O Lord. Encourage me along my way, not to satisfy my trivial ambitions but to strive toward that eternal and high goal in life which I do not see but of which I am conscious."

The literary world instantly recognized the merits of the Sevastopol stories.

"Tolstoy's story on Sevastopol is a miracle!" Turgenyev wrote from Spasskoye to Panayev on July 10, 1855. "My eyes were moist as I read it and I exclaimed: Bravo! I am flattered by his desire to dedicate his new sketch to me. Tolstoy's story has caused a general sensation here. . . ."

Sevastopol in December drew the attention of the court of Alexander II. It was said that the Tsarina Alexandra Fyodorovna wept when she read it and that the Tsar had ordered the story translated into French.

"I received a letter and my story from Panayev," Tolstoy entered in his journal for June 15. "I am puffed up to hear it was read to the Emperor."

By this time Tolstoy was already in Belbek where he had been transferred on May 19 for the formation of a mountain platoon.

His descriptions of military events, his psychological analyses of types among soldiers and officers—the mixture in them of slovenliness and strict sense of duty, cowardliness and unlimited valor—gave proof of his fine power of observation and deep understanding of the Russian soldier. For the first time, the gray masses of officers and men—cannon fodder—are brought to life and the reader, despite himself, comes to care about the fate of these Ivans and Pyotrs, he begins to share their sufferings and joys, to live with them.

But what did these soldiers and officers think of Tolstoy? For them he was a man of vagaries, an aristocrat, but simple and understanding, a good comrade.

"By his tales, his faculty for whipping up verses, Tolstoy enlivened one and all in difficult moments of their Army experiences," wrote one of his comrades in arms at Sevastopol (V. N. Nazaryev, "Life and People of Other Days," published in the *Historical Herald* for November, 1900). "He was, in the fullest sense of the word, the life of the battery. Tolstoy was with us and we did not realize how time flew, and there was no end to the fun. . . . But when the Count would be absent, when he would ride off to Simferopol, all spirits sank. One day would drag by, a second, a third. . . . Finally he would come back . . . just exactly like some prodigal son—despondent, with a drawn face, disgusted with himself. . . . He would take me off to one side and then his remorse would set in. He would tell me everything: about how dissipated he had been, about gambling, where he had spent his days and nights, and meanwhile, would you believe it, he tortured and punished himself as if he were an actual criminal. It was even pitiful to see him, he was so consumed with grief. . . . That is the kind of a man he was. In short he was strange and, to tell the truth, not quite comprehensible to me. But on the other side he was a rare comrade, the soul of honesty, and a man one could certainly not forget."

In those days Tolstoy was phenomenally powerful; he loved this physical strength and prowess in himself and developed it. He despised weak, flabby, cowardly men. He was tall, straight, magnificently proportioned; he held up his head with its broad high forehead, clean-cut chin and wavy hair.

Panayev wrote Tolstoy that all Russia was reading his stories. One comment was: "The article is written with such a degree of unrelenting honesty that it is awful to read."

[71]

Thus the artillery lieutenant, Lev Tolstoy, brought the horrors, the sufferings of war into the comfortable drawing rooms of Moscow and St. Petersburg; he made people from the Emperor down shudder, weep, laugh. . . .

On July 27 the Military Council decided to offer a conclusive battle to the enemy along the Black River. Thanks to the high command's irresponsibility and lack of organization, or perhaps because of the numerical preponderance of the enemy, the Russian attack was beaten back and the Russians suffered tremendous losses. Tolstoy did not take part in this engagement, but its lack of success had a depressing effect on him.

The matter was discussed among officers, who criticized the actions of individual generals. They poked sly fun at them and with the help of Tolstoy's sharply satiric humor they put all this into a song. He read the verses, rewrote them, someone fitted a tune to them, and picked out an accompaniment on the piano. With lightning speed the song spread through the officers' corps; other variations were added to this remarkable collective creation. It was an extremely bold thing in those days to mock at the high command, generals and grand dukes, and in the last variation of the song they all came in for their share.

Tolstoy's part in the composing of the ditty did not further his career. But it is not likely that he thought of this.

In August the Russian forces, after eleven months of heroic defense, surrendered Sevastopol. The forces were ordered to retreat. "The French flag was already flying from the Malakhov heights."

"The Sevastopol garrison, like an ocean in a dark and turbulent night, flowed and ebbed and broke in all its great mass, surging along the harbor over the bridge, along the North Side, slowly pushing through the impenetrable dark away from the place where they were leaving behind so many brave brothers—from the place all drenched with their blood, from the place where for eleven months they had held off an enemy twice their size and to whom now they were ordered to surrender without a blow.

"On reaching the other side of the bridge nearly every soldier took off his cap and crossed himself. Yet behind that impulse lay something else—a heavy, engulfing, deeper emotion, something akin to remorse, to shame and anger. Nearly every soldier as he looked to the north side of abandoned Sevastopol heaved a sigh from the unutterable bitterness in his heart and voiced a threat to his enemies." These last lines were written at the end of December when Tolstoy had already reached St. Petersburg.

❧ 11 ❧

"LEV N. TOLSTOY has arrived," wrote Nekrasov to Botkin on November 14. "What a pleasant person, and what a mind! He is a pleasant, energetic, noble-minded young man—a young falcon! Perhaps even an eagle! He impressed me as being even better than his writings and they are very good. . . . He is not handsome, but has a most agreeable face, full of energy and at the same time of gentleness and good nature. Whatever his looks I quite liked him" (*The Press and the Revolution*, 1928).

This twenty-seven-year-old eagle, set free after four and a half years of army service, swept around St. Petersburg like a hurricane, reveling in his position of a recognized author, delighting in intelligent conversation, alternately shy, embarrassed, hurt, and throwing the proper denizens of St. Petersburg into a state of alarm by the sharpness, the daring of his unexpected views, contravening as they did the truths generally accepted.

In an apparent effort to make up for lost opportunities he rushed from place to place. He spent his time in literary circles, in drawing rooms, enjoying the company of beautiful and intelligent women. He went to plays and concerts, mostly of serious music; for nights on end he caroused with gypsies. . . .

He stayed with Turgenyev, who received the young writer with open arms. But they both very soon realized how at variance their characters were. Turgenyev, somewhat sentimental, of a Western European cast, moderate in his habits, looked with concern at Tolstoy who, with his tumultuous many-sided nature, did not fit into any frame.

"Tolstoy is visiting me," Turgenyev wrote P. V. Annenkov. "You cannot imagine what a pleasant and remarkable person he is—

although his savage ardor and stubbornness have made me dub him a troglodyte. I have come to love him with a strange emotion rather like that of a father. He read us the beginning of his story *Youth* and also the beginning of another novel—they are magnificent."

But Tolstoy had no need of Turgenyev's paternal tutelage, and Turgenyev realized that it was impossible to tame the "troglodyte."

In January, 1856, this carefree, gay life suddenly came to an end. He received word from Orel that his brother Dmitri, to whom he had scarcely given a thought, was dying of tuberculosis. The journey down to him was a painful one.

"I was particularly repulsive at that moment," Tolstoy wrote in his memoirs. "I reached Orel from St. Petersburg, where I had been going around in society, full of empty vanity. I was sorry for Dmitri, but not much. I turned my back on Orel and left. He died a few days later" (Biryukov).

Why did Tolstoy leave without waiting for the end? Could it be that he did not realize how ill Dmitri was? Perhaps the surroundings in which his brother was living were intolerable to him? Tolstoy loved his brother Dmitri and valued his spiritual qualities very highly. Dmitri had always been peculiar, unlike anyone else, but toward the end he had gone to pieces, did nothing, and took to drink. Now he was dying of tuberculosis and was being cared for by a pock-marked prostitute called Masha whose freedom he had bought from a brothel and whom he had taken to live with him.

"He was dreadful to see," wrote Tolstoy. "His enormous hand was attached to the two bones of his forearm, his face was all eyes, and they, which had been so beautiful, so serious, were now all puffy. He never stopped coughing or spitting and he did not want to die." Perhaps the presence of the woman, a stranger, made it difficult for Lev to express to Dmitri those things which it is sometimes so necessary to speak of when a loved one is on the threshold of a new world. It had been only a short time before that he had written (March 13, 1954. *Complete Works,* jubilee edition):

"I have a picture of you now before me to which I am saying in my thoughts so many sincere and friendly things which for some reason I do not seem to write or even say to you when we meet. But I trust that you yourself know that I love you very much."

When he heard of Dmitri's death on February 2 he wrote in his diary: "Brother Dmitri is dead, I have just heard. From tomorrow

[74]

on I want to pass these days in such a way that it will be easy to look back on them."

But when he returned to St. Petersburg he plunged into the same old life. At that time all the literary lights in that city clustered around *The Contemporary*, just as in Moscow they clustered around *The Fatherland Journal*.

The Contemporary had been started in 1836 and one of its founders was A. S. Pushkin. Later on Nekrasov and Panayev bought it; all the best writers contributed to it and it rose rapidly to prominence.

It is probable that these writers did not realize their own significance in creating a whole era of Russian literature, Russian culture. They had been brought up on Western European literature, they had absorbed the power and sweep of the poetry of Pushkin, Lermontov, Griboyedov, the bold keen mind of Gogol. Yet each went his own way describing the life he knew best, creating new characters, types, working out his own individual style. . . . No one of them imitated another. Goncharov, Druzhinin, Pisemski, Nekrasov—they were all writers with great reputations, but the one considered the most distinguished was Ivan Turgenyev.

Tolstoy as a newcomer in the literary world was scrutinized, listened to. "This slip of an officer will gobble us all up," said Pisemski of Tolstoy (*Biographic Survey*, I. F. Gorbunov, A. F. Koni). Turgenyev early discovered that the young writer did not need his patronage. Gradually, without realizing himself what he was doing, the second lieutenant of artillery, with his Junker manners, as Turgenyev described them, edged the older man into a secondary position. For all his good breeding and impartiality Turgenyev found this hard to stomach.

Tolstoy was young, ardent, sharp, intolerant of any and all conventions. Turgenyev was shocked by his ill-conceived opinions, which ran counter to tradition, and sometimes even to common decency. "Not a word, not a gesture of his is natural," he said (*Golova-chova-Panyayeva Memoirs*). "He is forever posing in front of us and I am at a loss to understand how an intelligent man can have in him such stupid arrogance because of a shabby title of Count.

"You can soak a Russian officer in lye for three days but you won't soak out his Junker arrogance: no matter what veneer of culture you apply on the surface of your subject his bestiality is still bound to show through."

Meanwhile Tolstoy, sensing the patronizing "paternal" tone of Turgenyev, acted like a naughty boy who has slipped his bonds; he maliciously and persistently contradicted all and sundry, and he nettled his fellow writers by expressing opinions which threw even his own partisans into complete consternation.

Nekrasov, Panayev and others realized that Turgenyev was perhaps unconsciously suffering from a feeling of jealousy. They defended Tolstoy but even they were horrified when he, at a supper given by the editorial staff of *The Contemporary* where Turgenyev and other warm admirers of George Sand were present, took the opportunity to make an attack on the French novelist. L. V. Grigorovich, who had come to the supper with Tolstoy, tried to restrain him, but to no avail. For the first half of the evening Tolstoy had behaved himself with propriety and held his tongue, but toward the end of the supper he broke loose. Having heard the praise heaped on a new novel by George Sand he abruptly expressed himself as hating her and added that "the heroines of her novels, if indeed they really existed, should be, for the sake of public edification, put on the whipping block, exposed to the view of all St. Petersburg" (Biryukov).

Turgenyev was outraged and wrote an indignant letter to Botkin: "I nearly had a row with Tolstoy. No, my friend, such lack of education is bound to make itself felt. The day before yesterday, when we were dining at Nekrasov's, he expressed himself with a vulgarity and coarseness I cannot reproduce. The discussion went to great lengths—in short he upset everyone and made a poor spectacle of himself" (Correspondence between V. I. Botkin and I. S. Turgenyev).

But Tolstoy continued to outrage *The Contemporary*. "You would have heard your fill of marvels!" said Panayev to an acquaintance. "You would have discovered that Shakespeare is an ordinary hack writer, that our admiration for and delight in Shakespeare are nothing more than a desire to keep up with others and our habit of parroting their opinions. . . . Yes, this is very strange! The man does not wish to recognize any traditions, either theoretic or historic!"

Evidently Tolstoy's opinions were looked upon as merely a desire to cut a figure, to be original. As a matter of fact Tolstoy never did care for Shakespeare. In those early years he may not have analyzed his attitude sufficiently but later on, in his essay on Shakespeare written in 1903, he produced serious critical conclusions.

From his earliest childhood Tolstoy was impervious to generally accepted opinion. "Everyone thinks this, everyone does that" was never a law to him.

He was often impatient, almost rude, and, when carried away, would lose his customary shyness, say unpleasant things which he afterward regretted. In his quieter moments he realized that his harsh attacks were incapable of convincing people. In his notebook he wrote on December 3, 1856: "God forbid that one make a direct attack [on another person] any more than one would break open a cocoon and leave the worm naked; a worm must be fed until he outgrows his cocoon and sheds it of his own accord when he has already become a butterfly."

Although many were offended and estranged by Tolstoy, others loved him and forgave him his violent attacks: "Tolstoy has written a splendid story—'Two Hussars,'" Nekrasov wrote to Botkin on April 17, "and it shall be published in the fifth issue of *The Contemporary*. What a nice fellow this Tolstoy is! As a journalist I have been indebted to him of late for many pleasant hours, and as a man, too, he is fine, his exaggerations are wearing off."

On March 28 Botkin wrote to Nekrasov: "My greetings to Tolstoy; I have a strangely warm regard for him. . . . I cannot wait to see Tolstoy for whom my feeling of devotion grows deeper, unvoiced and beyond any consciousness."

In his later years Tolstoy did not like to remember this time. His dreams of founding a magazine, his enthusiasms and disillusions, the literary gatherings where they read new works fresh from the pens of Ostrovski, Aksakov, Turgenyev and others—all this he put out of his mind; all that remained was harsh criticism of his life and activities during that time. "Life in general goes on unfolding," he wrote in his *Confessions*, harshly criticizing himself and his fellow writers. "In that unfolding we are the principal participants, we the artists, the poets. Our vocation is to teach people. . . . I am an artist, a poet— I have written and taught without knowing what."

❧ 12 ❧

IN MARCH Emperor Alexander II addressed the Moscow Assembly of the Nobility on the necessity of abolishing serfdom. By this time a peace had been concluded and the government, under growing pressure for immediate reforms, responded to public opinion and met it halfway.

The abolition of serfdom became a foregone conclusion after the Emperor's speech and many of the leading nobles began to take steps toward freeing the serfs on their estates.

One of these landowners was Lev Tolstoy. The previous August, while he was still in the Crimea and mulling over his "Story of a Russian Landowner," he had made a note in his diary (August 2) to the effect that "no civilized landowner of our century can lead a rightful life if it includes keeping serfs."

The Emperor's speech gave further impetus to his thinking. "My relation to serfs begins to upset me very much," he wrote on April 23 (Diary); and the next day he called on a writer by the name of Kavelin, who furnished him with a great deal of information on the subject of serfdom.

"After seeing him I came back gay, full of hope and happy," he wrote on April 24. "I shall go down to the country with a plan all prepared."

As it turned out, however, the emancipation of the serfs was by no means an easy matter. Tolstoy met with a series of obstacles. Not only did he have to prepare a plan, but when he went with it to the Ministry of Internal Affairs he ran into the usual governmental delays, formalities, red tape, and this drove him to despair.

Finally, his finished plan in hand, he set out for Yasnaya Polyana. He was full of radiant hope, a sense of moral satisfaction.

On the way he stopped over in Moscow, where he made the acquaintance of the contributors to *The Fatherland Journal*. Aksakov received him in a friendly fashion, introduced him to Khomyakov, read him parts of his *Family Chronicle*. "It is good, very good," was Tolstoy's brief criticism.

Konstantin Alexandrovich Islavin took Tolstoy down to Glebovo-Streshnevo, the nearby estate of his sister Lyubov Alexandrovna, who had married a court physician Andrei E. Behrs. Tolstoy liked the simple, wholesome, well-ordered lives of the Behrs family, where his attention was first drawn to his future wife, and he wrote in his diary: "The children made a fuss over us, what sweet, gay little girls they are."

But Tolstoy's thoughts were already in Yasnaya Polyana. As soon as he arrived there, without even a day's delay, he called together the village assembly and announced to the peasants his decision to put through his plan for their emancipation.

The peasants looked upon their master's noble gesture with apathy, indifference and distrust. They regarded all landlords as sharpers, who kept them in serfdom for their own profit; if now they were offered some concessions it was only because the concessions concealed some gain which the peasants "because of their ignorance" could not fathom.

On June 3 Tolstoy wrote in his diary: "I found out through Vasili that the peasants suspect trickery, that everyone will be freed at the coronation of the Tsar, whereas I am trying to bind them by contract." Rumors were current that they would be given their owners' land for nothing: Tolstoy was asking for a slight compensation.

Still he persisted in reasoning with the peasants to accept their liberty.

"They do not want their freedom," Tolstoy wrote in his diary. "This evening I chatted with some of the peasants and their stubbornness drove me into a state of anger I found difficult to repress."

"Two powerful men are shackled together with a painful chain," he wrote on June 9. "They both suffer from it when either moves, involuntarily each wounds the other and neither of them has room enough to work."

This was the end of Tolstoy's second attempt to get into closer relationship with peasants.

Meanwhile, in the literary field he had finished *Two Hussars*, a story of remarkable depth and insight into two military types: a father—a dashing, reckless, extravagant, dissipated fellow, who naturally draws the friendly interest of the reader; and a son—a shallow, calculating, disagreeable personality. Also Tolstoy went on working with enthusiasm on *Youth*.

Life was bubbling up in him. Nature, music, beautiful women

acted on him like champagne, at times stirring him to creative activity and again inciting in him a poignant longing for personal happiness, the love of a woman.

He realized that the only healing remedy for his confused internal and external life was marriage. Marry—but whom? Marriage would bind him for all his life, and he feared to take such a decisive step. Embarrassment, shyness often checked him from approaching decent women and coming close to them.

Auntie Tatiana had her own point of view about his state and felt that he had long been ready for marriage.

A little over five miles from Yasnaya Polyana, not far from the Kiev highway to Tula, was the comfortable old estate of three young ladies, the Arsenyev sisters, who lived there under the tutelage of an aunt and a French governess. They were the most unexceptional young ladies, dreaming about potential Princes Charming. They were well brought up, pretty, spoke French, and came of a good family though not of the highest aristocracy. The most attractive was Valerie, and she was picked as a likely bride for Lev Tolstoy.

On his way back from Moscow he had stopped by at the Arsenyevs' and after that he became a constant caller there. Auntie Tatiana was delighted; at last Lev was being sensible and would marry a proper young lady. The Arsenyev girls received Tolstoy with joy, and showered him with so much attention that he could not make up his mind: Was this really *she*? The woman with whom he should bind up his whole life? Did she really love him? And did he love her? What did she have to offer? Would he find some still secret unfailing source of living waters? Or would he, on further examination, stumble only on an insipid, subterranean, muddy trickle, incapable of satisfying his thirst?

Sometimes on foot, sometimes on horseback, he made solitary excursions. On Sundays he took the two-mile short cut across the fields to the church where peasants and landowners from the surrounding villages gathered. The church, packed with people, was stifling, and reeked with incense. Children whimpered while their distraught mothers—peasant women in embroidered aprons, full pleated paneled dresses, and sleeveless velveteen jackets—stuffed bits of chewed bread into their mouths to keep them from howling. Around the outside of the church lounged the young men in their new highly polished and heavily oiled boots. And among the graves stood the brick family vault containing the remains of Tolstoy's parents.

[80]

On hot and sultry days Tolstoy used to ride over to his favorite Grumont. He would tie up his horse and take a dip in the little sun-warmed pond, fed by cold springs. He enjoyed the water, his good horse, the rippling of the animal's muscles between his powerful knees. He even enjoyed the strong smell of horse sweat, rubbed to a fringe of white lather along the saddle cloth, the pungent dampness in the woods, the fragrance of the hay, meetings along the road with peasants with whom he stopped for a chat. . . . Thoughts swarmed in his brain, images emerged; he had the happy, almost exalted consciousness of a growing communion with the world, with God. . . .

It was his hope that he would find someone who could understand him. If he had been really in love with Valerie he could not have refrained from marrying her. But evidently this was not the case.

"I spent the entire day with Valerie," was the comment in his diary for July 1. "She was in a white dress with short sleeves which showed her unattractive arms. This upset me. I began in my mind to feel her all over and I did it so brutally that she smiled irresolutely, but there were tears in her smile. Then she played for me and I felt better, but she was already quite upset."

At times his attitude toward her softened and he entertained dreams of the future; at others he was appalled by Valerie's shallowness, her frivolity, realizing in the bottom of his heart that she was an innocuous product without either substance or warmth in her, a kind of mush. Yet kind. And she had a smile, but it was painfully submissive.

In a letter dated August 23 he poured out his venom in a bitter and not altogether justified attack on the Arsenyev girls. They had gone to Moscow for the coronation of the Tsar and recorded their sweetly naïve impressions in letters to Auntie Tatiana Alexandrovna. They were having a gay time, dashing young aide-de-camps were making a great impression, in fact they almost crushed their best wine-colored dresses. . . .

"Can it be that a red dress even 'de toute beauté, haute volée' and an aide-de-camp will always represent for you the apex of all bliss?" he wrote to Valerie. "How cruel! Why did you write that?

". . . As for the aides-de-camp, there are about forty of them it seems and I know for a fact that there are only two of them who are not scoundrels and fools, perhaps there is no bliss after all. . . . How glad I am that your wine-colored dress was crushed during the parade. . . ."

There were, as he wrote her, two men inside him: the one clever, the other stupid. The stupid one at times was prepared to marry her. "You're happy," so this one reasoned, "when you are with her, when you look at her, listen to her, talk with her. . . ." But the "clever" one in Tolstoy poured cold water on the "stupid" one. "I spent a month of carefree happiness," he wrote to Valerie on his way to St. Petersburg whither he had gone to put his true feelings toward her to the test of separation, "and that has been the object to which I devoted myself before going away and yet I felt that I was acting badly, in a way which made me displeased with myself. There was nothing I could say to you except silly sweet nothings which I now have on my conscience. There will be a time for all that, and what a happy time! I thank you for instilling the thought in my mind and strengthening my determination to go away because I should never have been able to do it of my own will. I believe that He is guiding me for our mutual happiness."

In this way he was gradually preparing himself and her for marriage. One can easily imagine his state of mind when he suddenly learned that Valerie was flirting with a Frenchman, a music teacher by the name of Mortier. It may well be that this incident served as the main reason for his final break with Valerie. "It hurts, it hurts me dreadfully to lose now the feeling of devotion you have for me, yet it is better to lose it now than to blame myself forever for deceit which would be bound to bring you unhappiness."

Tolstoy continued to correspond with Valerie for a while, as though he regretted to break off the relationship he had built, to destroy the dream fashioned by the "stupid" man. Occasionally the exchange of letters stopped, then was renewed, and finally on January 14, 1857 as he was leaving to go abroad Tolstoy sent her a farewell letter:

"I have not changed in my relation to you, I feel that I shall never cease to love you *as I have always loved you*, that is to say in the way of friendship, for never has my heart been so disposed to any woman as to you. Yet what can I do? I am not able to give you those feelings which your good nature is ready to offer me. I always felt this vaguely, but now our two-months separation, my life amid new interests, activities, indeed obligations incompatible with family life, have fully convinced me. . . ."

❧ 13 ❧

THE first condition of an author's popularity, the means of making himself beloved, is the love he bears to all of his created characters. That is why Dickens' characters are the common friends of the whole world: they serve as a bond between a man in America and one in St. Petersburg." Tolstoy jotted that down in his notebook at a time when his own fame had so increased that all the magazines, *The Contemporary, Library for Reading, The Fatherland Journal,* were outbidding each other to get his works. He tried to satisfy them all but his obligations to them were burdensome to him.

"How I wish I could as soon as possible get away from these magazines so that I might write the thoughts I am beginning to formulate about art. This is, oh so exalted and pure," he wrote in his diary for November 23 in St. Petersburg.

Although he did not realize it, he was himself writing in the very way he described. He was putting into his heroes all the boundless love stored up in his soul, and making his readers love them as he did.

"When I was living in St. Petersburg after being in Sevastopol the then famous writer Tutchev did me, a young writer, the honor of coming to call. . . . I was struck by the fact that he, who has spent all his life in court circles, who spoke and wrote French more freely than he did Russian, should express to me his approval of my Sevastopol sketches and showed special appreciation of some soldiers' expression; I was extraordinarily astonished by his sensitiveness to the Russian language" (Goldenweiser).

Although he moved among writers and critics, he nevertheless did not feel himself close to them. He was irritated when they tried to saddle him with the label of a "man of letters." Like a high-spirited horse he balked at this curtailment of his liberty and insisted on having his head to pursue a course of his own, untrammeled by the guidance of others: "Literary stuffiness was more abhorrent to me than anything else had ever been" (diary for November 22).

Generally accepted conventions of liberalism, within a framework of partisan politics, theories and programs, were always alien to him. "There are two kinds of liberalism," he wrote in his notebook on November 18, 1856. "There is one kind calculated to make all others my equals, as well off as I am, and another which wants them all to be as badly off as I am. The first is based on a moral, Christian feeling, a desire for the happiness and welfare of one's neighbor. The second derives from envy and a desire for the unhappiness of one's neighbor."

It was by this concept of liberalism, based on "Christian feeling," that Tolstoy's subsequent philosophical outlook was colored.

Serfdom continued to disturb him: "Mark my words," he wrote in his diary for January 8, 1857, "in two years the peasants will rise unless they are wisely set free before that time." The empty chatter about the "good of the people" on the part of those sitting around in comfortably furnished homes, who had no conception of what "people" really meant, made Tolstoy indignant.

"They are all abhorrent to me," he wrote in a mood of anguish, "because I long for their affection, their friendship, and they are incapable of giving it. . . ."

The circle of "progressive men of letters" did not succeed in harnessing the racehorse.

On the 26th of November in 1856 Tolstoy had received his discharge from the army, for which he had waited so long. No longer tied by military service, by Valerie, with whom his relations had been finally cleared up, by the emancipation of his serfs, which had ended in such a fiasco, he decided to go abroad. Turgenyev was already in Paris and expecting him.

"Tolstoy writes me he is preparing to come here. . . . From his letters I can see that extremely beneficial changes are taking place in him and I am as delighted as an old nurse," he wrote to Druzhinin. And when Tolstoy reached Paris the "old nurse" was at first much pleased with his charge, to judge by the following letter he wrote to Polonski: "Tolstoy is here. A quite remarkable improvement has taken place in him. . . . This man will go far and leave a deep mark."

But Turgenyev was soon disillusioned: "It is impossible after all for me to be close friends with Tolstoy," he wrote Kolbasin, "our views are too divergent."

Nevertheless the two writers saw each other frequently; they made a trip together to Dijon. It would seem that some mysterious force kept drawing them together, making them clash and inevitably rebound from one another. "I dropped in to see Turgenyev," Tolstoy noted in his diary for March 4-16. "Morally I have no use for him, he is so cold and selfish, but artistically he is very clever and harmless."

Over and over Tolstoy decided that any rapprochement between him and Turgenyev was out of the question. "No, I avoid him. I have paid sufficient tribute to his merits and have tried to meet him on too many grounds ever to come really close to him—that's impossible."

Evidently he was right. Turgenyev was incapable of grasping Tolstoy's stormy incoherencies, his abrupt rejection of "accepted conventions," his doubts, his corrosive remorse after his falls from grace.

While he was staying in Paris Tolstoy did the best he could to put his life onto a better plane and to draw some profit from his journey abroad. He threw himself into studying languages, visiting museums; he made an effort to do some writing. Then suddenly an incident upset all his plans. In his diary for the period March 25-April 6 he wrote: "I got up at seven in the morning and went to witness an execution. A plump, white, healthy neck and chest. He kissed the Bible and then—death. What a senseless performance! It made a strong impression and one that will not pass without results. I am not politically minded. Ethics and art—those are the fields I know and where I achieve things. . . . The guillotine banished my sleep for a long time and it made me reflect about things."

From that day on Tolstoy's attitude on the subject of capital punishment was fixed: ". . . The sight of capital punishment was concrete evidence of the precarious instability of my belief in progress. When I saw the head part from the body and both at once fall into a basket I felt, not with my mind but with my whole being, that no theories about the reasonableness of existing progress could justify such an action. . . ." (*Confessions.*)

Also in his article "What Are We to Do?" Tolstoy again related the horror he felt at the sight of the guillotine. "At that moment I realized—not with my mind, not with my heart, but with my whole being—that all the rationalizations I had heard about capital punishment are wicked fabrications, that no matter how many people gather together to commit this murder it is still the worst crime in the world, and no matter what they call themselves, murder is still murder, and that here in front of my eyes this sin has been committed. By my presence and noninterference I had condoned the sin and participated in it."

The emotions he suffered from witnessing this execution were so oppressive, they so saturated his whole being with horror, that he was unable to bear the burden of them alone. That very day he wrote Botkin.

"I saw many horrors during the war and in the Caucasus, but even if in my presence a man were torn limb from limb it would not be so repugnant as this artful, elegant machine by means of which they brought instant death to a strong, robust, healthy man. In the former you have an unreasoning but a human passion, but here you have the acme of refinement in the quiet, convenient art of killing and there is nothing majestic about it. . . . Just in these last days there has been a spate of arrests, a plot to murder Napoleon in a theater has been uncovered. Undoubtedly there will be more executions. I shall not only never go to see them but I shall never serve *any government* anywhere."

All joy in life was dead, everything was tarnished, distasteful. . . .

The next day he "got up ill," read a little, then suddenly the simple, practical idea occurred to him—to leave Paris. He recalled that his cousins Alexandra Andreyevna and Elizabeth Tolstoy were in Geneva so he went off to see them.

❧ 14 ❧

THE father of Alexandrine Tolstoy was the brother of Ilya Andreyevich Tolstoy, Lev's grandfather. Consequently Alexandrine Tolstoy was Lev Tolstoy's first cousin once removed. She was still quite young, only eleven years his senior, and he jokingly called her and her sister Elizabeth "Granny."

Alexandrine had gone abroad with the Grand Duchess Maria Nikolayevna to whom she was attached as lady-in-waiting. And her sister Elizabeth was tutor to the daughter of the Grand Duchess Eugenia.

In his state of dark despondency Tolstoy remembered his "Grannies" and knew that he would find solace with them.

As he traveled by train he felt bored. But when he transferred to a mail coach, drew nearer to earth and nature, he was enveloped in magic moonlight. Then his mood changed to one of delight: "It all rolled away and I was flooded with love and joy. For the first time in an age I truly thank God that I am alive," he wrote in his diary.

Like a tornado Tolstoy swept into the life of his two lady-in-waiting cousins. In her memoirs Alexandrine gave an excellent account of his mood. And, of course, she did everything she could for him. She had a tender affection for Lev and he felt it.

"Our pure, unaffected friendship was a refutation of the generally accepted but fallacious opinion that friendship between a man and a woman is impossible," she wrote in her memoirs. But was this really so? Tolstoy himself believed differently, feeling that friendship between a young man and a woman inevitably developed into a more powerful emotion.

"It is great fun to be with the Tolstoys . . . great, great fun," he wrote in his diary for April 29. "I am so much on the verge of falling in love that it is simply awful. If Alexandrine were ten years younger! She has a delightful disposition. . . . Alexandrine has a marvelous smile"—this in his diary for April 12-13.

The letters she wrote to Tolstoy after they had separated show her tender attachment for him.

"When near you it was difficult not to feel happy. . . . I cannot tell you how much joy I derived from our times together, so many of them unforeseen, and how the memory of them buoys me up. Everything I loved vanished along with Switzerland. . . . When I see you I always feel I want to be a better human being and the thought of your friendship (perhaps it is a bit blind) has the same effect on me," she wrote him to Yasnaya Polyana on August 29, 1857.

These words sound almost like a confession. For who can say where the dividing line lies between friendship and romantic love? There is no doubt that they were drawn to one another and when together they were contented and gay. Where Tolstoy's relation to Valerie was artificial, unclear, that to Alexandrine was easy and unforced. With Valerie, Tolstoy had to make an effort to develop her, to find in her things that in reality were not there. But Alexandrine was intelligent, sensitive, mature; there was not a shade of affectation in her. She was subtly responsive to his intellectual requirements, his love of art, literature, nature, his interest in religion and philosophy.

They had frequent and lengthy arguments. He would not accept her rigid, submissive attitude toward the Orthodox Greek Church. She was pained by his insufficient observance of church rules and rites.

"Despite our different training and positions," she wrote in her memoirs, "we had the same general traits of character. We were both terrific enthusiasts and had searching minds, we truly loved good, but did not know how to go about accomplishing it properly; actually our searching minds stimulated our imaginations and had absolutely no effect on improving our lives. Even at this time Lev was already full of renunciation but it stemmed more from his head than his heart. His soul was really made as much as mine for faith, as much for love, and often, even when he himself did not realize it, he gave proof of this in various ways.

"Our conversations often turned to religious subjects, but it is not likely that we understood one another. How could I at that time comprehend all the many facets of his exceptional nature?"

From Clarens Tolstoy moved to Vevey. "My Grannies have been given a leave of absence by the Grand Duchess, two more young people have joined them and all this young gay crowd wandered from morning to evening in the vicinity of Vevey, stopping in small Swiss pensions, upsetting by their noisy gaiety the quiet of the placid, well-behaved tourists."

"What a wonderful trip," wrote Alexandrine, "and what a series of delightfully happy days."

Although the Grannies were accustomed to the strict etiquette of court life, they were wholeheartedly gay and delighted with the jolly pranks of their "nephew." He was tireless in his invention of all sorts of entertaining mischief.

"One morning we all set out on foot for Glion. We stopped at a hotel there to drink some tea. In the drawing room, in addition to our group of Russian travelers, there were some Englishmen, Americans and other foreigners. After tea Tolstoy, disregarding the large number of strangers, sat down at the piano and obliged his companions to sing. Alexandrine had a fine voice; one of the other women also sang extremely well. Two men provided bass voices and Lev conducted. This improvised chorus sang 'God Save the Tsar,' Russian and gypsy lyrics and songs. Their success was overwhelming. The foreigners sitting in the living room crowded around the singers, showered them with expressions of delight and gratitude, and implored them to continue their concert."

Alexandrine's vacation came to an end but the friends still met.

On one occasion Alexandrine took the children of the Grand Duchess on a trip into the Bernese Oberland. On the way they stopped over in Vevey at one of the fashionable hotels.

"We had scarcely taken our places at table," relates Alexandrine, "when the waiter came to tell me in a mysterious voice that someone was waiting for me downstairs. Guessing who it could be I hastily went down to the living room in the center of which they were all gathered again: Tolstoy and his friends wrapped in long mantles and with feathers on their fantastic headgear. Sheets of music were lying beside them on the floor, according to the custom of itinerant musicians, and they carried walking sticks in lieu of instruments. At my appearance an incredible cacophony burst forth, a real caterwauling, voices and sticks alternated in this *tapage infernal*. I nearly died of laughter and the royal children were inconsolable because they had not been present at the performance."

The children implored Alexandrine to invite Tolstoy aboard their boat so that he would be with them as they continued their trip. To their great delight this was done. They long remembered how he entertained them with all kinds of pranks and jokes.

"And what quantities of cherries he could eat!" they exclaimed in astonishment.

15

TOLSTOY was not content to stay still in Switzerland, he wanted to see everything, go everywhere, and he was constantly making excursions. He was bored by himself, so he either joined others or took companions with him. On one of these trips in the middle of May he had an eleven-year-old boy, Sasha Galakhov, with him and they set off to climb Mt. Jaman. In his notes Tolstoy left some magnificent descriptions of the climb and the view from the heights.

"Although we could not see the sun," wrote Tolstoy, "it cast its rays over us, to light a few pines and crags on the heights opposite. Below us we still heard the streams, while beside us the melting snows trickled down, and at turns in the path we began to see the lake again and Vallé at a dreadful distance below. The feet of the Savoy mountains were as blue as the lake, only darker, their crests, bathed in sunlight, were quite pink and white. There were other snow-covered mountains, they seemed higher and more varied. Sails and boats, scarcely distinguishable dots, were visible on the lake." His imagination makes us feel with almost physical impact the power of the mountains, their infinite distance, their size, but he himself remained indifferent.

"It is a strange thing," he wrote that day in his diary (May 15-27), "whether out of a spirit of contradiction or because my taste runs counter to the tastes of the majority, yet in my life I find that not one of the sights famous for beauty has pleased me. I am happy when the warm air enfolds me on all sides, then curling up, rolls off into the infinite distance; when those succulent grass blades, which I crushed when I sat on them, form a part of the endless meadows; when those leaves, stirred by the wind, shifting the shade falling on my face, become part of the line of the distant forests; when this same air which I breathe becomes a part of the deep, blue, limitless sky; when I am not alone to gloat over and enjoy nature, when around me there is a myriad of humming, milling insects, scurrying beetles, birds pouring out their songs. . . ."

He returned to Clarens, but not for long. Soon he went with Botkin to St. Bernard, visited Chillon, took a trip to Geneva, spent some time in Bern and on July 5 reached Lucerne.

He wrote little and in snatches. He attempted to work on *The Cossacks* but without success. His mood was constantly shifting. A gay mood was followed by a dark one; his intention of systematizing his life, from the point of view of his writing, was not carried out. Nature still affected him without fail, as did music and art, stirring him to think and create.

"I arrived in Lucerne," he wrote to his Auntie Tatiana Alexandrovna. "I am stopping over in order to spend several days in this charming town. I am again entirely alone and I must confess to you that this isolation is often very hard for me to bear, because the acquaintances one makes in hotels and trains do not give me any satisfaction."

He was sad, he again began to think that people did not like him, and dark thoughts began to enter his mind: "What if I am sick with tuberculosis?" On the other hand his room was cozy, he could hear "music from the lake, the weather is overcast, the ruins stand there in silence. On my window, against the dark background of poplars, curling tendrils of a grapevine are touched with the light of my candle as they peep in. . . ." The day after his arrival Tolstoy again attempted to do some writing but without result, so toward evening he went to dinner. The table d'hôte dining room of his first-class hotel was filled with strangers and foreigners. "At such meals," Tolstoy wrote in his story about Lucerne "The Journal of Prince Nekhlyudov," "I am always ill at ease, wretched, and in the end sad. I always feel I am for some reason to blame, that I am being punished as I was in my childhood, when they put me on a chair because of some prank and then said to me sarcastically: now be quiet for a bit, my pet!—while the blood was pulsing in my young veins and I could hear the happy laughter of my brothers in the next room.

". . . I was feeling downcast, as usual after one such meal. I had left the table without waiting for the dessert, and in a low frame of mind I went wandering through the town. I was feeling dreadfully chilled inside me, lonely and distressed . . . when suddenly . . . I was struck by the sound of some strange, but extraordinarily sweet and pleasant music. These sounds instantly produced an enlivening effect on me. They penetrated my soul like a shaft of clear, bright light. I felt at ease and gay. . . . Directly in front of me was a bridge from whence I had heard the sounds. My attention centered on it and I saw in the twilight a semicircle of people pressed together in the middle of the street, in front of them, at a slight distance, a tiny man in a black suit. . . . I drew nearer, the sounds became more distinct. I could distinguish the faint notes sweetly trembling in the night air, the full chords of a guitar and several voices, mounting over one another; they did not really carry the theme but somehow by humming the main passages they made one feel it. This was not a song, it was the light silhouette of a song. I could not think what it might be, but it was magnificent. The passionate chords of the guitar, the gentle, sweet melody, and the solitary figure of the black-clad little man against the fantastic setting of the dark lake illumined by the moon, the two huge pointed towers rising in silence, the black ruins in the park—it was all strange but inexpressibly lovely, or so it seemed to me.

"All the confused, intruding impressions of life suddenly acquired a meaning and charm for me. It was as though a fresh fragrance of flowers had filled my soul.

". . . The little man turned out to be a wandering Tyrolean. He used to take up his position outside the hotel windows, put one foot forward, throw his head back and, strumming his guitar, sing his graceful little song with varying inflections. I was immediately seized with a feeling of affection for this man, and gratitude for the change he had brought about in me. . . .

"From the balconies or windows of the best, most expensive hotels, a wealthy, well-dressed crowd listened to this little, and perhaps rather commonplace, man. They listened to him from their windows, they listened as they walked along the quay. Perhaps some of them really enjoyed his original and musical renderings of Tyrolean songs, but when the musician held out his cap to them, they gave him nothing. Three times he repeated the phrase: *'Messieurs, mesdames, si vous croyez que je gagne quelque chose. . . .'*

"Of all the hundreds of gorgeously dressed persons who crowded around to hear him, not one threw him a single coin. Their loud laughter was unfeeling. The little singer, so it seemed to me, grew even smaller, put his guitar in his other hand, raised his cap and said: *'Messieurs et mesdames, je vous remercie et je vous souhaite une bonne nuit,'* and set his cap on his head. The crowd laughed uproariously."

A storm of indignation and humiliation on behalf of the little musician overwhelmed Tolstoy. He felt as though he himself were the object of the insult and injury of these heartless rich. "I ran after him," he wrote in his diary, "and invited him to have a drink with me in the Schweizerhof. . . . While we were having our drinks the waiter smiled and the doorman felt free to sit instead of stand. This riled me and I exploded at them and was terribly upset."

Tolstoy's "Lucerne" is a short and little-known story. Its power lies not only in the vivid descriptions of nature but in the contrasts between the overfed, spoiled, wealthy crowd and the little singer who had suffered bitter need and humiliation yet possessed a gift— through his unpremeditated art—to arouse joy and hope in human souls.

"He did his work, he delighted you," Tolstoy wrote in "Lucerne," "and he begged you to give him something from your overabundance for his work which you had enjoyed. But you looked at him from the heights of your gleaming mansions as though he were an oddity. . . . Crestfallen he left you, and the thoughtless, laughing crowd blamed not you but him for your coldness, cruelty and dishonesty; for stealing the enjoyment he provided for you—and for that they humiliated him.

". . . Who is more human and who more barbarous?

"Meanwhile in the dead silence of the night, far, far way I heard the man's guitar and his voice.

"No, I said to myself involuntarily, you have no right to be sorry for him and indignant at the material wealth of a lord. Who has weighed the inner happiness which lies within the soul of each of them? Perhaps he is sitting somewhere on a muddy doorstep, looking into the shining moonlit sky and happily singing amid the quiet and fragrance of the night; in his soul there is neither reproach nor anger nor remorse. And who knows what is going on inside all those people behind the high expensive walls? Who can say that they enjoy a life as carefree, as full of gentle joys and reconciliation with the world as that which dwells within the soul of the little man? How infinite is the blessing and wisdom of Him who allowed and ordained the existence of all these contradictions."

Stirred by the night, the music and the thoughts teeming in his head, Tolstoy returned to his hotel: "The night is a miracle," he wrote in his diary. "What is it I desire, yearn for passionately? I do not know, except that it is not the blessings of this world. Not believe in the immortality of the soul? When you feel in your soul such measureless grandeur? I looked out of the window. Everything was dark, diffuse and luminous. If even one could die! Oh my God, my God! What am I? Where am I going? Where am I?"

Yet not two weeks has passed before Tolstoy was in Baden-Baden and writing in his diary: "From morning till night at roulette. What a swine. It's revolting, rotten."

He borrowed money from some Frenchman, lost it, borrowed more from Turgenyev, who had arrived in Baden-Baden, and he lost that. Finally he turned to Alexandrine for help. "Nothing has rankled in me like this for a long time," was his bitter condemnation of himself in his diary.

Harassed, exhausted by the pangs of his conscience, he rode off to Frankfurt in search of fresh consolation and sympathy from his priceless friend Granny Alexandrine. He wrote in his diary: "A wonder, a delight. I do not know a better woman."

On July 8, after stopping in Dresden to visit the museum, Tolstoy started back to Russia.

❧ 16 ❧

ALTHOUGH Tolstoy had expected to find greater freedom and tolerance in Europe, even if, as he emphasized in his notebook, "all governments are alike in their degree of good and bad" and "the highest ideal is anarchy," yet when he returned to Russia he was rudely shocked by the poverty, disorder, ignorance, thieving and, above all, the serfdom of the peasants.

He recorded his impressions immediately after his arrival in St. Petersburg (diary, August 6): "Russia is repulsive, I simply do not love her." And to Alexandrine: "In Russia everything is foul, foul, foul. In St. Petersburg and Moscow people scream and are indignant, they expect something to happen but down in the country the old patriarchal barbarity, robbery and lawlessness prevail. Can you believe that when I reached Russia I had to struggle for a long time with my feelings of revulsion against my own country, and it is only now that I am growing accustomed to all the horrors which are forever part of our daily lives. . . . If you had seen as I did in the course of a single week how a lady beat her maid with her cane out in the street, how a police officer sent word to me that I was to make him a present of a load of hay or he would not allow my valet to remain in town, or how under my very eyes some officials beat a seventy-year-old sick man half to death because one of them had been tripped up by him, or how my bailiff, in an effort to please me, punished a delinquent gardener by not only flogging him but also forcing him to walk barefoot along with the sheep over a field of stubble so that his feet were all cut—if you had seen all this and looked into other abysmal depths as well, you would believe me when I tell you that for me life in Russia is a constant, unending grind, a struggle with my emotions. . . ."

"Patriarchal barbarity" had corroded the Russians, including that kindest of beings Auntie Tatiana, who could not grasp why the household serfs need be liberated. Her views were shared by the neighboring landowners, his own bailiff, head gardener, and even the elder of the village council who, as Tolstoy wrote in his diary, "holds me in such deep contempt it is difficult for me to do anything with him."

Tolstoy suffered under all these conflicts. He wished to straighten out the management of his property, but could not without applying severity. This he recoiled from, not because of any theory of non-resistance—which he worked out much later—but because of the very nature of his being. He might strike someone in a fit of temper, but he was incapable of deliberately punishing people, of inflicting bodily suffering. He could not even reprimand anyone without being upset by it himself. When one of the serfs, Sashka, stole some butter the village elder insisted that the master punish him. But Sashka said "that he did not know what he was doing when he was drunk" and that "his feet were rotting away," and the master "had given him a talking to and even rewarded him." Commenting in his diary, Tolstoy wrote: "It was silly of me but what else could I do?"

Could such a master command the respect of a village elder?

Nikolai Tolstoy wrote about his brother: "Lev wants to accomplish everything at once. He does not want to give up anything, not even his gymnastics. So he has had parallel bars set up beneath his study window. Of course, aside from prejudices with which he wrestles so fiercely, he is right: gymnastics do not interfere with running an estate. But the village elder has a slightly different point of view: You come, says he, to the master for orders and the master in a red shirt is hanging upside down from a pole; his hair is all hanging around, his face flushed. You don't know whether to listen to orders or stand and gape at him" (*Memoirs of Fet*).

The household serfs were the easiest to liberate. These were landless peasants who worked in and about the house: cooks, housemaids, footmen, coachmen. They served their masters all their lives, some were born and died in the house, often fathers had passed on their work to their sons for generations. Tolstoy began to free them gradually. Yet even in this he ran into misunderstandings: the household servants did not wish to leave; they continued to work for their masters.

Tolstoy was much depressed by all the "human poverty and the

[95]

sufferings of dumb animals," as he said in his diary when he was visiting his brother Sergei at Pirogovo.

"It's a blessing that there is a salvation—the world of morals and art, poetry and personal attachments" (diary, August 20), "for one does not enjoy torments."

"I am sitting alone," he wrote Alexandrine Tolstoy (August 18, 1857). "The wind is howling, it is muddy and cold out of doors, and with my stubby fingers I make a poor attempt to play an andante of Beethoven, and drop tears of tender emotion, or I read the *Iliad*, or invent people of my own, women, I live with them, I scrawl over sheets of paper, or think, as I am doing now, of those I love."

He was thrilled by the *Iliad*, as though he had just discovered a treasure: "This is—a very marvel!" he wrote in his diary. Then a few days later, after a long interruption during which he had resumed his reading of the New Testament, he wrote: "How could Homer not know that goodness is—love! That is the revelation. There is no better explanation . . ." (diary, August 15).

At times he felt an unquenchable thirst for human companionship and then he wrote to Alexandrine as the only person who could understand him.

"Only genuine emotion, effort and work, based on love, are what is called happiness," he wrote her. "Fraudulent emotion based on self-love spells unhappiness. . . . I laugh when I recall how I used to believe and as it seems to me you still do believe, that one can build a happy and honest little world in which to live peaceably, without mistakes or remorse or confusions, live undisturbed and do, in a leisurely and sure fashion, only what is right. How ridiculous! *It cannot be done*, Granny. It can no more be done than a human being can remain motionless, without making a single move, and yet be healthy. In order to live honestly one has to strive, fight, falter, begin and stop, begin again and stop again, forever struggling and giving up.

"To strive, to falter . . ." All Tolstoy is in that statement. He was a steaming, growing pile of compost, gradually being converted into rich, precious humus.

His strong and healthy nature required constant action: he rode to fairs to buy horses, and he experienced a genuine satisfaction in mixing with the crowds, in walking down the rows of horses tethered to hitching posts or carts, in looking at their teeth, in bargaining, in driving off insistent gypsy traders. The gypsies outdid each other in boasting about their wares. They set their worn fur caps at a rakish angle and careened around on their nags after putting pepper under the animals' tails to liven them up. Tolstoy wanted to show the dealers that he knew horseflesh, but they probably cheated him in any case. The buyers and sellers yelled, slapped each other's hands in making their deals and finally agreed on a price. When this was paid the seller, according to custom, passed the horse to the new owner "on the sly"—holding the halter under the skirt of his coat as he handed it over. Cows, not milked for three days, stood tied to carts and lowed, their huge udders dripping milk onto the dusty ground. Young children chewed sunflower seeds and adroitly spat out the shells, which gradually lent a gray surface to the ground on the square. . . .

Tolstoy bought standing lumber to be cut; he set out trees. The bare hills were gradually covered with orderly rows of firs, birches and pines, many of which are still in existence. But this did not satisfy him; he wanted to reforest the whole province of Tula. He proposed a whole plan of forestation and took it up to St. Petersburg to Muravyov, the minister in charge of state properties. But nothing came of it and Tolstoy's thoughts, while in the capital, turned into other channels.

Plunged once more into literary circles he was bitterly disappointed to find that his reputation as a writer was losing ground: "it has fallen or is barely creeping along" he wrote in his diary (October 30). A critical review of his "Lucerne" had appeared in the *St. Petersburg Journal*, Turgenyev had called the story a politico-moral sermon, and in *The Contemporary* the reaction had been more than cool.

Now and then he worked on his *Cossacks* but at this time he was much more concerned with "The Lost One" or "The Musician," which was finally published under the title "Albert."

This image of a drunken, dissolute genius of a musician was so firmly lodged in his brain that he was unable to rid himself of it. To understand this, one must appreciate Tolstoy's attitude toward music in general. Music had a large place in his life. For him it was not mere enjoyment for the senses and mind. Music—whether a simple folk melody, an old gypsy love song, or a classical composition by Mozart, Haydn, Schubert or Chopin, whom he loved above all—was to him a divine manifestation of the human soul. As he listened his thoughts surged up with extraordinary power, new images flooded his mind, his own creative capacity was aroused.

A little wandering musician in Lucerne, a drunken, down-and-out musician in a saloon—both made an ineradicable impression on Tolstoy. He was stirred by the thought that at one and the same time such things could coexist in one being: commonplaceness, dissoluteness, futility, and a divine gift for creativeness capable of exercising great power over human souls.

"The notes of the theme flowed easily, delicately, after the opening, throwing a surprisingly clear, soothing light into the inner world of each listener," he wrote in "Albert." "Not a single false or obtrusive note to disturb the intentness of those present; all the sounds were clear, delicate and significant. All were silent, stirred by some hope, as they listened to them unfold. . . . Into the soul of one might come a serene contemplation of the past, into that of another a passionately happy remembrance, into a third boundless urge for power and splendor, to others came a sense of resignation, of unsatisfied love, of sadness. Now wistfully tender, now wildly despairing came the sounds in fluent alternation; they flowed on and on with such delicacy yet so powerfully and unconsciously that they were no longer heard as sounds; of its own accord a magnificent tide of poetry long since known but now expressed for the first time flooded the soul of each one present."

Experiences of this order were fraught with such significance for Tolstoy that he had to pour them forth himself. But who wanted to hear of them? These unfortunate musicians of Tolstoy, on whom he expended so much of his intellectual and spiritual force, all but ruined his reputation.

Yet he was not one to be seriously or for long disturbed by an uncomprehending public. New writings were under way: *The Cossacks,* "Three Deaths," *Family Happiness.*

"Now I am content," he wrote in his diary for October 30. "I know that I have something to say and the capacity to express it powerfully; as for the public, let them say what they like. One must work conscientiously, bend all one's strength to the task and then let them spit on the altar."

The winter of 1857-58 was spent by Tolstoy in Moscow, with his sister Maria, her children and Auntie Tatiana. His favorite elder brother Nikolai came to town often to visit them, and life flowed by easily and gaily, a real family life. Maria was a fine pianist. Sister and brother often played duets, sonatas of Mozart, Haydn, Schubert; the Tolstoy home was a center for musicians, and the circle of friends interested in music kept growing until it gradually became a Society of Music which numbered among its members Botkin, Mortier and others, and eventually served as a basis for the founding of the Moscow Conservatory.

Maria's daughters, Lizanka and Varenka, adored their jolly uncle. He was constantly in their society, inventing games, taking them to the theater, teasing them, joking with them. His youth and love of life also played their part. "Lyovochka put on his swallow tails," said his brother Nikolai, "and a white tie and drove off to a ball." He loved to make a fashionable appearance and dressed well. In Fet's memoirs, a comrade who had known Tolstoy in the Caucasus is quoted:

"At this time Tolstoy's interest in being elegantly dressed was obvious and when Borisov saw him in a new winter topcoat with a beaver collar, his curled dark reddish-brown locks under a shining new hat set at an angle, with a stylish cane in his hand, all ready to go for a stroll, he could not resist applying to him the words of the folksong: 'He sways upon a slender reed and boasts himself a lily fine.' "

Tolstoy's transitions from the serious to the frivolous were unpredictable: from wild sprees to the solving of the problem of serfdom, from the study of jurisprudence to exercises in his underwear on a gymnasium horse, from the life of a city dandy to the simple life of the country—swinging from joy to despair, to thoughts of death or his inability to cope with or achieve anything in life.

Occasionally he saw Alexandrine. Once he accompanied her as far as Klin on the road to St. Petersburg. In Klin he stopped off to see his mother's cousin, Princess V. A. Volkonskaya.

Her memories carried the old princess far back into the past. For Tolstoy her stories brought to life his mother, whom he never knew and yet so adored, and his grandfather. All that he heard he stored in the treasurehouse of his own memory to use as material when the time came.

It was here, while visiting Princess Volkonskaya, that he made the first outline for his story "Three Deaths." In it he described the death of a spoiled rich lady, a peasant postrider and a tree.

In a letter to Alexandrine, May, 1858, he wrote:

"This was my thought: three living beings die—a lady, a peasant and a tree. The lady is pitiful and repulsive because she had lied all her life and continues to do it when she comes to die. Christianity, as she understands it, does not solve the problem of life and death. Why die when you want to live? Her imagination and mind tell her to believe in the future life promised by Christianity yet her whole being resists it, and she has no other comfort to turn to (outside the pseudo-Christian)—there is no place to go. She is repulsive and pitiful. He [the peasant] dies calmly for the very reason that he is not a Christian. His religion is another, although as a matter of custom he has observed the Christian rites; his religion is nature, in the midst of which he has spent his life. He himself felled trees, sowed his rye and reaped it, killed sheep and helped them into the world, brought children into it too, saw the old people die, so he is familiar with the established law from which he has never flinched, like the lady, but which he meets squarely, simply looking it straight in the eye. . . . The tree dies quietly, honestly, beautifully. It is beautiful because there is no lying, no false gestures, no fear, no regret."

Tolstoy was right. The tree described in his story does die beautifully: "Down below the sounds of the axe were more and more muffled, the white, sap-filled chips flew out onto the dewy grass, after the blows a slight crackling was heard. The whole trunk of the tree trembled, it leaned over, then quickly righted itself, tremulously swaying on its roots. For a second all was still, then the tree leaned forward again, there was a cracking in its trunk, its branches broke and twigs fell away as it crashed to the damp earth. . . ."

This was written in what the critics and biographers called and still call a "down" period of his work.

They expected him to write things of political import, to throw light on contemporary, day-by-day events. A writer, in the opinion of the literary minded, should guide people, instruct them, but Tolstoy thought otherwise.

"No matter how great the importance of political literature, reflecting as it does the passing interests of society, and necessary as it is to national development, there is another literature which reflects the eternal interests of all mankind, the dearest and deepest creations of a people, a literature accessible to every people and of every age, a literature without which no people of power and substance has developed."

In this speech, made by him on February 4, 1859, when he was elected a member of the Society of Friends of Russian Literature, Tolstoy expressed himself as an artist. He wrote as he must, he could not write in any other way: "Let the others scoff, let them spit on the altar."

⚜ 17 ⚜

NO MATTER how strong a person may be in any game or sport he will be weakened if he plays against a weak opponent. A chess player lets down his guard if he does not feel strength in his adversary; he may even lose the game. Whereas in playing a formidable opponent he pulls himself together and learns new methods.

In his intercourse with people Tolstoy eagerly sought out those in whom he might find intellectual competition; he had the urge to broaden his own horizons, a need to find some rational, and even severe, criticism of his writings. "For some time now every question has assumed for me immense proportions," he wrote in his diary on March 20, 1858.

"I am much indebted to Chicherin," he wrote later on. "Now in dealing with each new object or circumstance, in addition to the conditions surrounding each object and circumstance, I involuntarily seek to find its place in the eternal and infinite scheme in history."

Boris N. Chicherin, with whom Tolstoy at one time was quite friendly, impressed him deeply with his mental capacity and cultivation. He was a scholarly lawyer. From his youth Tolstoy had always been interested in jurisprudence and when he met Chicherin he eagerly absorbed new ideas and information. But when Tolstoy, as he expressed it in his diary, "poured out to him [Chicherin] a flood of pent-up emotions" it appeared that Chicherin was unable to cope with the still somewhat inchoate thoughts with which Tolstoy overwhelmed him. Tolstoy had expected to find in him some unplumbed depths, but he soon drained him dry and struck the bottom, the limitations of a scholar's interests—and his own interest cooled. Here is what he wrote to Chicherin from Dresden on April 18, 1861:

"The memory of our recent correspondence and your two letters, which I found in Dresden, have made me consider seriously our relations to each other. We have been *playing at friendship*. That cannot exist between two persons as disparate as we are. You, perhaps, are able to reconcile scorn for a man's convictions with a feeling of attachment for him; but I cannot do this. . . . Therefore it is better for us to separate and go our own ways, respecting each other, yet making no attempt to enter into that closer relationship which can be achieved only where there is a unity of the dogmas of faiths, that is to say of fundamentals which are beyond intellectual processes. We differ entirely on these fundamentals. And I cannot hope to come around to yours because I have already had them. Nor can I hope that you will come around to mine because you have already traveled too far along your temptingly well-beaten road. It is strange to you that one can teach *dirty* children. It is incomprehensible to me how one can retain one's self-respect and express oneself on the subject of emancipation in an *article*. Can you say in an *article* even a millionth part of what you know and what should be said, or even anything new, or state one righteous thought, a truly *righteous* thought?"

The two friends continued to correspond and to visit each other until they were well on in years; they retained their respect for each other but their ways lay in different directions.

Alexandrine Tolstoy, Lev's brother Nikolai and A. A. Fet, each in some way and because of certain special qualities, were closer to him. Nikolai, who was not much given to conversation, poked good-natured fun at the external vagaries of his younger brother, but at bottom understood and appreciated him, and never offended him through insensitiveness.

Fet was an extremely intelligent man. He loved and valued Tolstoy all his life. Tolstoy in turn was drawn to Fet because of his artistic perceptiveness, his understanding of the beauty and the grandeur of creation, his love of nature. Tolstoy's mood when with him was always light and gay.

As a plant turns to the sun Tolstoy sought tenderness and affection. He ought to marry, but whom? The only person who could make him feel he was not alone, that there was someone to share his interests and give him love and understanding, was Alexandrine.

"Where do you get all that warmth of heart which brings happiness to others and lifts them up?" he wrote her on March 30, 1858.

"I love you" was his Granny's reply. "I love you with all my heart just as you are. I wouldn't say that I might not wish some changes in you—that would be untrue. . . ." Yet who but Granny could understand Lev's power of thought and emotion, which always boiled up in him with the renewal of spring.

"Granny, it's spring!" he writes her in April. "It is fine for good people to be alive; even such as I have our good moments. In nature, in the air, in everything, there is a hope, a future, an alluring future."

And in his diary he said: "I made a prayer before a Greek ikon of the Virgin. The little light in front of it was burning. I went out onto the balcony: the night was dark, starlit. Some stars were misty, some were bright, clusters of them, the brilliance, darkness, the outline of dead trees—there He is. On your knees before Him and be silent" (April 20, 1858).

These were not mere words. They hold the inner substance of Tolstoy.

But he could not tell his Granny what had happened to him. This secret he confided, as always, only to his diary: "I have fallen in love as never before in my life," he wrote on May 13th, referring to the vivacious black-eyed Axinia Bazykina.

Love-burdened nightingales, frogs in croaking chorus, wild cherries in bloom, the scent of young grass and lilies of the valley, the upturned furrows' of ploughed earth and the lovely Axinia—all melted into a single quickening melody.

But the spring went by and Tolstoy's passion for Axinia cooled, leaving only an occasional prick of remorse and self-disgust. Axinia went on living with her husband, although Tolstoy continued to see her at intervals.

Axinia had an only son, Timothy, whose likeness to Tolstoy was striking. In later years he was powerfully built, broad-shouldered, tall, with shrewd gray eyes, a reddish beard and strong features. He was not well educated but he liked to read books, and in the village he was respected as an honest man. His unusually pleasant voice and cultivated speech involuntarily attracted the attention of anyone who met him.

Nature and the management of his estate so absorbed Tolstoy this summer that he did little writing. In April he had worked on his *Cossacks* but during the summer he wrote and read practically nothing.

Auntie Tanya was horrified when he decided to do some plowing himself. His brother Nikolai, with his usual gentle humor, told Fet about it: "Lev was fascinated by the way Yufan bows his arms while plowing. Yufan has become the emblem of agricultural power, a kind of [epic] Mikula Selyaninovich. So he himself, his elbows spread wide apart now takes hold of the plow and 'yufanizes.' "

The words "Yufan" and "to yufanize" remained long in the Tolstoy family and his relatives twisted it slightly to make it mean "act like a fool." Actually his plowing was for Tolstoy the expression of a deep-seated sense of union with the earth he loved. In part he kept this feeling throughout his whole life. The closer he came to the "Yufans" the more he was tormented by their lot.

In the beginning of September the Tula Provincial Assembly of Nobles convened to elect members to the Committee for the Betterment of the Status of Peasants. Tolstoy took part in this. The following resolution was adopted:

"We, the undersigned, with a view toward the betterment of the status of the peasants, the protection of the property of the landed proprietors, and the security of both, consider it necessary to emancipate the peasants only on condition that each receive an apportionment of land together with the right to bequeath it and that the landowners, in yielding up this land, should receive full, fair cash compensation by means of some financial measure, which will not entail any obligatory relationships between the landowners and the peasants —relations which the nobility considers it necessary to abolish." This was followed by the signatures of 105 Tula nobles among which is that of "Count Lev Tolstoy, landowner, Krapivna District." (Biryukov).

Throughout the summer, he continued to have periods of great depression; yet at times he was carried away by a kind of boyish, riotous merriness. "Darling Fetinka," he wrote to the poet in Moscow on October 24, "truly, darling, I am awfully, awfully fond of you! That's all there is to it! To write stories is stupid and shameful. Verses? Well, perhaps. But to love a good man is very pleasant. It may be that contrary to my knowledge and consent there is inside me, and not yet ready, a story that compels me to love you. It almost feels like that sometimes. No matter what you are occupied with, be it manure or mange, you can't help going ahead and thinking up stories. Thank goodness, I am still not letting myself write and I will not do it. . . . Druzhinin begs me in the name of friendship to write a story. And to tell the truth I'd like to do it. But I would only write a worthless one. The Shah of Persia, he smokes his pipe, but I love you. What a joke!"

The story Tolstoy was preparing to write "between manure and mange" was *Family Happiness*. He had it in mind at this time but evidently it had not yet reached the point of fruition.

Toward the end of December the two Tolstoy brothers, Nikolai and Lev, on the invitation of a friend called Gromeko, went to Vyshny Volochok on a bear hunt. It almost cost Lev his life.

In his story for children "Freedom Is Stronger than Violence," Tolstoy describes the incident:

"In front of me there was a sudden sound—of someone whirling toward me, of snow showering down, of heaving breath. I looked ahead and there he was, plunging straight at me, along a path through a thicket of firs, and he was evidently frightened to death. At five paces I could see all of him: he had a black chest and a huge head with reddish whiskers. He rushed straight at me, his head down, scattering snow in all directions. I could tell by the bear's eyes that he did not see me but out of fright was crashing in any direction he could go."

Tolstoy fired, the first time he missed, but the second time he wounded the bear.

"He plunged at me," Tolstoy continues, "knocked me down and jumped over me. Well, thought I to myself, it's lucky he left me alone. I started to get to my feet, then felt something was pressing me and kept me from rising. He had been carried forward by his momentum and could not avoid jumping over me, but then he turned and hurled his whole weight on me. I could feel something heavy lying on me, feel something warm over my face, and then feel him take my whole face into his jaws. My nose was already in his mouth, I could smell it, it was hot and had the odor of blood. He pinned my shoulders down with his paws; I could not stir. All I could do was bend my head down to my chest, turning my nose and eyes away from his jaws. But he was expressly intent of getting at my eyes and nose. I could feel him sink the teeth of his upper jaw into my forehead near the hair and those of the lower jaw into my cheekbone below my eyes; he began to close his teeth and press. It was like knives going through my head; I struggled and tried to wriggle away, but he was in a hurry and gnawed at me like a dog, biting and biting. I tore myself away but he grabbed me again. Well, I thought, my end has come. Then suddenly I felt the weight lifted. I looked up and he was gone; he had jumped up off me and run away."

Tolstoy was saved by one of the hunters who ran up with a long switch in his hand and yelled at the bear, who thereupon abandoned his victim and fled into the woods.

Two weeks later they found him. Still later his skin was a rug in the Tolstoy home on Khamovnicheski Street in Moscow; the younger children loved to lie on it and lay their heads on the great broad head of the beast. The bear lacked one tooth—it had been knocked out by the bullet with which Tolstoy had wounded him.

During this period Tolstoy was writing a little on *Family Happiness*. "One should write slowly, calmly, without thought of publication," he noted in his diary for December 13, 1858.

This mood was obviously reflected in the story. Later on, in 1862, in writing about it A. Grigoryev said: "This is a tranquil piece of work, profound, simple and highly poetic, it is lacking in all affectation, and deals in a simple, unforced manner with the problem of the transition of passion into another kind of sentiment."

Yet *Family Happiness* did not create an impression in literary circles and Tolstoy himself was more than doubtful about the quality of his novel, calling it a "shameful piece of abomination." He even wanted to stop the publication of the second part and burn the manuscript. It was only Botkin who, with his usual sensitiveness, rallied to Tolstoy's support. In a letter to him dated May 13, 1859, he said:

"I read the proofs of the second part with the most hypercritical care and what happened! The result was not at all what I expected; I not only like the second part but I also find it magnificent in nearly all respects. In the first place it possesses a great inner dramatic strength, and in the second place it is a splendid psychological story, and finally it contains a deeply gripping portrayal of nature. . . ."

But Tolstoy's mood was based on the fact that when the novel came out not a single person gave him any understanding support. Even such a close friend as Alexandrine, although she found the novel charming, discovered in it elements that were "highly comical." Such a reaction, naturally, was worse than the severest criticism.

In April he wrote to Alexandrine: "I am beginning Lent and this time I shall try to go through it in such a way that I shall not be ashamed because of disappointing my own expectations or yours for me. Besides the weather now is such that you can see God in the sky and when you turn your eyes inward, if only for a little, you can hear Him in you."

But his Lenten project was not a success. Tolstoy wrote Alexandrine a remarkable letter: "Christ is risen! Granny dear. I say this not only because the weeks of Lent are over and I want to write but because I have a falsehood on my conscience and I must confess it. On Tuesday, when I wrote you I was carried away by the fact that the weather was fine and I thought I wanted to go through the Lenten course, that I was practically as saintly as that old woman of yours. It turned out, however, that to go through Lent alone and in the proper spirit was something of which I was incapable. So now you teach me what I must do. I could eat Lenten food, all my life if necessary, I can pray in my room, all day if you like, I can read the Gospel and for a while I can think this is all very important: but to go to church, to stand and listen to uncomprehending and incomprehensible prayers, to look at the priest and all the mixed crowd around me—that is absolutely impossible for me. For the second year in succession now that has dried up the springs of my Lenten fervor."

Granny was upset to the point of tears. Lev's lack of faith, as she saw it, his indifference to the church, were a great sorrow to her.

". . . If you truly believed in the Sacred Mysteries, you would not abandon your Lenten course so lightly—and only because the surroundings did not suit you. What pride, what lack of understanding, what indifference there is in your feelings—which you, in all probability, consider reverential and worthy of respect! At times it seems to me that you combine in yourself all the idolatry of the heathen, worshiping God in every ray of sunshine, in every phenomenon of nature, in every one of the untold manifestations of His grandeur, without realizing that you must penetrate the source of life in order to be enlightened and cleansed. What does 'observe Lent' properly mean and who of us can do it? We are unclean, repulsive, weak, callous and stained with sin. Because of this we must turn to Him Who wishes to heal us, to cleanse us and draw us nearer to Him: whereas you, in order to enter into communion with Him, wait for a moment when you are pleased with yourself or at least when you are in one of the states of exaltation when it seems to you that you amount to something. This is a fallacy, it is rank materialism carried to the point where you seek in your Lenten state first of all some individual and palpable satisfaction."

This rift between the two friends widened with the years until it became a deep chasm.

"Dear me, how you do go for me! Really, you don't give me a chance to get my breath! But joking aside, Granny dear, I am bad, a wretch, and I hurt your feelings, but need you punish me quite so severely? Everything you say is true and untrue. A man's convictions are not the ones he talks about but the ones he wrings out of life. It is hard for another to understand this and you do not know mine. And if you did you would not attack me so. . . . I was lonely and unhappy when I was living in the Caucasus, I began to think as one has the power to think only once in a lifetime. I have the notes I made during that time and now, as I reread them, I could not comprehend how a man can reach the degree of intellectual exaltation I reached then. It was painful but worth while. Never again, either before or after, did I reach the heights of thoughts, or see so far as during those two years. And everything I discovered I will retain as my permanent convictions. I cannot do otherwise. In those two years of intellectual effort I discovered a simple, old truth, but I know it better than anyone else: I discovered that immortality exists, that love exists, that one must live for others in order to be happy forever. These discoveries astonished me through their identity with the Christian religion, so I, instead of trying to find things out for myself, began to search in the Gospels but found little there. I found neither God, nor the Redeemer, nor mysteries—nothing; I searched with all, all, all the strength of my soul, I wept, I agonized, for I longed for nothing except the truth. For heaven's sake, do not believe that you can even begin to gather from these words all the effort and concentration that I put into my searchings of that time. This is a secret of the soul, it lies in each of us; yet I can say that I have rarely encountered in others such a passion for truth as that which possessed me then. That is what has remained my religion, and I am happy in it. . . ."

"May 3 . . . The point is that I love, I revere religion, I believe that without it man can be neither good nor happy, that I would rather possess it than anything in the world, that without it I feel my heart wither with every year, that I still hope, and for brief periods I seem to have faith, yet I have no religion and have no faith. Besides, with me life makes my religion and not religion my life. When I am living right I am closer to it, it seems to me that I am on the threshold, ready to enter that happy world; but when I am leading a bad life it seems to me that I have no need of religion.—Here in the country, I am disgusted with myself, I feel such an aridity in my heart, that I am disgusted and afraid, and then the need of it is more palpable. God willing, it will come to me. You laugh at nature and the nightingales. Yet for me it is—a conductor of religion. *Each soul has its own path*, an unknown path and it can only sense it down in its depths. . . ."

He had his own Tolstoyan path. This path he had to hew for himself; what he needed was sympathy, affection, warmth, not exhortation or moral instruction.

". . . Do you know what feelings your letters (some of them like these last in which you lecture me) arouse in me?" he wrote Alexandrine on June 12, 1859. "I feel as though I were a big baby unable to talk, and that I have a pain in my chest, you are so sorry for me, love me and want to be of help, that you rub me with balsam and stroke my head. I am grateful to you, I want to cry and kiss your hands in gratitude for your love and affection and sympathy; but that is not where it hurts and I am not able to tell you. . . ."

Tolstoy himself found the solution which was to give him joy, peace, a purpose in life and above all tremendous moral satisfaction. It was in teaching.

18

BEFORE he journeyed off to the Caucasus Tolstoy made his first attempt at teaching children in Yasnaya Polyana. He was twenty-one. But he was not fit for it then. He sensed that a school requires serious work for which he was not yet sufficiently mature, so he abandoned it.

A decade later popular education had moved ahead very little in Russia. The children in the villages were taught by half-baked parish deacons or semiliterate retired soldiers. The methods of these uneducated, ignorant teachers were the simplest. They gave their pupils prayers to learn by heart, the book of common prayer in church Slavonic. If they did not retain these properly, they were beaten, punished, made to kneel in the corner on hard dried peas.

Yet in this decade Tolstoy himself had changed. Disappointed in his own writing, he was in urgent need of some fresh activity as an outlet for his creative powers. With the inspired passion so much a part of his nature, he began to form a school based on his own free principles. Without any false or preconceived theories, without any scientific mumbo-jumbo, without any methods or considerations whatever he approached the problem of public education with breadth and boldness, with practical vitality and simplicity.

"There is no one method all bad or all good. . . . The shortcoming of a method lies in adhering exclusively to that one method, and the best method is an absence of all method, while possessing the knowledge and use of all methods and the ability to create new ones as emerging difficulties demand," wrote Tolstoy in the beginning of 1862.

"The best teacher is the one who is immediately prepared to explain whatever may be impeding the scholar. These explanations are provided to the teacher by his knowledge of the greatest possible number of methods, his capacity for evolving new methods and above all his refusal to follow any one method out of a conviction that all methods are one-sided, and that the very best would be one that would meet every conceivable obstacle in the path of the scholar, and that would mean not a method but an art and a talent."

"An art and a talent"; anyone who has been active in the field of pedagogy knows that everything is included in that. No matter how much an untalented teacher studies, no matter how many theories he applies, if he lacks a God-given capacity to understand children, he will never make a good teacher. Tolstoy had an inborn gift for teaching and his approach to children was simple and straightforward. Through his personal charm, the power of his creative spirit, he soon produced an atmosphere of contentment, almost of enthusiasm, among the children and some of the teachers.

"In the early autumn of 1859," wrote Vasili Morozov, one of Tolstoy's favorite pupils, in his memoirs, "we got word in the village of Yasnaya Polyana about the desire of Lev Nikolayevich—the Count as we called him—to open a school in Yasnaya Polyana, and about the fact that any children who wished to, could attend, that the school would be free. I remember what a storm that raised; there were village meetings, various interpretations and opinions were aired.

"Why was he doing it? What was the point? Might it not be some kind of a trick? It was contrary to nature to teach for nothing.

"Some parents even asserted that if they handed their children to the Count he'd train them and send them to the Tsar to be turned into soldiers, and they'd like as not be the very ones to fall into the hands of the Turks. Others argued more intelligently. . . . I don't care what you do, I'll send my child, said one man and this was repeated by a second, a third, and others followed, until they all agreed: and I'll send mine too."

As a rule peasant children stayed at home in winter warming themselves by the stoves. If they had to go out of doors they would seize any piece of footgear or clothing, belonging to mother, sisters or brothers. To go to school meant being properly dressed and many children had nothing to wear.

"They all set themselves to getting ready," Morozov continued, describing the first day: "they put on clean white shirts, new bast sandals, heads were smoothed down with oil or even butter, whatever was in the house. Look, there was Kiryusha dashing hurriedly into our cottage.

" 'Where's Vaska?' . . .

" 'Kiryusha', said I, 'I haven't anything to wear on my feet. I don't have any bast sandals.'

" 'As for mine, the heel is split. But I am going. What do you expect, that the master will be looking at your feet? Better see that your head is in good order!' . . .

"God pointed the way and I was soon ready. My thoughtful sister had long since gotten her own bast sandals and coat ready for me, although they were not at all my size: the sandals were too big and the coat too long, because I was skinny, thin as a slat, but I pulled up the coat, turned up the sleeves, slicked my hair with kvas [cider] there being no oil available.

"The children gathered in a lane with their fathers or mothers. Each parent brought his own [Vasya Morozov had a stepmother who did not like him, so his older sister took her place].

"The procession set off, with me in the rear accompanied by my sister. In a few minutes we were standing before the manor house. The children were whispering to each other. The parents told them what to do: 'As soon as the Count comes out you must make a bow and say: Good health to your Excellency.'

"I stood there like some bit of refuse, feeling that I was worse clad than any of the others, and even smaller and poorer and an orphan to boot. The thought came into my mind: What if they drive me away? Then my stepmother will dress me down again. But how wonderful it is here! I . . . never saw a house like this. . . . At the front door there appeared a man, the Count, our teacher. We all took off our caps and made a deep bow. My heart almost stopped beating; I clutched my sister's hand, steadying myself behind her as if she were a small fort.

" 'How do you do! You have brought your children to me,' said Lev Nikolayevich to the parents.

" 'Yes indeed, Your Excellency,' the older ones replied with a bow. . . .''

The children's fears were soon allayed. Tolstoy looked them all over, inquired of them whether they wanted to study, asked the parents to bring the girls too. Very soon the form of address of "Your Excellency," which their parents had taught them to use for the Count, was replaced by the simple "Lev Nikolayevich." Studies went swimmingly and inside three months the children read and wrote with ease. The first group of twenty-two had grown to almost seventy when Tolstoy divided them into three classes: oldest, middle and youngest.

Despite the fact that Vasya Morozov was the one to tremble most when he first met his teacher, Tolstoy immediately picked him out, smiled at him in friendly fashion and called him Vaska-cat (Russian equivalent of Tommy-cat). "We felt somehow as though we had met before," wrote Morozov, adding that he "loved school, and loved Lev Nikolayevich . . . we felt a most sincere, childlike affection for him and he had a most sincere affection for us. It was a community, but not an obligatory one, it was a community bound together by love."

In an article entitled "The Yasnaya Polyana School" Tolstoy gives a detailed description of his activities:

"The school is housed in a two-story stone building." This was the so-called wing, built originally in exactly the same style of architecture as the house in which Tolstoy lived to the end of his days. While the house in time was rebuilt and altered, the wing remained almost unchanged.

"Two rooms are occupied by the school, another is used as a study, and two by the teachers. At the front entrance, under the porte-cochere, hangs a bell with a cord tied to the clapper, in the entry there are parallel bars and a horse, and upstairs in the hall a carpentry bench. . . .

"In the village they get up by lamplight. From the school the lights in the windows have long been visible. Now within half an hour after the bell has rung, in fog or rain or in the darting rays of an autumn sun, dark figures appear on the hill (the village is separated from the school by a ravine) two or three in a group or singly. . . . It is no matter they have nothing to carry in their hands, they have nothing to carry in their heads either. There was no home work given out the day before, nothing to be learned by heart. There is no sense of oppression at the thought of the impending lessons. The schoolboy takes only himself along, his own impressionable nature and the confidence that it will be as much fun in school today as it was yesterday. He does not think about his class until the class begins. No one is rebuked for tardiness, and no one is ever tardy except perhaps older children retained at home by their fathers because of some chore. But later they run to school and arrive breathless. . . .

"The teacher comes into the room, some children are lying on the floor in a heap engaged in some noisy game. Those sitting at their books yell to them: 'Why are you making such a fuss! We can't hear ourselves think. Quit it!' The hotheads give in and all out of breath take up their books . . . the fighting spirit subsides and the spirit of reading settles over the room. With the same enthusiasm with which he pounded Mitka's head on the floor, one boy now reads . . . a book, his teeth practically clenched, his little eyes shining, unaware of anything near him except his book. It requires as much effort to tear him from his reading as it did earlier to tear him away from his squabbling. They sit wherever they like: on benches, tables, windowseats, the floor or in armchairs. . . .''

The longer Tolstoy worked with children the more fresh ideas came into his mind; his observations gave rise to new techniques, he reached new conclusions.

"School children are—people," he wrote in that same article "The Yasnaya Polyana School.'' "They may be small but they are none the less people, possessing the same needs as we and thinking along the same lines; they all want to study, for that purpose they came to school, and that is why they will always reach the easy conclusion that they must submit to certain conditions in order to be able to study. Not only are they people, they are society, bound together by the same idea: 'Wherever two or three are gathered together in my name, I am with them'! In submitting to rules that are natural, which derive from their own natures, they are not upset, they do not grumble; but when they must submit to your ill-timed interference they do not believe in the justness of your laws, schedules and rules."

Tolstoy could not be content to work on the problems of education merely in his own school. The brilliant results he achieved gave rise to thoughts of public education throughout Russia, and he wrote to the brother of the Minister of Public Education, Kovalevski, with whom he was well acquainted, asking what the minister's attitude would be toward the founding of a Society for Public Education.

"It must be startlingly evident," he wrote, "not only to us Russians but to any foreigner traveling a dozen miles in Russia what a numerical disproportion there exists between educated and uneducated people or, to be more precise, between literates and savages. Not to mention any comparison with the figures in various European countries. . . . This is a social evil which we are accustomed to recognize and explain in various ways, mostly as force, despotism, but which is none other than the force of overwhelming ignorance. Force cannot be inflicted by one man on many, only by a preponderant majority of those equal in ignorance."

In Tolstoy's opinion public education could be furthered only through private social initiative.

". . . The most urgent need of the Russian people is public education," he continued, in his letter to Kovalevski. "This does *not* exist. It has not even been started and it never will be as long as the government controls it. . . . To prove to you that it has not been begun we . . . could go together into my school and I could show you the ones who know how to read and write and who used to go to school to the priests and sextons. They are the only pupils who are utterly hopeless. There is nothing to laugh at in the arguments about whether literacy is worth while or not. This is a serious and tragic debate and I frankly take the negative. *Literacy*, the mere process of reading and writing, is harmful. In the first place, what do they read? That symbol of faith in old Slavonic, the prayer book, sermons (in old Slavonic), and in the second place a fortune-telling book, etc. Without actually checking on this practice it is difficult to conceive of the dreadful intellectual desolation it produces in the mentally capable, what ruin it brings to the moral outlook of the pupils. To make a success of public education it is necessary that it should be transferred to the charge of society."

In the same letter Tolstoy suggested a program for public education, and pointed out ways of raising the necessary money. Yet he was too well aware of the apathy of the government to entertain much hope for his plan and he ended on a pessimistic note:

"When you think of these things, you are ready to despair. What does the government fear? Would it be possible in a free school to teach things that should not be known? There would not be one single being in my school if I so much as hinted that relics are not as absolutely sacred as God Himself. But that does not keep them from knowing that 2 x 2 = 4. Well, what is to be will be: only let me know quickly, as quickly as possible."

From letters to his friends it is clear how his new teaching absorbed Tolstoy.

"By now I am useless as a writer. I am not writing, nor have I written anything since *Family Happiness*, and, so I think, I shall not write. I flatter myself at least with this hope. . . . Life is short and to spend my adult years writing novels of the kind I have been writing goes against one's conscience. I could and should and I want to undertake some job. Preferably it should be the kind that tires me out, demanding, a source of daring and power—that would be the thing. But at thirty-one to write very nice readable novels, good Lord, I really cannot raise a finger to do that!" so he wrote to Botkin.

Tolstoy's friends did not share his opinion or look with sympathy on his enthusiasm, feeling as they did that in burying himself in the country with his school children and abandoning literature he was destroying himself. In reply to the expostulations of his friend Chicherin, Tolstoy wrote: ". . . I do not say it is necessary to work, but one must choose work the fruits of which can be seen far enough ahead to make one able to devote oneself wholly to it: plowing land, teaching youngsters, being honest, etc. The self-conceit of so-called artists . . . is, for the person who comes under its spell, most abominably low and false. To do nothing all one's life, to exploit the work and gains of others for the purpose of eventually describing them is evil, low, perhaps even perverted and vile. . . . You ask, what have I been doing? Nothing special, no trumped-up work, something which is as natural to me as breathing and at the same time from its exaltation I often like to look down, I fear with a rather sinful pride, *sur vous autres*. You would love and understand this work of mine, it cannot be described, but come when you have finished your travels, to Yasnaya Polyana, and then tell me truly if you do not envy me when you see what I have done and the calm with which I go about doing it."

Never before had Tolstoy come so close to peasant life. It may be that his intimacy with Axinia Bazykina was one of the oblique reasons why he was absorbed by the peasantry, by the half-starved, undernourished little Vasyas, Ignatkas, Danilas in their homespun blouses, their patches, with their hands calloused from work. And at the same time that Tolstoy was opening new horizons, new delights and interests in life for them, he himself was discovering new and hidden treasures. . . . He was astounded by the mental capacity of these children, by their sensitiveness, by the ease with which they soaked up the knowledge he was giving them.

In these surroundings Tolstoy's theoretical ideas gave way to wholehearted convictions on the subject of serfdom, the inequalities and injustices under the existing structure of society.

By what right did the landowners enjoy the labor of the peasantry? What had they done for these people? What were the scholars, the writers, the journalists, doing? And why should millions of Russians live in slavery, poverty, ignorance, to provide food and drink for all these useless people?

The fire was kindled and never went out. But Tolstoy was to experience many things in the next twenty years, reach a peak of fame, before these thoughts burst forth in the bright flame of conviction which changed the course of his life.

❧ 19 ❧

THE children were sitting in the schoolroom as usual. They were working on a difficult problem with Lev Nikolayevich. When the problem was solved Teacher Tolstoy suddenly announced: "I am going away tomorrow, but keep on coming to your lessons. Other teachers will work with you."

The children were bitterly grieved.

"Lev Nikolayevich, will you be gone long?"

"I'll be back soon."

"How soon?"

"Well, I'll be gone about two weeks."

"Are you going far?"

"To a foreign country."

"It seemed to us," wrote Morozov in his memoirs, "that two weeks was a very long time. Why, when we did not see him for even an hour we felt as if we had been separated from him for a whole day. If he had said he was going away for a month I do not know what would have become of us; probably our whole school would have collapsed.

". . . He went away and we remained behind in an orphaned state. When we came back to school we could positively smell how empty it was—no games, no nonsense, nothing we learned stuck in our minds; it was as though we had buried him. One week passed after Lev Nikolayevich's departure, then another and still there was no Lev Nikolayevich. It was a long long time before he returned—I do not recall how many months, but it seemed like an eternity to us."

". . . It is spring and everything should be fine," Tolstoy wrote to Druzhinin on the 14th of April, 1860, "but a terrible grief is threatening me. You know that one of my brothers died of tuberculosis, and now this year the same symptoms are developing with terrifying speed in my brother Nikolai."

On July 1 of that year Tolstoy, together with his sister Maria and her children, set out for St. Petersburg, where they boarded a steamer for Stettin. His brother Nikolai, and Sergei too, were already abroad.

Nikolai had been in poor health for a long time; he was losing weight and coughing. However, probably because of his modest nature, he never complained, never paid particular attention to himself. It was only when the symptoms of his illness became obvious that his relatives took serious note of the state of his health.

Nikolai had been stationed on the Terek frontier on two occasions, and had spent two years in the Caucasus, where wine flowed in rivers, and he had acquired the habit of drinking.

Fet said in his memoirs: "Unfortunately, this remarkable man—of whom it is not enough to say he was loved by those who knew him, one would rather say he was adored—acquired the habit current among the military in the Caucasus of drinking strong spirits. Although I knew Nikolai Tolstoy at a later period and went hunting with him, where drinking was more accessible to him than at any evening party, yet in all the three years I was acquainted with him I never saw in Nikolai Tolstoy even a shade of drunkenness. He used to sit with his easy chair pulled up to the table and sip tea laced with brandy."

Turgenyev, as well as Fet, admired Nikolai Tolstoy and was cordially devoted to him. "That humility toward life," Turgenyev used to say, "that Lev Tolstoy theorized about, his brother applied directly to his own existence. He always lived in impossible quarters, almost in hovels, in some distant part of Moscow, and gladly shared all he had with the poorest of the poor. He was an entrancing conversationalist and raconteur, but writing was for him almost a physical impossibility."

The estates of Fet and Turgenyev were close by Nikolskoye-Vyazemskoye, the family home which Nikolai inherited as the eldest son, and they often visited each other in the rare intervals when Nikolai was not in Moscow or visiting his sister or brothers. Nikolai's old lemon-yellow, lopsided *calèche* with his three gray horses was a familiar and welcome sight to his neighbors. Everyone poked fun at his carriage. Because of its advanced age the left side wheels sagged out so far that the main part was all one-sided and the right wheels were pushed up against the body. Despite this the old *calèche* was sound, it never broke down, and continued to roll along the deep-rutted country roads, in the spring often sinking to its hubs in the black mud. Because of its extraordinary hardiness, Fet dubbed the carriage a "Symbol of the Soul's Immortality" and the name remained.

In his memoirs Fet wrote that "when Nikolai Nikolayevich used to stay in his wing of the manor house the drowsy, hungry flies would cling to the glasses, the plates, the walls. They would come to life again, buzzing and clustering on the food, falling into the vodka in our glasses, the soup in our plates. Lev Nikolayevich used to say: 'When my brother is not at home no food is brought into this part of the house and the flies, submitting to fate, settle silently on the walls, but as soon as he arrives the most vigorous ones among them begin to tell all their neighbors: There he is, he has come, he'll go right over to the sideboard and take some vodka to drink; soon he will bring in some bread and hors d'oeuvres. . . . Come along boys—z-z-z-z!' "

When these friends heard of Nikolai's illness they were disturbed.

Turgenyev wrote to Fet from Soden (June 1, 1860): "Can it be that this precious and sweet person is to die! Yet how can this illness be arrested? . . ." and added the postscript: "If Nikolai Tolstoy has not yet left, go down on your knees to him and then collar him and send him abroad. Here . . . the air is mild, the kind we never have anywhere inside of Russia."

When Lev Tolstoy reached Bad Kissingen with his sister and her children, he wrote home to his Auntie Tatiana: "We have had letters from my brothers, in which Nikolai writes that Soden would seem to have helped him."

Evidently Nikolai himself did not realize how ill he was. In a letter to Diakov on July 19 (New Style calendar) he wrote: "My health is improving, although not fundamentally. . . ."

It is not likely that Sergei would have continued to gamble away his money in roulette or Lev would have traveled carefree through Germany—visiting schools, attending lectures at the university in Berlin, going on walking trips—if they had dreamed Nikolai was soon to pass away. It was only after Sergei went to see him in Soden and sent word that Nikolai's illness caused him grave concern that Lev went to him and carried him off to the South of France, to Hyères. But it was already too late. On the 20th of September (New Style) Nikolai died.

"The black seal on my letter will tell you all," Lev wrote to Auntie Tatiana. "The eventuality I have been expecting from hour to hour for the last two weeks took place today at nine in the evening. He was conscious throughout; even a quarter of an hour before he died he whispered several times: 'My God, my God.' I believe he sensed his condition but deceived us and himself."

To his brother Sergei he wrote: "I feel sorry for you that you were not here, even if it was painful I am glad it happened in my presence and that it had the right effect on me. It was not the way Mitenka died . . . he mastered himself and was quite changed; he was gentle and kind; he did not groan, did not have a word to say against anyone, he praised everyone and kept saying: 'Thank you, *my friend.*' You can realize what that meant in our relationship to each other. . . . I am sorry for you, sorry this news will reach you when you are out hunting, diverting yourself, and it will not affect you as it has us. It has certainly cut deep. I feel something now that I had often heard, that when you lose a person as close as he has been to us it is much easier to think about death."

"Nikolenka's death was the most powerful impression of my life," Tolstoy wrote in his diary in 1860.

In the course of his life Tolstoy frequently spoke of his brother and he touched on his memory as if it were something high and luminous. "He was more intelligent and gifted than I," he used to say, "but because of his great modesty, his humility, he never was able to express himself."

This feeling for their brother was so strong that it permeated the whole Tolstoy family.

Whenever guests or visitors to Yasnaya Polyana looked at the bust of Nikolai Tolstoy, which stood in a place of honor, and asked who the thin, smooth-shaven man with such noble features might be, his close friends and members of the family used to reply:

"That was the elder, beloved brother of Lev Tolstoy. He was a remarkable man."

❧ 20 ❧

TOLSTOY did not wish, as he wrote his brother Sergei, to have people in Russia think that his teaching "bore the imprint of foreign countries," but he did desire "to be informed on all that had been done in this field." He undertook a painstaking study of European schools, visiting universities as well as undergraduate schools. He attended lectures in Berlin, conversed with pastors, with the lights of the educational world as well as with rank and file teachers. He went to Germany, Switzerland, France, England, Italy, Belgium, and was interested in the schools of America. Occasionally there are brief notes in his dairy on his impressions.

"Dreadful," he wrote about a German school in Kissingen. "Prayers for the king, thrashing, everything learned by heart, frightened, morally crippled children."

In these foreign schools Tolstoy was seeking confirmation of a theory which was becoming more and more a conviction with him. Education should be as necessary as daily bread. Study cannot be forced. What one must do, in answer to inquiry, is to present knowledge in such form that every student will eagerly seize upon it. But he met with disillusion everywhere he went.

To prove his theory that a person acquires knowledge easily, when the teaching contains no element of compulsion, he wrote, later:

". . . One need only get into contact and talk with someone from the populace in order to be convinced that . . . the French people are almost just what they believe themselves to be: perceptive, intelligent, sociable, freethinking, and in reality civilized. Consider an urban workingman of almost thirty; he will be able to write a letter, not with the mistakes he made in school, and often without any at all; he has some grasp of politics, therefore of most recent history, of geography; he knows something of the stories of various novels, he has some information on natural sciences; he often knows how to draw and he applies mathematical formulas to his trade." Where did he acquire all this? From books, on the street, from newspapers, in museums—that was Tolstoy's answer.

"Whether this is a good or a bad education—that is another matter," Tolstoy goes on, "but there it is, an unconscious education, how many times more effective than any compulsion; there it is, an unconscious schooling which has sapped the compulsory type of education and reduced its contents almost to nil. Nothing has remained beyond the despotic form, almost entirely lacking in content. I say *almost*—except only the mechanical skill of putting letters next to each other and producing words, the only knowledge acquired in five or six years of teaching."

Tolstoy was convinced that mechanical memorizing was harmful, and that wrong methods ruined the children.

In a conversation with the nephew of the famous pedagogue Froebel—a socialist revolutionary—Tolstoy astonished Froebel by his assertion that "the Russian people are not yet spoiled, whereas Germans are like a child who has been subjected for several years to the wrong kind of training," and "that education should not be compulsory, or if it is the need for it should arise of itself, like the need for food."

One can easily imagine the horror of the "civilized Europeans," who were taking such pride in their *Kultur* and Western thought, when they heard such opinions from the lips of Tolstoy!

We find even harsher condemnation in a letter he wrote to an "unknown": ". . . it is terrifying even to me when I sum up the conclusions at which I must arrive as the result of all I have seen, *Heraus damit*. Let us be frank. It is only we Russian barbarians who do not know positively, who hesitate and seek for solutions for man's future in life, for improved means of education, whereas in Europe all these are solved problems, and what is most remarkable of all they have been solved in a thousand different ways. In Europe they know not only the laws of the future development of humanity, but also the avenues which it will follow, they know the character of the supreme, harmonious development of man and how it is to be achieved. They know what science and what art are more or less serviceable and for whom. Nor is that all. They have taken the soul of man apart like some complicated substance, dividing it into memory, mind, feelings, etc., and they know just how much of which kind of exercise is needed for each part. They know what poetry is better than any other. Moreover, they believe and know what faith is the very best. With them everything is provided for, they have set up ready-made, unalterable molds for the development of human nature on all sides. And all this is not a farce, a paradox, a piece of irony, it is a fact of which any free person must become convinced who had in mind the purpose of observing one school after another, as I did, even if only in Germany. . . ."

". . . In a Protestant school you find that the teacher has not only a prescribed schedule concerning the sequence of subjects which he must accept, the number of hours which he must devote to prayers, to each subject, to each exercise, but also that even this is directed, that is to say, the methods which he may use are defined and laid down in advance. . . . One hundred, two hundred boys come in at a given hour, they say a prayer, they sit down on benches and all two hundred begin to do the same thing. A boy in school is unable to express what he does not understand, whether this or that is agreeable to him, or what his desires are. All variation of thought in the classroom is reduced to the simple expression of 'I can'—'I will,' which is done by the raising of a hand.

". . . All that you see is the bored faces of children, forcibly herded into an institution, impatiently alert for the bell and meanwhile awaiting with terror a question asked by the teacher for the purpose of obliging them against their will to follow the instruction.

"It is superfluous to prove that a school where they teach for three years what one can learn in three months is a school of idleness and sloth. A child, forced to sit motionless over a book for six hours, who learns in the course of a year what he could learn in half an hour, is artificially being inculcated with the most complete and vicious idleness."

Self-assurance, complete satisfaction in one's own achievements, were things Tolstoy never could tolerate; to him it was like slamming the door on all further improvement, all advance.

After ripping up the elementary and intermediate educational institutions of Europe, Tolstoy proceeded to criticism of the universities.

"Of the subjects taught not one is applicable to life, and they are taught the way one learns the prayer book. . . . I except only the experimental courses, such as chemistry, physiology, anatomy, even astronomy, in which the students are called upon to do work; but all the other subjects, such as philosophy, history, law, philology, they learn by rote with the single purpose of getting through examinations of whatever kind, incidental or final, it makes no matter."

Perhaps these were the thoughts going through Tolstoy's mind when he, as a nineteen-year-old youth, left the university. Then he was overburdened with the necessity of studying subjects that were both uninteresting and unnecessary to him, while being prevented from doing what he was actually interested in and what he could find of use in the future.

Tolstoy turned his attention to American schools. He wrote to the Minister of Public Education, E. P. Kovalevski, that he had ordered school curricula, publications and manuals in pedagogy from the United States sent in his care. Later on, certain thoughts expressed by Tolstoy in 1862 were widely introduced into American universities and even into intermediate schools. Tolstoy for his part was struck by the American system for the spreading of public education. In his "Outline of a General Plan for the Institution of Public Schools," he wrote: "America's success derives only from the fact that its schools developed in consonance with the times and the surroundings. It is exactly in this way, so it seems to me, that Russia should act: I am firmly convinced that in order to have the Russian system of public education no worse than others (and because of the circumstances of the times it should be better) it must be indigenous and unlike other systems. . . .

"As is generally known America is the only country in the world which does not have a peasant class *de jure* or even *de facto*. Because of this the distinctions in education and attitude toward it cannot exist in America as they do here between the peasant and nonpeasant classes. Moreover, America, in building its system, I assume, was convinced that it possessed the most essential element on which to base schools—the teachers. . . . If America, which began its schools after those in the European states, has gone farther in public education than Europe, the inevitable conclusion is that it has carried out its historic function and that Russia must in turn perform its function. If Russia transplanted to its soil the American compulsory (through taxation) system, it would be acting as mistakenly as America would have done had it adopted the German or English system of education when it first established its schools."

Tolstoy remained abroad for over nine months. He spent many hours with workingmen, artisans, peasants and many distinguished persons of the time. He learned much, but from his observations he often drew unfavorable conclusions.

"What has happened in these last four months?" he asked himself in his diary for April 13, 1861. "It is hard to say now. Italy, Nice, Florence, Leghorn, Naples. A first vivid impression of nature and antiquity. Rome—return to art. Hyères, Paris, rapprochement with Turgenyev. London—a blank; revulsion against civilization. Brussels—a gentle sense of family life. Eisenach—a journey —thoughts about God and immortality, God restored, hope of immortality. . . ."

The intensity of his grief-stricken resentment caused by the death of his brother slowly subsided. He was helped by his constant, burning interest in his brain child, his school project and everything connected with it. As always he sought out people capable of sharing in the thoughts forever surging in him, but he found very few. The majority shied away from the daringly revolutionary, moral and philosophical views on education, on life, which Tolstoy did not hesitate to express.

In London he met Alexander Herzen. He had long been interested in this writer who had been expelled from Russia because of his revolutionary activities. He made a brief note about him in his diary for July 23: "A turbulent mind, great ambitions, yet with breadth, shrewdness and kindness, a refinement that is Russian." In the beginning of their acquaintance even Herzen, for all the breadth of his views, inwardly recoiled from Tolstoy. Probably Turgenyev shared fully the views of Herzen, who wrote him: "Tolstoy is an intimate friend; we have already ceased arguing; he is stubborn and talks nonsense, but he is open-hearted and good. . . . But why does he not use his head instead of taking everything by storm and valor as he did at Sevastopol."

Through Herzen Tolstoy met distinguished revolutionaries—the famous French economist and scholar Proudhon, the Polish revolutionary Lelewel. The views of these men greatly impressed him. He was interested in them but their effect on him was by no means deep.

By contrast, in Dresden Tolstoy met a man whose views were so akin to his own that he felt like someone parched for spiritual communion who suddenly comes upon a spring of living waters. . . .

Tolstoy had read a story by the German novelist Berthold Auerbach called *A New Life*. In it he found ideas about the people and public education so identical with his own that they might have been expressed by him.

"You yourself are the best teacher. With the help of the children create your own method and all will go well. Any abstract method is an absurdity. The best that a teacher can do in a school will depend on him personally, on his own capacities."

In this story Auerbach described a titled aristocrat who, under an assumed name, goes off into a remote village and devotes himself to the service of his people by becoming a country schoolteacher.

"Auerbach," exclaims Tolstoy in his diary, "is the most enchanting of men. . . ."

His meeting with him was encouraging and made a profound impression. On his return to Russia he spoke of him to Nekrasov and suggested that he publish a translation of Auerbach's story.

Tolstoy was now eager to return home. "I am on fire to get back to Russia," he wrote Tatiana Alexandrovna (from Dresden on April 18, 1861). ". . . I have wanted to use my journey to fullest advantage. I believe I have done that. I am carrying away such a great quantity of impressions and information that I shall be busy for a long time before I can get it all straightened out in my head."

All that Tolstoy had accumulated abroad he put into his store solely for use in his work among his little barefoot friends, the "Taraskas and Marthas" in whose lives he had immersed himself, with whom he felt an almost blood relationship, as though they were his own family, all bred and nourished by the same Russian land in Tula.

If they had not been constantly in his mind, how could he, while

still abroad, have made the first draft of one of his best stories—
Polikushka?

How could he, while still abroad, have outlined a program and articles for a proposed pedagogical magazine *The Country School-teacher?*

On the 19th of February, 1861, a great event took place in Russia, one which stirred the entire country: a manifesto which proclaimed the emancipation of the serfs was published. It was signed by Emperor Alexander II, and concluded with these words:

"Shield yourselves under the sign of the Cross, O Orthodox nation, and together with us invoke a Divine Blessing on your free labor, the guarantee of your domestic felicity and social well-being."

It opened up for Tolstoy a new and large field of activity for which he was quite unfitted but into which he could not refuse to enter—in the role of mediator.

❧ 21 ❧

THERE were various kinds of landowners in Russia. There were the more civilized kind, who had tried even under the system of serfdom to improve the lot of their peasants, who were fair to their household domestics and concerned themselves with their welfare. These landowners welcomed the emancipation of the serfs and co-operated in carrying out the law. Others feared ruin, protested against dividing the best lands among the peasants and tried in every way to maintain their own advantages. Still others were simply bewildered by the new edict, and grasped nothing except the fact that the government had sadly let them down by taking away their serfs.

In carrying out the reform, misunderstandings were inevitable, and were often followed by litigation. In order to clear up all these matters the government appointed special officers—mediators— who were charged with straightening out the disputes which cropped up between the landowners and the peasants.

Tolstoy was named mediator for the First District of Krapivna in the province of Tula. His appointment brought forth a storm of protest from the Provincial and County Marshals of the Nobility and from many landowners. He enjoyed the reputation of being a free-thinking, brusque, plain-speaking man and many Tula landowners both feared and disliked him. The school he had founded on a new and free basis had only confirmed their opinion of him.

"Knowing the lack of sympathy toward him [Tolstoy] on the part of the Krapivna nobility," wrote the Provincial Marshal of the Nobility to Valuyev, Minister of the Interior, "because of his dealings on his own estate, the [County] Marshal fears that when the Count enters into his new office there may arise certain unpleasant clashes capable of impeding the peaceful execution of such an important undertaking."

From every point of view the Marshal of the Nobility considered that Daragan, the Governor, in appointing Tolstoy as mediator, had committed an error. When he received the above denunciation, the Minister instantly asked the Governor for an explanation. The Governor replied:

"Being personally acquainted with Count Tolstoy and knowing him to be a man of education, ardently devoted to the present undertaking, and having taken into consideration the explicit desire of certain landowners of the Krapivna district to have Count Tolstoy as mediator, I could not replace him with some other person unknown to me—the more so that Count Tolstoy was suggested to me by your Excellency's predecessor as well as by certain other persons who enjoy the highest repute."

Tolstoy's appointment was finally confirmed by the Senate.

A mediator was called upon to decide the greatest variety of matters: the peasants' cattle trampled the landowners' meadows, and the landowner demanded too large a compensation; or the peasants demanded an apportionment of land not belonging to them; or the landowners refused to let their serfs go free.

In reply to a complaint by a woman landowner Tolstoy wrote: "Mark [a former serf] will go away, on my order, wherever he likes, and take his wife along. I shall respectfully ask you to do the following: (1) compensate him for service illegally rendered since the time of the promulgation of the edict, three and a half months, and (2) also for the beating given his wife even more illegally. If you do not like my decision you have the right to appeal to the mediation assembly and the Governor's session."

It is easy to imagine the resentment and indignation on the part of the landowner accustomed to complete power over her serfs. She probably had only a hazy notion of the manifesto and she attributed any such unjust decision not so much to the law promulgated by the Tsar—Little Father himself—as to the freethinking ways of the mediator, Count Tolstoy, who did not shrink from insulting a poor, defenseless noblewoman.

There were many dissatisfied people. Not only did the reform itself demand great tact on the part of the government in relation to both parties; but neither the landowners nor the peasants had any clear conception of their rights and responsibilities. Tolstoy had an especially difficult time because the work was alien to his whole being. He was obliged to sit in judgment on people, make firm decisions, constantly refuse pleas, none of it easy for him. Yet he could not refuse to take on this heavy duty, being well aware of the importance of the reform which he himself had labored to bring into existence. He apportioned to his own peasants the major part of his lands and set the moderate price of four rubles a desyatin (2.7 acres) as the compensation.

To Alexandrine he wrote: "The mediation work is interesting and absorbing, but it is too bad that the nobility has come to hate me with all their hearts. . . ."

Nevertheless, in many instances Tolstoy did, in the interest of justice, take the part of the landowners and firmly reject illegal demands put forward by the peasants.

On occasion the landowners went into court against Tolstoy, but in the majority of cases his decisions were upheld. His contemporaries assert that he was a good mediator, honest and just; but when it came to the paper work, the red tape, he was incapable of coping with it so that complete disorder reigned in his office.

Tolstoy held the post of mediator for about a year. In May of 1862 the Senate "relieved Artillery Lieutenant Count Lev Tolstoy, for reasons of ill health, of the office with which he had been entrusted by order of the Governing Senate as mediator for Krapivna District." Tolstoy was glad. He was weary and the job was growing increasingly burdensome.

꧁ 22 ꧂

THE quarrel actually occurred in the spring of 1861, at the very time when Tolstoy was engaged in his activities as mediator. But the event, as we have seen, had been in the making for years.

Turgenyev and Tolstoy had both watched with a jealous eye every new product of the other's pen and hastened to express what seemed to them impartial criticism. But their output was so at variance in its very substance that no matter how objective each attempted to be in his approach to the other, he was bound to be prejudiced.

We do know that *A Sportsman's Sketches* exercised a great influence on Tolstoy as a youth. We also know that Turgenyev hailed *Childhood* and the *Sevastopol Stories* with enthusiasm but that Tolstoy's later works did not please him.

One has to admit that Tolstoy did not make friends easily. He was always a puzzle to his fellow writers.

On April 6, 1859, Botkin had written Turgenyev: "Tolstoy is still here and working on his story [*Family Happiness*]. . . . Yesterday I told him [Tolstoy] right out that I found it cold and dull. He is of quite a different opinion. I see him quite frequently—but I understand him as little as ever. His nature is full of passions, vagaries and caprice. And at the same time it makes for discomfort in relation to other people, and he is full of invention, theories, schemes which change almost daily."

There is but little doubt that Turgenyev fully shared Botkin's opinion.

"I have settled my account with Tolstoy," Turgenyev wrote to Botkin on April 12 of the same year. "As a human being he no longer exists for me. God grant him and his talent every good fortune, but as for me when I hail him I inevitably wish to bid him farewell and without further meeting. We were created poles apart. If I eat some soup and like it I can know that if for no other reason than that Tolstoy will dislike it—and vice versa."

One can further see Turgenyev's relations with Lev Tolstoy in a letter Turgenyev wrote to Fet:

[129]

"Kiss Nikolai Tolstoy," he wrote. "And to Lev my greetings, as well as to his sister." A postscript added: "There is no reason for me to write him; I know he had no love for me, nor I for him. We are made of too different elements: yet there are many paths in the world; we shall not seek to obstruct one another."

Tolstoy was unhappy, sensing as he did that his relationship to Turgenyev had come to naught. His heart was ready to love Turgenyev. In a letter to Fet he wrote: "Hang it all! I am fed up with loving him!" As for their "obstructing" one another, that is something that could not have entered Tolstoy's mind.

In his memoirs Fet set down what he called the "bull's-eye" remark of Nikolai Tolstoy: "Turgenyev cannot in any way accommodate himself to the thought that Lyovochka is growing up and leaving his tutelage."

Indeed Turgenyev found fault with absolutely everything Tolstoy did. When he heard that he had taken up teaching, Turgenyev wrote to Fet: "So Lev Tolstoy continues to have his vagaries. Evidently he was born to be that way. When will he take his last somersault and finally land on his feet?"

"I have read *On the Eve*," Tolstoy wrote Fet on February 23, 1860. "This is my opinion of it: writing novels is useless in general and even more so if those writing them are dispirited or do not have a good idea of what they want to get out of life. Incidentally, *On the Eve* is a great improvement over *A Nest of Gentlefolk* and there are two outstanding characters in it: the artist and the father. The others are not even types, their fictional concept, their circumstances are not typical, or else they are quite commonplace. Incidentally, this is a constant mistake of Turgenyev's. His girl is bad from the very start: *Oh, how I love you . . . and her eyelashes were long.* I am always astonished by Turgenyev, that with his intelligence and poetic sensitiveness he is not able to restrain himself from banality even in his style . . . if he has no pity for his most worthless characters, he should ridicule them in such a way as to make us laugh at them and not just vent his spleen and dyspepsia." Whereupon Tolstoy, anxious to be just to the last, adds: "Even if they are unsuccessful it should be said in general that no one is capable of writing such novels today."

In May, 1861, Turgenyev wrote Fet that he wanted to come down with Tolstoy to make him a visit on his estate Stepanovka.

"I want to see Ivan Sergeyevich [Turgenyev] but my desire to see you is ten times greater," Tolstoy wrote Fet when he received his invitation.

On the way to the Fets' Tolstoy stopped by at Turgenyev's estate of Spasskoye. The incident that occurred here was one that Tolstoy could not recall without horror to the end of his days. Turgenyev suggested that Tolstoy read the manuscript of his new novel *Fathers and Sons*. After a copious supper—Turgenyev liked to have good food for himself and his guests—he put Tolstoy in a soft, deep armchair in the living room, with his manuscript on a table nearby, gave him cigarettes, lighted the candles, making him as comfortable as possible, and left the room.

The warmth of the room after the long journey and the heavy supper produced their effect. Tolstoy started reading, but was soon overpowered by sleep and dozed off. . . . When he awoke with a start, he saw Turgenyev's back in a closing door: he was noiselessly tiptoeing out of the room.

What had he seen and noticed? Tolstoy was horribly embarrassed.

It is easy to imagine how deeply Turgenyev would have been offended by this lack of interest in his famous novel *Fathers and Sons* if he had really noticed.

The writers reached Stepanovka on May 26.

"At the usual time in the morning," Fet wrote, "that is to say eight o'clock, the guests came into the dining room where my wife was seated at the head of the table behind the samovar and I, in anticipation of the coffee, had taken my place at the other end. Turgenyev sat down on his hostess's right and Tolstoy on her left. Knowing the importance attributed at that time [by Turgenyev] to his daughter's education, my wife asked him if he were satisfied with his English governess. Turgenyev was full of praise for the governess and went on to tell how she, with English punctiliousness, had asked him to fix the sum his daughter might have at her disposal for charitable purposes. 'Now,' Turgenyev said, 'this Englishwoman requires my daughter to handle the shabbiest clothing of the poor, mend it with her own hands and return it to the owners.'

" 'And you consider that a good thing for her to do?' asked Tolstoy.

" 'Of course; it brings the benefactress into close contact with urgent needs!'

" 'But I think that a dressed-up girl holding dirty and evil-smelling and ragged garments in her lap is doing an insincere and theatrical piece of acting.'

" 'I beg you not to say such things!' ejaculated Turgenyev.

" 'Why shouldn't I say it if that is what I think?' retorted Tolstoy.

"Before I could call out to Turgenyev: 'Do stop!' he, pale with rage, said: 'Then I will silence you with an insult!' With that he jumped up from the table and, putting his hands to his head, staggered into the next room. In a moment he came back to us and turning to my wife, said: 'For heaven's sake forgive me for my rude behavior, which I deeply regret.' With that he again left the room."

The kind hosts were in despair. It was exactly as though an abscess, which had been forming for years, had suddenly burst. Easygoing Fet was incapable of controlling the ire of his two passionate and enraged guests. He realized that such a quarrel, between two of the greatest writers of the time, might lead to a duel, with the possible death of one of them. At that time every Russian still bore vividly in mind the keen sense of loss of Russia's two greatest poets—Pushkin and Lermontov—both killed in duels, at the very zenith of their powers, by worthless rivals.

It was necessary to take immediate action. Fet ordered Turgenyev's carriage to be prepared. Having dispatched Turgenyev he had his own horses brought around to send Tolstoy to his brother-in-law Borisov.

Fet felt that Turgenyev was to blame, that he should have asked Tolstoy's pardon and also that of his hosts in whose house he had precipitated such an unmannerly quarrel.

Turgenyev agreed and wrote as follows to Tolstoy:

"Lev Nikolayevich, dear Sir: I can only repeat what I considered I was obliged to say to you at the Fets': being carried away by a sentiment of involuntary hostility, the cause for which I shall not go into here, I offended you for no valid reason on your part and I ask your pardon. What occurred this morning has clearly proven that all attempts to bring together two such opposite temperaments as yours and mine cannot do any good; I therefore am all the more glad to do my duty with regard to you, since this present letter is probably the last manifestation of any relationship whatsoever between us. I wish with all my heart that it may satisfy you and I agree in advance to your making any use of it you see fit. And I beg to remain, dear Sir, Your respectful servant, Ivan Turgenyev. Spasskoye, May 27, 1861."

Turgenyev dispatched the letter to the Borisovs; but Tolstoy had stopped at the railway station of Bogoslovo. Not receiving any letter, Tolstoy became further enraged and wrote Turgenyev a letter in which he challenged him to a duel. He sent a man to the estate of his deceased brother Nikolai for weapons and ammunition. The duel was to take place in the vicinity of Bogoslovo on the edge of the forest. Tolstoy did not close his eyes that night; he was prepared to shoot in earnest, not sparing himself or his antagonist; his soul was in an angry turmoil. . . . But instead of Turgenyev a man finally arrived with Turgenyev's letter.

Nevertheless, it was a long time before Tolstoy could calm down. "I wish you good luck in your dealings with that man but I despise him, I have written him and thereby broken all contact with him unless he requires satisfaction. Despite all my apparent calm I have been inwardly disturbed, and I have felt that I must demand a more positive apology from him, Turgenyev, and this is what I did in the letter I wrote from Novosyolki. Here is his reply, with which I am satisfied except that I have answered that I exculpate him not because of our antithetical temperaments but for other reasons which he himself can conceive. Besides, I had in the meanwhile sent another rather harsh letter, with a challenge, and to that I have had no reply; but if I do receive one I shall return it to him unopened. This then is the end of a sorry story which, if it crosses the threshold of your house, should carry with it this supplement. L. Tolstoy."

In a second letter to Tolstoy, Turgenyev wrote: "Your man tells me that you desire a reply to your letter; but I do not see what I can add to that which I have already written. Should I recognize your right to demand satisfaction from me by arms? Yet you preferred to be satisfied by an expressed and repeated apology. That was your choice. I state plainly that I should be happy to face your fire in order to make amends for my truly insane remarks. The things I said so contravened the habits of my whole life that I can attribute them only to an exasperation evoked by the extreme and constant antagonism between our points of view. This is not an excuse, I do not mention it as a justification, but in explanation. And therefore, in parting from you forever—such occurrences are irrevocable and cannot be wiped out—I consider it my duty once more to repeat that in this matter you were right and I was in the wrong. I shall only add that there is no question of any courage, which I might or might not choose to display, and I admit your right to call me out in a duel, in the usual manner of course (with seconds), as well as your right to accept my apology. You have chosen as you saw fit and there is nothing left for me to do but bow to that decision. Again I beg you to accept the assurance of sincere respect. Ivan Turgenyev."

Several months passed. Tolstoy's anger against Turgenyev cooled and as always after he had quarreled with anyone, he began to feel oppressed by the hostile relations between himself and Turgenyev. He wrote Turgenyev a conciliatory letter. But at the very same time, unfortunately, rumors were reaching Turgenyev that Tolstoy was accusing him of cowardice in refusing to accept his challenge to a duel.

"Dear Sir," Turgenyev wrote Tolstoy from Paris, "On the eve of my departure from St. Petersburg I learned that you are circulating in Moscow a copy of your last letter to me and saying at the same time that I am a coward, that I refused to fight a duel with you, etc. It was impossible for me to return to Tula and I continued my journey. But as I consider such actions on your part, after all that I did to make up for my inadvertent remark, both insulting and disgraceful—I warn you in advance that this time I shall not let this go unnoticed and when I return next spring to Russia I shall demand satisfaction from you.

"I consider it necessary to inform you that I have sent word of my intentions to my friends in Moscow so that they will be in a position to refute the rumors spread by you. I. Turgenyev."

Of course, there was no basis whatever for the rumors. "As for Turgenyev," Tolstoy wrote on October 28, 1861, to Boris Chicherin, "all I shall say is that I am wholeheartedly sorry for him and I shall do all in my power to calm him down. I am as capable of fighting a duel with him, especially after a year has passed and we are separated by some 1,500 miles as I am of dressing up like a savage and doing a war dance on Tverskaya Street."

His reply to Turgenyev was brief: "Dear Sir, You wrote me that my actions were *disgraceful*; moreover you told me in person that you will 'punch my nose,' but I tender you an apology, admit that I am in the wrong, and abandon my right to challenge you. Count L. Tolstoy, October 8, 1861, Yasnaya Polyana."

Much water had to flow under the bridge before the two greatest writers of their time could meet again on friendly terms.

It was seventeen years later that Tolstoy made the first gesture of reconciliation toward Turgenyev.

❧ 23 ❧

WHERE Tolstoy did his work as a mediator out of a sense of duty, his work in the school was to him pure joy. "It is an idyllic, fascinating thing, from which it is hard to break away," he wrote to Alexandrine. "I tear myself from the office and from the peasants who pursue me at every step of the building. Then I go to the school where the lessons, since the classrooms are being done over, are held in the nearby garden. . . . The teacher instructs them according to my advice but is not altogether successful, and this the children sense. They are more fond of me. We talk on for three or four hours and no one is bored. . . . The building for the school is almost ready. There are three large rooms—one in pink, two in pale blue which are to serve as schoolrooms. In the same place there will be, in addition, a museum. On shelves running along the walls lie minerals, butterflies, skeletons, grasses, flowers, physics apparatus, etc. On Sundays the museum is open to the general public and Keller, a German from Jena (who has turned out to be a splendid young man), conducts experiments. Once a week we hold a class in botany and we all go out into the woods for flowers, grasses and mushrooms. There are four periods of singing in the week. Drawing six times (the German does this too) and that goes very well. Surveying is so successful that the boys are already being asked by the peasants to do it for them. There are three teachers besides me. And then there is the priest who comes twice a week. And you still think I am an atheist. Whereas I teach the priest how to teach. And this is how we do it: On St. Peter's Day we tell the story of Peter and Paul and the whole service. Then Feofan dies over in the village—so we tell them about the last sacraments, etc. And so, without any obvious sequence we go through all the mysteries, the liturgy and all the New and Old Testament holidays. The classes are scheduled from 8-12 and 3-6, but they always run on to 2 o'clock because we cannot drive the children out of school—they keep asking for more. . . ."

The network of schools in the district spread; new ones were opened in remote villages; Tolstoy sent to Chicherin in Moscow for teachers; he supervised instructors and arranged gatherings.

Tolstoy exercised a great influence on his student teachers, who were all fine, conscientious young men. Yet he was often driven to despair by their inability completely to absorb the methods which to him were so clear. For that they needed his talent. He himself made mistakes, but he learned by them.

"We begin with numerals with the oldest children and the older ones of the second class. The meaning of the signs for decimals, simple fractions and equations. Sashka can do nothing in a group. I handled it badly. Evidently nothing was accomplished."

On August 7, 1862, Tolstoy wrote to Alexandrine on the subject of his young assistants: "Of the twelve all but one turned out to be splendid people; I was so happy that they all agreed with me, and fell not so much under my influence as that of the surroundings and enterprise. Each one arrived with a manuscript of Herzen in his trunk and revolutionary ideas in his head and *each one*, with one exception, at the end of a week burned his manuscript, cast his revolutionary ideas out of his mind, and taught the peasant children sacred history, prayers, and gave them the Gospel to read at home. These are facts."

Tolstoy had special esteem for G. F. Keller, whom he had brought from Germany. "Keller's experiments are interesting and good," he wrote. "He's an agreeable and useful fellow."

The curriculum was all inclusive: in addition to reading and writing they taught grammar, sacred history, drawing, design, singing, natural history; moreover, the pupils had carpentry work and gymnastics. Tolstoy saw the children gradually develop, witnessed their dawning realization that life was not bounded by Yasnaya Polyana, that there were other peoples, countries, and customs. They learned about Christ and his teachings; they came to understand the beauty of art, poetry, music. Through his experiments Tolstoy became thoroughly convinced that any false note or exaggeration in art or literature was unacceptable to his sensitive audience. Everything sincerely beautiful they devoured with an insatiable hunger.

It was necessary for Tolstoy to share his experiences, his discoveries, to hear intelligent criticism, so he decided to publish a magazine *Yasnaya Polyana*, which he had had in mind while he was abroad, although he was forewarned that it would neither be successful nor draw many subscribers.

In his address "To the Public" he wrote:

"In entering what is for me a new field, I am apprehensive about myself and those ideas which I have worked out over the years and which I hold to be right. I am convinced in advance that many of them will prove mistaken. No matter how hard I try to study a subject I involuntarily approach it from only one side. I trust that my ideas will provoke opposing opinions. I shall be glad to give space in my magazine to all opinions. . . ."

The first issue of the magazine was released by the censor in January, 1862.

Tolstoy's articles on teaching produced the effect of a revolution in the pedagogic methods of the times. It is almost impossible to define his system because it was built on daily, living observation and subtle psychological analysis of the pupils. In the process of instruction the teachers themselves were learning. Lack of comprehension on the part of the pupils, boredom in class, stupid answers were laid to a wrong approach by the teacher or to bad, dull manuals and textbooks.

In an article entitled "The Yasnaya Polyana School During the Months of November and December" Tolstoy wrote:

"A teacher is always involuntarily moved to choose a method of teaching most convenient for him. The more convenient it is for him the more difficult it is for his pupils. The only true method of teaching is the one that satisfies the pupils."

In this same article Tolstoy spoke of the surplus of poor literature of no use to anyone, and the total absence of people's literature. And he expressed his thoughts on art: Refined art is created by and for people vitiated by progress.

"There are thousands of us but millions of them. . . ." wrote Tolstoy in attacking progress and its representatives. What had these people done for the millions?

Here again, in the thirty-four-year-old Tolstoy, we can see the beginnings of his thoughts on art, thoughts which were finally formulated thirty-five years later.

Scholarly pedagogues, men of letters, progressives could not fail to be indignant over such heresy. Tolstoy's magazine stirred a whole series of critical articles in reply. To one article on progress, published by a Mr. Markov in the *Russian Herald*, Tolstoy replied with an article entitled "Progress and a Definition of Education." With characteristic warmth, and disregarding the storm of resentment his article was bound to unleash among educated Russians, he attacked Markov and the so-called progress he defended with every ounce of his strength:

". . . In the first place progress may be recognized as leading to a state of well-being only when a whole nation affected by that progress will recognize its effect as good and sound, whereas in nine-tenths of the population, among the so-called plain laboring people, we constantly see quite the opposite. . . . The people, that is to say the mass of the people . . . maintain an attitude of constant hostility to progress, they constantly refuse to recognize its benefits whereas they definitely and consciously recognize the harm it does them. . . ."

"I ask any serious reader," Tolstoy went on, "to read through the third chapter of the first part of Macaulay's *History*. His conclusion is bold and decisive, but the basis for it is incomprehensible to any sane person who is not befuddled by faith in progress. The only significant facts are the following: (1) Population has increased, increased in a way that inevitably confirms the Malthusian theory. (2) There were no armies, now they are huge; the same is true of the navies. (3) The number of small landholders has decreased. (4) The cities have attracted the major part of the increased population. (5) The land has been denuded of forests. (6) Wages have increased by half, prices for everything have increased and there are fewer comforts. (7) Taxes on the poor have multiplied ten times. There are more newspapers, street lighting has improved, wives and children are beaten less and English ladies have learned how to write without mistakes in spelling."

At that time Tolstoy was concerned with only one thing: the fate, the happiness, the development and the well-being not of the "thousands but the millions." He threw his whole being into his school work; thoughts of living in a village, of marrying a village girl passed through his mind. He was so absorbed in his surroundings that all other classes of society vanished, as it were, from his life; even in his writings he often made use of folk expressions.

"What has this school done for me since I opened it? It has been my whole life, it has been my monastery, my church into which I escaped, finding refuge from all the anxieties, doubts and temptations of life"—so he wrote on August 7 to Alexandrine. His teaching, his intercourse with the children, gave him a tremendous sense of satisfaction and moments of unforgettable exhilaration, almost of rapture. This was the emotion he experienced when he had his children "compose."

He often gave his pupils varied themes for their compositions but the results were disappointing. The children did not write the stories as they told them but the way they thought would please the teacher. Tolstoy could not obtain what he wanted—a folk and children's artistry—although he felt that it lay dormant in his favorite pupils, as many other capacities and talents had lain dormant for centuries in the Russian peasant people. How to find this secret, unconscious, unmined store?

In the article to which he gave the title "Who Should Learn to Write from Whom, the Peasant Children from Us or We from the Peasant Children?" Tolstoy described how the children wrote the stories "A Spoon to Feed You, a Stalk to Poke Your Eye Out" and "Life of a Soldier's Wife."

When he suggested writing the children were indifferent to the idea.

"Well, said I: let's see who will do best; I'll write it down with you.

"I began a short story . . . and wrote the first page. Any unprejudiced person, with a sense of art and folk quality, who will read that first page written by me and then the following pages written by the pupils themselves will distinguish it from the others like a fly in milk: it is so false, artificial, and written in such poor language. It should be noted too that in its original version it was even more grotesque, it was improved in many ways thanks to suggestions from the school children.

"Little Syomka felt the need, predominantly, of concrete images: bast sandals, an old coat, an old man, a peasant woman, having scarcely any relationship to each other; whereas Fedka had to arouse a sense of pity, of which he himself was full. . . .

"His eyes glistened almost as if with tears; his dark, thin little fists were balled; he was annoyed with me and continually prodded me: have you written it? have you written it? he kept asking. His attitude toward all the others was that of an irate tyrant, he wished to speak to only one person, and not speak but recount, speak as one writes, that is to say cast the words in the artistic mold of feelings; for instance, he would not allow words to be transposed; he would say: on my feet there are wounds, and he would not accept: there are wounds on my feet. His soul, so softened and stirred at this time by a sense

[139]

of pity, that is to say, love, invested each image with an artistic form and rejected everything that did not correspond with a concept of eternal beauty and harmony. Whenever Syomka was moved to discourse at disproportionate length on details concerning the lambs in the stables, etc., Fedka would get angry and say: Drat you, you mess it all up! I had only to hint, for example, at what the peasant did when his wife eloped with his neighbor, and instantly into Fedka's imagination came a picture with lambs bleating in the stables, the old man groaning and the boy Serezhka in delirium; I had only to suggest an artificial or false image to have him retort angrily that it should not be used. I proposed, for example, a description of the peasant's exterior—he did not agree to it; but when I proposed a description of what the peasant was thinking when his wife eloped with the neighbor, the turn of expression immediately came to him: 'Oh, if only you'd picked on lifeless Sava, he'd have yanked your hair out for fair!' and he said it in such a weary, quiet, habitually grave yet good-natured tone, leaning his head on his hand, that the other children rolled with laughter. The essential element in all art —a sense of measure—was developed in him to an extraordinary degree. He was jarred by every superfluous line suggested by any of the boys. He was so tyrannical, and with every right to his tyranny, in supervising the construction of the story that the other boys soon went home, only he and Syomka, who would not yield the field to him although he was working along a different line, remained behind.

"We worked from seven to eleven o'clock; they were not aware of either hunger or fatigue and were even cross at me when I stopped writing. . . . He [Fedka] was excited for a long time and could not get to sleep, and I cannot describe the feelings of excitement, joy, awe and almost of remorse which I experienced in the course of that evening. I felt that from this day a new world of satisfaction and suffering was open to him—the world of art; it seemed to me that I had had a stolen glimpse of something no one should ever see— the unfolding of the mysterious bud of poetry. I was as awed and rejoiced as the searcher after precious things who might see the flower of a fern; I was rejoiced because suddenly, quite unexpectedly, I had found the philosopher's stone for which I had so diligently been searching for two years—the art of how to teach the expression of thoughts; I was awed because that art would stir fresh demands, a whole world of desires, incompatible with the surroundings in which the pupils were living, so it seemed to me at first. But there could be no mistake. This was not an accidental happening but a conscious piece of creation. . . .

"The following day I still did not believe in the experience of the day before. To me it was so strange that a half-illiterate peasant boy could suddenly manifest such conscious artistic power as Goethe in all the vast expanse of his development could never attain. It seemed so strange and wounding that I, the author of *Childhood*, who had earned a certain success and recognition from Russian public opinion, that I, in a matter of art, not only could not guide or help eleven-year-old Syomka and Fedka, but also that I should scarcely—and only in a fortunate moment of exhilaration—be able to keep up with and understand them."

♧ 24 ♧

THERE was one characteristic which Tolstoy kept until late in life—a childlike, spontaneous gaiety, an unaffected, almost passionate enthusiasm for sports, games, all sorts of pastimes. "A game is a serious matter"—this was a saying of Tatiana A. Behrs-Kuzminskaya which Tolstoy loved to repeat. When he was playing, wrestling, hunting, chasing his children, he did it in earnest, he threw himself into it with all his being and enjoyed it as much as his children. The Yasnaya Polyana school children were infected with his gaiety. There was no end to the things he thought up. For Christmas he arranged a tree, for New Year's masquerade, for Lent pancakes and excursions, after the Russian custom. They ate the pancakes with butter, sour cream, herrings. When they finally pushed away from the table the Count ordered several large, low sleighs harnessed and they all went out for a ride. Their joy was complete. The bells tinkled, the children's voices broke out in songs, in laughter, and in the first sleigh rode Tolstoy, the chief merrymaker and teacher. He drove himself; kindness and jollity shone in his deep gray eyes under his bushy brows; his broad bearded face, his strongly built body radiated a sense of power. To the children he was some kind of superlative, extraordinary being, not altogether understood. Their fathers bared their heads before him, but to them he seemed at times marvelously, inexplicably near.

In the spring of this year, 1862, Tolstoy was aware of fatigue, a lack of energy. He began to cough. As he, along with his brothers, had a tendency toward tuberculosis the doctor advised him to go to Samara for the kumys cure. Because he felt unable to tear himself away from the children, he took his favorites along: Vaska Morozov and Yegor Chernov, and with them his valet, Alexei Orekhov. They drove first to Moscow, then took a train to Tver, where they went aboard a steamer. The journey, made by steamer on the Volga from Tver to Samara, calmed Tolstoy, and in the steppe country of the half-savage Bashkir nomad camps he felt quite recovered. He soon made friends with the Bashkirs. They invited the "Prince" as they called him, into their tents, where rugs covered the earthen floor, and they ate lamb and horsemeat with their fingers, washing it down with kumys (made of fermented mare's milk). Tolstoy himself started games and wrestling matches with the Bashkirs, from which he always emerged the victor. "He was a powerful athlete and he had no rivals. Only one Bashkir equaled him in strength and Lev Niko- layevich was unable to get him down but neither was he able to get Lev Nikolayevich down," wrote V. Morozov in his memoirs. "Dur- ing the games all the Bashkirs young and old from all the tents gathered around . . . there was always a crowd around our tent in the evening twilight. . . ."

Meanwhile, in Yasnaya Polyana storm clouds were piling up.

All around revolutionary and atheistic ideas were current; the writings of Alexander Herzen were secretly being read, the partici- pants of the December uprising were being idolized, revolutionary proclamations were being printed. Among the teachers in Tolstoy's schools some had revolutionary pasts, and there had been briefly a young man by the name of Sokolov, who when he arrived at Yasnaya Polyana in December, 1861, was under police surveillance. He stayed in the school altogether a month and a half, yet this insignificant event set off a train of consequences which might have ended in catastrophe for Tolstoy.

Reporting on every movement Sokolov made, the police traced him from Moscow to Tula and from there to Yasnaya Polyana. A detec- tive named Michael Shipov, later known as Zimin, was then assigned to investigate the Yasnaya Polyana school. He was a former serf from the household of Prince Dolgoruki, head of the police in St. Petersburg, a worthless drunkard who boasted about his pretended acquaintance with his titled chief. On the 9th of June he himself was arrested for disorderly conduct and sent back to Moscow. There, racking his brains for a plan by which he could insinuate himself into the good graces of his superiors, he fabricated the following story: "Lithographic slabs with letters and some colors for printing forbidden writings" had been brought from Moscow to Yasnaya Polyana, and subsequently "all these slabs and instruments had been, for reasons of prudence, removed to the Kursk estate of Tolstoy, where printing will begin in August."

This was first reported to the office of the military Governor General of Moscow. Several days later Shipov sent supplementary information to the effect that Tolstoy frequently received visits from schismatics "from the village of Starodub" and that in August they were preparing to print a manifesto on the occasion of Russia's millennial celebration. Also, in the Tolstoys' house they had built "secret doors and stairs, and in general the house is heavily guarded at night."

No one can tell the source of these fantasies. The "heavy" guard consisted of one old night watchman, who made the rounds of the house with his club, and the rumor about the "secret doors and stairs" could only have been started by the somewhat unusual and strange architecture of the Tolstoy house. From the vestibule, where Tolstoy's manservant Orekhov slept behind a partition, there was a door into Tolstoy's study. This room was entirely cut off from all outside noise by thick walls and a vaulted ceiling, both of stone. Set in at fixed distances from each other were large, heavy iron rings. They say that in the days of Prince Volkonski this was the larder and home-smoked hams were hung on these rings. From Tolstoy's study a small, narrow door led to the tiny "stone" room where the floor was covered with unevenly laid flagstones. Out of it ran a narrow, dark wooden staircase to the next floor, to his aunt's apartments, the living room and the other large light rooms opening into each other.

On receipt of the Shipov report the Governor General ordered a "careful investigation to be made and the necessary steps to be taken." A search of Yasnaya Polyana was ordered and, if necessary, that of his estate in the province of Kursk to which parts of the secret printing press were purported to have been removed.

In those days the estate of a landowner was a self-contained little world. In the absence of Tolstoy with his boiling energies, life at Yasnaya Polyana was quiet, measured, unhurried. The passing years built habits. Of an evening Auntie Tatiana Alexandrovna laid out her solitaire, Maria played the piano, the servants went serenely about their chores.

Suddenly the estate was aroused—there were carriage bells coming nearer and nearer. . . . Someone was driving down the avenue lined with old birch trees . . . a troika was drawing up to the front door, then another; the courtyard was filled with carriages. . . . Who was it? People in uniform, a colonel of the police force, a district officer, policemen . . .

The servants came running, Auntie Tatiana Alexandrovna fainted; Maria was terrified; no one could understand what was happening. A messenger was sent post haste to the neighbors. A police search! The Count's estate was being ransacked by the police! . . . The rumor spread like lightning through the estate, and on to the village. . . . Meantime the police authorities stationed guards everywhere and began the despicable work: they rummaged through all the tables in Tolstoy's study, read all his intimate correspondence, his diaries, searched the school, tore up the floors in the stables, looking for the printing press on which Tolstoy was said to be printing revolutionary proclamations.

The search went on for two days, during which time the teachers were kept under arrest. One can easily imagine what an impression this police search made on them! Their revolutionary spirit, their resentment against the government, which had somewhat cooled while they were working with Tolstoy, now flared with fresh ardor.

Finding nothing of a suspicious nature, except for some quotations from Herzen in the effects of one of the teachers, the Colonel ordered a search on the estate of Tolstoy's dead brother, Nikolai, at Nikolskoye-Vyazemskoye. This search was also fruitless. All this happened on the 6th and 7th of July. About the 20th Tolstoy reached Moscow on his return from Samara.

"What worries you have been having on my account," he immediately wrote to Granny Alexandrine. "I kept wondering about this all of the time, and it is only now that I have received word from Yasnaya Polyana that I understand all about it. You have fine friends! They write to me from Yasnaya that on July 6 three troikas full of police drove up, ordered no one, including Auntie no doubt, to leave the premises, and began to ransack the place. What they were searching for we still do not know. One of your friends, a filthy colonel, read through all my letters and journals, which I had intended before my death to turn over to the friend who would be closest to me at the time; he read two sets of correspondence which I would have given anything in the world to keep secret—and then he drove off after asserting that he had found nothing of a *suspicious* character. It was my good fortune and also that of my friend that I was not there—I should have killed him. How lovely! How endearing! This is how the government wins friends for itself. If you recall what my political interests are you know that I have always been, and especially since I have been wrapped up in my school, completely indifferent to the government, and even more indifferent to the present-day liberals whom I despise with all my heart. Now I can no longer say this of myself. I am full of anger, revulsion, almost hatred for that sweet government which undertakes a police search of my home for lithographic and typographic presses for printing proclamations by Herzen, whom I scorn, and which bore me so I have not even the patience to read them through. . . . And suddenly I and my student teachers are subjected to a police search. . . . Your friends are lovely people! I have not seen Auntie yet but I can imagine her state. . . . Phew! How can you, such an exceptional person, live in St. Petersburg! That is something I shall never understand. . . ."

When he reached Yasnaya Polyana and heard all the details of the search from his aunt and sister, Tolstoy flew into such an insane rage that his family thought he might do something that would ruin his whole life. He wrote Alexandrine from Yasnaya on the 7th of August and expressed his anger and resentment with characteristic heat:

"I wrote you from Moscow; all I knew then was by letter; now the longer I am in Yasnaya the greater, the more painful is the injury done me and the more intolerable my ruined life seems to me to be. I am writing this letter carefully, trying not to forget or to add anything, so that you can show it to those various brigands, the Potapovs and Dolgorukis, who are deliberately sowing hatred against the government and undermining the Emperor in the estimation of his subjects. I am unable and *unwilling* to let the matter rest. All the activities in which I had found such happiness and serenity have been ruined. Auntie is so ill she is unlikely to survive. The common people look at me not as an honest man, an opinion I had earned from them over the years, but as a criminal, a firebrand or counterfeiter, who skinned out of trouble by cheating. . . . Please write immediately and let me know how to formulate and present a letter to the Emperor.

I have no alternative—how can I accept oral satisfaction, how can I submit to such an insult (it cannot be made good) save go into exile, and this I have firmly decided to do. . . . I shall blazon abroad that I am selling my estates in order to quit Russia, where I cannot know from one minute to the next that I, my sister, wife or mother may be put in chains or flogged—I am leaving. . . .

"Now you can imagine what rumors have begun to circulate after this throughout the district and province among the nobles. . . . The rumors were so positive that I was in prison or had escaped abroad that people who knew me and knew how I scorn all such secret goings-on, conspiracies, flights, etc., began to believe them. Now they (the police) have left, we are allowed to go from house to house, they did, however, take the students' passports away from them and refuse to return them, and our lives, particularly mine and Auntie's have been blighted. There will be no school, the common people are laughing us to scorn, the nobles are triumphant, and we involuntarily, whenever we hear any bells, think they are coming to carry us off somewhere. This policeman tried to calm us down by saying that if anything has been hidden away we can make up our minds that tomorrow he, in the role of our judge and master, may again appear along with the private inspector. However, if this is done without the Emperor's knowledge we must fight to the last and defend ourselves against such a state of affairs. It is impossible to exist this way. But if this is as things are supposed to be and it has been put to the Emperor that they cannot be otherwise then I must go to some place where I know that if I am not a criminal I can hold up my head, or else I must try to prove to the Emperor that such a state of things is impossible."

Poor Alexandrine, whom Tolstoy identified with the government only because she was a member of the court, and on whom he poured out all his indignation, was not offended. She wrote him:

"Lev, my dear, by all that is sacred to you I implore you not to undertake any steps, no matter what has happened, especially until you have calmed down completely."

On August 23 Tolstoy presented a letter to the Emperor through his aide-de-camp Count Sheremetyev complaining against the actions of the police department. Among other things he wrote:

"Because of the feelings inherent in the nature of any human being I am seeking to find whom I can blame for what has happened to me. I cannot blame myself: I feel myself to be more in the right than at any other time; I do not know the false informer; nor can I blame the functionaries who prosecuted and insulted me: they reiterated several times that they were not acting on their own free will but on orders from the highest authority. . . . So that I may know whom to blame for all that has happened to me I dare to appeal directly to Your Majesty. I ask only that all possibility of accusation of injustice be removed from Your Majesty's name and that those who have abused that name should be, if not punished, exposed."

The police search without any doubt had a deep effect on Tolstoy. It left a lasting feeling of bitterness. Before this Tolstoy had criticized actions by the government but his attitude toward it and the Emperor was entirely loyal; the undeserved insult, the arbitrariness of the search made him reconsider and gave rise to thoughts that became convictions in his later years.

The explanation given by Prince Dolgoruki to the Governor of Tula in response to Tolstoy's letter could not possibly have satisfied him.

"Despite the fact that several persons living at his house prove not to have proper passports, and one of them was found to have forbidden writings in his possession, it is His Majesty's pleasure that the measure undertaken (i.e., the police search) remain without any consequential effect on Count Tolstoy personally."

Although the school and the magazine *Yasnaya Polyana,* which had begun to be viewed askance, continued in existence for a while, Tolstoy from this time became inwardly indifferent to his beloved school work. Whether the search or other events were responsible, the whole tenor of his life was to change.

✿ 25 ✿

IT WAS growing increasingly difficult for Tolstoy to live alone. Coming home of a winter evening from the school, with the snow crunching softly under his felt boots as he walked along the narrow, beaten path, when the only sound to break the dead silence was that of a tree riven with frost—he was alone.

Striding in early spring through heavy mud, enjoying the sight of the brilliant greenery just freed from its sheath of snow, when his own sense of being alive made him want to shout with joy—he was alone.

Sitting in the living room, hearing the songs of the young folks over in the village, the gay cries of the children down at the pond, the croaking of frogs, the trills and runs of nightingales, smelling the air laden with the spicy fragrance of apple blossoms and cherry blossoms—when he passionately longed to love and be loved—he was alone.

In the scorching heat of summer, sweating and tired after haying all day with peasants, rejoicing in his own physical power, in his understanding with the peasants, in the weather, in the fact that the meadow had been mowed so quickly—and wanting to share all this with someone—he was alone.

"I am sad," he wrote in his diary, "I have no friends, none!"

At first he had no thought that he might find a wife for himself in the Behrs family. He visited them because he had known Lyubov Alexandrovna Islavina Behrs since he was a child; she was a great friend of his sister Maria; he was both fond of and admired her. He also knew her father, Alexander Islenyev.

In his youth Islenyev had been a great gambler. They used to say that in a single evening he would gamble away and rewin whole fortunes—he carried the gold coins away tied up in sheets—and also that he was a dashing, dissipated officer, a passionate hunter and a great fancier of gypsies. His unbridled nature recognized no obstacles. When he met Princess Sophia Kozlovskaya née Countess Zavadovskaya, and they fell in love with each other he decided to carry her off and marry her secretly, since Prince Koslovski refused to give his wife a divorce. The story caused a great deal of commotion in high social circles in Moscow. The marriage was declared invalid, the children of it were not allowed to bear his name but were given that of Islavin.

The Islenyevs lived together happily for fifteen years. Then Sophia died, leaving three daughters, the youngest of whom was Lyubov. After an emotional period of mourning Islenyev soon consoled himself with a second wife, and the lives of his three daughters, especially of the youngest, Lyubov, were not altogether gay under their stepmother's roof.

When Lyubov was fifteen she was seriously ill with brain fever and Islenyev called in young Dr. Andrei Behrs to attend her. He took care of her for several weeks and pulled her through. By the end of that time they had fallen in love with each other. Marriage with a doctor of German ancestry was looked upon as a misalliance. Islenyev protested but Lyubov insisted on having her own way. She turned out to be right for they lived happily together all their lives.

Andrei Behrs was a court doctor and in Moscow the family lived in the Kremlin. He was intelligent, gifted, virtuous, but hot-tempered and headstrong. His daughter Sophia inherited in part her father's fiery temperament. She used to say that when he was having one of his rages the whole house shook. Fortunately such tantrums were rare and as he grew older they ceased altogether; nevertheless he was feared and respected as the master in his house.

Many children were born to the Behrs: three daughters and five sons.

In their upbringing Lyubov Alexandrovna clung to the traditions of the circles in which she herself had been reared. There were resident governesses, the children spoke French and German. There were ten servants, footmen, chambermaids, a chef. . . . The family was received in many aristocratic homes in Moscow; on Saturdays, as was the custom, there were dancing classes, held either at the Behrs' or, more frequently, at Maria Tolstoy's where the Tolstoy children— Lisa, Varya and Nikolai—danced with the Behrs children. Lyubov Alexandrovna trained her daughters in housekeeping and, dressed in exquisite aprons trimmed with lace, they lent a hand in the kitchen or the dining room.

The older the Behrs girls grew, the more often Tolstoy came to call. Here he was not in search of answers to the problems which tormented him, but of something else: the coziness of family life, youth with its untrammeled pleasures, the society of fine, virtuous girls. Bursting out of what he termed his "hermit's existence" he was like a horse seldom turned loose; he had to "kick over the traces."

It was gay at the Behrs'. Although the atmosphere was that of a tranquil bourgeois family, the passions of the young people were already kindled. Tolstoy described it in the household of the Rostovs in *War and Peace*. The place was swarming with youngsters, the friends of Sasha Behrs, the eldest son. There were cadets, high school boys, boys from the Naval Academy. They were all in love. Sonya was in love with Polivanov, a young guards officer, who was courting her with ardor. Tanya was enamored of her cousin, Sasha Kuzminski. They sang, they danced, they gave plays. One might have thought that the thirty-four-year-old author, though he had already acquired something of a name, might have disrupted the high spirits of all these young people but actually Tolstoy's arrival was the sign for increased gaiety.

"We did not feel his age," one of the younger of the Behrs daughters, Tanya, said later on. "When he arrived everything livened up; he would take us for a walk in the forest, lose the path, tell us stories along the way. Footsore, weary, starved, we would get home late for dinner, of course. Mama would be displeased but Lyovochka knew how to put on such a mollifying expression, beg so hard for forgiveness that in the end she used to laugh and forgive us."

The young ladies of the Behrs family were brought up strictly, in the old-fashioned way. They were forbidden to go out onto the streets unaccompanied; not only was kissing a young man looked upon as a crime—it was considered improper even to shake hands with him. A girl was supposed to nod her head ever so little, curtsy slightly and pass modestly by. Lyubov Alexandrovna was horrified that among the educated classes there was a growing freedom on the part of nihilist, revolutionary females who walked around the city without their parents or governesses, sometimes in the company of men, who read novels, revolutionary pamphlets, articles by Herzen, who chose husbands to their own taste.

All three Behrs girls were very pretty. The oldest, Lisa, was eighteen when Tolstoy began to frequent the doctor's home. Lisa was the most cultivated. She wrote, read a great deal, was well versed in mathematics, was interested in philosophy. Tolstoy even tried to interest her in contributing to his pedagogic magazine. Lisa looked down on her younger sisters. "What, indeed, do these flighty young things know of life except silly games, flirting and sentimental reveries?" Her reasoning was always logical, her remarks sound, she was always right when she complained to her parents of the misdemeanors of her brothers and sisters; but this logic and righteousness was irritating to the younger members of the family and they rather avoided her.

Her youngest sister, Tanya, was exactly her opposite. She was slight, graceful, with regular features spoiled only by an overlarge, sensual mouth. Gay, mercurial, she was undoubtedly the most attractive of the three sisters. She feared no one in the house, not even her strict father, and was always the one to stir up the others, to think up all kinds of pranks. She read novels on the sly, was forever falling in love, and dreamed of being a dancer.

Of the three Sonya was the most beautiful. She was the same height as Tanya, slight of build, well proportioned, with especially narrow hips and a high waist, which any woman might well envy. Her legs and arms were slim and lovely; only her thick, stubby fingers were out of keeping. Sonya was not as generously prodigal with her smiles as Tanya but when she did smile or was convulsed with noiseless laughter—something which rarely happened—her dazzling white, healthy teeth would flash, her eyes would shine with joy and gaiety, and she was very attractive. Sonya was as lively as Tanya, her walk was as rapid and light, but her movements were not so graceful. Sonya was extremely short-sighted and for that reason she always appeared to be a little shy and hesitant. They did not wear glasses in those days—they were thought to spoil a girl's looks—but she did not squint as many myopic people do. She opened her great black slightly protuberant eyes wide, with a questioning look which gave a special quality of charm to her face.

Tanya (T. A. Kuzminskaya) wrote in her memoirs:

"Sonya never gave herself up completely to the gaiety or happiness with which her youth and early years of marriage were blessed. She somehow did not trust her happiness, did not know how to grasp it and exploit it to the full. It always seemed to her that any moment something would interfere with it, or that something else must be added to make her happiness perfect. This trait of her character remained with her as long as she lived.

"Father knew this trait in her character aand used to say: 'Poor little Sonya will never be entirely happy.' "

This quality of unfounded, imaginary sadness seeps through the lines of Sonya's diary: "I felt so full of contentment, solace and joy," she writes; and later on, without giving any explanation, she suddenly falls into a saddened mood: "But all this did not last, and now it seems so hard to go on with life in this world."

In Lisa there was no sentimentality, in Tanya there was little, but in Sonya this feeling was very strong. She was affected by a lovely flower, a touching book, by herself and her own emotions.

The whole Behrs family was very practical. The aim of the parents was to educate their sons in preparation for good careers, to marry off their three daughters to advantage.

In the Behrs household Tolstoy was called *le comte* and the parents fondly hoped that their eldest daughter Lisa would marry this man of aristocratic family, with something of a literary reputation, although he was not so very young.

Tolstoy once said to his sister Maria:

"Mashenka, I feel myself especially drawn to the Behrs family, and if ever I marry, it will be only one of them."

The more often he came to call there, the more the tongues in the Behrs household began to wag; the governesses, the nurses, the aunts, the friends, all began to make their own conjectures. For whose sake could *le comte* be coming to the house so frequently? There was really no doubt about it; of course he had his eye on the eldest daughter, that most reasonable and reasoning Lisa. Gradually those around her put that idea into Lisa's own head. Tanya immediately caught on to the fact that as soon as *le comte* was expected Lisa stood at great length in front of her mirror and in general began to take pains with her external appearance. This was not like Lisa; it was very amusing to see and Tanya continued to watch her with curiosity.

In his diary entry for September 22, 1861, Tolstoy wrote: "L[isa] B[ehrs] tempts me; but she will not be the one. She is all reason, and has no feelings." In a letter to Alexandrine Tolstoy on February 10, 1862, he confessed: "I have almost fallen in love." But he soon realized that his feelings were not genuine and he was rather oppressed by the conviction which had sprung up in the Behrs family that he should marry Lisa. On May 20, 1862, he noted in his diary: "I feel a little easier at the Behrs' now, they have given me a little more freedom."

In the beginning of August the family, consisting of Lyubov Alexandrovna, the three girls and little Volodya, were planning a big tour down to the province of Tula, to visit the Tolstoys at Yasnaya Polyana and Lyubov Alexandrovna's parents, the Islenyevs, at Ivitsy. There was no railroad then between Moscow and Tula so the Behrs hired a huge, so-called (Empress) Anna coach for the journey.

In Yasnaya Polyana Lyubov Alexandrovna was greeted by her friend Maria, who was just preparing to go abroad with her children, by Auntie Tatiana and the hospitable host, Tolstoy. One can well imagine the stir the visitors created in the quiet, almost patriarchal way of life in Yasnaya Polyana. There was a great bustle; everyone had to be lodged, to be fed, the servants were on the run, Auntie hurried about, but the host himself was the one who did the most fussing. Assigning sleeping quarters to all, he himself, with his large untrained hands, yet with unaccustomed tenderness, made up a bed for Sonya on his grandfather's chaise longue in the room "under the vaulting." He was happy that everyone was so contented, that gay young voices echoed through the house, that there were sounds of piano playing, of singing. He wanted to show the Behrs all his favorite spots in Yasnaya Polyana and environs, the meadows, the glades, the dreamy Forest Preserve, with its century-old oaks. Here in the State Forest, in a glade, they arranged a picnic. All this entertained the Behrs girls—riding horseback, taking walks, the hounds circling around the big house, and the remarkable "roller" droshky, an unusually long and jolting equipage, of special Yasnaya Polyana construction, capable of seating twelve people back to back, six on either side. Then there were the apples and pears ripening under the hot August sun, the young teachers inexpertly prancing around on horseback before the young ladies.

All this was wonderful, like a fairy tale—above all, to Sonya, who involuntarily, with her fine woman's instincts, sensed that *le comte* liked her and was paying her more and more attention.

From Yasnaya Polyana the Behrs went to the estate of the Islenyevs. There that once brilliant, handsome old man with a stormy past was quietly living out his days in the country with his second wife.

After the departure of the guests, Yasnaya Polyana seemed empty. Tolstoy himself was bored; a feeling stronger than the mere desire to be with other young people prompted him to follow them. Scarcely two days later he rode over to Ivitsy. Now things really became lively. Young people arrived from neighboring estates, filled with curiosity to see the young ladies from Moscow. Once more picnics were arranged; in the evening the young folks danced and their elders played cards.

Tolstoy sought out Sonya. Lisa, jealous, was angry with Sonya, as she saw the man she had tried so hard and so long to capture move farther and farther away from her.

The evening was almost over and Lyubov Alexandrovna was chasing her daughters off to bed when Tolstoy suddenly called Sonya. The older people had just finished their card games in the living room, there were still chalk marks on the green baize tables. Tolstoy beckoned Sonya to one of the tables, brushed off some of the card game scores and began to write down the first letters of some words, waiting to see if Sonya would grasp their meaning.

This scene is recorded in *Anna Karenina* and in Sonya's diary. It is difficult to say which account corresponds to reality. One thing is beyond question: they were both in the grip of an unexpressed emotion, of nervous tension; the desire to understand each other had reached its limits, so that when Tolstoy jotted down the letters, Sonya guessed the whole words. Sometimes she hesitated and Tolstoy prompted her and went on writing. It was almost a declaration of love. "Your youth and craving for happiness are too lively a reminder to me of my own age and incapacity for happiness. . . . In your family there is a mistaken attitude toward me and your sister Lisa. You and Tanya defend me," he wrote on, again using only the first letters of words. As Sonya read along, and the declaration moved toward its climax, there came the sound of her mother's angry voice, demanding that Sonya go to bed, and the scene was interrupted.

On their way home from Ivitsy the Behrs stopped over briefly at Yasnaya Polyana and then returned to Moscow. Tolstoy went with them.

In Moscow Tolstoy continued to frequent the Behrs home. His relation to Lisa obviously weighed on him: "My God! How perfectly unhappy she would be if she were my wife," he wrote in his diary on September 8, 1862. "I begin to hate her at the same time that I pity her," he wrote in his diary two days later.

Father Behrs grew angry. According to his ideas daughters should be married off in the order of their ages. There was nothing commendable about the fact that Tolstoy was obviously courting his second daughter, Sonya. Let Sonya marry and hop out of the nest, the next thing you knew her older sister would be stuck there. Lyubov Alexandrovna suffered on Lisa's account, and was disturbed on Sonya's. Tanya pitied Lisa, sympathized with Sonya, became more and more attached to *le comte*, while Tolstoy was riven with doubts, doing his best with his customary honesty to analyze the emotion which had taken possession of him. "Spent the night at the Behrs'," he wrote in his diary for August 23, 1862. "What a child! Or like one! What a great tangle! Oh, if only I could find my way to a clear and decent place to rest! I fear for myself: what if this desire to love is not love itself? I try to look only at her weak points and yet it is still there. What a child! How absurd!"

His own external appearance, his age, tormented him and he unceasingly asked himself: did she love him? When he discovered that Sonya kept a diary and was working on a novel Tolstoy begged her to let him see her writing. She refused to give him her diary but let him see her story. It was a naïve description of the life of the three Behrs girls, their flirtations. It described the romance between Sonya and young Polivanov, and even *le comte* figured in the story as Prince Dublitski, a man of "extraordinarily unattractive exterior."

"I started to work but I can't go on," wrote Tolstoy on September 9. "Instead of working I wrote her a letter, which I shall not send. Leave Moscow—I *cannot*, I *cannot* do it. . . . Did not get to sleep until three o'clock. I rhapsodized and agonized like a sixteen-year-old boy."

The entry of September 12 read: "I woke up on the 10th of September at ten in the morning, exhausted by my disturbed night. I was too lazy to work, I waited for evening to come as a schoolboy for Sunday. I went out for a walk . . . to the Kremlin, of course. She was not at home . . . when she returned she looked severe and grave. So I went away, my hopes dashed again, but more in love than ever. *Au fond* I do have hope. I must, I am compelled to cut this knot. Lord, help me! O God, show me what to do! Again a night of sleeplessness and torment for me who laugh at the agonies of those in love. The thing you mock becomes your master. How many the plans I intended to tell her . . . and all to no purpose. . . . Lord, help me, show me what to do. Mother of God, help me. I am in love, as I never believed one could love. I am insane, I shall shoot myself, if things go on any longer this way. I spent the evening at their home. She is charming in every way. And I—am a repulsive Dublitski. I should have protected myself earlier. Now I cannot check myself. Dublitski—very well, but I am magnificent in my love. Yes. Tomorrow I'll go to them in the morning. There have been moments but I did not make the most of them. I became shy when I should have simply spoken out. Now I want to go right back and tell everything to all of them. Lord, help me."

The tension mounted.

"Tomorrow I'll go as soon as I get up and I'll say everything or else I'll shoot myself," he wrote on the following day. "It is past three at night. I have written her a letter and I'll give it to her tomorrow, that is to say today, the 14th. My God, how I dread to die. But happiness, and such happiness, seems impossible. O God! Help me!"

On the 16th Tolstoy was as usual at the Behrs'; it was a Saturday. Sasha Behrs came home from Naval College, and a lot of young people foregathered. Tolstoy chose a moment when no one else was in the room to give Sonya a letter: "I wanted to talk to you," he began, "but I couldn't. Here is a letter, which I have been carrying in my pocket for several days. Read it. I'll wait here for your reply," he said to her.

Sonya hurried to the bedroom she shared with her sisters. But Lisa, who realized that something out of the ordinary was going on, ran after her. "What is he writing to you, what?" she teased. "*Le comte* has proposed to me," Sonya replied and ran off to find her mother. Lisa was beside herself. "Refuse him! Refuse him!" she cried after her.

"Sophia Andreyevna," Tolstoy had written, "I am in an intolerable state. For three weeks I have said every day: Now I'll tell her everything, and yet I leave with the same longing, remorse, terror and happiness in my soul. And each night, as tonight, I go over the past, I agonize and I say: Why did I not speak, and what I would have said and how. I am taking this letter with me to give to you, if once more I lack the opportunity or the spirit to tell you everything. . . . In Ivitsy I wrote: '*Your presence reminds me too much of my own age, you do especially.*' But both then and now I have been lying to myself. At that time I might still have torn myself away and returned to my monastery of solitary labor and absorption in my work. Now I am incapable of anything. I feel that I have been the cause of confusion in your family; that the simple, cherished relationship with you as with a friend, an honest human being, has been lost. Yet I can neither leave nor dare to remain. As an honest person, cross your heart, and without hurrying, for God's sake don't hurry, tell me, what am I to do? The thing you mock will become your master. I should have died of laughter if a month ago anyone had told me that I could suffer as I am suffering now, and as I am happy in doing. Tell me, as an *honest person*, do you wish to be my wife? But only if you can say *yes boldly*, with all your heart, or else it would be better to say *no*, if there is a shadow of doubt in you. For the love of God, question yourself thoroughly. It will be terrible for me to hear your *no*, but I am prepared for it and I shall find the strength to bear it. But if I as a husband am never to be loved as I love—that will be dreadful!"

Sonya did not reflect for even a minute. Like a hurricane she whirled into her mother's room where Tolstoy was waiting for her.

"Well, what is to be?" he asked.

"Of course it is *yes*," answered Sonya.

The wedding took place one week later. Lyubov Alexandrovna was horrified when Tolstoy insisted that the wedding be not put off for a single day. "What about a trousseau?" What significance could that have in Tolstoy's eyes? Sonya was always beautifully dressed, what more did she need? Nevertheless the trousseau was made and Tolstoy himself tried to be conscientious about doing everything expected of a bridegroom-to-be: he made presents, he ordered photographs, he bought a sleeping coach for their wedding journey. He did all this because it was considered the proper thing, but other thoughts were harassing him—his past life, his moral filth as compared with the crystal purity of this girl whom he had chosen to be his wife. What did she know of life? Did she suspect his past sins, his amorous lapses? "You have never been in love?" she once had asked him. What if she, on finding out the truth, gave him up? So he decided to give her his diaries to read. "He should not have done it," Sonya wrote in her own diary. "I wept a lot on looking into his past."

On the day of the wedding the bridegroom, according to custom, was not supposed to call on his bride. Great was Lyubov Alexandrovna's horror when, on going into Sonya's room, she found Tolstoy there and Sonya weeping bitterly. It turned out that at the last minute Tolstoy had had some qualms about Sonya's love and had come to clear matters up with her. "You chose a wonderful time to upset her," Lyubov Alexandrovna said reprovingly. "This is her wedding day, it's hard enough for her anyhow, and she has to start off on a journey, and now she is all tears." She sent Tolstoy away.

The ceremony was set for seven o'clock in the evening. Sonya, in her wedding dress, sat and waited for her bridegroom's best man, who was supposed to come and announce to her that the groom was in the church. Seven o'clock had struck and no one had come. Half an hour more went by, an hour. . . . Sonya, still under the influence of the difficult conversation with Tolstoy earlier in the day, was upset, harassed with doubts. At half past eight Tolstoy's valet, Alexei, arrived. It turned out that his servants had packed all his shirts and he had nothing to put on.

Finally the best man appeared. Amid the clouds of her tulle wedding dress Sonya was put in a coach with Aunt Pelagea Ilyinichna and her little brother Volodya—who was to carry the ikon—and they drove off to the court church.

Many guests were present, the church was crammed, but the wedding was not a gay one. Sonya was embarrassed and shy; Lisa avoided the bridegroom and was obviously suffering; Lyubov Alexandrovna could scarcely keep back her tears; there was the unexpected arrival of Polivanov, young and handsome in his officer of the guards uniform. Little Petya was in tears, the old retainers cried, and Tanya wept bitterly because she realized how lonely she would be without her sister.

After the ceremony the young couple, having received the congratulations of their friends, changed their clothes. Sonya looked thin and pale in her dark blue traveling dress. The new sleeping coach (*dormeuse*) drawn by six horses pulled up to the front steps. Alexei, Tolstoy's faithful servant, jumped on the footboard and the newly-weds drove off.

They made the journey in less than forty-eight hours. In Yasnaya Polyana they were ceremoniously received by Auntie Tatiana, carrying an ikon of the Mother of God, and by Sergei Tolstoy, bearing the customary bread and salt. The young couple bowed low in silence, crossed themselves, kissed the ikon and tenderly embraced Auntie Tatiana.

From that day forward everything was changed for Tolstoy, life took on a different purpose, a different meaning—for at his side he had a beloved and loving wife. He was no longer *alone*!

26

MUCH has been written about the relationship between Tolstoy and his wife. Most writers have unconsciously taken the side of the one or the other, blaming either Tolstoy or his wife for the drama of their forty-six years of life together. I believe that to write about it with impartiality is a task no one could fulfill, and if I lay the blame for this on the writers of the many books about Tolstoy, I do not exclude myself. I quite realize that in my earlier book *The Tragedy of Tolstoy* I made this same mistake. Now, however, with the advantage of greater maturity, I shall try as dispassionately as possible to explore the psychological shadings of these two complex, powerful, integral characters—though I recognize that it is always difficult for a daughter to write about the intimate life of her parents.

Sonya knew nothing of life. She had grown up in quiet family surroundings inside the Kremlin walls, played with the idea (as not so long since she had played with dolls) of a family life of her own, of her love story with "him," her future husband, young, handsome and poetic. What had happened to her was unexpected, like a stroke of lightning; it was not at all as she had dreamed it would be. A whirlwind had entered her life in the form of a man no longer young, not altogether comprehensible, powerful, who had seared her with his uncontrollable passion, had carried her off into his world, a world alien to her. Everything was quite, quite different. There was his little old auntie, her dependents with their inquisitive, hungry eyes watching and appraising the young countess. There were the new servants to whom she had to accustom herself and whom she had to win for herself. There were the coarse country women, the peasants, the stranger teachers, the silence, the sticky mud in the yards and along the roads—it was all uncivilized and unfamiliar.

The day after their arrival the village women, in accordance with ancient customs, arrived to do honor to the young couple. Their gay, loud song was audible all the way from the village. The crowd came nearer and nearer, moving along the avenue of trees toward the house. The women were all dressed in bright-colored *sarafans*, embroidered blouses trimmed with variegated gold, red and green ribbons. Two of them came out to the front holding in their hands a cock and a hen all decorated with bright ribbons.

The young couple stepped out onto the piazza before the front door. Sonya was bewildered. The women sang, clapping the rhythm, dancing a bit and showing their enthusiasm in all sorts of ways. "Our Count is a clever one! See what a fine young beauty he fetched home from Moscow!" Their straightforward, coarse remarks embarrassed the young Countess, made her cheeks flame. She had no idea what to do with the flapping, gaudy birds in her hands.

From the very first day Sonya made the utmost effort to adapt herself to her new life. She was as entertained as a child by going over her possessions or fixing up a cozy room. She made a dignified figure sitting behind the pot-bellied samovar, pouring tea like a real grownup, and she was rather proud of signing her letters Countess S. Tolstoy. "She is wearing a cap with crimson ribbons, not bad at all!"

Tolstoy added at the end of one of her letters to Tanya Behrs. "And this morning how she did play at being a great lady—a good likeness, well done."

He was as much in love as a seventeen-year-old youth. "What incredible happiness," he wrote in his diary for September 25, 1862. "It cannot be that it will last only for this life."

"Kind and dear friend, Granny," he wrote on September 28, 1862, to Alexandrine, "I am writing from the country and as I write I hear the voice upstairs, talking to her brother, of my wife whom I love more than anything on earth. I lived to be thirty-four without ever knowing that one could love so much or be so happy. When I am calm I shall write you a long letter—not that it will be a calm letter —I am calm now and clear-headed, as I have never been in my life —but when I shall be more accustomed to it."

The change in his life was so tremendous that he simply could not control himself. "Duckie little old Fet, my truly darling friend Afanasi Afanasievich," he wrote on October 9, 1862, "I have been married for two weeks and I am happy, I am a new, quite new man. I wish I could get over to see you but it does not seem possible. When shall I see you? Now that I come to think of it I hold you in great, very great favor. Do come over and get acquainted with me."

Yet there is no happiness without clouds. They began to gather, misunderstandings blew up, there were quarrels. Sonya was too young to accept her husband as he was: expansive and stormy as the sea, a passionate sinner with saintly interludes, toothless, no longer young, as gay and carefree as a child, sometimes simple and naïve to the point of primitiveness and yet so complex that even he lost himself in his own depths.

"Since long ago," she wrote in her diary, "I always dreamed of the man I would love as being a whole, fresh, *pure* person. I imagined, and these were childish fantasies which it is still hard to give up, that this person would never be out of my sight, that I would know his tiniest thought, feeling. . . . All his [her husband's] past is so terrible to me that I think I shall never be reconciled to it. . . . He does not realize that his past is a whole life with thousands of various feelings good and bad, which cannot belong to me, just as his youth, squandered God knows on whom or on what, cannot belong to me. Nor does he realize that I give him everything, nothing has been wasted, and it is only my childhood which does not belong to him."

Fundamentally their disputes did not destroy Tolstoy's happiness.

[160]

In his headlong enthusiasm he did not feel what she with her fine woman's instinct was beginning to realize. "I see," she wrote in her diary for October 9, 1862, " that it is true that I give him little happiness. I seem to be asleep and cannot waken. If I were awakened I should be quite another person. What I must do to bring this about, I do not know. Then he would see how I love him, then I could talk to him, tell him *how* I love him, I would see, as I used to, what is in his heart and would know what to do to make him entirely happy. I must, I must waken soon." Sonya's diaries are shot through with yearning, bitterness, unsatisfied spiritual cravings and childish helplessness. And this was only two or three weeks after her wedding day! "I do not want to fall into the general rut and be bored," she wrote in her diary for November 13, "and I won't do it. I would wish my husband had more influence over me. How strange, I am terribly in love with him yet am very little subject to his influence!"

"I sway back and forth between the past, the present and the future," another diary entry of the same date read. "My husband loves me too much to know how to direct me, it's difficult anyway, I shall have to work it out myself. . . ."

They had been brought up in different spheres. She was city bred. He, her husband, not only loved the country, he was part of it; by the very nature of his being he could not live away from it and be happy.

"For me he is revolting with his peasants," Sonya writes on November 23. "I feel he must choose either me, that is to say me as representing the family for the time being, or the peasants for whom he has such warm affection. This is egotism. Very well. I live for him, I live in him, I want it that way, otherwise I would feel cramped and stifled here, and today I ran away because everything, absolutely everything was so revolting . . . old Auntie, the students, and N. P. [Natalia Petrovna Okhotnitskaya, one of Auntie's hangers-on], and I almost burst out laughing with joy when I slipped out of the house. L. is not really revolting, but I suddenly felt that he and I were on opposite sides, that his peasants cannot *completely* absorb me, just as I cannot *completely* absorb him, as he does me. It's very simple. If I cannot absorb him, if I am a doll, a mere wife, and not a human being then I neither can nor wish to live this way."

Sonya was eager and cheerful in helping her husband with some spheres of the management of the estate which she understood and with which she could cope.

At that period Tolstoy was passionately enthusiastic about improving the economy of Yasnaya Polyana: at one time he undertook to raise bees in the copse beyond the Voronka River, where a hoary-headed, bearded old man took care of the hives; at another he set out trees, started an apple orchard, bought a flock of sheep or considered breeding some kind of extraordinary Japanese hogs, and he wrote to his father-in-law that he could not be happy if they did not get him "those little Japanese pigs." He had no steward; he himself laid out the plans for the workers, and Sonya was his right hand. She hung a large bunch of keys at her belt, doled out supplies from the storerooms and barns with a dignified and important expression; at one time she checked the milking of the cows, and she busied herself with household matters.

Her efforts were touching to him and he admired her for them. He did the best he knew how to entertain her. On still, frosty days or evenings he drove her around in a troika sleigh; he was delighted to see her wrapped in a fur coat and sheepskin rug, with rosy cheeks, full of childlike joy in his love, the beauty of nature, the swift movement of the sleigh. But there were few diversions. She missed her family, her young friends in the city. The peasant men and women were coarse creatures who, according to her point of view, existed only to work for their master; the teachers distressed her with their not altogether clean fingernails, and they ate with their knives; Auntie's dependents were a nuisance; and he, her husband, with his outside interests which drew him away from her, was incomprehensible and difficult.

"It is terrifying to live with him," she wrote in her diary. "Suddenly he will center all his love on the peasants again and I shall be lost, for he loves me in the same way he used to love his school, nature, the peasants, perhaps his own writings, all of them only to a certain extent . . . and then there is always Auntie, N. P., and once more Auntie, and again N. P., the students in between times. My husband does not belong to me even today."

On top of all that, as bad luck would have it, an unfortunate thing occurred. As was the custom, the peasant women from the village came up to the manor house to scrub the floors. One of these women was Axinia Bazykina. . . .

"It seems to me that sometime or other I am going to have enough of jealousy," Sonya wrote in her diary December 16, 1862, and further on she quoted with a sense of bitter irony from her husband's diary: "I love as I have never loved before!—and she is just a plain peasant woman, fat, pasty, horrible. . . . And there she is, a few steps away. I am like a madwoman. . . . I can see her now. That's how he loved her. If only one could burn up his diary and all his past life. . . ."

There followed a scene of jealousy, then one of reconciliation, passionate declarations of love. . . .

At times she felt that she was growing accustomed to her life. "I gradually am becoming reconciled to everyone, the students, the peasants, and Auntie—and of course to everything I used to scold about. Lev's influence is strong and I am delighted to feel his dominion over me."

There were moments when he longed for literary pursuits; he felt himself too bogged down by family life, by the management of the estate. He had already given up the school and the magazine, having made up his mind in October that the burden was too great. So when on November 5 he received the decision of the censor prohibiting the ninth issue of *Yasnaya Polyana*, containing the article "Who shall teach whom how to write?" he was not much distressed. His interests had shifted.

Despite the ups and downs of his domestic life he was happy and, what was most important, his marriage had calmed him.

"Where is this leading?" he wrote to Alexandrine Tolstoy. "I do not know, yet with every day that passes I feel calmer and better. . . . I have broken with all my past as I have never done before, I feel all my own vileness every second when I measure up to her, to Sonya, though I cannot blot the grievous lines. . . . It is so appalling to lead a responsible life, the two of us. . . . It is quite terrifying for me to go on living now, to feel life, to feel that every second is for keeps, not as it used to be—just for the moment."

Then on January 5, 1863, he wrote in his diary: "The thought often crosses my mind that happiness and all its peculiar traits are disappearing, that no one knows it or will know it, no one ever possessed it or will possess it, but I am aware of it. . . . I love her when I wake up at night or in the morning and see her looking at me, loving me. And no one, especially I, hinders her loving, as she knows how to love in her own way. I love it when she sits close beside and we know that we love one another, to the best of our ability, and then she will say 'Lyovochka' then hesitate—'why do the pipes in the chimney run straight?' or 'Horses don't die for a long time, do they?' and so it goes. I love it when we have been alone for a long time and I say: 'What shall we do? Sonya, what shall we do?' She laughs. I love it when she is angry at me and instantly her eyes, her thoughts, her words are sometimes quite sharp: 'Do stop, you're being tiresome.' In another moment she will be smiling shyly at me. I love it when she does not see me, is not aware of me, and I love her in my own way. I love it when she is a little girl in a yellow dress and pushes out her lower jaw, sticks out her tongue. I love it when I see her head thrown back, her face, sometimes serious, sometimes frightened, sometimes childlike, sometimes passionate. I love it when . . ."

They were insanely jealous each of the other. He was jealous of every man with whom she spoke, of everyone who dared to be charmed by her. She could not forgive him his past, she reproached him bitterly with his earlier passions, she was jealous of every young woman he was in the habit of seeing, even of her own sister Tanya.

Sometimes he could not bear it. "We are in Moscow," one diary entry read. "As usual I have wasted a whole day in an unhealthy and bad frame of mind. I was very displeased with her; when I compared her to others, I was on the verge of regret, but I knew it was only temporary so I waited and the mood passed."

A few days later he made the entry: "Sonya is very touching with her fears. . . . I shall always love her."

But the "ebb and flow," as Tolstoy called these alternating moods, did not keep them from a lasting love for each other. They were both honest to the very core of their beings, they both looked upon marriage as something sacred, inviolable, they both were made desperately unhappy by their quarrels and were overjoyed when each conquered the difficulties of his character and peace was restored.

There was one fundamental difference in their relationship. Tolstoy felt that he was old, a great sinner who had given in to temptation in the past, that he was unworthy of her. Sonya could not rid herself of the thought that she had sacrificed herself to an older man with an unclean past.

In his diary for January 23 Tolstoy wrote: "The fear remains, that she is young, and there is much she does not know and she does not love me and she suppresses many things in herself for my sake *and all these sacrifices are instinctively charged against me.*"

[164]

Side by side with this we see entries like this in his diary: "I love her more and more all the time. Married now seven months, and I have the feeling I had in the beginning and have not had in a long time, of being swept away in her presence. For me she is so unutterably pure, good and untouched."

Tolstoy's first son was born June 27, 1863, and they gave him the name of Sergei.

This event left a great mark on Tolstoy's soul and, as always happened, it was reflected many years later in his novel *Anna Karenina*, where they show Levin "this strange little red being, squirming and burying his head in the edge of his swaddling clothes." He was astonished that "he also had a nose, crossed eyes and sucking lips. . . . And suddenly: his old little face . . . became even more wrinkled, and the baby sneezed. . . .

"The feelings toward this creature which he experienced were not at all what he expected," Tolstoy went on. "There was nothing enlivening and joyous in his emotions; on the contrary there was a new, harassing terror. It was the recognition of a whole new area of vulnerability. At first this was so tormenting, the fear that this helpless little creature might be harmed was so powerful, that he did not notice the feeling of unreasoning joy and even pride which he felt when the child sneezed."

Now that he had calmed down Tolstoy returned to his literary work: he finished *The Cossacks*, wrote *Polikushka*, attempted a story drawn from peasant life, a kind of idyll, called "Tikhon and Melania"; he set down the history of the piebald gelding, "Kholstomer," in which he carries his readers, with a power of artistry all his own, into the psychology and emotions of the horse.

The success of *The Cossacks* was inspiriting to Tolstoy. He was especially joyful over the criticism of Fet, who wrote: "How many times I embraced you in absentia as I read *The Cossacks*. *The Cossacks* is a chef d'œuvre in its field."

The Cossacks brought a spate of critical articles. All the critics were unanimous in stressing the outstanding artistic merits of the story, and almost all of them decried the author's passionate protest against civilization. "Here you have a poem," wrote Eugenia Tur, "in which the praise is sung, not by any commonplace talent but a very real one, of daring, prowess, thirst for blood and booty, man hunts, the heartlessness and pitilessness of a beastlike savage. Side by side with this beast-savage is the abased, disparaged, broken, debauched representative of civilized society. . . . The author is at great pains to prove that savages are magnificent and happy, and cultivated people are low, petty and unhappy."

Turgenyev also expressed his delight over the story. "I have re-read L. N. Tolstoy's novel and was again delighted with it. It is really a remarkable thing and one of extraordinary power," he wrote to Borisov on the 5th of June, 1864.

Meantime Tolstoy wrote to Fet: "I live in a world so far removed from literature and criticism that when I received a letter like yours my first sensation was one of amazement. Who indeed had written *The Cossacks* and *Polikushka*, and what indeed was there to be discussed about them?"

In the autumn of 1863 he wrote to Alexandrine: "You will rec-ognize my handwriting and my signature; but you will ask yourself who and what I now am. I am a husband and a father, satisfied with my condition and so accustomed to it that in order to feel all my happiness I have to think how would it be without it. . . . My situation affords me tremendous intellectual latitude. I have never felt my intellectual and even my moral powers as free and as ca-pable of work. And the work I have. This work is a novel in the pe-riod 1810-1820. . . . Does this prove weakness of character or strength —I sometimes think it is both, yet I must confess that my point of view on life, the peasants and society, is now quite different from what it was the last time we saw each other. One can feel pity but it is difficult for me to understand how I could love so deeply. Nevertheless I am glad I went through the training; that last mis-tress was very educational. I love children and teaching but it is hard for me to think of myself as I was a year ago. The children come to see me evenings and to me they bring with them the memory of the teacher who was in me and who will no longer be there. I am now a writer with all the strength in my soul, I am writing and thinking harder than I have ever before written or thought."

⚛ 27 ⚛

ALL during her life my mother meticulously saved the rough drafts of my father's writings; she never threw away a scrap of paper written on by him. The manuscripts of *War and Peace* were laid aside in an unused room in the house at Yasnaya Polyana and for many years no one touched them. But it so happened that the oldest son Sergei, as he grew up, needed that room and in clearing out all sorts of rubbish he unthinkingly threw out the manuscripts of *War and Peace*. Fortunately, my mother noticed what he was doing and rescued them. In time she had twelve wooden cases made, in which she put, in no particular order, all the Tolstoy manuscripts and sent them for safekeeping to the Rumyantsev Museum in Moscow.*

The manuscripts were little harmed by the mishap. They were all sorted out, typed, and from them we can judge the grandiose scale of the work Tolstoy put into his novel.

By helping with the deciphering of my father's manuscript—not an easy task, since he wrote illegibly, put in an incredible number of corrections, crossed out passages, added others between the lines, in the margins and on the backs of pages—I succeeded in some measure in following the very process of his creativeness. This

---

* In 1918, at the very height of the revolution, I took an active part in the creation of a society to study the works of L. N. Tolstoy. Distinguished scholars and historians in the field of letters joined the society. These scholars, with the co-operation of several Tolstoyans and my brother Sergei, went over twelve cases of manuscripts, putting them in order, photographing them, copying and preparing for publication the first complete jubilee edition of Tolstoy's writings, which was later undertaken by the State Publishing House of the Soviet Union. It was expected that this edition, which would include all the letters and diaries of Tolstoy, would consist of about eighty-two volumes and would be brought out in 1928, the hundredth anniversary of his birth. Many years, however, have now passed and up to the present time the State Publishing House has issued only thirty-seven volumes of this exceptionally valuable edition, which is in reality a work of capital importance from the point of view of an analysis of Tolstoy's creative achievements.

In the twelve cases of my father's manuscripts preserved in the Rumyantsev Museum in Moscow and examined by the Society for the Study of the Works of L. N. Tolstoy were the manuscripts of *War and Peace*.

was confirmed by Professor A. E. Gruzinski, who worked on the editing of *War and Peace*.

In the first phase of creation Tolstoy did his thinking. Vague images and ideas occurred to him; he searched, felt his way, outlined, erased, added new touches. His images were still fluid, unclear, they were still being challenged. By degrees he accepted them and the characters began to live, think, feel, act, commit their sins. By then Tolstoy had them under control; he loved them. In a letter to Alexandrine he wrote, in January, 1865: "In a few days there will appear the first half of the first part of a novel laid in 1805. Give me your unvarnished opinion of it. I would wish that you might take these children of mine to your heart; there are some fine people among them, and I love them very much."

Some of the initial drafts are so weak from the literary point of view that one sometimes doubts that they were penned by Tolstoy. Carelessly, with no regard for style, he would sketch out events, scenes, draw the characters of the leading personages in a few phrases, all in haste, fearing to forget the thoughts, the fine, all but imperceptible points which only he understood. Thus, for example, we find this entry in his diary for September 16, 1864: "For the novel: (1) Loves to torment the one he loves—constantly harassing. (2) Father and son hate each other, avoid facing each other."

To whom does this refer? Perhaps to the elder Bolkonski and his son and daughter?

But there are excellent variants. You read them with such genuine aesthetic enjoyment that you wonder why he left them out. Only upon reflection do you realize that there was no place for them in the novel.

The history of the Decembrists always intrigued Tolstoy. He was interested in and moved by the self-sacrifice of the wives who followed their husbands into exile, the psychology of the Decembrists who returned from Siberia having lost the habits and vanities of social life. He had begun a history of 1825, but after writing three chapters he abandoned it and decided to write a novel that would begin in the year 1805.

"By 1825 my hero was already a mature, family man," Tolstoy wrote in one of the rough drafts for an introduction to *War and Peace*. "In order to understand him I had to put myself back in the time of his youth and that coincided with the glorious, for Russia, era of 1812. I reworked my beginning a second time and started with 1812, the very smells and sounds of which were still familiar and pleasing to us, yet it was a time so far removed from us that we could contemplate it with equanimity. But I abandoned my start a third time. This time it was not because it was necessary for me to describe the early youth of my hero; on the contrary, in the midst of the semi-historical, semi-public personalities, semi-fictitious major characters of that great epoch, the person of my hero receded into the background and in the foreground there were old and young people, men and women of those days, and all of equal interest to me. This third time I went farther back because of a feeling which perhaps will seem strange to the majority of readers but which, I trust, will be sensed by those whose opinion I value: I did it out of a feeling similar to uneasiness, which I cannot define in one word. I was conscience-stricken at the thought of writing about our triumph in the struggle with Napoleonic France and not describing our failures and our shame. Who has not had that secret and disagreeable feeling of uneasiness and skepticism when reading patriotic writings on the subject of 1812! If the reason for our triumph was not accidental but lay in the essential character of the Russian people and army, then this character should have expressed itself more vividly in times of failures and defeats.

"So it was that in 1856, having gone back as far as 1805, I intended to carry not one but many heroes and heroines through the historic events of 1805, 1807, 1812, 1825 and 1856. The unfolding of the relationships among these characters is not limited, as I look ahead to it, to any one of these epochs. Despite my efforts in the beginning to invent a romantic solution, I became convinced that this was not within my capacities, and I decided that I should, in describing these characters, keep to my own habits and powers. I tried, nevertheless, to have each part of the work maintain a separate interest."

In her memoirs Tanya Kuzminskaya tells how "in the evenings Lev Nikolayevich used to come to Auntie's room and lay out games of solitaire, forecasting aloud to this effect: If this game comes out I'll have to change the beginning—or: If this game comes out I'll title it . . . but he never gave the title. . . ."

The Behrs family was thrilled by the idea that Tolstoy was writing a novel about the 1812 era. "Yesterday evening," Andrei Behrs wrote on September 5, 1863 "we talked a lot about 1812 in relation to your intention of writing a novel set in that epoch." And, in order to encourage his son-in-law, Behrs began to collect material, books and letters for the years 1812-1814.

On September 18, 1863 he wrote to Tolstoy:

"It so happened that my father had much to tell about 1812; it was indeed a remarkable and interesting epoch. You have chosen a lofty subject for your novel. May God help you."

To Fet Tolstoy wrote on November 10, 1863: "You cannot imagine how difficult this preliminary work is, the plowing of the field on which I am compelled to sow. To dwell on, to think over and over again about what might happen to the future characters in this impending story, a very long one, and to weigh the millions of possible combinations in order to select 1/1,000,000th part of them, is terribly difficult. And that is what I am working on."

A year later he wrote to Fet: "I am in a state of dejection, I am not writing at all, my work goes along at a painful rate."

It is impossible to follow through the whole process of the creation and development of *War and Peace*, as impossible as it is to penetrate the soul of another person. Elusive shadings of thought, the reading of various literary works, family relationships, the people he met along the way—all this and much besides was stored up and gradually found its reflection in his own work. Who can tell whether Tolstoy would ever have been able to describe war if he himself had not taken part in battles; or describe the emotions of a gambler if he himself had not lost whole fortunes playing cards; or fathom the psychology of fashionable society had not he himself belonged to that class; or grasp the chivalrous honor of his heroes, their prowess, courage, dissipation, if he had not possessed in himself these traits? Could he have understood the love of risk, the passions of a hunter, if he himself had not often been swept with those emotions? Tanya, his sister-in-law, describes in her memoirs how on a hunting expedition her saddle slipped and she was hanging head downward. "Lyovochka, I am falling," Tanya yelled at the top of her lungs, just as he, Lyovochka, tore by her in mad pursuit of a rabbit. "Wait just a moment, dear," he called to her as he galloped past. Could Tolstoy have described Natasha Rostov, have penetrated the psychology of a girl in love, had he not observed day after day the romantic emotions of his attractive sister-in-law Tanya? Or have described Sonya, so reasonable and so boring, had he not observed those traits in Lisa Behrs? Could he have described the heroes of the war of 1812, and Nikolai Rostov, had he not from his childhood heard endless tales of 1812 campaigns from his father?

As early as November 11, 1862, his wife wrote to her sisters: "Girls, I'll tell you in confidence but don't repeat it, Lyovochka may describe us all when he is fifty."

Tolstoy did not like to be asked who the models for his leading characters were—whom he was describing in Natasha Rostov. We cannot, however, keep from noticing that there were many of Tanya Behrs' traits in Natasha, much of her character, and even a whole series of episodes drawn from Tanya's life. "I took Tanya, did her over in combination with Sonya, and out of that came Natasha." It is difficult to say whether Tanya Behrs-Natasha Rostov was intelligent or not, good or bad, beautiful or not, but there was in Tanya such subtle charm, such fire, such enjoyment of the life that she swept everyone along with her—old and young—and wherever she went she enlivened the atmosphere.

If people were quarreling Tanya would rush into the room like a whirlwind, and, without thinking what she was doing, would say something amusing, chide the quarrelers good-naturedly, be sorry for them, and peace would be restored. If a child was crying, Tanya would pick it up, sing to it, dandle it or give it a little slap—and the child would stop; if an old nurse was grumbling, or parents were cross, or guests were bored all Tanya had to do was to appear and everyone would feel gay, unrestrainedly joyful.

Tanya was at all times the faithful companion of Tolstoy. In early spring she went woodcock hunting with him, rode horseback, hunted to hounds cross country with him. Tanya loved sports, games, whereas Sonya was completely indifferent to them. When Sonya, to be sociable, went hunting she would admire nature, fall into a reverie, look with indifference through the lorgnette she carried for her short-sighted eyes at a rabbit scurrying past, and unleash the dogs too late when the quarry had safely slipped away. To the great disgust of the real hunters, Sonya was delighted when the poor rabbit escaped. In the evening Tolstoy played the piano and Tanya sang. In her singing, in her voice there was the same subtle charm, melodiousness and suppressed passion that permeated her whole being. It was not surprising that Fet dedicated one of his best poems to her, "You Sang Until the Dawn."

Tolstoy after once hearing grandfather Islenyev sing remarked, with regard to the whole Islenyev-Behrs race: "Oh what a vital energy, this Islenyev blood, and it flows in all of you too, the black

Behrs!"—that is, those who had dark eyes and hair. In a letter to his wife on December 8, 1864, Tolstoy commented:

"All the black ones in your family are awfully nice and attractive. Lyubov Alexandrovna is awfully like you. The other day she was making a shade for a lamp, just the way you do; when you take up a piece of work nothing can pry you loose from it. You even have bad traits in common. I hear her sometimes beginning to talk with confidence on subjects of which she knows nothing, making positive assertions and exaggerating—and I see you in her. But you are adorable in all ways for me. I am writing in my study and before me are pictures of you at four different ages. Darling Sonya! How clever you are in everything on which you care to put your mind. That is why I say that you are indifferent to intellectual interests, and not only are you not limited but you have a mind, a big mind. And you all have that, my especially attractive black Behrs. The black Behrs are: Lyubov Alexandrovna, you, Tanya, Petya; and the blonds—are all the rest. In the black Behrs the mind is dormant—they have the power but not the will, that is why they are so self-assured, often embarrassingly so, and possess tact. And the reason the mind is dormant is that they love so strongly and also because the fountainhead of the black Behrs—Lyubov Alexandrovna—was not educated. The blond Behrs have a great love for intellectual interests but their minds are too weak and shallow. Sasha is motley, half blond."

It is not strange, in this period of Tolstoy's greatest creative work when the entire family of Behrs was very close to him, that he borrowed incidents here and there from the human dramas being enacted around him. Tanya's adventures were especially colorful.

Tanya's childlike love for Kuzminski did not satisfy her. He was a handsome, well-built youth, straightforward and honest, but narrow and rather dry, and he could give her nothing of what drew her to the Tolstoy home. Tanya was happy whenever she was in Yasnaya Polyana, at her sister's or at Pokrovskoye, Maria Tolstoy's, with whose daughters Lizanka and Varenka she was very friendly. At home Tanya was bored.

When, for the first time in her life, her father took her to St. Petersburg, she met a distant cousin, Anatol Shostak. Tanya characterized him this way: "He was one of those people one often meets in society. He was self-confident, unaffected and free of all embarrassment. He loved women and was popular with them. He knew how to approach them directly, caressingly and boldly. He knew how to make them think that the force of love endows one with rights, that love is the greatest satisfaction. No obstacles existed for him. He was not good but he was good-natured. In money matters he was honest and even generous. In society he was witty and brilliant. He was adept at languages and had the name of being an intelligent youth."

Anatol fell in love with Tanya and never doubted for a second that she shared his feelings. He acted as if it were a sure thing. His attentions rather turned the head of the sixteen-year-old girl. Hearing that Tanya was in Yasnaya Polyana, Anatol went there. The Tolstoys watched with uneasiness. In her memoirs Tanya describes how, while out riding, she and Anatol lagged behind the others and how, in the woods, he kissed her. For those days this was an inexcusable liberty. Tanya was unable to conceal her "crime," especially from her brother-in-law, who saw right through her. The Tolstoys were indignant over Anatol's behavior, knowing that he had no intention of marrying her, and they suggested that he leave Yasnaya Polyana.

The episode, in an altered form, was described by Tolstoy in *War and Peace*.

Tanya's stormy albeit superficial fascination with Anatol passed quickly and this time was replaced by a serious passion which was to last, as she said, for all her life—she fell in love with Sergei Tolstoy.

Love flared between them with incredible speed. Without consideration or reflection Sergei, madly in love with Tanya, proposed to her and they decided to be married regardless of obstacles, the seriousness of which she had not even imagined. Deep down in his heart Sergei felt that he did not have the right to do as he wished. He had a family. For many years he had been living with Masha, a gypsy woman—a small, gentle, swarthy little person, who had won his affections through her marvelous singing voice. They had already three children. Besides, the law forbade the marriage of two brothers to two sisters. . . . But Sergei was bereft of the power to reason logically and unwittingly deceived both himself and Tanya, hoping no one knows for what, and torturing himself and her.

One night brought them especially close. Tanya was visiting Maria Tolstoy in Pokrovskoye. Sergei invited Tanya to drive over with him to Pirogovo, his house across the river. When they were ready to return a terrible thunderstorm blew up, lightning flashed, thunder rolled and the rain came down in buckets. It was impossible to get back. Sergei and Tanya were alone in his new little house. Sergei kept trying to go upstairs to his own room but Tanya was afraid. They sat talking for half the night and finally Tanya dropped off into the serenely sound sleep of a child, while Sergei sat up all night near her but behind a screen, alone with his perturbing and joyous thoughts.

The Tolstoys were keenly aware of and upset by this drama between the two people closest to them, and the elder Behrs felt it even more keenly.

In the end, after agonizing over it and having learned the whole truth about Sergei's family, Tanya definitely refused him.

Like a bird that has been shot, Tanya furled her wings, her song was stilled, she grew thin, pale, began to cough. They feared for her lungs.

Tolstoy wrote from Pirogovo to his wife about the break between his brother and Tanya: "I slept downstairs, it must have been on the very same sofa where Tanya made him [Sergei] stay with her. And the whole poetic and sad story came to my imagination. They are both fine people, both beautiful and good: the one an aging man and the other almost a child, and both are now unhappy; yet I can understand that the memory of that night—when they were alone together, in an empty, charming house—will remain for both of them the most poetic memory. . . ."

Anyone reading *War and Peace* carefully must unconsciously compare Tanya Behrs with Natasha Rostov, with all her fascination, striking voice, sensuality, stormy emotions, her yearning for Prince Andrei.

"Lyovochka," Tanya once said to Tolstoy, "I can see how you are able to describe landowners, fathers, generals, soldiers, but how you can insinuate yourself into the heart of a girl in love, how you can describe the sensations of a mother—for the life of me I cannot understand."

Yes, it is difficult to understand this, except by keeping in mind that Tolstoy had been a daily witness of Tanya's emotions, had himself gone through tempestuous experiences with her, and had observed the psychology of a wife and mother in his own wife.

Toward the end of 1863 Tolstoy temporarily was distracted from

War and Peace and for the first time tried his powers in what was for him an entirely new field of creative activity.

He never had any use for the emancipated women who cut their hair short, looked like men, smoked and deviated—as he used to say—from their true destiny as wives and mothers, or in roles of service where their gentleness and feminine instincts could be brought into play. Such women were drawn to socialism, nihilism, revolutionary work, and to the movement described as "going to the people." Tolstoy was out of sympathy with this tendency, it was obnoxious to him, and in his five-act play *Infected Family* he made fun of these "advanced" people. It was the story of a cultivated, respected family swept away by new ideas. But this comedy, Tolstoy's first effort in dramatic art, was not produced. He took it to Moscow early in 1864, but the dramatist and director, A. N. Ostrovski, did not choose to stage it at the Maly Theater. "When I was just getting well again," Ostrovski wrote Nekrasov on March 7, 1864, "L. N. Tolstoy dragged me over to his place and read me his new comedy; it is such a monstrosity that my ears positively wilted off from listening to it."

Tolstoy was very anxious to get the play before the public as quickly as possible. "What are you in such a hurry for?" Ostrovski asked ironically, "Are you afraid that people will grow intelligent?"

It is difficult to tell whether his opinion, and that of other contemporary writers, was based exclusively on the literary defects of the comedy or whether a major reason for its rejection stemmed from Tolstoy's negative attitude toward the liberal currents of the time.

Sonya at this time was weighted down with maternal cares. Sergei was not yet two and in October a second child was expected. Tanya was in a state of gloom. Tolstoy again took up the burden of writing his novel. "It will soon be a year that I have written nothing on this book," he said in his diary for September 16, 1864. "Yet it has been a good year. The relations between Sonya and me have grown finer, stronger. We love, that is to say we are dearer to each other than to anyone else in the world, and we look at each other with clear eyes. We have no secrets and no cause for remorse. Since then I have begun a novel . . . but now I am in the stage of correcting and recasting. It is torture. My interest in teaching has receded far. My son is not at all close to me. . . ." Just as Sonya could not share in his passion for dogs, horses, hunting, farming, Tolstoy did not enter sufficiently into her interests which centered in the nursery. His paternal feeling for Sergei was not immediately aroused.

In the summer of 1864 Tolstoy was away frequently, hunting, visiting neighbors, Fet, his brother Sergei. He wrote in snatches at times with enthusiasm and power.

On one of his cross-country rides, Tolstoy was thrown when his horse stumbled in a rut. In a half-fainting condition, doubled up with pain in his shoulder and arm, he dragged himself to the highway, where he was picked up by some peasants and put to bed in a cottage in the village. He was afraid that the news of his accident would frighten the pregnant Sonya.

His dislocated arm recovered quickly, but his collarbone proved to be broken. The Tula doctors set it but did not do it well so that the bone healed badly. Tolstoy continued to have pain in it and had poor use of the arm.

Despite all the upset a healthy little girl was born to the Tolstoys on October 4 and they gave her the name of Tatiana. Life began to slip into its normal groove. Tolstoy again took up his novel—he felt the urge to write. But his arm ached, he had difficulty in raising it and, after faithfully trying out all sorts of household remedies, he decided to go to Moscow for treatment.

In Moscow he stayed with the Behrs. On the advice of Dr. Behrs he showed his broken collarbone to several physicians; he did exercises, had massage, but there was no improvement. Finally, after a series of consultations, Tolstoy decided on an operation. On November 29 he dictated this letter to his wife:

"Here is the account for you of two days. When they told me, and I believed them, that just exercises would benefit me I began to wave my arm and, I must confess, put it into a very bad condition. I was very dejected and in that state of dejection I went to Redlich; when Redlich, who would have had a material advantage in getting money from me for the exercises, said that I must have the bone straightened, I finally made up my mind; to tell the real truth I had made it up the evening before in the theater, when the music was playing, the ballerinas were dancing, Michel Bode was using both his arms while I felt, looked lopsided and pitiful, with an empty sleeve, and an ache; but above all the nervous tension, under the influence of which I had come up from Yasnaya, left me and I recalled your words: not to obey your father, that he would bully me; and that is what happened.

"That day I was particularly busy going around the bookstores, to the doctors and, although I felt that I had upset all the Behrs by my decision to have the bone straightened, was very merry; I went to the opera, I was in a pleasant mood from the music, from seeing so many gentlemen and ladies, who are all types to me. I was embarrassed even to think of being afraid of the chloroform and the operation, despite the fact that you have such a low opinion of me; I felt it was disagreeable to be deprived of my arm a little on my own account, but truly more on yours, especially after a conversation with Tanya which convinced me all the more of this. I had to face the probability that they could not straighten the bone, but I did it in order to be free from reproaching myself in the future. . . ."

At this time the manuscript entitled *1805* had already been delivered and was to appear in the first issue of the *Russian Herald* in 1865.

Tolstoy's letter continues: "I almost forgot to describe the meeting with Lyubimov before the opera; he came from Katkov and announced, again with his slobbery smile, that Katkov accepted all my terms, so the silly bargain is made, that is to say, I agreed to three hundred rubles apiece for each sheet for the first part of the novel which I brought with me. But when my *portefeuille* was emptied and slobbering Lyubimov carried off the manuscript I was sad and just because of the thing that angers you, that I cannot make any more changes and improve it still more."

On the 8th of December Tolstoy wrote his wife: "How sweet of you to understand my feelings when I turned in the manuscript. Traits like that are all important to me and the best proof of your good love for me. . . ."

For about two weeks Tolstoy continued to nurse his collarbone under the supervision of his doctors. But he did not waste any time; he visited libraries, collected books and, with the help of the three sisters, he continued to work on his novel. Sonya copied the manuscript at home in Yasnaya Polyana. He never liked to dictate; it embarrassed, impeded him, but the urge to write was so powerful that he from time to time dictated to the Behrs sisters, especially to Tanya who was closest to him.

"Yesterday I explained to Tanya," he wrote his wife on December 1, "why it is easier for me to bear the separation from you and the children (I do feel here that I still love them too little); it is that I have a constant affection and concern for my writing. If it were not for that, I feel I should certainly not be able to spend a single day without you, and you understand this correctly because what writing means to me is what the children must mean to you."

But, as always with Tolstoy, these moments of exaltation alternated with disillusion, and in the same letter he wrote Sonya:

"I am always susceptible to praise, and your praise of the character of Princess Maria pleased me very much. But today I read over what you had sent me [the clean copy] and it seemed pretty foul to me, and I felt the lack of my hand; I wanted to correct, to scribble in, something—and I was unable to do it; in general I was disillusioned today about my talent, especially as yesterday I dictated some awful nonsense to Lisa. I know that this is only a temporary mood, which will pass. . . ."

Nevertheless, by the end of 1864, thirty-eight chapters of the novel *1805* had been written and turned over to be printed. The destiny of this greatest of all Tolstoy's works, *War and Peace*, was already cast. He could not now abandon his child. He was compelled to pour the entire creative power of his genius, all his intellectual energy and vitality, all his experience, into this child which by an unknown and complex process had been conceived in him.

On January 22, 1865, Tolstoy again wrote to Fet: "You know, what a surprise I have to tell you about myself; when the horse threw me to the ground and I broke my arm, when I came to after the anesthetic, I said to myself, I am a man of letters. And I am a literary man, but a solitary, slow-poke writer."

❧ 28 ❧

THE opening installment of Tolstoy's novel made a tremendous impression. People were carried away by it and waited with impatience for the continuation. A whole series of critical articles about it appeared. And although Tolstoy did not like the critics, he was not indifferent to them, he even appreciated very much the opinions of certain individuals. He wrote, for example, to Fet (January 23, 1865):

"Please write me in more detail your own opinion, yours and also that of the person I love less and less as I grow up, yet whose opinion I cherish—Turgenyev. He will understand. The things I have published heretofore I consider only trial tests of my pen; what has been printed, although I like it better than my earlier writings, still seems weak yet without it there is no beginning. What follows may be—a catastrophe! Write me too what you hear said in the circle of your acquaintances and especially what the effect on the general public is. Probably it will pass unnoticed. I expect that and would wish it so; if only they do not scold, because scolding upsets me.

". . . I am very glad that you are fond of my wife, even though I love her less than I do my novel, still, you know, she is my wife. . . ."

Tolstoy waited in vain to get from Turgenyev directly an impartial and just evaluation of his work. But on March 25, 1866, Turgenyev wrote Fet: "The second part of *1805* is weak, it's all so shallow and contrived, and don't these endless discussions, about am I or am I not a coward, bore Tolstoy? All this is battle—morbidity. Where in it are the traits of the times? Where the historic colors? The character of Denisov is dashingly drawn; it would be fine as a pattern against a background, but there is no background."

In a letter written June 8, 1866, Turgenyev expresses himself even more severely: "Tolstoy's novel is bad not because he too has been infected with 'ratiocination'; he has nothing to fear from that: it is bad because the author has not studied anything, knows nothing, and under the names of Kutusov and Bagration he puts forward some slavishly copied portraits of contemporary pigmy generals."

Later, as was more than once the case with Turgenyev and his attitude toward Tolstoy's writings, he gave an entirely different estimate of *War and Peace*. In the year 1868 we find this in his letters:

"I have just finished the fourth volume of *War and Peace*. There are some intolerable things in it and some which are admirable, and the admirable ones, which on the whole predominate, are so magnificently good that nothing better has been written by anyone in Russia, and probably nothing so good has ever been written. . . . The third volume is altogether a chef d'œuvre.

"There are tens of pages which are solidly admirable, first class—all the parts concerning native life, descriptions—hunting, driving at night, etc. . . . there are things in this novel which no one in all Europe except Tolstoy could write, and which have given me both the chills and fever of delight."

Tolstoy craved impartial criticism, sought it and, like a sponge, soaked up all the reasonable, kindly suggestions of his friends.

"There is an important lack which checks the kind of fervent interest with which one reads great writings. . . ." Fet wrote to Tolstoy on June 16, 1860. "I do not think that Prince Andrei was a pleasant companion, or person with whom to converse, etc., and even less than that a hero, capable of providing the thread on which to string the attention of the readers. . . . As long as Prince Andrei was at home, where his decent character was an achievement in contrast with his fiery old father and silly wife, he was interesting, but when he left, when he had to do something, then Vaska Denisov wins over him hands down. It seems to me that I have found the Achilles' heel of your novel. However, who can tell."

After considerable delay, yet with exceeding kindness and consideration, Tolstoy replied: "I did not answer your last letter of a hundred years ago," he wrote Fet, "and I am all the more to blame because as I recall you wrote things about my novel in that letter which were of great interest to me and more than that you wrote as *irritabilis poetarum gens*. But I am not of them. I recall that I on the contrary was delighted by your criticism of one of my heroes—Prince Andrei—and drew a lesson for myself from your criticism. He is monotonous, boring and no more than *un homme comme il faut* for all the first part. That is true, but he is not to blame for that, I am. Besides the pattern of characters and their movement, besides the pattern of conflict of characters, I have a historical pattern which complicates my work to an extraordinary degree, and which I am not going to be able to carry out, so it would seem. That is why in the first part I was engaged with the historical angle and the characters stand still, do not move. But that is a shortcoming which I clearly recognized after reading your letter and I hope that I have corrected it. Please write me, dear friend, everything you have in mind about me, that is, the bad things about my writing. This is always of great benefit to me and I have no one else but you. . . ."

It is not worth while to cite the innumerable critical reviews of the novel. Side by side with the favorable ones there appeared articles by conservatives reproaching Tolstoy for having belittled the great Russian commanders and demoted the political leaders from their pedestals. There were reproaches too from the intellectual liberals because their circle was not described at all. Tolstoy was taken to task also for historical inaccuracies, for using too much French, and for many other things. At one time he stopped reading the criticisms—in some respects they hampered his work as a painter is hampered by

The only existing likeness of Tolstoy's mother, taken at the age of nine years

Tolstoy's father

Tolstoy as a student

Tolstoy in 1848

Tolstoy as an officer

Tolstoy in 1856

Tolstoy in 1862, the year
of his marriage

The four Tolstoy brothers:
Sergei, Nikolai, Dmitri, Lev

Countess Tolstoy as a bride

Tolstoy at the time he began
writing
Anna Karenina.
From a portrait by Kramskoy

Tolstoy's house in Yasnaya Polyana

View of the Yasnaya Polyana estate. On the right one can see the roof of the main house. On the left, the view of the wing—former Tolstoy school. In the foreground—the Volkonski house and the stables

Tolstoy's study room

Drawing room and a view of the living-dining room—the "hall"

Tolstoy and his brother Sergei's wife

Tolstoy's sister

Tolstoy's daughter Masha
From a portrait by Repin

Tolstoy's daughter Tanya
From a portrait by Repin

Alexandra and Vanichka

Tolstoy with some schoolchildren

Tolstoy with Repin

Tolstoy and his daughter Alexandra

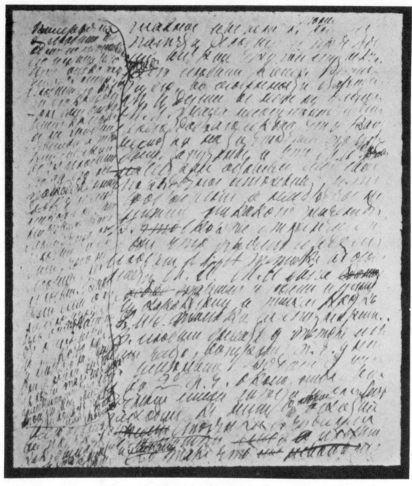

A page of the manuscript of *The Kreutzer Sonata*

N. N. Gay
A self-portrait

T. M. Bondarev
From a portrait by Volguzhev

Tolstoy with V. G. Chertkoff

Tolstoy with his grandchildren Ilya and Sophie

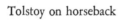

Tolstoy on horseback

Hadji Murat playing chess
From a portrait by G. G. Gagarin

Tolstoy with Chekhov

Tolstoy with Gorki

The family circle at Yasnaya Polyana
From left, back row: Dushan Makovitsky, Alexandra Tolstoy, Elizabeth
Obolenski (Tolstoy's niece), V. G. Chertkoff, Lev N. Tolstoy, S. A. Tolstoy;
front: J. I. Igumnova ("Jooly-Mooly"), M. N. Tolstoy (Lev Tolstoy's sister)

Tolstoy driving with Tokutomi and his daughter Alexandra

A late portrait of Tolstoy smiling

Tolstoy with Dr. Makovitsky

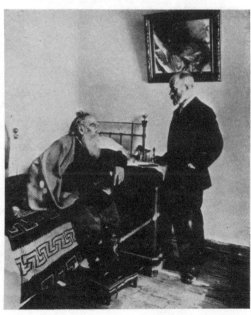

Countess Tolstoy denied admission to the house where Tolstoy lay dying

Tolstoy's grave

an onlooker who watches his canvas with curiosity and begins to discuss the details of an unfinished painting.

Tolstoy worked on *War and Peace* for about seven years, beginning with 1863 when he first conceived the novel and up to December, 1869, when he published the sixth and final volume of it. The longer he wrote, the closer he came to his leading characters, to their lives, to the currents and moods of the time.

"I immersed myself in the history of Napoleon and Alexander," he wrote in his diary for March 19, 1865. "I am now caught up in a cloud of joy and the consciousness of the possibility of doing a great piece of work, by the thought of writing a psychological history of the story of Alexander and Napoleon. All the meanness, all the empty words, all the madness, all the contradictoriness of the people surrounding them and of the men themselves. Napoleon as a man lost his way and was prepared to abdicate to the assembly on the 18th of Brumaire [Revolutionary calendar]. *De nos jours les peuples sont trop éclairés pour produire quelque chose de grand.* Alexander the Great could call himself the son of Jupiter and people believed him. The whole Egyptian expedition was—French vainglorious wickedness. All the *bulletins* were deliberately false. The Peace of Pressburg was *escamotée*. On the bridge at Arcola he, and not the standard, fell into the mud puddle. He had a bad seat on a horse. In the war in Italy he carried off paintings, statues. He loved to ride around on the field of battle. The dead and wounded inspired him with—joy. His marriage with Josephine was—a social success. He wrote three accounts of the battle of Rivoli—and he lied in all of them. He was still a human being at first, and powerful in his self-sufficiency—then he lost his grip—turned fatalist! How? You are just plain people, but I see my star in the sky. He is not the point of interest, but the crowds which surround him and whom he affects. At first there is his self-sufficiency and the *beau jeu* in comparison with the Marats and Barras, then feeling his way—self-confidence, good fortune, and then madness—*faire entrer dans son lit la fille des Césars.* Complete insanity, deterioration, and annihilation on St. Helena. The lies and the grandeur existed only because of the scale, but the course was brief and came to nothing. And the death was ignominious!

"Alexander was intelligent, kindly, sensitive, striving to embrace all from his superior heights, striving for human eminence. Abdicating his throne and giving his approval, not interfering with the murder of Paul (this cannot be so). Plans for the revival of Europe. Austerlitz, tears, the wounded. Naryshkin betrays him. Speranski, liberation of the serfs, Tilsit—the overwhelming effect of greatness. Erfurt. The space of time up to 1812 I am not familiar with. The nobility of the man, vacillation, victory, triumph, *grandeur* which frightened even him, and the search for human loftiness—for his soul. Confusion in external things, clarity inside. Yet combined with military harshness—maneuvers, strictness. External confusion, clarification in his soul. Death. If killed, that would be best.

"I must write my novel and work toward that."

In the first part of the third volume of *War and Peace* the fatalistic point of view is quite clearly defined. Had Tolstoy lived on into our times he might have been convinced again of the rightness of his outlook. Is it not true that now, as 125 years ago, history is fatally bound to push to the top not only weak, insignificant, and short-visioned politicians but also criminals who run the world regardless of the desires of the masses whom they govern? Is it not true that our contemporary historians are seldom able to evaluate the events of our times, but must wait for future historians to arrive at a true estimate?

"To us the descendants, who are not historians, not absorbed in the process of research, and therefore capable of contemplating the events with unclouded common sense, myriad reasons for them appear," wrote Tolstoy. "The farther we investigate reasons, the more of them we discover, and each reason taken separately or a whole series of reasons seems in itself justifiable, yet misleading because it is so insignificant in comparison with the tremendous size of the event and equally misleading by its inability (without the participation of all the other coincident reasons) to produce the event which occurred.

"If Napoleon had not been offended by the demand that he withdraw behind the Vistula, and had not ordered his troops to advance, there would not have been any war; yet also had all the sergeants refused to serve a second term there could not have been any war either.

"Also there could not have been any war had England not intrigued, had there been no Prince Oldenburg, had Alexander not taken offense, and if there had not been an autocratic government in Russia, and if there had not been any French Revolution with the subsequent dictatorship and empire and all that produced the

French Revolution, and so on. Lacking any one of these reasons nothing could have happened. Evidently all these reasons—billions of them—coalesced in order to produce what happened. Consequently no one reason was the exclusive cause of the event, and the event had to take place only because it was destined to do so. Millions of men renouncing their human sentiments and their minds had to leave the West and go East to kill others of their own kind, just as, so many centuries ago, people left the East and went West to kill others of their own kind. . . .

"Fatalism in history is inevitable in order to explain irrational phenomena (that is to say those whose rationality we do not understand). The more we strive to explain these phenomena of history by means of reason the more irrational and incomprehensible they become. . . ."

And although Tolstoy applied his own interpretation to the historical events of 1812 he was extraordinarily careful to be accurate with his facts. He said to himself: "Whenever in my novel historic personages speak and act I have not invented anything, I used materials of which I have a whole library full. I see no necessity of giving the titles here but I can always refer to them."

Yet historical figures came to life under his pen. To make them do so he had to know that Napoleon had short, puffy hands, that he had a cold in his head at the time of the Battle of Borodino, that he was a poor horseman. He had to know that General Kutuzov, when his feelings were affected, gushed with emotion, that now and then he liked to indulge in good Russian oaths, that he had a hard time hoisting himself onto a horse, etc., etc. . . . And as Tolstoy read he used his own rich imagination to fill out the characters of his leading actors, who live their own special, individual lives. As one reads the novel one shares with them, as with one's own family, their love, tears, laughter, sufferings, hatreds. . . .

From the manuscripts we know what great significance Tolstoy laid on even such a small detail as the family name of a leading character. Thus "Rostov" began by being "Prostov" in the early versions, and then Tolstoy eliminated just one letter. That name was somehow right for the type of family he had in mind. Pierre Bezukhov looks dark blue in Natasha's mind, he could not be anything else, and Natasha is offended when the old Countess does not at once comprehend what it is she means by that.

Tolstoy avidly grasped at any piece of information about the epoch he was describing. He even placed an advertisement in the *Moscow Journal*: "For 2,000 silver rubles I wish to acquire a complete set of the *Moscow Journal* with all its supplements. Deliver to Tverskaya Street, Golyashkin Chambers."

Living witnesses of the times offered an even greater interest to him. In his own household were several who had lived through the 1812 period: both his aunts Alexandra and Pelagea, Auntie Tatiana Alexandrovna, and the housekeeper Praskovia Isayevna, a former serf of Nikolai Volkonski.

For a long time Tolstoy was unable to portray the scene in Moscow when the Commander in Chief of the City, Rostopchin, desirous of distracting the grumbling and unruly mob, let them butcher young Vereshchagin who had been arrested on suspicion of spying. Tolstoy asked N. P. Peterson, a former teacher in his school, to hunt up all the material bearing on this incident. "I collected such a quantity of tales about the incident, from newspapers and other sources," said Peterson," that it was necessary to set up a special table for it. Leo Nikolayevich did not come around for some reason or other for a long time, and when he did come and I showed him the literature about Vereshchagin he said he did not intend to read it because he had discovered some old man in a lunatic asylum who was an eyewitness of the event and he had been telling him how it all occurred."

Tolstoy had to see with his own eyes the places where this or that event described in his novel had taken place. It was not difficult to picture Lysy Gory, the pond where the soldiers bathed, or where the elder Bolkonski with the aid of an Italian architect put up his stone buildings, with a shady park. For that Tolstoy described Yasnaya Polyana. He knew the house on Povarskaya Street where the Rostovs lived. But how could he tell of the Battle of Borodino, not having been on the spot, not having imagined the deployment of the troops? So Tolstoy went to Borodino with his brother-in-law, Stepan Behrs.

"I have just come back from Borodino," he wrote his wife on September 27, 1866. "I am very pleased, very, with the trip and even with the way I stood it given the lack of sleep and decent food. If only God will give me good health and tranquillity, I'll write the best Battle of Borodino yet!"

Sonya was distressed to have her husband away from her so frequently, and because he was little interested in the life which completely absorbed her—the poor health of Seryozha, who at times suffered from diarrhea or a cough, of little Tatiana whom she was nursing herself, and the arrival (May 22, 1866) of a second son, Ilya. Love of the children, especially of black-eyed, vivacious Tanya, gradually grew in Tolstoy as they gave evidence of intelligence and individuality. If anything serious happened in the absence of her husband, Sonya was quite lost.

In November, 1866, the Tolstoys acquired an English governess for the older children. "She is very young," Sonya wrote her husband in Moscow, November 12, 1866, "rather sweet, a pleasant face, even very pretty, but our mutual ignorance of languages is terrible. For the time being her sister is staying over with us, to translate, but what will happen later on—God only knows; I quite lose my head, especially with you away, dear one. For once I remembered your rule, to think how all this will seem so easy and insignificant a year from now. But right now it's even very difficult. The children accepted her, Tanya sat in her lap and looked at pictures, told her some kind of story, Seryozha raced with her and kept saying, 'See how she plays with me!' Later on, in the nursery Tanya imitated the way the English governess talked. Probably everything will get straightened out but for the time being it all seems so unnatural, difficult, awkward and alarming."

Everything was straightened out shortly with the English governess, because in her next letter Sonya wrote that all went sleighing and "Hanna was so happy she jumped up and down in the sleigh and kept saying 'so nice' which is to say, probably, that it was all right. And then and there in the sleigh she explained to me that she loves me and the children and that the country is beautiful and that she is 'very happy.' I can understand her rather well but only with difficulty and concentration. She sits and sews panties for the children and the children are put to bed by the old nurse. When they are transferred to her charge it will be much better and otherwise she has only half work to do. By contrast I gain from it; I shall learn quickly, I am confident; and that would be very pleasant. For the time being she is also dining and taking tea with us. Until you come back I shall make no change, we shall have time to do that. But she is anxious, so it seems, to take on her future duties and she understands them. Yet she is not a nurse, she carries herself quite as a member of the family, but she is not fazed by any work and is very good-natured, it would seem."

Sometimes Sonya was jealous of her husband though always without reason. In her diary for July 19, 1866, she had written: "We have a new steward and his wife. She is young, pretty, a *nihilist*. Lyova and she have long animated conversations about literature and convictions in general; she has long, unseasonable conversations which are tormenting to me and flattering for her. He preaches that in the family, in the *intimité*, one should not introduce an extraneous person, especially a beautiful and young one, yet he is the first to do it himself. I of course do not show by my looks that this is unpleasant to me but already my life knows not a moment of peace. . . .'"

That autumn, however, Sonya's jealousy ended rather abruptly: What brought this about was a play Tolstoy wrote for the young people who were accustomed to gather at Yasnaya Polyana. It was called *The Nihilist*, and its theme concerned a husband stupidly jealous of his wife because of a student—a nihilist. The younger people were delighted and began at once to prepare the production. Sonya played the husband, Tanya played the wife, Lisa Tolstoy played the hero, the nihilist student, and Maria Nikolayevna, that veteran entertainer, played a vagrant. For her Tolstoy simply indicated her cues and she improvised her lines as she played, doing it with such talent that he, sitting out with the spectators, was absolutely delighted and doubled up with laughter. Unfortunately, no full text of this comedy is extant. After the performance, however, Sonya's jealousy of the beautiful "nihilist" faded out.

In the intervals between her maternal cares, nursing babies, taking walks, attending to household matters, Sonya sat at an old mahogany secretary desk, topped by a bookcase, and copied her husband's novel in a clear round hand, following its development with excitement. She wrote on one side of the paper, leaving large margins for the corrections with which Tolstoy was wont to sprinkle his manuscripts. So it was she copied *War and Peace* approximately seven times. Only a small part of the book was copied by an amanuensis specially engaged for the purpose.

Whenever Tolstoy went up to Moscow there was always a lively exchange of letters between him and his wife. Sonya wrote about the children, the household. Tolstoy wrote about the events connected with his work.

"Tomorrow I shall go to Bashilov's," he wrote her on November 11, 1866, "to the printer and to the Rumyantsev Museum to read up on Freemasons."

Bashilov was a painter, a connection of the Behrs, and Tolstoy was negotiating with him about some illustrations to go with *War and Peace*, which he had decided to publish himself.

Tolstoy did the major part of his writing at Yasnaya Polyana and went to Moscow only for the winter months. By late November, 1867, the novel was in proof.

"I have an awful fog in my head," Tolstoy wrote on November 26 to P. I. Bartenev, who had undertaken to proofread it. "This is the fourth day that I have been at work without even stretching myself and now it is after midnight."

Meantime a number of things had happened in the Tolstoy family.

In January, 1865, Maria Tolstoy had lost her husband. To be sure she had not been living with him, because he was frequently unfaithful to her. He was a frivolous person, but there was a time when Tolstoy and he had been friends and his death was found to leave a mark.

The stormy romance between Tanya and Sergei Tolstoy came to an extraordinarily prosaic conclusion. In June, 1867, Sergei married his gentle little gypsy Maria Shishkina and Tanya returned to her childhood flame, marrying her cousin Sasha Kuzminski on July 24, 1867.

In this period Tolstoy was leading a double existence: he was living in 1812 and he also had his life with his family, looking after the estate, hunting. There were days and weeks when he did not touch his novel. At other times his personal life faded into the background as he worked so intensively that he was quite cut off from everything surrounding him. He would write until he was completely exhausted, with such absorption that his head was racked with pain. Sometimes his thoughts ranged far beyond the limits of his novel. Russia, war, government, injustice, stupidity, the futility of so-called public opinion, the poverty of the peasantry would engage his mind, and, it would go on working while he slept.

On August 13, 1865 he had had a dream which he recorded in his notebook: "The universal, national goal of Russia consists in bringing to the world the idea of socialized organization without landed property.

" *'La propriété c'est le vol'* will prove a greater truth than the truth of the English Constitution until such time as there will exist a human race. This is an *absolute* truth, but there are also certain relative truths which derive from it—supplemental truths. The first of these relative truths is the attitude of the Russian people toward property. The Russian people rejects property as something very lasting, something quite divorced from labor, and above all that property which hampers others in their right to acquire property—that is to say landed property. This truth is not a dream—it is a fact, expressed in the peasant and Cossack communes. This truth is equally understood by the educated Russian and by the peasant who says: let them make Cossacks of us and the land will be free. . . ."

In the summer of 1866 an infantry regiment was garrisoned near Yasnaya Polyana. Some officers of the regiment told Tolstoy that Vasili Shibunin, a former staff clerk and noncommissioned officer, had been court-martialed. According to the information gathered by Tolstoy, Shibunin's superior officer was a cold, cruel Pole who had taken a dislike to his clerk, kept finding fault with him, and had unfairly demoted him to the ranks. Shibunin had been unable to bear the unjust nagging and in an outburst of anger had struck his officer. Shibunin was now threatened with being shot and Tolstoy undertook to defend him.

The only argument that might save Shibunin from execution was the recognition of the fact that he was not normal and this Tolstoy attempted to prove in his speech. But the case was lost, the court condemned Shibunin to be shot and Tolstoy's petition, forwarded by Alexandrine to Milyutin, Minister of War, was also rejected. Shibunin was executed on August 9.

As so often happens this execution did not enhance the authority of the top officers. Many who were present at the execution wept and the people spoke of the "martyrdom" of Shibunin. While he was under arrest the peasants had provided him with all necessities, and after he was shot his grave became a goal for pilgrimages, and masses were said until the authorities interfered. Services were prohibited and his grave was leveled.

The question of the right of one man to kill another was again facing Tolstoy. It may well be that the execution of Shibunin had an indirect influence on *War and Peace*. In the sixties and the seventies we still sense some contradictions in Tolstoy. The traditions of his class, of military circles, and loyalty to the Emperor were still strongly rooted in him, but in *War and Peace* as well as in the earlier *Sevastopol Stories* we already feel his aversion to war. All the positively good characters in *War and Peace* either directly or obliquely feel the crime of killing in a war. In them all there is a living part of Tolstoy.

The richer and more varied the nature of a man, the more facets and qualities he possesses, the more he can absorb of the thoughts and feelings of other beings and understand them. The good and the bad traits of Tolstoy himself are embodied in his leading characters. Yet despite this each one of them preserves the traits which are peculiarly his own. Some of Tolstoy's qualities are intensified, some reduced; of others only a glancing shadow falls on the characters, but the seeds of Tolstoy are in all of them.

More than eighty years have passed since Tolstoy wrote the last word in his novel. Yet *War and Peace* is still being translated and printed and read in all the countries of the civilized world. One is unconsciously prompted to ask: Why is this so?

Since Tolstoy's day the technique of writing has made a great advance, many events close to him have receded far into the past, customs, habits have changed, the face of civilization itself is changed. Why does this novel of Tolstoy still offer interest?

It is because in its pages Tolstoy raises questions which are eternal. He sought for the truth by his own Tolstoyan standards, and he was not disturbed when it failed to coincide with public opinion.

"The great Emperor's final leave-taking from his heroic army," writes Tolstoy, "has been presented to us by the historians as something tinged with grandeur and with genius. Even this last act of flight, which in common parlance is called the ultimate degree of baseness and which every child is taught to shun, is presented by the historians in the saving guise of greatness. . . .

"And it never occurs to anyone that this recognition of greatness, the immeasurable measure of good and evil, is only the recognition of one's own insignificance and immeasurable littleness.

"For us who have Christ's gift of the measure of good and evil there is nothing immeasurable. And no greatness exists where there is no simplicity, goodness and truth."

🐉 29 🐉

A FOURTH child was born to the Tolstoys on June 20, 1869. He was named Lev for his father, yet by a strange freak of fate he was the least like him.

Although the children were still very young their characters were already well defined. The eldest, Sergei, was a grave, thoughtful boy with pale blue, short-sighted eyes; he was truthful to the point of naïveté, clumsy and shy. He never tried to exculpate himself, and black-eyed, vivacious Tanya ordered him around although she was a year his junior. Tanya knew how to approach their English governess, Hanna, and get from her whatever she chose, she also knew how to please Papa, how to be the first to climb up on his shoulder, how to wheedle an extra ten minutes out of Mama when it was bedtime. She was the quickest of all at learning to chatter in English, quicker than Mama and Seryozha, and Hanna adored her. When Hanna used to croon "Home, Sweet Home" in a low voice and weep as she thought of her beloved England, Tanya would take up the tune and weep with her. Pink-cheeked, light-blue-eyed Ilya was the healthiest and chubbiest of all. He was rarely ill, he loved his food, scarcely ever fussed or cried, and caused his mother few worries. In contrast, young Lev was ill almost from birth. Many were the nights without sleep that his mother passed by his crib caring for this sickly, nervous child. Because of this she became in a way morbidly attached to him—and this exceptional attachment lasted throughout her life. In his face, his capacities, his tastes in life, Lev resembled his mother.

During these years the Tolstoys had changed both outwardly and inwardly. Sophia Andreyevna was more experienced, poised. She had learned a great deal. She knew how to distinguish between a rash and scrofula as she examined her children with her near-sighted eyes; she knew how to administer an enema or give a timely dose of castor oil. In appearance she was slightly stouter, and her beauty was even more expressive. At times she was a little hurt that her husband entered so little into the interests of the nursery and was not upset that Seryozha had diarrhea, that Lelya (Lev) had not slept and cried all night. Everyone was delighted when he did take a hand with the children. He would lift them up, set them on his powerful shoulders and carry them around the room. Tanya, her tiny hands clasped around his neck, would squeal with joy and terror.

The children throve in the healthy country atmosphere. Hanna took them for walks in all weathers, and bathed them in cold water, to the horror of their Russian nurse, Maria Afanasyevna. There was one bath tub, no plumbing, water had to be heated in big iron kettles and carried up in pails.

Tolstoy wanted his children to know horses and as soon as they were able to stay in the saddle they began to ride alone, but when they were little, he would hold them on the horse in front of him and take them to bathe in the Voronka River. In the winter they went ice skating. And there again in teaching the children Tolstoy was carried away with enthusiasm and learned how to cut figure threes and eights on the ice.

During this period Tolstoy wrote little. He made attempts, began things, but quickly threw them aside because he felt they were not really what he wanted. It would seem that, having emptied himself in the creation of *War and Peace*, he could not start a new piece of work until he had replenished his reservoir of thought. He searched avidly for fresh intellectual and spiritual nourishment. On the 30th of August 1869, he wrote to Fet:

"Do you know what this summer has meant to me? Unabated enthusiasm for Schopenhauer and a series of spiritual satisfactions which I never before experienced. I sent for all his writings and have read and am reading him (I have also read Kant). And truly no student has ever studied so much for his courses or found out as much as I have in the present summer. I do not know whether I shall change my opinion or not but now I am convinced that Schopenhauer is a man of greatest genius. . . . Would you not undertake to translate him? We could publish it together. As I read him I cannot conceive how his name should have remained unknown. There can be only one explanation, that is what he so frequently repeats, that there are scarcely any people on earth, except idiots."

Nor were the German philosophers all. Tolstoy plunged into the literary classics: Shakespeare, Goethe, Molière, Pushkin, Gogol. Again he attempted to write for the theater. But in this he met with no success.

His wife wrote in her diary December 9, 1870: "Today he began for the first time, and seriously, so it would seem. I cannot express what has been going on in his head during all this period of inaction. . . . At this very minute L. is sitting with a seminary student in the living room and is taking his first lesson of Greek. He suddenly was seized with the thought of studying Greek. All this time of inaction, of what I should have called intellectual repose, he has been much tormented. He has kept repeating that his conscience bothered him because of his idleness, before me, others, and people in general. Occasionally he seems to think that he is being inspired again and then he is happy. At other times it seems to him—but this always occurs when he is out of the house and away from the family—that he will go mad, and his fear of insanity becomes so intense that afterward, when he has told me about it, I too am terrified."

In this entry she was evidently alluding to the "Arzamas depression" which overtook Tolstoy on one of his journeys when he was considering buying an estate in the province of Penza.

"The night before last I stopped over in Arzamas," Tolstoy wrote his wife, "and something unusual happened to me. It was two o'clock at night, I was terribly tired, I longed to sleep and I was not in any pain. But suddenly I was overcome by depression, fear, terror such as I have never experienced and which I hope no one else may have to suffer."

In his "Notes of a Madman," an unfinished piece of writing dating from the 1880's, Tolstoy describes this sensation: ". . . How silly, I said to myself. Why am I depressed? What am I afraid of? Of me—came the inaudible voice of death—I am here. A chill ran over my body. Yes, of death. It will come—there it is, and it should not be. . . . My whole being felt the urge, the right to live and at the same time the approach of death."

The impression left by this terrifying night—who, alone in a strange city, has not experienced something similar?—was so profound that Tolstoy could never forget it. From then on every dark mood was known in the Tolstoy family as an "Arzamas depression."

His preoccupation with Greek was neither a foolish idea nor a passing caprice. He made a really serious study of the language.

"I am not writing, I am only studying," he wrote to Fet in December, 1870, "yet how happy I am that God inspired me with this fancy. In the first place I am enjoying it; in the second place, of all that is truly fine in human utterance I have until now known nothing —like all the rest (except the professors who, although they know about it, do not comprehend it); in the third place, I am not writing and never will write a lot of redundant rubbish. . . . For God's sake, explain to me why it is that no one knows the fables of Aesop, nor even delightful Xenophon, not to mention Plato and Homer who are still in store for me. As far as I am at present able to judge, Homer is only defiled by our translations taken from the German. As a trivial but natural comparison, take boiled or distilled water—and water from a spring, to shatter your teeth, full of brilliance and sunshine, and even with chips and particles in it to make it even purer and fresher. You may well exult: without a knowledge of Greek— there is no education."

"Lev Nikolayevich took it into his head to learn the ancient Greek tongue," wrote Stepan Behrs in his memoirs, "and to get acquainted with the classics. I know it for a fact that he learned the language and read the writings of Herodotus in a period of three months whereas up to then he knew no Greek at all. When he was staying in Moscow at this time he called on the late Professor P. M. Leontyev of the Katkovski High School to tell him his impressions of ancient Greek literature. Leontyev was reluctant to believe in the possibility of such quick mastery of the ancient language and proposed that they read together *à livre ouvert*. In three places they disagreed about the translation. After these were cleared up the Professor admitted that Lev Nikolayevich's opinion was correct."

For a while in this interval of "inactivity" he considered doing a novel laid in the days of Peter the Great. With characteristic conscientiousness he undertook a study of materials concerning the period, but the idea was abandoned. It may have been that as he became more closely acquainted with the personality of Peter he was repelled; moreover he found it difficult to transpose himself into those times, to write in the language, and after *War and Peace* he evidently could not make up his mind to undertake another such colossal piece of work.

On February 12, 1871, a second daughter was born to the Tolstoys. After her confinement Sophia Andreyevna was very ill with a fever and almost died. The little girl, who was tiny and thin, with pale blue eyes and a broad brow, received the name of Maria.

Sophia Andreyevna was exhausted by childbearing and by her illness. Tolstoy himself was slightly unwell at this time; he had pains in his face and in his legs. By spring he had developed a dry, stubborn cough which was extremely wearing. Something like a cloud lay over the relations between them; they were both tired and at times irritated each other. In reality each in his own way was lonely. Sophia Andreyevna did not get sufficient sympathy from her husband. She was still very young, at times she longed for a different, more social city life, with its pleasures, music and spectacles, and she missed her sister Tanya with her buoyant carefree gaiety. She was bored with having to remain forever in the nursery, with bearing and nursing children. She tried to understand her husband. She loved the writer in him, the artist; her heart comprehended this side of him, but there were other aspects of his mind which she could not comprehend.

Was there anyone who could take in completely the many facets of his thought, his spiritual life? Every book he read, whether it was the Lives of the Saints, epic poems, or ancient Greek classics, precipitated a swarm of thoughts and of moods. As early as 1865, he wrote to Alexandrine Tolstoy: "We writers have some arduous sides to our work, yet we also have what you probably are not familiar with, a certain *volupté* of thought—you read something, one side of your mind comprehends it, but another thinks about it and in general lines imagines to itself whole poems, novels, theories of philosophy."

There were a few friends with whom he shared his thoughts but even they probably did not plumb his depth or his variety.

Afanasy Fet-Shenshin was one of the friends who understood and appreciated Tolstoy and it was to him that Tolstoy frequently poured out his heart. Fet was a genuine artist, despite the fact that his exterior was anything but poetic. He was large and heavy in build, wore a full beard, had heavy features, a protruding lower lip and huge ears—a very ugly man. Nor did he have the gift of fluent speech. Each phrase he uttered began with "m-m-m-m-m," and the more excited he became the more frequently his speech was punctuated by this mooing sound, which started on a low base note, rose and slid back down again like a wail, depending on his state of agitation. Fet loved good food and his wife, Maria Petrovna, a cozy, roly-poly woman, had a reputation for providing unusual and delicious foods.

Another friend was Prince Sergei Urusov. I do not think that there was any really deep relationship between them. "He was a very strange and individual man," wrote Ilya Tolstoy in his memories of his father. "In size he was almost a giant. During the Sevastopol campaign he commanded a regiment and they say that he distinguished himself by his absolute fearlessness. He used to go out of the trenches and, dressed all in white, stroll about under a rain of shells and bullets." And Lev Tolstoy, in a letter to the "Swedish Advocates of Peace" written in 1899 recounts the following incident connected with Prince Urusov:

"I recall one time, during the siege of Sevastopol, I was sitting in his reception room with the adjutant of General von Sacken, commander of the garrison, when in strode Prince S. S. Urusov, a very brave officer, a most original person, and at the same time one of the best chess players of the day in all Europe. He said he had business with the general. . . . He had come to von Sacken in order to propose that we challenge the English to a game of chess for the first-line trench in front of the Fifth Bastion, a trench which had already changed hands several times and cost many hundreds of lives."

It may have been just this originality of Urusov's, his difference from all other people in his circle, that pleased Tolstoy.

More recently Tolstoy had become deeply attached to Nikolai Strakhov. This friendship lasted until Strakhov's death. He was a scholarly mathematician, a philosopher, and at the time *War and Peace* appeared the editor of the magazine *The Dawn* (*Zarya*). His brilliant reviews of the novel in four different issues were a source of tremendous joy to Tolstoy.

When in November, 1870, Strakhov wrote Tolstoy to ask him for a contribution to *The Dawn*, Tolstoy did not wish to refuse, yet at that time he was planning to write his *Primer* and *Reader*; he was not engaged in any literary work. All this he told Strakhov, and urged him to stop off at Yasnaya Polyana if he were passing by on the Moscow-Kursk railway.

The first time Strakhov visited the Tolstoys was in August, 1871, and from then on he was one of the constant visitors at Yasnaya Polyana. He was one of those rare persons who had not only a deep understanding of Tolstoy but—and this was something Tolstoy valued highly—a genuine and profound affection for him. In their natures they were quite different. Strakhov never became worked up or irritated, as he listened to Tolstoy's heated, flaming speeches. His large, tender eyes would rest on his friend, his lips under his thick mustache and beard would curve slightly in a quizzical and wise smile. Then, unhurriedly, he would reply to Tolstoy in his quiet, even voice.

As time passed Strakhov became more and more involved in Tolstoy's interests. He helped him in the work of putting together his *Primers* and his *Readers*, and he was one of his few admirers to whom Tolstoy would listen.

But friends, family, intellectual interests, which would have satisfied Tolstoy at another time, were no solace when he felt unwell. In the spring following Maria's birth, after much pleading by his wife, he finally decided to take some notice of his failing health. So on June 11, 1871, with Stepan Behrs, he went off to the province of Samara to take a cure of his favorite kumys.

[195]

He had no taste for doctoring himself, and in the beginning he was bored.

"I have settled down," he wrote his wife on June 15, 1871, "in a tent. I bought a dog for fifteen rubles, and am preparing to endure my ordeal with patience. But it is very difficult. I am depressed, and I ask myself: why was I brought here, far away from you and the children. . . ."

"We live in a tent," Tolstoy wrote in his next letter, on June 18, "we drink kumys (Stepan too, everyone invites him to do so), but the inconveniences would horrify your Kremlin heart: there are no beds, no china, no white bread, no spoons. To look at us would make it easier for you to bear the disasters of an overroasted turkey or a too slightly salted kulich."

But gradually Tolstoy accommodated himself to his surroundings and began to make a life with new interests. He looked over property with an eye to purchase, went hunting, duck shooting, drank kumys in vast quantity, ate lamb with his fingers, among the Bashkirs, and discovered the greatest charms in the endless expanse of the steppes.

The Bashkirs received him everywhere with enthusiasm. "When one arrives," Tolstoy wrote his wife, "one's host kills a plump fat-tail sheep, sets out an immense tub of kumys, lays some rugs and pillows on the ground, puts his guests on them and does not let them go until they have eaten the entire sheep and drunk up the kumys. He invites his guests to drink out of his hands and with his fingers (no forks) he puts bits of meat and fat in their mouths, and one cannot offend him."

The nearer the date of his return, the more tender were Tolstoy's letters to his wife.

"Your letters, however," he wrote on July 16, "probably are more harmful to me than all the Greeks because of the disturbance they create in me." And he closed with these words: "Now I want to weep, I love you so."

Sophia Andreyevna was convinced that one cause of her husband's overexhaustion was his absorption in his Greek studies. In one of her letters she asked: "Are you drinking your kumys, are you putting on weight, and have you given up those hateful Greeks?" And in her next she said: "If you are still poring over the Greeks, you will never be cured. They are the ones who have brought on you this depression and indifference to current life."

"Not to see you for an extra day, I would not postpone coming for anything," he declared in his last letter on July 20. "So family life is hard on me! And the cries of the children, you suppose. I cannot wait to hear the duets of Lev and Masha. . . ."

Whether it was because Tolstoy loved the steppes, the Bashkirs and the kumys, or because he had a passion for acquiring new property, or a desire to build up some capital for the benefit of his growing family, his trip to the province of Samara ended with his making a most advantageous purchase of 2,500 desyatins (6,750 acres) of land in the Buzuluk district of the province of Samara, for 20,000 rubles.

✤ 30 ✤

TOLSTOY proved to be a poor teacher when he came to instruct his own son Sergei. They were both nervous; the father was upset by the son's slowness, and the son made such an effort, strained himself to such an extent, was so afraid of not satisfying his father, that he in the end was slow-witted. Yet working with his son renewed Tolstoy's interest in teaching. He was struck by the poor quality of the textbooks, the paucity of reading material.

Ever since Tolstoy had given up his work with the village children he had more than once come back to his ideas about a school; he longed to systematize and expound the experiences he had gained in his school in the 1860's. In September, 1868, Tolstoy received the visit of the United States Consul, Mr. Eugene Schuyler. Their conversation touched on education. In his memoirs Schuyler wrote:

"One thing that constantly preoccupied him [Tolstoy] and especially drew his attention was the question of finding the best method for teaching children to read. He questioned me at length about new methods used in America, and at his request I was able to obtain for him—I believe it was done through the kindness of Mr. Garrison of *The Nation*—a good selection of American methods of instruction in reading for the use of beginners and elementary schools. In one of them, I recall, the pronunciation of various vowels and consonants was depicted vividly with letters whose general appearance was that of ordinary letters but with distinctive changes which immediately were obvious. These books Tolstoy tried to adapt when he composed his *Primers*. . . ."

At this time Tolstoy was evidently thinking hard about the makeup of the *Primer*. In the Archives there is a notebook in which one whole page is sprinkled with crude designs: under *W* was the phrase "Wolves love lambs" with a picture showing a wolf chasing a lamb. Under the letter *m*: "We found mushrooms," and again there was an amusing drawing—three large mushrooms and two little girls hunting them, etc. But his serious work on the *Primer* was begun only three years later in September, 1871, and then he plunged headlong into it.

On January 12, 1872, he wrote to Alexandrine Tolstoy: "But I have nothing to write: my external life is always the same, that is to say it goes on according to the saying *'les peuples heureux n'ont pas d'histoire.'* All goes well too in the household, there are five children and so much work there is never any time. These last years I have been writing on my *Primer* and now I am printing it. It is very difficult to tell you what this work of many years, this *Primer*, has meant to me. This coming winter I hope to send it to you, and you, out of friendship for me, may perhaps read it. My conceited ideas about this *Primer* are these: that if only two generations of all Russian children, from royal to peasant, will study this primer and will receive all their first poetic impressions from it, and that, having written this *Primer*, I can die in peace."

This forecast was partially correct for in their corrected and abridged forms his *Primer* and *Reader* became the favorite books not only of children but also of teachers, and millions of copies were spread throughout Russia.

"My work advances farther and farther," wrote Tolstoy to Alexandrine in April, 1872. "If anyone had said to me twenty years ago: think up work for yourself for twenty-three years, I could not, with all the strength of my mind, have thought up enough work for three years. And now you may tell me that I shall live my life multiplied by ten and each one a hundred years long, yet we should not have time to make the changes in everything where they are necessary. At one end my *Primer* is being printed, while at the other I am still writing it and making additions. This *Primer* alone may provide work for a hundred years. To write it one should know the Greek, Indian, Arabian literatures, one needs knowledge of the natural sciences, astronomy, physics and the work on the language itself is terrific. It must be beautiful, brief, simple and, above all, clear."

The first, uncorrected version of the *Primer* was put together as follows: (1) the alphabet, instruction in reading and writing; (2) the *Reader*; (3) instruction in Church Slavonic according to a method invented by Tolstoy, together with excerpts from the Lives of the Saints, the Bible (Old and New Testaments), prayers; (4) arithmetic—numerals in old Slavonic, Roman and Arabic forms.

The stories Tolstoy put in his book were interesting and of artistic merit, often rich in meaning yet never moralistic. The moral truth, in short, flowed naturally from the text. Tolstoy's wide reading, his enthusiasm for the Greek language, stood him in good stead; he remembered and used everything that had impressed him: Russian tales, "The Bishop and the Thief" taken from Victor Hugo's *Les Misérables*, Aesop's *Fables*, oddments from Plutarch, from Indian, Turkish, Arabian tales, one story of Hans Christian Andersen, two important and many minor stories of his own. His two long stories are: "A Prisoner in the Caucasus" and his profoundly significant "God Sees the Truth." Children still read both with absorption.

In teaching the children to read, Tolstoy used his own original method, which was contrary to the phonetic method generally accepted by the pedagogues.

In the general remarks to the teacher, which Tolstoy put at the end of the book, he explained and clarified once again the principles on which he had founded his school in the early 1860's.

"In order that the pupil may study well," he wrote, "he must study gladly; in order that he study gladly the following is necessary: (1) that the material he is being taught be comprehensible and interesting, and (2) that the inner powers of the pupil be in the most advantageous state possible. To that end it is necessary:

1. That there should be no new, unfamiliar objects about him where he is studying.

2. That the pupil should not be embarrassed before his teachers or comrades.

3. That the pupil (and this is very important) should not fear punishment because of bad work, that is to say failure to understand. The mind of man can operate only when it is not oppressed by external influences."

Farther on Tolstoy speaks of the fact that the pupil must not be overtired, and that his capacity must be taken into account.

"The easier it is for a teacher to teach, the harder it is for a pupil to learn. The harder it is for the teacher, the easier for the pupil. The more the teacher himself studies, thinks over each lesson and takes into account the capacities of his pupil, the more closely he watches the working of his pupil's mind, the more he provokes him to question and answer, the easier it will be for the pupil to learn."

Tolstoy also worked out his own special system for the instruction of arithmetic.

"I am working myself into a stupor finishing up arithmetic," he wrote to Strakhov on August 7, 1872. "Multiplication and division are done and I am finishing fractions. You will laugh at me for having undertaken something out of my field but it seems to me that the arithmetic will be the best thing in the book."

Tolstoy loved mathematics and was thoroughly familiar with it.

In order to test the accuracy of his theories Tolstoy reopened his school in January, 1872. He not only taught the children himself but he gathered together teachers from the whole district to show them in practice his method of teaching how to read.

"When I was six," wrote Ilya Tolstoy in his memoirs, "I recall how Papa used to teach the country children. They were taught in 'the other house' and sometimes downstairs in our house. The country children came to us and there were a great many of them. When they came it smelled of sheepskin jackets and they all taught them together, Papa and Seryozha and Tanya and Uncle Kostya [a cousin once removed of Sophia Tolstoy]. While the lessons were going on it was very gay and lively.

"The children conducted themselves quite freely, sat wherever they chose, ran around from place to place and answered questions, not one at a time but all at once, interrupting each other and pooling all their forces to remember what they had read. If one of them missed anything, immediately a second would rush in, a third, and the story or the problem was put together by common effort.

"Papa was particularly appreciative of vividness and originality in his pupils. He never demanded the literal reproduction of expressions in the book and he particularly encouraged whatever was one's 'own.' "

"Tanya and Seryozha are doing fairly well," wrote Sophia Andreyevna to her sister Tanya on February 2, 1872. "Within a week they knew all the letters and the syllables by ear. We teach them downstairs in the vestibule, which is huge, in the small dining room under the stairway, and in the new study. The main thing is that they are taught to read and write, that there is such an urge to do it and that they study with such pleasure and enjoyment."

Despite themselves everybody became infected with Tolstoy's enthusiasm. They all taught, Tolstoy himself, his wife, children, guests. Regardless of the difference in social position, the children of landowners and of peasants often formed friendships, which in the case of Tolstoy's family usually endured. They used the informal second person singular in addressing each other, and later the Tolstoys acted as godparents to the children of these childhood friends.

When the *Primer* was ready Tolstoy decided to appeal to his new friend Strakhov to help with the printing of it.

"Kind Nikolai Nikolayevich," Tolstoy wrote him on May 19, 1872, "I have a great favor to ask of you. I should like to pile up introductory remarks about how conscience-stricken I am to do so but the matter will have to speak for itself. If you find it possible and you choose to do me a great kindness you will do it. This is it. I have long since finished my *Primer*, and sent it to be printed, but in four months the printing not only is not done but it is not even begun, it never will begin or ever be done. . . . I have now decided to take it away from Ris in Moscow and print it in St. Petersburg where, so they say, there are more typographies and they are better. Would you be willing to supervise this work?"

Since Strakhov was the kindest of men and adored Tolstoy, he, of course, agreed. "I do not expect to make a huge lot of money from this book," Tolstoy wrote him. ". . . the first edition will go immediately and then the peculiarities of the book will enrage the pedagogues, the whole contents will be filched for anthologies and the book itself will not be a success. . . ."

But Tolstoy was to have a bitter disappointment. The first edition did not sell. The blow was especially painful because he felt with all his being that he understood things which the teachers, the scholars did not. . . . Their knowledge was theoretical, their attitude toward the peasants condescending. He knew that the peasant children would not stand for the superficial, the elaborate, the hypocritical, and he felt that the intellectuals should listen to the demands of the people, and try to give them what was genuine and classic, the best of wisdom and simplicity.

Tolstoy made two other efforts to contribute his mite to the cause of popular education.

On the 15th of January, 1874, he spoke before the Moscow Committee for Literacy in defense of his teaching methods. He offered to make experiments: to institute a competition between two Moscow schools. In one school they would teach by the phonetic method, in the other according to the Tolstoy method. Tolstoy himself did not take part in the test but the lessons were conducted by his pupil Morozov. The tests were not successful and the defenders of each system stuck to their own opinions.

In a letter to Alexandrine Tolstoy in December, 1874, Tolstoy expressed graphically his feeling about popular education: "I do not reason about it, but when I go into a school and see this crowd of tattered, dirty, emaciated children with their shining eyes and often angelic expressions, I am overwhelmed with a sense of agitation, terror, such as I should feel at the sight of drowning persons. Oh my, if only I can pull them out, and whom shall I save first, whom next. What is being drowned is that most precious thing, that spiritual something, which so often flashes into the eyes of children. I want education for the people only in order to save the drowning Pushkins and Lomonosovs. Every school is teeming with them. . . ."

Tolstoy's last attempt to put his impress on public education was made in 1876. He dreamed of founding a peasant teachers seminary, "a university in bast sandals" as he expressed it, where peasant teachers would be trained who could better approach the peasant children. Tolstoy's application to the Minister of Public Education for the opening of such a normal school was approved; the Tula provincial council was prepared to meet him halfway; and it seemed as though the project would be realized. But when it reached the district councils it was blocked and so came to nothing.

Tolstoy abridged his *Primer* and it was published under the title *New Primer*; also four *Readers*. In their new form they enjoyed a great success. Hundreds of thousands of Russian children learned to read and write out of the *Primer*, into which Tolstoy put so much love and the power of his constructive genius.

❧ 31 ❧

VARIOUS important events had occurred during the time that Tolstoy was immersed in his *Primer*, which, as he wrote to Alexandrine Tolstoy, "is being printed at one end while at the other it is still being written and enlarged."

Tolstoy added a large two-story structure to his house. In the lower part there was a roomy entry and a large room with a stone balcony, his study; upstairs there was one large room with six windows facing southwest and southeast. This room served at once as a living and dining room for the family and was called the "hall." The building was thoroughly well constructed; the walls were of the same foot and a half thickness as those in the sleeping quarters, and the waxed parquet floors delighted the children, who slid on them. The furnace downstairs in the butler's pantry heated the upstairs room with hot air. Tolstoy's study was divided in the middle by bookshelves; in the center was the door of the partition, and over the door a lintel. In this study Tolstoy put his writing table, leather-covered furniture and a leather sofa on which all his children were born; in a recessed niche was the bust of his favorite elder brother Nikolai. This is how Ilya Tolstoy describes the room in his memoirs:

"On the wall there are antlers brought by father from the Caucasus, and one deer's head stuffed. On the antlers he hangs his towel and hat. Next to it on the wall there are portraits of Dickens, Schopenhauer, Fet in his youth and a famous group of writers from the circle of *The Contemporary* in 1856. In it are Turgenyev, Ostrovski, Goncharov, Grigorovich, Druzhinin, and Father, still very young, without a beard and in an officer's uniform."

Here, in this study, Tolstoy was secluded from the general noise of family life. From the windows, across a lawn, over the trees in the park sloping down to the ponds, one could see the fields and the trains flashing by on the newly built railroad. Tolstoy took delight in his new building, as he took delight in a fine young horse, a successful hunt, a young apple orchard he had planted.

But, as always in life, his joys alternated with his troubles. In the summer of 1872, when Tolstoy was in Samara putting his newly purchased estate there in running order, an unfortunate thing happened at Yasnaya Polyana: a young bull gored a herdsman to death. On his return the court investigator had Tolstoy sign a paper promising not to leave the premises, and a suit was pending. Feeling that he was not to blame, Tolstoy was indignant; he stormed and raged, prepared to write to the newspapers, and in the heat of his fury even decided to move to England to live.

But the matter was cleared up, Tolstoy cooled off and, as always after such outbreaks of irritation and hot temper, he was ashamed of himself.

"You inquire about the matter of the bull," he wrote to Alexandrine in September, 1872. "It ended with the investigator's being in error in lodging an accusation against me. . . . In slight justification of myself I can add that recently, having finished my *Primer*, I began a large piece (I do not like to call it a novel) over which I have been mulling for some time. And when this humor comes over one, as Pushkin so aptly described it, one is especially vulnerable to the barbarities of life. Imagine a person listening in complete darkness to the rustling of nature, watching for rays of light in the gloom and suddenly someone sticks some foul-smelling Bengal fire in his face and blares a discordant march on a trumpet. It is excruciating. Now I am back in the quiet and dark, I listen, I look, and if only I could describe a hundredth part of what I hear and see! It is a great satisfaction. . . ."

As early as February 24, 1870, Sophia Andreyevna had written in her autobiographical notes: "Yesterday evening he [Tolstoy] told me that he had in mind a type of woman who is married, in high society, but who ruins herself. He said that his problem was to make this woman only pitiful and not guilty, and as soon as he found her type, then all the other characters and male types he had thought of earlier fell into place and grouped themselves around this woman." The next day Tolstoy made the first outline of *Anna Karenina*.

Yet evidently this pearl of his creation was not yet ready; he put it back in hiding in his treasure chest. He was "listening and watching."

In January, 1872, Anna Pirogova, who was living with Alexander Bibikov, a close neighbor of the Tolstoys, committed suicide.

On the 18th of January Sophia Andreyevna wrote to her sister Tanya: ". . . We have had another dramatic incident here in Yasnaya. You remember Anna Stepanovna over at Bibikov's—. Well, she was jealous of all the governesses. . . . She threw herself under a train and was crushed to death."

More than a year passed, the tragic incident of the real Anna was beginning to be forgotten but the bewitching image of the other Anna had already been born in Tolstoy's imagination. Perhaps he already knew her whole life and tragic end when she, Anna, "threw aside her red handbag and, pressing her head down between her shoulders, fell under the train."

On the 19th of March, 1873, quite unexpectedly for his wife and perhaps even for himself, Tolstoy began to write a new novel.

"Yesterday evening," wrote Sophia Andreyevna in her Notes, "L. suddenly said to me: 'Well I wrote a page and a half and it would seem to be good.' Thinking that this was a fresh attempt to write about the times of Peter the Great I did not pay special attention. Then afterward I discovered that he had begun to write a novel laid in his own times." Later she went on to tell how this happened.

Their oldest son Seryozha kept pestering his mother for something to read to Auntie Tatiana. Sophia Andreyevna gave him Pushkin's *Tales of Belkin*; Auntie soon dozed off, and the book was left lying on the window sill. Next morning Tolstoy began to thumb through the pages and was carried away by it. "I learn a lot from Pushkin," he said, "he is my father, he is the one to learn from."

In the Tolstoy family they often recalled this episode and used to tell how Tolstoy, after reading the first line of one of Pushkin's unfinished pieces, "The guests were gathering at the country house," was so enthused that he went to his study and began his novel *Anna Karenina* with the words: "Everything was at sixes and sevens in the home of the Oblonskis." But actually it did not happen so. The novel, in its first draft, began with words much closer to those of Pushkin: "After the opera the guests gathered at the home of young Princess Vrasskaya. . . ." This later became the beginning of the sixth chapter of the second part of the novel. The sentence with which the novel begins in the final version, "Everything was at sixes and sevens in the home of the Oblonskis," only convinces us once more of the influence of Pushkin on Tolstoy's work. "The forte of Pushkin," said Tolstoy, "is in his ability to plunge the reader immediately, without superfluous words, superfluous description, into life, action."

Having begun the writing in the middle of March, about the 16th of May he wrote to Strakhov "the rough draft of the novel of *Anna Karenina* is finished."

We know how the spring season affected Tolstoy. Until he was very old, his appetite for life, his creative power and buoyancy were stirred afresh. "It is spring. Evening," he wrote in his notebook. "The ragged clouds of dawn. It is still, noiseless, dark, damp, fragrant . . . violet hue. . . . The cattle are shaggy, but underneath the shagginess there are bright patches where the hair is shedding. . . ." For those who know and love the country these scant, fragmentary words make a whole picture, stir up a swarm of recollections.

Of May he writes: "The leaf on the birch is full grown, like a tender little kerchief. There are mounds of pale blue forget-me-nots, yellow fields of wild garlic. . . . A gray-black bee hums, weaves its way, and feasts. Burdocks, nettles, the pipestems of rye push upward hour by hour. Yellow primroses. The dew is iridescent on the sharp-pointed tips of grass. They are plowing for the buckwheat. It is dark, strange. The peasant women are pounding the hemp and spreading their gray sacking on the grass. The songs of nightingales, cuckoobirds and peasant women in the evening . . ."

And so Tolstoy, with the door on his stone balcony open to the garden, wrote out the story of *Anna Karenina* in a spurt of two months. Then, as suddenly as he began it, he threw it aside.

That summer the Tolstoys went off to their new estate in the province of Samara. Sophia Andreyevna rather dreaded the wild steppes but Tolstoy was so anxious to go and took such pains to make life there agreeable for his family that she gave in and they all moved, with governesses and tutors and servants, down the Volga to the new estate.

"For what purpose my fate has carried me down here, I cannot tell," Tolstoy wrote Fet. "I have listened to speeches in the English Parliament (that, you know, is supposed to be very important) and I felt bored and worthless; but what is there here: flies, filth, Bashkir peasants, and I listen with intense respect, with awe, I observe closely and feel that this is very important."

The last years in the province of Samara had been hard ones; after three seasons of drought and crop failures, the population lay under the threat of famine. Tolstoy was not in a mood to write novels. He had to save lives.

He traveled throughout the area within a radius of some forty-two miles and became convinced of the impending catastrophe. In a letter to the *Moscow News* he appealed for help for the starving people—so eloquently that contributions in 1873-1874 amounted to 1,887,000 rubles and 21,000 puds (756,000 pounds) of grain.

When Tolstoy returned to the province of Samara in 1874, a good harvest had removed the threat of famine.

In the spring of 1873 the Tolstoys shared keenly their sister Tanya's first great grief in the loss of her eldest daughter Dasha. And in the autumn of that year they themselves were to suffer the first loss in their family. Their youngest son, Peter, who was eighteen months old, died. "On the 9th of November," wrote Sophia Andreyevna in her diary for November 11, "at nine o'clock in the morning my little Petyushka died of a throat infection. He had been ill for two days and nights. He died peacefully. I nursed him fourteen and a half months; he was born on the 13th of June, 1872. He was a healthy, sunny, merry boy."

In a letter to Fet Tolstoy wrote: "One may take consolation in the fact that if one had to choose one of us eight, this death is the easiest of all and for all to bear; but a heart, especially that of a mother, is a wonderful manifestation of the Divinity on earth, it does not reason, so my wife is much stricken."

Tolstoy worked on his revisions of *Anna Karenina* at great intervals. On September 25 he wrote to Fet: "I am beginning to write, that is to say I shall soon be finishing the novel I had begun." Evidently at that time he had no notion of the tremendous work which lay ahead of him.

While he was writing Tolstoy needed absolute quiet, concentration. The slightest disturbance in his surroundings destroyed his working mood. When the famous painter named Kramskoy came to Yasnaya Polyana, having been commissioned by the Tretyakov Gallery to do his portrait, Tolstoy was not at all pleased. He did not like to pose. But he agreed to do so at the insistent request of both Kramskoy and Sophia Andreyevna, who urged that Kramskoy do two portraits—one for the gallery and the other for the Tolstoys.

The portrait was a success. The artist was able to get a likeness, to convey the strength, the vigor of the ugly face with the deep-set, penetrating eyes looking straight out from under the heavy eyebrows, and the quiet power of the whole figure in the gray blouse, gathered into a leather belt.*

* This portrait still hangs in Yasnaya Polyana in the hall of the museum.

The middle of February, 1874, Tolstoy announced to his friend Strakhov that the first part of the novel was ready for the printer. This news was the occasion of great rejoicing on the part of Strakhov.

"The undertaking now in course in Yasnaya Polyana," he wrote, "is so important, so precious to me that I am almost afraid of something or other, the way you are when you are fearful, not believing that a woman really loves you. Yet you write that it is all ready; for God's sake take care of that manuscript, do not hand it over to a printer. I shall not believe in my good fortune until I see the printed lines."

Apparently it was about this time that Tolstoy reconsidered the end of *Anna Karenina* because in July, 1874, Strakhov wrote to him: "Your novel does not leave my mind. . . . The unfolding of Anna's passion—is miraculous. For me, the inner history of that passion is the main point and clarifies everything. Anna kills herself with egoistic intent, subservient always to that passion, it is the inevitable way out, the logical conclusion of the course set from the very beginning. Oh, it is so powerful, so unutterably clear!"

From the moment that Strakhov became a close friend he never let pass a single word written by Tolstoy. With extreme consideration, with delicacy and affection, he noted each fine shading and twist in the spiritual and intellectual life of his friend. In Strakhov Tolstoy possessed at last a sensitive, intelligent friend to appreciate his creative work.

On June 20, 1874 the Tolstoy family again suffered a great loss: Auntie Tatiana Alexandrovna passed away.

"Yesterday I buried Auntie Tatiana Alexandrovna," Tolstoy wrote to Alexandrine on June 23, 1874. . . . "She was a wonderful being. Yesterday, as we carried her through the village we were stopped at every door: a peasant man or woman came out to the priest, gave him money asking him to say a prayer, and took their farewell from her. And I knew, I knew that each stop was the recollection of many kind deeds she had done. She lived here for fifty years and never caused injury to anyone, not even any unpleasantness. Yet she feared death: she did not say that she feared it, but I saw she did. What does this mean? I think that it is humility. I have lived all my life beside her and to me life without her seems frightening."

We must remember the lonely childhood and youth of Tolstoy, and his life before his marriage, in order to understand what Auntie Tatiana meant to him. Until the end of his days he loved to remember her. "How could I have begrudged her any sweet, have forgotten her or ever been angry with her? When she died I was unutterably sad that I had not been kind enough to her when she was alive," he used to say.

Shortly before Auntie died, the Tolstoys had another son, born April 22, 1874, to whom they gave the name of Nikolai in memory of Nikolai Nikolayevich Tolstoy. He lived only ten months and died of dropsy. And this death, like that of Petya, had a profound effect on Sophia Andreyevna.

"Dull apathy," she wrote in her diary, "indifference to everything today, tomorrow, the coming months, year—it is all the same. You wake in the morning but you don't get up."

She was harassed by the thought of the lack of purpose in all the childbearing, nursing of babies, all the work, the illnesses. . . . For what? Death seemed senselessly cruel, unnecessary for anyone.

"What will invigorate me, what is in store for me?" she wrote later on in her diary. "In the evening it's the same old mending of holes, with Aunt [Pelagea] and Lyovochka laying out eternal, hateful games of patience. Reading provides a brief pleasure—but how many good books are there?"

"God knows," she went on, "how I have wrestled this year with this shameful sense of boredom, how I by myself, in my heart, have conjured up all that was good, fortifying myself with the main thought that for the sake of the children, for their moral and physical well-being, country life is the very best thing, and I was able to silence my personal, self-centered emotions, yet now I see to my horror that this is transformed into terrible apathy, and such an animal-like dull indifference to everything. . . ."

She tried to interest herself in her husband's affairs: the Samara estate, the school, in which he was especially busy during the winter of 1874, his writings. She zealously copied his manuscripts. But that was all bound up with *him*. *Her* job was the children; she had lost two, and she was tired of both carrying and nursing them. At times she was infinitely depressed in the country. She longed for the social world, music, people. . . .

At a time when he felt that he needed to live a hundred more lives to carry out all he had in mind, she was bored, did not know what to do with herself, or where, except in the family, to find something to fill up her life.

Was he conscious of this? Could he have helped her? Perhaps
not. Life for him was crammed with so many interests that he could
not have imagined even if he wanted to why she felt this emptiness
in her life.

❧ 32 ❧

TOWARD the end of January, 1875, the *Moscow News* carried
an announcement of the publication of the first fourteen chapters
of a novel by Tolstoy in the first issue of the *Russian Herald*.

Despite brilliant reviews from the critics, the encouraging comments of his friends, the enthusiasm of N. N. Strakhov, Tolstoy
himself was at times in a mood to abandon the novel.

In February, 1875, he wrote to Fet: "You praise *Anna Karenina*,
that is extremely pleasant for me and, so I hear, others also praise
it, but probably no author has ever been as indifferent to his success, *si succès il y a,* as I am."

Often in letters to his friends he claimed that he was disgusted
and bored by *Anna Karenina.*

"For two months I have not soiled my fingers with ink or my
heart with thoughts about it," he wrote to Fet on August 26, 1875,
"but now I am taking up this tiresome, trivial *Anna Karenina* with
the one wish: to make room as quickly as possible for leisure to do
other things, and not just for the occupation of teaching which I
love but which I want to give up because it absorbs too much time."

He used almost the same words in writing to Strakhov—he must
"make room," have some "leisure."

When he read the first book of Vladimir Solovyov, *The Crisis of
Western Philosophy—Opposition to the Positivists,* it gave his thinking still another goad.

"My acquaintance with Solovyov, the philosopher, added very little
that was new to my knowledge, but it was a great stimulus, it caused
philosophic ferment in me and confirmed many things, in clarifying
thoughts of paramount necessity for the remainder of my life and
for my death, thoughts that were of such comfort to me that, had I
the ability and time, I should try to pass them on to others."

These were thoughts about God, the soul, death, the purpose of life, subjects to which he continually returned, and which several years later completely possessed him and became the cornerstone of his whole outlook on life. But they had not yet acquired definite form. His deepest religious and philosophic impulses and ideas were still clouded by worldly concerns: ideas about how to increase his estate, the desire to have his children associate with aristocratic families, unreasoning outbursts of anger and at times even purely boyish amusements.

In the summer of 1875 the Tolstoys again went off to their Samara estate. The untrammeled, wild life of the seminomadic Mongol tribes, with their special habits and customs, the wide horizon, the expanse of the steppes carpeted with soft feather grass, the special breed of Kirghiz horses with their thick manes and tails—all this attracted Tolstoy. He liked the mettle, the strength and the spirit of these horses of the plains, and he even considered setting up a stud farm on his estate to crossbreed them with racehorses.

Tolstoy was so carried away by his enthusiasm for horses that, to the delight of the population and his own children, he conceived the idea of getting up some races. Word was spread, and on the appointed day people began to arrive from all quarters with their sheep, their camp equipment, kettles, tubs of kumys: the local peasants, Kirghiz, Bashkirs in quilted coats, in clean white shirts and loose trousers, sheepskin caps, in fezzes and soft leather boots. Four distinguished Mohammedan women, who normally would have remained in seclusion, were driven to the races in the Count's carriage.

The crowd of several thousand persons spread out their rugs, installed themselves in picturesque, colorful groups and orderly fashion along the heights from where they could see the races. Plaintive Oriental songs were intoned, bagpipes were played and dancing alternated with wrestling. Twenty-two of the best horses were entered on a circular course of a little over three miles. Only four reached the goal; the rest fell out. Prizes were triumphantly presented to the winners: a watch with a portrait of the Tsar, a coat, silk handkerchiefs. Two days later they all went home in a happy and jolly frame of mind. Everything had gone off to perfection, without the slightest unpleasantness, and without any help from the constabulary, which pleased Tolstoy very much.

When he returned home from Samara he did not at once take up his work on *Anna Karenina*.

"The Tolstoy who writes novels has not yet come. I am awaiting his arrival with particular impatience," he wrote to Fet in October. He was not able to make himself settle down to his novel.

"Our kind of work is a dreadful thing," he wrote to Fet a few days later. "No one else knows this. In order to work we have to have a scaffolding grow up under our feet. And that scaffolding does not depend on us. If we start work without it we merely waste material and foolishly topple walls that cannot be kept up. You feel this especially when your work is already under way. You keep thinking: why not continue, take hold here, take hold there, but you haven't a hold, so you sit and wait. That is what I have been doing. Now, so it seems, the scaffolding has grown up under me and I am rolling up my sleeves."

As always, he received the greatest help from Strakhov.

"You are not a moralist," Strakhov wrote him on November 23, 1875, "you are a true artist. . . . Art has often been reproached, and with justice, for its lack of morals. Art sings the praises of passion, of the beauty of life, and therefore it is always the companion of enjoyment. . . . But when *you* begin to create figures you give evidence of an infinite and incomparable sensibility with regard to their moral purposes; you are the judge, at once pitilessly penetrating and altogether merciful, with the capacity to weigh everything in appropriate scales. . . ."

But Tolstoy was not to succeed in doing any writing that autumn. Sophia Andreyevna fell gravely ill with peritonitis, having scarcely recovered from the whooping cough which she had caught from the children.

At the sight of any member of his immediate family in a state of suffering Tolstoy lost his head, was tormented, rushed around from one spot to another and did not know what to do with himself. As a result of her illness, Sophia Andreyevna was prematurely delivered of a little girl on November 1. She lived only long enough to be christened with the name of Barbara.

When finally life began to resume its normal course death came once more to the Tolstoy family. On December 22 Tolstoy's own aunt—Pelagea Yushkov, former guardian of the Tolstoy brothers—passed away. The old lady had been living in a convent and, as though she sensed her approaching death, she came that year to die among her own people.

Having been brought face to face with death in his own family, which had lost three children and two aunts in recent years, Tolstoy began to think about it more and more frequently. The loss of his Aunt Pelagea in itself did not upset him much, for he had never been very close to her. What struck him about her death was something different—the lack of humility, fear of the end, insubordination to the will of God. He himself was tormented by the "mystery of death," as he wrote in *Anna Karenina*, when he described the death of his brother Nikolai. "He felt himself less able even than formerly to comprehend the significance of death, and its inevitability seemed even more terrible than ever."

"Nothing is left in life but to die. I feel this constantly," he wrote his brother Sergei on February 21, 1876. And he was "constantly" reverting to these thoughts.

"You say," he wrote to Alexandrine Tolstoy in April of that year, "that you do not know what I believe in. It is strange and terrible to say: I do not believe in anything that religion teaches us to believe in; yet at the same time I not only hate and scorn unbelief, I cannot see any possibility of living without faith, much less dying without one. So I am gradually building up my beliefs but they are all, even if firm, still very indefinite, lacking in distinctness and capacity for consolation. When my head challenges them they give cogent replies; but when my heart aches and longs for a reply, they offer neither support nor consolation. With my intellectual demands and the answers given by the Christian religion, I find myself in the position of two hands trying to clasp each other but whose fingers stand in the way. I yearn to believe but the harder I try the worse off I am; and yet I know that the possibility is there, the one is made for the other."

It was only in the middle of winter that Tolstoy went back to writing on his novel. He was obliged to finish it. The first part of it had been published in the first four issues of the *Russian Herald* for 1875, but not until January of 1876 did it begin to appear again in the magazine.

In March, 1876, Tolstoy wrote to Alexandrine: "My Anna has become a bore, insipid as a bitter radish. I have to worry along with her as one would with an ill-natured pupil; but do not speak ill of her or, if you must, do it with *ménagement,* for after all I have adopted her."

There is no doubt that the circumstance of Tolstoy's having obligated himself to the *Russian Herald,* and begun to print the novel before he had finished it, was a psychological error. He could not, as was his constant habit, correct what had been printed and this restriction hampered him.

In the beginning of April he wrote to N. N. Strakhov: "I realize to my terror that I am going into my summer state: I am repelled by what I have written and now I have here the proofs for the April issue and I fear I shall not be able to correct them. Everything about them is bad, everything should be done over, and everything should be done over that has already been printed, and everything should be rubbed out and everything thrown away. I should give it all up and say: it's my fault, I will not do it again, but try to write something new, not so incoherent, so indefinite. That's the state I am getting into and it is very pleasant. . . . And don't you praise my novel. Pascal got himself a belt with nails against which he pressed his elbows every time he felt he was enjoying praise. I'll have to get such a belt. Prove your sincere friendship for me: either do not write anything about my novel or else write only about what is bad in it. And if, as I suspect is the case, I am running down then, please, write me. Our vile author's function is corruptive. Each writer has his atmosphere of praise which he carefully carries around with him so he cannot have any conception of his real importance or the time of his decay. I would wish to avoid this error and not become further corrupted. Please help me in this. And, especially, do not be inhibited because your severe reproof might impede the activity of a person who has talent. It is much better to stop with *War and Peace* than write 'The Watch' and the like." *

"Anna Karenina appears to be stalled," Sophia Andreyevna wrote with distress to her uncle K. A. Islavin. She had not yet recovered from her illness; she was still coughing and losing weight. The death of the three children had undermined her otherwise vigorous morale. Had Tolstoy begun to write again she would have had an occupation in her work as copyist; it would have distracted her from her grief. The pessimism which was native to her disposition increased, everything was difficult for her and she forced herself beyond her strength to take care of the children and not be irritated by them.

In the beginning of June Tolstoy took his wife up to Moscow to see a doctor. But the doctor found nothing seriously wrong with her and gradually her health began to improve.

As usual, Tolstoy scarcely wrote at all during the summer. He read, he argued philosophical questions with N. N. Strakhov, who

---

* "The Watch" was a story of Ivan Turgenyev, written in 1850.

was a frequent guest at Yasnaya Polyana, he went off to the provinces of Samara and Orenburg to purchase horses, and it was only in September that he settled down at Yasnaya Polyana and waited for inspiration.

Toward the end of November he began to write hard and in the middle of December he took the next chapters of *Anna Karenina* up to Moscow for the December issue of the magazine.

While he was in Moscow Tolstoy went several times to call on P. I. Tchaikovski.

According to the composer's brother, Tchaikovski all but adored Tolstoy. "Because of his impressionability and imaginativeness it was characteristic of him," wrote the brother, "to attribute fantastic dimensions to what he loved but could not grasp. Therefore the author of *Childhood* and *Youth, The Cossacks*, and *War and Peace* seemed to him to be not a human being but, as he expressed it, a 'demi-god.' " Tchaikovski himself referred to his awe of Tolstoy: "I had the feeling," he wrote in his diary for 1886, "that this great seer of the heart could with one glance penetrate the secret places of my soul. From him, so it seemed to me, it was impossible to hide all the filth accumulated in the lower depths of my soul and to show him only the outer side."

Tchaikovski requested Nikolai Rubinstein, then director of the Moscow Conservatory, to arrange a special evening of music for Tolstoy.

We know the impression always made on Tolstoy by good music. What he experienced was far more complex than mere enjoyment. Music penetrated the deepest recesses of his soul, it stirred his whole being, it released in him sources of thoughts and emotions of which he was not himself cognizant. Waves of delight, joy, fear of losing these seconds of almost divine uplift, flooded him, suffocated him. He felt like crying and laughing all at once and then, without wasting a moment of time, like creating a great work.

"I cannot recall what was done for me in that rotunda [of the conservatory] without shuddering," Tolstoy wrote to Tchaikovski from Yasnaya Polyana.

And Tchaikovski made this note in his diary: "It may be that never in my life have I as a composer been as flattered and touched as I was when Lev Tolstoy, sitting beside me and listening to the *Andante* of my quartet, burst into a flood of tears."

In the same letter in which Tolstoy expressed his gratitude to

Tchaikovski, he asked him to convey his thanks to Rubinstein. He thanked him too for the magnificent impression he had received from the whole circle of musicians to whom he had been introduced. On the same occasion he sent Tchaikovski a collection of folk songs, begging him to make use of them in his compositions. Tchaikovski replied with exquisite politeness, but criticized the collection of songs. With that the relationship between them was broken off.

On December 9, 1876, Sophia Andreyevna wrote to Tanya: "We are now really at work on *Anna Karenina,* that is, writing without interruption. Lyovochka is in a lively, concentrated state of mind; he adds a whole chapter each day. I work hard on the copying and already, lying under this very letter, I have the fresh copies of the pages of the new chapter he wrote yesterday."

The last part of *Anna Karenina* was to be printed in the first four issues of the year in the *Russian Herald*. But a disagreement occurred between Katkov, the editor of the magazine, and Tolstoy on the subject of a rising in Serbia.

As he did so often, Tolstoy took the unpopular side and maintained that it was not necessary for Russian volunteers to go fight the Turks. "There is not and cannot be any such spontaneous feeling about the oppression of the Slavs," says Levin in *Anna Karenina,* to prove that the masses of the Russian people could have no interest in a war between the Serbs and the Turks.

Katkov demanded an alteration of the text.

"Apparently," Tolstoy wrote to Strakhov on May 22, 1877, from Yasnaya Polyana, "Katkov does not share my views nor could this be otherwise because I am condemning just those people like him, and he, hemming and hawing, asks that I soften this or delete that. I am awfully sick of it all and have told them that if they do not print the text exactly as I wish I shall not let them publish it at all. . . ." Accordingly, on Strakhov's advice, Tolstoy decided to bring out the eighth and last installment of the novel in a separate edition.

The novel was finished and the success it achieved was great. *Anna Karenina* was the talk of the town not only in Moscow but in St. Petersburg as well and, as was to be expected, it was both praised and criticized.

Tolstoy did not want to let himself be affected by the corrupting influence of praise. He tried not to forget Pascal's belt with the nails and whenever he was praised he tried, mentally, to press against the nails. In the spring Strakhov sent Tolstoy some laudatory articles about *Anna Karenina.* He burned them without reading them.

Nevertheless, in a letter to Strakhov he said that "the success of the last installment of *Anna Karenina* has, I must confess, pleased me. I did not at all expect it."

Turgenyev watched with impatience for the appearance of the novel and, having read it, hastened to express his opinion of it to other writers. "I do not like *Anna Karenina,*" he wrote to the poet Polonski, "although there are in it some truly magnificent pages (the races, the harvest, the hunt). But all this is stale stuff, it reeks of Moscow, old maids, Slavicism, patricianism and so forth."

Whereas Dostoyevski wrote: *"Anna Karenina,* as an artistic product, is perfection . . . nothing in the literatures of Europe at the present time compares with it."

There is hardly need to mention the enthusiastic comments of Tolstoy's friends Strakhov and Fet. The latter, in a long letter to Tolstoy about his novel, wrote: "But what artistic daring—the description of a birth. No once since the creation of the world has done it or will do it. The fools scream about the realism of Flaubert, but here all is idealism. I was so overjoyed that I read it until I wore two holes in it; I broke into the spiritual world, into Nirvana. These are two visible and mysterious windows: birth and death. But how would you expect them to be interested in such things!"

Readers often wonder who is who in Tolstoy's novels. Always Tolstoy's leading personages are composite, molded out of several types whom he had come across in life, and then enlarged. Tolstoy met Anna Karenina at an evening party in 1868. "Who is she?" he asked his sister-in-law Tanya. She proved to be M. A. Hartung, the daughter of Pushkin. Her thoroughbred appearance, her fascination, the adorable curls in the nape of her neck, her beauty—all struck him. With this image of Pushkin's daughter he blended the traits of other women, perhaps among them those of a lady called Diakov-Obolenski, to whose charms he was at one time not indifferent.

Stiva Oblonski in *Anna Karenina* reminds one of Leonid Obolenski (the husband of Maria Tolstoy's daughter Lizanka) in his frivolity, recklessness, extravagance, but in his external appearance and disposition Stiva is more reminiscent of a certain Perfiliev, a jovial *bon vivant* and friend of Tolstoy.

Nikolai Levin with his mistress Masha, his illness and death, are a vivid reminder of Tolstoy's brother, Dmitri.

Kitty, the description of her first confinement, the scene in the forest where Kitty and the child are overtaken by a thunderstorm—all this was taken from the lives of the Tolstoys.

Perhaps more than in any other of his works we sense Tolstoy himself in his hero Konstantin Levin. His attitude toward life, his preoccupation with farming, his desire to help the peasants, his negative point of view toward the Zemstvos, his jealousy of his wife, his enthusiasm for the movement to resettle the peasants—all these traits are undoubtedly autobiographical. The main similarity, however, is to be found in Levin's search for an all-embracing creed, something for which the author of *Anna Karenina* too was searching at that time with much anguish.

At the end of the book, almost the final words, are clearly revelatory of Levin-Tolstoy:

"It was already quite dark, and to the south, where he was looking, there were no clouds. The clouds were on the opposite side. From there came the flashes of lightning and distant thunder. Levin listened to the steady drip of the rain from the lindens in the garden and looked up to the familiar triangle of stars, to the Milky Way and its spreading train as it passed through the center of them. With every flash of lightning not only the Milky Way, but even the brighter stars disappeared, yet as soon as the lightning was gone, as though reset by a precise hand, they re-emerged all in their same places.

" 'Then why should I be disturbed?' Levin asked himself, with a premonition that the resolution of all his doubts, although he did not know it, was already prepared in his own soul.

" 'Indeed, the one patent and positive manifestation of God is the law of good which is given to the world by revelation, which I feel in me, and by the recognition of which I am united, whether I choose or not, with others into a society of believers that we call the church."

To search until the day of his death, to search and gradually attain to the eternal, immutable things for the sake of which a man lives—that was the urge in Tolstoy's soul in all these years. "Nor shall I understand with my mind why I pray," he wrote in conclusion, "but I will pray—and now my life, my whole life, regardless of whatever may happen to me, every minute of it, is no longer lacking in purpose as it was, but it has an indubitable purpose of good which I have the power to put into it."

❧ 33 ❧

W AR with Turkey was declared on April 15, 1877. "The thought of war puts a cloud over everything for me," Tolstoy wrote to Strakhov on August 9. "It is not the war itself but the question of our own irresoluteness, which at any moment must be solved, and of the reasons for this irresoluteness which daily become more apparent to me."

Despite his inner aversion to war he was still affected by the old emotion. As a former army man and patriot he suffered from wounded pride; the thought that the Russians might lose the war was intolerable to him.

"My feeling concerning the war has already passed through many phases," he wrote to Strakhov again in September, "and now it is evident beyond all doubt that this war can result in nothing except the most cruel condemnation, one far more searing than in 1854."

"Lyovochka has had a strange attitude toward the Serbian war," Sophia Andreyevna wrote to her sister. "For some reason or other he did not take the point of view of everyone else, but had his personal, partly religious one; now he says that the present war moves him." Throughout Tolstoy's life, as we have seen, he often adopted a "strange" or critical attitude toward established and fashionable trends. He had a dread of the stereotyped and trivial, the commonplace in every department of art.

As for the spell cast over public morality, Tolstoy feared that even more. Under the idealistic cloak of liberty, equality, fraternity, public welfare, those in places of power had plunged whole nations into fratricidal wars, revolutions, internecine quarrels. At such times, he knew, logical thinking is absent—people are blinded, they take lies for truth, villainy for nobility, brutality, treason and vengeance for courage.

"In all that constitutes human life, such as how to live, whether to go out and kill others or not, condemn them or not, educate their children this way or that—the people of our world willingly give themselves into the hands of others who know no better than themselves why they live as they do and make others live thus and not otherwise."

Faith in God, without which he could no longer live, was the rock to which Tolstoy clung.

". . . a faith in what life should be, drawn from the teachings of Christ," he wrote in his *Confession*. "No matter how they persecuted them [the believers], defamed them, yet they were the only ones not to give in without a struggle to whatever they were ordered to do, and that is why they are the only ones in our world who have not an animal but a reasoning existence, they are the only true believers."

He felt that the road to salvation was the road to God.

"You speak to me for the first time of Godhood—of God," he wrote to Fet that same spring that war was declared. "But I have long been thinking uninterruptedly about this principal problem, and if we are incapable, as others are, *of thinking about this,* we are obliged to find a way to do it."

And he did search.

He sensed the great power of faith resident in the Russian peasantry. This faith helped the peasants to endure poverty, disease, taught them how, without demur, to accept the will of God, face death. Tolstoy often walked out to the Moscow-Kiev highway, which ran about a mile from Yasnaya Polyana. There he encountered the itinerant pilgrims traveling to Kiev. They walked in groups or singly, mostly in sandals made of plaited bark, with canvas knapsacks on their backs in which they carried all their worldly possessions: a change of linen, extra sandals, a New Testament and prayer book, a chunk of black bread. They were on the road for months, stopping along the way at the homes of peasants, who rarely refused to harbor them. "God's people," the peasants called them. "It would be a sin not to take them in for the night." So they made them sit down to a dish of hot cabbage soup, and cut them a piece of bread. The pilgrims underwent many hardships along the way—they fell ill, their feet became sore, they were soaked by the rain—yet nothing shook their faith; they were prepared to suffer all privations, if only they could lay their hands on the sacred relics in Kiev, and say their prayers in the holy places. Other pilgrimages took them to Jerusalem, to the Troitsa-Sergeyevskaya Abbey, and other holy places.

What was it that drew these people? For Tolstoy it was not enough to understand; he had also to feel the impulses that quickened their faith. He himself began to attend church more often and decided to make the visit to Optina Pustyn which he and Strakhov had long been planning.

According to tradition Optina Pustyn Abbey was founded in the fourteenth century by a regenerate brigand. It attracted many famous people and writers. It was visited by Gogol, Dostoyevski (who described it in his *Brothers Karamazov*), the philosopher Vladimir Solovyov, the poet Alexei Tolstoy. Other writers lived and some were buried there. It was to be Lev Tolstoy's fate to go to this monastery four times; the fourth and last time was when he left his home just before his death.

For those unfamiliar with Russian monasteries it may well be impossible to imagine the feelings stirred by the approach to the monastery walls. Built up over a period of centuries, it drew people from all over Russia. As you enter its enclosure you seem to feel the accretion of those centuries; you sink back into the ancient patriarchal world of early Russia. Since the 1820's Optina Pustyn was famous for its elders. These elders, devout and wise ascetics who had rejected all rewards of earthly life, attracted the unhappy, the dissatisfied, the sick, the erring, those who in their grief sought words of solace. And the elders prayed with them, consoled them, admonished them.

It was with a feeling of profound hope that Tolstoy set out for Optina Pustyn.

It was August. Against the background of the thick greenery of a huge forest, the white walls of the monastery and the churches with their light-blue cupolas and gold crosses glinting in the hot sun stood out in bold relief. On the near side of the monastery were low-lying meadows cut across by a narrow but deep stream called the Zhizdra. There was no bridge. The pilgrims, with their knapsacks slung across their shoulders, the carriages bearing the well-to-do, peasant carts with their high seats stuffed with straw and covered with matting—all were loaded onto an open ferry. On either side of the ferry stood two monks and slowly, hand over hand, they pulled the heavy rope cable.

Having crossed the river the traveler set foot in a new, entirely isolated world.

At this time the Abbot of Optina Pustyn was the famous Elder Ambrosius, and it was from him that Tolstoy hoped to gain the power of faith for which he yearned. But he did not find what his

[221]

soul was seeking. Perhaps the holy fathers did not understand him, perhaps he himself did not have the right approach to them, for the only person who made any impression on him was not Ambrosius but his cell attendant, a deeply religious, simple man called Father Pimen, who found the conversations he listened to so boring that he quietly dozed off in his chair.

Tolstoy made a good impression in the monastery. An acquaintance of Strakhov, whom he quoted to Tolstoy after they had been in Optina Pustyn, reported back "a whole batch of conversations about you and even about me. The fathers were unusually loud in their praise of you; they find you have a splendid soul. They compare you to Gogol, and recall that he was terribly proud of his mind, whereas you are quite lacking in that pride. They fear that the literary world will strike at you for the eighth part [of *Anna Karenina*] and cause you distress. Father Ambrosius called me a 'tightlip,' and in general they believe me to be steeped in impiety, but you are closer than I am to faith. Father Pimen praised us too (he it was who spoke of your splendid soul) and this it pleased me to hear. . . ."

But Tolstoy was seeking outside the church as well for the answer to questions that tormented him. He had to find out everything the great thinkers, the prophets and the wise men of the world had attained, and in his quest read one philosopher after the other.

Many of his answers he found in the *Pensées* of Pascal. Some of that writer's thoughts coincided with his own. "Our virtue," says Pascal, "lies in our thinking. It is through that we must raise ourselves, and not by means of space and time which we cannot fill. Let us try to think well; there lies the beginning of virtue."

"For both these and the other books, I cannot tell you how grateful I am," Tolstoy wrote Strakhov on December 18, 1877. "I have already completely immersed myself in them, that is to say in Strauss, Renan, Proudhon, Max Mueller, and I now have Burnouf. I still need one more—that is Kant on ethics, *Critique of Practical Reason,* but I think I ordered it. I have hesitated before Solovyov's article for a long time, fearing to tackle it."

But when he finally decided to "tackle" it he was pitiless in the criticism of it which he sent to Strakhov.

"It appears," he wrote, "that the fundamental bases of good (according to Solovyov) are abstract and concrete, and the concrete have power when they are recognized as possessing a divine basis . . . it is necessary to decide whether or not those principles are

[222]

legitimate which cannot exist without God or, on the contrary, are those principles legitimate which are without God. . . . I am carried away," he went on, "by my attempt to say what I think and I am unclear, but my objection to Solovyov and to all philosophical articles of this kind remains in full force: it is impossible in discussing fundamental knowledge to introduce a concept of God as an incidental feature, useful in establishing a category."

Even as devoted and sensitive a friend as Strakhov could not fathom to the depths the process going on in Tolstoy's soul.

On August 16, 1877 he wrote to Tolstoy: "Your good letter brought you so vividly to my mind, invaluable Lev Nikolayevich. In these last two months I have, of course, come to know you better than during all my earlier visits. My feeling of affection for you has grown stronger and stronger, also my fears for you. I see how each day you go through experiences that would fill up another's life for a year, that you think and feel with ten times the power of others. It is obvious that you seek and do not find rest, that dark and harassing thoughts sometimes assume inordinate proportions in your mind. You have a remedy at hand: Live more moderately, do not throw yourself with such intensity either into your music, your writing or even your hunt, which intoxicates you and in which you pursue not snipe and ducks, but thoughts. Filling the brain to excess with blood makes a man too impressionable, beyond measure irritable; therefore do not work with your brain.

"I write this to you but I really think that I love you for this very responsiveness which has no limit, for the never-ending work to which you devote yourself."

Meanwhile life at Yasnaya Polyana pursued its course. On December 6, 1877, a son named Andrei was born to the Tolstoys. Six children of varying ages were the source of many cares, much attention, and great expense. They had to be trained and educated, there were tutors and governnesses to be hired. Tolstoy tried to increase his income; he bought up property, attempted to improve the economy of Yasnaya Polyana and to get as much money as possible from his own writings. At this time Tolstoy was elected a member of the provincial Zemstvo, but public work did not appeal to him. For relaxation, he often went off by himself with his dog and roamed for days through the forests and marshes, shooting woodcocks, ducks, snipe. Sometimes he would take along the older boys, Sergei and Ilya, and ride into neighboring fields to chase foxes and hares.

Yet whatever he was doing his thoughts constantly reverted to that main theme, the meaning of life and death. "Is there in philosophy any definition of religion except that it is superstition, and what form is there of most purified Christianity?" he wrote Strakhov, and not finding an answer he himself attempted an Exposition of the Christian Catechism and a Definition of Religion.

"I wanted to expound what I believe in the form of a catechism, and this is what I have attempted to do," he explained to Strakhov. "And this attempt has proved to me how difficult and—so I fear— impossible it is for me."

In her diary for December 26, 1877, Sophia Andreyevna wrote that "L.N.'s mood changes very much with the years. After a long struggle between unbelief and desire to believe, he has suddenly calmed down since the autumn. He has begun to observe fasts, goes to church and prays."

"I like his argument," she noted on this same date, "which he puts forward on behalf of Christianity for all who argue that the laws—social laws—of all the communists, socialists appear superior to those of Christianity. . . . If there were no teachings of Christianity which for centuries have been instilled in us and on the basis of which we have shaped our whole existence as a society, there would be no laws of morality, honesty, no desire to distribute the good things of this earth more equitably, none of the desire for good, for equality, which resides in those people."

At this point Sophia Andreyevna could not guess how far Tolstoy would go along this path, on which she was gradually, with great suffering and heartache, to lose him.

Early in January of the year 1878, Tolstoy did something to delight his wife: he began to work on a historical novel *The Decembrists,* laid in the time of Nicholas I.

From January 13, 1878 on, we find a series of notes relating to *The Decembrists.* From the notebook we can follow the tremendous work Tolstoy planned, and had already begun.

As always Tolstoy had a wide approach to his novel. The resettlement of peasants, the meeting between Decembrists and the new settlers in Siberia, the self-sacrifice of the families who followed the Decembrists to Siberia, all had to be woven together to include whole areas and spheres of Russian life.

Toward the end of January, 1878, Tolstoy wrote to Alexandrine: "I am now deep in my reading about the 1820's and I cannot tell you the satisfaction I derive as I picture those times to myself. It is strange and pleasant to think that a time I can remember, the 1830's, has already passed into history. So you see, the wavering of the figures in this picture is ended and they all find a fixed place in the triumphant tranquillity of truth and beauty. I have the feelings of a chef (a poor one) who has come to a richly furnished market place and, as he looks around at the vegetables, meats and fish, offered to him for his use, he dreams of the repast he could make out of them. That is how I am dreaming, although I know how often one dreams magnificently and then spoils the broth or does nothing at all!"

Tolstoy met some of the Decembrists; he studied a mass of relevant material, and went himself to the prison fortress of Peter and Paul, where the Decembrists had been incarcerated. His friends all helped him in getting the data he needed.

The fortress of Peter and Paul made a tremendous impression on him. On March 14 he wrote to Svistunov, one of the Decembrists: "I was in the fortress of Peter and Paul and there they told me that one of the criminals threw himself into the Neva and then ate glass. I cannot tell you the strange and strong feeling that came over me at the thought that you were that person. It was like the feeling I had when they brought me the handcuffs and leg irons of 1825...."

As always in the summertime Tolstoy did little work. He went off to his Samara estate and in the autumn returned to his writing. "Lyovochka said today that his thoughts have clarified," Sophia Andreyevna noted in her diary for November 11 of that year. "The types are coming to life, he has just been at work and is gay, he has faith in what he is doing. But his head aches and he coughs a little."

Tolstoy discovered that in the Third Section of the police headquarters in St. Petersburg they had preserved the secret findings of the Decembrist affair, their portraits and general data which would be invaluable to him. He asked first Strakhov and then Alexandrine Tolstoy to try to obtain permission for him to familiarize himself with these materials, but it was not granted. Access to the Third Section required special permission from the Tsar.

Along with his current work Tolstoy also conceived the idea of a novel of eighteenth-century life in which the main character would be his great uncle, Vasili Nikolayevich Gorchakov, who was exiled to Siberia. Tolstoy again appealed to Alexandrine for help in gaining access to the secret archives of the Ministry of Justice and simultaneously he wrote an application to the Administration of the Moscow Archives for permission to study the documents there.

But the work did not advance. After writing several snatches of his novel laid in the times of Peter the Great, Tolstoy more and more rarely returned to his thoughts and plans for it. We know what difficulty he found in finishing *Anna Karenina*, how his thoughts kept wandering off into another realm—that of religion and philosophy. He could not write a second *War and Peace* until he had solved the fundamental purpose of his existence. Why do we live? What is the main meaning of our life? Of what does our faith consist? And . . . therefore what are we to do?

❧ 34 ❧

UNLIKE most people, Tolstoy did not look upon the confession of mistakes as a sign of weakness. He was not afraid of losing his dignity when he asked forgiveness from a servant at whom he had been angry, or admitted a mistake before his pupils in his school, before his wife and his own children, when he had been unfair in his treatment of them. It was much easier for him to repent than to go on living in an atmosphere of conflict, even if he was not the only one at fault.

His relations with Turgenyev had long weighed on his mind and in one of his moments of insight, which came over him with increasing frequency, he wrote him a letter.

"Forgive me if I have been at fault in any way with regard to you," he wrote to him in Paris in the spring of 1878; and he begged Turgenyev to forget everything, to keep only the memory of the good things which had brought them together in the early days of their acquaintanceship.

"I received your letter," replied Turgenyev. "I was much pleased and touched by it. It is with the greatest delight that I am prepared to renew our former friendship and I warmly grasp the hand you have extended to me."

In early August, when the Tolstoy family returned from Samara,

Turgenyev hastened over to Yasnaya Polyana to call. His arrival was an exciting event. By his animation, his vivid eloquence, his brilliant and witty stories, Turgenyev charmed them all. Apparently he himself was extremely happy over this visit.

"I had the very clear impression," he wrote Tolstoy, "that life having aged us has not passed in vain, and that both you and I have grown to be better men than we were sixteen years ago."

Yet despite the passing of the years and the external reconciliation, the two writers were at heart so different that no true friendship could exist between them. Turgenyev remained the same aesthetic person, the admirer of the Western world, the romanticist, little concerned with religious and philosophic questions; while for Tolstoy these questions now, more than ever before, formed the basis of his whole life. He attempted to share his most intimate thoughts with Turgenyev, to admit him to his holy of holies, but Turgenyev could not penetrate Tolstoy's soul; he interpreted Tolstoy's attitude in his own superficial terms.

"I am glad that your physical health is good," wrote Turgenyev to Tolstoy, "and I trust that your intellectual malady, of which you write, has passed. I too have experienced it: sometimes it came on in the guise of inner ferment at the inception of a piece of work; I suppose that that kind of fermentation has gone on in you too."

Clearly Turgenyev took Tolstoy's "malady" to be merely an author's "pangs of creativeness," rather than what it was—a search for the meaning of life.

Turgenyev understood and appreciated Tolstoy as an artist and, after the reconciliation, he did not doubt that in seizing every opportunity to praise his works, especially *War and Peace*, he was gratifying Tolstoy. He was incapable of grasping the fact that once Tolstoy had finished and published a work he did not care to hark back to it, and that at this particular time he was unable to take any interest in novels.

The path of the man who seeks God is always a lonely one, apart even from those nearest to him. His wife, Strakhov, Fet—none of them could help Tolstoy. They could grasp certain thoughts and feelings which were accessible to or inherent in themselves, but they could not plumb the secret recesses of this complex, many-faceted being.

What were the questions to which Tolstoy so stubbornly sought the answers? They were: "(a) Why am I living? (b) What is the reason for my existence or that of anyone? (c) What is the aim of my or anyone's existence? (d) What is the meaning and purpose of the division between good and evil which I sense in myself? (e) How should I live? (f) What is death? The most general and complete expression of these questions would be: How am I to achieve salvation? I feel that I am being destroyed. I live and I die, I love life and fear death—how can I save myself?"

". . . moments of what at first was indisposition began to come over me," Tolstoy wrote in his *Confession*. "They were stops in my life, as if I did not know how to go on living, what to do, and I was bewildered and depressed. But that passed, and I went on living as before. Later these moments of indisposition began to repeat themselves more and more frequently and always in the same way. These stops in my life always took the form of the questions: For what purpose? and afterward, what?

". . . I sensed that the thing on which I was standing had given way beneath me, that I had nothing to stand on, that what I had been living by no longer existed, that I had nothing to live by.

"My life came to a stop. . . .

". . . If a fairy should come and offer to grant any wish I should not know what to say. Even if I had no wish but the habit of wishing I had formed in my intemperate days, still I know, in my sober moments, that this is a delusion, there is nothing to wish for. I cannot even wish to know the truth because I have already guessed of what it consists. The truth is that life is nonsense. It is as though I had lived, lived and walked, walked, and came to an abyss, I saw clearly that there was nothing ahead, except destruction. . . .

". . . What has happened to me is that I, a healthy, happy person, have come to feel that I cannot go on living—some indefinable force has drawn me to the point where somehow I must rid myself of my life. I cannot say that I *desire* to kill myself.

"The force which has drawn me away from life was more powerful, more complete, more sweeping than desire. . . . The thought of suicide came to me as naturally as earlier the thoughts about improving my life. . . ."

He roamed over Yasnaya Polyana, sometimes with dog and gun, and still the same thoughts pursued him: death will come, and what of it? Why do I live? "I myself did not know what I wanted," he wrote in his *Confession*. "I feared life, attempted to get away from it and yet, at the same time, I still hoped for something out of it." Tolstoy stopped going out hunting with his gun—he did not trust

[228]

himself, as he put it, "not to be enticed by the too easy means of getting rid of my life."

Sometimes he was plunged into such despair that, in looking at the wooden partition dividing his bedroom from his study, he wondered if it would bear the weight of his body, and he "hid cords for fear of hanging myself on the crossbeam between the bookcases and my room, where I spent my evenings alone . . ." (*Confession*). But could Tolstoy choose this path—the path of the weak? He was cognizant of God, even though he had not yet chosen the path by which he could come closer and more directly to Him. He could not violate His will by destroying life, the grandeur and beauty of which he so loved. And this life force in him was without limit. He not only loved God's world, he was part and parcel of it.

"The nightingales, the frogs, the tree toads are making music at the top of their bent," he wrote on April 9, 1879, in his notebook. "The grass in the forest is about two inches high, dandelions, mullein, yellow ones too, are all over the place. Rain on and off all day, warm in some spots, cold in others, as in summer."

On October 13: "It is still. A mist is moving and coming down. It is bright out, moonlight with a golden cast. Drops hang transparent on the tips of buds and fall onto the wet, slate-colored leaves. That is in the woods. In the fields everything is quiet, so still you can hear every sound; a mist is stirring, it moves along in bands."

Meantime, his children were growing up, his estate was increasing, his books were being published . . . and that was his life, which he himself had built up, *his* family which he was surrounding with the glory of his fame, esteem, prosperity . . . and gradually all this which he had built up with great effort ceased to interest him. Because of habit, he still participated outwardly in this life, but inwardly he was withdrawing from it.

What had happened to Lyovochka? his wife asked herself. He had taken her when she was scarcely more than a child and she could not imagine other surroundings than those in which she had been brought up. What has happened to Papa? the children asked. Why had he grown so different?

Tolstoy was writing his *Confession* and his wife was upset: "Lyovochka has now buried himself in his writing," she wrote to her sister in November, 1878. "His eyes are fixed in a strange gaze, he scarcely talks, he has quite left this world and is absolutely incapable of thinking about everyday matters."

In another letter she wrote: "Lyovochka is working all the time.

as he calls it, but, alas, he is writing some kind of religious discourses; he reads and thinks until he has headaches, and all this in order to prove that the church is not in accord with the teachings of the New Testament. There will scarcely be ten people in all Russia who will be interested in this. But there is nothing to do about it. I care only about one thing which is that he will finish it as quickly as possible and get over it like a sickness."

But the "sickness" or "indisposition," as Tolstoy called it in his *Confession*, did not pass. Instead it grew worse and worse. About this time he engaged V. I. Alexeyev as a tutor in mathematics for the older children, Sergei and Tanya. Alexeyev was a member of a group of socialists, an intelligent, enterprising and splendid teacher. Together with other Russians belonging to a revolutionary group, he had gone to America where they attempted to establish an agricultural commune in Kansas. But the colony in America fell apart, and on his return to Russia Alexeyev was in a state of great poverty; when he was offered the post of tutor in Tolstoy's home he was dubious about accepting it because Tolstoy was a Count. Nevertheless, simple, friendly relations were soon formed between the two men. Alexeyev, as a socialist, rejected the Orthodox faith, and he and his employer had long talks on religious themes. At that time Tolstoy had not entirely broken away from the Orthodox faith; he was still trying to find inside it the answers to the questions tormenting him.

In the summer of 1879 Tolstoy went to Kiev.

"All morning and until three in the afternoon I walked around among the cathedrals, the catacombs, the monks, and I am very much disappointed with my trip," he wrote his wife on June 14. "It hasn't been worth while. At seven o'clock I went back to the abbey to see Father Antonius, but I found little that was instructive."

In December he visited Archbishop Nikander of Tula, spoke of his desire to distribute his estate to the poor and enter a monastery. But the Archbishop, evidently sensing the instability of Tolstoy's frame of mind, urged him not to do this, to wait.

The Tolstoys by now had a large family. In 1880 the oldest child, Sergei, was seventeen and was preparing to enter the university. Pretty black-eyed Tanya was sixteen. Blue-eyed, good-natured, broad-shouldered, tall Ilya, the passionate hunter and horseman, was reaching fourteen. Lev, his mother's favorite and very like her with his black eyes, slight build and nervous temperament, was eleven. Little

Masha, unloved by her mother, unattractive, with a broad intelligent brow and deep-set, thoughtful eyes like her father's, was nine. Three-year-old Andrei, who had a large head and was always ailing, was the cause of constant worry to his mother and she was morbidly attached to him. Then, in 1879, on December 20, a fifth son, Michael, was born—a quiet, well-poised, healthy child.

Seven children meant a constant round of cares and Sophia Andreyevna found it increasingly difficult to follow the inner experiences of her husband.

". . . This morning, after a bad night with nightmares and dreams, I drank my tea with Lyovochka," she had noted in her diary within the year. "This happens so seldom, and we got into a long philosophical conversation about the meaning of life, death, religion and so on. Such conversations with Lyovochka always have a morally soothing effect on me. I'll have to go my own way to achieve his wisdom in these questions and I shall find the points on which I can remain firm, with which to console myself in times of doubt. I would expound his views except that I am unable to, especially now when I am tired and my head aches."

Such conversations were rare. Sophia Andreyevna was preoccupied with the question of the children's education. They must move to town, yet for Tolstoy the very idea of city life, especially in his current frame of mind, was death dealing. The children themselves began to feel the urge toward a city life. They were depressed by their isolation, their separation from their contemporaries. In the summertime it was different—Aunt Tanya came with her numerous family and Yasnaya Polyana was lively and gay; but in the winter!

In Sophia Andreyevna's diary was this note: "Seryozha and Tanya are always dreaming about *gaiety* and I feel badly that I can provide so little of it for them, but I shall bend all my efforts to do so." And again: "This evening I played a quadrille for the children, they danced in a very gay fashion, first the older ones and then the younger ones joined in."

Sophia Andreyevna, in her own way, was lonely too. She was still quite young, only thirty-five, and like her older children she yearned for a little *gaiety*. Her pregnancy had put her in a more acutely despondent state; she felt smothered; the children and the whole household were tense.

Her world as pictured in her diary was a very special one: "Andryusha is two years and two months old," she wrote on February

[231]

11, 1880. "Misha is seven and a half weeks old. Andryusha got up at seven, drank his acorn coffee with milk, he wet once during the night, dressed himself in an open-necked blouse, a light dimity vest, undershirt, trousers, stockings with garters. . . ."

"Misha is husky," she wrote on the 19th, "he is being swaddled, but is being taken out dressed in a flannel vest, a cap and bib. We bathe him every day except Sunday, in a bath of thirty degrees. He is frequently constipated and we have to give him enemas of warm water and oil. . . ."

"Andryusha has a cough and a head cold."

". . . Misha's second tooth is coming through. . . ."

". . . I do not have much milk for Misha," and so on.

Although she was sometimes bored, her life was a full one. Yet for some time now, whenever she lifted her large short-sighted eyes from the diapers, the sicknesses, the children's lessons, and directed her gaze on her husband—so unlike anyone else in the world, so close to her and yet so far away—she was frightened.

Why did he write strange discourses on religion that no one cared about? Why did he not begin a new novel, one like *War and Peace* or *Anna Karenina*? What ails this big powerful man? Why do his deep-set gray eyes light up so seldom now with mirth, affection and gaiety? Why do his lips beneath his thick reddish mustache and beard smile so seldom?

So she prayed God that "*this* will pass, like a sickness."

But the "malady" did not leave him and its symptoms grew more and more evident.

🐚 35 🐚

IN JANUARY, 1880, Tolstoy made a business trip to St. Petersburg, where he saw Alexandrine Tolstoy. He was ruthlessly harsh in expressing his doubts to his Granny, telling her that her faith—that of the Orthodox Church—was founded on falsehood. Their conversation was so tempestuous that Tolstoy lay awake for half the night and left St. Petersburg without saying good-by to her. But before he left he wrote her a letter.

"I know," he said toward its conclusion, "that I am asking the almost impossible of you—to recognize the true meaning of a teaching which negates all the surroundings in which you have spent your life, on which your affections have been centered, but I cannot talk to you and refrain, as I do with others, from saying all, for it seems to me that you cherish a true love of God, of good, and that you cannot fail to realize where He is.

"For my irritability, my coarse offensive ways, forgive me, and farewell, old and dear friend, until my next letter or we meet again, if God wills."

Alexandrine was hurt. "Such outbreaks are unpleasant enough, even in a young person, but at our age not to offer one's hand in farewell, when every separation may be the last, is simply unpardonable, and it is very hard for me to forgive you," she wrote him. But their correspondence did not end there; Alexandrine wrote Tolstoy a long letter in which she expounded her Orthodox faith.

". . . The main point is that your profession of faith is that of our church," Tolstoy replied. "I know it and I do not share it, but I have not a word to say against those who believe that way. Especially when you add that the essence of the teaching is the Sermon on the Mount. I not only do not reject that teaching but, if I were asked: What do I wish, to have my children be unbelievers, as I was, or that they *believe* in what the church teaches, I should, without hesitation, choose the *faith* in accordance with the church. . . . But to believe in what appears to be false—that is impossible. Nor is that all; to assure myself that I believe in something in which I cannot believe . . . is an act in absolute opposition to faith. . . . The first condition of faith is love of light, truth, God—and a pure heart without lies. . . . And just as I feel myself to be in complete harmony with sincere believers from the people, so do I with those following the paths of the Church, with you, when that faith is sincere and you look directly at God with your own eyes, not through glasses, not squinting. . . ."

"To remember God, one's soul, every day and every hour, means putting love of one's neighbor above mere animal existence. There is no trick at all about this, it is just as simple as that to shoe a horse one must be a blacksmith. And that is why it is God's truth, because it is so simple that nothing can exceed its simplicity, and at the same time it is so important and great and such a blessing to all people, that nothing can be greater."

While working on his *Confession*, Tolstoy undertook a study of the dogmas of the Orthodox Church. By now he took nothing "on faith"—he had to understand and know. Among the theological works he studied was the widely distributed book of Metropolitan Makari.

"Tell me the truths as you know them, tell them if you will as they are stated in the symbol of faith, which we all learned by heart," was his challenge to the theologians. ". . . But do not forget that whatever you say will be telling me God's truth, put into words, and words in turn have to be comprehended with the mind. Explain these truths to my mind. . . ."

We must believe, says the church; I must comprehend with my mind what I am to believe, said Tolstoy.

He believed in God the Father, by whose will he lived, whose will he knew and must carry out. But he was unable to believe in God in three aspects, the Trinity of God the Father, the Son, and the Holy Ghost, and, not comprehending it, he once and for all rejected this concept for himself.

Yet in rejecting the faith into which he had been born, trained and grown up, he had to replace it by a faith of his own, something that would serve him as a guide, and so he began a detailed reading of the New Testament. Yet even here, although he accepted *in toto* the teachings of Christ as an obligatory rule of life, he still could not find explanations for the miracles. He stumbled on contradictions between the teachings of Christ and their interpretation by the church. "Do not kill," said Christ; yet the church prayed for the believing warriors.

"He has a wonderful understanding of the ideal Christian," Strakhov wrote to Danilevski, "and it is strange how we pass by the New Testament without ever seeing its most straightforward meaning. He has immersed himself in a study of the New Testament text, he has explained a little of it to me with astounding simplicity and subtlety. I very much fear that because of his lack of practice in expounding abstract thought . . . he will not succeed in putting forward his ideas briefly and clearly; yet the contents of the book he is putting together will be truly great."

Tolstoy was working on a translation and study of the four Gospels. He was so steeped in his work that when Turgenyev came to Yasnaya Polyana to persuade him to take part in the Pushkin celebration on the occasion of the unveiling of a monument to Pushkin in Moscow, Tolstoy seemed to think that this was utterly unimportant in comparison with the decision he was trying to reach, and he refused to go. Turgenyev, as all the world of letters, was thunderstruck. How could Tolstoy, the author of *War and Peace*, a pillar of Russian literature, not take part in the ceremonies dedicated to the greatest of Russian poets!

Dostoyevski intended to go to Yasnaya Polyana but Turgenyev assured him that Tolstoy was in such a frame of mind that it was impossible to converse with him—that he was absorbed in some religious question or other and not interested in anything. Grigorovich expressed the same thing in harsher terms: "Tolstoy has all but lost his mind and indeed he may have lost it altogether. . . ."

On the 28th of May Dostoyevski wrote to his wife: "Katkov too has confirmed the fact that Lev Tolstoy has quite gone out of his mind. Yuryev has been urging me to go down to Yasnaya Polyana to see him. . . . But I shall not go, although it would be a curious experience. . . ."

At that time Dostoyevski did not enjoy an authoritative standing among the liberal writers. Looked upon as a Slavophile, he stood, as Strakhov put it in a letter to Tolstoy, "aloof in hostile surroundings."

Everyone was therefore all the more struck by his success at the Pushkin celebration, where his speech surpassed anything said about Pushkin up to that time. Its style, brilliance and profound understanding of the poet made Dostoyevski suddenly the very center of attention. In a storm of enthusiasm and applause the audience picked him up and carried him off on their shoulders.

More than once, later on, Tolstoy expressed his regret at not having gone to the celebration, heard Dostoyevski's speech and made his acquaintance, especially as that proved to be their last opportunity to meet.

On September 26 of this same year Tolstoy wrote to Strakhov: ". . . I continue work along the same line and, it would seem, not without result. These last days I have not been well and I have been reading *House of the Dead*. I had forgotten a great deal of it and so was rereading it, and I do not know of a better book in all modern literature, including Pushkin.

"It is not the tone but the point of view which is astonishing— sincere, natural and Christian. It is a good, an edifying book. I enjoyed myself yesterday as I have not enjoyed myself for a long time. If you see Dostoyevski tell him that I love him."

Strakhov gave the letter to Dostoyevski and it was a source of great joy to him. On January 28, 1881, Dostoyevski was dead. . . .

Strakhov wrote Tolstoy in February: "Since the minute I heard of Dostoyevski's death, dearest Lev Nikolayevich, I have not been able to throw off a sense of emptiness. I have the feeling that half of St. Petersburg has given way, that half of literature has died."

"How I wish I could say all that I feel about Dostoyevski!" Tolstoy replied to Strakhov. "You, in describing your feelings, express a part of mine. I never saw the man and never had any immediate relations with him; and suddenly, when he died, I realized that he was someone very close, dear and necessary to me. . . . I felt him to be my friend and never dreamed but that we should meet, just that this had not yet happened, but was in store for me. And suddenly I read—he is dead! A kind of support to me had broken off. I was bewildered, and then I saw clearly how I had loved him and I wept and now I am still weeping. Recently, before he died, I read *The Humiliated and Insulted* and was moved. . . ."

Dostoyevski went his own way as did Tolstoy. What he wrote was described as "corruption" and "lunacy." In his youth he had been carried away by revolutionary ideas which he later abandoned. Faith in Christ and the closeness of the Russian people to Christ formed the basis of his life and writings. It was for that very reason that he was closer to Tolstoy than to any other of his contemporaries in literature.

Tolstoy, as it has been said, was never attracted by the revolutionary tendencies of those times. Even during the liberation of the serfs his approach was his own; he did not share the general liberal attitude. The revolutionaries considered the people ignorant masses who could be roused against their oppressors—the Russian government. The words "people," "people's" on the lips of those who had no conception of the essential being of the Russian people only irritated Tolstoy. He lived with the people, ignorant, poor and oppressed, he knew them, he learned from them, and in them he sought support for his own growing consciousness of Christianity. In the peasant he sensed a spiritual power, a true faith, a beauty, from which he drew sustenance.

For the past decade the revolutionary movement had been growing apace.

In 1870 the first volume of *Das Kapital* of Marx appeared in a Russian translation. In Western Europe and in America Karl Marx had long since acquired fame. In 1847 Marx and Engels had entered into a secret international union of Communists and composed the "Manifesto of the Communist Party." This did not prevent the *New York Tribune* from having Karl Marx as a regular contributor on economic questions during the 1850's and early 1860's. The development of communist ideas was seen in the establishment of the Paris commune of 1871. In Russia the revolutionary movement took the form of a series of terroristic acts.

On January 24, 1878, a revolutionist, Vera Zasulich, attempted to assassinate F. F. Trepov, the Chief of Police. She was arrested, tried three months later by a jury and acquitted. A series of attempts to assassinate the Tsar followed. Finally, on the 1st of March, 1881, all Russia was shocked by the terrible murder of the Liberator— Tsar Alexander II. "Today, March 1, 1881, in accordance with the decision of the Executive Committee reached on August 26, 1879, the execution of Alexander II has been effected by two agents of the Executive Committee," ran the proclamation released by the party of "Land and Freedom."

"What a blow, dearest Lev Nikolayevich!" wrote Strakhov. "I am still so upset I do not know what to do. They have brutally murdered the old man who dreamed of being the most liberal and benevolent Tsar in the world! It was a theoretical murder, not done out of malice, not out of any real necessity, but because as an idea it was a very good thing. Everything gets on my nerves: the calm, the malicious satisfaction of others, and even the pity. . . . No, we shall not return to our right minds. It will take dreadful catastrophes, laying waste whole regions, fires, the blowing up of whole cities, the killing of millions of human beings, to make the people return to their right minds. Now we see nothing but flowers."

In his memoirs Ilya Tolstoy tells how the family heard the news of the murder.

"On the first of March Papa, as usual, went for a walk along the highway before dinner. After the heavy rains of winter a thaw had set in. There were already deep ruts in the roads and the hollows were filled with water. Because of the bad weather we had not sent in to Tula and there were no newspapers.

"On the highway Papa met some kind of a wandering Italian with a barrel organ and a fortunetelling bird. He was coming on foot from the direction of Tula. They fell into conversation—'Where from? Where to?'

" 'From Tula, bad business, I had no food, my bird has not eaten, they killed the Tsar.'

" 'What Tsar? Who killed him? When?'

" 'The Russian Tsar, St. Petersburg, threw a bomb, we got the papers.'

"When he came home Papa immediately told us about the death of Alexander II and the newspapers which arrived the next day confirmed the news, giving precise details.

"I remember the depressing effect on Father of this senseless murder. Aside from the fact that he was horrified by the brutal death of the Tsar 'who had done much good and always wished people well and was a good old man,' he could not take his mind off the murderers, off the execution being prepared, and he thought not so much about them as about those who would participate in their killing, and especially about Alexander III."

For several days he went around preoccupied and gloomy. Finally he wrote a letter to the new Emperor.

"Your father, the Russian Tsar, who did so much good and always wished for the welfare of his people, a kind old man, has been barbarously mutilated and murdered, but not by his personal enemies," he wrote, "but by enemies of the existing order of things: they killed him in the name of some sort of notion of benefiting all humanity.

"You have taken his place; before you there are the same enemies who poisoned your father's existence and destroyed him. They are your enemies because you occupy the place of your father, and for the sake of the supposed general benefit for which they must desire to kill you too.

"Toward these people you must have a feeling of revenge in your heart, as the murderers of your father, and also a feeling of terror before the obligation which you have had to take on yourself. No more terrible situation can be imagined, all the more terrible because one cannot imagine a greater temptation to commit evil. 'They are the enemies of our fatherland, of the people, contemptible youngsters, godless creatures, who are upsetting the peace and lives of millions of trusting people, the murderers of my father. What else can I do with them except to cleanse the Russian earth of this contagion, crush them as one would loathsome serpents? I am obliged to do this not because of my personal feelings, not even out of revenge for my father's death, I do it because it is my duty, all Russia expects it of me'!" Thus Tolstoy wrote to the Tsar:

". . . To your lot has fallen the most dire temptation. Yet no matter how terrible it is, the teaching of Christ destroys it: the whole net of temptations which enfolds you will crumble away to dust before the man who executes the will of God.

"In Matthew 5:43 you have heard what has been said: love thy neighbor and hate thine enemy: but I say unto you: love your enemies . . . do good to those who hate you . . . and you will be the sons of your father which is in heaven. . . .

"Your Majesty! If you did that, if you called these people before you, gave them money and sent them off to some spot in America and wrote a manifesto headed by these words: 'But I say unto you: Love thine enemies!' I cannot speak for others but as for me, poor subject that I am, I would be your very dog, your slave. I would weep for gladness, as I weep now every time I hear your name. Yet what am I saying: 'I cannot speak for others!' I do know what a flood of love and goodness would flow from your words all over Russia. . . .

"Just the one word of forgiveness and Christian love, spoken and carried out from the heights of the throne, only the path of Christian rule upon which you must now enter, can destroy that evil which is corroding Russia. Like wax before a flame, all revolutionary opposition will melt away before the Tsar-Man who fulfills the law of Christ."

Pobedonostsev, who was asked to transmit this letter to the Tsar, refused to do so and returned it. The letter was again dispatched through other channels, and the Tsar received it.

They said that after reading it Alexander remarked: "If this crime concerned me personally I should have the right to pardon the guilty persons, but for my father's sake I cannot do so."

On the 3rd of April all participants in the murder of the Tsar-Liberator were executed.

Tolstoy's appeal to Alexander III proved to be a voice crying in the wilderness. Tolstoy was infinitely depressed. Even those nearest to him could not understand his mood.

"They should be hung, they should be flogged, they should have their teeth knocked in without witnesses. . . ." Such were the phrases heard in the Tolstoy family circle. "The people wouldn't mutiny then—they'd be afraid. . . ."

But in his diary for July 6 Tolstoy wrote: "The economic revolution is not only possible, it is inevitable. It is surprising it is not here yet."

❧ 36 ❧

IN THE summer of 1881, as always happened when Aunt Tanya and her numerous Kuzminski family were in Yasnaya Polyana, there was a surge of life.

The two mothers, Aunt Sonya and Aunt Tanya, as they were called, were put to it to keep track of all the children. On a sudden impulse they might run off into the fields to find their favorite horse Kavushka, and three or four of them would mount him at the same time; or they would disappear into hidden corners of the thick and leafy woods. Ilya, with gun and hound, might be absent for days and nights on end, roaming the forests and marshes in search of snipe, wild ducks, woodcocks, while his mother worried; someone would fall in love with black-eyed Tanya or Masha, and again the mothers worried. The children quarreled among themselves, fought and raised such a howl that Aunt Tanya would grab them, knock their heads together and bid them make up. Sometimes the whole horde, eight to twelve of them, drove off in the long katki or droshky through the forest along the muddy road (which never dried out because it ran through the shady Forest Preserve) to bathe in the Voronka River, and the mothers had to watch to see that no one fell under the horses' hoofs, or choked in the water or caught cold.

There were constant celebrations of name days, of birthdays; cakes were baked; the mothers discussed the superiority of each other's cakes and watched to make sure the "little folks" did not overeat on sweets. . . .

The chefs roasted chickens, lamb, beef, prepared unusual fruit ices, fancy desserts—whole cottages with windows made of waffles and served with an extraordinary cream sauce. The housemen polished a battalion of dirty shoes, they waited on table, cleaned the house; the chambermaids starched collars, ironed clothes; the coachmen curried the horses, busily harnessed or unharnessed them to the calèches, troikas, droshkies, tarantases, and saddled them for riding. Each one had his favorite horse. Slim, graceful, adroit Tanya and broad-shouldered, powerful Ilya adored horses and rode beautifully —their master in the art of riding was their father.

Aunt Sonya rarely rode, and when she did they gave her the most obedient mount. Aunt Tanya also rode rarely, but she had a sure and easy seat on a horse and was not afraid.

But that summer "Papa," or "Uncle Lyalya" as the Kuzminski children called him, was not a party to the gay life of the young people. In simple dust-stained clothes and plaited bark sandals Tolstoy, in company with two fellow travelers, his servant Sergei Arbuzov and the Yasnaya Polyana teacher, was making a pilgrimage to the monastery of Optina Pustyn.

From his journey Tolstoy wrote his wife: "It is two o'clock in the afternoon. . . . Did not arrive in as good shape as I expected. Rubbed blisters, but slept, and from the point of view of health I feel better than I expected. Here I have bought some hemp sandals, they will be easier on the feet. It is pleasant, worth while, very instructive (this trip). If only God grant we may all meet again in good health, the whole family, and that there will be nothing untoward with you, or with me, or else I shall never be able to regret enough that I went away. One cannot imagine how new, important and worth while it is for the soul (for one's outlook on life) to see God's world, the great real world, not the one you and I have arranged, which we never step out of, even if we travel to the ends of the world. . . ."

This effort to sever himself from the everyday limited world in his search for God shows through in the end of this letter as well: "The principal new feeling is to be aware of oneself, in one's own consciousness as well as in the eyes of others, as you really are, free from any dependence upon your usual background.

"I hope the children big and little are not upsetting you. If only you don't have any unpleasant guests; if only you keep yourself well; if only nothing happens, if only . . . if I did nothing but what was good, and you too, then everything would be fine."

On June 12 Sophia Andreyevna wrote her husband a long letter describing her life: "Tanya's children are husky. I have just given orders now to take Misha too out for a walk. We go bathing; the berries are getting ripe; it is very hot and lonely without you. I think you must be having a hard time of it walking with a pack in this heat, and I am worried about your head. I do hope that in the hottest part of the day you will sit in the shade or sleep, and that when you are perspiring you will not drink anything, or bathe; that's very harmful, you might get a stroke . . ."

When the dirt-stained travelers from Yasnaya Polyana, in their hemp sandals and peasant kaftans, arrived at Optina Pustyn, the monks would not let them enter the clean hostel but directed them to the general dormitory in a hut where all the poor people stayed. It was only at the insistence of Tolstoy's servant Sergei that they were taken to a private room.

But the next day, when the monks discovered that Count Tolstoy was among their guests, they were upset and insisted that he move to the very best room.

"Since they have recognized me," Tolstoy said rather ruefully to his servant, "there's nothing to be done about it. Give me my leather boots and a different shirt and I'll change. . . ."

On this visit Tolstoy again talked with Father Ambrosius, but the elder's admonition to repent and return to the bosom of the church had no effect. Tolstoy's stay in Optina Pustyn pushed him even farther away from orthodoxy.

"I'll tell you frankly what I think I am," Tolstoy wrote to the educator S. A. Rachinski on July 15 in this same year: "I think I am a Christian. The teachings of Christ are the source of my life. If I doubted them I could not go on living; but conscious orthodoxy, bound up with the church, the state, is for me the source of all sacrilege; it is a sacrilege which hides God's truth from people."

On his return Tolstoy did not remain long in Yasnaya Polyana. At Turgenyev's invitation, he spent two days with him at Spasskoye, and then, on July 13, he went off to Samara with his eldest son, Sergei.

Externally Tolstoy's life continued in the same channels. He was still interested in expanding the income from his Samara estate, his horses: "The grain is in good condition," he wrote his wife on July 20, "although not in all places. Ours is very good. . . . The stud horses, about ten in number, are fine. I did not expect to find such good ones. Probably I'll bring some home in the autumn to sell and some also to keep. The horses have been a remarkable success, despite the famine years, during which they starved and much was spent on them. These are cheap horses, in my opinion, at three hundred rubles and over. The prospects for income, over ten thousand, seem to me right; but I have been mistaken so often that I am afraid to believe the figure."

In the course of his journey to Optina Pustyn Tolstoy had visited some Old Believers. In the province of Samara he became interested in the sect of the Molokans. In the simplicity of their teaching and the great weight they accorded the teachings of Christ, Tolstoy felt that they were nearer to him and more comprehensible than the Old Believers.

In a letter to his wife he said: "I was at their prayer meeting, and present too at their discussion of the Gospels, and I took part in it, and they asked me to expound my interpretation and I read them some extracts of my Exposition, and the seriousness, the interest, the sane, clear sense of these half-literate people were amazing."

Meantime Sophia Andreyevna was having her own worries. It was necessary to move to town, so she went to Moscow where, with characteristic energy, she hunted for a house to which the whole family could come for the winter. The move took place in September.

The oldest son, Sergei, now eighteen, was entered in the natural sciences department of Moscow University. Seventeen-year-old Tanya, who had inherited her mother's gift for drawing, attended the Moscow School of Painting and Sculpture, and sixteen- and thirteen-year-old Ilya and Lev went to a private Polivanov school.

For Tolstoy life in the city was the most cruel of torments. "Stinks, stones, luxury, poverty, corruption," he wrote in his diary for October 5. "The wicked have gathered together, robbed the people, collected soldiers and judges to guard their orgies—and they feast. There is nothing left for the common people to do but prey on their passions, to get back some of that which has been stolen from them. The peasant men are more adept at this. Their womenfolk stay at home but the men scrub floors and bodies in the baths and hire out as coachmen.

"A month has passed. The most agonizing of my life. The move to Moscow. Everything is being organized. When will they ever begin to live? All this is not for the sake of living, but to do as others. Poor people. It's no life."

One ray of light was his acquaintance with a peasant from the province of Tver, one Vasili Syutayev. The previous summer, in

Samara, Tolstoy had met a man called Prugavin, who was making a study of the life of the various Russian sects.

"With avid curiosity Lev Nikolayevich quizzed me about my impressions and observations obtained from my knowledge and personal study of these or those sects in the areas where they were distributed," wrote Prugavin in his book on *Lev Tolstoy and the Tolstoyans*. "But what interested him particularly was the personality and the teaching of Vasili Syutayev, a peasant from the province of Tver, who had just come to the fore, and who preached love and brotherhood among all people and nations and complete communism of possessions."

In October, after he was settled in Moscow, Tolstoy went to the province of Tver to see Syutayev. His acquaintance with Syutayev was a revelation to him. Here again in the midst of "dark" peasantry he found true religious exaltation, a faith in the teachings of Christ, in God. He wrote in his diary that this was for him a "consolation." Syutayev believed in the fraternal commune; he did not recognize private property. Tolstoy said: "Syutayev expressed his faith in very simple phrases: 'All is in you and all is love.' "

Sophia Andreyevna wrote to her sister: "Lyovochka fell not only into a state of depression but even into some kind of desperate apathy. He did not sleep or eat, he *à la lettre* cried at times, and I thought I should simply go out of my mind. Then he went to the province of Tver, met some old acquaintances, then he journeyed to a village to see some kind of a dissident, a Christian, and when he came back he was less dejected. Now he has made arrangements to do his work out in the ell of the house, where he has rented two small, quiet rooms for six rubles a month; then he goes to Devichie Pole, crosses the river to the Sparrow-Hills and there he saws and chops wood with the peasants. That is healthy for him and makes him lighthearted."

Submerged as she was in the life of the family, Sophia Andreyevna could not understand why Lyovochka moped. She realized how hard on him it was to live in the city, yet what could she do? In the society in which she had been brought up children should be educated and trained in certain ways; she had to introduce Tanya to the fashionable world; she had to have a proper home, clothing, servants.

"I stayed at home with the boys, the two Olsufyev boys came over, they drank tea very properly; then Countess Keller came to ask if I would allow the boys to go to the circus tomorrow," she wrote to her husband on March 3, 1882. "I agreed and they are going to the opera matinee. This excitement will last a long time. On Saturday there is dancing at the Olsufyevs', on Friday the Obolenskis have invited us; some need shoes, some need dresses, some need other things. . . .

"My little boy is always ailing and he is so sweet and pitiful. You and Syutayev may not have a special love for your *own* children, but we common mortals cannot, and perhaps we do not want to, pervert ourselves and justify our lack of love for a particular person by some sort of love *for the whole world*.

"Enjoy the quiet, write me and don't get upset: after all it is quite the same here whether you are here or not, except that there are fewer guests. I see you rarely even in Moscow; *our lives are sundered*. What kind of a life is it anyway—it is a kind of chaos of work, vanity, lack of thinking, time, health and everything else *that men live by*."

The "little boy" mentioned by Sophia Andreyevna was their son Alexei, born October 31, 1881.

Tolstoy had small interest in society; he wanted to find out how the poor people lived in the city. When he went to Khitrov market that winter he for the first time came face to face with the horrifying, sickly, consumptive city paupers and their doss houses, and having seen them he was revolted.

"City poverty," he wrote in his article *What Then Must We Do?*, "is less honest, more exacting, and more brutal than country poverty."

In order to come closer to these people Tolstoy offered his services to help take the census, a task to be carried out within a three-day period. He undertook this work with the intention of helping all the unfortunate people he could meet. For that purpose he chose as his district the poorest one in the city. But he very soon became convinced that the task he had set himself was beyond his powers to carry out.

"The object of the census is scientific. The census is a piece of sociological research. The object of the science of sociology is the happiness of the people. This science and its methods are in sharp contrast to those of all other sciences. . . .

"The census taker comes into a doss house; in the cellar he finds a man dying of malnutrition and he politely asks: Your last name, first name, patronymic, type of employment; and after some slight qualms about whether or not he should be entered on the lists of the living, he registers him as alive and goes on with his job." This is what Tolstoy wrote in an article on the census in Moscow. At the close he made an appeal for help for these unfortunate beings, and not just in money.

But he very soon realized that his was a voice crying in the wilderness. The whole setup, the economic class divisions, the temptations of urban life—all gave birth to poverty. Help to individuals was either impossible or useless. In individual cases, when Tolstoy gave money, the people spent it on drink, they refused to work; the prostitutes, unused to working, preferred to live the lives to which they were accustomed.

"At the sight of this hunger, cold, poverty, among a thousand people, I realized, not with my mind or my heart but with my whole being, the existence of tens of thousands such in Moscow, while I, along with other thousands of educated people, dined on tenderloins and sturgeon, kept warm blankets on our horses and rugs on our floors—let not all the scholars in the world tell me that this is a necessity—I realized that this is a crime, not committed once but constantly being committed, and that I, with my luxury, am not only an accessory, but a direct party to it," he wrote in his article *What Then Must We Do?*

Tolstoy could not alter the lives of a million persons. He could alter only his own.

"If a man truly does not like slavery and does not want to be a party to it the first thing he will do is to refuse to make use of the labor of others, either by means of service to the state, or by the possession of land, or by means of money," he wrote in this same article.

This conclusion, which with the years grew clearer and clearer to Tolstoy, and which he decided to apply to his life, sounded like the most cruel sentence to his wife.

❧ *37* ❧

SOPHIA ANDREYEVNA still hoped that Tolstoy's ardent interest in religious questions would cool, that he would again become what he had been, a solicitous, albeit strict father, a tender husband, a writer of immortal works of art which would bring him constantly fresh fame. And he, in the depths of his soul, cherished the vague hope that she would come to share his convictions and follow in his path.

Each of them lived and thought in his own way; each was right and incapable of living and thinking otherwise.

"Here all the streams have swollen so it is hard to get through," Tolstoy wrote his wife from Yasnaya Polyana on February 27, 1882. "But now it is freezing and it is blowing so that I have had to heat up a second time. I was just looking over to the Kuzminski house and thinking: why does he torture himself? He works in a place where he does not want to be, and they all do, and we too. They should decide, all of them, to live in Yasnaya summer and winter, bring up their children there. But I know that this is crazily possible and reasonably impossible. Good-by, darling, kisses to you and the children."

"I was in the worst apathetic, depressed state; but I do not regret it nor am I complaining," he wrote again on March 1. "Like a man who has been frozen and regains consciousness and feels pain, so I, in all probability am morally *regaining consciousness*—experiencing all sorts of unnecessary impressions—and I am returning to the control of my own self."

Sophia Andreyevna's letter of March 2 is filled with concern for the health, the nerves of her dear Lyovochka: "When I think of you (which is practically all day) my heart aches, because the impression you make nowadays is that you are unhappy. I am sorry for you and at the same time bewildered: why is this so? For what purpose? All around you everything is all right and happy.

"Please do try to be happy and gay, ask anything of me to that end, anything of course in my power and to the hurt of none but me. There is only one thing that I want now: that is your peace of mind and happiness. Good-by, my dear one; if I had not come to the end of the sheet I would have written a lot more. I kiss you."

They were deeply bound to each other. Sonya knew how hard it was for him to live in the city, but she sincerely believed that there was no other way to organize the life of the family. "Good-by, take a rest, love me, do not curse me for having gotten you into such a state because of Moscow, I kiss you," she wrote him. She advised him to take "care of his health."

"You were in this sad state before, a long time ago; you said: I wanted to hang myself because I 'lacked faith.' But now what? You are not living without faith, why are you unhappy? Didn't you always know that starved, sick, unfortunate and wicked people exist? You would do better to look around; there are also gay, healthy, happy, kind people. May God help you, for what can I do?"

In Yasnaya Polyana Tolstoy found life incomparably easier for him than in Moscow. There, in the midst of nature, he slowly revived, his thoughts clarified, his nerves calmed.

"I lay out solitaires," he wrote his wife on March 2, "I read and I think. I'd like very much to write the article I began. But even if I do not do it this week I shall not be upset. In any case it is healthy for me to get away from all that strenuous city life and withdraw inside myself; to read the thoughts of others on religion, listen to the chatter of Agafia Mikhailovna, to think not about people but about God. Just now Agafia Mikhailovna has been entertaining me with stories about you, and about what sort of a person I would have been if I had married the Arsenyev girl. 'And now you've gone and left her, with her eight children—do as you see fit, but there you sit at home and smooth your beard.'"

Agafia Mikhailovna, or Gasha as we called her, had been a serf belonging to Tolstoy's grandmother, Pelagea Tolstoy. There are no more types like Agafia Mikhailovna. She was proud, headstrong, witty; it was hard to believe that she had been a serf, she bore herself with such independence and authority. Tolstoy prized her and loved to chat with her about the past, when she had been very beautiful and much courted, about dogs and the household economy.

In her old age Agafia Mikhailovna was in charge of Tolstoy's hunting dogs, and was nicknamed the "kennel governess." Toward the end of her life she became so attached to animals that she even fed the mice which got into her room. She had a dim notion of the drama going on between the Tolstoys and she was wholeheartedly on the side of Sophia Andreyevna.

That summer Tolstoy, at the instance of his wife, bought a house in Moscow on Dolgokhamovnicheski Street. He did not look for a place in the aristocratic sections of the city, with a handsome façade and front entrance; he hunted for greenery in the city and found not only a house, but a whole manor.

It was a two-storied wooden structure which stood in the middle of a large court, shut off from the street by a high enclosure; it had all kinds of outhouses—wings, porter's lodge, carriage house, cowshed, stables, kitchens—which formed a more or less complete square. Beyond the house there was a large park with old trees, avenues, flowering shrubs, and a large mound in the center. A winding, shady path led to the top where there was a platform and view over to the immense neighboring park of Count Olsufiev, whose family were great friends of the Tolstoys.

"What a lovely garden," he wrote his wife. "You sit by a window looking out into the garden, and you feel lighthearted and calm. You go into the street; you feel depressed and agitated."

At the far end of the land, for the length of a neighboring brewery building, there was a beaten path leading to a well, the only source of water on the premises. The water was pumped up into a large tub and hauled to the house. In the autumn and spring it was carried in buckets on a yoke, in winter on a sledge.

In the early autumn Tolstoy, wishing to relieve his wife of some of the cares connected with the house, moved to Moscow with the two boys, Sergei and Lev, and the rest of the family remained in Yasnaya Polyana until the repairs were finished.

There were many things to be attended to: the kitchen had to be done over, the stove moved, wallpapers chosen, stairs rebuilt, floors repaired, the cellars put in readiness to store provisions moved up from the country—apples, vegetables, tubs of sour cabbage and pickled cucumbers, jams and marinated foods. Tolstoy worried and had his doubts about the renovations. Would Sonya like the arrangement of the rooms, the choice of wallpapers, the balusters on the stairs?

Meanwhile the news of the change in Tolstoy's mood quickly spread. Some of his articles had already been printed. He continued to work on his *Study and Translation of the Four Gospels, A Critique* of *Dogmatic Theology,* and *What Then Must We Do?* The preface to his *Confession* had already appeared in *Russian Thought,* but the article itself had been banned by the censor.

A tacit watch was put on Tolstoy, especially because of his relations with various sects, principally the Molokans in the province of Samara.

But this did not prevent people who were searching for the truth as he was from seeking communion with him. They came from all walks of life. In Moscow Tolstoy made the acquaintance of aged Rabbi Minor and began to study Hebrew under him. He decided he must study the Bible by reading it in Hebrew.

The spring before the Tolstoy family had acquired a new friend. "As a spark touches off a fire this word has set me all aflame. I realized that I was right, that my childhood world had not faded away, that it had been preserved for my whole life and I owe to it the best I have, whatever has remained in my soul that is sacred and whole. I am going to Moscow to embrace this great man and work for him. . . . I have a boundless love for this man who has opened everything to me. Now I can put a name to what I have loved all my life—he gave it the name, and above all he loved the same thing." This from the notebook of the famous painter and member of the Academy, Nikolai Nikolayevich Gay.

Gay and Tolstoy became instant friends. Faith in Christ's teachings was the basis on which these two unusual men came together. Yet it was not only his deep religious faith and artistic power that drew people to "Grandpa Gay," as the Tolstoy children called him. His childlike, crystal purity, his sincerity and goodness attracted people irresistibly. His kind, pale blue eyes shone with affection, his soft southern speech rang with kindness. His whole body, as smooth and clean as that of a child, his handsome, regular features and rosy cheeks, his round bald spot, edged with an aureole of thick, graying hair, all expressed the one thing: "I like everyone, I wish everyone well, I wish everyone would like me too."

"The famous painter Gay," Sophia Andreyevna wrote to Aunt Tanya about his visit, "is doing my portrait in oils, and very good it is. What a nice, naïve fellow he is—adorable! He is fifty, bald, has clear light blue eyes and a kind look. He came to make Lyovochka's acquaintance; he immediately declared his affection for him and wanted to do something for him. When Tanya came in, he said to Lyovochka: 'Allow me to paint your daughter,' to which Lyovochka replied: 'Better do my wife.' So now I have been sitting to him for a week and he is painting me with an open mouth, in a black velvet bodice with my Alençon lace on it, my hair simply dressed, a very severe and beautiful style of portrait."

Despite the fact that Sophia Andreyevna herself and the rest of the family considered the portrait a success, "Grandpa" was not satisfied and one fine day destroyed it. "It is impossible," he said. "You see a fine lady sitting there in a velvet gown, and it is obvious that she has forty thousand in her pocket. I should paint a woman, a mother. And this one is nothing like."

Four years later Gay painted Sophia Andreyevna with her youngest daughter in her arms. This portrait still hangs in the living room in the Yasnaya Polyana Museum.

Having become one of the family, Grandpa easily established a common bond with Sophia Andreyevna and very soon began to call her "Mamenka."

Under the influence of Tolstoy, Gay painted a series of pictures variously entitled: "What Is Truth?," "The Last Supper" and "The Crucifixion," as well as many others depicting the life of Christ. In these he broke away from the commonly accepted methods of portraying Christ as God. The zealots of the Orthodox faith reproached Gay for having brought Christ down to earth, for having identified Him with *Man*.

In the picture called "What Is Truth"? from the point of view of the ordinary observer, Christ is a harassed, exhausted man. He has been flogged, mocked at; He is suffering, one pities Him, there is no divine majesty in His aspect. The crude strength of earthly physical power is portrayed in Pilate, in the imperious gesture of his hand, his majestic pose, in his whole self-satisfied, full-fleshed figure. "What Is Truth?" asks Pilate with a derisive smile.

In the nineteenth century just as centuries earlier, the existing powers were convinced that only they, the rulers, were given the ability to attain the truth, and they did not recognize the majesty of Christ in His very humility and persecution. The picture when exhibited was ordered removed and any further showing of it was banned.

All this time, through the period of religious searching, Tolstoy had nothing to do with literary activity of an artistic nature. One of the people most distressed by this was Turgenyev. To him Tolstoy sent his *Confession*, which had been banned, and after reading it, Turgenyev wrote Grigorovich:

"It is a remarkable thing in its sincerity, truthfulness and power of conviction. But it is based on false premises and in the end leads to a most gloomy rejection of all human life. . . . And yet Tolstoy is probably the most remarkable man of contemporary Russia."

Turgenyev was ill then, and Tolstoy was sincerely grieved by the news. Later, a letter came from him dated June 27-28, 1883. It was his last.

"Dear and cherished Lev Nikolayevich!" he wrote. "I have not written you for a long time for I have been and am, to speak frankly, in a dying state. I cannot get well and it does no good to think about it. I write you, really, to tell you how happy I am to have been your contemporary, and to express to you my last request. My friend, return to your literary activity. You have, you know, that gift from whence all other things come. Oh, how happy I should be if I could think that my request would have its effect! . . . I am done for, the doctors do not know even how to call my ailment, my *névralgie stomacale goutteuse*. Not to walk, nor eat, nor sleep, nor anything! It's a bore even to list them all over. My friend, great writer of our Russian land, do heed my request. Let me know if you receive this note, and allow me to embrace you once more affectionately, and your wife, all of you. . . . I cannot write any more. . . . I am tired."

On August 22 Turgenyev was dead. The giants of Russian literature of those times had passed to eternity; Tolstoy remained in lonely solitude.

Out of respect for Turgenyev, or out of a desire to pay him a last honor, Tolstoy began to reread Turgenyev's works. When the question arose of an evening devoted to his memory, he readily agreed to take part. But the government was alarmed for fear that Tolstoy would make a speech rather too free-thinking in character. The Governor General of Moscow, Prince V. A. Dolgorukov, called in S. A. Yuriev, president of the Society of Friends of Russian Literature, and ordered him to announce (under some plausible pretext) that the meeting dedicated to the memory of Turgenyev had been indefinitely postponed.

Meanwhile, on April 23, 1883, nearly the entire village of Yasnaya Polyana had gone up in flames. Tolstoy was there at the time.

A fire in a Russian village was a terrifying event. There was no water supply, no fire brigade. In each village of about seventy-five to one hundred families there were two or three wells from which water was drawn by a wooden bucket on a hand-cranked crane or rope. It was almost impossible to check a fire in one house; it spread with lightning rapidity from one straw-thatched roof, one wattle fence, one wooden-beamed cottage to another. Children howled, the peasant women shrilled, the cattle driven out of the sheds bellowed. . . . The smoke- and soot-stained peasants, with an expression of patient suffering on their faces, hauled out the last sticks of furniture from what an hour ago had been dwellings. All was confusion, people milling around, yelling, scolding.

Tolstoy tried to evolve some kind of order; tubs were brought down on a wagon from the manor house, workers came to help. Now here, now there, one could glimpse his tall broad-shouldered figure, giving orders, pouring water on the fire. But it was impossible to check the raging flames.

"I feel so badly for the peasants," Tolstoy wrote to Sonya. "It is difficult to picture to oneself what they have been and still are going through. All their grain is burned. If one could calculate the loss in money it would be more than 10,000 rubles. There will be about 2,000 of insurance money, and the rest will have to be scraped together by the destitute, as they will have to scrape together whatever is needed to keep themselves and their families from dying of cold and starvation."

On the same day he wrote to her again: "I have just been over the burned-out places. It is pitiful and terrible and magnificent—this power, this independence, this confidence in their own strength, and calm. The main need now is for seed oats. Ask my brother Seryozha, if it is not inconvenient for him, to give me an order on Pirogovo for one hundred quarts of oats. The price will be the same, the highest at which he sells it. If he is agreeable send me the order or bring it. You might even telegraph me whether or not Seryozha will give me the order for the oats, because if he is unwilling to do it I must make other arrangements to buy it."

It is very possible that if it had not been for his wife's protests and his sense of duty to his family, Tolstoy would have distributed all his property, which was beginning to disturb him. In order to rid himself of the weight of material cares, the next month he gave his wife full power of attorney to conduct all matters connected with his property, and he himself went off to the province of Samara to liquidate his holdings there. He sold his cattle and horses, and rented out all the land. He was no longer interested in it. Conversation with peasant settlers, his talks on religion with Molokans, the study of the Bible in Hebrew—those were what occupied his thoughts.

Meantime

> Down Yasnaya Polyana way
> Any fine and lovely day
> We were happy, we were gay. . . .

That was the beginning of a comic jingle written by him for the so-called "Post Box." This box hung on the upstairs landing in the main house, near the big old clock with the chimes. Each person wrote whatever came into his head—stories, anecdotes, jokes about each other, verses—and all were put into the box. On Sundays the box was ceremoniously opened and a reading took place. Everyone tried to guess the authors, as there were no signatures; the articles and verses of the head of the house were always the source of the greatest enthusiasm because they were so telling and witty. Ilya Tolstoy, in his memoirs set down one of Tolstoy's contributions:

"Aunt Sonya and Aunt Tanya and in general what Aunt Sonya and Aunt Tanya like."

". . . Aunt Sonya wears a gray bathing suit and goes down into the water slowly, step by step, the cold making her catch her breath; then once in, she plunges properly and with even strokes swims off to a distance.

"Aunt Tanya puts on a tattered checked bonnet, with pink calico strings, jumps recklessly into the deep water and instantly throws herself on her back and floats motionlessly about.

"Aunt Sonya is frightened when the children jump into the water.

"Aunt Tanya rows the children if they are afraid to jump.

"Aunt Sonya, when she is in a difficult situation, thinks: 'Who needs me any more? To whom am I of any use?'

"Aunt Tanya thinks: 'Who can be of use to me? Whom can I send where?'

"Aunt Sonya washes herself in cold water. Aunt Tanya is afraid of cold water.

"Aunt Sonya loves to read about philosophy and converse on serious subjects and astonish Aunt Tanya with terrific words, and she is completely successful in this.

"Aunt Tanya likes to read novels and talk about love. . . .

"Aunt Sonya, when she plays croquet, always finds things for herself and for others to do, such as: sprinkle sand over rocky places,

[254]

mend mallets, and she says that she is too active and not accustomed to sit with folded hands.

"Aunt Tanya plays the game with fury, hating her opponents and forgetting all else.

"Aunt Sonya adores babies, Aunt Tanya is far from adoring them.

"When the little ones get a bump Aunt Sonya caresses them and says: 'Dearie me, darling, just wait and we will bump that old floor —there, there!' and together she and the little tots bang the floor with might and main.

"Aunt Tanya, when a child gets a bump, begins to rub the spot furiously and says: 'May the —— take you, why were you born anyway, and where are the nurses, may the —— take them! Get me some cold water at least.'

"When the children are sick Aunt Sonya broods gloomily over medical books and prescribes opiates. Aunt Tanya, when children are sick, gives them a good scolding and castor oil. . . .

"Aunt Sonya, whenever she is having a good or gay time, immediately has to feel a little sad. Aunt Tanya throws herself wholeheartedly into enjoyment. . . .

"We still haven't decided whose foot is smaller, Aunt Tanya's or Aunt Sonya's. . . ."

One joke that enjoyed an enormous success was a skit also written by Tolstoy and entitled "The Register of the Psychopathic Ward of the Yasnaya Polyana Hospital."

"No. 1 (Lev Nikolayevich). Sanguine nature. Belongs in the peaceful category. The patient is affected by a mania, defined by German psychiatrists as *Weltverbesserungswahn*. . . . The patient's special obsession is that he believes it possible to alter the lives of others by means of the word. General symptoms: dissatisfaction with the existing order, condemnation of everyone except himself, exasperatingly loquacious, without regard to his audience, frequent alternation from anger and irritability to unnaturally tearful sensitiveness. Personal symptoms: occupation with unsuitable and unnecessary work, cleaning and cobbling shoes, grass mowing, etc. Treatment: complete indifference to his speeches on the part of those who hear him, occupations of a nature to absorb all the strength of the patient.

"No. 2 (Sophia Andreyevna). Is in the division of tractables, but at times must be isolated. The patient is affected by the mania *petulanta toropigis maxima*. The patient's special obsession is that she thinks everyone asks her to do everything and she does not have time to get through it all. Symptoms: the solution of problems no one has ever proposed, replies to questions before they are asked, the satisfaction of demands not made. Treatment: intense work. Diet: dissociation from mundane people.

"No. 6 (Tatiana Andreyevna Kuzminskaya). The patient is obsessed by the rather rare mania known as *mania demoniaca complicata*, and offers little hope of a cure. The patient belongs in the dangerous category. Origin of malady: unmerited success in her youth and the habit of having her ambitions satisfied while lacking a moral basis for her life. Symptoms: terror of make-believe, personal devils and a special partiality for all their doings, for every kind of temptation: idleness, luxury, malice. Preoccupation with the life to come, indifference to the life at hand. The patient believes herself to be at all times in the toils of the devil; she enjoys being in his toils and at the same time is afraid of him. . . . The treatment is twofold: either she must admit herself entirely to the devil and his doings, so that the patient can gain a full knowledge of the bitterness inherent in them, or she must be completely divorced from the devil. In the first case it would be well to have two large parties to discredit coquetry, a fortune of two million, two months of absolute idleness and a lawsuit for some offense before the justice of the peace. In the second case: bear three or four children, nurse them, have a life full of occupation and intellectual development. Diet: in the first case: truffles and champagne, all lace dresses, three new ones every day. In the second case: cabbage soup, porridge, on Sundays cheese cakes of sweetened curds, a dress of one color and style, to do for her whole life."

There was a lot of fun poked at the pleasures of the young people and the weaknesses of their elders in the "Post Box" communications. No one was ever offended; all waited with impatience for Sunday to come around. The main purveyor and the soul of the institution was Tolstoy himself. His writing and his preoccupation with religion did not deter him from participating with almost childlike gaiety in the games of the youngsters often laughing with them till he cried over some successful prank.

This same summer of 1883 Tolstoy finished his article on "In What Does My Faith Consist?" and at the end of September he sent it to be printed. But again, as was his inveterate habit, he made many alterations and it was only at the end of January, 1884, that it was finally ready. This article met with the same fate as his *Confession*; the censor banned it, and it was distributed in hectograph or mimeograph copies.

"In What Does My Faith Consist?" showed more than anything previously written by Tolstoy his inexorable break with the church, his profession of the teachings of Christ, that is to say nonresistance to evil by force, as his guiding principle.

"I do not wish to expound the teachings of Christ, I wish only to tell how I came to comprehend what there is in the teachings of Christ that is simple, clear, understandable and beyond doubt, what is addressed to all the people, and also how what I did not comprehend gave me a change of heart, peace and happiness," he said.

"I could not understand this life. It seemed to me to be dreadful. And suddenly I understood the words of Christ, I understood them, and both life and death ceased to seem evil, and instead of despair I experienced the joy and the happiness of life untouched by death.

"The passage which to me was the key to everything else, is in the 5th chapter of Matthew, verses 38-39: '. . . It hath been said, An eye for an eye, and a tooth for a tooth: But I say unto you, That ye resist not evil.' Suddenly for the first time I understood these verses directly and simply. I understood that Christ says the very thing he intends to say. And immediately it was not that anything new appeared, but that everything which obscured the truth fell away, and the truth stood before me in all its meaning. 'Ye have heard that it hath been said by them of old time, An eye for an eye, and a tooth for a tooth. But I say unto you, That ye resist not evil.' These words suddenly seemed to me quite new, as if I had never heard them before."

Tolstoy's theory aroused all sorts of derision and criticism. Many people deliberately distorted the meaning of this principle by ignoring the words "by force." They asserted that Tolstoy refused to fight evil; they called him an anarchist, a revolutionary, an atheist. There were only a few who thought through all the way his interpretation of the Gospels. These few were drawn to Tolstoy, seeking support and the solution of the doubts which beset them.

In September, 1883, Tolstoy was called into court in the county seat to act as a juror. On the 29th, he wrote to his wife: "I have just come from Krapivna. I went there on a call for jury duty. I arrived before three o'clock. The court was already in session, so they fined me 100 rubles. When they called on me I said I could not be a juror. They asked: 'Why not?' I said: 'Because of my religious convictions.' Then they asked me again whether my refusal was final. I said I could not act under any circumstances, and left. Now they will probably fine me another 200 rubles and I do not know whether it will end there. I think probably it will. But please do not be cross with me because I did not tell you I had been appointed a juror. I would have told you had you asked: but I did not want to tell you on purpose. You would have been upset; it would have agitated me, and I was already agitated enough. I had to exert all my strength to calm myself."

Sophia Andreyevna was not angry. Uneasiness and tender affection shine through the letter she wrote in reply: "I imagine this will not reach you and you evidently will be arriving here soon. God grant you will. The whole matter with the jury did upset me awfully after all. I wanted to go at once to F. Perfiliev and ask what they might do to you, but I was afraid you might not like me to. Not having had any reply to my telegram I began to be uneasy for fear they may have arrested you.

"How much trouble lies ahead! And how could you conceal anything from me! That distressed me. Perhaps I would have gone with you myself. And now I think perhaps you will soon get here, if there is only a fine, it is no matter. But if they sue you it will be bad. I do not know what I would have done in your place. I do not think I would have found in myself the fervor of a youngster on behalf of some truth or other. Most likely I think I would have thought about how not to distress anybody too much. I am writing awfully incoherently; I still haven't digested what is in your letter; and besides the babies, Kostenka, the children, the noise—all this makes me stupid. Misha has slobbered over and messed up this letter, while I was trying to teach Andryusha to read.

"Good-by, see you soon, I trust. If only everything turns out well. I kiss you. Sonya."

Tolstoy perceived with joy and gratitude every expression of understanding and sympathy on the part of his wife.

"I have just received from Kozlovka your two letters and telegram: two wonderful letters," he wrote her. "From both of them I see that you are in the good mood I love, in which I left you, and in which, with small interruptions, you have been for a long time.— Read this letter when you are alone. I have never thought about you as I do now, so much, with such good and quite unmixed feelings. From every angle you are dear to me."

And though their inner divorce seemed inevitable, their deep devotion to each other and their love for the children gave rise in both to the hope that any moment there might be a change and life would resume its old course.

But this hope was never to be realized.

❧ 38 ❧

IN THE autumn of 1883 Tolstoy made the acquaintance of Vladimir Grigoryevich Chertkov.

Chertkov came from a very wealthy, aristocratic, liberal family. He was more than usually handsome and well built. One needed only to look at him, observe the proud carriage of his head, his huge, protruding cold eyes, his high-bridged nose, to realize that this imperious young man could never pass unnoticed. When, in the stunning uniform of a cavalry guards regiment, he made his appearance at court balls, the ladies went mad about him; and the colder, the more indifferent his manner to them, the greater his success. The story was told that a lady from the imperial family went up to him at a court ball during a waltz, indicating her desire to dance with him. Chertkov bowed politely and said that he was not dancing. This was a piece of unheard-of audacity. The court circles were horrified, and the social busybodies were thrilled to pass the story around.

Chertkov was witty. He told anecdotes and made jokes with an impassive expression, while those around him rocked with laughter. He spoke French and German extremely well, and English like an Englishman, with a slightly exaggerated British accent, but like many aristocrats brought up on European languages he spoke Russian badly, with a strong foreign accent.

In 1879 Chertkov wished to resign his commission, but his father, who had spent his life in service at court, first as aide-de-camp to Emperor Nicholas I, then as adjutant-general to Emperor Alexander

II and Alexander III, and who dreamed of a brilliant court career for his son tried to persuade him to take a leave of absence and go to England. Chertkov had known Emperor Alexander II since childhood. The Emperor used to come informally to call on Chertkov's mother, and his murder made a powerful impression on the young man. However, despite his father's opposition, Chertkov did resign his commission and decided to make a radical change in his life.

Chertkov's mother, an exceptionally intelligent, tactful and beautiful woman, had great influence over her son. Her family was closely associated with the Decembrists, and her sister married a wealthy landowner, a retired colonel in a cavalry guards regiment, named A. V. Pashkov. In 1874 Pashkov had met Lord Radstock, an English preacher, and been so carried away by his teaching—salvation from sin by faith in redemption, in Christ's blood given for man—that he withdrew from mundane society and devoted himself to spreading the teachings of Radstock and of his own sect, which acquired the name of "Pashkovtsy." One of the convinced followers of the Pashkovtsy was Chertkov's mother; consequently freedom of thought, which passed beyond the bounds of autocracy and orthodoxy, was not new to young Chertkov.

Cards, carousing, women, all that constituted the interest of the gilded youth of St. Petersburg, were obnoxious to Chertkov. He like Tolstoy began to search for the meaning of life. He went off to his estate in the province of Voronezh, and did what he could for the peasants. At the house of a friend he met N. V. Davydov, prosecuting attorney for the Tula district court, who had been to Yasnaya Polyana; and through him Chertkov discovered that his views were close to those of Tolstoy. Shortly thereafter he went up to Moscow to see him.

For Tolstoy the meeting with Chertkov was an occasion of great joy. It was evident at once that there was no serious divergence in their views. In his memoirs Chertkov tells about the meeting.

"In Lev Nikolayevich," he wrote, "I met the first person who with wholehearted conviction shared the attitude I had toward military service. When I put my usual question to him he, in reply, began to read to me from a manuscript lying on the table—'In What Does My Faith Consist?'—his categoric rejection of military service from the Christian point of view, and I was filled with such joy. . . ."

"As far as I know he also found in me his first adherent to that view." Chertkov was mistaken in saying he was the first, because Tolstoy had already found in the peasant Syutayev and N. N. Gay others who shared his views. However, Chertkov was the first follower who devoted his life to spreading Tolstoy's writings. At this time Gay, after a year's acquaintance with Tolstoy, was quite at home in his house. He was such an intimate friend that Tolstoy allowed him a privilege not enjoyed by even those closest to him. He allowed him to come into his study while he was working. Tolstoy's study was a very particular place. The ceiling was low; you could touch it with your hands. The furniture was upholstered in black oilcloth—a sofa, a big armchair. At the window was a large writing table with an open work rail on three sides. It was quiet in the study, the windows opened onto the garden, family life was far away—the dining room, the nurseries were down in the other half of the house.

His protruding lips moving, Tolstoy would sit and work on his article "In What Does My Faith Consist?" While on tiptoe, for fear of disturbing his friend, "Grandpa" Gay would steal into the room with palette and paints. Both would remain completely silent, each absorbed in his own work.

Gay's portrait is about the best ever painted of Tolstoy. The pose, the angle of the head, even the magnificently drawn right hand holding the pen—all convey a profound concentration of thought.

The number of Tolstoy's followers grew. Despite the fact that his religio-philosophic articles were banned by the censor, they enjoyed a wide distribution throughout Russia. A copy of one of his articles penetrated the precincts of the Nicholas Institute for Wellborn Young Ladies in Moscow, an arch-monarchical and Orthodox establishment, where it fell into the hands of two of the preceptresses—Olga Alexeyevna Barshteva and Maria Alexandrovna Schmidt. It had a tremendous effect on the two ladies. They decided to read everything Tolstoy had written about religion and, without delay, went to call on him in the hope of obtaining from him the *Study and Translation of the Four Gospels*.

Tatiana wrote in her memoirs that Tolstoy "received the ladies very graciously, had a good talk with them and they immediately felt in him an intimate and dear person."

"After that," she added, "Maria Alexandrovna and Olga Alexeyevna began to come frequently to our house. They were called

'Papa's *dames de classe*.' Everyone treated them with friendliness and affection."

These ladies, who had spent their entire lives in institutional and city surroundings, knew nothing about the country or manual work. Yet, their hearts aflame with enthusiasm, they converted all their city possessions into cash, took the sum of their not very considerable savings and set out for the Caucasus. On the way they were robbed of all their money. But they soon consoled themselves. They were intent on simpler ways, on life and work on the land; they had no need of money. Olga Alexeyevna unable to stand the hard life, passed away; Maria Alexandrovna, after the death of her companion, continued her laborious existence in the neighborhood of Yasnaya Polyana.

It was not easy for the Tolstoy children to find their way around in the complex emotions being experienced by their parents. Their father's new friends sometimes were the source for them of good-natured merriment. They were as anxious as everyone else to live simply, but they could not escape their father's dissatisfaction and it worried them, each one in his own way.

In the winter of 1883-1884, when she was twenty, Tanya began to go into society. Everyone had great regard and affection for her. When her parents quarreled, Tanya did her best to calm and console them; when her brothers were rude to their mother, she shamed them and they heeded her. The little ones clung to her. Ilya was proud of and admired his sister; her opinion of him was far from a matter of indifference. Even the oldest, Sergei, who was already twenty-one, recognized Tanya's authority. She was fond of painting and made good progress in the School of Painting and Sculpture. She had a remarkable gift for getting likenesses, and Grandpa Gay loved to help her with technical advice. Tanya liked people; she bewitched them. Unlike Sergei, who hid kindness often under a rude exterior, she was not afraid of showing her feelings and she felt an equally ardent affection for each of her parents.

The emergence in the social world of the wife of the famous writer, herself beautiful and still young, together with her pretty daughter, caused a stir in Moscow. They were invited everywhere. Both in society and in her school Tanya had admirers. Her father did not approve of her idle life, and frowned on her admirers. Her mother was overjoyed by Tanya's success and kept an eye out for a good match for her favorite daughter. Tanya was not beautiful; she was attractive. She had a wonderful complexion, brilliant dark-brown eyes, a short, sharply chiseled pert little nose, wavy chestnut hair, a slim, graceful figure and with them talent, wit and a buoyant charm. She was pleasing to old and young. In social circles she enchanted everyone with her tact, her ability to handle herself, her wit and gaiety; simple people were attracted to her by her goodness and unaffected manners.

"You are probably just getting ready to go to a ball. How I pity you and Tanya," Tolstoy wrote his wife on January 30, 1884, from Yasnaya Polyana, where he went with increasing frequency.

On the same day Sophia Andreyevna wrote her husband: "Today I and Tanya, who slept in my room, got up at one o'clock in the afternoon. The ball yesterday was wonderful, we were prudent and expected to leave after four o'clock. But the carriage wasn't there and we had to wait an hour. Too bad! Otherwise we should not have been tired at all. Dolgorukov was there in person; he again urged us to come to his ball tonight. It's a bore but we shall go, but later."

Prince V. A. Dolgorukov was at that time Governor General of Moscow and it was a great honor to be invited by him to a ball.

"Yesterday at the ball," Sophia Andreyevna wrote the following day, "Dolgorukov was more amiable than he has ever been. He had a chair brought so that he could sit beside me, and chatted for a whole hour, which even puzzled me a little. He said a quantity of agreeable things to Tanya," and then, as if to comfort him, she added: "Yet we did not feel exactly gay yesterday, no doubt we were too tired."

To her sister Tanya, Sophia Andreyevna described a ball at the Samarins': "It was a wonderful ball and supper, a gala that no other ball has matched. Tanya wore a pink gauze dress with plush roses, I had on a lilac velvet dress with yellow pansies of all shades. Then there was a ball at the Governor General's and an evening with a play at the Teplovys', and then the Christmas tree for the little ones, and today another ball at Count Orlov-Davydov's, and Tanya and I are going. She has a wonderful dress—tulle illusion, greenish-pale blue and covered with lilies of the valley of a pinkish cast. Tomorrow there will be a big ball at the Obolenskis, more dancing. They have simply run Tanya and me off our feet."

Meanwhile in Yasnaya Polyana Tolstoy continued to live simply, without footmen and chefs. He chopped wood and learned to cobble shoes at the local shoemaker's.

"I am well and happy," he wrote to his wife. "I am reading Montaigne, I go skiing for no good reason, but I get very tired, I cobble shoes and meditate and try not to offend anyone. I do not even try to do anything useful for anyone that is impossibly difficult. I did a lot of work today (cobbling), I went to the baths and I am very tired."

The bathhouse was a simple thatched and timbered little cabin near the pond. On Saturdays the water was hauled in pails to fill the caldrons on the iron stove. The floor was spread with clean straw which smelled of rye bread. When the stove was red hot, pails of water were splashed on it to sizzle and form a heavy, thick cloud of steam. The bathers perspired for hours there, scrubbing themselves and perspiring again. Sometimes in the winter when they were overcome by the steam they would rush out and roll in the snow and then return to steam themselves again. The baths were a relaxation, a pleasure and a necessity. Not everyone, even a rich peasant, had a bath in his own home. Sophia Andreyevna had insisted on having a bathroom installed at Yasnaya Polyana, but there was no running water (nor was there any in their home in Moscow) so that whenever any member of the family took a bath the porter had to drive for nearly half a mile to get the water in tubs.

In the forenoons he wrote. In the afternoons, depending on the season, he worked out of doors or in the fields: plowing, sawing, mowing. His evenings were spent in reading. In this period of especially intense thinking, during the eighties, he reread a great many books, from Marcus Aurelius, Epictetus, Confucius and Lao-tse, to Pascal, Montaigne, Parker and Emerson. "I must compile a reading circle," he wrote in his diary for March 15, 1884.

He continued to urge his wife to exchange the luxurious, idle life of the family for a simple, useful one. He was tormented by the fact that his children were being brought up in idleness, not knowing even how to wait on themselves, that they did not inquire seriously into life, had no deep interests.

His relations with his wife were growing more and more strained. "Qualms of soul are terrible, not only sad, painful, but also difficult," he wrote in his diary on May 3. "It is just as though I alone am not mad, I live in a madhouse run by madmen," he wrote on May 28. Meantime Sophia Andreyevna was expecting her twelfth child.

She did not wish to have any more children and in the beginning of her pregnancy she did everything to get rid of the child. The endless births, the nursing, the illnesses, had exhausted her and shattered her nerves.

Frequently during the spring of this year Tolstoy thought of leaving home. But love for his wife, despite their inner discord, and love for the children restrained him. During the night from the 17th to the 18th of June a terrible quarrel took place between the Tolstoys. Tolstoy could no longer restrain himself and left. Then remembering that his wife was on the verge of her confinement, he reconsidered and returned.

"I cut some grass around the house in the evening," he wrote in his diary. "A peasant came to see me about the estate. I went to bathe. Came back in a buoyant, gay frame of mind, and suddenly my wife began to make some silly reproaches about the horses which I don't need and which I won't get rid of. I said nothing but I became very much depressed. I went out and wanted to go away entirely, but her confinement made me turn back when I was halfway to Tula. At home two bearded men—my young sons—were playing whist. 'She's on the croquet ground [we had no lawns], didn't you see her?' sister Tanya said. 'I don't want to see her.' I went to my room to sleep on the sofa, but I couldn't, I was so unhappy. Oh, how hard it is! And yet I am sorry for her. I had just fallen asleep after two o'clock when she came in and wakened me: 'Forgive me, the baby is coming, perhaps I'll die.' Then she went upstairs. The birth began— what should have been the most joyous happy event in a family all went by like something unnecessary and hard. A wet nurse has been called in. If someone runs the affairs of our lives I would like to put some blame on him. It's all too difficult and ruthless. Ruthless with regard to her. I can see that she is moving at an increasing rate of speed toward destruction and suffering—frightful, spiritual sufferings. I fell asleep at eight. Woke up at twelve. So much came back to my mind I sat down to write. When my brother arrived from Tula I for the first time told him the whole burden of my situation. . . ."

Toward morning on June 18 a third daughter was born to the Tolstoys and they named her Alexandra in honor of Alexandrine Tolstoy, who had agreed to be her godmother.

It is difficult to picture the complex inner struggle which was going on in Tolstoy during this period of his life. He was searching for a way out and could not find it. Go on with a life which to him appeared wicked—of that he was incapable. Yet he felt he did not have the right to abandon his wife and his children, and there was no one who could advise him intelligently.

One of the causes of the Tolstoys' quarrel was that Sophia Andreyevna had categorically refused to nurse her new daughter, and had hired a stout, healthy peasant woman from a neighboring village who simultaneously nursed Sasha Tolstoy and her own child.

"All is well with us physically speaking," Tolstoy wrote to Chertkov on June 24. "My wife has given birth to a little girl. But my joy has been poisoned by the fact that my wife, despite my clearly stated opinion that to hire a wet nurse away from her own child to feed a stranger is a most inhuman, unreasonable and unchristian act, nevertheless and without any reason took a wet nurse from her living child. All this happens somehow without our understanding, as if in a dream. I wrestle with myself, but it's hard. I am sorry for my wife."

And later on in the same letter he wrote: "Poor people that we are, how far we have strayed. There are a lot of people here now —my children and those of the Kuzminskis—and I often cannot look without horror at this immoral idleness and gluttony. There are so many of them, and yet they are so big and powerful. I look at them and I know how much farm work there is to do all around us. But they go out riding, soil their clothing, their bed linen, their rooms. Others do all the work for them, and they do not do anything, not even for themselves. Yet this seems the most natural thing to everyone, and so it did to me; and I took part in introducing this order of things. I see this clearly, nor can I for a minute forget it. I feel that I am a kind of killjoy for them, but they, so it seems to me, begin to sense that there is something not quite right. We have occasional talks—good ones. This happened awhile back: Our youngest daughter, Masha, was ill, I came to see her and I and the girls began to talk about what they did all day. They were a little ashamed to tell, but they did tell and even told the bad things they did. We repeated this the next day and once after that. I did so dreadfully wish that I could draw them into the way of getting together every evening to tell about their day and their sins! It seemed to me this would be wonderful, on condition, of course, that it was done quite freely. . . ."

The two daughters—attractive Tanya and skinny thirteen-year-old

Masha—listened responsively to their father. His influence over them was imperceptibly making itself felt; they tried to live better lives, to be less idle; they decided to take care of their own rooms, give up eating meat. Tolstoy himself had become a vegetarian, and he was trying to give up smoking.

Masha was like her father. She had the same deep-set intelligent, soul-piercing gray eyes, the unbecoming wide mouth. The first thought one had on seeing this thin, sickly little girl, with her pigtail, especially in contrast with Tanya, was: "Poor little thing, how ill-favored and colorless she is. . . ." And Masha, as though she sensed this, always kept in the background. She was not spoiled by too much affection from her mother. Lev, born a year before her, ailing Andryusha, and Tanya were the mother's favorites. The penetrating eyes of the little girl often rested on her father; his words, frequently not quite comprehensible to her, lodged in her heart. Masha took in a great deal, although the grownups did not realize it, and with her whole being craving affection, she was shyly drawn to her father.

At times the family squabbles subsided. Tolstoy, absorbed in writing his *Study and Translation of the Four Gospels*, gave in and did his best to adjust himself to the life of the family.

"We are living in the country," he wrote to Chertkov on October 3, 1884, "I, my wife, two daughters, the three little boys and the newborn baby girl. *And I am not in error in saying that we are very well off*—everything is in the open, friendly and not unrighteous. In the course of the summer I have enjoyed many quiet but great pleasures. In my family there is a big drift toward me, and the happiness I feel I cannot convey to you. The joys I have never experienced are to see the softening of hearts, the renouncing of former ways, the recognition of the truth, and the feeling that one has had a part in this. The elder boys are in Moscow and so by inertia, no doubt, we shall go up there. My wife says it will be about the 20th. But life in Moscow will be different. There is no talk about society. I still don't see how I can go. I feel that I don't need to go anywhere. . . ."

And in the end, when the rest of the family went up to Moscow, he remained in Yasnaya Polyana. On October 23rd Sophia Andreyevna wrote: "I realize that you stayed in Yasnaya not because of that intellectual work which I set above all else in life, but in order to play at some sort of Robinson Crusoe game. You sent away

Andrian, who was crazy to stay out the month, you let the chef go who would have been glad not to receive his pension for nothing, and from morning to night you are going to be doing footless physical work, which among the simple people is done by young men and women. So it really would be better for you to live with your children. You will say, of course, what kind of life is that— you mean according to your beliefs, and that you are well off as it is; in that case all I can say is: 'Enjoy yourself,' and yet I can but feel distressed that such brains are being wasted on chopping wood, lighting the samovar, cobbling shoes—all of which is fine as relaxation or change of work, but not as a special occupation."

The next day, Tolstoy outlined to his wife his plan to manage the estate of Yasnaya Polyana without a steward.

". . . I have come to see clearly," he wrote in explanation, "that if what I consider the truth and a rule of life for people is really to become the rule, it can only be accomplished if we, the rich, the oppressors, will arbitrarily renounce wealth and oppression; and this will be accomplished not suddenly, but by means of a gradual process leading to that end. . . ."

Sophia Andreyevna replied: "I myself have thought exactly that: that is to say, in relation to the estate where you live more than half the year, it is lacking in conscientiousness not to manage it yourself and especially because of the relationship with the common people; you can get the same profit, I think even a larger one, and all that is otherwise lost, stolen, wasted through mismanagement, all this one can use intelligently to distribute as help for, and to divide with, the peasants. The relation will be most agreeable—the profit from Yasnaya has been so trifling it is not worth mentioning, but with your skill and brains (when you choose to apply them) you can manage anything extremely well. . . . I do not know whether I have understood you but I am answering you as I have been able to understand you."

So the Tolstoys' family life flowed on. At times it seemed as though all was calm and that they could, living together, each follow his own path. Perhaps this might have been possible had there been no children, but to Tolstoy the circumstances of their upbringing were intolerable—even though he knew himself to be in part to blame.

At times, when he felt especially depressed, he would go away— as he did in March, 1885, to the Crimea with his friend Prince L. D.

Urusov. Urusov had been ill and the doctors had ordered him to a mild climate. It was the first time since the Sevastopol campaign that Tolstoy had been in the Crimea.

"We drove over the places which had seemed inaccessible, where the enemy were situated, and it was strange: the memory of the war is linked with a feeling of buoyancy and youth," he wrote to his wife. All the time he was away he wrote to her almost daily. As always, he enjoyed nature, took long excursions, sometimes on horseback, sometimes on foot, but his attention was not concentrated on the beauties of the Crimean landscape. What he saw everywhere was the people, the poor, the aged, ill-treated by the rich Tatars.

Sophia Andreyevna had to spend August of that summer in Moscow because of the examinations Ilya and Lev had to retake. Her worries and responsibilities were increasing. By now she was attending to the publication of her husband's writings, which afforded a constant and rather large income. She handled the proofs; she kept track of income and expenses. To his mother's great distress, Ilya failed his examination. Science did not interest him; his dream was to work on the estate, and live in the country. He decided to quit school, and went off to Yasnaya Polyana, while his mother remained in Moscow with Lev, who was more successful in his second examination.

That autumn while Tolstoy was in Yasnaya Polyana with Tanya and the younger children, a Jew by the name of Feinermann appeared, settled in the village and began to teach the children to read and write. The local authorities put a stop to it. In order to obtain a license to teach, Feinermann had to accept the Orthodox faith. He was baptized in the local church with Tanya acting as his godmother—to the horror of the children's governess, Madame Seuron, whom the Tolstoys had nicknamed *la grande dame* because of her manners. Sophia Andreyevna's indignation, when she heard about this, brought forth a fresh dispute between her and her husband.

Tolstoy wrote about the matter to Chertkov on August 29: "I do not condemn Feinermann's conversion to orthodoxy. I do not think I should have been able to go through with it because I cannot picture to myself a situation in which it would not be better to speak and act the truth. . . ."

Tolstoy remained in Yasnaya Polyana until late in the autumn, after the young people had rejoined their mother in Moscow. He made no plans; he "lived" as he wrote his wife, "as long as life was possible."

But his sense of peace did not last for long. When he arrived in Moscow and found himself enveloped by the idle, aristocratic life of the city, he again began to be unhappy. By the end of December he reached his limit of despair and exasperation.

"There happened," Sophia Andreyevna wrote to her sister Tanya, "what has already happened so many times: Lyovochka got into a state of extreme nervousness and depression. Once I was sitting there, writing, and he came in: I looked at him, his face was terrible. Up to this point we had been getting along beautifully: not an unpleasant word had been said, literally, not a single thing. 'I came to tell you that I want a divorce, I cannot live this way, I am going to Paris, or America.'

"You can realize, Tanya, that if the whole house had tumbled down about my ears I should not have been so astounded. I asked with amazement: 'What has happened?'

" 'Nothing, but if you pile more and more on a load the horse will get up, but not pull it.'—What has been piled up I do not know. But then the fracas began, reproaches, harsh words, it grew worse and worse, but I was patient, went on being patient and scarcely made any reply. I saw that the man was mad and when he said, 'Wherever you are the air is polluted,' I sent for a trunk and began to pack. I intended to come to you for a few days. Then the children ran in and howled. Tanya said: 'I'll go away with you, what's it all for!' Then he implored me to remain. I stayed but suddenly there was an outbreak of hysterical sobbing, it was simply awful, imagine Lyovochka all trembling and twitching with sobs. Thereupon I was sorry for him, the four children, Tanya, Ilya, Lelya, Masha, were all howling at the top of their lungs: I was overcome by a kind of stupor, I couldn't speak, couldn't cry, all I wanted to do was talk nonsense and I was afraid to do that, so I was silent for three hours, I couldn't for the life of me utter a word. That was how it all ended. But the sadness, the grief, the explosion, the painful sense of estrangement—all that has remained with me—you know, I sometimes ask myself over and over until I am quite beside myself: now then, what's it all for? I do not set foot out of doors, I work on the publications until three o'clock in the morning, I am quiet, I always loved everyone so much, and I have been thinking about them all this time as never before, and to what end?"

"What is it best to do?" Tolstoy wrote Chertkov between the 9th and 15th of December: "Suffer and lie, as I lie now with all my life—whether I am sitting at a table, in bed, allowing my writings to be sold, signing papers on electoral rights, allowing fines to be paid by the peasants and authorizing their prosecution for stealing my property. Either I must break this all up—or deliver myself up to exasperation. To break up everything, free myself from lies without being irritated, is something I am still unable to do. I pray—that is I seek God to find the path to a solution and do not find it." (This letter was never sent. A.T.)

After the painful scene Tolstoy and his daughter Tanya went off to the nearby estate of their friends the Olsufievs.

On December 20, after he had calmed down, Tolstoy wrote his wife: "I have said and I repeat this one thing: you must discriminate and decide *what is good and what is evil, and in what direction you should go*; but if you do not clarify this you must not be surprised if you will suffer yourself and others will suffer. As to the necessity of doing something at once—there is nothing to say because there are no compulsions for the people who have money, a roof, and food—they have nothing to do except weigh things and live as is best. But for God's sake let us never speak of this again. I will not."

39

THOUGH Tolstoy had long since given up his school work, the necessity of educating the peasantry continued to weigh on his mind. In those days in Russia there was a "bast books" literature (named from the bast sandals worn by Russian peasants in lieu of boots or shoes). Book peddlers went from house to house, village to village, selling chromos in vivid colors, primitive poetry, dream and song books. This vulgar, inartistic literature had not contributed either to the moral or intellectual development of readers among the people. And despite their limited literacy, the workingmen and peasants were extremely discriminating in their taste; they liked and appreciated good pictures and honest writing and sensed the meretriciousness of the pseudo-popular literature served up to them.

On February 5, 1884, Tolstoy wrote to his wife from Yasnaya Polyana: "Pyotr Osipov [Pyotr Osipov Zyabrev was a peasant in Yasnaya Polyana. He worked all his life to educate himself, read a great deal, collected books] is very interesting on the subject of popular reading. He brought me his library—a box of books; these were the *Lives* [of the Saints], *Catechisms, Our Native Tongue, History, Geography,* the *Russian Herald,* Galakhov's *Anthology,* and some novels. He stated his opinion on each kind of book. And all this was most interesting to me, and it made me think about many things and revise my ideas of popular reading."

A few days later he wrote to Chertkov: "I am more and more drawn to the idea of publishing a book for the education of Russians. I purposely avoid the word 'people' because the essence of the idea is that there should be no division into those who are of the people and those who are not. . . . I dare not believe it will come off, I fear to believe it because it would be too wonderful if it did."

The writer Danilevski included in his memoirs a conversation with Tolstoy on this subject.

". . . These millions of literate Russians stand before us like so many young daws with open mouths," said Tolstoy, "and they say to us: 'Gentlemen, writers of our own land, throw us some mental food worthy of yourselves and us: write for us who crave living, literary works, rescue us from the cheap Eruslan Lazareviches, stories about lords, and other market-place wares.' The simple honest Russian people deserves an answer to this cry from its fine and true heart."

"I have thought a great deal about this," Danilevski added, "and decided, so far as in my power lay, to make an effort in this field." But good will was not enough.

"Prisoner in the Caucasus," "God Sees the Truth but Waits," "What Men Live By," "Where Love Is, God Is" and other stories flowed naturally from Tolstoy's pen. He did not "make an effort," to write. He could not but write.

When, in the autumn of 1884, a publishing house called The Mediator (Poszrednik) was founded, one of the chief difficulties which faced those working on its staff was the choice of books both artistically valid and fit for general consumption. Chertkov applied himself with great zeal to the task. He secured the agreement of the better-known writers and artists to collaborate with The Mediator and suggested to the editor, Ivan Dmitriyevich Sytin, that he print and distribute pictures and little books for the peasants, instead of the cheap material he was publishing in great quantities.

[272]

Sytin himself had been a peasant; he went through the four years of a village school, but had little other education. However, he was intelligent and resourceful—the kind of businessman of whom they say, "He won't take what belongs to another, but neither will he give up anything he has." It was thanks only to him that Tolstoy was able to break into the mass public. As a boy Sytin had worked temporarily in a bookstore, where his parents had placed him. He studied the business and later opened his own bookshop, which gradually grew and turned into one of the largest book publishing houses of Russia. He also published the newspaper the *Russian Word (Russkoye Slovo)*, which had one of the widest circulations in Russia.

When Chertkov first began to talk to him about the necessity of popular education for the workers and peasants, the idea that public welfare or Christian duty demanded it, was new and strange to him. Sytin had been accustomed to look at any business from the point of view of what the figures showed. But Chertkov impressed him by his aristocratic bearing, his stubborn insistence, his commanding manner. The names he mentioned of writers such as Tolstoy, Leskov, Garshin, Korolenko, and artists such as Gay, Repin, Kramskoy and others— as contributors to the future popular publishing house—were well known to Sytin; and, after a slight hesitation, he agreed to put out cheap booklets at eighty kopecks a hundred for wide distribution among the peasant masses.

Toward the end of 1884 Chertkov introduced his friend P. I. Biryukov to Tolstoy. Biryukov came from the gentry in the province of Kostroma. He had gone through the Naval Academy and had the prospect of a brilliant career in the Navy. But he was not interested in that. When he became familiar with Tolstoy's ideas, he threw himself ardently into working with Chertkov to establish The Mediator.

It was not easy. They demanded in the material they published not only literary merit of a high order, but an approach in harmony with their own basic ideas.

Out of this activity grew a lively correspondence between Tolstoy and Chertkov on religious and philosophic questions in general, and an exchange of views about Tolstoy's own works. Hence it came about quite naturally that Chertkov should undertake the distribution and translation into foreign languages of Tolstoy's writings, and gradually become the chief editor of his works. He did this work conscientiously, and saw to it that Tolstoy did not indulge in the slightest contradiction or deviation from his principles. Though he valued Tolstoy as an artist, his main interest lay in the principle of nonresistance expressed in Tolstoy's writings. Tolstoy could not but love the peasants—to him they were the basis, the essence of Russian life. Chertkov had no knowledge or understanding of them and no affection for them—he saw the peasantry only as a "laboring" and unfortunate class in Russia.

There is no moralizing in Tolstoy's artistic works, and very little in his popular tales. One may draw various conclusions from their contents, but there is nothing artificial in them. A good piece of writing, as Gogol put it "sings itself out of you," it is something all of a piece, with the positive and negative features of the types described. As in musical composition, every false note destroys the harmony. Did Chertkov realize this?

In a letter to Tolstoy, written after he had just read "Prisoner in the Caucasus" for the first time, he said: "I liked it immensely. But I must speak of one thing quite frankly . . . On page 20 it says: 'The Tatar fell ill, so they came to Zhilin: "Go cure him," they said. Zhilin had no notion of how to cure anyone. He went over, looked at him and thought to himself: "Chances are he'll get well by himself!" Then he went out into the shed, took some water and sand and mixed them. In the presence of the Tatars he murmured words over the water and gave it to the sick man to drink. To his good luck the Tatar recovered.' And then again on page 23. 'Zhilin, wishing to spy out the surrounding country, said to the youngster who was guarding him: "I shan't go far, I'm just going to climb up that mountain: I have to find some herbs, to cure your people." '

"If one looks at Zhilin as representing a living person with his virtues and defects, then, from the literary point of view, the introduction of negative features may, perhaps, add reality to the type described. But I look at the book from the point of view of its practical influence on a sensitive reader, and I am sure that these two passages are bound to evoke in such readers an approving smile and consequently to give them one more push in the already too easy direction of thinking that it is incomparably more practical not to choose one's means too carefully in gaining one's ends. That is why I should so much like to obtain your permission to delete these few lines in the popular edition. . . ."

To this letter Tolstoy made the following reply: "I gladly accept and thank you for your proposal to cut out the passages about which you wrote. But do this yourself." As an artist Tolstoy himself could not make such corrections.

But what importance would Tolstoy ascribe to these trivial points in comparison with the devotion and self-sacrifice with which Chertkov followed his religious views? Tolstoy was lonely. Chertkov's sympathy and aid filled him with deep gratitude. He was thoughtful and tactful in accepting his suggestions.

The extent of Tolstoy's craving for the support of those close to him is evident in a letter he wrote to Chertkov about this time: "How pleasant it would be to lay my troubles before a court of people who hold the same faith as I, and then to carry out whatever they told me to do. There are times when you pull yourself up and feel forces within yourself, but there are also times when you wish, not to rest, but to give yourself up to others in whom you trust and let them direct you."

The strenuous work on his article "What Then Must We Do?," which Tolstoy somehow could not finish, exhausted him. He yearned to go back to literary work.

"I want to begin and to carry to a finish something new. Either the death of the judge, or 'The Notes of a Madman,' " he wrote in his diary for April 27, 1884.

The Death of Ivan Ilyich or *The Death of the Judge* was a novel Tolstoy had begun in 1882. The theme was brought to his mind by the death of a member of the Tula District Court. He wrote it in bits, put it aside, went back to it again at intervals and finished it only in March, 1886.

There were vast numbers of bureaucratic families like that of the Judge Ivan Ilyich. They lived like all the other people in their class, they had regular careers, received their salary the 20th of every month, spent their free evenings at the theater or visiting friends, and they fell ill and died. Judge Ilyich was dying. His sufferings were unbearable but the terror he was experiencing derived not so much from his physical pain as from his consciousness of the inevitability of death. In his despair he groaned and struggled. His wife and his son suffered with him, out of pity for him, and because of their utter inability to help him. So it went for three days.

Then, quite unexpectedly for the reader, a new angle of interest is introduced. Out of the drab, uninteresting envelope of a petty official the immortal soul of a human being emerges. It was toward the end of the third day, two hours before he died. His schoolboy son crept quietly up to his father's bed. The dying man was constantly crying and wringing his hands. One hand fell on the boy's head. The boy caught his father's hand, pressed it to his lips and burst into tears. . . .

Suddenly everything was clear to the father, everything that had been exhausting him and to which he could find no issue, everything suddenly was resolved, in two ways, in ten ways, in all different ways. He was sorry for them, he must do something so that they would not suffer. He must deliver them and himself from their sufferings. "How good and how simple," he thought. "And the pain?" he asked himself. "Where has it gone? Well now, where are you, pain?" And he began to listen.

"Yes, there it is. Well, never mind. Let the pain be."

"And death? Where is that?"

He sought his previous fear of death and could not find it. Where had it gone? What death? There was no fear, because neither was there any death.

Instead of death there was light.

"So that is how it is!" he suddenly said aloud. "What joy! . . ."

In this period of from 1884-1886 Tolstoy wrote a series of popular stories for The Mediator: "What Men Live By," illustrated by N. N. Gay, "Two Old Men" and "Three Elders" ("Three Hermits"). Sometimes Tolstoy drew his themes from popular legends, sometimes from real life; others he simply invented, as for instance, "The Tale of Ivan-the-Fool." The themes for the Mediator series came from a peasant from Olonets called V. P. Shchegolenok, with whom he had become acquainted in 1879.

Many years later, when Tolstoy was asked which of his works he considered his best, he used to answer: the popular tales "What Men Live By" and "Where Love Is, God Is." The latter grew out of a story Chertkov sent him, entitled "Uncle Martyn," published in the magazine *The Russian Worker*. Tolstoy did not know that the story had been written originally in the 1880's by a Frenchman named R. Saillens, and he was deeply distressed and apologetic when Saillens, in 1888, accused him of plagiarism.

Tolstoy touched on many themes in his popular writings: the vanity of amassing possessions in "How Much Land Does a Man Need?," the evil of drunkenness in "The First Distiller," love, God, forgiveness, but in no place is his philosophy expressed with such vividness as in "The Tale of Ivan-the-Fool." From the lips of the simple-minded Ivan come the accents of truth. Ivan harbors no malice, lives without affectation according to God's will, trying not to offend anyone and to live in peace with all. One of his brothers, Semyon-Warrior, tries to conquer the world, but the Emperor of India proves stronger than he is: "The Emperor did not permit the armies of Semyon to fire a shot; he sent his women through the air to throw explosive bombs down on Semyon's soldiers. . . . Semyon's army ran away and Tsar Semyon was left all alone." ("The Tale of Ivan-the-Fool" was written in 1885, when airplanes were not even thought of.) Ivan's other brother, Taras-Pot Belly, piles up a large fortune for himself and is ruined by a merchant. Tempted by the devil, these two brothers get more and more involved, whereas Ivan-the-Fool lives quietly in his empire, populated by just such fools as himself. The fools refuse to fight; they have no need of money. They work, they feed themselves and give shelter to all who wish to live peacefully. The complexities of human existence with its civilization, its wars, the division of empires, the accumulation of capital—all that is a closed book to them. They are fools, and as fools they are not even capable of perceiving the wisdom and right-eousness of their own philosophy.

The attitude of the writer I. S. Aksakov to Tolstoy's folk tales is interesting. It is mentioned in a letter Strakhov wrote to Danilevski in 1885 on the subject of Tolstoy's tales: "The Candle" and "Two Old Men":

"In his tales, according to Aksakov, it is evident that Tolstoy's attitude toward Holy Truth is so sincere and wholehearted, and the secret of this is so far beyond our analysis, that it puts the author outside our competence to judge him. Evidently he has his own open account with God."

The collaborators in The Mediator continued to work with zeal. V. M. Garshin collaborated with Tolstoy in writing the text for Repin's picture "The Sufferings of Our Lord Jesus Christ." Tolstoy was thrilled by this picture. As he wrote to Chertkov: "If you see Repin, tell him I always loved him, but that his image of the face of Christ has bound me to him even more closely than before. When I call to mind that face and that hand the tears well."

N. N. Gay did the illustrations for "What Men Live By" and the fairy tale about Ivan-the-Fool. In addition to Tolstoy's writings, The Mediator published a small book by A. M. Kalmykova, called *Socrates—The Greek Teacher*, on the rewriting of which Tolstoy put a great deal of work; they also put out a number of lives of saints and many other things. These little books were printed by the hundreds of thousands and spread all over Russia.

For Tolstoy, however, it was not enough to improve the cultural status of the peasants by providing them with education—it was necessary to raise the material level of their lives. Yet how was this to be done?

Here Tolstoy read *Progress and Poverty* by the American economist Henry George, who proposed to solve this problem by the nationalization of all landed property and the establishment of a single state tax on land, levied in proportion to its value. George's theory interested Tolstoy. It provided a direct, logical solution to the inequalities existing between the rich landowners and the laboring peasantry.

"I was absorbed by George, by his last and first book, *Progress and Poverty*," he wrote to Chertkov on February 24, 1885, "which made a very powerful and gratifying impression on me."

In this same year Tolstoy received an article written in longhand by a peasant, T. M. Bondarev: "Diligence and Sloth or the Triumph of the Farmer." Bondarev's views on peasant labor coincided with Tolstoy's, who wrote a preface to the work.

"Labor to earn one's bread, according to Bondarev, is the panacea to save humanity! Let man recognize this primary law of God . . . and all men will then be united in faith in one God, in love toward one another, and they will destroy the poverty which oppresses men. All will work and eat the fruit of their labors, and bread and the things of prime necessity will not be subject to purchase and sale."

Bondarev impressed Tolstoy by his superior mind, the firmness and clarity of his thinking. "Do you know what I am going to tell you?" Tolstoy said to A. S. Prugavin. "I owe more to two simple Russian peasants, scarcely able to read and write, than I do to all the learned writers of the whole world."

He had in mind Syutayev and Bondarev.

Tolstoy wanted to print Bondarev's article. However, censorship made this extremely difficult. The government was taking increasingly severe measures about the distribution of the free-thinking writing of Tolstoy and his followers, fearing that the circle of those who shared his thoughts might grow. People were leaving the fold of the Orthodox Church, and were refusing to accede to government requirements. Only the year before, in 1884, a young man named Zalyubovski had written to Tolstoy that he was thinking of refusing to do his military service on grounds of religion. Tolstoy did not reply to the letter because he did not think it possible to influence a young man in such a serious matter. Nevertheless Zalyubovski refused to shoulder a gun. He was arrested, imprisoned and sentenced to two years in a disciplinary battalion.

"What your brother has done and is doing," Tolstoy wrote to Zalyubovski's brother, "is the greatest thing a man can accomplish in his life. I do not know whether I could have stood up to it, but I could wish nothing better for myself or my children."

In writing to V. V. Stasov, a St. Petersburg art critic, to ask him to do all in his power on behalf of the young man, Tolstoy said: "The matter about which I write is of tremendous significance; nothing has ever been closer to my heart or more important to me than this."

It was not only in Russia that Tolstoy sought support for his religious doctrine. He was interested in the views of people in other countries, and he was delighted to receive a letter from the son of the defender of Negroes in America, William Lloyd Garrison, Jr., who professed, as Tolstoy did, the theory of nonresistance to evil by force.

❧ 40 ❧

ON JANUARY 18, 1886, the Tolstoy family was overwhelmed by a new loss. Their youngest son died of a throat infection accompanied by a terrible fever which took him in thirty-six hours. It was as though a dark cloud had settled over the household, for they all loved little four-year-old Alyosha. Sophia Andreyevna, who never left the child's bedside, said that just before the end Alyosha opened wide his large, gray eyes with their heavy lashes: "I see, I see. . . ." he said and so he died with an expression of surprised delight on his little face.

The same day Tolstoy wrote to Chertkov: ". . . There is nothing to be said about this. I know only that the death of a child, which earlier seemed to me incomprehensible and cruel, now seems to me to be a reasonable and blessed thing. We have all been united more affectionately and closely by this death."

But to his mother the little boy's death was senselessly cruel. It was a long time before she became reconciled to her grief. She tried to deflect her tormenting thoughts by constant, intense work about the household, the sale of books. Only her husband could understand and pity her, but she felt that he was slipping farther and farther away.

"All the people in the house, especially Lev Nikolayevich, and with him all the children, like a herd of sheep, foist the role of taskmaster on me," she wrote in her diary later that year. "They put onto me all the weight and responsibility for the children, the household, all money matters, education, although they get more out of the estate and the material side of things than I do; and then all dressed up as benefactors, they come to me with cold, official, prejudiced expressions on their faces and request the use of a horse for some peasant, money or flour, etc. I do not run the farm, I have neither the time nor the capacity for it—and I am not able to know whether the horses are needed for work on the estate at a given time or not, and these official requests, coupled with my lack of understanding of the state of affairs, upset and anger me."

In July Tolstoy hurt his leg while loading some hay. They thought it was not serious but the leg became very much infected, his temperature rose and it turned out that he had erysipelas. He was confined to his bed for over two months.

"These last two months—of Lev Nikolayevich's illness—have been," Sophia Andreyevna wrote in her diary of the same date, "strange to say, a partly distressing and partly happy time for me. I have cared for him night and day; I had such a happy, clear task to perform—the only one I can do well—that is to sacrifice my personal being for the sake of someone I love. The harder it was on me, the happier I felt. Now he is up and almost well. He has made me feel that he no longer needs me, that here I was cast away like some useless object from whom only one thing is asked—as it has always been in my life and family—that vague, impossible renunciation of property, of convictions, of the education and well-being of the children, something which I am incapable of doing, and not only I, although I am a woman not without energy, but thousands of others, who are as convinced of the rightness of these convictions."

Toward the end of this same year Sophia Andreyevna lost her mother—Lyubov Alexandrovna Behrs. But the death of her aged mother, whom she saw only rarely, caused less pain than what was happening in her immediate family. For by now the members were split into two factions.

The two elder daughters were drawn to their father. Sophia Andreyevna and the boys had their own interests. Tolstoy's views, his new friends, upset them. But the girls found it easier to accept their father's views and carry them out in their lives, though for Tanya it was more difficult than for Masha, who was still very young. Unnoticed, with quiet modesty, Masha gradually made herself necessary to her father, first by carrying out his simplest requests; with light steps she would fetch a glass of water, a book; and later, with Tanya, she copied his manuscripts. The more difficult the task assigned to her the more willingly Masha carried it out.

Her father's guests, who were ill at ease in their greasy, smelly sheepskin coats, muddy felt or leather boots, felt less embarrassed when they met this plain and simply dressed young girl with the welcoming, friendly look in her eyes, and were led by her into her father's study.

The majority of Tolstoy's guests were peasants and workingmen, interested in his ideas on religions, landholding, on the organization of Christian agricultural communes. Occasionally Tolstoy read them some new article or story of his, or the works of other authors, or discussed the fitness of this or that work for popular consumption.

Sophia Andreyevna did not like the Tolstoyans. Someone of the family, whether Aunt Tanya or Aunt Sonya, nicknamed them the "dark people," and the nickname stuck.

"Who is with the Count?" Sophia Andreyevna would sometimes ask one of her menservants.

"I cannot say, Your Excellency," the servant would reply. "Some dark person or other."

The servants did not like the "dark people" either. They never gave any tips, they brought in a lot of dirt, they made spots on the parquet floors, they reeked of tar and they always managed to insinuate themselves right into the Count's study.

The Countess' friends were quite another matter: they were clean, well-fed, they drove up in their carriages, sometimes with footmen, and some of them gave generous tips. So gradually the circle of friends was split into the bright and the dark, and only a few of the "dark"—Biryukov, Chertkov, M. A. Schmidt, Grandpa Gay—entered the household as friends of the Tolstoy family.

The majority of their society acquaintances never had any contact with the "dark people," but there were some families who worshiped Tolstoy as a "literary genius" and so "forgave" him his erring ways; they took a condescendingly friendly attitude toward the "dark people" and liked to visit the Tolstoys. Count Olsufiev and the family of the Stakhoviches belonged to this group.

The Olsufievs were exceptionally well-educated and cultivated people. Tanya was on friendly terms with Lisa and her two brothers, Misha and Mitya. Among the younger set it was supposed that Tanya was in love with the elder brother, Misha, while the younger brother, Mitya, was in love with her. They were all very fond of the good-natured, agreeable old Count, but Tolstoy made a special friend of his Countess, Anna Mikhailovna, an uncommonly sensitive, intelligent woman who had a subtle appreciation of Tolstoy, although she did not share his religious views. When Tolstoy sometimes wished to get a rest from his many visitors and from the family surroundings, he would take Tanya and go for a long stay with the Olsufievs in their country home.

The second family on terms of intimacy with the Tolstoys, the Stakhoviches, were wealthy, cultivated and brilliant. Two of them were particularly attached to Tolstoy: Zosya Stakhovich idolized him as an artist; she knew whole chapters of *War and Peace* by heart. An independent, proud beauty, with severely classical features, a year older than Tanya, she had even more admirers than Tanya, but she looked down on all young men and was thought cold and inaccessible.

Mikhail Alexandrovich Stakhovich (Misha) sometimes spent weeks on end at Yasnaya Polyana. He was a genuine lordling who dressed beautifully, took great care of his handsome appearance, strewed money right and left, and gave tips, not of silver, but of gold coin. For a while Misha fell under the spell of Tolstoy's influence, used to go with him to help the peasants plow or mow and take in the hay, but the influence was not a profound one. Misha Stakhovich was in love with Tanya and hoped to earn her regard by "simplifying" his life. Sophia Andreyevna was fond of Misha and secretly hoped that Tanya would marry him; it was a "good match."

Evidently their father—Alexander Alexandrovich Stakhovich—had instilled in both his children a love for literature. He enjoyed reading aloud, and did it splendidly. Sometimes, of an evening, the family and guests at Yasnaya Polyana would gather around the big mahogany table in the living room; Sophia Andreyevna would mend the children's stockings or knit coverlets for her numerous brood, while the younger children wound the balls of soft, fluffy wool; Tanya would sit in the corner, drawing someone's portrait, and Stakhovich would read aloud from Ostrovski or Gogol. Tolstoy would listen in delight. Indeed, he derived more enjoyment from this than anyone else. He particularly liked *Poverty Is Not a Vice* and *Live Not as You Choose*. He dreamed of publishing Ostrovski in The Mediator, and not long before the playwright's death asked his permission to print his dramatic works in a popular edition; but Ostrovski died before he could reply.

Stakhovich had read *Live Not as You Choose* aloud in the autumn of 1866. When later he returned to Yasnaya Polyana, Tolstoy said to him: "How glad I am that you have come. Your reading stirred me into action. After you left I wrote a drama . . . either it is because I haven't written anything for the stage for a long time or else it really is a *wonder!*"

Toward the end of August Tolstoy had received a letter from the head of a people's theater *(Skomozokh)* with a request for his support. Perhaps this was what originally prompted him to begin *The Power of Darkness*; the Ostrovski reading supplying an additional impetus. It may also be that when he was lying in bed with his infected leg, he passed the long days mulling over various themes, among them the one on which this play was based and which had been suggested to him back in 1880 by Nikolai Vassilyevich Davydov, prosecuting attorney of the Tula District Court.

Why was it that this particular story made such an impression on Tolstoy? There are many evil acts, crimes and murders committed in the world; yet Tolstoy was deeply stirred by the fact that a handsome young peasant, one Koloskov, after committing a series of crimes, including the smothering of an infant his stepdaughter bore him, did not fear publicly to confess his sins.

"It's a damp, dull autumn," Sophia Andreyevna wrote in October of 1886. "Andryusha and Misha have been skating on the lower pond. Tanya and Masha both have the toothache. Lev Nikolayevich has undertaken to write a drama about peasant life."

On October 26 she noted in her diary: "Lyovochka has written the first act of a drama. I am to copy it. Why is it that I have lost faith even in his literary power?"

On October 30 Sophia Andreyevna copied the second act and in less than three weeks the rough draft of *The Power of Darkness* was finished. Only the polishing remained to be done, the pointing up of certain colloquial peasant expressions, the rewording of several scenes and acts.

At the end of November *The Power of Darkness* was handed in for the approval of the censor.

The ink was scarcely dry on this new work when news of it spread over Moscow and St. Petersburg. Mme. Savina, a famous actress in the Alexandrinski Theater, wrote to Tolstoy for permission to have the première take place there as a benefit for her.

But *The Power of Darkness* was banned both for production and for publication.

Sophia Andreyevna was upset and wrote to the head of the Department of Publications, E. M. Feoktistov, requesting that the drama be passed. He replied that the play would be "bound to have a most depressing effect on the public, that it put on the stage a whole series of adulteries and murders," that it was dreadful in its cynicism, etc. In the opinion of the chief of the department of publications and drama censorship, the play should be banned "because of its licentiousness and lack of literary quality."

Meanwhile, Stakhovich, who admired the play warmly, read it aloud in court circles in St. Petersburg; and on the 27th of January, 1887, he gave a reading of it at the house of Count Vorontsov-Dashkov, Minister of the Court of Emperor Alexander III. The Emperor, the Grand Duchesses and a number of persons connected with the court were present. This is how Stakhovich described the occasion:

"The fourth act made a tremendous impression; it was obvious that everyone was stirred by it; one could tell this in the intermissions by the varied but general expressions of approval. After the end of the fifth act there was a long silence, until the voice of the Emperor broke it with these words:

" 'A wonderful thing!' "

The Emperor's praise unloosed the tongues of all the rest. The arguments began and enthusiastic exclamations echoed on all sides.

Not long after this the Alexandrinski Theater prepared to produce the drama. Seventeen rehearsals were held; people went down from the theater to Yasnaya Polyana to study the peasant setting—the cottages, the clothing, the way of life.

Simultaneously, in early February, *The Power of Darkness* was published in Tolstoy's collected works, edited by Sophia Andreyevna, as well as by The Mediator. The first printing was of twelve thousand; then another of twenty; and finally one of forty thousand copies was distributed at the price of three kopecks (approximately a cent and a half) for each little booklet.

But the Alexandrinski Theater was not destined to produce *The Power of Darkness*. When Feoktistov heard of the Emperor's flattering estimate of the drama and his desire to have it put on in the Alexandrinski Theater, he wrote an indignant letter to Pobedonostsev, the all-powerful Procurator of the Synod, and sent him a copy of the play to read.

Pobedonostsev was enraged and wrote a letter to the Emperor: "The day on which this drama is produced in the imperial theaters will mark the final downfall of our stage," he declared.

The Emperor could not bring himself to oppose the wishes of the Procurator of the Synod, so he agreed that "it is impossible to stage this drama; it is too realistic and dreadful in its subject matter."

So the play was banned.

Beginning with 1888 *The Power of Darkness* ran in various theaters throughout Europe: in France, Switzerland, Italy. But not until 1895, during the reign of Nicholas II, was Russia permitted to see on its own stage this work by one of its great writers.

There was nothing surprising in the fact that the censor found it difficult to pass Tolstoy's drama. The futility of all human punishment is blazoned forth in *The Power of Darkness*. What meaning can police sergeants, prisons, forced labor have in comparison with God's chastisement, with the torments of a man's own conscience?

❧ 41 ❧

IN JUNE of 1887 Tolstoy wrote to Chertkov: "The very best state for one's soul is—not to be guilty but to feel guilty."

And these were not merely words. He actually felt guilty in regard to his wife, to the peasant he met when he went out for a walk, to his children and to the Tolstoyans.

He felt worst about his wife, for he could not change his convictions, and thus could not remove the cause of her suffering. In 1887

Sophia Andreyevna was in her forty-third year. She was very young looking. Her complexion, untouched by powder or paint, was one any beautiful woman might envy. There was not a wrinkle on the delicate pink skin of her face. Her figure had filled out, grown stout, from constant childbearing, but her movements were quick and light. Her whole manner, even the way she put her lorgnette up to her short-sighted eyes, bespoke a quiet self-assurance. She never wore a pince-nez or spectacles, in order not to spoil her appearance, and she was so short-sighted she often missed the expression on the face of the person she was talking to, the winks of the children bent on some mischief, or the frown on her Lyovochka's brow. For the same reason she sometimes did not recognize people, or mistook them for others, and thus seemed tactless.

Tolstoy himself could not in any way be looked upon as old at this time. Although he was in his sixtieth year he was hale and hearty. Sophia Andreyevna loved to talk about her youth and his age, but in reality she did not feel the disparity. She would have loved him anyway—if only he would not torment her with his strange convictions.

She now carried the whole burden of publishing his works, which constituted the main source of revenue for the family. Poverty to her was the most terrible thing in the world and she was in a constant state of worry for fear he would manage his affairs badly and they would be ruined. The fact that this was precisely what Lyovochka wanted exasperated her. What had become of Lyovochka the writer, the gentleman, the hunter? This "real" Lyovochka had been taken over by the "dark people," with Chertkov at their head. They made demands on him, they reshaped him into a strange figure of a teacher who preached self-renunciation, love for one's neighbor, all kinds of self-control and the rejection of private possessions. This teacher had renounced the Orthodox Church and attacked the government which she had been accustomed to respect since childhood, when her father had been court doctor in the Kremlin; he condemned smoking, drinking, meat eating and all sorts of innocent entertainment for the children: dances, plays and good clothes. He had even reached the point of preaching complete continence and she, his wife, somehow was classed as a sin and temptation.

"I shall not move to Yasnaya Polyana before May 20," Sophia Andreyevna had written from Moscow that spring. "The prospect of sharing my life with Feinermann is so burdensome that I'd rather not come at all."

Feinermann was one of the "dark people" Sophia Andreyevna particularly disliked. Despite his conversion to Christianity, which he undertook with the idea of becoming a village teacher, the government had not confirmed him in his teaching job, and he was now living at Yasnaya Polyana, having decided, as a genuine follower of Tolstoy, to hire himself out as a shepherd to a peasant for the summer. Tolstoy communicated the fact of Feinermann's intention to Sophia Andreyevna, and added that he very much envied Feinermann because he would be pasturing cattle.

"There is nothing to envy Feinermann for," Sophia Andreyevna replied. "What you do in the world no Feinermann will ever do. He is not capable of doing anything, he will even be a bad shepherd. Such people have no notion of what real work is. They do what is easiest to them, which is really not work."

Sophia Andreyevna did not like Tolstoy to take their daughters and go down to Yasnaya Polyana; she was slightly jealous of them because now it was they on the whole and not she who copied his manuscripts. Moreover she worried about his health, believing that no one else knew how to feed him or take care of him properly. He was having more and more frequent attacks, probably from passing gallstones. The pains would be so severe that he would break out in a cold sweat, and groan aloud. Once Sophia Andreyevna found him in the living room, writhing on the floor, dragging along a heavy chair and literally howling with pain.

In order to calm his wife Tolstoy had his cook come over occasionally from the village—a former serf who was very weak and frail, so that more often than not it was the Tolstoys—father and daughters and their visiting friends—who did all the work: the cooking, dishwashing and chamber work.

That spring Professor Masaryk came to Yasnaya Polyana. One of the professors of philosophy at the Moscow University, N. J. Grot, had introduced Masaryk to Tolstoy while he was in the city and Masaryk had called several times.

In his letter of April 30 to his wife Tolstoy wrote: "Masaryk has been visiting me for two days. I have enjoyed being with him," and at the end of this letter he added: "I walked with Masaryk to Kozlovka. Received two good letters from you. I am always so happy when I feel that you are in a good mood and that all is cheerful with you. Masaryk knows how to start a samovar, he is a good blower, but he also thinks and understands well."

On the 3rd of May Tolstoy wrote again: "We are having all kinds of weather now: thunderstorms, heat, nightingales, violets, the forest is half in leaf, how lively, how good God's world is! Yesterday I plowed for half a day. I was good and tired, but that is the best way to feel and it was fine. . . . Today I have been at work on my writing. Don't think that I am uncomfortable and badly off—it's wonderful. Except that I miss you all."

For the greater part of 1887 Tolstoy was working on his article "On Life and Death," which after several months he called simply "On Life"—for there is no death; the human soul is immortal.

This essay expresses a point of view diametrically opposed to materialistic atheism. Life makes sense, said Tolstoy, only in that it is not physical but spiritual in nature. When a man's "reasoning consciousness" is awakened it is impossible for him to "continue his personal existence" and live only for the sake of achieving a personal well-being. "There occurs something," wrote Tolstoy, "which is similar to what occurs in the material world at any birth. The fruit is born, not because he chooses to be born, or knows that it is good to be born, but because he has matured and cannot continue his previous existence; he has to submit to a new life, not so much because the new life calls him as because the possibility of his previous existence is destroyed. Reasoning consciousness . . . grows to the point where life in his own person becomes impossible."

Life, the meaning of life, can lie only in the renunciation of the physical, in service, in love toward people.

"Love thy God with all thy heart and all thy soul and all thy understanding. This is the first and the greatest commandment."

"Love thy neighbor as thyself."

And Tolstoy added: "True love is life itself . . . only the man who loves is alive."

His article "On Life" is known scarcely to anyone and yet, perhaps more than any other of Tolstoy's works, it provides an understanding of what took place in him: the seed sprouted and personal life ceased to have any significance for him. The main meaning of life lay now in the constant growth of spiritual awareness.

Did Sophia Andreyevna grasp the essential meaning of this essay? At least she liked it, for in it Lyovochka did not, thank goodness, scold the government or the church. She not only copied it for her husband, she also undertook to translate it into French, which pleased him very much.

Tolstoy intrusted the checking of the essay to Professor N. J. Grot, who had recently become one of Tolstoy's constant visitors, and who was delighted with his assignment. Conversations with Grot and with N. N. Strakhov—both scholars, philosophers and theoreticians—had done much to strengthen Tolstoy's convictions, though their deliberations were purely abstract, whereas Tolstoy was concerned with the immediate and practical application of his views to life.

He noticed the underground birth and growth of the new and terrible force of militant atheism among the Socialist Revolutionaries, the Marxists, the people promising a new and free life to the populace. But Tolstoy knew that this force, negating as it did man's divine origin, was more terrible than the tsarist government. He saw too that the so-called intelligentsia had nothing with which to oppose this force. They did not even really know the masses of the Russian people.

In his article "School Holiday," Tolstoy made a severe attack on "the intellectuals who look down . . . on 'the people' " . . . and "consider the peasant a 'lower order of being.' " "And how do they," he continued, "these educated persons, celebrate the University's holiday [the traditional St. Tatiana's day]? [They] . . . can think of nothing else to do than for hours on end to eat, drink, smoke, and bellow nonsense. . . . Worst of all, the people who do all this are so befogged by their own conceit that they are not able to distinguish between good and evil, the moral and the immoral."

Having given up smoking himself, Tolstoy felt a great relief—as he put it, a "catharsis"—and he was anxious to help people free themselves from their sins of drunkenness and smoking. He wrote a whole series of articles on this subject—"Why Do People Stupefy Themselves?" was finished in the summer of 1890—and he decided to found a society called Fellowship to Combat Drunkenness. This society gradually increased its membership and by 1890 741 people belonged to it.

In one of his letters to Chertkov, Tolstoy drew a straight line—the shortest distance between a man's consciousness and perfection; "but a man cannot walk any other way," wrote Tolstoy. "I wish to go straight and I sin, a sin appears which I recognize and of which I repent, but I do not compromise, or deceive God. And deception is much worse than sin—it is a sacrilege against the Holy Ghost."

Tolstoy felt that so-called educated mankind had lost its bearings. The voices of the atheists, the socialists, were more bold and loud, and educated people were increasingly indifferent to questions of religion. Yet the millions of Russian peasantry continued to live under the guidance of their own old, perhaps primitive, religious traditions. It was not without reason that he appealed to all writers to contribute their work toward the education of the Russian people, who craved education like so many "hungry young daws."

Out of these thoughts his essay "What Is Art?" had its inception, although it was not written until later.

"Any education," wrote Tolstoy in the conclusion to this essay, "not founded on a moral life never was and never will be education, but will always do nothing more than obscure and debauch."

42

DURING these years, while communication between Tolstoy and his wife grew more and more difficult, his influence was reaching out to people all over the world. In pérson and by letter those seeking spiritual enlightenment turned to him for guidance. As a result, life at Yasnaya Polyana was an extraordinary medley which allowed little privacy for the most intimate family concerns.

Two events of major importance were a birth and a marriage, which Tolstoy reported to Grandpa Gay in a letter dated February 13, 1888: "All is going well with us—I might even say very well. My wife is expecting a baby in another month. Ilya is getting married to the Filosofov girl (you surely know her—a sweet, unaffected, healthy, pure girl) on February 28, and he is in that irresponsible state of mind common to those in love. Life for him is standing still, it is all in the future. . . ."

When informed that a sixth son was born to the Tolstoys on March 31, Gay replied: "I kiss the newborn Ivan—God grant he have something of John the Theologian, the beloved writer and man, in him." From birth Ivan, or John, was a thin, frail, sickly child.

Around Tolstoy at Yasnaya Polyana milled a horde of relatives and guests, including transient visitors who were often complete strangers.

The large Kuzminski family came each summer to live in a wing of the house. Of the two daughters, Big Masha—as they called her to distinguish between her and Little Masha Tolstoy—was slightly younger than Tanya; Vera was Masha Tolstoy's junior. They and the three boys, Misha, Sanya, and Vasya, contributed greatly to the liveliness of the household, for there was scarcely any separation between the families. All the members played together, studied together, fought together; and when autumn came they separated for the winter, the Tolstoys going to Moscow, the Kuzminskis to St. Petersburg.

There were others who had literally put down roots in Yasnaya Polyana, among them Grandpa Gay and his son Kolechka who, as the years passed, became practically at home there. No one could help loving Grandpa. Everything he did was done easily and simply, with joy; he never sought to lecture others and never forced anyone, beginning with himself and his own children. Grandpa never said he had given up personal property; he went around in a frayed suit and tried to live according to the teachings of Christ. He really loved Him and painted Him as he comprehended Him, not as God, but as the greatest Teacher of the world, radiating joy and goodness, and demonstrating by His whole appearance that it is far easier and happier to be good and kind than it is to be wicked.

Grandpa could not tolerate pretense, affectation, high-sounding words. He looked slightly askance at Chertkov because of his moralizing, and he was not at all ashamed of his own weaknesses. He loved sweets and often came to Sophia Andreyevna, asking in his soft Ukrainian accent: "Mamenka, do you happen to have some tasty little thing or other?" And Mamenka would go to her room, open the old mahogany chiffonier where she kept the candy, and bring some out as a treat for Grandpa.

His son Kolechka Gay had just as sweet and sunny a disposition, and a wonderful way of laughing. Sergei Tolstoy loved to make puns and tell anecdotes. Kolechka would listen with serious mien, then as the story progressed the skin on his face would begin to go into deep creases like the folds of an accordion, especially on his forehead; until suddenly his face would relax and his whole body would begin to shake noiselessly. He would laugh sometimes with the tears rolling down his cheeks, until he was quite helpless. If the children were there when this happened they all burst out laughing whether they understood the story or not—especially Sasha, who was always ready to seize any opportunity to roar with laughter.

Chertkov had a very different place in the circle. The Tolstoy family stood in awe of him. Although the older boys addressed him with the intimate second person pronoun, Chertkov embarrassed them and they avoided him. This was not Chertkov's fault. He tried very hard to be friendly, but he did not know how. One cannot say that he was insincere. He served Tolstoy with self-sacrificing zeal, he faithfully promoted his teachings, did a great deal of work for The Mediator, at the same time that he helped to edit and print Tolstoy's writings, which were now being published abroad, principally in England. Perhaps it was his aristocratic manner, his handsome face, his anglicized accent which embarrassed people, perhaps too his desire always to instruct. At any rate, the young people felt a strain in him which was absent in Grandpa Gay, in M. A. Schmidt, in Biryukov.

The Tolstoy boys poked fun at him on the sly. They liked to tell stories about him, recalling, for example the time when the whole village and all the members of the Tolstoy family, with Lev Nikolayevich at the head, were hauling hay at the height of the farming season. Exhausted and streaming with sweat, they suddenly met Chertkov walking along in a long red Russian blouse hanging down below his knees, and asked him where he was going. He replied in his broad British accent that he was "going to the village to converse with the peasants."

In 1886 Chertkov had married Anna Konstantinovna Dieterichs. In order not to hurt their parents' feelings the young couple were married in church. Anna Dieterichs was a college girl, a populist of advanced liberal views. Although she came of a conservative family she met Chertkov through The Mediator. She shared her husband's views completely, but like him she lacked buoyancy. She had pretty, regular features, a Cupid's bow mouth, dark curly hair and great black eyes. Yet there was something morbidly tragic in her good looks, as though she would break any moment under the weight of life, as though her frail body could not sustain the burden.

Another of the very few "dark people" who were accepted by Sophia Andreyevna was P. I. Biryukov, or, as everyone called him, Posha. The fact that he was a well-brought-up young man from a good family meant a great deal to her. He was simple, friendly and modest, conscientiously devoted to Tolstoy and his teaching. In Sophia Andreyevna's eyes he was not just an idler. She was quick to detect insincerity in people and could not tolerate it. But her attitude toward him was slightly shaken when, early in 1889, he proposed to

Masha and she accepted him. Sophia Andreyevna was not in favor of this marriage, feeling that Masha was not in love but had decided to marry Posha in order to lead a laboring life in accordance with her father's principles.

Tolstoy also was afraid of this marriage, but his feelings were far more complex. He did not really know how genuinely Masha might be in love, but if she did not marry he feared it would be because of him, her father, because she wanted to stay with him—which was what he in his own heart desired. With each year he had become more and more strongly attached to this daughter, and to lose her would not be easy.

To Chertkov he wrote that spring: "I have a feeling of great tenderness toward her, only to her. Somehow she makes up for the rest."

To the general relief of all, except Posha who remained inconsolable for a long time, the engagement was broken off.

About this time a new follower of Tolstoy's, Ivan Ivanovich Gorbunov-Posadov, came to work for The Mediator and joined the larger family circle. In time he became the editor in chief and publisher of the firm. Upon meeting him, Tolstoy noted in his diary: "Very intelligent, and gifted and clean." When he came to know him better, Tolstoy might have added: also kind, supersensitive, even sentimental and modest. Ivan Ivanovich idolized Tolstoy. He drank in his every word and sometimes, when Tolstoy read aloud from his own works, he would purse his lips out like a child, wheeze and unobtrusively wipe his kind, affectionate eyes with a not-too-immaculate handkerchief. Occasionally, in order to cover up his emotions, he would jump up during a break in the conversation and pace heavily up and down the room, wiping the perspiration from his broad Russian face.

Leonila Annenkova slipped quietly into the Tolstoy household and was immediately accepted as a close friend; without any effort on her part she won the affection of the entire family. She was soft and plump, had a soft, southern accent, was pleasant as the soft fluffy wool of which she was forever knitting various things. She said little, listening rather to her beloved teacher, and imperceptibly, tacitly, put into practice what he said.

Still another follower, was Gavril Andreyevich Rusanov. "Tolstoy gave me happiness and I became a Christian," wrote Rusanov. But Rusanov gave a great deal to Tolstoy too. Although Tolstoy rarely saw him because Rusanov was afflicted with locomotor ataxia and was confined to his chair, he corresponded with him frequently and followed his advice and suggestions with regard to his writings. Rusanov suffered much and like people who have been through a great deal he attained great spiritual heights. Tolstoy looked upon him as one of the best persons he had ever met; he loved and respected him.

One day a new follower, called Klopski, turned up. Sophia Andreyevna sooner than anyone else found out his real nature, but he made her a great deal of trouble.

"Klopski has arrived," she noted in her diary. "He is awfully repulsive. Some kind of a dark creature."

A day later she wrote again: "What a keen struggle is going on now. This morning the children were studying downstairs, Klopski was there, and he said to Andryusha: 'Why do you study and ruin your spirit? Your father, you know, does not wish that.' The little girls immediately took up the idea, they were ready to shake his noble hand for such talk. The boys came running to tell me about it."

Still another category of Tolstoy's friends cannot be described either as belonging to high society or to the "dark people." Professor Grot, for example, was not a follower of Tolstoy's, but he became a constant visitor and friend in his household. This friendship was further promoted by the fact that the Grots, with their numerous family, lived next to the Tolstoys in Moscow; their children played together.

Tolstoy's friendship with the painter Repin dates also from this period. It had begun when Repin illustrated Tolstoy's popular tales, but in due course Repin made friends with the entire family, and often visited them in Yasnaya Polyana.

In 1887 Repin while there painted two portraits of Tolstoy: Tolstoy with a book sitting in a Voltaire chair, and Tolstoy plowing. Tolstoy could not bear to pose: not only was it a boring waste of time, but more important, it underscored his "fame," which weighed on him and hampered him in his eternal struggle with "the sin of ambition," as he called it. But he did not wish to upset Repin. Despite the fact that Repin himself was a famous person, he was extremely modest and by that quality had won Tolstoy. A kindly, half-sad, half-quizzical smile scarcely ever left his face. When Tolstoy was talking he listened in concentrated silence. It was difficult to paint Tolstoy plowing, for he absolutely refused to pose when he was doing what he considered a vital piece of work. Holding the heavy plow in his muscular and powerful hands, he moved along without stopping, treading down the soft earth, while Repin ran around him from one end of the field to the other, trying to catch him on paper. The painter tried to plow himself, but the horse would not obey his orders.

In this same year of 1887 (in April) Leskov came to visit Tolstoy. His story, *Christ Visiting the Peasant*, was one of the first works to be published by The Mediator with the permission of the author. It sold for one and a half kopecks (less than one cent) at retail. In a letter to Chertkov Tolstoy wrote: "Leskov has been here. What an intelligent and original man!"

A famous lawyer, A. F. Koni, arrived in the summer of that year. He was a man of exceptionally brilliant mind and a broad outlook, a lively and gifted conversationalist. Tolstoy took him for long walks. This was a privilege extended to very few people and only to those for whom he felt a special interest or sympathy, because usually he liked to go walking alone. It never entered Tolstoy's head that these walks were beyond the physical capacity of a sedentary denizen of St. Petersburg. "With a flexibility and lightness remarkable for his age, Tolstoy would run uphill and he jumped across ditches with the quick and firm movement of one who has springs in his shoes," wrote Koni in his memoirs.

Their conversation ranged over literature, which both he and Koni knew well, and Koni's legal practice. One of his cases made a deep impression on Tolstoy and he asked Koni to write it out for him. This case served as the theme for his novel *Resurrection*.

Another summer visitor to Yasnaya Polyana, after a long interval, was Granny Alexandra Andreyevna Tolstoy. Old friends though they were, she and Tolstoy very seldom met. And when they did, or even when they exchanged letters, they always argued. Though Granny admired Tolstoy as a great artist, she was utterly unable to comprehend his new outlook on the world, his rejection of the church and his negative attitude toward the state. Nevertheless their old bond remained; above all they retained a deep-rooted respect for each other.

This is how Granny described her stay in Yasnaya Polyana: "I very much loved these morning hours. Lev, revived by sleep, was in fine fettle and unusually nice. We chatted quite quietly: he often read me his favorite verses of Tutchev, and some of Khomyakov, which he particularly liked; when at any place the name of Christ was mentioned his voice trembled and his eyes filled with tears. . . . The memory of this still comforts me; without himself being conscious of it, he has a deep love for the Redeemer and, of course, feels in Him an extraordinary man; it is difficult to understand in him the contradiction between his words and his emotions.

"When he went off to work in his study he usually left me all the magazines, books, letters he had received the day before. One can scarcely imagine the pile of stuff that is brought in nearly every day, not only from Russia but also from all the countries of Europe and even from America—and all of it reeked of incense. . . . I often was amazed that he was not suffocated by it and I even gave him the greatest credit for this."

Whenever Tolstoy was in a great hurry to have something copied he would divide the work up: Sophia Andreyevna, the daughters, the guests—everyone copied. So it was when Tolstoy finished his article "On Life" on August 3, 1887. Among the copyists were Granny and A. M. Kuzminski.

"The reading of it took about two hours," Granny wrote in her memoirs. "I understood far more than I had expected to; there were magnificent parts, but my heart neither trembled nor took fire. I had the feeling that either I was in a dissecting room, or else I was running around in crooked alleys in an ill-lighted labyrinth and kept losing my way, becoming confused, and unable to breathe freely. . . . Naturally, I did not tell anybody about this. . . ."

Among Tolstoy's foreign correspondents was a young man, a student at the Ecole Normale in Paris, who wrote to ask him how to build his life, how to organize manual labor. His name was Romain Rolland, and Tolstoy replied in a long and full letter which at one time he considered reworking into an article.

Tolstoy received all the leading magazines and newspapers, foreign as well as Russian; and kept up with most of the significant books being published abroad. Alice Stockheim's book *Tocology* made a powerful impression on him. He insisted that it be translated into Russian and he himself wrote an introduction to it.

"The questions of abstinence," Tolstoy wrote about her book, "from any stimulating drinks, including the giving up of tea and tobacco, the questions of a nutrition which does not involve the slaughter of living beings, vegetarianism, questions of sexual abstinence in family life, and many others, some of which have already been settled or partly worked out and which are the subject of a large literature, have not even been raised by us, and that is why the Stockheim book is particularly valuable for us: it instantly carries the reader out of our moribund realm into the world of a living, human movement."

While he was reading "The World's Thought" he came across an article by George Kennan about the Fortress of Peter and Paul in St. Petersburg and Siberian exile. Kennan went to Siberia to see for himself the system of forced labor and wrote a book entitled *Siberia and the Exile System*. While in Russia he went to see Tolstoy.

Other Americans visited him over the years: Isabel Hapgood, later a translator of his works, the journalist William Stead, among many. But Tolstoy's greatest joy was in communion with people who professed the same Christian teaching he did—nonresistance to evil by force. One book, Adin Ballou's *Christian Non-Resistance* was sent him by a Unitarian minister named Wilson, in June of 1889. In his diary he made the note: "excellent," and writing to Posha Biryukov several months later he again expressed his enthusiasm.

As Tolstoy's fame grew, and as his correspondence increased, the government became more and more uneasy. Tolstoy's influence must be curtailed—but how? The government could not take the same measures with him as toward an ordinary political criminal. If Tolstoy were exiled, if he went away to Europe or America, it would not only arouse the resentment of civilized countries; it would also increase his popularity in Russia. To put him in prison or pack him off to Siberia might cause convulsions inside Russia, student riots and strikes, and again would serve only to increase his fame.

In the end, the government chose two courses: the persecution of Tolstoy's followers and the banning of his books. The retail sale of *The Power of Darkness* in a cheap edition was banned. His folk tales, which, as we know, were deeply Christian in feeling, were attacked by the government. When they were being considered for interdiction, Archimandrite Tikhon, spiritual censor of publications, summed them up as follows: "They are all permeated by the same buffoonery, and although they appear to have a morally instructive character they will tend to affect the reader not in a way to edify him, but rather to upset his moral well-being."

Thereupon the Committee on Publications banned an anthology

which included the stories, as well as individual editions of "God Sees the Truth," "What Men Live By," "Where Love Is, God Is," "Three Elders," "Does Man Need Much Land?" "The Seed," "The First Distiller," "Two Old Men," and others. But these repressive measures in no way diminished Tolstoy's influence over the young people of his time. Besides being attracted by the teaching itself—a Christian life of total abstinence, with its elements of self-sacrifice and asceticism—they were undoubtedly drawn also by his revolutionary ideas protesting the existing order. They clustered around The Mediator, they argued, they hungrily devoured all of Tolstoy's new writings. And, since they did not care simply to talk, they gathered in groups to form Tolstoyan Christian communes. In these communes the land was recognized as common property, all were obliged to work, the food was simple, vegetarian, and relations between the sexes platonic. Unhappily, the communes did not flourish, breaking up on the shoals of misunderstandings, personal property disputes and general recrimination.

"A-n came to see me this autumn," Tolstoy wrote to Grandpa Gay. "He and the rest are living in a remarkable fashion. Take for instance the question of sex: they solve this by total abstinence, they live like saints. But—may the Lord forgive my sin—it left a depressing effect on me. It is not because I envy them the purity of their lives from the depths of my own filth, there is none of that; I recognize the heights they have achieved and am as happy about it as if I had done as much, but there is something lacking. Dearest friend, do not show them this letter, it would distress them; and perhaps I am wrong."

As early as the end of 1887 a police search was made in the home of M. A. Novoselov, a follower of Tolstoy. Tolstoy's article "Nicholas Stick" (an exposé of Emperor Nicholas I) was found on the premises. Novoselov was arrested. The Minister of the Interior, Count D. A. Tolstoy, in reporting on the affair to Emperor Alexander III, spoke of the inefficacy of persecuting Tolstoy for his antigovernment writing. He added that the article had been written "without any criminal connections or intentions, and purely under the influence of religious fanaticism, and if he were subjected to examination this would provoke entirely undesirable notions and results."

The Minister proposed to Dolgorukov, the Governor General of Moscow, that he "invite Count Tolstoy to call on him and, after delivering the necessary cautionary remarks, suggest at the same time that Tolstoy hand over without delay all remaining copies of the article." The Emperor approved the Minister's report.

Tolstoy's response to the invitation to call on the Governor General could easily have been foreseen. Through an acquaintance, who was at the head of the Governor General's secretariat (Istomin) he sent word that he refused "to appear of my own free will to discuss any questions relating to my writings . . . since such an invitation implies intrusion into my spiritual domain." Moreover he said that he had never seen any copies of the article. Dolgorukov considered that the matter should be dropped. "Any repressive measure, taken with regard to Count L. Tolstoy," he said, "would surround him with a halo of suffering and hence would serve to spread all the more his thoughts and teachings."

After some time Novoselov was released, but the repression of the Tolstoyans continued.

In the village of Yasnaya Polyana there was a miserably poverty-stricken parochial school, where the children were taught by half-literate teachers. The Tolstoy girls, following in their father's footsteps, started classes to teach the village children to read and write. Occasionally Tolstoy visited the classes, gave his daughters advice, and at times became so enthused that he fell into his old habit of working with the youngsters himself.

The government did not like this and the Governor of the province was obliged to close the school. At the time the Governor was N. V. Zinoviev, a near neighbor of the Tolstoys and a frequent visitor at Yasnaya Polyana. It was extremely unpleasant for him to carry out this order, but he had no alternative. In March of 1890, after Tolstoy had refused to receive the inspector of public schools, Zinoviev drove over to Yasnaya Polyana and in a very delicate manner requested the Tolstoy girls to discontinue their teaching, since the government could no longer countenance the existence of an *illegal* school.

Tolstoy himself continued to ignore the government's displeasure. He was distressed when his adherents were persecuted, but he continued to express his views quite freely and openly. And no matter what the government did, it was not able to stop the growth of Tolstoy's influence.

❧ 43 ❧

IT WAS spring and they were in their house in Moscow. Among a group of guests gathered there were the painter Repin, the actor Andreyev-Burlak, a student at the Moscow Conservatory, the tutor of the Tolstoy boys Andryusha and Misha, and Lasoto, a violinist. Seryozha and Lasoto were asked to play.

Seryozha was different from all the other Tolstoys because of his great shyness and reserve. He often concealed his emotions, his outbursts of tenderness or passion, under a cloak of deliberate rudeness, or brusqueness. The most serious-minded and industrious of all the Tolstoy brothers, he had his own separate existence; he did not lean toward either his mother, or his father, and he rarely confided his thoughts to the members of his family. It was only when he sat down to the piano and for hours played his beloved Chopin, Beethoven, Bach, Grieg, or attempted to compose something himself, that everyone listened to him. It was said that Seryozha had a remarkable touch. As a matter of fact it was only to the piano that he laid bare his heart: in sounds that were tempestuously passionate or tenderly singing one sensed the sadness, the inner struggle of this ill-favored and reserved youth.

It must have been that on this spring evening the young man played the Beethoven sonata dedicated to Kreutzer with especial verve. The first part, which Tolstoy particularly liked, strongly affected everyone present. They spoke of how fine it would be if Tolstoy wrote a story on the theme of the Kreutzer Sonata, and Repin illustrated it and Andreyev-Burlak acted it. This idea was never realized; Andreyev died shortly afterward. But in Tolstoy the idea continued to mature. It is difficult to say exactly when the theme of *The Kreutzer Sonata* first entered his head—that evening, under the influence of the music, or very much earlier, when in the 1870's he sketched out and then abandoned a story called *The Murderer of His Wife*.

On April 3, 1889, when Tolstoy was visiting his friend S. S.

[300]

Urusov in his country place, he jotted down in his diary: "It is early, I intended to write something new, but I reread just the beginnings and settled on *The Kreutzer Sonata*." And on the 5th of April he wrote: "I wrote a great deal on *The Kreutzer Sonata* and it was not bad."

But Sophia Andreyevna wrote in her diary in December, 1890, that "the idea of making a real *story* was given to him [Tolstoy] by Andreyev-Burlak, an actor and wonderful storyteller." Then Sophia Andreyevna added: "It was he who told about how once in a railroad train a man confided in him the misfortune of his wife's unfaithfulness and this was the subject used by Lyovochka."

In creating his main character, Pozdnishev, there is no doubt that Tolstoy drew upon various aspects of his own relations with his wife: the periods of tenderness and coolness, the discord, the quarrels, and faithfully described some of Sophia Andreyevna's more annoying characteristics fully aware of this, she did not care for *The Kreutzer Sonata*.

"There were words and expressions of hatred because of the coffee, the tablecloth, the carriage, a lead in a card game—all things without any importance to either of them," Tolstoy has Pozdnishev say in *The Kreutzer Sonata*. "In me, in any case, hatred toward her boiled furiously. I watched her sometimes as she poured tea, swung her foot, carried her spoon to her mouth, noisily sipped the liquid, and I hated her as much for this as for the worst kind of act. I did not notice at that time that the periods of resentment came over me quite regularly and at equal intervals and corresponded to the periods of what we called love. A period of love—a period of bitterness—a spirited period of love—a long period of bitterness— a weaker manifestation of love—a brief period of bitterness. . . . We were two prisoners who hated each other, fastened to the same chain, ruining each other's lives and trying not to see it. I still did not know at the time that nine-tenths of married people live in this hell in which I lived and that this cannot be otherwise."

Tolstoy's ideas about marriage and continence were upsetting to Sophia Andreyevna.

"You are harassing and killing yourself," she wrote him on April 19, 1889, to Yasnaya Polyana. "I . . . have been thinking: he does not eat meat, nor smoke, he works beyond his strength, his brain is not nourished, hence the drowsiness and weakness. How stupid vegetarianism is. . . . Kill life in yourself, kill all impulses of the flesh, all its needs—why not kill yourself altogether? After all you are committing yourself to *slow* death, what's the difference?"

The writing of *The Kreutzer Sonata* took almost two years. Tolstoy wrote in spurts; at times he lost interest in it and then he would take it up again with enthusiasm. In a letter to his friend G. A. Rusanov, he wrote (March 14, 1889): "The rumor about a novel has some foundation. As early as two years ago I wrote the rough draft of a novel dealing with the theme of sexual love, but I did it so carelessly and unsatisfactorily that I did not even revise it, but should I become interested in the idea I would make a fresh start." Earlier Tolstoy had written in his diary: "Have been revising *The Kreutzer Sonata*. . . . Have gotten bored by *The K.S.*"

When Tolstoy wrote that he was "bored" by one of his works it meant that he was nearing the finish of it. Before he had quite concluded the novel he began to write the Epilogue, and meantime the novel was being passed around. Tolstoy received varied reactions: bewilderment, condemnation, friendly criticism, enthusiasm.

In his Epilogue he attempted to reply to the many questions he had been asked.

"Given the ideal of chastity," he wrote, "one must consider that the only departure from it on the part of any two people must be to form a unique, indissoluble union for life, and then it will be clear that the guidance given by Christ is not only sufficient but also the only one possible."

In a letter to V. I. Alexeyev Tolstoy wrote: "The contents of what I have written are as new to me as to those who have read them. In this respect the ideal revealed to me is so far from my own actions that at first I was terrified and said nothing, but then I became convinced, repented, and rejoiced at the joyful advance in store for others and for me."

N. N. Strakhov, although he criticized *The Kreutzer Sonata* from the point of view of the external handling of the novel, wrote Tolstoy an enthusiastic letter about its substance.

Tolstoy replied: "From the artistic point of view I am well aware that the writing is beneath all criticism: it was based on two mentally inharmonious methods, hence the formlessness you sensed. Nevertheless I am leaving it as it stands and have no regrets, not because I am lazy, but I cannot correct it. I also have no regrets because I know somehow that what is written is true, and not only not useless but surely beneficial to people, and in part it is new.

If it were to be written in artistic form, which I do not repudiate, I would have to start all over again and at once."

Chertkov criticized it: "The novel in its present state can do no more than arouse in the reader questions, doubts; it does not clarify them to the degree which you are capable of clarifying them, by injecting into the novel the core of Christian convictions which so far is lacking. . . ."

This reaction on the part of his friend evidently distressed Tolstoy, who noted in his diary: "He makes a valid criticism of *The Kreutzer Sonata*, and I'd be glad to follow his advice, but I have no urge to do so. I feel only apathy, sadness, despondency."

Was Tolstoy really in need of such criticism? He was more severe on himself than anyone else. "I am writing on *The Kreutzer Sonata* and 'What Is Art?' and they are both negative, wicked, and I want to write what is good," he said in his diary for June 24, 1889.

During this period of artistic creativeness any polishing of his writing, his style, seemed a superfluous luxury to Tolstoy. To him the important thing was to have time to express thoughts from which readers might benefit.

His main concern was his own conscience. "All I want is to be in a state of cleanliness, that is to say, clean of all lustful appetite," he wrote to the elder Gay, "of all delights, wine, smoking, sexual lust and human fame, to be humble, that is to say, be prepared to have my work scored and myself slandered."

And Tolstoy was both scored and slandered. Now, people said, after having enjoyed a stormy life, in his old age he preaches chastity and abstinence.

"To struggle, that is one's very life," Tolstoy wrote in his "Thoughts on the Relations between the Sexes," and later on he said: "Man must not make chastity his goal, but an approach to chastity."

The Kreutzer Sonata was banned, despite the fact that everyone everywhere was talking about it and it was being passed from hand to hand.

"It is difficult to imagine," wrote Alexandrine in her memoirs, "what happened when *The Kreutzer Sonata* and *The Power of Darkness* appeared. Although they were not yet licensed to be printed, these works were copied by the hundreds and thousands, they were passed from hand to hand, they were translated into all languages and were always read with incredible emotion; it seemed as if for the time being the public abandoned its private cares and lived only on the writings of Count Tolstoy."

When on February 25, 1890, the whole of Volume XIII of the complete works of Tolstoy, the one in which this novel appeared, was held up, Sophia Andreyevna appealed to Durnovo, the Minister of Internal Affairs. Her request that the ban be lifted was refused; but Sophia Andreyevna was not one to give up easily. The greater the obstacles, the greater her energy. After consulting with Granny and with A. M. Kuzminski, she decided to go to St. Petersburg and in person request the Emperor to allow the publication of the novel. The Emperor proved to be more liberal-minded than any of his subordinates, and he granted Sophia Andreyevna permission to issue Volume XIII. By now it was April, 1891. Sophia Andreyevna came back from St. Petersburg gay and satisfied. The ban on Volume XIII had been the cause of serious financial loss. Moreover, she appears to have been flattered by the reception and attention accorded her by the Emperor, for she enjoyed talking about it to all her relatives and acquaintances.

Many people missed the deep significance of *The Kreutzer Sonata*. They made it trivial, they distorted it. One of the states in the United States proved to be less liberal than the Russian Tsar; it banned the novel as being pornographic, and in Germany a publisher, hoping to make money, launched a vile advertising campaign and printed a naked woman on the cover of the book.

All during this period Tolstoy was absorbed by the question of sex. Having wrestled with the temptations of lust all his life, he was well aware of its great power which leads men to crime and sometimes to complete moral collapse. Before he had finished *The Kreutzer Sonata* he sketched out within two weeks' time a novel called *The Devil*, in which he described with all the creative power at his disposal the frightful animal passion of a man for a peasant woman and his battle with it.

The Devil, or, as Tolstoy called it at first, *The Story of Fredericks*, was told to him by the sister of the main character in it. This was a piece of writing which so enthralled him that he wrote it in one sweep. There is this note in his diary for November 10, 1889: "After dinner I quite unexpectedly began to write *The Story of Fredericks*." On November 19 he again made a note: "I wrote all morning on *The Story of Fredericks*." But once it was blocked in in rough draft he put it aside and scarcely ever went back to it. It was twenty years later that he wrote another version of it, first called *Irtenev*, and in its final edited form, *The Devil*.

At the time Sophia Andreyevna knew nothing about this novel. Tolstoy purposely concealed it from her, knowing that it would evoke a storm of jealousy over his past love affair with Axinia. It is true that this affair, about which Sophia Andreyevna had learned only after her marriage and which had made such a painful impression on her, served in part as the theme of *The Devil*.

Another story of this period—*Father Sergius*—which was first outlined in a letter from Tolstoy to Chertkov on February 3, 1890, describes the fall of a monk from his holy state, seduced by a woman.

In February Tolstoy, with his daughter Masha and Vera Kuzminskaya, went to the Shamordin Convent where his sister, Maria Nikolayevna, had taken the veil. The monastery of Optina Pustyn, where he had been many times, was only a few miles away. He again went to see Elder Ambrosius and had lengthy talks with two monks, Shidlovski and Leontiev. It is likely that this visit gave him a great deal of material for *Father Sergius*.

In a letter to one of his followers, E. I. Popov, later that year Tolstoy wrote: ". . . In our struggle with temptation we are weakened by setting victory as our goal; we set ourselves a task beyond our powers, a task which it does not lie within our power to fulfill or not fulfill. We, as a monk does, say to ourselves in advance: I promise myself to be chaste, with the understanding that I mean by that, external chastity. And this, in the first place, is impossible because we cannot imagine in what circumstances we may be placed and in which we would not resist temptation. And, moreover, this is bad; bad because it does not help to achieve the goal—the approach to greater continence—but on the contrary. . . .

"There can be only one aim: to achieve the greatest degree of continence given my character, temperament, the circumstances of my past and present—continence, not in the eyes of people who do not know what I have to contend with, but in my own eyes and those of God. . . ."

With these words Tolstoy expressed with particular clarity the thought which he often repeated to his fervent and often unreasonable followers, who boldly, ardently, and with the self-assurance of youth, were convinced that they could achieve perfection, and who set themselves aims beyond the reach of their powers.

[305]

A series of plots were revolving in Tolstoy's mind. He began to write a novel on a theme given him by Koni. Tolstoy called this one the "Koni novel"—it was to become *Resurrection*—but the plot was too broad, so he put it aside. *Father Sergius* exercised an obviously stronger pull on him. He also had to finish an article on nonresistance—"The Kingdom of God Is Within You." Concurrently he was revising a novel in the Tolstoyan mood that he had sketched out in the eighties, called *Walk in the Light While Light Remains*.

At the same time he experimented with a new story form which employed a succession of people into whose hands a *counterfeit coupon* falls. But neither did that work out. He grew tired, for *The Kreutzer Sonata* and "The Kingdom of God" absorbed the major part of his energy. Then quite unexpectedly, perhaps even to him, in March of 1889, he began to write a comedy which originally was called *Themselves Outwitted* and later *The Fruits of Enlightenment*, which he had sketched out and then abandoned three years earlier.

No matter how hard Tolstoy tried to ignore artistic form and finish he could not cease to be an artist, and as an artist he was carried away by this new medium. The writing of a comedy about spiritism —at which he scoffed all his life—was a relaxation.

But perhaps even then the play would never have been finished had it not been for his daughter Tanya, who, with Seryozha, had just returned from a journey abroad. "The children wanted to stage a comedy," Tolstoy wrote Chertkov on December 22, 1889. "They asked if they could take mine (*The Fruits of Enlightenment*). I agreed and began to revise it. Now I have finished. It's a very weak piece, but it can, I believe, do some good. Incidentally, I feel rather conscience-stricken over occupying myself with such trifles when there is so much that is needed. The only thing I am happy about is that I am rid of it."

But the gaiety and liveliness of the young people involuntarily affected Tolstoy too. The preparations were legion, a stage was built in the big room, many people came from Tula. The arch instigator, Tanya, stirred up everyone in the household; she undertook the production of the performance with ardor. The President of the Tula District Court, N. V. Davydov, directed the play. Samarin, Tsinger, Lopatin and others divided up the parts. During the rehearsals Tolstoy often took the text away from the actors and carried it into his study in order to enter some corrections. In places where the audience rocked with laughter, the one who laughed loudest and most infectiously was the author himself. The two Tolstoy sisters played magnificently; there was no doubt that Tanya in particular had acting ability.

In April 1890 N. V. Davydov produced the play in the city of Tula for the benefit of a reformatory. On the basis of Emperor Alexander III's decree, according to which the play was judged unsuitable for the public stage, the censor allowed it to be performed only in amateur productions. Later on permission to produce the play was granted, after special applications had been made in individual cases, but it was only in 1894 that a separate circular was issued which sanctioned the performance of *The Fruits of Enlightenment* in all theaters of the Russian Empire.

44

TOLSTOY'S article on nonresistance, eventually entitled "The Kingdom of God Is Within You," slowly took shape. It was begun in 1890 under the influence of Adin Ballou, whose death upset Tolstoy as much as that of a close friend. To find people thinking along the same lines as he was, to find them even beyond the seas, was one of the greatest consolations in Tolstoy's life.

He wrote "The Kingdom of God" with interruptions. His interest was deflected by other schemes, the translation and adaptation of Guy de Maupassant's story "Françoise," the writing of an article entitled "Why Do People Stupefy Themselves?," and other literary work. The middle of November, 1890, Tolstoy wrote to Rusanov: "I have been cudgeling my brains about this (the article on nonresistance) for a long time, but I can neither finish it nor tear myself away from it in order to devote myself to other artistic plans which attract me"; and on November 19, he noted in his diary: "I'd like to do something free, something artistic, but I refuse to let myself go until I have finished this."

On March 2, 1891, Sophia Andreyevna made this entry in her

diary: "Lyovochka is downcast. I asked him the reason; he said his writing was not going well. But on what subject? On nonresistance. I should think it wouldn't! This question has put everyone, even him, on edge; it's been twisted and considered from every angle. What he yearns for is *artistic* work, but it is difficult to start on it. This is no place for *moralizing*. When the flood gates of true artistic creativeness will be opened in him he will not be able to stem the tide, so he is afraid to let go and meantime his heart is heavy."

Eighteen ninety and 1891 were years of especial tension in the relations between Tolstoy and his wife. In the winter of 1890 the Yasnaya Polyana peasants cut down and carried off some trees from the forest planted by Tolstoy. They were arrested and haled into court at the instigation of Sophia Andreyevna. This incident upset Tolstoy. Never had he felt so keenly the divergence between his convictions and the actual state of things. Because of his property, which he renounced, some peasants would be handed over to a court and put into prison for having cut down trees, perhaps out of their dire need. . . .

"I am losing my balance," wrote Sophia Andreyevna in her diary. "It's easy to say that, but every single minute I am concerned with my children who are studying or ill, with the state of health and spirits of my husband, with the older children and their affairs, with debts, the small children and the servants. . . ."

Ilya was young, inexperienced, his home was not being successfully managed; he raised hunting dogs, bought good horses, lived beyond his means; his wife was expecting a second child. Lyova was sickly, nervous, variable in his interests, and his mother worried about him. Masha was still trying to make up her mind to marry Biryukov and this angered Sophia Andreyevna. She had no sympathy for Masha's leading the "simple" life, doing her own laundry, wearing herself out with physical work. The boys were not doing well in their studies. Tanya did not seem able to make a life for herself; she could not find a man she was willing to marry; she made friends with Popov, one of the "dark people," who was obviously in love with her. Vanichka was ailing.

"And so that is how we have the kind of incident which occurred last night," she wrote in her diary about the scene between her and her husband when they could not calm themselves but went on until five o'clock in the morning heaping reproaches on each other. "I see that I made a mistake, that I have lost some kind of focus, and that I hurt Lyovochka inadvertently. *The incident*, as one might have expected, grew out of the sentencing of some peasants to six weeks' arrest because of cutting trees in the plantation. When we lodged the complaint with the rural magistrate we intended to pardon them after they had been sentenced. It turned out to be a *criminal* offense, a pardon was absolutely ruled out, and Lyovochka was plunged into despair by the thought that because of his property Yasnaya peasants would be put in jail. At night he could not sleep, he kept jumping up, pacing the floor in the living room, raging, reproaching me, of course, and his reproaches were terribly brutal."

Tolstoy wanted to leave home for good. "I think I must announce to the government," he wrote in his diary for November 18, "that I do not recognize property and rights, and leave it to them to act as they choose." By "them" he meant the family.

After this occurrence Tolstoy began to consider more and more seriously how to rid himself of the burden of property. His older sons, who wished to be independent, especially Ilya, supported him in his decision. And so, in April, all the family came together. The property was appraised and divided into nine parts. The last born, Vanichka, received by tradition half of Yasnaya Polyana, including the main house, Sophia Andreyevna being given the other half and one wing of the house; the elder son, Sergei, was given the family estate of Nikolskoye-Vyazemskoye. Masha, following her father's principles, refused any share in the property. Ilya received Grinevka, the Chernskoye estate; Lev, the Moscow house; Tanya, the Ovsyannikovo estate, seven versts from Yasnaya Polyana (between five and six miles away) and part of the cash; Andrei, Misha and Sasha (Alexandra) were given the Samara estate.

Tolstoy's intention of giving up all his author's rights and of transferring them to public domain met with a sharp objection from Sophia Andreyevna. Again she saw herself confronted by "poverty," as she expressed it, and a change in her whole way of life for which neither she nor her children, with the exception of Masha, were adapted. How was she to bring up the "infants" and how was she to train "the little ones"? How to give them an education? She was not prepared for such sacrifices. She *could* not accept them.

She might have agreed without a struggle to giving up for the public benefit all the writings about which Tolstoy particularly cared and which he had written after 1880: his folk tales, his articles. She might have given them up promptly and gladly, which would have soothed Tolstoy, but she could not bring herself to do it. All the children were by now fully provided for, and with what joy, what gratitude, Tolstoy would have accepted this sacrifice!

On July 12, 1891, Tolstoy wrote to his wife: "I have been thinking all this while of composing and publishing an announcement about my renouncing my rights to my most recent writings, but I have not been able to think it out; now it occurs to me that it might be well, with regard to being reproached on your account by the public for exploitation—as a member of a labor association would say— for you to print an announcement in the papers on your own behalf, perhaps in the form of a letter to the editor.

" 'My husband Lev Nikolayevich Tolstoy renounces his rights to royalties from his latest writings and offers them for publication without remuneration to him, to anyone who cares to print and publish them. The writings are as follows: [here follows a list of all folk tales, his latest articles, *The Fruits of Enlightenment*, "Why Do People Stupefy Themselves?," *The Kreutzer Sonata*, "Epilogue."]

" 'In making this announcement, I beg that those who choose to print such writings use the text published in my edition. Yours truly, Countess Sophia Tolstoy.'

"I think that this would be well," Tolstoy added in a postscript, "but if it does not appeal to you, do not do it, do not print the announcement in your name, but in mine, and then it would read:

" 'Dear Sir: I renounce my author's rights to my latest writings and offer them to anyone caring to print and publish them. . . . The writings included are the following. . . . Yours truly, etc.' "

Sophia Andreyevna received this letter in Moscow, where she had gone on business connected with his books. When she returned he again raised the question of giving up his income from his books.

Sophia Andreyevna was quite beside herself and reproached her husband with not caring for his family, with putting on her alone the whole burden of the household, the estate management, the publications. She told him he was egotistical and that he was driving her crazy with his "dark people" and his whims and that she no longer wished to live.

In the course of one of these stormy conversations when Sophia Andreyevna was in no state to listen or reason she ran out of the house and down to the station with the intention of throwing herself under a train. She did not of course realize what she was doing. A. M. Kuzminski, who was quietly taking his daily stroll, ran into her out on the highway. He instantly sensed that something had happened, calmed her and led her back to the house.

The children saw all this and, each one in his own way, suffered because of it. Tanya strove to reconcile her parents. She was very fond of her mother, but she sympathized with her father's views and she pleaded with her mother to make some concessions. Sergei tried to get away from it all. Ilya was absorbed in his own material cares and family. Lev was inclined to his mother's side. Masha was on bad terms with her mother; wholeheartedly devoted to her father, she suffered more than anyone else on his account.

Sophia Andreyevna once wrote in her diary: "Masha anyhow is a cross sent by God to bear. From the day of her birth she has never caused me anything but torture. In the family she is aloof, in her faith she is aloof, in her love for Biryukov, an imaginary love, she is incomprehensible."

This was the daughter of whom Tolstoy said: "She somehow makes up for all the others."

Following in her father's footsteps, aflame with renunciation and self-sacrifice, Masha mortified her flesh, slept on hard boards covered with a thin layer of felt; she lived on a vegetarian diet, worked from morning to night in the fields, teaching children, helping the sick, the unfortunates, or visiting peasant families. Almost everyone called her by her first name and used the familiar "thou" in addressing her. In the evenings she copied her father's manuscripts in her fine, neat hand. And this life was not easy for her. She liked other things too, tennis and gypsy songs. She played well on the guitar, sang with a true if not large voice, and she, as well as Tanya, had many suitors. Despite her lack of beauty, she had a great deal of charm.

On the 16th of September, after much hesitation and argument with his wife, Tolstoy decided to execute his intention.

"Gentlemen," he addressed the heads of the newspapers. "As the result of the many requests I have received for permission to publish, translate and produce on the stage various works of mine, I beg you to place in the paper you publish the following announcement:

" 'I herewith grant to all who wish it the right without remuneration to publish in Russia or abroad, in Russian or in translation, as well as to produce on the stage, all my works printed in Volume XII being issued this year, 1891, as well as my published works which may be issued later on, that is to say from this day forward.' "

While all this internal drama was in progress in the Tolstoy family, one might have supposed they would be in no mood to entertain guests, yet the way of life at Yasnaya Polyana was not altered. Every day ten to fourteen sat down at the long dining-room table. The usual picnics went on, there were horseback parties for the young people, numerous neighbors came, the Figner couple came to sing —they lived on a neighboring estate and were artists from the Imperial Opera—there were the same nurses, children's digestive upsets, quarrels and caprices; painters, sculptors, Professor Grot, various foreigners came to visit. . . . In the evening there were singing to guitars, readings, conversation. . . .

In the forenoons Tolstoy would withdraw from all the noise and activities to his new study. He now worked in a room called "under the vaults," which in the days of N. S. Volkonski had been a storeroom. The vaulted brick ceiling shut out every sound; light came in through two high grated windows. Near one of the windows stood the writing table; on the walls were various tools—a scythe, a saw— and in the corner was a basket with cobbling tools. The walls were bare, the furniture was simple, covered with leather.

But even here Tolstoy could not escape people. In one corner, in absorbed silence, sat I. E. Repin, palette in hand, painting. He was joined by the sculptor Ginsburg, who was visiting at Yasnaya Polyana for the first time.

Near the village station a fine grade of clay of various colors had been found, and Yasnaya Polyana was swept by an enthusiasm for modeling. The artists modeled—Gay, Repin, Ginsburg—also Sophia Andreyevna and Lyova, while the children modeled animals and mugs.

Tolstoy patiently posed. This is how Ginsburg described it in his memoirs: "We began to arrange ourselves, I settled myself beside I. E. Repin, who was finishing his work; I was enchanted by his painting: the setting of the room, the light falling from the window and indeed the figure of Lev Nikolayevich—all painted with astonishing truthfulness and artistry." Ginsburg was right. "Tolstoy in His Study" is probably the best portrait done of Tolstoy.

"To tell the truth it was difficult for me to work," Ginsburg goes on. "I was so afraid of making a sound that I had to remain in one place without stirring, yet to make a bust in the round it is necessary to move and observe your model from different angles. It seems to me that our presence bothered Lev Nikolayevich."

Ginsburg was not mistaken; the presence of outsiders did hamper him in his writing. Ginsburg, like a rambling convolvulus, wound himself around his bust, jumping up, sitting down, crouching on his heels and squinting, as though he were drawing a bead on Tolstoy. He literally was incapable of sitting still in one place for a single minute. Ginsburg soon became a familiar member of the household at Yasnaya Polyana, usually arriving with his friend Vladimir V. Stasov, a literary critic and chief of one of the divisions in the St. Petersburg Public Library.

It would be difficult to imagine two people more different in appearance than these two friends. Ginsburg, a modest man, was short, swarthy, bald, with fiery black eyes, tiny hands, a thin voice. Stasov was a man of tremendous stature, of heroic proportions, with a long beard and a thick head of hair. When he spoke it was not with simple tones but with the utterance of a prophet, attracting the attention of all.

Of the three busts which are still in Yasnaya Polyana, Tolstoy felt that the best was the one done by N. N. Gay, but some of the experts prefer Ginsburg's. Repin's bust was also very successful, but it was overshadowed by his painting of "Tolstoy in His Study."

During that summer there was talk in Yasnaya Polyana of a famine. Sophia Andreyevna, who was still in Moscow, wrote to her husband in September:

"Dunayev and Natasha have been here about the starving people and again my heart was wrung. I wish I could forget and close my eyes to it, but that is impossible, the need is too great. But how is it we see nothing of it in Moscow! Everything is as usual, the same luxury, the same fine turnouts and stores, and everyone is buying and arranging, as I do too, to keep his own silly corner tidy from which we shall look out into the far distance where people are starving to death."

In the months that followed both she and her husband were to devote much of their time and effort to helping the starving, and in this work they were, if only for a time, to find each other again.

❧ 45 ❧

TOLSTOY was always revolted by philanthropy as practiced by the idle rich in self-justification. In his youth he had almost fought a duel with Turgenyev because of a dispute they had on the subject.

"The children sometimes give the poor some bread, sugar or money," he wrote in his diary toward the end of June, 1891, "and are pleased with themselves . . . believing they have done something good. Children do not know, they cannot know, where the bread and the money come from. But grownups should know and understand that there can be no good in taking from one to give to another. Yet there are many grownups who do not understand this."

". . . Kind acts cannot be done suddenly because there is a famine; if anyone does good he has already done it yesterday and the day before that, and he will do it tomorrow and the day after tomorrow, and during a famine and when there is no famine." So Tolstoy wrote to Leskov in reply to a question about the threat of famine in the provinces of Samara, Ryazan and Tula.

As early as midsummer of 1891 it was obvious that the wheat and the rye crops had failed, and that this failure constituted a dreadful threat. Just as rice and beans are the staple food of the Chinese and Japanese, bread, potatoes, buckwheat and millet form the basic food of the Russian peasant.

Despite all his arguments about the senselessness of temporary help, the famine began to upset Tolstoy more and more. An acquaintance of his, Ivan Ivanovich Rayevski, arriving from one of the starving districts in the province of Ryazan, implored him to do something for the peasants. In September another friend visited him with stories of the famine. "I could not get to sleep until four o'clock —I kept thinking about the famine," Tolstoy entered in his diary on September 17. Two days later he went to his brother's estate, Pirogovo, which was on the edge of the steppe area affected by the failure of crops, and from there he proceeded through other regions in the steppes. Returning to Yasnaya Polyana for a few days, he took five hundred rubles from Sophia Andreyevna for initial relief and again went off to the famine areas in the provinces of Tula and Ryazan.

It was out of the question for Tolstoy to remain inactive. With his customary ardor he now set to work. He wrote an article about the famine which he sent to Grot to print, while he and his daughters, Masha and Tanya, and his niece Vera Kuzminskaya, traveled to Begichevka, the estate of Ivan Rayevski. At the same time his son Lev went down to the famine areas in the province of Samara.

In her diary for October 8, 1891, Sophia Andreyevna wrote: "When he arrived home and announced to me that they were not going to Moscow, but were going to live in the steppes, I was horrified. The thought of being separated all winter, and with them thirty versts [over twenty-two miles] from a station, with Lyovochka and his attacks of stomach and intestinal pain, the young girls so isolated, and with me left to my eternal worries about them, upset me so I became really ill. I hardly get one problem solved with difficulty, when there is a new one, and a fresh decision to be made. Meanwhile Lyova, not knowing about the decision to go to Rayevski's, wrote that we should all remain at Yasnaya, that my arrival in Moscow would distract the three in their studies, and that I am not at all needed. For twenty-nine years I have lived *only* for my family: I gave up everything that spells enjoyment and the fullness of life to any young person, and now I have reached the state of not being needed *by anybody*. How I cried! Evidently I must be very wicked, yet how was it that I poured out so much love, and love is looked upon as a good sentiment?"

Tanya also had little sympathy with her father's plan in the beginning, as she made clear in her diary: "We are on the eve of setting out on our journey to the Don River. I am not happy about the trip and I have no spirit at all. That is because I find that Papa's actions are not consistent and that it isn't proper for him to handle money, to accept contributions and take the money from Mama to whom he has just given it. I think that he himself realizes this. He says and he writes, and I agree with him, that all the misfortunes of the people derive from the fact that they have been robbed and driven into such a state by us, the landowners, and the whole crux of the matter lies in the fact that one must stop robbing the people. That, of course, is just and Papa acted on his own words—he ceased to rob them. Accord-

[315]

ing to me there was nothing else for him to do. But to take this stolen money from other persons and dispose of it, that is something I think he should not do. . . ."

But the doubts of the mother, as well as those of the daughter, were soon swept away. Sophia Andreyevna addressed herself to the task with all her characteristic fervor and energy.

On November 3 she wrote an appeal to the editors of the *Russian News,* asking for contributions to relieve the starving people. This letter was reprinted in all the newspapers of Russia and also abroad. She concluded by quoting a letter from her daughter which gave figures to show how the peasants lived.

"Consequently," she said in closing, "for thirteen rubles ($6.50) per year one can save a person from starving to death."

Sophia Andreyevna had scarcely time to turn around before contributions began to pour in. In less than two weeks more than 13,000 rubles ($6,500) were donated. In addition, people sent and brought in dry biscuits, clothing materials. . . . To Sophia Andreyevna's many occupations was now added that of a colossal correspondence and the accounts for the monies received.

"I do not know how all of you look upon my performance," she wrote to her husband. "But I was annoyed to be sitting here without any part in your work and since yesterday I even feel better physically; I enter the amounts in a book, give receipts, write letters of thanks, talk with people, and am glad that I can help to extend your work even if it is with the money of others."

In the beginning of November Tolstoy sent a second article to the *Russian News,* in which he touched on the question that was tormenting him: Is there sufficient grain in Russia to feed us through to the next harvest?

But he had no reason to worry—there was plenty of grain in Russia and very soon he became convinced of it.

The deeper Tolstoy and his helpers became involved in the condition of the peasantry, the more complex and varied became their activities. Tolstoy opposed giving out flour, feeling that it made for bad feelings and jealousy. The opening of canteens for the starving was both more practical and fairer, for it was possible thus to a certain degree to establish what the needs were and to feed only those who had absolutely no grain at all. There were other problems: the lack of fuel, of hay for the horses, which were dying of hunger, the need to find a secondary means of earning a living for the peasants. Foodstuffs, such as rye, wheat, dried pulse, potatoes, were ordered from other provinces. Work was in full swing.

At first there was a lack of helpers, but gradually people who were thinking along the same lines as Tolstoy were drawn to him: students, young people aflame with the desire to help in the general disaster. The two Tolstoy sisters threw themselves into the work. Tanya's doubts soon vanished and she worked wholeheartedly despite the fact that it was more difficult for her to adjust to the surroundings than it was for Masha, who followed her father without criticism and for whom the deprivations and hardships provided the very thing her soul craved—self-sacrifice and service to her father and the people.

During this autumn the family lost two close and devoted friends: Tolstoy's childhood friend, D. A. Diakov, and Ivan Rayevski, the owner of Begichevka, who had taken the Tolstoys in and come close to them in the general work of the famine.

No good work has ever been done without great difficulties, ill will or without arousing some unpleasantness. The government thought it sensed in Tolstoy's activities an intention to overthrow the existing powers. Pobedonostsev wrote to the Emperor:

"Abroad the haters of Russia, whose name is legion, the socialists and anarchists of every variety are basing the wildest kinds of ideas and speculations on the famine—some speak of sending their emissaries to stir up the people to revolt against the Government. . . . But even here at home there are many who . . . are taking advantage of the famine to spread their form of faith, their social fantasies, among the people in the guise of relief. Tolstoy has written a crazy article on this subject, which will, of course, not be published in the magazine where it is supposed to be printed but which they will, of course, attempt to distribute in manuscript copies. . . ."

In the *Moscow News* there were articles on "The Family of His Excellency Count L. N. Tolstoy," "The Plan of Count L. N. Tolstoy," and "A Message to Mischief Makers."

Sophia Andreyevna was annoyed: "Today the *Moscow News* all but made a revolutionary of you because of your article," she wrote to her husband on November 9. "How vile of them to think there is political scheming behind this. I have been scored too because of my letter. Evil is all this newspaper lives by."

She could not calm herself. "Today I am writing a letter to the Foreign Minister about the article in the *Moscow News*. I think they are setting a match to a revolution by their articles, identifying Tolstoy, Grot and Solovyov with some sort of supposed liberal party which by making capital out of the national catastrophe hopes to accomplish something of a political nature."

In another letter she wrote: "Lyovochka dear, you live in a calm place down there and do not suspect what a storm has been loosed about us up here. Grot has just been here and he says that the main government office on publications has been sent an order not to publish *anything* by Tolstoy, anywhere. The *Moscow News* branded you as a revolutionary because of your 'The Terrible Question' and there are no bounds to anger in the circles of the government and of the *Moscow News*. How is it the government does not see that the *Moscow News* people are systematically preparing the revolution. . . ."

There was good reason for Tolstoy to write all his friends—Gay, Chertkov, Rusanov—that in the work of feeding the famine sufferers he had come closer to his wife "than ever before." Like a mother eagle defending her brood, Sophia Andreyevna was ready to pounce on anyone who attacked what her family was doing.

"But now this is the problem," she wrote in this same letter of November 17. "An article on the canteens is urgently needed. I read publicly excerpts from your letters and everyone is terribly interested. Your articles are banned. There are two solutions: let an article be signed Tatiana Tolstoy. She, after all, also wanted to write, or else let me send it to the Emperor for his personal censorship. Only be sure to put a lot of *feeling* into the article, you used to be be able to do that when you were an artist; stir him up—and forget about all *your* nonsense and preferences. How even the smallest amount of *feeling* arouses an instant response—it is amazing! The little peasants from Samara were delighted that I was able to house them; and I am delighted. I wrote Masha yesterday. Sasha is still running a fever, all the others are well. There's a heavy snow."

The next article appeared over the signature of T. Tolstoy. A district police officer made an investigation in Begichevka, and two priests were suddenly sent down by the Tula church to check on Tolstoy's activities. The black reactionary press became more and more vociferous. Excerpts from his article on the famine, which Tolstoy had sent to Dillon for translation and publication in England, were retranslated into Russian—and distorted in the process—by the *Moscow News* and printed with comments. "The letters of Count Tolstoy," wrote the *Moscow News*, "need no commentary. They are open propaganda for the overthrow throughout the world of the existing social and economic order, which, for a very comprehensible reason, the Count attributes only to Russia. The Count's propaganda is the propaganda of the most unbridled socialism, beside which our underground propaganda pales. . . ."

All the little people who cluster around the seats of the mighty were thrown into a state of agitation. There was talk of arresting Tolstoy, of shutting him up in the Suzdal Monastery. Police searches were instituted, his adherents were arrested. Strict supervision of Tolstoy and his helpers was put in force by the local police. Local priests spread rumors to the effect that Tolstoy and his followers were the "offspring of the Antichrist," that they did not believe in God, did not pray, that they had appeared on the scene of the famine "to tempt the people," and that it was necessary "to get rid of them." The young girls had no conception of the campaign against them going on behind their backs and of the dangers that threatened them. But the peasants with their native intelligence took a different view. "What kind of Antichrist offspring are these—they are God's angels, sent by the Lord," said one peasant.

Even Granny Alexandrine was disturbed. "I shall not attempt to describe what a storm was raised all over Europe by the article," she wrote in her memoirs, "and how many punishments were thought up by the Moscow journalists to be visited on poor Lev Nikolayevich: they predicted for him Siberia, incarceration in a fortress, exile from Russia; they almost went so far as to mention the gallows. . . .

"And so," she continued, "when I found out what danger Lev Nikolayevich was in I decided to exert all my influence in order to save him. I wrote to the Emperor that I very much needed to see him and requested that he fix the time for me to do so. Imagine my joy when I suddenly received the reply that the Emperor himself was coming to call on me that very day.

"I was extremely excited while waiting for his visit and mentally begged God to help me. Finally the Emperor came in. I saw that his face was tired and that he was disturbed by something. But this did not alter my intention and only increased my own firmness. To the Emperor's question what it was I had to tell him I answered directly:

" 'In a few days you will receive a report proposing to incarcerate in a monastery the greatest genius in Russia.'

"The expression on the Emperor's face instantly changed: it grew severe and profoundly grieved.

" 'Tolstoy?' he asked curtly.

" 'You have guessed it, Sire,' I replied.

" 'You think he is plotting against my life?' asked the Emperor.

"Yet when he realized what the matter was the Emperor gave orders that Tolstoy was not to be touched.

" 'I have no intention of making a martyr of him and of bringing universal condemnation on myself. If he is guilty, so much the worse for him.' "

But the ferment continued. Count Lamsdorf, a councilor in the Ministry of Foreign Affairs, wrote in his diary that there were requests from all quarters for the issue of the *Moscow News* containing the Tolstoy article, which "one could not find at any price: they say in Moscow they are offering up to twenty-five rubles a copy."

Sophia Andreyevna, still agitated, went to the Grand Duke Sergei Alexandrovich (then Governor General in Moscow) and asked him to order the *Moscow News* to print a retraction of their article on Tolstoy. Sergei Alexandrovich replied that Tolstoy must do that himself.

On February 25, 1892 Tolstoy wrote to his wife:

"How sorry I am, my dear, that you are so upset by the stupid talk about articles in the *Moscow News* and that you went to see Sergei Alexandrovich. Nothing new has happened. What I wrote in the article about the famine I have said many times before and in much stronger language. What's new in that? It's all a question of the mob, of hypnotizing the mob, of rolling up a snowball. I have written the denial. But please, my dear, *do not change or add a single word,* and do not allow this to be done by anyone. I have thought over each word carefully and I have told the whole truth, and I have completely refuted the false accusation."

But Sophia Andreyevna was not satisfied. She told her husband that "they say here that the young people are all upset, have lost faith in you, are tearing up pictures of you, etc. That is the sad part of it and the thing that should be redressed." She also wrote to the press abroad to clear up the rumor that Tolstoy had been arrested: "The highest authorities have always been especially favorable in their attitude toward our family."

"Please do not take on this tone of one being accused," Tolstoy wrote his wife on February 25, 1892. "That is a complete reversal of roles. One can be silent. If one cannot be silent, then one can only accuse—not the *Moscow News,* who represent no interests, and not individual people, but the conditions of life which make possible what is possible in our country."

Despite all the difficulties, the whole Tolstoy family engaged in famine relief experienced a sense of joy in their work. The best people in Russia sympathized with Tolstoy and helped with contributions, each according to his capacity. Contributions also came from abroad—from England, America. There was no end to the volunteer helpers, including a number of Tolstoy's followers—Biryukov, Popov, and others—and many who were untrained, ignorant of country life. But what was easy and natural to Tolstoy came hard to the city folk. They did not know how to approach the peasants, how to understand or be understood by them, they were afraid to go to outlying villages during a blizzard or heavy frost, they did not know how to drive horses, to harness or unharness them, how to get a horse and sleigh out of a snowdrift. But gradually they learned.

They lived like a large family. In the evenings they came together, read aloud, chatted, exchanged the experiences and impressions of the day, played chess. In the forenoons Tolstoy continued to work on his essay "The Kingdom of God Is Within You," and his two daughters, as always, copied his manuscripts.

The storm clouds which had gathered over Tolstoy's head passed all but unheeded by them—they were too absorbed in the needs and griefs of the people they were serving.

The young people clustered around Tanya and Masha. Youth took its natural course. Petya Rayevski, a handsome young man, a medical student who loved hunting and gypsies, lost his heart to Masha and she was favorable to his courtship. Popov suffered; he did not dare openly to declare his devotion to Tanya because he was married. Masha made friends with a young woman medical student, Vera Velichkina, who had come down to help the famine sufferers. Vera Velichkina was one of those self-sacrificing, somewhat ecstatic girls of whom there were many in Russia. For the most part they were unattractive in appearance; they came from poor but educated or partially educated families, and from their tenderest years they yearned to serve the common people. Some of them became schoolteachers, others nurses, a third group joined the revolutionaries and found both their calling and their aim in the overthrow of the existing system by revolutionary means. The endurance, the self-sacrifice and the resoluteness of this type of woman was amazing. No matter in what field they worked, they gave themselves without stint, never saving their strength, their time, their health. Vera Velichkina gave herself up to the service of the starving with the same fervor with which later she threw herself into the revolution when she joined the Bolshevik wing of the Social Democratic party.*

As they had come to Yasnaya Polyana, the visitors now flocked in numbers to Begichevka—American journalists, English Quakers, tourists, cranks, and many genuinely anxious to help. Among the oddities was a seventy-year-old Swede who had lived for thirty years in America and been in China, Japan and India.

"He has long, yellowish white hair," Tolstoy wrote to his wife, "a beard of the same, is small of stature, wears a huge hat; he is somewhat tattered, looks a little like me; he is an advocate of a life lived in accordance with the law of nature. He speaks excellent English, is very intelligent, original and interesting. He wants to live somewhere (he has been in Yasnaya) where he can teach people how one person can feed ten persons by himself on four hundred square sazhens [a sazhen is seven feet] of land, without draught animals, using only a spade. I wrote to Chertkov about him and want to send him to him. But for the time being he is digging the ground for potatoes and preaching to us. He is a vegetarian, takes no milk or eggs, and prefers everything raw. He goes barefoot, sleeps on the floor, puts a bottle under his head etc. . . . ."

This Swede not only foreswore meat, fish, milk and eggs, but "when the big samovar was brought in at breakfast," wrote Skorokhodov, one of Tolstoy's followers, in his memoirs, "the Swede rose and, like a prophet, pointed to the samovar and said with a reproachful tone: 'And you bow down before that idol! I am entrusted with a mission from the Chinese who are suffering because their best lands are pre-empted by tea plantations and they have nowhere to sow their essential grain. You should refuse to use tea if you know that by its use you are accessories to robbing our Chinese brethren of their daily bread.' Lev Nikolayevich with some embarrassment translated this appeal from the English and suggested that we act on it. He himself ceased to drink tea; in place of it he took barley coffee, and the samovar was taken away."

The Swede settled into the Rayevski home and had no intention of leaving. His hosts began to feel burdened but Tolstoy was interested in him. He found that, like the prophet Jeremiah, he was right on many points. Tolstoy was so taken with his theory that he

* She later married Vladimir Bonch-Bruyevich, Lenin's personal secretary.

gave up milk and butter and decided to eat only raw foods. This experiment ended up with his having violent pains in his abdomen. Sophia Andreyevna, who had come down to Begichevka for a few days, was horrified when she saw the filthy, tattered, barefoot, half-naked old man sleeping on the floor under a table. "And what are these bare legs?" she asked.

"He lies on the grass like a cow, digs in the earth, rinses himself in the Don River, eats a lot, lies in the kitchen—and that's all. We told him very gently that . . . he must go away, and he promised to leave," Sophia Andreyevna wrote to her daughter Tanya, who had gone off for a rest in the home of her friends, the Olsufievs.

It proved impossible to dislodge the Swede from Begichevka, and to Sophia Andreyevna's horror he turned up later on, trailing Lev Nikolayevich, at Yasnaya Polyana. From there he moved to Ovsyannikovo, a small estate belonging to Tanya, and it was only the departure in the fall of the whole family and the coming cold that finally obliged him to quit the place, from which he disappeared without a trace.

In the middle of April, 1892, Tolstoy published the report of his work in famine relief for six months:

The opening of 187 canteens in which some 10,000 persons were fed.

The distribution of firewood to the population.

The distribution of linen and bast to be worked up.

Feeding stations for children from infancy to three years of age.

The distribution of seeds and seed potatoes to the peasants.

The purchase and distribution of horses.

Collection of 141,000 rubles (70,500 dollars) of which 108,000 rubles was expended.

Beginning with the end of May, Tolstoy divided his time between Yasnaya Polyana and Begichevka, but the relief work was continued in several districts in the provinces of Tula and Ryazan. Lev Tolstoy, Jr., and Biryukov were working in the province of Samara.

In the autumn of 1892 the crop failed again and the grain bins of the peasants were bare. Typhus was rampant. It was necessary to continue the relief.

"What then is the situation?" were Tolstoy's closing words in his autumn report. "Can it be there are starving people again? Starving people! Canteens! Canteens! Starving people! After all this is an old story and so terribly boring.

"You have been bored by it in Moscow, in St. Petersburg, but down here there are people standing under our windows, at our doors, from morning until night. You cannot even go out for a walk without hearing the same phrases over and over: We haven't had any food for two days, we ate up our last sheep. What will you do? The very end has come. It means we shall die.

"To be sure we are weary of it. Yet these people, as much as we ourselves, want to eat, to live, they yearn for happiness, for love. . . ."

Beginning with the autumn of 1892 the main management of famine relief in the Begichevka region was turned over by Tolstoy to Posha Biryukov. Sophia Andreyevna insisted that her family come home. Typhus was raging in the villages and she was afraid they would catch it. That autumn Maria Petrovna Behrs, Stepan Behr's wife, died of the disease.

Tolstoy's emotional experiences in connection with the famine relief were complex, as complex as all the rest of his personal life had been in recent years. From the human point of view, from the point of view of the general public and even of some of his followers, Tolstoy's life was nothing but a compromise; only he, standing stripped before his God, could judge whether or not he followed the dictates of his conscience or his own personal, egotistical impulses.

From the very minute when he realized the urgency and magnitude of the national disaster, his theories about money and property had to be laid aside; he did what he was incapable of not doing, though he knew that many, even those closest to him, did not understand and would condemn him.

"There will always be enemies," he wrote in his notebook. "One cannot live without having enemies. On the contrary, the better life one leads, the more enemies one has.

"There will always be enemies; but one must manage not to suffer because of them. And this can be done. One should act so that enemies are a source not of suffering, but of joy.

"One must love them, and that is easy.

"I am alone, yet there are so terribly many human beings, they are so different, it is impossible to come to know them all—all the Indians, Malayans, Japanese, or even those who are always with me, my children, my wife. . . . Among all these people I am alone, completely lonely and alone. . . ."

☙ 46 ☙

THE Kingdom of God is at hand—it is at the gates.

"I cannot think it otherwise and I shall die with the consciousness of it, and also live; above all I wish to live out the time still left to me to live, in a way to harmonize with that realization.

"It may well be that I am not doing what I should toward that end; perhaps I am on the wrong path: still I know that it is only a life which brings about the Kingdom of God, a life spent in searching for the Kingdom of God and for truth, that has any meaning for me."

The idealism and optimism of Tolstoy knew no limits. "There are three degrees in life," he wrote to Obolenski. "(1) life for the sake of one's animal nature, (2) life for the sake of earthly glory, (3) life for the sake of God."

Tolstoy firmly believed that people in the end will realize that they must live for the sake of God.

Nothing gave him as much joy as the evidence of divine qualities in a person. ". . . It is clearer and clearer to me that only one thing is needed," he wrote to Popov, "to keep watch over one's divine 'I' and make it grow so that one may pass over into one's other life increased in stature—the trace it leaves behind in this life is only the inevitable result of this growth—this moving toward perfection. I fear that this may seem nothing but words: yet for me it is a deed, and not only a deed but my only tie with life. Only thus can one live with buoyancy, energy, after one has renounced, at least in one's conscience, external terrestrial joys as the goal of life. Only when one does not set them as a goal are terrestrial joys added to one."

When he came into contact with human evil Tolstoy suffered more than from keen physical pain. He could not restrain his tears, he groaned out loud. The lowering of moral standards, the corruption of people, especially the youth, depressed him. He suffered when he read a novel of Baudelaire, which he had to do "in order," as he wrote Sophia Andreyevna, "that he might realize the degree of the fin-de-siècle profligacy."

He suffered when he saw the Yasnaya Polyana recruits who, in order to keep up their brave fronts, got drunk, and in that drunken state rioted and quarreled.

Tolstoy saw humanity rushing madly toward an abyss. The atheists and revolutionaries were more and more forcibly laying hold of the minds of the young, who were drawn to the radical, swift path of revolution with its noble slogans, its conspiratorial atmosphere, and its call for instant sacrifice, courage, heroism. Whereas Tolstoy's call to attempt to live according to the teachings of Christ, to strive for self-perfection, to meet evil with passive resistance was, in the eyes of most people, sheer Utopia.

Tolstoy was working on his essay "The Kingdom of God Is Within You" for the third year. He wrote to Chertkov that no piece of work had ever required such an effort on his part, and it was only at the end of April of 1893 that he sent the manuscript to Germany and France to be translated.

This essay was a revelation of Tolstoy's world outlook.

"The history of humanity is nothing but a gradual transition from a concept of life that is personal, animal, to one that is social, from one that is social to one that is divine," he wrote. "The whole history of ancient peoples, covering a period of thousands of years and ending with the history of Rome, is the history of the substitution of a concept of life based on society and state for one that is based on the person, the individual animal"; and farther on he says: "The situation of the Christian part of humanity—with its prisons, forced labor, gallows, with its factories, accumulations of capital, with its taxes, churches, saloons, brothels, constantly increasing armaments, and millions of confused people ready like trained hounds to attack anyone against whom their masters set them—this situation would be terrible if it were the product of coercion, but it is above all the product of public opinion. And what has been established by public opinion not only can be destroyed by it, but is being destroyed by it."

Tolstoy saw the harsh, one-sided policy of a narrow-minded government, and the no less brutal, narrow-minded propaganda of the revolutionaries. His work among the starving peasants had made clearer than ever to him the abyss dividing these infinitely patient, downtrodden people from the rich. He saw the self-assurance, the egotism and indifference of the rich, their unshaken conviction that they had an inalienable right to luxury, land and servants, while millions were forced to live from hand to mouth, work from morning to night, possessing nothing.

He knew that this could not continue. He foresaw the possibility of revolution and feared it. Only faith in God and adherence to the teachings of Jesus could save humanity.

"The Kingdom of God is attained by striving. . . ." That was the path which Tolstoy chose for himself.

Why then did he not renounce his family, leave the wealthy surroundings amid which he lived, and build his life according to his convictions?

It is difficult for his critics to understand that this was what constituted his cross. Which was easier for him: to leave his family, shake off the circumstances of life which oppressed him, and which he had rejected in his heart, and settle in some village, surrounded by his beloved peasants, where he would earn his bread on equal terms with them—or to remain at home without breaking up the family, without wounding them further, without depriving his children, to whom he was so profoundly attached, of their father?

It would have been easier for him to leave. But he considered it his duty to remain. And in remaining he bent every effort to convince those closest to him of the things that were so clear to his mind. In each of his children he sought out the good and tried to develop the best of their qualities. He loved them all, each in his own way, and always, with his inborn sensitiveness and affection, he knew how to reach them when they were little and when they were grown.

"What's the matter with Andryusha?" he asked his wife in a letter dated November 18, 1892. "Why are you in such a state of despair about him? To me, on the contrary, he always seems better than he might possibly be."

"What about Sasha?" he asked in his next letter.

And he had quite special feelings about Vanya. To his wife he wrote: "I did not have a chance yesterday to write you quite fully. Vanichka has just been here for tea and I told him you were not well. I saw how this distressed him. He said: 'And what if she were really ill?' I said: 'Then we should go to her.' He said: 'We'll take Rudnev [the family doctor in Tula] with us.' Then Lyova came and sent him to Tanya to ask for your letter of yesterday. You should have seen how he understood it all, how readily he ran off to do the errand, how upset he was that Lyova thought he had not transmitted the letter. He is very sweet, he is more than sweet—he is good" (September 15, 1893).

In Begichevka, to which Tolstoy now paid only flying visits, he had grown unaccustomed to the life of the idle rich. His relations with Sophia Andreyevna had worsened because of her attitude—"We Tolstoys have done enough, let others bestir themselves." She was loud in her protestations whenever Tolstoy or one of their daughters, more often Masha, went down to Begichevka. The temptation to leave home tormented him ceaselessly. He was especially oppressed in summer when all sorts of idlers came to visit, when all sorts of gaiety, noise and foolishness went on around him. The autumns he enjoyed, when they all went away and left him alone with his two daughters.

Tatiana Kuzminskaya told about how she went down once to have a look at the "recluses" as she called them. Auntie was fond of food and when she was offered only a vegetarian diet she was indignant, said she could not eat any old filth and demanded that they give her meat, chicken. The next time she came to dinner she was astonished to find a live chicken tied to her chair and a large knife at her place.

"What's this?" asked Auntie.

"You wanted chicken," Tolstoy replied, scarcely restraining his laughter. "No one of us is willing to kill it. Therefore, we prepared everything so that you could do it yourself."

"I find it very agreeable here," Tolstoy wrote his wife, "after the fatigue of my morning's work—I tire more nowadays—to have the quiet of the evenings. No one to distract or disturb me. I have a book, a game of solitaire, tea, letters, thoughts on good, on serious subjects, thoughts on that great journey before me to the place from which no one returns, and I feel content. Except that it is awfully sad that, according to your letters, the recent one to Tanya, you are so downcast. If only you could have the sense of tranquillity, of joyous, contented, grateful tranquillity which I sometimes feel."

Throughout 1893, despite the opposition of Sophia Andreyevna, Tolstoy continued to concern himself with the suffering caused by the famine.

". . . I went to Yasenka (over five miles from Yasnaya Polyana) to see the clerk and foreman, to stir them into sending off the peasants' applications for food allotments and to get the details about those in need, and we shall distribute flour," he wrote to her in February. "There is no general distress as there was in Begichevka, but some of them are in a frightful situation. Masha received the same impression. So we shall go to Begichevka as soon as Tanya arrives, if she wants to come."

In July, while on another visit to Begichevka, he wrote again:

"Yesterday in Tatishchev I had a most painful impression. No village is worse off. I was surrounded by emaciated people, aged and young, mainly children, in old caps—they were haggard, but smiling. There was especially one pair of twins—. We arranged with the elders to get them milk in addition to that for the nurseries. This is necessary in view of the new epidemic extent of diarrhea. Also I arranged for the homeless for a year. So I shall spend all the money. There will not even be enough."

By the autumn the situation had improved, though there was still dreadful need in some villages. After correcting the report drawn up by Biryukov, Tolstoy sent it to the *Russian News*, where it was printed over their joint signature—Tolstoy and Biryukov—on October 19, 1893. One may consider that this date marked the end of Tolstoy's famine relief work. He was now able to devote far more time to his writing and, having finished "The Kingdom of God," he began a new essay under the title of "Religion and Morality."

Reading a newspaper account of the Toulon celebrations in October, 1893, Tolstoy was struck by the pseudo-patriotic, pompous tone of the speeches, the insincerity of everything said by those who ruled the land in the name of a people ignorant even of the existence of Franco-Russian friendship. Tolstoy poured these thoughts out in an article called "Christianity and Patriotism."

As always he was reading a great deal. Many books in many languages flowed into Yasnaya Polyana, sometimes in autographed copies.

"I have been absorbed by a story of Potapenko in the *Northern Herald*, it's astonishing! A boy of fourteen discovers that his father has a mistress and his mother a lover, he is indignant about it and expresses his feelings. And it turns out that by so doing he has destroyed the happiness of the family and acted wrongly. How awful! It has been a long time since I read anything so shocking. The awful part of it is that all these writers, the Potapenkos, the Chekhovs, the Zolas, the de Maupassants, don't know what is good and what is evil; for the most part what is evil they hold to be good, and by this means, under the guise of art they feed it to the public and debauch it," he wrote to Sophia Andreyevna.

Out of this flood of books Tolstoy chose the things which now constituted the main interest of his life. When he received the *Tao Tê Ching* of Lao-tse in German he was thrilled and with the aid of E. I. Popov he set about translating it.

About this time Professor Grot introduced Tolstoy to a Japanese named Konissi, a candidate for a degree in the Kiev Theological Seminary and a member of the Moscow Psychology Society. Konissi, who was extremely well versed in Chinese and Russian, was translating the *Great Science* of Confucius and the *Tao Tê Ching* of Lao-tse.

He was a very agreeable young man who wished to be on pleasant terms with everyone, but he ran into difficulties with his translation of Lao-tse. One evening in Moscow, he came into Tolstoy's low-ceilinged study with his manuscript. Tolstoy glanced through it.

"This is untrue, it is a mistake," exclaimed Tolstoy. "Lao-tse could not have said this," and he read the following sentence aloud: "Whosoever conducts a war out of love for humanity, he shall conquer his enemies. If he protects his people, his defense will be strong."

"But it is written in his own words," said the Japanese shyly.

"Cut it out!" said Tolstoy firmly.

"But I cannot. . . ." Tolstoy was dreadfully upset and would not listen to Konissi.

"Cut it out, I tell you; Lao-tse could not have thought any such thing; he was against war."

Konissi was quite bewildered and asked Professor Grot's advice.

"You cannot rewrite *Tao Tê Ching*," said the Professor. "Leave it as it is, but say nothing to Tolstoy."

"You should have seen how distressed Tolstoy was when he saw that Lao-tse's words about war were kept in the printed text," Konissi said. "I was sorry for him."

In a letter to Professor Grot, Tolstoy wrote: "You say I do not know Aristotle. Yes, and the reason I don't know him is that he does not have what I need to know. But I know more of Lao-tse and Confucius, who are not far removed from him, and I cannot help but know them."

It was about this time, in November, that Tolstoy read Paul Sabatier's *Life of Francis of Assisi*. As he read excerpts from it aloud he was moved to tears.

"I have received a lovely book about Francis of Assisi," he wrote Chertkov. ". . . I have been reading it for three days and am appalled by my own vileness and weakness, although by the reading I have been made better. . . ."

Tolstoy felt a deep satisfaction whenever he received confirmation of his philosophy from the wise men of the world. It was like the joy he experienced from communion with people who shared his teaching. Yet this joy was not unclouded. Increasingly his followers were investigated by the police, arrested, and even deported. Since everything he wrote was banned, people were sometimes arrested simply for having his manuscripts in their possession, although the government did not dare touch him personally. When he heard that Biryukov and Popov had been subjected to a police search, Tolstoy wrote in his diary: "This hurts my conscience! And to think that I go scot free!" Herein lay his ordeal.

On January 27, 1894, a country teacher, E. N. Drozhzhin, who had refused to do military service because he had been influenced by Tolstoy's writings, died in prison in Voronezh. In a preface to a small book about him, Tolstoy wrote: ". . . as a result of education our way of life has been so altered that power, in the sense in which it was formerly accepted, no longer has any place in our world, nothing remains except gross violence and deceit. And to submit to violence and deceit is impossible; not out of fear but out of conscience."

Drozhzhin suffered and died as the early Christians suffered and died. From the disciplinary battalion, to which he was first sent, he wrote to his family and to his friend Izyumchenko, who also refused to do military service: "But we are not downhearted although we, who are not guilty of anything, are being sent where people go for stealing, for robbery, and we are not afraid of anything because all lies within the will of God: they kill and let them do so, then we shall not have to answer for anything to God; the one who has killed and condemned others will have to answer and take all our sins on him. I do not in the least regret that I have been locked up for a year and a half, because the Apostle said that 'when a man suffers he ceases to sin.' That means that every day we live we must count as good or bad, and whoever is in prison or suffering an ordeal in any other way is not responsible for himself."

When he read Drozhzhin's letter Tolstoy wept tears of joy that such people exist and tears of sorrow that he could not share his lot. "I am incessantly nagged by the thought of following his example," Tolstoy wrote to T. M. Alekhin.

As long as Drozhzhin lay dying in prison the doctors and the prison personnel were amazed by his endurance.

"How long were you in solitary confinement?"

"I was fourteen months in the battalion."

"You had a hard time of it there?"

"No, I was all right there," Drozhzhin replied in his quiet voice.

"How can a man be all right when he is deprived of his greatest blessing, freedom?"

"But I was free."

"How do you mean—free?" the doctor cross-questioned.

"I thought what I chose," said Drozhzhin. With that the doctor left.

Of the Tolstoy sympathizers persecuted by the government those who suffered most unexpectedly and cruelly were Prince D. A. Khilkov and his wife. With their two small children they were sent into exile to the Caucasus. At one time Khilkov attempted to found a Christian agricultural community, and he participated actively in the Neo-Stundist movement. Later, he and his wife broke with the Orthodox Church and they did not have their children baptized. Khilkov's mother, a person of the old school, devoted to the Tsar and the Orthodox faith, was horrified. She conceived a hatred for Khilkov's wife, Cecilia Viner, and after receiving the blessing of Father John of Cronstadt, with the help of a policeman and an order from the highest authorities, she took Khilkov's children and carried them off to her home.

". . . It would be senseless for me to write to you, a mother, about the sufferings of a mother forcibly separated from her children, or about the other unhappy circumstances of this affair," Tolstoy wrote to her, "because I am convinced that you know and have considered all this better than I, so that if you acted thus you must have had some special and obscure reasons. Therefore all I permit myself to beg of you is that, if you consider it worth while, you will tell me why you acted as you did, what forced you to act thus and what desirable consequences you foresee as a result of this."

But neither this letter nor an appeal transmitted to the Emperor by Biryukov through a court minister was of any avail.

"Drozhzhin's death and the seizing of the Khilkov children are two events of paramount importance which challenge us all to make greater moral demands on ourselves," Tolstoy wrote to a friend.

Yet neither the sufferings of his friends nor his own position— the inviolability of his person—which seemed false from the worldly point of view, could stop Tolstoy. He continued to write and say what he believed.

"Seek ye the Kingdom of Heaven and His truth, and all else shall be added to you."

"Nor will the Kingdom of God come in any perceptible way. People will not say: here it is, or there it is. For the Kingdom of God is within you."

Tolstoy believed quite sincerely that the martyrdom of such Christians as Drozhzhin would not pass without leaving a trace, that the time was at hand when people would come to their senses and make an ever greater effort to bring about the Kingdom of God on earth.

❧ 47 ❧

CHOOSING not to upset his wife more than necessary, Tolstoy continued to spend at least part of the winter months in Moscow trying to make the period bearable by hard work and physical exercise.

He used to get up early in the morning, put on a short fur coat and felt boots, and go outdoors for an hour: he hauled buckets of water from the well in the garden or he chopped the wood used to heat the many stoves in the house or for cooking. If there was no work to do, he went for a walk. He loved to wander through the deserted streets down to the river, past the barracks of the Sumskoy regiment which stood on the place at the end of Khamovnicheski Street. There was even more open space down by the frozen river, buried under the snow—there were narrow, beaten trails, little huts, in which simple working people lived; it was quiet. Sometimes he went out to Devichie Fields and down to the river on the other side, near the Devichie Convent. From there he could see the historic Sparrow Hills, described in *War and Peace*, from whence Napoleon looked down on conquered Moscow and demanded that the boyars of the city come to him.

Returning home he would shut himself up in his study. None of the children ever entered this room of their own accord—it was the "holy of holies," and they set foot in it only on very important occasions when Father wanted to "talk" to them—and that was a great and exciting event. As soon as he had finished his work Father went out again for a walk and in the evening "dark people" came to see him. These did not attract the children who were rather terrified by their dark blouses, ragged clothes, long beards.

The young children were delighted when Father played with them. In one of their favorite games the soiled linen was dumped out of the covered basket and Vanichka, or sometimes Sasha—although she was soon too heavy for it—was dragged through the house by Father and his friend Dunayev; whenever the basket stopped, the child inside had to guess where he was; and no one could tell who had more fun out of this game, the child or Father.

The two boys, Misha and Andryusha, were routed out of bed every morning by the footman, who respectfully shook them by the shoulders and said: "Be good enough to get up, it's after eight o'clock, you'll be late to school again!" Hastily splashing water on their faces and hands, the boys swallowed some coffee without sitting down, ate their buttered rolls as they ran off in their black belted jackets and white starched collars, to the private Polivanov School. Mother slept until noon. A nurse took care of Vanichka. Sasha had lessons from a Mademoiselle Detras, a fidgety Swiss governess with a thin face, large hooked nose covered with purplish veins, and heavy posterior. Sasha ran her ragged with her disobedience, inattention, and ceaseless efforts to get into the garden, where in autumn and spring she tore around with the neighborhood boys and dogs and in winter went skating. To walk sedately along the street, as all well-trained girls did, and talk French with Mademoiselle Detras, was the greatest possible torture.

A host of teachers frequented the house. Mother wished to do everything possible for her children and their education. Tutors came for the boys who, especially Andryusha, were poor scholars. Without exception, they failed their spring examinations and had to take them over in the autumn. Misha had a violin and Sasha a piano teacher. Both were musical but did not study and were slack about practicing exercises and scales.

All the children had friends, drawn largely from so-called society. There were constant parties in one household or another with charades and entertaining *petits jeux*. In the spring they climbed into a barouche drawn by a pair of black horses and drove out into the countryside for picnics. The chef, Semyon Nikolayevich, baked meat

[334]

pies, roasted young chickens, made hard-boiled eggs, and all this was wrapped in starched napkins and packed in convenient hampers. On these excursions the children strolled around, picked lilies of the valley and forget-me-nots, played tag and hide-and-seek.

But the children's balls were the most fun. Evening dresses were made, dancing slippers and white kid gloves were bought, even a French hairdresser, Théodore, was sometimes called in to curl everyone's hair. Then they drove to the ball in a large carriage, with a footman on the box: Mother, Andryusha, Misha, Sasha and Vanichka.

Although he was so young, Vanichka could dance beautifully, especially the mazurka. He flew around the ballroom, scarcely touching the floor—a slight, graceful little figure. He stamped the rhythm with his heels as he stood in his place, he skillfully clicked his feet together off the ground, he dropped to his knee and promenaded his lady, always taller than himself, in a circle around him. His pale face was flushed, his eyes shone, his long golden curls danced about his shoulders. But in the carriage driving home, sometimes after midnight, Vanichka suddenly became quite small; his little face grew pale and drawn and he curled up on his mother's lap and went to sleep.

The Tolstoys too had to give an evening party at least once a year and one that would stand out from all the others. No one was so inventive as Tanya and she gladly took on this happy task.

One year the young people were dancing the mazurka with gaily colored balloons floating in the air while the grownups sat along the wall of the ballroom admiring the beautiful spectacle, when suddenly, everything stopped. Into the room came a group of men not at all dressed for a party: there was bearded Tolstoy in a peasant blouse, his hands thrust in his belt, and beside him the imposing figure of Vladimir Solovyov, Repin stroking his pointed beard with a swift gesture of the hand, Anton Rubinstein with his lion's mane. At first no one understood what was going on. Then a side door was opened into the corridor at the end of which was Tolstoy's study—and into the ballroom stepped a second Tolstoy. To the accompaniment of general merriment on the part of the youngsters, the two Tolstoys politely shook hands. Tanya had persuaded her friends Lopatin, Vasili Maklakov and Tsinger to make themselves up and come to the ball. The affair was a glorious success and was much talked about in Moscow.

But Tanya's pleasure in it was blunted. The preceding evening when she had been busily rushing about the house she ran into a plainly dressed woman who wanted to see her father. Tanya had waved her aside, saying it was impossible. What was her dismay when she learned that this was the wife of Khilkov, whose children had been taken from her, and who had come to seek help and consolation from Tolstoy.

Despite the gaiety in which Tolstoy sometimes was obliged to participate, he tried not to get involved in the life around him, avoiding lectures, concerts, literary evenings. Wherever he did go he usually was recognized; people would begin to whisper and often, as at one of Professor Tsinger's lectures, he would be given an ovation. Unable to endure Moscow life for long, he would finally give up and go back to Yasnaya Polyana.

There M. A. Schmidt and Posha Biryukov joined him during the winter of 1894. Later Grandpa Gay arrived in a state of excitement. He was extremely anxious to show Tolstoy his large painting of the Crucifixion which he had just completed. When this group of friends returned to Moscow, Grandpa took Tolstoy to his private studio where the picture stood. Biryukov described the scene:

"Lev Nikolayevich walked into the studio and stopped before the picture, fixing his penetrating eyes on it. N. N. Gay could not bear the strain of this and ran out into the vestibule. A few minutes later, L. N. went out to him, found him there humbly awaiting the judgment of Tolstoy, who held out his arms to him, and they embraced each other. One could hear the low, restrained sobbing. They both were weeping like children and through their tears I heard Tolstoy's words: 'However could you do it that way!' N. N. Gay was happy. He had measured up to the test."

But the members of the imperial household did not share Tolstoy's opinion of the "Crucifixion." When the Grand Duke Vladimir Alexandrovich, President of the Academy of Art, visited the exhibition of the picture in St. Petersburg he was indignant. "This is sheer carnage," he said, turning away. And the fate of the "Crucifixion" was sealed: it was removed from the exhibition.

The old man's heart could not bear the strain of all the excitement. On June 2, 1894, the watchman from the Zaseka railway station brought a telegram with the sad news of the sudden death of Nikolai Nikolayevich Gay.

"I cannot recall any death that has affected me so powerfully,"

Tolstoy wrote his friend L. F. Annenkova. "As always when one comes close to the death of a dear person, one's life becomes a very serious matter . . . and one is truly sorry that there is one less friend, helper, worker in this world."

For some time the Tolstoys had been much worried about the condition of their son Lev. He was thin, nervous, always searching for something yet never able to find himself. At one time he was close to his father, helped him in his work, became a vegetarian, stopped smoking; then he grew closer to his mother and criticized his father's acts and views. Finally his nerves became completely unstrung and he fell ill. But the doctors were unable to diagnose his illness—which consisted of pains in the stomach and weakness. They sent him abroad, to Paris, but the loneliness of a big city evidently had a bad effect on him. The French writer, Charles Salomon, the friend and translator of Tolstoy, wrote disturbed letters begging some member of the family to come. So Tanya went to her brother, but she did not remain long; both soon returned home.

This same spring—1894—Tolstoy received word of the serious illness of Galya Chertkov, whose health had been unstable ever since the death of his first child, a little girl of twenty months. Chertkov begged Tolstoy to come to visit him and his wife on their estate in the province of Voronezh. The meeting of the friends was very happy. "I feel spiritually so close to them, we have so many interests in common, and we see each other so rarely that we both are happy," Tolstoy wrote Sophia Andreyevna on March 30, 1894.

Before going back to Moscow, Tolstoy and Masha, who was traveling with him, went to see his beloved and ailing friend Rusanov. Tolstoy experienced a deep joy in his communion with men like Rusanov and Chertkov, who understood him almost without words, who lived with the same thoughts he did.

Among the growing number who shared Tolstoy's views was an American, Ernest Crosby. As early as 1891 Tolstoy had received a letter from him, and in May, 1894, Crosby came to visit him. Crosby was a handsome man, well-dressed, well-nurtured, with a great sense of humor, gay and witty, in appearance the absolute opposite of the bearded Tolstoyans in their often grubby blouses. Crosby would probably have been astonished had anyone told him that an unkempt appearance to some of the "dark people," was one of the necessary attributes of Tolstoyanism. In Crosby, Tolstoy found a serious fellow

[337]

thinker who had grasped his teachings and was firmly determined to spread those teachings in America.

Another American who had an influence on Tolstoy around this time was Henry George.

Distressed as always by the poverty of the peasants living next to estates of wealthy landowners, Tolstoy often reflected on how to remedy this injustice. The revolutionary method of forcible confiscation of the landowners' property by the "workers" was unacceptable to him. When he learned about Henry George's system of the single tax, he took it up because he considered it the only painless and just solution to the land question.

All land, according to George, should be subject to a tax, depending upon its usefulness. The more valuable the land—city property used by commercial enterprises, buildings providing rentals—the higher the tax. Peasants engaged in manual labor on the land would pay a minimum tax. Landowners dependent on hired labor would pay a maximum tax that would in many instances make it unprofitable to hold on to their property.

Under the influence of their father, Tanya and Masha too were carried away by their reading of Henry George's *A Perplexed Philosopher* and *The Single Tax,* and Tanya decided to apply the principle of the single tax to her estate of Ovsyannikovo. Her father helped her. Perhaps his conversations with the villagers at that time served as raw material for the scene described in *Resurrection,* where Nekhlyudov explains to the peasants the theory of the American economist.

As introduced at Ovsyannikovo, instead of rentals for the land, the peasants paid in money to a special fund which was used for their public and social needs.

Tolstoy and Henry George cherished a profound regard for each other. In a letter to an American correspondent named McGahan, Tolstoy asked that he convey "to Henry George gratitude for his books" and to express to him his "delight in the clarity, brilliance, mastery of exposition" of one who was "the first to lay a sound basis for the structure of future economy" and whose name "will be forever remembered by humanity with gratitude and reverence."

Henry George replied to this letter early in March, expressing his gratification, and asking Tolstoy whether he could come to meet him on his trip to Europe. Tolstoy replied with enthusiasm but the meeting never took place.

The autumn of 1894 saw the death of Tsar Alexander III. It seems preposterous to say this but Tolstoy had a feeling of affection and respect for the Tsar, in whose name his writings were banned, his followers persecuted, their children taken. Tolstoy never felt the hatred of the monarch which burned in the hearts of the revolutionaries, nor the resentment, the thirst for vengeance. The sense of devotion to the Tsar on which Tolstoy had been brought up and which he ascribed so vividly to Nikolai Rostov in *War and Peace* was transmuted in Tolstoy to one of pity for the Emperor who, in his view, harmed himself by unjust and cruel acts.

Just before the end, Tolstoy wrote Chertkov: "I am much moved by the Emperor's illness. I am very sorry for him. I am afraid it will be hard for him to die and hope that God will find him and that he will find the way to God, despite all the obstacles which the circumstances of his life have erected between him and God."

The Russians were excited: what changes could Russia expect from the accession of Nicholas II? Would there be a manifesto of amnesty for political prisoners? Would there be a lessening of repression? Would the young Tsar give Russia more liberty?

But from the very start of the reign of the young Emperor it was clear that the awaited "liberty" was not forthcoming. Nicholas II's speech to the nobles on January 17, 1895, in which he announced that he would conserve the principle of autocracy as firmly and inflexibly as his father had done, showed that no great change in government policy was impending.

In his diary Tolstoy wrote: "There is frenzy and baseness on the occasion of the death of the old and the accession of the new Tsar."

Toward the end of 1894 Tolstoy was writing his "Catechism"—the exposition of his faith. As with all his religious and philosophical essays, he wrote with difficulty, made untold corrections, alterations; for a while he would be in despair, then inspiration would return. In the midst of this work, to the surprise of those close to him and perhaps also to himself, one morning as he lay in bed there came into his mind the idea for a new literary creation.

Many admirers of Tolstoy consider "Master and Workman" one of the most powerful things he ever wrote. The impact of the story lies in the unexpected awakening of God's spirit—which, Tolstoy believed, exists in every human being—in a simple merchant who had spent his life trying to make money. There is a blizzard, they lose the road, the horse stops. The master, the workman and the horse are all freezing. Death is at hand. At the very last minute the merchant with his own heavy body covers the workman and saves him from freezing to death.

To Tolstoy this story of the "Master and Workman" seemed like a plaything, "rather insignificant" (as he wrote in his diary) in contrast to his religious and philosophical essay, his "Catechism."

He wrote to Leskov: "I was on the point of continuing a piece of literary work but, would you believe it, I felt some remorse at writing about people who never existed and did nothing. Something is wrong. Perhaps the novel as a literary form is dying out or I am. Do you sense anything similar?"

When "Master and Workman" was published early the next year, the critics expressed themselves enthusiastically. But Tolstoy's mind did not change, as a diary entry indicates: "As I do not hear the adverse criticisms but only praise of the 'Master and Workman' I get the impression of much noise. It makes me think of an anecdote about a preacher who remarked, after a round of applause had greeted one of his phrases: Did I say something stupid? I feel the same way, and I know that I have done something stupid in spending the time on the literary polishing of a foolish story. The idea itself is not clear, it is labored—not simple. It's a bad story. I rather wanted to write an anonymous criticism of it, if I had the leisure for it."

Through a Slovak from Austria-Hungary, Dr. Dushan P. Makovitski, who visited at Yasnaya Polyana in 1894, Tolstoy came to know of Dr. Shkarvan who was refusing military service because of religious convictions. This acquaintance led to a lively correspondence. And about the same time Tolstoy heard that in the Caucasus a strong Christian movement had originated among the Dukhobors, who were refusing en masse to do military service.

The leader of the Dukhobors, Peter Verigin, was arrested. He was transferred to Moscow and directly from there was sent into exile in Siberia. Tolstoy did not succeed in seeing him but he, together with Biryukov and Popov, met three Dukhobors who were friends and followers of Peter Verigin.

These were simple, unlettered people; they were peasants, healthy and powerful in spirit and body. "Ye have heard that it was said in old times, Thou shalt not kill; and whosoever shall kill shall be in danger of the judgment." That was what the Dukhobors believed. It was what Tolstoy believed. They were not interested in the fact that

Tolstoy was a celebrated writer; probably they did not even know it. To them he was a wise old man who interpreted the teachings of Christ in the same way as they did.

ℳ 48 ℳ

A SENSE of oppression lay over the whole house. The younger children quieted down; they watched their mother with apprehension. Even Vanichka was sober-faced. Father was scarcely to be seen. He spent more and more time in his study, had his luncheon alone and when he came out to dinner he was downcast, taciturn. . . . Masha frowned and did not look in the direction of Mother.

The quarrel had been precipitated by trivial occurrence. At Chertkov's request Tolstoy had had his picture taken with Chertkov, Biryukov, Gorbunov, and others of his friends and collaborators on The Mediator, by one of the best photographers in Moscow. When she heard of it, Sophia Andreyevna was extremely annoyed. Through closed doors one heard her harsh, demanding hysterically pitched tones and the muffled, martyred voice of Tolstoy. The photograph was torn to bits, the negative destroyed, and only then did Sophia Andreyevna subside.

One can imagine how Tolstoy felt in relation to his friends. Yet he was prepared to make any sacrifice if only he could avoid these angry and hysterical attacks by his wife.

The quarrels were repeated more and more frequently. By now her completely unfounded and indiscriminate jealousy had become morbid. During these stormy outbreaks she lost all poise; she saw insults and offense where they did not exist. With the passion characteristic of her nature, she gave free rein to her imagination and became lost in a maze of her own confused emotions. She suffered keenly and made everyone around her suffer as well.

One of the most terrible quarrels had to do with the story "Master and Workman."

Of all the many magazines being published in Russia Tolstoy liked best the spirit of *The Northern Herald,* the editor of which was a Madame L. Y. Gurevich. One of his short stories, "Karma," was printed in this magazine and Tolstoy promised to give Madame Gurevich "Master and Workman" for a later number.

But the thought that her husband had at last written something literary, something good, and then would not give it to her, his wife, for the complete edition of his works, produced in Sophia Andreyevna a fresh storm of anguish, offense, jealousy.

There ensued a dreadful scene. Her reproaches, sobbing and screams penetrated through the walls of the bedroom, and the whole house fell silent. The old housekeeper, Dunichka, trembled with fright and crossed herself. The menservants and maids tiptoed off to their rooms for fear of falling under the eye of the Countess.

"Lev Nikolayevich has written a wonderful story, 'Master and Workman,'" wrote Sophia Andreyevna in her diary. "But an intriguing half-Jewish woman called Gurevich, by means of clever flattery, has kept begging for something for her magazine. Lev Nikolayevich is not accepting any money now for his writings. . . . He did not let me have it for Volume XIII so that I might not get some extra money; why should Gurevich have it? . . .

"The idea of a woman was the first thing that occurred to me. I lost all control over myself and in order not to let him leave me first I ran out of doors and along the street. He came after me. I was in my dressing gown, he was in his trousers with no shirt on, only a vest. He begged me to return but I had no other thought in mind but to make an end to my life one way or another. I sobbed and I recall that I screamed: let them take me to the police station, to the insane asylum. Lyovochka dragged me along, I fell in the snow, my feet were bare inside my slippers. I had only a nightgown on under my dressing gown. I was soaking wet and, evidently, caught a chill. Now I am ill, not normal. I feel as though I were all bottled up, everything is confused. . . ."

The next day there was a similar scene: "a feeling of jealousy, vexation, chagrin because he *never will do anything for me*: that old feeling of grief because of the little love Lyovochka bears me in exchange for my great love for him—all this rose in me with terrible desperation," Sophia Andreyevna wrote in her "history." "I threw the proofs down on the table, put on a light fur coat, galoshes and a cap and left the house. Unfortunately, or perhaps not, Masha noticed my disturbed expression and followed me, but I did not notice her at first, only later. I walked toward the Devichie Convent and wanted to go off and freeze to death, somewhere in the Sparrow Hills, in the woods. I liked the idea, so I recall, that in the story Vasili Andreyevich [the merchant in "Master and Workman"] froze to death and that I too would freeze to death because of that story. . . ."

What did she want? Did she really mean to drown herself in the Moscow River, or was she only trying to frighten him, to get her way? Or was this perhaps the beginning of insanity?

"My despair did not cease for two more days," she continued. "I again wanted to go away; the next day I picked up a cab in the street and drove to the Kursk railway station. How the children at home could have guessed that that was where I had gone—I do not know. But Seryozha and Masha intercepted me and brought me back home."

No one was able to help Sophia Andreyevna, neither her family nor the doctors who examined her. Perhaps it was a temporary imbalance brought on by the menopause.

How could Tolstoy prevail over her? Only by love. And he gave her all he could. But she wanted something far greater; perhaps even she did not know what it was. In recalling his past love for her, she wrote in her "history": "When I wept very hard he would come into the room and bow down to the very ground, and on his knees he would make vows to me and beg me to forgive him. If only a drop of that love which was in him then had remained for long—I could still be happy."

"Help me not to depart from Thee, not to forget who I am, what I am and why I am. Help me . . ." wrote Tolstoy in his diary for February 7, 1895.

The idea of leaving home was frequently in his mind, but he did not go for reasons made clear by this diary entry for May 5 that year:

"One thing is true; it often happens that a person enters into life's worldly relationships which call only for just dealing; not to do to another what you do not want to have done to you, and then, finding that these demands are difficult, he frees himself from them under the pretext (in which he sometimes believes quite sincerely), that he is aware of higher Christian demands and wishes to serve them. He marries and decides, after he has learned the burden of family life, that he must 'leave wife and children and follow Him.' "

On February 15, having sent "Master and Workman" to the *Northern Herald,* he simultaneously gave it to Sophia Andreyevna for Volume XIII, and also to The Mediator. He wrote in his diary: "God helped me: His help albeit feebly was manifested in me in the form of love, love toward those who do us evil, that is to say, the only true love. And as soon as this feeling did manifest itself in me, at first it overwhelmed me, fired me, and then touched those close to me, then it all passed; that is to say, the suffering passed. . . . All I had to do was to love her again and I understood her impulses, it was not that I forgave her but it proved that I had nothing to forgive."

The thoughts put on paper by Tolstoy during this period undoubtedly had their source in his wife's condition. "Insanity," he wrote, "is egoism . . . on the part of people who lack the urge to serve others. . . . There is a vast number of this type of insane persons. . . ."

Grownups are mistaken if they think children do not understand anything. The Tolstoy children, even if they were not aware of the details, nevertheless sensed that there was something untoward happening in the family.

No matter how tightly nurse closed the doors and guarded Vanichka's room, everything could still be heard through the wooden wall which separated the nursery from the parents' bedroom. "Lord have mercy on us sinners," whispered the old woman, stopping her work on the white stocking she was knitting. "Oh, Lord! They surely will awaken Vanichka."

Sasha tried to avoid her mother; she clung to her nurse, because nurse understood everything. She was not like the foreign governess. But Vanichka went boldly to his mother, caressed her: "Are you sick, Mama?" he would ask her. "You're not just your everyday self." She kissed him and wept. "Have pity on Mama," she said. His little transparent hand passed over her head in a gesture of comfort, smoothing and straightening the hair on both sides of her part. Her hair was still quite black, with no gray in it.

Vanichka had his father's eyes; they were pale blue, deep; they saw and understood more than a child could express in words. No one realized then what an important place this little creature held in the family circle. Often he was an unintentional lesson to the grownups, merely through instinct and an inner recognition of good.

When his mother said in pointing out to him the surroundings of Yasnaya Polyana: "Look, Vanya, all this belongs to you," Vanichka frowned and said: "Don't say that, Mama; everything is for everyone."

Vanichka was joyful when he saw good and was upset by every

manifestation of evil. "Mama, why does nurse get angry?" he would ask with tears in his eyes. "Don't you dare hit Sasha," he would cry at Misha when that husky, powerful tease cuffed his sister. "Why did you scold him?" he would ask his mother when she reprimanded a maid or manservant. Why were people bad? Why did they spoil their lives when they could live happily and well? Why?

Unhappily, Vanichka was constantly ailing. He was crammed with quinine and other medicines, but they did him no good—he stayed thin and pale. Despite this, he was a truly merry child; he loved to make jokes and was very good at it, and he was enthusiastic about games. When he and Sasha were left with their father in Yasnaya Polyana, as they occasionally were, Vanichka used to dictate letters to his mother:

"Dear Mama, Sasha was sick and now she is well. Tanya and I wanted to go to Kozlovka today but it was cold and Papa and nurse wouldn't let us go. Sasha is still hurrying, trying to make you some kind of a present but she thinks she will not have time enough. We have finished reading *Robinson Crusoe* and we are waiting for you to come: so we can read it again from the beginning because you remember we began reading in the most interesting place. We finished *Robinson Crusoe* and another little book and we have begun *Captain Grant*. And one page was very, very interesting about red wolves. I was very scared. Now Papa is riding to Kozlovka, so I am writing you a letter. I went to waken Tanya, to go to Kozlovka, and I had just wet my finger to sprinkle her—and she woke up. Good-by, Mama dear. I expect to come soon to Moscow. Kiss Andryusha, Misha, Lyova and all the others who are there, and you I even hug. Vanya."

When the children went off to Moscow, Tolstoy wrote letters to all of them—to each about what was of greatest interest: to Sasha about her friend Varka, the cook's daughter; to the boys about the horses and dogs—but the letter to Vanichka was the most serious and also the longest.

"I caught three rats downstairs, and one got its tail pinched, and its tail was thicker than your finger. And Masha and Nadya Ivanova carried it away to let it out. They were so frightened that they climbed up on a bench by the Kuzminski house and let it out there, but they themselves squealed. I set mine free on the avenue and they made bounds over two feet long and buried themselves under a tree. Maria Alexandrovna [Schmidt] also let rats go down in the Caucasus and a German told her that as soon as they were let go they would get back to her house before Maria Alexandrovna did. But that is not true: I watched their tracks; they stayed in the garden. Tanya said yesterday that they brought a sheep from Ovsyannikovo because all the people wanted some meat. Stakhovich and Nadya Ivanova too, so they brought the sheep and slaughtered it. That's *principles* for you. . . ."

Vanichka knew that Papa had principles, that to kill animals and eat sheep was a sin. And probably he would have been glad not to eat the meat they so diligently crammed into him.

For some months Vanichka had been ill with a fever but in the middle of the winter of 1895 his temperature fell and he began to get better. No one was prepared for what happened. As always in such cases the disaster occurred with the speed of lightning. He was taken ill again. Even with an alarmingly high temperature he thought of others. "It isn't anything, Mama, don't worry," he said to her in his intervals of consciousness. "It will all turn out well. Nanny, don't cry, why are you crying?"

But the physician, Dr. Filatov, diagnosed the case as virulent scarlet fever for which there was no cure. Inside of thirty-six hours Vanichka was no longer of this world.

His little coffin stood in the now deserted nursery amid a smothering fragrance of hyacinths. Throughout the house there was a sense of inexorable emptiness, and instinctively everyone, young and old, clung together in an effort to fill the void. In the presence of this death all discord, hard feeling, misunderstanding vanished like smoke. In his heart each tried not to think of his own grief but that of the others. Masha went through the house with a light, noiseless step. She cared for her mother, her father, was the first to discover that Sasha was ill, had a fever and sore throat, probably a light case of scarlet fever. The boys tried to be well behaved; they remained at home and studied their lessons. All the affection, the tenderness, the concern of the family, especially Father's, was concentrated on Mother. Father was, as always, self-controlled, outwardly calm. No one can tell which had the more harrowing effect on the feeling of the children, Father's silent tears, the terrible guttural sounds he choked down, or Mother's loud sobbing, which went on all day long.

"Why?" she would cry, beating her head against the wall, tearing her hair, rushing from one side of the room to the other. "Why was he taken from me?" And then the next moment—"It's not true! He is alive! Tell me, why don't you speak? He didn't die, did he? You tell me: God is good. Why then did He take him from me? Why?"

Did those near her understand why? Father did.

"The only aim in every person's life," he wrote in a letter to Granny, "lies in enlarging one's own power to love and, having developed it in oneself, to infect others so that it will grow in them too. And when life itself posed the question 'why did this boy live and die without rounding out even a tenth part of the ordinary span of a human life—the answer is the same for everyone. It is the one to which I have come without thinking at all in terms of children, and I did not come to it in relation to this death but through the very nature of what has happened to all of us; that is what confirmed the rightness of this answer. He lived in order to enlarge his capacity for love, to grow up in love, because that was necessary to Him who sent him and in order that in leaving life he would go to Him who is love, yet leave in us all the love that flourished in him, thus binding us together. We have never been so close to one another as now, nor have I ever felt in Sonya or in myself such a need of love, such an aversion to all disunion and evil. I never loved Sonya as I do now. And because of this I am at ease."

The same thoughts were expressed by Tolstoy in his diary for March 12: "It is one thing or the other: either death, hanging over all of us, has power over us and can divide us and deprive us of the blessing of love; or there is no death, there is only a series of changes, consummated in us all . . . one of the most significant being death, and these changes come about in us all in varying conjunctions, some earlier, some later, like waves.

"The death of children from the usual point of view is: Nature tries to give the best and when she sees that the world is not yet ready for them she takes them back. But try she must in order to advance. Just as the swallows who come too soon are frozen. But still they must come. So it was with Vanichka.

"But this is objective, foolish reasoning. A more sensible way to reason is that he did God's work: by establishing the Kingdom of God through the enlargement of love to a greater extent than many are able to who live for half a century or more."

⁊ 49 ⁊

SOPHIA Andreyevna wrote in her diary: "We had come back as orphans to our empty house, and I remember how Lev Niko-layevich, down in the dining room, sat on the sofa weeping and said:

" 'I had thought that Vanichka was the one of my sons who would carry on my work on this earth after my death.'

"Another time he said almost the same thing:

" 'But I had hoped that Vanichka would continue God's work after me. What can one do?' "

To her sister she wrote: "Lyovochka is quite bowed down; he has aged, walks about sadly, with shining eyes, and it is evident that the last shining light of his old age has gone out. The third day after Vanichka's death he sat and sobbed and said: 'For the first time in my life I feel hopeless.' "

Still, no one close to Tolstoy had any doubt that no matter what he suffered as a father he would accept the new ordeal laid on him by God. But they were concerned about Sophia Andreyevna. Would she be able to accept this new loss as God's cross, become reconciled to it? Would she find a meaning in continued existence? Would there be opened to her that world of the spirit toward which her little son, now vanished into eternity, was half unconsciously draw-ing her?

In early spring Tolstoy did not, as was his habit, leave for Yasnaya Polyana. He remained with his wife in Moscow, trying to deflect his grief by work. He always had more work on hand than he could cope with. How often he used to say: "It would last me for three lives." In his diary for March 12, 1895, he spoke of wanting "to write something literary in nature—to finish something which had been begun and thought out: (1) The Koni story (*Resurrection*), (2) *Who Is in the Right?*, (3) *Father Sergius*, (4) *The Devil in Hell* (*The Resurgence of Hell*), (5) *The Coupon* (*The Counter-feit Coupon*), (6) *The Notes of a Mother*, (7) *Alexander I* (*The Deathbed Notes of Elder Fyodor Kuzmich*), (8) A play (*The Light That Shines in the Darkness*), (9) *The Migrants and the Bashkirs.*"

All during that spring Tolstoy was hard at work on *Resurrection* and by the first of July he had finished the first draft. "The finishing touches on the Koni story are done," he jotted down in his diary for July 4.

Considering the condition of his wife, Tolstoy now had less hope than ever of altering the external circumstances of his life. He continued to live among his family but they oppressed him, and he brooded constantly, seeking some solution. These thoughts he poured into the form of a will which he put in his diary for March 27, 1895. Masha copied it out and preserved it for herself. He actually signed his will only on July 23, 1901.

These were the fundamental terms:

". . . Bury me where I die, in the cheapest cemetery, if it is in the city, in the cheapest coffin, as they bury beggars. Put no flowers, no wreaths, make no speeches. If possible, let it be without priests and funeral rites. But if this is distasteful to those who will bury me then let them bury me in the ordinary fashion, with rites, but let it be done as inexpensively and simply as possible. . . .

"Give all my papers to be looked over and sorted to my wife, Vladimir Grigoryevich Chertkov, Strakhov, my daughters Tanya and Masha. . . . I exclude my sons from this charge not because I do not love them (I have, thank God, in recent times come to love them more and more) and know that they love me, but because they are not fully aware of my thoughts, they have not followed their course. . . . I ask that my diaries of my bachelor days be destroyed, not because I would like to hide my evil life from people—my life was the usual worthless life of young people without principles—but because these diaries, in which I entered only what tormented me when I realized its sinfulness, would produce a falsely one-sided impression and pretension. . . . However, let the diaries stand as they are. Out of them it will at least be seen that despite the frivolity and worthlessness of my youth I still was not deserted by God and that at least when I grew older I did, if only a little, learn to understand and love Him. . . . Of the remaining papers I make this request of those who will sort them—that not all be printed, but only those which will be of public benefit.

"The rights to the publication of my works to be the same as formerly: the ten volumes and the *Primers* I request my heirs to turn over to the public, that is to say, to relinquish the author's rights in them. But I make this only as a request, and not as a term of my will. It would be a good thing to do. It will be good for you too—if you do not do it, that is your affair, it will mean you are not ready to do it. The fact that my writings have been sold for these last nine years has been for me the hardest thing in life to bear.

"And now this above all, I beg all, both those who are close to me and those who are not, to refrain from praising me (I know they will do it because they have done it in my lifetime in the worst way), but if they choose to interest themselves in my writings then let them probe into those parts of them in which I know that the Divine Force spoke through me, and let them make use of those parts in their own lives. Often I myself was so impure, so full of personal passions, that the light of truth was overcast by my own darkness, yet sometimes that truth did pass through me and those were the happiest moments of my life. God grant that these truths have not been profaned in passing through me, so that people, despite the shallow, impure character they have received from me, can be nourished by them. Therein alone lies the significance of my writings, and therefore I am only to be blamed for them and not praised at all.

"That is all. Lev Tolstoy."

In the beginning of June the Tolstoys moved to Yasnaya Polyana. The Kuzminskis no longer came to spend the summer in the wing of the house. A shadow lay over the relations of the two families which had earlier been so friendly. The cause was Misha, the oldest Kuzminski son, an unprincipled and dissolute youth, whom the older Tolstoy children, especially Lyova, feared would have a vicious influence on their younger brothers. The so-called Kuzminski house in the wing was occupied by a professor from the Moscow Conservatory of Music, the pianist and composer S. I. Taneyev.

For this summer Chertkov, his wife and their little son Dima settled in a small house Tolstoy found for them three miles from Yasnaya Polyana. Tolstoy saw his friends nearly every day and it was a great joy to him to have them so near. Chertkov kept daily track of what Tolstoy wrote, helped him with the copying, answered some of his correspondence for him, and entered wholly into his life. Tolstoy's family were politely pleasant to Chertkov, rejoicing in the fact that their father was happy with him, but they did not have any great affection for him. Probably the reason for this was Chertkov's imperiousness. He seemed to take possession of all Tolstoy's thoughts and writings, interpreting them in his own way exactly as if they belonged to him.

In the beginning of August Tolstoy received his first visit from Anton Pavlovich Chekhov, who had just written his *Seagull*. The two writers were immediately drawn to each other, and an easy, simple relationship sprang up between them. "He is very gifted," Tolstoy wrote to his son Lev in Sweden, "and he must have a good heart, but up to now he has no definite outlook."

In his diary for August 7, Taneyev wrote: "Lev Nikolayevich spoke of Chekhov, approving of him greatly as a writer. He said: 'If it were possible to combine Chekhov with Garshin we would have a very substantial writer. Chekhov has little of Garshin's trait of always knowing what he wanted, for Chekhov does not always know what he wants.'"

Apparently Chekhov was also satisfied with his visit to the Tolstoys. "I spent a day and a half with Tolstoy," he wrote to Suvorin. "The impression was marvelous. I felt as much at ease as in my own home, and my conversations with Lev Nikolayevich were easy. . . ." And later, in his next letter: "Tolstoy's daughters are very attractive. They worship their father and cherish a fanatic belief in him. And that means that Tolstoy is indeed a great moral force, for if he were insincere and not above reproach the first to be skeptical of him would be his daughters, because daughters are like sparrows: they are not to be caught with chaff. . . . You can fool your fiancée or your mistress to the top of your bent, and in the eyes of his beloved even an ass appears to be a philosopher, but daughters are a different kettle of fish."

Among the visitors who came to see Tolstoy at this time were the English philologist Marshall, and Paul Boyer, Professor of Russian at the University of Paris, a great intellect and a brilliant conversationalist, with whom the Tolstoys maintained friendly relations for many years.

Yet no matter how interesting and agreeable some of these guests were, the constant presence of outsiders in the house was a burden. Neither at meals nor in the evenings beside the big round table in the living room could they sit by themselves, talk about who was reading what, who had fallen in love with whom, how the day had been passed, who had what new clothes—in a word, they were deprived of that thing which every family prizes: personal life. They lived in the sight of everyone, under a glass bell. The people who surrounded Tolstoy jotted down what he did and what he said.

For example, Tolstoy with his characteristic, almost boyish, spirit of enterprise and interest in everything around him, became fascinated by bicycling. This brought him a tremendous amount of pleasure but . . . the unimportant diversion was frowned on. "Tolstoy riding a bicycle! Is that proper? Does it not contradict his views as a Christian?" Chertkov was disturbed.

Auntie Maria had an excellent insight into all this. She shared her brother's breadth, his sensitiveness, and buoyancy. She did not have an easy time of it when she left the quiet of her retreat in the Shamordin Convent to pass this summer in such strange and mixed society. It was not easy to reconcile herself to the views of her brother who had left the Orthodox Church and was surrounded by people who had done likewise. Yet between this brother and sister there existed a different bond: the blood kinship that could not be replaced by anything else and, despite the divergence in their ways of life, a profound understanding of the meaning of human existence. They avoided conversation about their differences. She knew how powerfully her brother was affected by the death of his beloved little son but they did not speak of this; they understood each other without words. Tolstoy hoped that his sister would sustain his wife in her grief, help her to find solace through her Orthodox Church and faith. Sophia Andreyevna was fond of "Mashenka," as she called her, and Mashenka's attitude toward her brother's wife was one of solicitude and sympathy.

To an outsider a nun in the Tolstoy entourage probably seemed strange. For Maria Nikolayevna's whole appearance was nunlike, with her black gown, her black headdress which half veiled her wide, intelligent brow, the rosary which her long fingers constantly handled. She was strict in her observance of fasts and spent long hours at prayer in her room, yet there was in her no affection of convent austerity. She was interested in everything, she listened with enjoyment to music, which she knew well, being herself an accomplished pianist, she loved nature, flowers, and relished a joke. Everyone was delighted when Auntie's snapping brown eyes flashed with mirth and her toothless mouth melted into a sly, artful smile as she made some uproariously amusing or pat remark.

The peaceful existence of Tolstoy and his friends was interrupted during this summer by news that profoundly disturbed them. Tolstoy's follower Prince Khilkov, who had been exiled to the Caucasus, wrote to him about the repressive measures taken by the government against the Dukhobors because of their refusal to do military service. He also sent Tolstoy an article which he begged him to print as written. The article did not inspire Tolstoy's confidence, so Posha Biryukov decided to go to the Caucasus in order to check the facts and get the details of the situation.

At the time the sect of the Dukhobors was little known although it has been in existence since the middle of the eighteenth century. It was first persecuted in 1792 when its members were exiled to Siberia, but in the beginning of the nineteenth century, during the reign of Alexander I, they were resettled in the Caucasus. It is interesting to note the reasoning in the report to St. Petersburg of the Governor of Ekaterinoslav province. He wrote that "all are affected by iconoclasticism and unworthy of human treatment, for this heresy is especially dangerous and seductive to followers because the Dukhobor way of life is founded on the soundest rules, their greatest care is for the general good and they hope for salvation from their good deeds."

The main dogma of Dukhobor teachings consists of service, worship of God in spirit and in truth, and they reject all externals as not needed in the work of salvation. They do not recognize any authority as higher than that of God and His law. If ordered to commit acts contrary to the law of God they refuse. Christ said: "Ye have heard that it was said of old time: thou shalt not kill and whoever shall kill shall be in danger of the judgment. But I say unto you that whosoever is angry with his brother without a cause shall be in danger of the judgment." So the Dukhobors refuse to kill or to be taught how to kill by doing military service.

From time immemorial the people in the Caucasus had carried arms—daggers, shotguns—as a defense against warring tribes, bandits, and wild animals. Having acquired the conviction that all killing is sinful the Dukhobors became vegetarians and decided that they did not need any weapons. In Elizavetpol province, in the Kars region and in the Akhalkalak district of Tiflis province, where the main Dukhobor settlements were, they gathered all their arms, put them on an immense pyre and for two days kept a fire going while they melted away to the accompaniment of the solemn chant of Psalms. At the same time great numbers of them began to refuse military service.

[353]

Neighbors sent exaggerated reports of the events to the authorities, who decided that this was a mutiny and sent Cossacks to "pacify" the Dukhobors. The Dukhobors were brutally flogged, four were killed, about two hundred were arrested and put in prison; their property was looted, their land was seized, and about four thousand were resettled in far-off Armenian and Georgian villages.

Tolstoy was stunned by these events. Only a deep faith in God could enable people to stand such suffering with fortitude and patience. Tolstoy saw in the Dukhobor movement the start of a resurgence of true Christianity in the Russian people. He was deeply indignant that at the end of the nineteenth century, in a so-called civilized world, such atrocities were perpetrated against people whose only guilt was their desire to carry out the commands of Christ and to live according to the dictates of their conscience.

Of course it was impossible for the Russian newspapers to print anything about the persecution of the Dukhobors. Biryukov wrote an article entitled "Persecution of Christians in Russia," which was edited by Tolstoy, who also wrote an introduction to it. It appeared in the London *Times*, and was widely circulated in manuscript form in Russia.

People began to talk about the Dukhobors; the Quakers of England and America became interested in them. In the eyes of the government, which unjustly ascribed the whole Dukhobor movement to Tolstoy, his actions seemed increasingly dangerous. They say that when Pobedonostsev heard about the article in the *Times* he was terribly upset. Many of Tolstoy's friends, among them Biryukov, were put under police surveillance.

In April, 1896, after a series of fresh arrests, when people were put into prison for nothing more than reading or forwarding Tolstoy's forbidden writings, Tolstoy could bear it no longer. He wrote to the Ministers of Justice and Internal Affairs, begging that the persecution of his adherents be directed against him: ". . . If the government is determined not to remain quiescent but rather to punish, intimidate and suppress what it considers to be evil, then the least unreasonable, the least unjust thing it can do is to direct all measures of punishment, intimidation and suppression against me, all the more so because, as I proclaim in advance, I shall go on doing to the day of my death what the government considers evil and what I consider my sacred obligation in the eyes of God."

Tolstoy's influence grew both in Russia and abroad. In one country after another—in Holland, England, America, Germany and even in Japan—there emerged strong figures, proponents of Tolstoy's teachings.

From America Ernest Crosby wrote to Tolstoy seeking support, and Tolstoy sent him a long letter containing his interpretation of the teachings of Christ and of nonviolent resistance to evil.

"There is no moral rule," wrote Tolstoy, "against which it is not possible to set up some proposition rendering it difficult to decide which is the more moral: to deviate from the rule or carry it out. The same is true of the question of not resisting evil by force: people know that this is bad; but their desire to live by coercion is so strong that they bend all the force of their minds not to comprehend the evil created by man's right to exercise coercion on his fellow men but rather to defend that right."

It was widely, but erroneously, believed that Tolstoy used moral pressure to persuade people to live one way or another: to distribute their property among the poor, not to marry, not to eat meat, not to perform military service. Many who scoffed at Tolstoy's views said that he taught "nonresistance to evil," but they purposely omitted the words "by force," thus completely distorting the meaning of his teaching.

Actually, Tolstoy, who was a student of the subtleties of human psychology and well aware of the difficulties involved in each step a man takes in his spiritual development, feared impulsive, unreasoned action, especially on the part of the young who, overconfident of their strength, attempted to clear several hurdles at once, and hurt themselves. He tried to restrain them.

From Holland a sympathizer wrote to him for advice on what a youth who had been called up for military service should do.

"I consider it useless and in part harmful," wrote Tolstoy in the course of a long reply, "to preach certain action or abstention from action, such as the refusal to perform military service and the like. It should be that all acts derive not from the desire to follow certain rules but rather from the absolute impossibility of acting otherwise. Therefore, when I am in the position in which you find yourself with regard to this young man I always advise that they do whatever is required of them—go up for military service, serve, take oaths, etc.—if it is morally possible to them to do so; not to abstain from anything so long as it does not become morally impossible, as impossible as it would be for a man to lift a mountain or raise himself into the air. I always say to them: if you wish to refuse to do military service and are willing to suffer all the consequences of that refusal, then try to attain that degree of confidence and clarity which will make it as utterly impossible to take oaths or do military exercises as it would be impossible for you to strangle a child or anything else of that nature. But if it is possible for you, then do it, for it is better that there should be an extra soldier than an extra hypocrite or backslider, which is what occurs when a person undertakes things beyond his strength."

In the school where Tanya was studying painting she made the acquaintance of a very sweet and gifted young man, L. A. Sullerzhitski—his friends called him Suller. A painter, an actor, an interesting talker, a wonderful singer of Ukrainian and gypsy songs, he was a general favorite, who brought gaiety with him wherever he went. When he was called up for military service, he refused to go and was put in prison. All his friends, among them Tolstoy, were with cause disturbed by his act. In prison Suller fell into a state of complete collapse, so the authorities transferred him to a military hospital in Moscow for examination. Tolstoy went to see him and persuaded him to put on his soldier's uniform. He did so, agreed to go through with his term of military service in the Navy and went on a distant voyage. Neither Tolstoy nor Chertkov nor other friends blamed him for being weak; rather they were particularly kind and understanding. Tolstoy wrote Suller: "Continue to live with as much zest as you did among those who surrounded you, and humbly, truly—and everything will turn out well." To this he added in postscript: "My affection for you is incomparably greater since your sufferings."

In December Tolstoy conceived the idea of writing a new play —*And a Light Shines in the Darkness*. He began with enthusiasm, dreamed about the play at night, sketched out almost all of it, but thereafter it did not go well and he dropped it without finishing it.

Perhaps the idea of writing another play was the result of the success of *The Power of Darkness*, on which Emperor Nicholas II had just lifted the ban. Tolstoy was once more convinced of the strong impression which the dramatic form could produce.

The first production of *The Power of Darkness* was put on by a popular Moscow theater, Skomorokh. It was also given in October and November, 1895, by the Imperial theaters, in St. Petersburg by the Alexandrinski, in Moscow by the Maly. In each of these productions the directors of the play, the scene and costume designers were all meticulously conscientious in carrying out their task; they traveled to Yasnaya Polyana, made sketches of peasant izbas (cottages), bought up peasant women's costumes, took photographs and learned the correct pronunciation of various folk expressions.

In all the theaters *The Power of Darkness* scored a smashing success. On November 29, after the performance of the play in the Maly Theater, a crowd of students gathered in the courtyard in front of Tolstoy's Moscow house. He was not at home at the time but when he returned they followed him into the vestibule. One student jumped on a chair and made an ardent speech of thanks. They gave Tolstoy a thundering ovation and kissed his hands. Had he been able to do so, Tolstoy would have escaped, for all such expressions of enthusiasm, such ovations, were intolerable to him. He was so excited that for the first few minutes he was incapable of uttering a single word.

At the time the university students were in a constant ferment of antigovernment activity—there were demonstrations, meetings. In Tolstoy they saw not only a famous writer but also a revolutionary, an ally, a fighter against the Tsarist government they hated. An abyss separated Tolstoy from the revolutionaries; the path of peace, through faith and God, the gradual perfection of humanity, the path of resistance to force which the Dukhobors followed, were approaches which these people deliberately ignored.

50

THE two younger Tolstoy boys, Audryusha and Misha, did not like to study, a fact no less distressing to their father than to their mother. It was not that Tolstoy placed much importance on their graduating from school; what distressed him was their lack of perseverance, of self-discipline, their moral dissoluteness, the inner vacuity of their lives. Yet no one was to blame for that. Life fell into that pattern. Could the boys—in 1895 Andryusha was eighteen, Misha sixteen—follow their father's way of life? They were keenly affected by the discord in the family—the clash of two outlooks on life—and since they lacked a father's firm hand they followed the line of least resistance, giving full rein to the ardent nature they inherited from both their parents. The older children had grown up in a normal environment of strict discipline and order during a period when their father had been concerned with their training. It was harder for the younger sons, who were subject to temptations on all sides: their companions were rich, idle, used to carousing. The boys were reckless of money, especially Andryusha. He squandered all his money on the gypsies and the next day was ill-natured, rude to his mother, and then wheedled more money out of her.

Tolstoy knew that idleness and easy money spelled ruin for the boys. Only the discipline of hard work, the compulsion of work could keep them from succumbing to the temptations to which he himself had yielded—the carousing, the amorous interests in peasants and gypsy girls. Thinking about his sons, Tolstoy suffered, and became so depressed he could not work.

"I kiss Andryusha," he wrote. "May God help him to find a way, bringing him closer to Him. May he, above all, take pity on and preserve his own immortal soul and not obscure it."

Andryusha left school to volunteer for military service in Tver. Sophia Andreyevna, determined that Misha, at least, should graduate, transferred him from the gymnasium, where he was apparently stuck in the sixth grade, to a lyceum school. She found to her dismay that even there Misha did not study; he cut his classes or went unprepared. It was all the more distressing because he had an outstanding intellect and was gifted in music. For his age, he played excellently on the violin, and his teacher, with whom he played Beethoven and Mozart sonatas, predicted a brilliant future for him. But Misha preferred to pick out gypsy love songs by ear on the piano, singing softly to himself in his true though small tenor voice.

Toward the end of October Tolstoy wrote his son a long letter, in which he sought to make clear that "there is an immense difference between believing that the satisfaction of the lusts, toward which you are impelled, will bring you happiness, thus enhancing the lusts; and on the contrary, knowing that their satisfaction will push you away from true happiness, thus weakening the power of the lusts."

In the same letter he cautioned Misha against amorous interest in a peasant girl: "In order that falling in love may be pure and lofty, it is necessary that both lovers be on the same high plane of spiritual development; besides, falling in love has a beneficent effect when the lover must make a great effort, perform feats, so that the object of his affection will return his love; but, as in your case, where there is no need of obtaining a return of affection, no need of anything except agreement and honey cakes . . . you do not need to raise, but lower yourself to her. Such falling in love is nothing more than animal lust, enhanced by the charm of the primitive quality of peasant life. . . ."

"Misha received your letter," wrote Sophia Andreyevna. "Andryusha and he were reading it when I came in. Andryusha looked through the letter very carefully to find something he could disagree with, and he retained one thing so that he did not feel humiliated by agreeing with it all. Misha was somewhat affected by this. . . . When Andryusha went out I took up the letter and tried to explain, clarify your thought to Misha, because otherwise he was beginning to talk about and see things quite differently. In general he is quite malleable material and if we stick to his training we can, by influencing him, make a decent fellow of him. Today his violin teacher told me that the longer he teaches him the more convinced he is that Misha had great musical talent. It will be a pity if Misha blocks or buries his capacities—we really must help him."

It was not only the younger sons who caused their parents anxiety. Lyova was in ill health, living in Sweden under the care of a famous physician, Westerlund. Ilya was becoming more and more involved in material worries. His estate did not bring in enough income to pay for his living, and his family was growing; he now had three children—Anna, Misha and Andrei, the youngest, who was constantly ill.

The family found one cause for rejoicing, however, when in July of 1895 Sergei was married to Manya Rachinski, daughter of the director of the famous Petrovski Academy of Agriculture.

It is difficult to portray the ill-favored, shy, taciturn Sergei, so embarrassed to show any of his feelings, engaged in a courtship of pretty, attractive Manya Rachinski. She was a friend of Tanya's, charming, intelligent, educated, with an English university background.

One day several months before their marriage, Tolstoy had walked into Tanya's room and, as he wrote to his wife, found Manya there:

"I thought, perhaps she is getting dressed, so I wanted to shut the door. No, you are not disturbing us, she said, whereupon embarrassed Seryozha stepped forward from the wall and also insisted I was not disturbing them. They were both embarrassed, and I was convinced something was going on but unfortunately, when I returned from my bicycle ride, Seryozha said that she was leaving, and when I asked what was going on between them, he said: 'A ticklish conversation.' She has now left for England."

But Manya soon returned, and their marriage was celebrated at Petrovosko-Razumovskoye, near Moscow.

In October, 1895, the relations between Tolstoy and his wife reached another crisis. Through unflagging affection and concern Tolstoy had tried to maintain in his wife the religious surge which had come over her at the time of Vanichka's death. With characteristic optimism he hoped that she would fill the void created by the loss of the child with spiritual interests, with love for her other children, for him, for people generally, and he gave her constant support.

"Not to be upset one must pray," he wrote her on October 4. "You know this because you yourself pray now. Still I prefer not to pray by the book, in the words of others, but in my own words. I call prayer the thinking over of the situation, not from the point of view of world events, but from that of God and death, that is to say in the eyes of God and death, i.e., the transition to Him or to some other habitation of His. This is very soothing to me and strengthening when I understand vividly and realize that I am only here for a while and for the carrying out of some purpose needful to me. If, while here, I do all in my power to carry out that purpose, then what untoward thing can happen to me. Either here or beyond. I know that for you your main grief is—your separation from Vanichka. Yet therein too is salvation and consolation: drawing nearer to God—and through God—to him. That is why in the grief caused by our losses, by death, we turn—to God, and why we feel that we are united with them—only through Him."

Anxious for her calmness of mind and prepared to make any sacrifice to maintain a loving and peaceful relationship with her, he must have been distressed and, at first, perhaps indignant, when he received his wife's letter of October 12.

"Why do you always, when you mention my name in your diaries, speak so ill of me?" wrote Sophia Andreyevna. "Why do you want all future generations and our descendants to hold my name in contempt, as that of a *frivolous*, ill-tempered wife, who caused you unhappiness? Of course if it adds to your glory that you were a *victim*, yet how much this does to destroy me! If you simply scolded or even beat me for what I do that is wrong in your eyes, why that would be immeasurably easier on me; that would pass—but this remains. . . . You promised you would strike out the bad words about me in your diaries. But you did not do it; quite the contrary; or is it you are indeed afraid that your glory after your death will be diminished unless you show me to have been your tormentor and yourself as a martyr, bearing a cross in the form of your wife?

"Forgive me for having done a mean thing and having read your diary. I was impelled to do it by chance. I was tidying up your room —in brushing the dust and cobwebs off your desk, I knocked off a key. The temptation to take a look into your soul was so strong that I did that very thing. And there I came upon such words, more or less, as these: 'S. arrived from Moscow. She intruded into the conversation with Boll to show off. She has become even more frivolous since the death of V. I must *bear my cross* to the end. Lord, help me. . . .'

"When you and I are no longer alive that *frivolousness* will be interpreted in all sorts of ways and all will besmirch my name as you by your words urge them to do. . . .

". . . If it is not very difficult for you to do so—please delete from all your diaries all the mean things about me. After all this is only the *Christian way to act*. I cannot ask you to love me, but please, if you can, have pity on my name, but anyhow, do as you please in this too. Once more I attempt to reach your heart. I write this with pain and with tears. I shall never be able to speak of this. Farewell. Each time I leave, I instinctively wonder: shall we see each other again? Forgive me, if you can. S. Tolstoy."

It is probable that even Sophia Andreyevna did not expect the effect produced by her letter.

"All these last days I could see that something was bothering Sonya," wrote Tolstoy in his diary for October 13, 1895. "This morning it was explained. She had read the angry things I had written about her in a moment of desperation. On some occasion or other I became exasperated, recorded it immediately and then forgot about it. Down deep inside myself I felt that I had done a mean thing. And now she's read it. And the poor thing has suffered dreadfully and yet, the sweet thing, instead of being incensed, has written me this letter. Never before have I felt myself so guilty and affected. Oh, if only this would bring us closer to each other. If only she would free herself from belief in nonsensical things and would believe in her own soul, her mind. In looking through the diary I found a place—there were several of them—in which *I repent of the angry words I had written about her—these words were written in moments of exasperation. Now I repeat once more for the benefit of all who may chance on these diaries.* I was often exasperated by her because of her hot, thoughtless temper, but, as Fet used to say, every man has the wife he needs. She—so I now see—was the very wife I needed. She was an ideal wife in the heathen sense of loyalty, devotion to family life, self-sacrifice, family affection, yet heathen as she is, she has in her the possibilities of a Christian friend. I saw that after Vanichka's death. Will it develop in her? O Father, help her. This most recent incident is only a source of joy to me. She saw and she will see the power of love—of her love over me."

". . . All these last two days I have been reading over my diaries for the purpose of destroying whatever is untrue in them, and I found only one place, and that is far from being as disgusting as the one which upset you," he wrote her on November 3.

No one in the family, except Masha, knew what had happened. Masha was profoundly troubled by the thought that the destruction of the documents would throw a false light on her father's life with her mother and that future history would, therefore, have a one-sided picture of their relations. Tolstoy himself never gave it a thought. He only blamed himself for having harbored any unkind sentiments toward her.

"I had wanted to write you, my dear," he said in a letter from Yasnaya Polyana dated October 25, 1895, "on the very day of your departure, under the fresh impression of the feeling I experienced, but a day and a half have already passed and I write you only today. The feeling which I experienced was one of strange tenderness, pity, and an entirely new love for you, such a love as enabled me to identify myself completely with you and feel exactly what you were feeling. This is such a sacred, good feeling that one should not speak of it, yet I know that you will be glad to hear this, and I know that it will not be altered because I have expressed it. On the contrary, having begun to write you, I experience it again. This is a strange feeling of ours, like an evening glow. Only occasionally your disappointments in me and mine in you dim this light. I keep hoping that they will resolve before the night and that the sunset will be quite bright and clear."

She sent an immediate answer to this letter:

"The little clouds which, as it seems to you, still darken at times our good relations—are not at all terrible. They are purely external —the result of life, habits, reluctance to change, weakness—but they do not in any way derive from inner causes. Inwardly, the very basis of our relationship remains serious, firm and harmonious. We both know what is good and what is bad, and we both love each other. God be thanked even for that! And we both have our eyes trained on the same point—on the way out of this world, we do not fear it, we go forward together and seek the same goal—the divine one. What paths one travels is of no importance. I am rejoiced that you are all well and living happily. I feel a little envious because you are not involved from morning to night with upholsterers, printers, governesses, the noise of carriages, policemen and the spending of money. Amid this chaos it is difficult to remain in an attitude of contemplation of God or a peaceful, prayerful mood. Anyhow I shall strive to extricate myself from this earthly crust so that I shall not be altogether mired in the mud. But it is difficult!"

It was indeed difficult for Sophia Andreyevna to break through the earthly crust in which she was held by the life she herself had made.

In the winter of 1895 the Tolstoys had as a guest in their Moscow home Elizaveta, the eldest of the three daughters of Tolstoy's sister Maria. Sophia Andreyevna was very fond of them, and the families were often together.

Of the three sisters, Lizanka (Elizaveta) was the most sensible and placid; Varenka (Varvara) was the general favorite. People instinctively began to smile when Varenka approached them, so much affection and goodness shone in her black eyes. Her husband, Nagornov, was a man of modest means, a civil servant, and when he died Varenka, with her large family, had a difficult time of it. But her spirits never flagged; somehow or other she managed to exist and to educate her children.

It was about Varenka's absent-mindedness that the Tolstoys loved to tell stories. At a formal dinner party Varenka was sitting next to an old general covered with medals. Her knee itched, so unobtrusively she put her hand under the table to scratch it, but somehow it did not relieve the itch. Suddenly she saw to her horror a deep flush spread over the general's face, as he looked at her with popping eyes. It turned out that she had been vigorously scratching not her own knee but his.

Sophia Andreyevna liked the story of the time Tolstoy received his royalties for *War and Peace* and gave his nieces each a five-thousand-ruble note (approximately $2,500). Sophia Andreyevna went to call on Varenka and saw a broken pane of glass in a window, stuck together with a strange-looking piece of paper. On closer inspection it proved to be a five-thousand-ruble note.

The third daughter, Lenochka, was much younger than her sisters and an unhappy person always. Her father was a Swede, whom Maria Nikolayevna had met abroad. They say that he was a fine, sensitive man. Lenochka was born out of wedlock and educated abroad. It was because Maria Nikolayevna was so tormented by her sin that she had become a nun.

The two elder sisters, especially Lizanka, were devoted to their uncle. She had hoped to be helpful by staying with Sophia Andreyevna, but after a few days she moved to the home of some other friends.

"The Tolstoys are very nice, affectionate and cordial," she wrote to her eldest daughter, Masha Maklakova, "but they lead such noisy, unhomelike, restless lives; from the morning until the afternoon at five there is no one at home; for dinner there are two or three outsiders; in the evenings they are either out again or more outsiders come in. Tanya is very busy with her school, Aunt Sonya has undergone a great change which is displeasing to everyone. She has become restless, never stays at home, she has begun to dress up a lot, that is to say rather that she is preoccupied with her external appearance, she has begun to go to the theater, to concerts, and in general she makes the impression of a person who is living with terrible speed and not losing a minute. She explains this by saying that after Vanichka's death she could not lead the same life as before, and also she had suddenly developed a fondness for music. But we all think that it is simply her dread of old age and desire not to appear an old woman. I believe this is purely a physiological process. She is a woman in whom the body always outweighed the soul. I should be more severe in my attitude toward her were it not that I am so sorry for her; she recognizes this herself and says: 'I lead a somewhat disjointed, restless life, like a lost soul, yet I cannot do otherwise.'

On another occasion I deliberately spoke to her of Vanichka, in order to point out to her the shallowness and emptiness of the contents of her life in comparison with that grief, and I regretted that I did this: she began to sob dreadfully and begged me never to speak to her of Vanichka. Her daughters are fine with her; it is very hard on them, especially on intelligent and sensitive Tanya, to see their mother in this state, yet they are gentle and tender with her; to be sure they treat her a little condescendingly, as if she were a child, but it is difficult to ask that they do otherwise. Lev Nikolayevich is mild and wise; no matter how much one may criticize him, he is still a great mind and spirit. I have seen little of Masha, but as far as I could see she is kind and gentle. . . ."

It was true that the change in Sophia Andreyevna did not please the family. No one criticized her for it, but they regretted it; and imperceptibly she lost the respect which her children, despite their outbursts of rudeness and disobedience, had always felt for her. And outwardly it seemed that there was nothing for which to criticize her. Was there anything wrong with their mother's being carried away by music, going to concerts, entertaining musicians in her home? Could there be anything reprehensible in her beginning to study music, or in the fact that she preferred to spend her time with S. I. Taneyev, that nice, talented composer and pianist?

There was nothing either wrong or reprehensible in the conduct of their mother, yet in her attraction to music and to Taneyev they sensed a kind of show, an insincerity, and all the Tolstoys, old and young, were made to suffer by the change in her.

Let us glance for a moment at twelve-year-old Sasha, a naïve, undeveloped girl, not pretty, awkward, morbidly shy, with the clearly defined inferiority complex of a child left almost entirely in the care of governesses and an old nurse.

Of an evening in the Moscow home when there were many guests, tea was served in the formal reception rooms upstairs. If there were only a few intimates, the tea table was laid in the downstairs dining room, where the family usually took their meals. This was a large room with a parquet floor, a huge sideboard, simple oak chairs, upholstered in a dark material, and a cuckoo clock on the wall.

When she had finished her lessons Sasha would run to the dining room in the hope of snatching up an apple, a piece of candy, or anything tasty. Sasha was already aware of the fact that on the days when her mother drove out to Hunters Row, and returned with numberless hampers in her sleigh, delectably smelling bags, and boxes from Tremble's all tied up with ribbons, guests could be expected. And indeed she would find the table with a white cloth laid in the lower dining room, and on the table various preserves, cakes, fruits, candies, sandwiches with anchovies, hard-boiled eggs, soft caviar, and a slim-waisted samovar fuming and sputtering on a silver tray.

"Are guests coming today?" Sasha would ask the housekeeper, Dunechka.

"How should I know, the countess does not report to me. . . . I suppose that musician, the fat one, will be here. . . . Don't you touch those figs! Now who did that? I don't doubt it's you who made a spot with the caviar on the tablecloth! You go on out of here!"

"But may I take a sweet?"

"Take it and get along. . . . You all make me nothing but trouble. . . ."

Toward nine o'clock, rubbing his frost-chilled hands, Taneyev would arrive. His red, shiny, jolly face literally beamed with good nature.

"It's time to go to bed," her mother would say. "Go along, go along, do you hear?"

As she went out Sasha would give an angry pouting glance at Taneyev. "They did not even give me a piece of candy; all that food can't be just for him!" Then she could not go to sleep. Nurse snored. Somehow she was irritated by the presence of that man, by his high-pitched, hoarse laugh . . . her soul was filled with a feeling of offense . . . at whom?

Taneyev was very sweet with Sasha. It was extremely jolly to play with him at shuttlecock and laugh with him at his own awkwardness. It was an immense pleasure to listen to him play, especially when he was performing Chopin or Mozart—his own compositions were sleep inducing. Sasha would have been glad to go to the concerts with her mother; the music, which she could grasp, transported her into an imaginary, beautiful world of marvelous fantasy and happiness. Yet all this was poisoned. By what? She could not have replied to that question. It was only with time that a feeling of hostility toward her mother was to develop and take on more definite shape. It was difficult for her to wrestle with this feeling; it tormented her, it poisoned her adolescent and younger years. In time Sasha found that going to concerts grew to be a burden, especially when her mother's season tickets put them in the sixth row next to Taneyev, for it seemed to Sasha that her mother's remarks during the performance interfered with Taneyev's listening to the complicated symphonic music in a serious, scholarly way.

Sasha tried not to brood over these complex, and to her incomprehensible, feelings. She had her own amusements—best of all the skating that went on in the garden of their Moscow home. Sasha and the sons of an artisan made a rink which they flooded by hauling water from the well. They all skated, but Misha was the star performer. He could spin around like a top, cut fancy figures, skim down a slide on one foot and do a Spanish leap with incredible agility. Sasha practiced for hours on end trying to imitate him.

Sophia Andreyevna was admittedly not well, and was under treatment by Dr. Snegiryov. But aside from the fact that she was going through the menopause, aggravated in her case by nervous, psychiatric troubles, there did not seem to be anything serious the matter with her. The solitary life, the introspection of her husband, seemed ever more intolerable to her. She longed for movement, music, social life, people.

"What can I tell you, dear, of my inner life?" she wrote him from Moscow in March, 1896. "I know nothing about it and dare not own up to it because there is no good in the vanity amid which I continue in order to drown out everything that torments me in life and all that still hurts. While I was praying and fasting during Lent I was better off: but now I am either seeking distractions and sensations or I am overwhelmed with a wave of depression and nervousness and then I rush out anywhere—away from my home, away from myself. Recently I have had, thank God, a great deal to do—I was going to write to Tanya, but now I have written to you again, anyhow I love her too, think about her and kiss her most affectionately. I am very glad if you are all happy, but I do not like the quiet—alas! and solitude even less."

Once more Tolstoy, with his usual attentiveness answered his wife's letter:

". . . I should like to tell you that your desire to lose yourself, very natural as it may be—is not sound: that if you do lose yourself you only postpone the solution of your problem, it will still remain the same and it is just as necessary to solve it, if not in this world then in the next, that is, after our physical death. . . . One must inevitably solve the question of life and death for oneself and those

[367]

nearest one. I should like to tell you all this, but shall not do so because you must come to it yourself through your own experience. I shall say only one thing, which is that one has a sense of marvelous well-being when one sees clearly . . . that life is not limited by this existence, that it is infinite. This instantly alters one's evaluation of all things and emotions, it is as though one stepped out of a cramping prison into the light of God's day, the true light."

In May of that spring Sophia Andreyevna's love of social life was satisfied to a degree. With Misha and Sasha she went from Yasnaya Polyana to Moscow for the coronation of the new Tsar. All society was there; the city was filled to overflowing and very gay. But the incident on Khodynski Field, when three thousand people were trampled to death during an ill-managed outing, clouded the ceremonies. It was predicted by all that the reign of Nicholas II would end in tragedy.

In the middle of the same month, the Tolstoys' son Lev married the daughter of his Swedish physician, and Tanya and Misha traveled to Sweden for the wedding. At first the family did not know whether to be happy or sad over the event; but both Tanya and Misha were delighted not only with Sweden but also with their seventeen-year-old, rapturous sister-in-law, who was so much in love with Lev.

Although Lev's marriage, to a foreigner who was at first unable to speak Russian, was successful, Sergei's turned out to be a cause of great distress. No one knew the real reason why Manya, who had been received into the family with so much affection, and to whom Sergei was so devoted, suddenly left him. There was much speculation on all sides, Manya was blamed, there was a lot of vicious gossip. Sergei said nothing. He remained aloof in his little house in Nikolskoye-Vyazemskoye, played the piano, composed, and poured his heart out in his music. Manya bore a son who was named Sergei. After her confinement she contracted tuberculosis and soon died.

During the summer of 1896 the wing of the Yasnaya Polyana house was inhabited by Taneyev and his aged nurse, an old woman with sore feet, a wrinkled, almost entirely freckled face. Taneyev took part in everything; he went on all family excursions, joined in croquet games, played chess in the evening with Tolstoy and delighted everyone with his magnificent piano playing. Probably he did not possess the technique of a professional pianist, but he did have a knowledge of music, a subtle understanding of it and the ability to communicate the musical compositions of others to a striking degree. He had only to sit down at the piano, strike the first chord, and he was completely transformed. He saw no one or anything around him, he became entirely engrossed in the sounds, he lived in them and carried everyone along with him. He was particularly successful with Beethoven, his favorite *sonata passonata*, as his old nurse called it. In listening to him it was hard to believe he was the same man who had roared so absurdly and idiotically when Sasha deliberately poked her shuttlecock into his fat belly.

Taneyev never had the slightest notion that Sophia Andreyevna had any special penchant for him. The attentions she showed him he accepted as a matter of course. He was accustomed to attention. His close friends the Maslovs—three spinsters and their old bachelor brother—showered him with the same attentions. A decent and kind-hearted fellow, Taneyev would at once have broken off all relations with Sophia Andreyevna had it ever occurred to him that his presence was unpleasant to Tolstoy.

That same summer Lizanka Obolenskaya came to Yasnaya Polyana for another visit with the family. On September 26 she wrote to her daughter Masha:

"Aunt Sonya arrived on the last day of my stay in Yasnaya Polyana. She looked young, gay, was well dressed and beautiful. For the first time I did not find her very agreeable. Her strange attitude toward Taneyev (I call it strange because I do not know how to define these feelings on the part of a fifty-two-year-old woman) reached such a point that finally Lev Nikolayevich could not stand it and began to make a scene: of jealousy, outrage, offense and indignation. Whereupon she started off in the direction of Kozlovka station, with the idea of throwing herself in front of a train; she was gone all night in the garden, and in general raised a dreadful fuss and quite exhausted everyone. Tanya went to the Olsufievs, Masha became quite ill from the constant nervous tension. I can see that one cannot respect such a mother. This has not just happened, it was during the summer, in August, after the departure of that 'sack with sounds' as I call him. All this slid off her like water off a duck's back; she was as gay and chipper as ever, has taken season tickets for all the concerts and is impervious to everything!"

Lizanka was right. There could be no question of jealousy. But Tolstoy was hurt; it was a bitter thing for him that his wife, the mother of grown children, could put herself into such a humiliating, unnatural position.

In a later letter to her, written on February 1, 1897, he mentioned her trip to St. Petersburg for the première of an opera by Taneyev:

"You told me not to be excited and then you said you would not go to the rehearsal. For a long time I could not think: what rehearsal. I had never given it a thought. And all this is so painful. It was unpleasant, worse than unpleasant . . . for me to discover that despite all the time you have spent on planning and preparing, deciding on your trip to St. Petersburg, you have chosen the very time when you should not go. . . . I know that nothing can come of the fact that you are going now, yet you are unconsciously playing with this, stirring yourself up. . . . This game, I must confess, is horribly painful and humiliating to me and morally frightfully exhausting. You will say that you could not arrange your trip in any other way. But if you will reflect and analyze yourself, you will see that this is not true; in the first place there is no particular need for the trip, in the second place you could have gone sooner or later—during Lent. But you do this unconsciously. It is dreadfully painful and humiliatingly embarrassing that a complete stranger, a person of no use, of no kind of interest [Taneyev] should be directing our lives, poisoning the last years or year of our life; it is humiliating and agonizing, that we must be governed by when he goes where, by what rehearsals, by when he plays. It is horribly, horribly disgusting and shameful."

Yes, and Sophia Andreyevna realized very well that something not quite right was going on in her, and in her own way she suffered. On July 18, 1897 she wrote: "I know that painful feeling, when one is not illumined by love, when God's world is darkened, when it is *wrong, impossible*—yet I have not the strength to alter it."

It was not possible to alter it. With every year the Tolstoys drifted farther and farther apart.

℘ 51 ℘

"I AM still absorbed in my work," Tolstoy wrote his wife in September of 1896. "I have been wrestling with one part about sin: yesterday it seemed as though I had cleared it up, but now it's all fallen apart and confused again. I'd like to write something else but I feel that I should work on this, and I think I am not mistaken about my peace of conscience when I am occupied with this and my lack of peace of conscience when I allow myself to do anything else. It is a great blessing to have something to do about which one has no doubts. If I finish this, then as a reward I shall take up what I have begun and wish to do."

Tolstoy was finishing his essay, "How to Read the Gospels," and "A Letter to Liberals," which he wrote on the disbanding of the Literacy Committee, whose activities in spreading education among the masses had developed parallel with those of the publishing house, The Mediator. This letter grew into an article.

As had been the case in recent years, Tolstoy felt that literary expression was a luxury, not work, but he loved it and allowed himself to engage in it only after he had executed what he conceived to be his duty. Chertkov it was who encouraged him to carry out his duty; Sophia Andreyevna, Stakhovich, Stasov and other worldly friends were always delighted when he used his pen in literary expression. It was only N. N. Strakhov, who, adoring Tolstoy, accepted with equal interest everything he wrote. But Tolstoy lost his friend, this subtle and intelligent critic: Strakhov had died early in the year after suffering terrible pain from cancer of the tongue.

What Tolstoy called his "reward" was the story *Hadji Murat*.

"Yesterday I was walking across a fallow field of black earth divided into two parts," he wrote in his diary for July 18, while he was visiting his brother Sergei. "As far as the eye could reach there was nothing to see but black earth—not a single green blade of grass; then on the edge of the dusty, gray road there was a clump of thistle. There were three shoots on it: one was broken and a white, muddy flower hung from it; another was broken and splashed with mud, the stem was shattered and dirt-stained; the third shoot stuck out sideways, it was also dark with dust, but it was still alive and the center of it was turning red. It reminded me of Hadji Murat. I'd like to write about it. It clings to life right up to the last, it is the one thing in all the field and somehow it has clung to it."

So he sketched out the story of Hadji Murat.

The picture of the Caucasus with its majestic beauty, the customs of its half-savage, indigenous, high-spirited tribes, in the conquest of whom he himself had taken part, and the figure of the attractive, powerfully built Chechen horseman, young Hadji Murat, ran through his mind. It was hard to pluck the thistle:

"More than that, the stem pricked in all directions, even through the handkerchief which I wrapped around my hand," wrote Tolstoy in the preface—"it was so strong that I struggled with it for five minutes, pulling off one fiber at a time . . . and yet what energy and capacity for life, I thought to myself as I recalled the effort it cost me to pull that flower. How stoutly it defended its life and how dearly it sold it."

The story of Hadji Murat was laid in the 1850's. Toward the end of December, 1852, when Tolstoy was in the Caucasus and wrote to his brother Sergei, he mentioned "the outstanding and dashing young horseman of all the Chechens," Hadji Murat. At the time of the conquest of the Caucasus, Hadji Murat, in an outburst of revenge against the Imam Shamil (the highest arbiter of the spiritual and communal life of his people) for having killed his father and brothers, gave himself up to the Russians. Hadji Murat declared to Prince Voronstov, Viceroy of the Caucasus, that he was prepared to serve the Russians faithfully and truly under one condition— that the Russians would rescue his wife and children from Shamil. Hadji Murat knew that if his son remained a prisoner Shamil would either kill him or put his eyes out.

Time went by. There was no word of his family.

So Hadji Murat decided to leave the Russians. After knocking out his guard he galloped off into the mountains with five henchmen. A troop of soldiers overtook them; they were surrounded, but Hadji Murat and his henchmen decided they would not be captured alive. Mortally wounded in his side, Hadji Murat still fought on— "he crawled out of a ditch and holding his dagger he walked, limping badly, straight out to meet his enemies. There were several shots, he staggered and fell. Several soldiers ran with triumphant yells toward the fallen body. But what had seemed to be a corpse suddenly moved. First he raised his blood-stained, shaven head, from which his fur cap had fallen, then his body, and, grabbing hold of a tree, he drew himself to his feet. He seemed so terrible that his conquerors stood still. But he suddenly quivered, staggered away from the tree and, like an uprooted thistle, he fell full length to the ground and moved no more. . . ."

In 1902 Tolstoy received a letter from Karganov, son of the colonel who had had custody of Hadji Murat. Tolstoy immediately wrote him a series of questions: "Did Hadji Murat live in a separate house or in the house of your father? What was the layout of the house? Was his clothing distinguishable from that of the ordinary mountaineers? On the day he escaped did he and his henchmen ride out with rifles on their shoulders or without them?—There are so many things I'd like to ask but I am afraid of bothering you. . . ."

Although Tolstoy returned periodically to his *Hadji Murat* until 1904, he still did not look upon the story as being in finished form.

In addition to his essays "How to Read the Gospels," "Carthago Delenda Est," he made a beginning late in September of 1896 on an essay entitled "What Is Art?"

During Taneyev's visit that summer he had played a great deal on the piano. Tolstoy loved the classical music, especially Chopin, Mozart, Haydn. But when Taneyev played the works of contemporary composers Tolstoy was indignant and argued fiercely with Taneyev about music and art in general, proving to him that art is real only when it is comprehensible and accessible to all. It is possible that these arguments were what moved Tolstoy to write this particular essay. When in the spring of that same year he had heard the opera *Siegfried* at the Bolshoy Theater he had run, as he wrote his brother Sergei, "out of the place like a crazed person. It is a stupid, pretentious show, nothing but affectation and no music at all."

Tolstoy quickly finished a rough draft of the essay and put it in final form toward the end of 1897. Other concerns deflected him from writing. The persecution of the Dukhobors was on the increase.

On October 31 Tolstoy wrote his wife: "Yesterday I received letters from Chertkov and Tregubov with a description of the sufferings of the Dukhobors. One man, they write, was flogged to death in a disciplinary battalion and their families are ruined and dying off, they write, from lack of shelter, from cold and starvation. They have written an appeal to the public for help and I have decided to send them 1,000 rubles [approximately $500] out of our charity funds."

At the end of the letter he added: "This news has been the principal event for me during this time."

I. M. Tregubov had met Tolstoy back in 1891 and since then had been a firm follower of Tolstoy's teachings. A short man with small features, a round little beard, dark blue glasses, he was modest and retiring, and somewhat inclined to mysticism, about which he often argued with Tolstoy. And he had a heart of gold. He took a warmly sympathetic attitude toward the work of helping the Dukhobors, and to the end of his life he remained a convinced Christian. After the Revolution he was persecuted, according to rumors, by the Soviet government, was deported to one of the camps in North Russia where he died, unable to stand the severe privations.

Chertkov, Biryukov and Tregubov addressed a joint appeal to the public—"Give Help!" Tolstoy edited it and wrote a preface. The appeal was reproduced and distributed among influential officers of the government and people active in public life; and it was printed abroad.

The greater the persecutions the stronger the spiritual exaltation of the Dukhobors became. The severe tortures to which they were sub- jected did not daunt them; on the contrary, they went through their sufferings for their Christian faith with the endurance of the early Christians. In his article "Where Is Thy Brother?" Chertkov told how one Dukhobor replied when asked by the police chief what orders by the authorities they would submit to and what they would not: "Put into our hands the tiniest stone and order us to throw it at a human being—and we shall not be able to do it; but order us to move the heaviest stone from one place to another and we shall gladly do it."

The article "Give Help!" evoked a series of repressive measures against the Tolstoyans. Chertkov's apartment was searched; Tolstoy and all his adherents were put under police surveillance.

On January 31, 1897, Tolstoy and his daughter Tanya drove over to the estate of the Olsufievs' where, in quiet surroundings, under the care and affection of his friends, he could relax in spirit and write. On February 5 Sophia Andreyevna arrived, and the next day Gorbunov-Posadov brought Tolstoy the sad news that Chertkov was being sent into immediate exile abroad and Biryukov to the province of Courland. That same day Tolstoy left with Sophia Andreyevna for St. Petersburg to say good-by to his friends.

Had it not been that the reason for his going to St. Petersburg was to part from his friends, and also that he was depressingly aware of his own immunity, Tolstoy would have found his stay agreeable in St. Petersburg, where he had not been for fully fifteen years. He walked with interest through the streets of the vastly enlarged city, finding it difficult to recognize some of them.

The news of Tolstoy's arrival spread through the city with lightning rapidity; his friends invited him to their houses; everyone wanted to see him.

In his memoirs A. F. Koni wrote:

"One evening at eleven o'clock, having just returned from some meeting or other, I sat down to my work. . . . My aged maid told me that some old peasant was asking to see me. To my question as to who he was and what he wanted at so late an hour she returned with the information that his name was Lev Nikolayevich. With affectionate respect I led the 'peasant' to my study and we talked for a whole hour, during which he astonished me with his loftiness of spirit, his all-forgiving attitude toward what had been done to Chertkov. Not a word of reproach, not the slightest expression of indignation broke from his lips. He made the impression on me of one of the first Christians, who could look without trembling into the eyes of agonizing death and by their meekness conquered the world."

Tolstoy stopped in at the Public Library where Stasov headed the Art Department. He called on his old literary colleague Grigorovich; he visited Repin's studio.

"A group of close friends devoted to Lev Nikolayevich gathered together in my huge studio," Repin wrote in his memoirs. "They clustered around the teacher and wanted to hear what he would say as he stood in front of this or that picture. The lucky painting was 'The Duel.' Tears came into Lev Nikolayevich's eyes as he stood in front of it and he talked a great deal about it and was delighted. They all looked at the picture and hung on his every word. After the inspection by the whole group we went down the Academy stairs to the street, where a sizable crowd was waiting for us. Joining forces we filled the whole sidewalk and moved toward the Bolshoy Prospect, to the horsecar. The conductor of the horsecar, a man no longer young, when he saw Lev Nikolayevich, was somehow suddenly dumbfounded, his eyes opened wide and he all but shrieked: 'Oh bless my soul, brothers, why that's Lev Nikolayevich Tolstoy!' and he reverently doffed his cap."

In the surveillance record of the St. Petersburg Security Department each step Tolstoy took and even his clothing were described. On the first day: "Count Tolstoy was dressed in an open-necked, lined sheepskin coat, patched in places, held in by a gray belt, dark-colored trousers, worn outside his boots, with a dark gray knitted cap on his head, and he had a cane in his hand." ". . . L. Tolstoy, Biryukov, and the above-mentioned peasant walked toward the Anichkov Bridge, from there they rode by horsecar to the Academy of Arts; meanwhile Count Tolstoy sat on the top benches of the car and then near the Kazan Cathedral he changed to the interior of the car. Various university students who were inside the car immediately approached him and in the course of their conversation they urged him to come to their university speech day, to which he agreed: at which one of the students kissed the Count's hand.

"After the Academy, together with the same persons and Vladimir Chertkov, retired captain in the cavalry guards, who was under special surveillance, they all went to Chertkov's mother's. . . ."

When he went to the Winter Palace Tolstoy exchanged his patched sheepskin coat for a more suitable dress and the police report read: "On his way to the Winter Palace Tolstoy was dressed in a cloth overcoat with lambskin collar, dark trousers and a gray felt hat."

From this same police description we know that Tolstoy, in company with "P. I. Biryukov, retired Collegian secretary under special surveillance," went into a pastry shop on the Nevski Prospect, was in several bookstores, had his hair and beard trimmed at a barbershop. . . ."

It was during this stay in St. Petersburg that Tolstoy broke with Granny Alexandrine. Granny could no longer understand her old friend.

Saddened by the exile of his friends, weighed down by the suffering of the Dukhobors—all in the name of the Tsar, to whom Alexandrine was so devoted—Tolstoy found himself irritated by the luxury of the Winter Palace where Granny lived, by the court atmosphere that surrounded her, and when he met her at the Shostaks' he was harsh in expressing his opinions. When Granny, after a sleepless night, decided that at their next encounter she must "save poor Lev" and reveal the truth to him, he was even more upset.

"It is dreadful to come out with it," wrote Granny in her memoirs. "On the one hand there are a love of truth, love of human beings, love of God and even of that Teacher, all of whose grandeur he does not choose or is unable to recognize, and on the other hand there are pride, ignorance, unbelief, the abyss. . . ."

As for Tolstoy he found Granny "lifeless, unkind and pitiful" and, so it seemed to him, "possessed of a dreadful pride."

Tolstoy returned to the Olsufievs', in whose house he had stayed while in St. Petersburg. And he went on writing his essay on "What Is Art?"

Although the Olsufievs belonged to the highest aristocratic circle of society, their simplicity, cordiality and friendliness attracted everyone around them. People of all classes and professions streamed into their home: doctors, teachers, community nurses. They gave musicales, masquerade parties, plays, dances. The stocky Count, always radiating good humor, danced the mazurka with his employees, and Tolstoy confessed that in looking at such jollity he himself longed to join in the dance.

Back in Moscow, Tolstoy was again caught up in the maelstrom of city distractions, endless visitors and worries.

Aylmer Maude arrived from England. A member of an English agricultural community, who knew Russian extremely well, he had become interested in the ideas of Tolstoy; later he was one of his best translators.

Disturbing news continued to arrive from the Caucasus: I. M. Tregubov was arrested and exiled for five years to the province of Courland.

About this time there was talk of the Nobel prize. A rumor was current that it would be awarded to Tolstoy, as a proponent of world peace. From Tolstoy's point of view, no one had done so much for peace as the Dukhobors and he felt that in all justice the Nobel prize should go to them. He wrote an article on the subject and sent it to the Swedish newspapers.

In the spring (1897) some members of the Molokan sect arrived in Yasnaya Polyana from the district in Samara where Tolstoy had once lived while taking the kumys cure. The government authorities had taken the children away from sixteen Molokan families on the ground that they were not baptized, and had sent them to religious institutions to be brought up. The Molokans begged Tolstoy to intercede for them. As with the majority of these Russian peasant sectarians, Tolstoy sensed their inner power, their tranquil firmness and faith in their own righteousness, and their stories had a strong effect on him.

The next day he wrote to the Tsar:

"Sire: In reading this letter I entreat you to forget anything that you perhaps may have heard about me and, having set aside all prejudice, to see in this letter nothing but a desire for the welfare of innocent sufferers, together with an even greater desire for the welfare of that person whom it is so natural to blame for those sufferings.

"A month ago in the village of Zemlyanka, Buzuluk township, a village sergeant in the company of policemen entered the house of the peasant Chipelev, a Molokan by religion, and ordered him to waken his children so that they could be separated from their parents. The frightened and puzzled boys—one is thirteen, the other eleven —were dressed and led outside, but when the sergeant attempted to take a two-year-old girl, the mother seized her daughter and did not want to let her go. Thereupon the police chief told her that he would be obliged to bind her should she not release the child. The father persuaded his wife to give up the child, but demanded a receipt from the officer which explained on whose orders the children were taken. . . .

"A few days later in another village . . . the sergeant and policemen arrived and ordered two little girls, one twelve years old, the other ten, to be prepared to leave. . . .

"The same thing happened in the same village that same night in the family of a peasant . . . from whom they took his five-year-old son. The seizure of the child was signally brutal. This boy was the joy and hope of the family as after many years he was the only son who had remained alive. When they seized the child he was ill and had a fever. It was cold out of doors. His mother begged that he be left for a while longer. But the police chief would not agree to that and, in accordance with the opinion of a doctor who decided there was no risk to the child's life in his removal, he ordered the sergeant to seize the child and take him away, but the mother pleaded successfully with the police chief to allow her to travel with her son as far as the town of Buzuluk. In the town they took the boy away from his mother, and she did not see him again. . . .

"It is said that this is being done in the support of the Orthdox Church, but the greatest enemy of the Orthodox Church could not have invented a surer method to alienate people from it than these deportations, prisons, the separation of children from their parents . . .

"Sire, dismiss if only temporarily these, I shall not call them wicked, but rather, erring people who are persuading you mistakenly that it is necessary to persecute people for their faith; and you yourself, by the virtue of your kind heart and upright mind, decide how the faith you hold to be the true one should be professed and how one should treat people who profess another faith. . . .

"Seize this opportunity to do the good deed which you alone can do, and which it is evident you are destined to do. . . ."

P. A. Boulanger offered to carry the letter to St. Petersburg himself. He had been a frequent visitor and recently had become more and more interested in Tolstoy's teachings.

As far as is known the letter was put into the Emperor's own hands, thanks to the efforts of Tolstoy's friends such as Koni, Olsufiev, and Alexandrine. Did the Tsar ever read it? Did he comprehend that Tolstoy harbored no feelings of resentment or irritation, but wanted only to open the Tsar's eyes to the barbarities and stupidities being committed in his name? Who can say?

In the course of four months the children had not been returned to their families. Tolstoy wrote in vain to his friends in St. Petersburg begging them to help. In the beginning of 1898 Tanya, who was visiting friends in St. Petersburg, received a telegram from her father. He told her that the Molokans had left for the capital to make a plea on behalf of their children, and he asked Tanya to help them.

Tanya went to see Pobedonostsev. Whether Pobedonostsev had received an order from the Emperor concerning the return of the children, or was himself alarmed over the excessive publicity, we do not know. The Russian press was silent out of fear of repressive measures, except for the ultra-conservative *Citizen* which expressed indignation. The foreign press, on the other hand, gave the brutal facts wide circulation. Whatever the reasons, Pobedonostsev's reception of Tanya was amiable; he promised that the children would be returned to their parents and on her return home Tanya received the following letter from him:

"Dear Madam: I should advise the Molokans not to remain here in expectation, but to return and inform themselves of the matter in, let us say, Samara, from the Governor to whom I have today written concerning them, and I believe that in all likelihood the children will be returned to them. Your obedient servant, K. Pobedonostsev."

Pobedonostsev kept his word and the children were returned to their parents.

This never-ending defense of the oppressed took much of Tolstoy's strength. Yet service to others, along with his religious and philosophical writings, was what he considered the main concern of his conscience.

❧ 52 ❧

NO ONE knew what Tolstoy suffered, what the bitterness, pain, perhaps even jealousy, that gnawed at his lonely, proud soul. . . .

To lose his two close friends Chertkov, Biryukov was as nothing compared to what he now had to go through. Masha . . . Masha who glided noiselessly into his study with her father's freshly copied manuscript, who caught every fleeting thought, who lived his life, his interests; Masha who sensed so fully the joy of service; Masha, the sensitive, the spiritually minded . . . what had come over her? Why should there appear at her side a youth steeped in lordly ways, a handsome, extremely attractive creature—Prince Nikolai Obolenski? What was there between them?

Nikolai was the son of Lizanka, Tolstoy's own niece, and was two years younger than Masha. He had been living with the Tolstoys at Sophia Andreyevna's suggestion, because Lizanka had great difficulty in supporting her family. Kolya went through the university and law school, although he did not attend lectures and worked only just enough to enable him to pass his examinations. He was a sweet, honest, intelligent fellow, who neither drank nor gambled. He got up late in the morning, in time for luncheon, he smoked in a slow, charming way, blowing rings, gracefully waving his well-manicured hand; he was fond of food, gave lordly tips although he never had any money, pronounced his "r"s with the aristocratic foreign inflec tion. Kolya was an aristocrat with princely ways, a sybarite. And Masha was lost to her father, to all around her. She now spent hours on end in conversation with Kolya. A soft, warm light came into her gray, pensive eyes, she had a new, almost guilty smile. Masha fell in love, passionately in love, without rhyme or reason, and nothing could keep her from this marriage: neither the stormy protestations of her mother, nor the pained bewilderment of her father. Yet he did not attempt to dissuade her. His personal grief over the loss of Masha as a helper and friend was too keen; he was conscious it might have influenced his attitude toward her marriage, and he wished for her happiness not his own.

"Masha . . ." he wrote her, "there is nothing I have to say against your intentions, called forth, as I can see, by your yearning for marriage . . . Judging by your life recently, which has been more thoughtless and luxurious than formerly, and judging by the life and habits of Kolya, you are not only not going to live like Maria Alexandrovna [Schmidt] but you will need a lot of money. . . . One of the main precipitating causes for you . . . is children. And children spell need. This is very difficult and indeed too obvious—the exchange of independence, tranquillity, for the most complex and painful sufferings. How do you weigh this? What does he think about it? . . . Do you intend to ask that your inheritance be given you? Does he intend to take a job and, if so, where? And please put aside any thought that if he went into government service my attitude toward him would be altered, or that your rescinding of your intention not to accept your inheritance could change my estimate of you. I know and love you beyond and deeper than that, and none of your weaknesses can change my understanding of you and the love for you bound up with it. I have been myself and still am full of weaknesses and therefore I know how sometimes and indeed often they gain the upper hand. But there is just one thing: I may lie under his weight, under my enemy, I am in his power, yet I still cry out that I will not surrender, and once I can deal with him again I shall battle him. I know that you too will act in the same way, so do it. Only one must think, one must think hard."

Masha's marriage was preceded by a series of difficulties. The priest refused to perform the ceremony because one had to produce a certificate of confession and communion, and Masha had not performed her church duties for many years. Kolya wanted to bribe the priest and Masha told her father about his intention. In May, just before the wedding, Tolstoy made a definite statement of his opinion:

"To get married in church without believing in the sacrament of marriage is as wicked as to confess and take communion without believing in it; this quite aside from your inducing another person . . . a priest, to lie in order to free you from a lie, and by bribery too; aside too from throwing away 150 rubles on a bribe in order to free yourself of an onerous procedure—all this is very bad. After all you can omit your church duties when you have to because you are unable to fulfill them. But if you are able to go through the church ceremony of marriage and even commit bribery there is no reason why you cannot go to confession and communion."

And Masha went to confession.

The second compromise was no easier. At the time of the division of property Masha had renounced her share. Kolya Obolenski had nothing, he neither knew how nor wished to work, and the young couple had nothing on which to subsist. So that it fell to those who had the more valuable property—Sophia Andreyevna and Seryozha —to cut from their portion what was Masha's share and give it to her in money, which was very complicated. Her mother and brothers tried not to show their displeasure over the "tricks" which, they said, Masha played, but the unpleasant aftereffects of this incident remained.

On the 2nd of June, 1897, Masha married Kolya Obolenski. At the ceremony were only their two attendants—Misha Tolstoy and one of Kolya's brothers. They walked to the church as they were dressed, in ordinary clothes.

Tanya's affairs too now became a source of distress to Tolstoy, who for some time had felt that Tanya was gradually drawing away from him. Even so he had not dared to guess what might lie behind her restlessness, her constant trips away, her loss of interest in his inner life, his friends, in the handsome Tolstoyan with the sheep's eyes—E. I. Popov, with whom she had been for many years on a footing of what was called an *amitié amoureuse*.

What attracted Tanya to M. S. Sukhotin? Probably she could not have explained it herself. Those around her simply could not entertain the thought that Tanya, who had such a tremendous success among the young men who courted her in droves, could be seriously, irrevocably in love with, as Sasha called him, an old man.

Sukhotin had been married, he had six children, of whom the

eldest, Lev, was a contemporary of Misha Tolstoy. Rumor had it that the Sukhotin couple had not been on good terms, that they had been unfaithful to each other. Some called Sukhotin a rake. As a matter of fact Sukhotin was a man who, no one knew why, fascinated women. As soon as one met his intelligent, gray, quizzical eyes one knew that this man would not say anything stupid or banal. At the same time there was not a soul in the Tolstoy family who was not hostile to him. A widower, old, with children!

At the time of his wife's death, Tanya had suffered pangs of remorse. She tormented herself with the fact that even while his wife was alive they had talked of love, although she never allowed him any intimacies, never even allowed him to kiss her. Tanya hid her feelings from her father for a long time, and he was glad not to notice, not to believe that his crystal pure, talented, all-comprehending, sensible Tanya was going to fall into the embrace of this shopworn, worldly old widower. This thought caused him keen, almost physical pain.

Sophia Andreyevna stormed and raged. Even gentle Maria Alexandrovna Schmidt who adored "dear, darling Tanichka," as she called her, never for a moment took seriously Tanya's infatuation. "Forget about it, dearie," she used to say when Tanya told her about her feelings for Sukhotin. "Forget it, you just invented some nonsense. What kind of love can there be here, what kind of a mate is he for you?"

On July 10, 1897, Sophia Andreyevna wrote in her diary: "I have been through a painful, painful experience. The thing I feared so dreadfully about Tanya has taken definite form. She is in love with Sukhotin and has discussed marriage with him. We got on the subject accidentally and naturally. Apparently she felt the need and the desire to express herself. Lev Nikolayevich also had had a talk with her. When I first told him the news he was dumbfounded, it immediately . . . reduced him to despair. Tanya has wept a great deal all these days, but she seemed to think that this would be her undoing and she refused him."

It was a painful summer. Tolstoy was very lonely. Masha was not at home, and she was the only one who knew how to give him simple, heart-warming affection.

With his wife relations were still confused and restless. . . . "Our life is tainted," we read in Sophia Andreyevna's diary, "and frankly Lev Nikolayevich worries me somewhat: he is getting thin, his head aches—and then this morbid jealousy! Am I guilty? I do not know. As I came to know Taneyev better it often occurred to me, how good it would be to have such a friend for my old age: a quiet, kindly, talented man. I liked his relations with the Maslovs, I wanted to have the same thing. . . . And what happened!"

Her strange, unnatural attitude toward Taneyev continued.

"Taneyev played two of Mendelssohn's 'Songs Without Words' and my heart turned over within me," ran another entry in her diary. "Oh, these songs! One of them particularly is graven on my heart."

For hours Sophia Andreyevna, with a kind of stubborn desperation, played scales and Hanon exercises, vainly hoping thereby to develop her fingers. Sasha, who had a good ear and who was also studying music, knew the melodies of the "Songs Without Words" by heart; she knew where her mother would slow the tempo in an effort to give a special singing quality to the notes, also where she would stumble. . . . Oh, those songs! Sasha hated them!

On top of all that Sophia Andreyevna now demanded that her husband turn over to her the rights to all his works. She did not suspect how close he was to giving up everything and beginning to live as he thought it necessary to live if he were to be quite consistent. She was constantly underscoring her purity, innocence and the sacrifice she had made of her youth and talents. She did not grasp the fact that a sacrifice has a value only when it is made joyously and voluntarily and when one does not mention it.

Tolstoy had aged very much in this year under the weight of events. His doubts tormented him: Should he continue to carry the burden of a life distasteful to him in every sense for the sake of his wife, of his family, of not destroying love, or should he go away?

On the 8th of July he wrote a letter which Sophia Andreyevna received only after his death. Masha, and after her death her husband Kolya Obolenski, kept it.

"Dear Sonya," he wrote. "For a long time I have been tormented by the disparity between my life and my beliefs. I cannot oblige you to alter your life, your habits, to which I have trained you; nor have I been able until now to leave you, believing as I did that I would thereby deprive the children, while they were small, of even the small amount of influence I might have over them, and I would distress you. Yet to go on living as I have lived for sixteen years, struggling, and irritating you, or else falling into the temptations to which I am accustomed and by which I am surrounded, is likewise something I can no longer continue, and I have decided now to do what I have long yearned to do—go away. In the first place, I with my increasing age find this life more and more burdensome, I long more and more for solitude, and, in the second place, since the children are grown up, my influence in the home is no longer needed, and all of you have livelier interests which will make my absence unnoticed. But the main point is that as the Hindus when they reach the age of sixty go off into the forests, as every aged person of religious cast wishes to devote the last years of his life to God, and not to jokes, puns, gossip, tennis, so I, entering now on my seventieth year, long with all the strength of my soul for that tranquillity and solitude and, to have if not complete harmony between my life and my conscience, at least not a crying discord between them. If I did this openly there would be pleas, arguments, complaints, and I might weaken, perhaps I should not carry out my decision, yet it must be carried out. And therefore, please forgive me if my act is painful to you, and in your heart, especially you, Sonya, let me go of your own free will and do not seek for me and do not be unhappy because of me, do not reproach me.

"The fact that I have left you does not prove that I was dissatisfied with you. I know that you could not, and that you literally cannot alter your life and make sacrifices for the sake of something you do not feel. Therefore I do not reproach you; on the contrary I remember with love and gratitude our thirty-five long years together, especially the first half of that time, when you, with the maternal abnegation which is a natural part of your character, were energetic and firm in bearing what you believed you were destined to bear. You gave to me and to the world what you were capable of giving: you gave much maternal love and self-sacrifice, and it is impossible not to prize you for that. But in the latter period of your life—the last fifteen years—we have drifted apart. I cannot believe that I am to blame, because I know that I have changed not for the sake of other people but because I was incapable of doing anything else. I cannot blame you either for not following me, still I am grateful to you and I remember you with love, and I shall remember you for what you gave me. Farewell, dear Sonya. Your loving Lev Tolstoy."

Yet he did not make up his mind to go away.

In August he wrote to Chertkov in England: "How happy I should be if I could end my days in solitude and above all in circumstances not distasteful and tormenting to my conscience. Yet evidently, it must be thus. In any case I know of no way out."

For the first half of the summer Masha lived with her husband at Ovsyannikovo, but in August she was stricken with peritoneal typhus and was brought to Yasnaya Polyana. Then in the autumn she and Kolya left for the Crimea, where Tanya also went with little Andrei Tolstoy, Ilya's three-year-old son, who was fading away with tuberculosis.

In October Tolstoy wrote to Masha in Yalta: "I am indeed given to loving you and being loved by you. . . . Do I feel the break since your marriage? Yes, I feel it but I do not wish to feel it and I will not. . . ."

Tolstoy had no opportunity to get over his sorrow in quiet; hosts of strangers, often alien to him, continued to crowd the house. Lombroso, the famous psychiatrist, who had been attending a congress of physicians, came down from Moscow. "A narrow-minded, uninteresting, unhealthy little old man," Tolstoy wrote to Biryukov. Sophia Andreyevna made this diary note on August 11: "Lombroso arrived this morning. A little man, very weak on his feet . . . I had asked him down for a talk but he gave me little of interest. He said that crime was everywhere on the increase, except in England, that he did not trust Russian statistics about crime, because there is no freedom of the press in Russia."

Lombroso used to tell the story that when he was preparing to go down to visit Tolstoy the "good chief of police" in Moscow warned him that Tolstoy was not quite right in the head. When he came back, Lombroso said the police chief asked him how he had found Tolstoy.

"It seems to me," replied Lombroso, "that he is a madman who is far more intelligent than the stupid people who hold the power."

During this summer Tolstoy was finishing his essay "What Is Art?" At the same time art in all its aspects was flourishing in Tanya's studio at Yasnaya Polyana. Here, where Repin worked at one period and where the famous pictures of Gay hung, Ginsburg, the sculptor, was now doing a statuette of Tolstoy, and Kasatkin was painting. This studio of Tanya's was converted into something like a club—in the afternoon guests, artists, pianists, members of the family, all gathered there. And in the evenings, in the big living room, Taneyev and Goldenweiser played, sometimes on two pianos. Occasionally, after evening tea, Tolstoy read aloud from his essay on art.

They praised the essay but without warmth. The new tendency in music, literature, the visual arts was spreading like a contagion. How could people from the world of art accept Tolstoy's revolutionary view that as soon as art ceased to be an art for all the people and became art only for the rich, it was changed into a trade?

"The art of our time and our group has become a prostitute."

"A true product of art appears only rarely in the soul of an artist, like the fruit of life already lived, just as the child is conceived by the mother. Imitation art is put out by journeymen, artisans who turn out a product without stopping, as long as there are consumers."

"The basis for the emergence of a true art is an inner compulsion to express accumulated feeling. The basis for imitation art is greed, just as in prostitution."

"It may be that in the future science will reveal to art new and higher ideals, and art will give them life; but in our time the purpose of art is clear and definite. The aim of Christian art is to bring about the brotherhood of man."

Tanya, who had acquired a novelty in the form of a Remington typewriter, and Sophia Andreyevna copied and recopied the essay an untold number of times.

Sophia Andreyevna was bored by having to copy Lyovochka's arguments. On September 4 she wrote in her diary: "I have begun to look for some interest related to my inner life. I began to love music, to read it and, above all, to perceive those complex human emotions embedded in it; but at home they were not at all sympathetic to my music, they attacked me cruelly for it, and so now I am left again without any content to my life and I sit, bent over for hours on end, copying a boring essay on art ten times over, and I try to find joy in the doing of *duty*, but my vital nature rebels, it seeks some personal life. . . ."

With Sophia Andreyevna feeling that way, any trivial occurrence gave sufficient ground for a quarrel. Whether the pretext was the dispatch of an article to the *Northern Herald* without her authorization—the preface to *Contemporary Science* by Carpenter—or a frank entry by Tolstoy in his diary, Sophia Andreyevna would get angry, reproach her husband without pity, and would leave home without telling anyone where she was going.

"Today he wrote in his diary that I had admitted *my guilt* for the first time, and what a joy that was!" said Sophia Andreyevna in her diary. "Good God! Help me to bear this! Again he feels he must appear as a *martyr* before future generations and I as the *guilty one*! L. N. was angry because I went with Uncle Kostya a month ago to visit Sergei Ivanovich [Taneyev], who was laid up in bed with a bad leg. Because of this L. N. was terribly angry, he would not go to Moscow and he calls that *guilt*."

Toward the end of December Tolstoy received a threatening letter which upset Sophia Andreyevna.

"Count Lev Nikolayevich," wrote the anonymous correspondent, "Undoubtedly your sect is growing and putting down deep roots. Lacking in basis as it is, you have nevertheless, with the aid of the devil and thanks to the stupidity of people, fully succeeded in giving affront to our Lord Jesus Christ, who must be avenged by us. To fight you underground we too have formed a secret society, The Second Crusaders, whose aim is—to kill you and all your adherents—the leaders of your sect. . . . The lot has fallen to my unworthy person; It is my duty to kill you! I set the day for you: April 3, 1898. . . .

"You may easily put this logical question to me: why this agitation against just your sect? To be sure, all sects are an abomination in the sight of the Lord! Still the men who make their laws are pitiful incompetents—not on a par, Count, with you; in the second place: you are an enemy of our Tsar and our fatherland! . . . and so, until the third of April. [Signed] Second Crusader, number one lot caster. December, 1897. Bold Village."

Tolstoy was unperturbed. "God's will exists for everything," he said to his wife.

Now and then Tolstoy rode on Boy, his dark gray Kabarda horse to see elderly Maria Alexandrovna Schmidt in Ovsyannikovo.

By taking forest trails he could cut the distance. At places he had to lean over to avoid the branches; he went by a deep ravine, past the railway station of Kozlovka, avoiding the summer cottages which had grown up on either side of the big highway, skirting the village of Ovsyannikovo, then across the fields, across the mill dam of a small pond, to arrive at a brisk trot before the home of Maria Alexandrovna. When she saw him at a distance, his beard flying in the wind, his calm, broad figure, clad in a white blouse, riding easily, almost a part of his horse, Maria Alexandrovna would run out to meet him.

"Lev Nikolayevich darling . . ." and her large, gray, deep-set eyes would shine with joy. She was sunburned, emaciated, her cheekbones stood out prominently in her haggard face, she wore a simple gray homespun dress, and her whole being radiated integration, purity and an ardent spirit.

Maria Alexandrovna worked the livelong day. Her main income was derived from "Manichka" her cow, and her strawberries. She had a moderate-sized garden, but she raised vegetables only for her personal use. The strawberries were the principal item of revenue. Her beds were kept in perfect order, neatly weeded and strewn with straw. Every day all summer Mironych (Tanya's caretaker, who looked after her estate) hitched the black gelding—called "Five Kopecks"—to the farm wagon and Maria Alexandrovna would load it with milk cans and baskets of berries and drive off to peddle her products to the cottagers of Kozlovka. They took her for a simple peasant woman, addressed her in the familiar second person and sometimes were quite rude to her. Kozlovka was scarcely two miles from Ovsyannikovo but Maria Alexandrovna's trip took a great deal of time and energy. Five Kopecks was an inordinately phlegmatic creature and despite the long switch which Maria Alexandrovna waved threateningly and her vociferous pleas he plodded along at his own slow gait. He had learned long since that Maria Alexandrovna was opposed to all forms of coercion and that she would not beat him, so all he did was to swish his sparse tail, snarled with burdock burrs, but never add an iota to his rate of speed. After the day's work Maria Alexandrovna would sit down in the evening to copy by hand the forbidden writings of "dear Lev Nikolayevich," which she then distributed among her friends.

Of all the Tolstoyans, Maria Alexandrovna was probably the one true follower. Despite the fact that she was physically emaciated, scarcely able "to keep body and soul together" as her peasant neighbors said of her, she was happy. In her tiny cottage, which she called her "palace," everything was very clean and cozy. Along the walls were bookcases, pictures of Tolstoy, a rough bed. In the center stood a table, always neatly covered with a snowy white cloth, and in the corner a Russian stove in which she baked large loaves of sour-sweet rye bread.

Everyone loved Maria Alexandrovna: her peasant neighbors, on whom she had a great and beneficent influence, their children who came to her for little books, and both the "dark" and the society friends of Tolstoy. To all she was affectionate and hospitable.

In "old lady Schmidt" there was no element of preachiness, no holier-than-thou attitude; she simply was devoid of all pretense. Her old schoolmarm manner, her exclamatory enthusiasms and abominations only amused people, but were not in the least irritating. She herself laughed at her own weaknesses. Although a strict vegetarian she could not resist the temptation to eat a bit of pickled herring, which she adored. "Sophia Andreyevna darling, you must leave me alone," she would exclaim. "There you have tempted me again, oh, what wickedness!" Or she would confess to Tolstoy: "Oh, dearie, Lev Nikolayevich, I was so angry, so angry, those naughty boys stripped my strawberry plants, the good-for-nothing, unscrupulous creatures. . . ."

It was in the "palace" of "old lady Schmidt" that Tolstoy found a resting place for his spirit, an inner warmth and peace of which he was deprived in the surroundings of his own home.

ᴂ 53 ᴂ

IF ANYONE had told Tolstoy that he was a "public figure" he would probably have rejected the epithet rather harshly—he could not endure routine labels: social worker, progressive, liberal. . . . Yet as a matter of fact all his life he was preoccupied with questions of "public" import—his school, the Mediator work, the famine, the Dukhobor movement, the fate of the Molokan children and the Molokans themselves, who turned to him for help to emigrate to Canada, following the pattern of the Dukhobors.

In the spring of 1898 famine was once more raging in the provinces of Tula, Orel, Samara, Ufa and Kazan, and Tolstoy was showered with requests for aid. As he had before, Tolstoy went into action at once. With Sophia Andreyevna, who was anxious to see her grandchildren, he went down to Ilya's estate in the heart of the famine-stricken area, where he rode through the villages to determine the degree of need. Appeals for aid were published, contributions poured in and a network of soup kitchens was set up. Tolstoy, dissatisfied with this stop-gap aid, tried to get at the basic reason for the frequent and recurrent famines in Russia in an article called "Famine or No Famine." It was published in the newspaper *Rus*, which thereupon immediately received a warning from the Ministry of Internal Affairs.

As usual, the government agents acted stupidly and short-sightedly throughout the crisis. In some cases, the distribution of relief was forbidden, in some villages police officials threatened to close existing soup kitchens, prohibited the opening of others, or forbade the peasants to visit them.

"What is going on in the heads and hearts of people who think they must prescribe and execute such measures, who without really knowing what they do, take the bread of charity out of the mouths of hungry old people and children!" exclaimed Tolstoy.

Disturbing news came too from the Caucasus. Captain St. John, an English friend and follower of Tolstoy, who had helped the Dukhobors, was to be sent out of Russia, and another Tolstoy adherent named Nakashidze had been arrested.

The Dukhobors' desire to emigrate was finally recognized and official permission received. It then was necessary to decide to what country they would emigrate and where they could get the money for the move.

Tolstoy carried on a correspondence with a number of persons on this subject. Several offers came: to resettle the Dukhobors on the island of Cyprus, in Texas in the United States, in Chinese Turkestan, in the Hawaiian Islands. In London the Quakers, whose views approximated those of the Dukhobors, became interested in their plight and undertook to help move them. Money had to be collected but it was impossible to raise it through the press. The only newspaper which dared to print anything about contributions being gathered for the benefit of the Dukhobors was the *Russian News* and for its daring it was ordered to suspend publication for two months.

Tolstoy, although it was an unpleasant task for him, sent personal letters to wealthy people asking them to contribute money. Some sent 500 rubles (*circa* $250), other 1,000, and one merchant, Soldatenkov, himself brought 5,000 rubles to Tolstoy. Tolstoy's appeal for aid was published abroad, the Quakers gathered funds in England, money was sent from America. Yet there was still not enough, whereupon Tolstoy decided to earn the balance needed.

"Since it is now evident," he wrote Chertkov about the middle of July, "how much money is still needed for the resettlement of the Dukhobors, this is what I propose to do. I have some unfinished novels, *Resurrection* and others. I have recently been working on them. So I should like to sell them on the best possible terms to English and American newspapers and use the funds received for the resettlement of the Dukhobors. . . . The novels in themselves, although they do not meet with my own requirements of what art should be—they are not simple and accessible enough in form—in content are not harmful and may even be salutary for people. Therefore I plan, after having sold them for the highest possible figure, to publish them now, without waiting for my death, and to turn over the money to the committee for the resettlement of the Dukhobors."

Tolstoy himself began negotiations with Marks, the publisher of the magazine *Niva*, for the sale of *Resurrection* and even bargained with him. Marks promised to pay a thousand rubles a page for the first serial rights, agreeing to Tolstoy's stipulation that after the novel had finished running in *Niva*, it would come onto the open market.

Sophia Andreyevna did not like it.

"I cannot accept in my mind and my heart," she wrote in her diary for September 13, 1898, "that this novel, after L. N. has renounced his author's rights to it in a public statement in the newspapers, should for some reason now be sold at a tremendous price to Marks and *Niva* and that the money should be given not to our grandchildren, who do not even have any white bread to eat, nor to our children who are in need, but to rank outsiders, to Dukhobors, whom I cannot possibly come to love more than my own children. On the other hand the whole world will hear of Tolstoy's participation in the aid to the Dukhobors, and the newspapers, and history, will write about it. But our grandchildren and children will eat black bread!"

"I do not know whether this is good or bad but I am steadily absorbed with *Resurrection*," Tolstoy wrote Chertkov in the autumn of 1898. "I hope to express much that is of importance. It seems to me at times that there will be a great deal that is good and needed in *Resurrection* and at other times I feel that I am giving in to my passions. At present I am definitely incapable of working on anything but *Resurrection*. As a bombshell falls to the ground with ever-increasing speed, so it is with me now that I am almost at the end: I cannot think of anything—no, I cannot—I cannot and I even believe I do not want to think of anything else."

But to write for a deadline was painfully difficult. The magazine *Niva* was to publish the novel in weekly installments, so Tolstoy was unable to go over his writing the usual infinite number of times. There were occasions when he received the final proofs and, carrying them off to his study for "a minute" to look through them once more, would bring them back with a guilty look several hours later. On the galleys there would remain not one place untouched, whole sentences would be deleted, the margins and the space between the lines would be covered with writing, and on the back of the galleys there would be an entirely new text.

Marks was in despair, telegrams were rushed to the publishers abroad. Often the new, corrected text was delayed and the first edition in Russian differed from the foreign one. Everyone who was capable was drafted to copy the text: Tanya, Masha and her husband, various guests—and Alexander Petrovich Ivanov.

Ivanov, a retired lieutenant, had copied Tolstoy's texts for years. Tolstoy had discovered him in Khitrov Market when he was taking the census in the slums of Moscow. Ivanov, who was a hard drinker, lived for periods of time at the Tolstoys'. He used to come to the house in dirty, threadbare, ragged clothing, in patched and torn shoes. They would give him clothing, shoes, food, and Ivanov would solemnly declare that he was not drinking and would not drink any more. Then, pushing his glasses to the very top of his nose he would set to copying Tolstoy's manuscripts in a careful clerical hand. With this occupation, he would acquire a dignified, supercilious appearance, and he would always insist that he was better than anyone else at deciphering Tolstoy's difficult handwriting. There were instances when Tolstoy would shyly ask Ivanov: "Alexander Petrovich, would you please give me my rough copy; there is something here that does not seem quite right, a mistake. . . ."

Having looked up the original, Alexander Petrovich would testily stick his finger on the spot and, lifting his dull, gray eyes above his glasses to Tolstoy, would cry out in a thin voice full of indignation, "A mistake . . . what mistake is there here? There can be no mistake here. God knows what you wrote in this place, and I had to straighten it out."

But Ivanov never could stand this virtuous life for long. As soon as he was paid for his work, he would disappear. Before long he would be seen drunk in some village. The money, the new clothes, boots had been squandered on drink and the hapless retired lieutenant would start off again on his lonely wanderings along the high roads, begging his way, and spending his nights in filthy flophouses.

An example is contagious. One might have thought that the members of the Tolstoy family would approach the profession of writing with considerable caution. Dumas-*père*–Dumas-*fils* is something one does not often find in the history of literature. The first one to try his luck was Lev Lvovich, whom one witty writer nicknamed Tiger Tigerovich (Lev means "lion" in Russian). In imitation of *The Kreutzer Sonata* he wrote *A Prelude of Chopin*. But this work, like all his other things, was weak and did not enjoy any success. Sophia Andreyevna wrote a novel called *Song Without Words* and, quite unexpectedly, Tanya began to write a drama in collaboration with an untalented writer named Sergeyenko, who had been coming often to the Tolstoys' for the purpose of writing a life of the "great" writer. *Sandra*—as the drama was entitled—was not a success. Tolstoy remained silent, but his brows knit when literary efforts of his family were mentioned.

Toward the end of 1899 *Resurrection* was printed in *Niva* with censorship deletions, and was published unabridged by the Svobodnoye Slovo (Free Word) publishing house organized abroad by Chertkov and Biryukov.

The appearance of *Resurrection* after such a long interval (Tolstoy's last novel was written in the seventies) aroused great interest. As always the criticisms were both favorable and unfavorable. Tolstoy was reproached for moralizing, for expounding his ideas on landed property—the theory of Henry George—for attacking the church, militarism and so on. Abroad, *Resurrection* was received also with great interest. Nevertheless, and strange as it may seem, the publishers abroad also exercised a kind of censorship. In America, for example, they deleted everything touching on landed property and pacificism; in France the translator feared to offend the Catholics, so in the first edition everything touching on the church was left out. In England and Germany *Resurrection* appeared in complete form. In Japan it met with immense success and became Tolstoy's most popular book. The Japanese even composed a song called "Katyusha," after the heroine.

The novel achieved its purpose; the money was finally collected, and the first party of Dukhobors left for the island of Cyprus early in August of 1898. This resettlement proved unsuccessful. There was little land, the climate was unhealthy; many fell ill and died. It appeared that the Canadian government was willing to grant land in the district of Assiniboia, about thirty miles from Yorktown in Saskatchewan.

On the first ship which sailed for Canada Sullerzhitski went along to help and interpret. Sergei Tolstoy went with the second shipload and Vladimir Bonch-Bruyevich went with the third, which sailed in April, 1899.*

Although the mass emigration of the Dukhobors was ended there still remained the problem of those left in prisons, exile or in penal companies. St. John, the Englishman, and Sullerzhitski, back from Canada, remained in the Caucasus and kept Tolstoy informed.

Tolstoy was also disturbed about the fate of those who had gone to Canada. He was far from confident that they would know how to adjust to life in a new country, or be able to establish good relations with the people and the government who had given them the opportunity to emigrate. Tolstoy wrote to the Dukhobors in Canada: ". . . instead of incurring the hatred and hostility of the people surrounding you, instill in them a sense of respect and kindness toward you. . . . It has been said: 'But seek ye first the kingdom of God and his righteousness and all these things shall be added unto you.' To every man is given the chance to prove the truth of these words. You know that they are true, and yet you begin to seek the blessings and joys of this world: nevertheless you will not acquire them and you will lose the Heavenly Kingdom."

Unfortunately Tolstoy's apprehensions were to a certain degree confirmed. Although the attitude of the Dukhobors has remained unaltered, as far as war and killing are concerned, the younger generation are gradually sloughing off the old traditions of the Dukhobors: they drink, smoke, have abandoned vegetarianism. One group of Dukhobors, so-called "Independents," have caused the Canadian government a great deal of trouble. They have organized demonstrations, appeared naked on the streets, refused to send their children to school, and there have even been instances of their burning the schoolhouses. Many Dukhobors have been infected by Soviet propaganda and even dream of returning to their Motherland where "freedom" is at last to be found.

In August, 1898, the month the first boatload of Dukhobors sailed

* Vladimir Bonch-Bruyevich wrote a great deal on the subject of sects in Russia. Later on he became head of the office of the Communist All-Russian Central Executive Committee and a close assistant of Lenin.

for Canada, Tolstoy was seventy years old. The celebration of this three score and ten years, the guests, the telegrams, the letters of congratulation overburdened him. He had difficulty enough in ordinary circumstances handling his constantly enlarging correspondence. There were always serious questions to which, whether he would or no, he felt obliged to react.

What did Tolstoy think about the manifesto of the Tsar on the subject of world disarmament? A cablegram arrived from an American paper, the *New York World,* to this effect: "We congratulate you in connection with the results of your struggle for universal peace, achieved by means of the Tsar's mandate. Kindly reply." To which Tolstoy answered: "The result of this manifesto will be words. Universal peace will be achieved only through self-respect and the refusal to obey a government which requires taxes and military service for the purpose of organized violence and murder."

54

THE Tolstoy nest was gradually being emptied. Left at home with the parents were Tanya and the two youngest: "difficult Misha," as Sophia Andreyevna said, and "naughty Sasha." These two were a source of tribulation to their mother—Misha by his dissipations and refusal to study until he went off as a volunteer in the Sumskoy regiment; Sasha by her aloofness toward her mother, her rudeness, her disobedience toward a succession of governesses, only one of whom—a kind and gentle Englishwoman by the name of Miss Walsh—could get on with the child. But Miss Walsh came to Yasnaya Polyana only for the summer season; she had her own music school in Moscow.

Andrei was married early in 1899 to Olga Dieterichs, the sister of Galya, Chertkov's wife. Under Olga's influence there had recently been a great improvement in him. He no longer dissipated or consorted with gypsies but stayed at home and came much closer to his father. A girl of healthy principles, Olga was eight years older than Andrei although she seemed younger and fresher. With her black, smoothly brushed hair, a wonderful complexion, affectionate, merry brown eyes, she was extremely pretty.

On Andrei's request the Samara estate, which had been given to the three youngest, was sold and he bought an estate near Tula, not far from Yasnaya Polyana, where he and Olga settled down.

On the 14th of the following November Tanya married M. S. Sukhotin and the next day the couple went abroad. This wedding was more like a wake. Despite every effort to restrain their emotions, all wept surreptitiously: the parents, Sasha, the old nurse, the housekeeper Dunechka, and Tanya herself.

"This event has caused us as parents the most heartfelt grief, such as we have not known since the death of Vanichka," Sophia Andreyevna wrote in her diary. "Lev Nikolayevich's outward calm completely vanished: in saying good-by to Tanya, looking exhausted and distressed in a plain gray dress and hat before she went upstairs preparatory to leaving for church—Lev Nikolayevich sobbed as if he were parting from all he held dear in life. We did not go to the church, nor could we remain together."

Tolstoy missed his daughters. He saw Masha frequently but lacking her daily care and companionship it was not the same. Pirogovo, where Masha lived, was almost twenty-seven miles from Yasnaya Polyana. The huge village was situated on the steep banks of the river—on one side of which was Masha's farm and on the other, the large estate of Sergei Nikolayevich Tolstoy. The Obolenskis were happily married. Kolya continued idle while he spent Masha's money, but he was tamed by her influence and he and Tolstoy were better friends than formerly. That God had deprived Masha of children was a sorrow. After carrying a child seven to eight months, all movement ceased, and the child died. The first time this was explained as accidental, but the same thing was repeated with her second and third pregnancies—all her children were stillborn. And the same thing happened to Tanya in her first pregnancy. It was dreadful to see the sisters when, after carrying a child for several months, they watched with bated breath, fearing that signs of life would stop. Both young women passionately desired children.

Tolstoy saw Tanya much less often. In the winter the Sukhotins went abroad and the summer they spent at Kochety, their estate. In Vienna Tanya received treatment for the sinusitis which had been torturing her for a long time and causing excruciating headaches. But the doctors could not help her, so when she returned to Moscow in the spring following her marriage, she decided to have an operation—a trepanning of the skull.

"Just this morning the dreadful operation on Tanya took place," Tolstoy wrote to Masha. "I had stayed at home, but I could not bring myself to stay there. . . . I went to the clinic hoping to get there when it would be over. An hour passed, two, and still it was not over. . . . Mikhail Sergeyevich and I went upstairs, glancing in at the door. The surgeon asked: 'Lev Nikolayevich, would you like to see the operation?' I was beckoned to, I went in, there lay a corpse yellowish-pale, not breathing, with the feet higher than the head and in the thrown-back head there was a hole in the skull this big [drawn] all bloody and deep, three fingers deep and a crowd of people in white and one of them digging. . . ."

When Tolstoy left the operating room they had to take him by the arms; he was as white as a sheet and staggering.

The end of 1900 was a period of gloom for the family. Lyova and Dora lost their first son Lyovushka. Tolstoy wrote in his diary on December 29: "Lyova's child has died. I am so very sorry for them. In all sorrow there is spiritual compensation and tremendous gain. Sorrow means—God has visited you, remembered you. . . . Tanya's child was stillborn, but she is very fine, reasonable."

The family of Sergei Nikolayevich, whom Tolstoy always visited when he went to see Masha across the river, was even more unfortunate. The only son and eldest child quarreled with his father, left home and married against his wishes. The little Tolstoy girls, as they were called, led shut-in lives while they were growing up, never went out, scarcely saw anyone.

The second daughter, Varya, was of diminutive stature, almost a dwarf. She fell in love with a cook, married him secretly and went away. The third daughter, Masha, married a half-literate landowner, a hunting man.

But it was his eldest daughter, Vera, whom Sergei Nikolayevich loved the most. She was Tanya's friend, a charming girl, who took care of her father and was devoted to the ideals of her Uncle Lev. Unfortunately, she was weak, frail, with a tendency toward tuberculosis. In the hope of helping her, her father sent for some Bashkirs to make kumys, which was thought to cure lung trouble. Among the Bashkirs was a handsome and sweet youth with narrow black eyes, broad Mongolian cheekbones and a yellowish cast to his complexion. Vera, who had her father's passionate nature and the hot gypsy blood of her mother, fell in love with him, became pregnant and without her father's knowledge went off to a lying-in home. When she came back carrying in her arms a child with a yellowish-bronze complexion and narrow slit eyes, Sergei Nikolayevich was at first under the impression that the child was adopted. But when he realized the truth, they feared he would have a stroke. The old man was prostrate with grief, crushed by it. He could not be reconciled or forgive Vera.

"My God! My God! Why have you done this to me? Oh . . . oh . . . oh!" he would sob.

But a miracle came to pass. Sergei Nikolayevich not only took back his daughter, but he gave Vera such proofs of love and affection that she grieved all the more because of the unhappiness she had caused her father. Still, a long time had to pass before the old man was willing to see his grandson. He lived in a separate wing of the house and never set foot in the women's and children's quarters.

Tolstoy, who understood his brother's suffering, wrote to his daughter Tanya: "I am sending you, Tanichka dear, the letters of Masha and Vera, over which I wept and always weep when I read them over. . . . I know nothing beyond what is in the letters, and, strangely enough, I have no desire to know anything. A lot of good is summoned forth by this terrible business. How beneficent unhappiness is."

In reply to a letter from his brother Lev, Sergei Nikolayevich wrote: "It is a punishment for pride. I counted on my children not being able to do anything of the kind. Were it not for that, all this could have been stopped two years ago, but my pride stood in the way, it placed them so high: what, *my* children? That is how I am to blame and why I was punished."

⁂ 55 ⁂

IT MAY seem strange to many that the war between the English and the Boers (1899-1900) had great repercussions in Russia. Volunteers joined the Boer army, the Red Cross sent units of Russian nurses to care for the Boers, in the villages and among industrial workers one heard on all sides the song: "Transvaal, Transvaal, my own dear land, you burn as in a fire. . . . Under a leafy little tree a Boer sits plunged in thought. . . . My sons, all nine of them, are killed in the war. . . ."

Tolstoy, in his heart, was sympathetic to the Boers. When a correspondent interviewing him asked how he felt about the Transvaal war he replied: "Can you imagine how far I went? . . . When I took up the morning newspaper I passionately wished to read that the Boers had beaten the English. . . . But I have controlled myself. . . . And this fighting, you notice, is going on after the Hague Conference which caused such a stir."

This interview was no sooner printed than Tolstoy was instantly besieged with letters and questions, among others from his supporter and translator, Aylmer Maude: How could he, who condemned war in general, take the part of any one side?

The answer to the doubts of his "friends" is found in a letter written by Tolstoy to Prince Volkonski. In it Tolstoy elaborated ideas coincident with those in *War and Peace*. It is not the Napoleons, the Wilhelms, or the Chamberlains who are to blame. "All history is a series of just such acts, on the part of all politicians, as the Transvaal war. . . . As long as we use exceptionally great riches at a time when the masses of the people are overburdenend with work, there will always be wars for markets, for gold deposits, etc."

These same thoughts occur in Tolstoy's article, "Thou Shalt Not Kill," written after the assassination of King Humbert of Italy, in "The Serfdom of Our Times," "Patriotism and Government," and "The Only Means," written somewhat later. In describing the condition of the working people he again and again reiterated the thought of man's subjection to only one law—that of God. Only in fulfilling the will of God can a people free itself from the control of government, manufacturers, landowners.

Beginning again in 1900 Tolstoy kept a diary with regularity. Everyone should keep a diary, he used to say. It helps one to move forward, it develops the brain as gymnastics develop our muscles. His diary was a thick blank book in which at the end of the day he entered his thoughts and some incidents. But in addition to his diary he always had with him, day and night, his little notebook. On horseback, or on waking in the middle of the night, he would jot down a thought or some detail that occurred to him in relation to his writing. These notes, sometimes in more developed and precise form, were copied into the diary. The diary for this period showed in evolution his philosophy of death, God, love, and his constant struggle with his sins—ambition, unkindness. Here too he often wrote criticisms of books he had read, commenting on their influence on himself. After reading *The Life and Teachings of Confucius* and *The Life and Works of Mencius* (Legge) Tolstoy thought of writing a message to the Chinese. His reading of John Ruskin, Descartes, Emerson, and other philosophers gave him satisfaction, for in them he frequently found sympathy for his own views. Sometimes, in concluding an entry, he would set down the date of the following day and beside it the letters "D.V.," if God wills, or the initials of the words meaning "If I am spared," to remind himself that he must fulfill the will of God and constantly think of death.

Although Tolstoy was quite overburdened with his philosophical work, he could not fail to take an interest in contemporary literature. Of the classic writers of the nineteenth century who had brought about the flowering of Russian literature, only he was left. He often used to say that he did not wish to be like the old-timers who recognized only the old forms in literature and criticized all that was new. He showed great kindness and concern in his dealings with young writers.

At this time art in Russia had risen to a high level. In St. Petersburg, under the aegis of A. N. Benois, a whole artistic center was founded around the magazine *Bygone Years*. Chaliapin emerged in the opera, and such scene designers as Korovin, Bilibin, Dobuzhinski and others. Ballet was raised by Diaghilev to hitherto unknown heights. In Moscow, alongside the famous Maly Theater, the new Art Theater of Stanislavski and Nemirovich-Danchenko completed its revolution and evolution. In music there appeared after Tchaikovski such composers as Rachmaninov, Scriabin, Stravinski. In literature the most popular writers were Chekhov, Gorki, Bunin, Andreyev, Merezhkovski. Tolstoy gradually made their acquaintance.

Gorki called on Tolstoy for the first time early in 1900. It is probable that Gorki approached the "aristocratic" home of Count Tolstoy with prejudice, and was irked by the menservants, the gleaming parquet floors, and the entire "bourgeois" setting. Gorki himself was dressed in a black Russian blouse, with trousers stuffed in his boots. His chestnut hair, which he wore long, kept getting in his eyes, and he was constantly throwing it back; in his movements, in his face with its broad, prominent cheekbones, in his gait, there was something awkward, unkempt.

At the beginning of the conversation Gorki seemed to feel he was being examined. But Tolstoy treated him with so much consideration and cordiality that that impression was soon erased. Tolstoy was frank in criticizing some of Gorki's works; he praised others, and in the end, as they were parting, he paid him what was from the Tolstoyan viewpoint a great compliment: "You are a true peasant. You will find it hard going among the writers, but don't be afraid, always say what you feel; it may be coarse in expression but never mind! The intelligent people will understand."

Soon after this encounter Gorki wrote Tolstoy a letter: "For everything, for everything that you said to me my thanks, my heartfelt thanks, Lev Nikolayevich! I am glad that I saw you and am very proud of it. I knew in general that you are simple and warm in your relations with people but I confess I never expected that you would treat one so well."

To which Tolstoy replied: "I was very, very glad to see you and glad that I liked you. Aksakov used to say that some people are better (he said more intelligent) than their books and some are worse. I liked your writing, yet I found you better than your writing. There's a compliment from me the main value of which lies in the fact that it is sincere."

Later Tolstoy wrote in his notebook: "Gorki had something to say and that is why he succeeded. He exaggerates untruthfully but he loves, and we recognize our brothers where we have not seen them before."

It was at this time that Chaliapin sang for Tolstoy in Moscow. Chaliapin had come up out of the same surroundings as Gorki but there was nothing "proletarian" in his tall, graceful figure, in his kindly, simple, typically Russian face, or in his manner of carriage or speech. He was unaffected, buoyant, his light blue eyes shone with mischief, jollity; there was nothing pompous or theatrical about him. On the contrary, he had a conquering, imperial, truly aristocratic way with him: "He came, he saw, he conquered."

With Goldenweiser to accompany him he sang "The Flea," "Nach Frankreich Zogen Zwei Grenadiere," and other songs; everyone was delighted. But the greater the enthusiasm expressed by those present the greater was Tolstoy's reserve. It was only when Chaliapin sang the Russian folk song "Nochenka" ("The Night") to Misha's sketchy accompaniment that Tolstoy's ardor was ignited.

"Marvelous, wonderful," he kept repeating.

From his diary one can see how works of other writers occasionally exercised an oblique influence on Tolstoy's own work. On May 7, 1901, he wrote: "I had a dream about a type of old man which Chekhov has already anticipated. The particularly good thing about his old man was that he was almost a saint and yet he was a drunkard and quarrelsome. I for the first time realized the power which certain types acquire from boldly laid on shades. I shall do this in *Hadji Murat*."

Tolstoy was literally enraptured by Chekhov's talent as a storyteller. Some of his stories like "Darling" he read aloud several times. Later he wrote a preface to the story and used the story in the weekly reading list of his *Circle of Reading*. "Chekhov," he used to say, "has given us an ideal type of woman in 'Darling'—self-sacrificing, kindly, whose main attribute is love, and without thought of self she serves to the end the person she loves."

"This is what Lyovochka likes," Sophia Andreyevna said with indignation. "A type of woman—a she-animal, slave, lacking in all initiative, interests! Wait on your husband, serve him, bear and feed children!"

"The ideal woman," wrote Tolstoy in his diary, "is the one who will bear children and bring them up in a Christian way, that is to say, so that they will serve God and people and not be parasites on life."

The question of woman's role was one which provoked constant argument in the Tolstoy family, with Sergei siding enthusiastically with his father against mother and sisters. Tolstoy was sometimes quite harsh in expressing himself against women, believing that all depravity stemmed from them, that a woman should not engage in any public, scientific or other duties—her calling was exclusively in the family.

Tolstoy's admiration for Chekhov's work did not include his dramas. Nevertheless, one of Chekhov's plays had an oblique influence on Tolstoy's play *The Living Corpse*.

Tolstoy saw *Uncle Vanya* played by the Moscow Art Theater early in 1900 and, as he wrote in his diary, was much "upset." "There is no real action, movement, toward which all the endless conversations of the neurasthenic intellectuals tend. It is incomprehensible what Chekhov wanted to say anyhow."

Yet having seen *Uncle Vanya*, Tolstoy was suddenly seized with the desire to write a play which had been in his mind since the middle of the nineties. He immediately made an outline, based on a story told to him by N. V. Davydov and involving A. F. Koni. It concerned a decent, upright woman married to a weak man, a drunkard. Abandoned by him, in love with another man, the woman persuaded her husband, when he reappeared, to pretend suicide in order that she might remarry. When the fraud was discovered, she was charged with bigamy and was only at the last minute saved from life exile in Siberia.

"It seems to me," Tolstoy wrote in his diary, "that in the drama *The Living Corpse* there are notes inspired by Chekhov's work. Such is the secret of artistic creativeness."

The news that Tolstoy was writing the drama found its way into the newspapers, and Tolstoy was showered with requests from magazines which wanted to print it. Nemirovich-Danchenko came to ask for the production rights for the Moscow Art Theater. But to everyone Tolstoy said no, and he never completed the drama. The main reason had to do with two visitors who sought Tolstoy out. One was a tattered, disreputable, hapless creature who confided that he was the very person, the "living corpse," described in the drama. Tolstoy was sympathetic, helped the man in material ways, extracted a promise that he would stop drinking, and through friends found him a job which he held to the end of his days. The second visitor was the son of the woman tried for bigamy, who came to beg Tolstoy not to publish his play and so stir up once more the tragic history of these several lives.

In abandoning the play, Tolstoy wrote to Chertkov on December 11, 1900: "I have written a rough draft of a drama as a joke—or rather as a distraction; but I not only do not intend to finish and publish now but also I very much doubt whether I shall ever do it. There are so many more urgent things on my conscience."

This was in the nature of an apology, for Tolstoy knew that Chertkov was more interested in his essays than in his creative writings.

Now, after two and a half years of exile, Tolstoy's follower Boulanger returned to Moscow. He was an ardent person easily carried away by new ideas. It occurred to him to found and edit *Morning*, a magazine to which Tolstoy and all the well-known writers would contribute. Soldatenkov, who had given 5,000 rubles to the Dukhobors, agreed to put up the money for the magazine. But nothing came of the project. Soldatenkov died and Boulanger was unable to raise the necessary funds. The affair brought Tolstoy two sharp, reproachful letters from Chertkov (January 3 and 5, 1901), which read in part: "I wish to point out to you all the compromising, all the immorality, all the betrayal of our Master, involved in obtaining a permit and submitting to all the demands connected with this foul affair. . . . All who go to apply for governmental permits are guilty of committing a series of servile, degraded acts to do which a man must be bereft of all human dignity and have become a willing toady." And in conclusion: "To take part in an organization subject to censorship is as bad as or even worse than to have a part in a brothel inasmuch as spiritual prostitution is worse, more revolting and debasing than the physical."

To this Tolstoy replied, as always, with a mild letter—he loved "accusation." But, on second thought, he wrote that "I am not altogether in accord. . . . I was much attracted by the fact that this, i.e., the magazine, would have incited me to write literary pieces which I otherwise shall not write."

Chertkov seems to have forgotten that he himself founded The Mediator in his day and personally had to do directly with the government censor.

✥ 56 ✥

A S EARLY as 1888 the question of Tolstoy's excommunication from the church was raised. Pobedonostsev's intention was confirmed in a letter to S. A. Rachinski in 1896, and in 1900 the Sacred Consistory met to hear the reasons for excommunication enumerated by the ranking member of the Holy Synod. A secret part of this decree mentioned that:

"The performing of a requiem and funeral rites for Count Lev Tolstoy, in the event of his death without repentance and reconciliation with the church, would undoubtedly disturb the true children of the Holy Church and be the cause of temptation, which should be precluded. In view of this the Holy Synod has decreed that it forbids the performing of memorial and requiem masses, funeral rites for Count Lev Tolstoy in the event of his dying unrepentant."

The decree of the Synod was officially published on February 22, 1901:

". . . In our days, under God's sufferance, a new false teacher has arisen, Count Lev Tolstoy. A writer known to the world, Russian by birth, Orthodox by baptism and training, Count Tolstoy, seduced by his proud intellect, has arrogantly defied our Lord and His Christ and His holy legacy, he has openly renounced the mother who nourished and trained him, the Orthodox Church, and has dedicated his God-given, literary talent to spreading among the masses teachings contrary to those of Christ and the church, and to uprooting in the minds and hearts of people their fathers' faith, the Orthodox faith, which has been accepted as universal, by which our ancestors lived and were saved by virtue of which our Holy Russia until this day has been maintained and kept strong. . . ."

This document was signed by Antonius, the Metropolitan of St. Petersburg and Ladoga, and by two other Metropolitans and four bishops.

It is probable that the government, especially Pobedonostsev, was not prepared for the effect produced. There were demonstrations protesting the decree in the large cities of Russia from Kiev, where the Kuzminskis lived, to Moscow. Most of them were led by rebellious students who saw in Tolstoy a revolutionary hero.

On February 24, when the newspapers carried the news, crowds numbering in the thousands gathered in the squares and streets of Moscow. Tolstoy, taking a walk according to his custom, happened to enter Lubyanskaya Place where someone recognized him and yelled: "Look, there is the devil in the shape of a man!" Instantly a mob surrounded him, yelling, crowding him, until with difficulty a mounted policeman helped to extricate him and he was put in a cab and driven home.

The action of the students in exploiting the excommunication in order to exhibit Tolstoy as a victim of the regime they hated placed him in a difficult position. He could not refuse to defend the young people, who were severely punished for their disorders, nor could he refuse to condemn them for proposing to use violence and terror to seize the power for themselves.

"The people who are concerned with masses and their well-being," he wrote in his diary, "ascribe quite wrongly, as I do too, some importance to the student disturbances. Actually this is a clash between oppressors, between those who already are oppressors and those who still only wish to become such."

In the Tolstoy home there was a violent reaction to all this. Everyone, young and old, was indignant over the "excommunication." Sixteen-year-old Sasha and her contemporary Misha Sukhotin, Tanya's stepson who lived with the Tolstoys, were filled with a spirit of stormy protest and revolutionary ardor; they thirsted for action, dreamed of impossible heroic sallies against the government. It was disturbing yet gay. Sophia Andreyevna wrote in her diary: "For several days there has been a kind of holiday atmosphere in the house; there have been visitors from morning until evening—whole crowds. . . ." (March 6, 1901.)

Sophia Andreyevna shared in the general mood. With quick, light steps she ran through the house in a state of great agitation, talking without stopping, expressing her indignation. Then she wrote a letter to the Holy Synod:

"There is no limit to my grievous resentment," she protested. "And not because my husband is spiritually doomed by this piece of paper; that is not the affair of man but of God. The life of a human soul from the religious viewpoint is unknown to anyone except God; it is unknown and, fortunately, not subject to anyone. . . . For me the order of the Holy Synod is incomprehensible. It has occasioned not sympathy (except possibly in the *Moscow News*) but resentment among people and great affection and sympathy for Lev Nikolayevich. We are already receiving such testimonials of this—and there will be no end to it—from all over the world. I cannot keep from mentioning, moreover, the grief I feel over the absurd thing I heard earlier: the secret order of the Synod to priests not to perform funeral rites for Lev Nikolayevich in the event of his death. Whom do they wish to punish—the dead man who no longer feels anything or those close to and surrounding him who are faithful believers? If this is a threat, against whom and what is it directed? Can it be that I should not be able to find a decent priest to perform the funeral rites for my husband and pray for him in church, a priest who is not afraid of men in the face of the true God of love, or else a dishonest one whom I shall bribe with large sums of money for the purpose?. . ."

The reply of Metropolitan Antonius was not satisfactory to her; Tolstoy did not even read it. The atmosphere continued to be charged with excitement. Sophia Andreyevna's letter was published in many foreign newspapers. In Moscow fables about "The Seven Doves" (the seven church dignitaries), "Pobedonostsev," and "The Donkey and the Lion" (Lev), were current, all poking fun at the government. The fable of "The Donkey and the Lion" began in this fashion: "In a certain country governed by donkeys, a lion appeared. . . ."

If the purpose of the Synod was to humiliate Tolstoy, to lessen his influence, the excommunication accomplished quite the opposite effect. It was particularly unsuccessful as it coincided with demonstrations taking place throughout Russia. The revolutionaries were not dormant. On March 4 there was a large demonstration on Kazan Square in St. Petersburg. The police attempted to drive off the crowds; many were beaten; various distinguished public men and writers were hurt. Prince Vyazemski, a member of the Imperial Council, came out in defense of those who were beaten, thereby incurring the disapproval of the authorities.

A protest against the actions of the police on this occasion was addressed to the Minister of Internal Affairs and signed by 155 writers, after which the civil governor of St. Petersburg sent an order closing the Union of Writers. This act aroused public opinion even more and the Union of Writers received a greeting bearing many signatures, the first being that of Lev Tolstoy. Moreover, Tolstoy wrote a letter to Prince Vyazemski, to express his respect and gratitude for the Prince's having taken the part of innocent people. Also in St. Petersburg, at the Circulating Exhibition, a large group gathered in a spontaneous ovation in front of the portrait Repin had painted of Tolstoy in Yasnaya Polyana (the one of his whole figure showing him barefoot—a portrait, incidentally, which Tolstoy disliked very much). One student jumped on a chair and made a speech. To cheers, the portrait was decorated with flowers, wreaths; but when the demonstration was repeated, the portrait was ordered removed from the wall.

Among those who were persecuted for protesting was Gorki. He was put in prison and Tolstoy wrote to St. Petersburg urging his release.

Misha Sukhotin and Sasha finally found an outlet for their energies. In all the free time they had from their lessons they copied the political fables, Sophia Andreyevna's answer to the Holy Synod, various banned works of Tolstoy. On each copy they wrote in large letters at the top: PLEASE CIRCULATE. But the work was tedious, nonproductive. One evening Misha, with a mysterious air, dragged something heavy up to his room. It was a hectograph—a machine forbidden for private use at that time by the government.

They worked at night. The place was like a printing shop. They issued hundreds of copies of forbidden writings. Then one night when scores of sheets with their wavering purple lines were laid out on Misha's bed, on the chairs, his bureau—in walked Sophia Andreyevna. A terrible storm was unleashed, some of the sheets were burned, the hectograph was carried out of the house and a strict watch was set over Sasha and Misha.

There is the following entry in Sophia Andreyevna's diary for March 30: "Things have turned out most unpleasantly with Sasha. She has not joined me in the Lenten observances; once she excused herself, another time she scraped her leg, and then she flatly refused to go. This is a fresh step in our break."

Moscow was gay in the spring. The streams flowed again, children swarmed on their banks, floating tiny paper boats, the sun was already getting warm, the bells rang, their sounds intermingling from one end of the city to the other. People went into the white churches with the golden cupolas, crossed themselves; their faces were serious. Many went to confession. The Tolstoys, mother and daughter, were in a melting mood, a mood of repentance, and they both strove to evoke in themselves a feeling of affection and closeness to each other. In their church the priest, ignoring the poor and the aged, had the Countess taken first to the confessional.

"Even here, in God's temple, everything is done for the rich, the well known, there is no equality, no justice. That is what Father has been saying, and this same church has excommunicated him—Father, the kind, just man who has always taken the part of the weak, the humiliated."

Sasha asked herself which of her parents was right. Her father, who rejected the church yet by his whole life professed the teachings of Christ? Or her mother? Her father or the church which excommunicated him? These thoughts were primitive, childish, prompted largely by emotion. Yet Sasha was no longer touched by listening to the mass—everything now aroused critical, hostile feelings in her. Even when, kneeling, she heard the choir of blind girls sing her favorite hymn, she wept bitterly, she could no longer pray. Something in her heart had snapped.

From that day there was a change in Sasha—in me. Sasha—I— was no longer a child. I realized that I had to choose my own path, and that evening I went to my father in his study to talk with him. This was my first significant conversation with my father. When I told him of my decision not to go to church any more he was not happy as I had supposed he would be; he was alarmed. He knew, as I did not, that my decision had been dictated by emotion, it was not thoroughly thought out as he would have wished it to be. He asked me to go to church; he did not want me to distress my mother. And indeed my mother reacted violently to my decision. She reproached my father for having corrupted her last daughter, although she had always known that Sasha was a stupid creature, interested in nothing—and she said many other things before I succeeded in calming her by agreeing to accompany her to church.

In Father's diary there is this brief note: "I am now using in my life my own prayers for every occasion. I spoke with Sasha about this."

Tolstoy had now reached a peak of celebrity, with the help of the Holy Synod and the government. Messages—a few of them abusive —poured in by the thousands, by letter and telegram. All this excitement undermined his health, affected his heart; he lost a lot of weight, aged. The more people expressed their sympathy with him, the more they wrote and talked about him, the more strongly he felt his obligation toward the people as a whole.

In the first draft of a letter addressed "to the Tsar and his Ministers," in which he once more implored the Tsar to let up on the repressive measures and to grant more freedom to the Russian people, he concluded: "No matter how difficult it is to believe that you have a kind heart, if one judges by the horrors which are ceaselessly committed in your name—still I believe in you. And when you were ill, I was sorry for you, I feared you would die and that without you things would be worse. For some reason I have hope in you."

At first Tolstoy hesitated to reply to the decrees of the Synod. Then on March 24 he made a first draft of a letter.

"I believe in God," he wrote, "whom I understand to be Spirit, Love, and the First Principle of everything. I believe too that He is in me and I in Him. I also believe that the will of God is most clearly, most intelligibly set forth in the teachings of the human being, Christ, to accept whom as a God and to pray to him—I look upon as a great sacrilege. I believe that man's true bliss lies in his fulfilling the will of God. His will is that men should love one another and consequently that they should do unto one another as they would be done by, as it is said in the Gospels, that therein lies all the law and the prophets."

At the close Tolstoy quoted Coleridge to the effect that: He who begins by loving his Christianity above truth very shortly will love his church or sect above Christianity, and will end by loving himself (his own peace of mind) above all else in the world.

"I took the opposite way," he went on. "I began with loving my Orthodox faith more than my peace of mind, and then came to love Christianity more than my church. Now I love truth above all else in the world. And up to now truth has coincided for me with Christianity as I understand it. And I profess that Christianity, and, in the degree to which I do profess it, I live happily and approach death joyfully."

It was this spring that I began to take a more active part in my father's work. After my sisters married there was no one who could do the systematic copying of his essays. Occasionally Julia Ivanovna Igumnova (Jooly-Mooly, as she was nicknamed), a classmate of Tanya's at Art School, would do some of it and also, at rare intervals, Alexander Petrovich Ivanov. But Ivanov was increasingly critical and abusive of Tolstoy, especially when he was drunk, as Tolstoy once noted in his diary: "Alexander Petrovich came, and I received him very coldly because he railed at me. But after he left I was uneasy. Where was that love, that devotion to love as an aim in life, which you profess, I said to myself; and I calmed myself when I had set myself right."

In the beginning of May the family was ready to move for good to Yasnaya Polyana. No one needed to go to school any longer. Misha had finished his military service in the Sumskoy Regiment and married a girl he had been in love with since he was a child—Lina Glebova. I did not wish to study any longer. I was prepared for an examination except for Sacred History which I had intentionally and as a form of protest left out of my studies (approximately a gymnasium program). I was far more interested in Father's work than in lessons with the English lady, Miss Walsh, or in reading Racine and Corneille with Mother. The examination was postponed until autumn but I never had to take it. Little by little, rather haltingly and poorly, I began to copy Father's manuscripts.

Father was very feeble and Boulanger arranged for a private railway car to move him to Yasnaya Polyana. Many friends, joined by a host of cheering and waving strangers, accompanied him to the station. Lyova and his wife were living at Yasnaya, he busy with his mediocre writings and with the management of the estate. Masha and her husband were also there.

But there was no respite in Yasnaya Polyana either from visitors or from the flood of messages which must be sorted and copied. The majority were sympathetic, as the one which read: "You have aroused the Orthodox from their slumbers and stirred the clergy who have been mired for centuries. It is natural that the first thing to emerge from this mire should be mud—but time will pass, the slime will settle but the springs you have brought into being will cover it with streams of living waters, for life is movement."

But occasionally another view was expressed. "To the beastlike Lev in a human hide," wrote one person. "May you from henceforth be anathema, you accursed offspring of hell, spirit of darkness, old fool. . . ."

In his diary Tolstoy had written: "I am seriously convinced that the world is governed by people entirely mad. Those who are not insane either stand aside or cannot participate [in its government]."

This bold, extreme judgment was supported in a measure by the statement of Mr. Lebedev, legal adviser to the secretariat of his Majesty, who summed up the situation in these words:

"I have just read the decree of the Synod with regard to Tolstoy. What a piece of stupidity. What bit of satisfaction of personal vengeance. It is, of course, obviously the hand of Pobedonostsev and it is he who is avenging himself on Tolstoy. . . . Perhaps tens of thousands of people in Russia have been reading Tolstoy's banned works, but now hundreds of thousands will read them. Earlier they did not understand his false teachings; now the Synod has underscored them. When he dies Tolstoy will be buried as a martyr for an idea, and with special pomp. People will go to his grave to honor him. What distresses me is the absence among the bishops of the spirit of love and the application of the truth of Christianity. . . . They dress themselves up in rich vestments, they carouse and feast, they accumulate capital as monks, forget about the poor and the needy; by not conforming to the works of the teachings of Christ they are the heretics. If Tolstoy is guilty of distorting the teachings of Christ by his words and his teaching, at least he is innocent in deed. He follows the teaching in his acts and he applies it by helping his neighbor. But they have withdrawn from the people, they have built palaces, they have forgotten their cells. . . ."

Others all over the world, in all walks of life, agreed.

[412]

❧ 57 ❧

WHILE the controversy over the excommunication raged, Tolstoy had not been idle. The essay on "What the Majority of the Working Masses Wish Above All" was gradually expanded, to take the title "The Only Means." In addition, he wrote a series of short articles: "A Handbook for Soldiers and Officers," which was a protest against war and military service; a preface to Polentza's novel *The Peasant*, which had made a powerful impression on him; a long letter to Biryukov on free education; and he made a start on an essay on the essential nature of religion.

His correspondence took a great deal of time. A sympathetic letter from the Rumanian Queen Carmen Sylva must be answered, a long letter written to a Paris correspondent Pietro Mazzini on the subject of the Franco-Russian alliance, toward which he maintained an attitude of indifference. An exclusive alliance favoring one people above others, he argued, could only result in drawing a nation into hostilities and perhaps war.

From time to time he posed—a tiring obligation—for painters and sculptors: for Repin, Pasternak who did a study of the family, Aronson, and Paolo Trubetskoy. Trubetskoy, a Russian educated in Italy, did some splendid little statues of Tolstoy—one of him on horseback. Father was very fond of him. A sweet and childlike person in addition to his great gifts, he read practically nothing, spoke little, all his life was wrapped up in sculpture. As a convinced vegetarian he would not eat meat but cried: *"Je ne mange pas de cadavre!"* if anyone offered him some. In his studio in St. Petersburg there was a whole zoo: a bear, a fox, a horse, and a vegetarian wolf.

A visit from Trubetskoy was a pleasure. But there were less agreeable visitors to Yasnaya Polyana, and one was a prison chaplain named Troitski who always happened to arrive when Father was ill—as he did at the end of June, 1901. Father received him but was quite frank in saying that if he had come on orders from his superiors it was a bad thing to do and asked him not to come any more.

About this time Father was taken with a severe form of malaria and for ten days lay between life and death: his pulse was 150, and intermittent, his breath was short. Doctors were called. All the children gathered; Aunt Maria Nikolayevna arrived. His temperature dropped but his breathing was labored and his heart was weak. The physicians diagnosed the trouble as angina pectoris and urged a change of climate, mentioning the Crimea.

Countess S. V. Panina, one of the wealthiest women of Russia, active at that time in work among the poor in the suburbs of St. Petersburg and founder there of one of the first People's Houses (*Narodny Dom*), offered Father her house on the south shore of the Crimea, near the village of Gaspra. In family council it was decided to accept her invitation for the winter.

All was bustle and excitement, plans were laid, luggage was packed, the families of Semyon, the cook, and Ilya, the footman, were reduced to tears over their departure with us.

Only Father remained aloof from all the agitation. In his diary he wrote: "My illness made for a complete spiritual holiday, for increased spirituality, and calm at the approach of death, and the expression of love on all sides. . . ."

We drove away from Yasnaya Polyana one damp, dark autumn night in two barouche carriages: Father, Mother, Masha, Kolya, Boulanger and I. The horses went at a walk, picking their way with care for the mile of rutted country road leading to the highway. Filechka, the groom, lighted the way with the bright yellow flame of a kerosene torch. We were in a mood of uneasiness. Father was so weak that he could scarcely stand. Only Boulanger was full of courage and put heart in everyone. He had managed to arrange with the Moscow-Kursk Railway for a private car which was to carry us from Tula to Sevastopol. The car was magnificent, including a kitchen, dining room, separate sleeping compartments. But Father's appearance alarmed us all—he seemed so exhausted and ill. They took his temperature. He had fever. What to do? How could we go on? Again it was Boulanger who persuaded us: it would be more difficult to drive the dozen miles back to Yasnaya Polyana than to ride the six hundred miles to Sevastopol with all the conveniences of the railway car, and down there were sun, warmth. . . . At three o'clock in the night the train moved out of the station. By morning Father's temperature had fallen, he was contented, and was already dictating to Masha.

Toward evening the train drew into Kharkov with its gleaming, clean, white plastered houses, its gardens, mild air. We intended to dine in the station restaurant, but that proved impossible. What was this uproar? A sea of human heads . . . a milling crowd bearing down on the train, hats being doffed. . . . I stepped out onto the platform of the car.

"Tolstoy! Lev Nikolayevich! Is he there? Here's a delegation! Let us come aboard! Hurrah! Tolstoy!" the crowd yelled.

I was terrified and rushed back into the car. "Father will die of excitement! His heart can't stand it . . . what shall we do?" were the thoughts that flashed through my head.

"Tolstoy! Hurrah! Hurrah!" boomed the crowd. Boulanger conducted one delegation in to see Father, then another. Tolstoy spoke with them in a friendly fashion but he was pale, his hands trembled, his breathing was spasmodic. Finally the seemingly endless twenty-minute stop at Kharkov was nearly over. "Let Tolstoy show himself, please come to the window!" yelled the crowd. Supported in back by Mother and Boulanger, Father stood up by the window, waved his hand. There were beads of perspiration on his face. The train slowly pulled out. Father wiped away some tears. When he was finally put back to bed he had a heart attack, he gasped for breath, his temperature went up. This Kharkov demonstration might have cost him his life!

The next morning we reached Sevastopol. A moderate-sized crowd was gathered at the station. The police kept order and Father was immediately helped into a hackney coach which was to take us to the best hotel in the city. There was sunshine, soft southern air, numerous ships about the bay, cutters, fishing smacks. Father revived, looking about him with interest. "Where's that Fourth Bastion?" he asked the driver. This was the Fourth Bastion which he, as a sublieutenant of artillery, had defended in 1855. During the twenty-four hours we spent in Sevastopol Father strolled around the city, trying to find his Fourth Bastion; he even came across the son of an old Sevastopol comrade, and he visited the military museum.

We traveled to Gaspra by post coaches, in two barouches. The Obolenskis and Goldenweiser, the pianist, had joined our party in Kharkov. The first part of the road was smooth, through settlements, fields, and steppe country. But then it rose higher, higher, until we reached Baidar, gates on the crest of a mountain range, in the midst of a beech forest. It was picturesque but not extraordinarily so. While

Mother was arranging for luncheon I ran out, beyond the gates, and found myself suddenly rooted to the spot—for the first time I really felt the vastness of the sea opening out before my eyes way down there at our feet. The vivid green shore, the gardens, with the mountain range of Yaila on the left—it was magnificent and I yearned to be carried on and on into that magic sphere.

Darkness was falling as we drove up to the Panin residence. The gravel in the courtyard crunched under the carriage wheels, a fountain was playing, in the twilight one could barely discern two towers, the dark granite walls, the cupola of a family chapel. . . . At the door, with the customary bread and salt offering of hospitality in his hand, stood Karl Christianovich Klassen, the aged little German steward of Countess Panina.

Although Father began slowly to recover he continued to think about death and prepare himself for it. His old friend Count Adam Vasilievich Olsufiev had died. "Soon it will be my turn," he wrote to his brother Sergei on November 6. "In the morning he went for a walk, ten minutes before it happened, he knew that he was dying, he said good-by to everyone, gave advice to his children and repeated over and over: I had no idea it would be so easy to die."

In two weeks Father was able to take walks, and then we rode on horseback together to Alupka and to the seashore.

The Obolenskis moved to Yalta and I began to copy Father's manuscripts. But at first I could not decipher them at all. His letters were slanting, the big ones ran together. I could not guess at them by the sense as I did not understand it all—at that time Father was working on his essay "What Is Religion and What Is Its Essential Content?" Try as I might my efforts were rewarded with little success: there were gaps, my lines were crooked, here and there the ink blotted, there were smudges from tears. I was ashamed to take what I had written to Father; I cursed my own ineptness, stupidity, youth.

Gradually I became accustomed to the work and soon went over to copying the manuscripts on a Remington typewriter—that entertained me. In between times I managed to ride to Yalta, run down to the seashore, pick a lot of wonderful black Isabella grapes from the vines hanging all over the lower marble terrace, play games with Gorki and his son Maximka who lived near the sea and often came to see us.

Father lived downstairs next to the living room. The furniture, the windows were in the Gothic style, there were deep marble embrasures, rugs, a view of the sea from the windows and from the broad terrace across the greenery of a dense park; there were cypresses, walnut trees, oleanders, magnolias. . . . None of us was accustomed to such luxury; in Yasnaya everything was poor and gray in comparison with Gaspra.

"I am living here in a most luxurious palazzo," Father wrote in his diary, "such as I have never been in before: there are fountains, sprinkled lawns in the park, marble staircases and so on; and in addition to this there is the startling beauty of the sea and the mountains. On all sides there are rich people and various grand dukes whose luxury is eighteen times greater." In a letter to Chertkov he said: "There are five of us living here: I and my wife, Masha and Kolya, Sasha. The beauty here is startling and I should be completely happy were it not for my conscience."

Gaspra bordered on Ai-Todor, the estate of Grand Duke Alexander Mikhailovich, where at this time his brother Nikolai Mikhailovich was visiting. Having heard that Tolstoy's heart was in bad condition, the Grand Duke offered him the use of his "horizontal path" on which there were no ups and downs and which led all the way to Livadia where the Tsar's palace was.

The Grand Duke Nikolai called on Tolstoy. When he came a second time Tolstoy greeted him with the words: "I am very glad to see you, I have been waiting for you, because my conscience has been bothering me. I want to ask you whether you were aware of what you were doing when you came here the first time. You see I am like scarlet fever, I am severed from the church, people fear me, yet you come to me; I repeat, I am scarlet fever, contagious, you may run into unpleasantnesses because of me; people will look at you askance that you should go calling on a politically suspect person." They chatted for a long time and parted well content with each other.

Naturally, the Grand Duke could not admit the antigovernmental and antichurch views of Tolstoy but he did not approve either of the people surrounding his cousin's son, Emperor Nicholas II. Father liked the unaffected, lively, probing mind of the Grand Duke.

The end of December Tolstoy again wrote a letter to the Tsar and asked the Grand Duke to place it in the Emperor's hands providing he chose to be the intermediary in such a matter.

In the letter he warned the Emperor that if he did not grant freedom to the Russian people there would be "fratricidal spilling of blood. . . . Autocracy is an outmoded form of government, capable of supplying the needs of some people in darkest Africa, cut off from all the world, but not the needs of the Russian people who are getting more and more enlightened along with the general enlightenment of the world: therefore it is only possible to support such a form of government and the orthodoxy linked to it, as is done now, by means of all sorts of violence, increased policing, executive deportations, executions, religious persecutions, the banning of books, newspapers, the distortion of education and in general all sorts of wicked and brutal things. . . . One can oppress a people by measures of violence but not govern them. . . ."

Grand Duke Nikolai Mikhailovich received the letter and transmitted it to the Tsar after begging him out of respect to Tolstoy not to give it to any of his Ministers to read. "After all," the Grand Duke wrote Father, "our Emperor is a very kind and responsive human being, and the whole trouble lies in those who surround him. . . ."

Chekhov was living in Yalta at the time of our stay in the Crimea and used to come over to see Tolstoy. They had last met in Moscow while Chekhov was hospitalized there under treatment for tuberculosis. As always their conversation inevitably turned to the subject of immortality. Because Tolstoy was fond of Chekhov in spite of a difference of views, he was distressed by the thought that Chekhov lived without God. He was troubled also by Gorki's lack of religious faith. For he respected the talent in these two men. Chekhov he put on a par with Maupassant; Gorki he considered a more significant writer, as he was opening up a whole world and life of people no one had hitherto paid any attention to—the world of barefoot men, proletarians, the downtrodden.

"I am glad that I find both Gorki and Chekhov agreeable," he wrote in his diary for November 29, "especially the former." And to Chertkov: "I am seeing Chekhov here, a complete atheist, but a good-hearted fellow, and also Gorki who has far more *fond*."

But he was soon disappointed in Gorki, principally because of his *Lower Depths* which, with the help of the Moscow Art Theater, won him great fame.

"Gorki is—a false impression," he commented in his diary. Insincerity, bombast, stilted style in literary expression—these were things Tolstoy could not endure, and it was this lack of sincerity which Tolstoy felt in Gorki. He used to say that the fame which raised him to such heights ruined him.

By contrast he came to appreciate Chekhov more and more, realizing that he, like Pushkin, had made an advance in form that was a great service. "Chekhov!" Tolstoy exclaimed once in conversation—"Chekhov—is Pushkin in prose. Just as in Pushkin's verses everyone can find something he has experienced himself, so it is in Chekhov's stories, in some one of them the reader is bound to find himself and his own thoughts. . . ." The understanding between the two writers was such that on one occasion, discussing literature in general, Tolstoy suddenly embraced Chekhov affectionately and said to him: "Old man, please don't write any more dramas." And Chekhov was not offended.

This true artistic sincerity was what Tolstoy prized in Kuprin, whom he also considered very gifted. The insincerity which was its opposite, Tolstoy felt in Leonid Andreyev whose fame was just beginning to grow. After reading his sensational *Bottomless Pit* Tolstoy was indignant. "It's all made up, bombast," he said, "as if he were trying to astonish and frighten everyone. But here I am not in the least afraid, yet I am somehow as embarrassed as I would be by a false note."

Little by little life in the Crimea settled into a routine. Father wrote, Mother was extremely active in photography, we took walks, rode horseback, in the evenings our cook Semyon Nikolayevich would arrive with his little account book, various things were discussed and meals were planned. Our seamstress Olga, to the despair of all, started a love affair with Semyon, who had children and a wife we adored at home. The footman, Ilya Vasilievich, who waited on table and had charge of Father's room, was homesick. Sometimes he and Semyon would drown their sorrows in drink and pour their complaints out on each other: "Where in the world have they taken us —on the one side is the sea, on the other the mountains—nowhere to go!" The servants were very sympathetic to Sophia Andreyevna who detested the Crimea, was bored there and longed to go home.

In the evenings there was a game of cards: Father, Klassen the German, Boulanger whenever he was there for a visit, and Kolya Obolenski. When they were short of partners, they included me to make a fourth. Klassen played in the classic manner; Boulanger's game was gay and shrewd; Father took risks and played poorly. He overbid and invariably had to pay penalties. Klassen was serious about the game and got angry with Father. "Dweadful, dweadful!" he would groan, with a German accent, rolling his sweet eyes toward the ceiling. "Another slam with four cards missing! Dweadful!" And they all laughed.

Mother was cross. "I loathe cards!" she used to say. "And they are spoiling the girl teaching her to play cards."

But the quiet was soon to be broken. Father fell ill again, and seriously.

Our brothers and sisters came to Gaspra. Sergei lived with us most of the time, the Obolenskis came over frequently from Yalta, Andrei and Olga with their little daughter, Sonechka, took up quarters in one of the wings.

The new year of 1902 did not usher in joy for us. Father's old stomach trouble began to plague him again and he had not had time to recover from that before he was taken with a sudden chill, pains in his side, a rising temperature and slight cough. The local doctors were called in, the famous Dr. Shchurovski arrived from Moscow, and the Emperor's physician, Dr. Bertenson, came from St. Petersburg. Together they diagnosed the illness as catarrhal pneumonia, judging the condition almost hopeless. Everything looked dark. All our thoughts were concentrated on the one question: Could Father's emaciated, aged body, weakened by illnesses and strain, stand this new, dreadful sickness?

Whatever else went on around us did not matter. It did not matter that the Governor of the province had received orders from St. Petersburg to the effect that if Tolstoy died he should not permit requiem rites or offices to be performed; nor that he in turn gave orders to the Moscow-Kursk Railway that in the event of Tolstoy's demise the train carrying his body to Yasnaya Polyana must not make stops in populous places.

The Holy Synod was uneasy. Metropolitan Antonius even wrote to my mother begging her to persuade her husband to make his peace with the church. When he heard of it Father said only: "From Thee I came, to Thee I go, and this is my last prayer: Thy will be done."

Mother wrote in her diary: "These spiritual sovereigns helped, indeed eased L. N. out of the church and now appeal to me to get him back in again. What lack of foresight!"

There were always two persons on duty at Father's bedside, a physician and one of us. I took Mother's place at four in the morning. The doctors were in constant consultation. We looked upon them as saviors, watched for them, pestered them with questions. And Mother was in a state: "What can we do for them? It is dreadful. No one will accept any money!"

The illness dragged on—the focal point of infection would clear up in one place only to break out in another. Father prepared himself for death and considered all the fuss about him unnecessary. I remember once during my watch, when Boulanger and I were in the room, Father turned to him saying: "What is finer than our folk expressions? Listen:

The little old man he began to choke,
The little old man he began to croak.
Time to get into his little old shroud,
His little old shroud and his little old grave.

"Isn't that wonderful?" he asked, smiling and swallowing his tears at the same time. "That's my case too: it's time for the little old man to get into his little old shroud! Among the peasant folk it's so simple, natural, no doctors, no fuss at all."

But I could not grasp why the little verse should move and delight him; the thought of a little old grave could draw only tears, not ecstasy, from a seventeen-year-old girl.

The night of the crisis I shall remember all my life. Moving about like dark shadows there were Tanya and her husband, Seryozha, somber Ilya, Lev, Misha, Andrei, Masha. Mother never left Father's side. The physicians were obviously avoiding us. They had scarcely any hope. Only Volkov, the regional doctor, probably because he saw the complete despair on my face, gave me some encouragement. No one slept. Two doctors kept close watch over Father's heart until, toward morning, they announced that the crisis was passed.

As Father began to recover they let me go more often into his room. Now I was allowed to help him in the morning, combing his soft hair, bathing him, rubbing his thin legs. He could not stand up, and was so weak that it was dreadful to see. But as the spring sun grew warmer they put him in a wheel chair and moved him over by the window so that he could look out at the sea, at the trees turning green.

On February 2 Father asked Masha to enter the following thought in his diary: "Fire destroys and warms. So does an illness. When you are well and try to lead a good life, freeing yourself from vices, temptations, you have to make an effort and even so it is as though you were only relieving one hard-pressed side and all the rest still weighs on you. An illness all at once releases the whole filthy scum and your spirit is lightened; still it is dreadful to think that, as I know by experience, once the illness is gone, the whole weight will bear down again."

But, though he had escaped his illness and was slowly mending, thoughts of death never left him. Several weeks later he wrote in his diary: "I am leaving this life according to the will of Him Who gave it to me. I submit to it in all serenity, knowing that it is the source of the highest bliss—life."

In the middle of February I was taken sick with a stomach ailment, accompanied by high temperatures and great weakness. Father was now lying in the large room with the terrace upstairs and I lay beside him. Mother was depressed. She longed to go back to Moscow, to hear the concerts. Although she cared for Father with self-sacrificing devotion and did everything in her power to restore him, their inner relationship was broken.

Little by little Father began to dictate. "I have work ahead of me," he wrote in his diary for March 2. "(1) On the true meaning of Christianity; (2) an address to the clergy; (3) to young people." He dictated a letter to Grand Duke Nikolai Mikhailovich on the project of Henry George. He did some thinking about an article on the ruthless suppression of a peasant movement in the provinces of Kharkov and Poltava; he wrote letters.

The relatives began to leave—Tanya and her husband, Andrei and his family. Sophia Andreyevna was happy to think that we should soon be leaving her detested Crimea. I was on my feet and able to help Father a little again. We had bright spring days, the almond trees blossomed, roses bloomed and the magnolias. But our happy mood did not last long. Father again fell ill with fever and pains in his abdomen which the doctors pronounced peritoneal typhus. Once more Tanya, Ilya and Boulanger arrived. Again hope alternated with despair. It seemed that surely his exhausted organism could withstand nothing more.

But toward the end of the second week the danger was over. Father's appetite revived, he felt a desire to get out into the air and sunshine. My sisters, Ilya, Boulanger left; there remained only Seryozha, who had amazed everyone by his attentions to Father and with whom I had become close friends during this time. Father gradually took up his life, began to write, read magazines, receive visitors. We took him on drives in the surrounding countryside. Occasionally Seryozha and our servant Ilya rolled him in his leather chair along the horizontal pathway to Ai-Todor, the Grand Duke's estate.

Once Boulanger and I drove him in a barouche down to Oleiz beside the sea, where some Turkish fishing smacks lay at anchor. After consulting with the fishermen, Boulanger said, "Lev Nikolayevich, would you like to go out on the water?" I protested: Father was scarcely able to walk and for him suddenly to put out to sea with some unknown Turks who could hardly speak a word of Russian struck me as outrageous. But Father was overjoyed—he loved unusual adventures. And indeed we all had a very gay time. When we went home, like children who have misbehaved, we dreaded to confess our escapade to Mother.

We left Gaspra for Yasnaya Polyana on June twenty-fifth. I had been taken ill again with fever and loss of weight, and was so weak that I could not walk. But Mother was determined not to remain longer in the Crimea. Seryozha carried me downstairs and throughout the journey he cared for Father and me with tender solicitude.

This time we made the trip to Sevastopol by boat. It was on this steamer trip that Father made the acquaintance of the writer Kuprin. In Sevastopol the private car of the director of the Moscow-Kursk railway was awaiting us.

As before, at the big stops groups of people appeared, bringing flowers and yelling greetings. In Kursk, where a congress of teachers was in session, some teachers gathered with the Zemstvo leader, Prince Peter D. Dolgoruki at their head. It was tiring for Father—and indeed for all of us, for we had been through an arduous time.

Back in Yasnaya Polyana, Father wrote to his brother, Sergei Niko-layevich: "We arrived the day before yesterday. I got here in good shape. My situation is this: I can walk two hundred paces on even ground and all bent over. My knees and arm joints ache, I sleep very little, but I can work. I understand and feel everything and can say, I am content. . . . Since my illness death has come very close to me, and I thank God for my illnesses in the course of which I came to understand many things."

In his diary for July 1, 1902, he made this entry: "My last illness was painful travail but now I am given a respite in which to gather my forces for the next one, so that it may bear fruit."

❧ 58 ❧

FATHER often said that in order to write well one must *learn* how to write. He was indignant when he heard something like this: "Have you written anything?" "No, I've never tried yet." He used to say: "How absurd it would sound if to the question: 'Do you play the violin?' you received the answer: 'No, I haven't tried.'"

Talent, he reasoned, is not enough; one must have a sense of truthfulness, polished language, style, a knowledge of the given background, a capacity for research. How can one put faith in a writer who describes Easter on a moonlit night? Or one who undertakes to write about the country and does not know that a peasant will not hew down an oak tree to make shafts or a shaft bow? He must *know* that for shafts and shaft bows the only wood used is elm.

When he returned from the Crimea Father started to work again on *Hadji Murat*. "I have been writing on *Hadji Murat*," he noted in his diary for August 5, 1902, "partly with pleasure, partly against the grain and with shame."

Despite his reluctance, he did the most detailed work on the data of the period: habits, customs, dress, religion of the Chechens; the personality of the local commandant Vorontsov and the circle about him. He gave special attention to Emperor Nicholas I.

Stasov sent data from the St. Petersburg library. Father requested Grand Duke Nikolai Mikhailovich to look up the correspondence between Nicholas I and Prince Vorontsov in Volume X of the Acts of the Caucasian Military Commission; he asked help from Alexandrine and received a detailed character sketch, a description of the Emperor's childhood and his relationship with his grandmother, Empress Catherine II. For the end of 1902 and during all of 1903, with intermissions, Tolstoy worked with youthful ardor on *Hadji Murat*.

Meantime he was correcting his story *The False Coupon*, the essay called "Address to the Clergy," memoirs of his childhood for Biryukov's biography, and the legend of "How Hell Was Destroyed and Resurrected." This legend, the essential meaning of which my mother did not grasp, put her into a state of indignation.

[424]

"This piece of writing," she wrote in her diary, "is saturated with a truly diabolic spirit of negation, with mockery of everything on earth, beginning with the church . . . and the children, Sasha, still unreasoning, and Masha, who is alien to me in feeling, added their fiendish laughter to their father's malicious laughter when he finished reading his diabolical legend, but I wanted to sob. That I should live to see *such* work! God grant his heart will be softened!"

In the autumn of 1902 my mother, who was preparing to reissue all of Father's writings, and for the publication of which she had to invest 50,000 rubles (about $25,000), demanded of Father that he return to her the testament which Masha had copied and he had signed. After a stormy scene, which caused his heart to race again, Father as always acceded to her wish.

Kolya Obolenski wrote to Biryukov: ". . . the existence of this will with its signature would give food for thought to such of his heirs as would wish to make use of his writings. . . . I say 'heirs,' but actually I am speaking only of Sophia Andreyevna, who is without shame or conscience; I have no right to include anyone else here since I do not know their opinions, except for Seryozha, Tanya, Sasha and Masha. . . . The other day Sophia Andreyevna went to Lev Nikolaye- vich and said she requested him to take this paper away from Masha and give it to her because she was harboring hard feelings against Masha and then they would pass. Lev Nikolayevich did not feel he could oppose her, so he took the paper and gave it to her. I attempted to talk to Sophia Andreyevna about this but, of course, I was unable to get anywhere. . . . One thing she stated quite clearly: 'I have now spent 50,000 rubles on the new edition, and if Papa dies and this paper is published, I shall not get any money back, and for that reason I took this paper and shall give it to no one.' When I tried to tell her that she nevertheless could not make it disappear from the face of the earth, since it was incorporated in the diaries, she replied brazenly that the diaries were in the museum, that she had the key to them, and that she would lock them up for fifty years along with her own."

Masha and Kolya were living at this time in the "Kuzminski House." "She will be the death of Father, Sasha," Masha used to say, pacing the floor in her excitement. "If I die, you must publish the whole truth. You must know that out of deference to Mother's wishes, Father deleted everything he had written about her in his diary; you must remember his will. . . ." Suddenly she stood still and her deep-set gray eyes, so like Father's, pierced mine—I was transfixed. "You are indeed very young . . . but still I shall tell you a secret . . . you should know it . . . Mother writes her diaries *post factum,* basing them on Father's, so that she can justify herself."

The doctors insisted that it was necessary for Father to live upstairs—because it was "sunnier, drier." They did not take in the family state of affairs and that was their error. They did not realize that the bedroom to which Father moved was separated from Mother's only by a small space. My mother immediately began to come in and out of the new quarters and he was deprived of the quiet he had enjoyed "in the vaults."

All the furnishings of his study were carried upstairs—the family couch of leather, armchairs with wooden backs made at home by a domestic cabinetmaker, the family portraits—to a room formerly used as the nursery where for some reason they neglected to remove from the walls two engravings of Raphael angels which were rather out of place. Glass French doors led out onto an open balcony facing southwest, with a view of the park, the distant fields, the railway. From the study one door led to the bedroom, where there was a narrow bed, a footstool, a wooden washstand with a basin and water pitcher, a slop pail which he, when he had the strength for it, carried outdoors himself. The other door led into the living room and big reception room.

One evening (September 11, 1902) we were sitting in the reception room, the samovar on the table had ceased to boil, and we were preparing gradually to go to bed. But from somewhere came the smell of burning. No one paid any attention to it—one might have smelled smoke from any place. But Sophia Anreyevna would not be reassured. A small door on the landing of the staircase, which was next to the hall, led to the attic. There, under the staircase, Mother was in the habit of developing photographs. When she opened this door a thick cloud of smoke enveloped her and filled the room.

As fast as I could go, I ran out to the barns, roused the steward and the workers. We had no fire hose at the manor, nor any water pipes. We drew water from the well and passed the buckets along a chain of people, all the way up to the attic. The fire was put out.

It turned out that some bricks in the chimney had been dislodged and had fallen out. If Mother had not discovered the fire in time the heavy oak beams would have burned through and the ceiling would have crashed down just above Father's bedroom.

In his diary for November 4, 1902, Father wrote: "The important things for this period are: the trial of Afanasi, the arrest of Novikov."

Afanasi Ageyev was arrested for scoffing at ikons and the Orthodox faith. His wife, a simple, illiterate peasant woman from Yasnaya Polyana, indifferent to her husband's ideas, comprehended just one thing: her husband was being deported, stripped of all property rights. Wiping her eyes with the corner of the black handkerchief in which her head was bound up, she begged Father to help them in their plight. But Father's intervention through various friends in St. Petersburg had no effect. Afanasi was deported for resettlement and his wife followed him.

Novikov was another peasant and Tolstoyan who suffered for his convictions. He possessed great native intelligence, had excellent use of his pen, read widely and thought a great deal. Because he was out- standing in his circle, he was invited to take part in a Special Council to Study Peasant Needs which was organized on the initiative of Count Witte, Minister of Finance. Novikov agreed and wrote out a sensible and bold memorandum of the needs of the peasantry, on the necessity of public education, etc. As a result, he was arrested for free thinking, but was subsequently released and deported to the province of Tula following an exchange of letters between Father and Count Witte.

In contrast to Novikov, whose spiritual power and sensitiveness made him akin to Father, Peter Verigin, the leader of the Dukhobors who had just returned from exile on his way to Canada to join his coreligionaries, was primitive in the spiritual sense. There was some- thing narrow, limited in this man despite his power of body and personality. Elderly Maria Schmidt wrote of him: "He is a very sweet, warmhearted fellow . . . but Lev Nikolayevich said of him: 'He is very good and can exercise a strong influence on people, but he is a man not yet born in the spirit.' "

On the 7th of December Father fell ill. Doctor Nikitin, our home physician, believed that he had a fresh attack of malaria. But my mother explained it differently: "I am tormented by the thought that God did not want to prolong his life because of the legend he wrote about the devils."

Again he was watched over day and night, there was a continual sense of fear, the whole house was intent on the degree of his fever, the state of his pulse. . . . "Today I have an unpleasant feeling of regret because of the amount of strength wasted on the care of Lev

[427]

Nikolayevich," wrote Sophia Andreyevna on December eighth. "This is the day of Nikisch's second concert in Moscow—it was my fondest hope that I could be at those two concerts—and, as always, I was deprived of this innocent pleasure, so I am sad and spiteful over my fate."

Fortunately, the illness did not last long. Father recovered and returned to his activities.

In the beginning of April, 1903, news of the Jewish pogroms in Kishinev spread with lightning rapidity, arousing the educated classes and the better representatives of the aristocracy to an uncommon state of indignation. Hundreds of letters and telegrams were sent to Tolstoy asking his help or the use of his name in protest. Many Jews wrote, begging him to express himself.

"My attitude toward the Jews cannot differ from my attitude toward my brothers, whom I love," he answered one, "not because they are Jews but because we and they, as all human beings, are the sons of the one God and Father, and this love does not require any effort on my part as I have met and I know many very good Jews."

Replying to the Jewish writer Sholem Aleichem (Rabinowitz) Tolstoy said that he would be glad to write something for the benefit of those who had suffered in Kishinev.

On June 18, 1903, he made this note: "I have thought of three new things: (1) The cry of the deluded people of our times: the materialists, positivists, Nietzscheans, the cry, 'Let *us* alone; what have we to do with thee, thou Jesus of Nazareth? Art thou come to destroy us? I know thee who thou art, the Holy One of God.' (This would be very good.) (2) For the Jewish anthology: a gay ball in Kazan, I am a man in love with Koreisha, a beautiful girl, daughter of a military commandant—a Pole, and I dance with her; her handsome old father takes her affectionately away, and they do a mazurka. In the morning after a sleepless night of being in love, there are sounds of drums and a Tatar made to run the gauntlet, and the military commandant orders them to flog him unmercifully. (This would be very good.) And (3) Describe myself with complete truthfulness, as I am at present, with all my weaknesses and stupidities, alternating with what is worth while and good in my life. (This would also be good.)"

This story "After the Ball" Father decided to turn over to Sholem Aleichem. But, before finishing it he wrote the fairy tales "Tsar Asarkhadon" and "Three Questions," which he sent in for the anthology to be published for the benefit of Jewish victims.

On August 28 Father turned seventy-five. He could not endure celebrations, and this day was no exception. Nearly all his children and grandchildren gathered. We wanted to be alone as a family, but many guests arrived for the "Tolstoy Jubilee," there was a formal banquet, at which speechmakers tossed around words like "the great writer," "the writer of the Land of Russia" (with allusions to Turgenyev's famous expression "great writer of the Russian land").

This expression "Land of Russia" was one we used at home in an ironic sense with regard to certain time-consuming people who thought of Tolstoy merely as a celebrity. P. A. Sergeyenko, for example. There are some people who are exceptionally clever in insinuating themselves into your home. They know how to bring some useful, unusual present, they flatter the lady of the house at just the right time. Sergeyenko was one of these. He was forever giving Father unusual gifts: a walking stick with a folding seat, a little lantern, a gramophone and so on. Tolstoy felt a kind of revulsion against the soft voice, the tall stooped figure, the long, almost tentacle-like fingers, and above all against the flattery. If I said to Father: "How repulsive Sergeyenko is!" he would counter with "More repulsive than you are?"—"Oh yes, yes, far more repulsive! I may be more wicked and stupid . . . but he is more repulsive!" Yet I knew that in the depths of his soul Father agreed with me.

Sergeyenko was among the guests on this occasion. But there were pleasant guests too: old Maria Alexandrovna Schmidt, and the radiantly happy Ivan Ivanovich Gorbunov, who brought Father his most precious birthday present: *Thoughts of Wise People,* an anthology collected by Father and published this day by The Mediator.

On September 3, 1903, Father wrote in his diary: "The 28th was difficult to get through. Congratulations are really a burden and unpleasant—they are hypocritical in saying writer of 'the Land of Russia' and all that nonsense. . . ."

How little people understood Tolstoy! Some called him a revolutionary, others a conservative, an aristocrat; they reproached him for his "luxury," which was in fact very relative. On whose side, in the last analysis, can we say he was? Not on that of the government, nor that of the revolutionaries. Only recently he had made his position clear on both issues.

On the weaknesses of the Tsar, he wrote earlier that year: "People address the Tsar advising him to do this or that for the general good, and I do so too. They expect help from him, action, but he can scarcely maintain himself. One might as well advise a man, scarcely clinging by his hands or his teeth to a branch over a precipice, to help lift a beam for a wall."

And on socialism: "In trusts and syndicates the socialists see the realization, or a movement in the direction of the realization of the socialist ideal, i.e., that people should work jointly and not separately. But they work jointly only under the pressure of force. What evidence is there that they will work the same when they will be free and what evidence is there that the trusts and syndicates will pass into the hands of the workingmen? It is much more likely that the trusts will produce slavery, and after freeing themselves from it these slaves will destroy the trusts not built up by them. . . . The partisans of socialism are people who envisage principally the urban population. They know neither the beauty nor the poetry of rural life, nor its sufferings."

Father condemned those to the right and those to the left, even his own followers, whose reproaches he often incurred.

"All our strivings, our efforts, the impulses of our hearts, all the cries from our lips, all our embraces—are in vain, all in vain . . . we are always lonely," wrote Guy de Maupassant in his story "Loneliness," which Father held in high esteem.

Yet Tolstoy possessed a tremendous power, invisible to others, which enabled him to love the hapless Tsar, as well as the erring revolutionaries, the Tolstoyans and the Sergeyenkos, and he was not "lonely."

"More and more frequently, in moments of displeasure, of doubt, I remember that I must please only God, to Whom I go, and not people. Then I feel much better and easier in my mind," he had written in the spring preceding his seventy-fifth birthday.

❧ 59 ❧

BEGINNING in 1884 when Tolstoy made a note in his diary about the necessity of getting together a "Circle of Reading" based on the thoughts of Epictetus, Marcus Aurelius, Lao-tse and other wise men, the idea never left him; he was constantly returning to it. Then during his illness in the Crimea, he began to realize his dream. The anthology *Thoughts of the Wise* was a start, but he was not satisfied. Gradually it was expanded into the Circle of Reading with weekly excerpts for Sundays. He never abandoned this work to the end of his life, and it afforded him deep spiritual satisfaction.

In literature, as in other fields, Tolstoy's views were often unorthodox, diametrically opposed to those generally held. He did not care for Goethe or Shakespeare, for example; on the other hand felt himself very close to Schiller.

"I read Goethe," he noted in his diary, "and I see the whole deleterious influence of this trivial, bourgeois and egotistical man of talent on the generation I have met—especially on poor Turgenyev with his raptures over *Faust* (an entirely bad piece of writing) and Shakespeare, and the especial importance he ascribed to certain statues, to the Laocoöns, the Apollos, and certain verses and dramas. How hard I tried, when I was fond of Turgenyev, to be fond of the things he held in high regard. I tried with all my strength but could not do it. What a terrible harm stems from the authorities, the so-called great, and especially the pseudo ones!"

Shakespeare's fame seemed to him artificial, affected. As he wrote Stasov, he had long wished to express about Shakespeare the things that had been in his mind for half a century. To his brother, Sergei Nikolayevich, he wrote that he wanted to prove that Shakespeare "not only was no writer, but was a terrible impostor and piece of filth."

Early in 1904, an essay on Shakespeare was among the manuscripts on Father's desk. In it he undertook to prove that Shakespeare's outlook on life "is the most degrading, trivial . . . it rejects not only all religious but also even humanitarian strivings." Furthermore that Shakespeare lacks technique which lends an external beauty to art, "there is no naturalness of situation," or of language, "no sense of measure," and "sincerity is completely lacking."

Besides this essay two other works were in progress. One was "The Divine and the Human," a story drawn from the life of a former revolutionary. Of this Tolstoy wrote in his diary for February 23: "I want to write a continuation of 'The Divine and the Human' . . . I like it very much." The other was a novel never finished, *The False Coupon*. In form it was an entirely new experiment: there were no central characters, but many people shown deteriorating under the

[431]

impact of external temptations and then by devious ways returning to God.

P. I. Biryukov returned from exile later this year and began to write a life of Tolstoy. He asked Father to describe his childhood himself, but Father, unfortunately, devoted little time to *Memories of Childhood*. He was too absorbed in his other work, especially the expanded anthology.

We were living quietly down in Yasnaya Polyana during this period, seeing few visitors. William Jennings Bryan came with his son, and was so agreeable to Father that he gave up his morning occupations, something that never happened. Bryan was to have an audience with the Tsar in Tsarskoye Selo, but he was so carried away by his conversation with Father that he sent a wire to say he could not make it. They talked of many things, including passive resistance to evil. Bryan mentioned the usual example which was always used against Tolstoy: What if a monster in front of your eyes were to torture a child? "I have lived in this world for seventy-five years," said Tolstoy, "and I have never yet seen such a monster. Yet I see how millions of people, women, children, are being destroyed as the result of the wickedness of governments." Bryan smiled—he understood.

Julie Igumnov and Doctor Berkenheim, who took the place of Doctor Nikitin, lived with us now. Father had entirely recovered, he took walks in the morning, worked a great deal, rode horseback. My mother often went up to Moscow, where she heard music and was occupied with the publication of the books. She was now much concerned with the preservation of Father's manuscripts for future generations and began to write the history of her life. It was her intention to turn over her diaries and Father's to the Moscow Historical Museum on condition that they would not be accessible to anyone for fifty years.

No one gave thought to a war with Japan and when it came Father was more shocked by it than anyone else. For several days he could think and speak of nothing else until he had unburdened his feelings by writing a new article against war—"Bethink Yourselves." This article, printed abroad, caused a stir. The London *Times*, in giving it nine and a half columns, commented: "This is at one and the same time a confession of faith, a political manifesto, a picture of the sufferings of a peasant soldier, a pattern of the thoughts going through the heads of many of these soldiers and, finally, a curious and instructive psychological study. In it one is vividly aware of the great chasm which divides the entire spiritual make-up of the European from the intellectual frame of mind of the great and influential Slavic writer who has not fully enough grasped several of the random expressions of European thought. . . ."

The *Daily News*, by contrast, was enthusiastic in its endorsement: "When Carlyle was talking about poverty-stricken, voiceless Russia as a country which had never produced a world voice, he was still unaware of the fact that at that very time amid the young officer class there was indeed a voice crying to which everyone listened. Yesterday Tolstoy published one of those great epistles to humanity, which bring us back to the first fundamental principles, and which are striking in their amazing simplicity."

To a telegraphic question sent him by the *North American* newspaper as to whose side he was on—that of Russia or that of Japan—Tolstoy replied: "I am not on the side of either Russia or Japan, but on that of the laboring people of both countries, deceived by their governments and forced to fight against the interest of their own welfare, their conscience, and their religion."

Despite this reply, and although he longed to be impartial, Tolstoy's emotions were morbidly involved with each account of a Russian defeat. He could scarcely wait for the Moscow papers, received by mail a day late, and sometimes he rode over to Tula to obtain fresh news of the course of the war.

On June 2 Father wrote: "The war and the recruiting of soldiers upsets me." And on June 6: "The poor deserted soldiers' wives keep coming. I read the newspapers, and it would seem that all these battles, the consecration of flags, are such solid facts that it is useless to protest, and sometimes I think I wrote my article for nothing, that all it did was stir up enmity; but then I look at the people, the soldiers' wives and I regret I wrote so little and so feebly."

To Tanya Father wrote: "The war weighs on everyone. The recruiting of the reserves makes a dreadful impression." And to Grand Duke Nikolai Mikhailovich and Dr. K. V. Volkov he said much the same thing.

My mother's diary, however, throws an entirely different light on things: "In the quiet of our village this war is exciting and interesting to everyone. The general exaltation of spirit and sympathy with the Tsar—is remarkable. This is to be explained by the fact that the attack of the Japanese was audacious and unexpected, and neither on the part of Russia nor of the Emperor nor of anyone was there desire for war, the war was *forced.*"

In our family it was my brother Andrei who went to war. Poor Olga had not succeeded in getting him to settle down. He was attracted to another married woman, left his wife and two small children, Sonechka and Ilya, and having completely involved himself he went to the Far East and joined the combat troops. My mother, Ilya and his wife Sonya, Lyova and Misha accompanied Andrei to Tambov, from which point his cavalry regiment was to leave.

Both my parents suffered because of his weaknesses, but they were fond of Andrei. Mother described her son with pride in her diary for August 8, 1904: "The orderlies rode out on horseback, and my Andrei in the lead in a light sand-colored shirt, a cap of the same, and on his charming mare. It all made an imprint on my memory: the mare's legs bound round with some white material, Andryusha's wonderful seat on horseback, and the words of an old woman: 'Your son sits on a horse like a—picture, it's as though he were at home in his own study.'"

In this year Tolstoy lost two persons who had been close to him from childhood: Granny and his brother Sergei. Alexandra Andreyevna Tolstoy, my godmother, died in March. The year before, already seriously ill, she and her beloved Lev, who had grown so far apart, exchanged cordial letters. She thanked Father for his affection, she was happy to feel in his letter "the very, very sincere note that had always been struck" between them.

"Dear friend Alexandrine," Father wrote on January 26, 1903, "the older I grow the greater and greater the tenderness I would like to show you . . . to tell you that I love you very, very much. Yes, it is probable that we shall not see each other again in this world; that is God's will, so I suppose it is right. Nor do I think we shall see each other over there in the sense that we mean meeting again, yet I think and indeed I am positive that all the kind, affectionate and good things which you gave me in this life will remain with me, perhaps even a few crumbs from me will remain with you. In general, as I draw nearer to the inevitable and good end . . . the stronger and firmer is my faith that life does not end here, but that a new and better one begins over there. So that all converges in faith in God's magnanimity—all that is of Him and from Him, all that is blessed. Just as I came from Him in being born, so I go to Him in dying and there can be nothing but good in this. 'Into Thy hands I commit my

[434]

spirit!' Farewell, dear, dear friend, in brotherly affection I kiss you tenderly and thank you for your love."

And on February 9, 1903: "Thank you, dear friend, for your reply to my letter. In your heart, your responsive heart, you sense the sincerity and tenderness of my feelings for you and so you responded to them. . . . That is a joyous thing. This letter will be transmitted to you by my Sasha. She is a very good person, or rather she has the serious desire to be good. In coming to see you she is embarrassed, as I too am slightly, by her non-orthodoxy. Do not judge either her or me severely because of this. I have deliberately refrained from influencing her yet instinctively she has subjected herself to me externally. Yet, as you know, at her age religion is not yet a necessity. Much lies in store for her. And when the real urge for religion will come she will choose what she needs.—In any case I am ashamed of writing this to you as if I did not know your sensitive heart. . . ."

When he reread in the last year of his life his correspondence with Granny, Father said: "As when in a dark corridor a light shines from under some door or other, so, in looking back over my long, dark life my memories of Alexandrine are always like a band of light."

Toward the end of August, 1904, Uncle Sergei Tolstoy died of cancer of the tongue, which caused him severe pain. Father visited him often during his illness and was present at his death. Just before, he confessed and took communion. Father was glad of this.

On August 26 Father wrote in his diary: "Seryozha has died. He went quietly without being conscious, clearly conscious, that he was dying. This is a mystery. No one can say whether it is worse or better that way. He did not achieve a workable religious sense; perhaps I still deceive myself, but it seems not. But he was content. Something new and better opened for him. So it was with me. What is valuable, important is the degree of enlightenment, yet on what point of the infinite circle it rests—that is immaterial."

That summer I was twenty. Like a sponge I was absorbing Father's ideas, but they did not penetrate deep into my consciousness as they did with my sister Masha. In me there was none of that self-sacrificial instinct, the asceticism which had existed in her before her marriage. Nor did I have the single-mindedness of my sister Tanya—I had no dreams of family, although the stuff of romantic novels and thoughts on moonlit nights of some extraordinary hero did revolve in my head.

Father was distressed by my lack of good looks, but he rejoiced in my skill in sports and my limitless gaiety and love of life. I thought I was following his ideas by being a vegetarian, dressing simply, spending money on a dispensary for peasants—but that was the very philanthropy which he considered pseudo-goodness. In the winter I taught a class of children in Tanya's old studio and helped Dr. Nikitin receive his patients. But Father soon put an end to these activities. "I beg of you not to go to the dispensary any more," he said. I protested, I wanted to know why. "I am asking this of you," was all he would say. So I never learned the reason for the restriction. Did he fear that I might catch some horrid disease or that I would flirt with the doctor? . . .

The end of 1904 saw the arrival of Dr. Dushan P. Makovitski, a friend and follower of Father's, who was to stay on at Yasnaya Polyana for many years. With him I again began to visit the dispensary, but his methods of treatment were so strange that my interest in medicine quickly evaporated. He so mangled the Russian language that, standing in the pharmacy where I was weighing up powders or preparing some ointment, I laughed till I cried.

Dushan was all but a saint. From morning till night he visited the sick, helped Father and . . . wrote. In his pocket he kept a quantity of tiny pencils and stiff little sheets of paper. While Father talked, Dushan would stick his right hand in his pocket and jot down his words. His protuberant gray eyes were fixed on a single point, his whole head would be transfixed in concentrated immobility. This writing habit and the saintliness of Dushan rather irked me; I used to tease him mercilessly and interfered with his taking notes. Now I am ashamed to remember it.

In those years I did not even comprehend how far I was from Father's teachings. Actually I should have distributed my property, but I was loath to do that. The horses, which I knew and loved so well, the saddles, the well-tailored English riding habits, the tennis rackets, the skates, the skis—all that cost money and I was not at all prepared to give them up.

Father wrote in his diary for June 18, 1904: "I have thought this about myself: (1) that I am perhaps fooling myself in praising poverty. . . . I see this in looking at Sasha. I am sorry for people of her kind, I am fearful of what they would do without their coaches, their cleanliness, their riding habits. To explain and justify is one thing: I do not love poverty, I cannot love it, especially for others, but I love less, I hate, and I cannot but hate what wealth brings: the ownership of land, banks, interests. The devil has gotten at me so cleverly that I do see clearly before me all the privations of poverty, but I do not see the injustices which rid one from it. All this is hidden, and all this is approved of by the majority."

In the winter Father often rode to the rink where I, with an army of peasant children—some of them my own pupils—was skating, and I knew that he admired me and rejoiced that I was gay. His entry in his diary for January 21, 1905, is characteristic: "I was listening to political discussions, arguments, diatribes, and I went off to another room where they were singing to a guitar and laughing, and I was clearly aware of the sacredness of gaiety—gaiety, joy—that is all one of the fulfillments of God's will."

I often distressed him by my lack of self-control with regard to my mother, my stupidity, and my lack of affection for the "dark people." But what distressed him most of all was when I, out of personal caprice and desiring to possess my own bit of land, bought the neighboring estate of Telyatinki—consisting of about two hundred acres. I thought that by giving the peasants a larger part of the land through the Peasant Bank, and having lost a rather heavy sum of money in the transaction, I was doing a good act. But again this was "philanthropy."

In his diary for April 21, 1905, Father wrote: "Yesterday I went to Pyotr Osipov's and he reproached me severely because I go on talking yet buy up land. It was both painful and good for me. I felt how healthy, how strengthening condemnation is, especially when one does not deserve it, and how undermining, debilitating, are praises, especially those that are undeserved (and they're all undeserved)."

Pyotr Osipov had in mind the land I had bought. Among the peasantry it was inconceivable that a daughter could do anything without the knowledge of the head of the family—the father.

"The worse off a man is physically, the better he is spiritually. Therefore a man cannot be badly off. I have searched long for a comparison to express this. The comparison is of the simplest: a pair of scales. The greater the weight on the physical side, the worse off one is physically; and in the sense of worldly fame (which is also physical) the higher the scales rise on the spiritual side, the better off one's soul is."

⚘ 60 ⚘

O N DECEMBER 20, 1904, the newspapers announced that General Stoessel had surrendered Port Arthur, together with its garrison of fifteen thousand men and all their arms, to the Japanese.

In our family this news affected Father most of all. The Russian patriot, the former military man, expressed themselves through him. He confessed this in his diary: "The surrender of Port Arthur distressed me, I felt hurt. This is patriotism. I grew up with it, and I am not free from it, just as I am not free from personal egoism, family egoism, even the aristocratic kind. . . . All these egoisms reside in me, yet in me there is a consciousness of the divine law, and that consciousness holds these egoisms in check, so that I can keep from being subservient to them, and gradually these egoisms atrophy."

The news from the Far East became ever more menacing. The Japanese sank the Russian navy. The third son of Auntie Tanya Kuzminski, Vasya, a naval officer, was among the missing. Later we learned that he was in the water for twenty-four hours, then picked up by the Japanese and made a prisoner.

"Yesterday came the news of the destruction of the Russian fleet," Father wrote in his diary for May 19, 1905. "This news, for some reason, affected me most powerfully. It became clear to me that it could not and cannot be otherwise: although we are bad Christians it still is impossible to reconcile the profession of Christianity with war. . . . In a war with a non-Christian people, for whom the highest ideal is the fatherland and military heroism, Christian peoples must be defeated. If, up to the present time, Christian peoples have defeated uncivilized peoples, that was due solely to preponderance of technical military improvements on the part of the Christian peoples (China, India, peoples of Afghanistan, Khiva and Central Asia); but, given technical equality, the Christian peoples are inevitably doomed to defeat at the hands of the non-Christians, as it happened in the war between Russia and Japan. In several decades Japan has not only equaled the European and American peoples in technical improvements, but outstripped them. This success of the Japanese in the technique not just of war but also in all material improvements has clearly demonstrated how cheap these technical improvements are, and what is called civilization. To imitate and even to make further inventions is easy enough. What is precious, important and difficult is the good life, purity, brotherliness, love, the very things taught by Christianity and which we neglect. This is a lesson to us.

"I do not say this in order to console myself in the defeat inflicted on us by the Japanese. The shame and disgrace will remain as great. But they do not lie in the fact that we have been defeated by the Japanese, but in that we undertook to do something which we do not know how to do well and which in itself is wicked."

Father could not calm himself. Before him already there yawned the abyss toward which not only Russia was heading, but also all humanity, lured by material advantages.

"This is the destruction not of the Russian army and navy, not of the Russian state," he wrote in his diary for June 18, "but it is the destruction of all pseudo-Christian civilization. I feel, I sense, I understand this with the greatest clarity. How good it would be to know how to express this with clarity and power.—This destruction began a long time ago: in the struggle for money, the struggle for success in the so-called scientific and artistic fields of activity, in which the Jews and not the Christians have outstripped all Christians in all countries, and provoked universal jealousy and hatred. Now the same in military matters has been achieved by the crude force of the Japanese."

The revolutionaries had not been napping. The soil was extraordinarily favorable for them: the defeat of Russian arms, the discontent of the workers, the pressure of the government, the lack of land among the peasants. In January the rumor was current that during the annual Procession of the Cross, celebrating Christ's baptism in the Jordan, in front of the Winter Palace, there had been an attempt made against the life of the Emperor, and that a policeman had been killed by the explosive.

On January 9, 1905, under the leadership of a priest, Father Gapon, a crowd of workers numbering fifteen thousand marched on the Winter Palace in St. Petersburg with a petition. They were not allowed to approach it but were dispersed by the police, soldiers and the elite guards. A number of persons were killed and wounded.

This same month my brother Lev had an audience with the Emperor and talked with him for an hour and a half. At that time I was in St. Petersburg visiting Lev and his Swedish wife and children, to whom I was devoted. Lev told me about his interview with the Emperor and I wrote Father about it:

"The Tsar told Lev that he was glad he had received a deputation of workers, over whom he had wept, that the *Zemski Sobor* [National Assembly] should be summoned but not now while the war lasted. . . . Lev spoke to him about vegetarianism, wine, tobacco, and promised to send him his writings on a hygienic way of life."

"They keep teaching, teaching, [people like] Lyova, Stakhovich," Father said to Makovitski; "but they themselves don't know how to do anything for themselves, they don't know how to light a samovar."

When Mother came down from Moscow February 1, she said the Tsar was reported to have remarked to Lev: "Your father is a great man, but at the same time a dreamer, for instance with regard to the land."

In February Grand Duke Sergei Alexandrovich was killed by a bomb in Moscow. I was in Moscow then and brought the news home to Father. He was indignant, groaned out loud, and was harsh in his condemnation of the revolutionary terrorists.

"The revolution cannot in any way repeat what happened one hundred years ago," he wrote. "The revolutions of 1830, 1848 failed because they had no ideals, they were inspired by remnants of the great revolution. Now the people who are making the Russian revolution have none at all: economic ideals—are not ideals."

Father did not believe that any changes would be brought about by the introduction of a constitution. The moderate liberals—Stakhovich, Vasili Maklakov, the Princes Dolgorukovas—who came to see Tolstoy depressed him because they could not comprehend his indifference to their efforts to introduce a constitution in Russia.

"There is only one way for humanity to progress," he kept saying, "and that is in the spiritual field, in the self-perfection of each individual human being. And a human being can perfect only himself, and not others, by means of state reforms. . . . The number of factors which influence the progress of humanity is tremendous, and these factors are very complex, so that one can foretell nothing; it is ridiculous to ascribe to any given internal reform an important influence on the progress of humanity."

Most distressing of all to Father were his arguments with Sergei. They did not understand each other. Sergei was a "liberal," a constitutional democrat. He was indifferent to religious questions and held that the most important thing was to acquire a constitution and freedoms in Russia.

"A constitutional subject who imagines he is free," wrote Tolstoy, "is like a man in prison who imagines that he is free because he can elect his jailer. The people of constitutional countries have lost the concept of freedom. A person who lives in a despotic country—such as Turkey, Russia—may be more or less free although he is subject to the power he has not established, but the member of a constitutional state, by always recognizing the legality of power under which he lives, is always a slave."

From his youth Tolstoy nourished a distaste for the intellectual liberals, considering them ignorant of the core of Russia, the peasantry, and of the religious foundation on which peasant life was based. His attitude toward the liberals is vividly expressed in his diary for December 24, 1905:

"Now, in these times of revolution, three sorts of people have clearly emerged with all their good qualities and shortcomings. (1) The conservatives, the people who desire quiet and the continuance of a life agreeable to them, and who do not wish any changes. The shortcomings of these is—egoism; their good qualities—their modesty, humility. The second ones are the revolutionaries—they want changes and they are impertinent enough to undertake to decide what change is needed, and they do not shrink from violence in carrying these changes into effect, or from their own deprivations and sufferings. The shortcomings of these people—their impertinence and brutality; their good qualities—energy and the readiness to suffer in the accomplishment of their aim, which in their eyes is represented as a blessing. The third group is the liberals—they lack the humility of the conservatives, and the readiness for sacrifice of the revolutionaries, yet they possess the egoism, the desire for peace of the first and the self-assurance of the second."

Father considered the peasants immeasurably superior to and wiser than the intellectuals who were undertaking to instruct them and organize their life, as he noted earlier in the year: "The intelligentsia have brought a hundred times more evil than good into the life of the peasantry."

It was with uneasiness then that he watched the growing revolutionary mood among the peasants. More and more often he was coming into contact with people who spurned God, with materialists like the revolutionaries, and conversations with such people always upset him.

"A Jew has just been here," he wrote in his diary for September 9, "a correspondent of *Rus*. At the end of our conversation and as a consequence of my disagreement with him, he said: 'Therefore you consider the killing of Pleve a bad thing!' I said to him: 'I regret that I have talked with you,' and I went away irritated, that is to say, I acted badly."

Things grew more and more alarming. . . . Strikes, student disorders. Father was receiving an increasing number of accusing letters containing demands that he distribute the land, which he did not own, to the peasants.

September 23, 1905: "I have finished *End of a Century*. Just now—it is morning—a letter came from an educated son of a peasant, with a vicious reproach, in the guise of praise for 'The Great Sin,' because I do not give up my land. This has reached a point of being very painful. Yet it proved all to the good. I realized then that I had forgotten that I live not for the sake of the good opinion of this writer, but in God's sight. I felt relieved, and indeed very much. Yes, one should never forget all the import of life."

Such thinking prompted Father to write Grand Duke Nikolai Mikhailovich the following letter, dated September 14, 1905:

". . . there is a certain unnaturalness in our relations, perhaps it would be better to put an end to them. You—are a Grand Duke, a rich man, a close relative of the Emperor, I—am a man who rejects and condemns the whole existing order and authorities, and frankly state this. For me there is an awkwardness in my relations with you because of this contradiction which we, as it would seem, deliberately avoid. I hasten to add that you have always been exceptionally kind to me and I can only be grateful to you. Yet there remains this unnatural something, and in my old age it is always particularly hard for me not to be simple. And so let me thank you for all your kindness to me and in farewell clasp your hand in friendship."

The Grand Duke answered on October 1, from St. Petersburg:

". . . I submit completely to your decision, although I do it with a sense of profound pain, because I love you with all my heart and I shall ask your permission, if only at intervals, to turn to you for spiritual succor in our times of desolation. You are completely right, there is something unspoken between us, yet I dare assure you that despite my family ties I am far closer to you than to them. It is

only because of a sense of delicacy of feeling on account of my kins-
man that I am obliged to be silent on the subject of the 'existing order
and authorities,' and this silence is all the harder to bear because all
the sores of the regime are obvious to me and they can only be healed
as I see it by a thoroughgoing breaking up of all that now exists. . . ."*

Exactly a month later Father made this note:

"The revolution is in full swing. There are killings on both sides.
A new, unexpected element, absent in former European revolutions,
has emerged—'the Black Hundreds,' 'the Patriots': in essence these
are people who brazenly, wrongly, represent the masses while going
against their demand not to use force. The contradiction lies, as
always, in the fact that these people wish by force to restrain force.
In general, the levity of the people making this revolution is astounding and revolting: it is childishness without the innocence of children."

The manifesto promulgated by the Tsar on October 17, in which
the people were granted a constitution, freedom of speech, press and
meetings, evoked at first stormy demonstrations of solidarity and
enthusiasm in the big cities, but the turmoil did not die down. In
Moscow there were armed clashes between the police and the revolutionaries, barricades were erected in the streets, people killed each
other.

There was no mail, no delivery of newspapers. There were strikes
on the railroads. Trains were stalled at the station of Kozlovka, distracted, hungry passengers roamed through the neighboring villages
searching for food.

We were fed on rumors, always exaggerated as they passed from
mouth to mouth. Among workingmen whom one had occasion to
meet, and even among some peasants, there was a notable change—
the respectful homage to older people had vanished, there was a new
tone of jaunty self-assurance in the air.

"The revolutionaries will hang us on the first birch tree," I
thought. My brother Misha, who was expecting his third child in
December, could not manage to get to Moscow where his family was.
Finally he succeeded in hiring some horses. Having gone half the
distance he called up a friend to inquire about his wife's health.

* Two years later Father wrote to the Grand Duke: "February 28, 1908 . . . I
am now ashamed to recall my letter written in 1905. . . . Now I would not write it.
You cannot imagine how life changes as one approaches old age, i.e., death. . . .
Now what I prize most is affectionate intercourse with all people, regardless of
what they are, Tsars or beggars. . . ."

"Everything is fine, twins!" replied his friend. To the accompaniment of gunshot, at the very height of the revolution, twins had been born: a boy and a girl.

April 27, 1906, saw the opening of the First Imperial Duma, with S. A. Muromtsev the presiding officer. Among our close friends, S. Sukhotin and A. Stakhovich were elected members of the Duma.

Yet a feeling of unrest persisted. Repressions were still being practiced by the government, in the cities strikes were in progress, the dissolution of the Duma was expected (it was dissolved on July 9, 1906). Among the peasantry tongues wagged, tales were told of outrages committed during the war, generals were covered with abuse. But the peasants wanted just one thing—more land; some placed their hopes in the Tsar, others on the Duma.

Father sent Chertkov his pamphlet on *The Government, the Revolutionaries and the People,* for publication in England, but Chertkov held it up while he begged Father to soften his condemnation of the revolutionaries. The article was published a little later on and with very minor changes by *Obnovlenie,* the undercover press of Felten, a Tolstoyan.

Just at this time Father was under the influence of a pamphlet written by the Slavophile Khomyakov, which he considered "magnificent." Russia must follow her own path. The path of the Western peoples would spell ruin for the Slavic peoples. On July 3, 1906, he wrote in his diary:

"If the Russian people are uncivilized barbarians, at least we have a future. Whereas the Western peoples are—civilized barbarians and they have nothing to look forward to. For us to imitate the Western nations would be the same as for a healthy, hard-working, unspoiled young man to envy a gilded and balding Parisian youth, sitting in his house. Ah, *que je m'embête!* One should not envy or imitate, but pity."

A month before the opening of the Duma, Tolstoy had expressed in his diary a thought which amplifies his views on the futility of external forms of freedom where there is no inner spiritual maturity, and at the same time sounds a prophetic note.

"How vividly the revolutionaries, when they began to lay their hands on the power, typified all the customary corruptive effects of power: conceit, pride, ambition and, above all, a disrespect for man. They are worse than their predecessors, because they are fresh at it."

❧ 61 ❧

WHILE larger events in Russia took their course, life in the family went on with its ups and downs. Father wrote as usual, engaging the help of all who happened to be in the house.

There were days when he worked on nothing but the *Circle of Reading*. This involved making a systematic arrangement of religious and philosophical teachings in units of days, weeks and months, a tremendous labor necessitating checking, sorting, reshuffling and translating. The Remington was placed on the table in the reception room and all the material laid out in folders. Masha, Julie, a Tolstoyan by the name of Chrisanph Abrikosov, who made frequent and long visits to Yasnaya Polyana, all lent their services.

In addition, Father had the idea of writing a Catechism for Children, which would provide them with religious and moral principles. Maria Alexandrovna Schmidt had started him thinking about it when she told of the time she asked a young herdsman's boy: "Where is God?"—"Up in heaven," replied the boy. "No, He is in our souls," she corrected him. "He must have a tough time of it in there," retorted the boy.

Father laughed hard over the story, then put it to use. When Tanya and her husband went abroad, her stepdaughter Natasha and stepson Dorik made long visits in Yasnaya Polyana. Dorik at nine years old was just the age for the instruction Father had in mind and the two worked together every day. They read the Gospels, Father explaining their contents, and they talked about religion and morals. Later Dorik was joined by several children from the village. So the plan for a course of religious instruction for children took hold of him, until gradually he evolved the new *Children's Circle of Reading*.

It was due to the *Circle of Reading* for adults that Father wrote several literary pieces toward the end of 1905 and early in 1906. Two of them were vivid in their power—"Korney Vasiliev" and "Alyosha Gorshok"—and were drawn from peasant life. "What

For?" was laid in the historical period of the Polish uprising. Then there was a short story called "Berries."

In addition to these, Father unexpectedly became excited about the history of Elder Fyodor Kuzmich who, according to legend and in the opinion of several historians—among them Grand Duke Nikolai Mikhailovich—was Emperor Alexander I in his later years after he abandoned his throne. Father found the theme "enthralling," as he noted in his diary, but after working on it for a couple of years, he abandoned it for lack of leisure to continue.

"It may well be that historically speaking it is impossible to identify the personality of Alexander with that of Kuzmich; nevertheless, the legend remains, with all its beauty and truthfulness. I began to write on this theme, yet not only is it unlikely I shall finish it, but I may even not find the leisure to continue it. I have no time, I must get packed up for my impending departure. I very much regret it. It's a charming figure."

It was my favorite occupation to copy Father's manuscripts, especially the literary pieces. I could stay up all night long when his work was urgent. Sometimes he insisted that I have some rest. Then I would get into bed with my clothes on and pretend to be asleep when he came by to check on me. But as soon as he had returned to his study I would go back to my Remington. In the morning after such an all-night session, when I brought Father the freshly typed sheets, double-spaced and with wide margins for multiple corrections, he would smile affectionately and thank me—and I was filled with delight.

I suffered from a keen sense of jealousy toward all who sought to replace me. I was jealous of Abrikosov, of Kolya Obolenski, Julie, everyone, with the exception of Masha. By now I had learned how to unriddle his handwriting and could even read things that he could not decipher. Like Lieutenant Ivanov, I conceitedly thought that no one could meet Father's needs better than I. I was especially jealous of Julie, who was much older than I and in her manner patronized while she poked fun at me. I was irritated by her low voice, her bobbed smooth hair, her insipid jokes and her endless conversation about politics with Kolya Obolenski, carried on as she lay stretched out on a couch in the reception room. I was jealous even of Father's dog Belka, a wonderful white Eskimo dog, who ceased to accompany Father on his walk after Julie trained him to go walking with her.

Yet Julie was a sweet and useful person in our home, always ready

[446]

to lend a hand where one was needed, and both Tanya and Masha prized her. She had the habit of doubling words, beginning the second one with "M," which was why we nicknamed her Jooly-Mooly. Occasionally when she conquered her inertia and remembered that she was an artist, she made very acceptable drawings of Father on horseback.

Tanya, again pregnant after several miscarriages, spent the autumn of 1905 with us. She was under the care of a Swiss physician who, as we laughingly said, had put her on a "macaroni diet," consisting exclusively of farinaceous foods and milk dishes. To everyone's delighted relief, she passed the fateful seventh month, when her child usually died, and carried the baby to full term. On November 22, in a quick and easy delivery, a little girl was born. "A great event!" Father wrote in his diary. "Tanya has been delivered of a child."

But what a tiny, wrinkled, dark blue and red creature it was! Her grandfather insisted that she be named Tatiana, so she naturally came to be called Tatiana Tatianovna—after her mother, instead of using her real patronymic, Mikhailovna.

That winter Tanya and the baby stayed in Yasnaya Polyana, but Sukhotin, whose heart could not stand the cold, went abroad with the Obolenskis. I joined them in the hope of enlarging my mental horizons and extending my education, but my stay abroad did not give me what I expected. It was not enough that I conscientiously ran around all the museums of Paris and Italy, Baedeker in hand, saw all the sights; I was alone. Masha did not feel well, Kolya was too lazy to go out with me, and Sukhotin had already seen everything ten times over. I was glad to get back to Father, to my work, the horses, the dogs.

In addition to the birth of Tatiana Tatianovna, there were other family happenings.

Quite unexpectedly, my brother Sergei, whose wife Manya had died several years earlier, was married a second time to Countess Maria Zubova, the niece of Count Olsufiev. A not good-looking but very sweet girl, she was a little younger than Tanya. We had known her for a long time and considered her well suited to Sergei in age and in interests. As we all hoped, the marriage proved to be a happy one.

In the summer of 1906 Kenjiro Tokutomi, a famous Japanese writer, editor of the magazine *Independence*, came to visit Father. He was a liberal, enthusiastic about Father's views. With his wife, he had settled in the country near Tokyo, where he worked his vegetable garden with his own hands.*

I had reason to discover that Tokutomi did not belong to those Tolstoyans who were unable to handle a pitchfork and could not tell rye from wheat. One day father called several of us from a tennis game to help Masha, the pregnant wife of our cook, get in the hay for her cow. In the group was Tokutomi, unusually picturesque in his white, wide-brimmed hat and white kimono. Working, we could scarcely keep up with him, his movements were so quick, skillful and trained. Before we could look around, all the hay was gathered in.

This same summer the government allowed Chertkov a brief stay in Russia to visit his aged mother. He was extraordinarily gay and amiable, and his stay was the source of great joy to Father.

I think I have never seen anyone's face vary as Chertkov's did. At times he was well-bred, sociable, gay, endearing, with an exceptionally attractive smile and a contagious laugh. In such moments my mother, who seldom showed amusement, rocked with noiseless laughter as she listened to his anecdotes and jokes. But if anyone disagreed with him, deep furrows would appear on his forehead, his aristocratic, curved nose would wrinkle unpleasantly, his large gray eyes would flash and his whole face assume a baleful expression. He could not tolerate opposition. His social manner and humor, his stubbornness and despotic ways, the boldness and the narrowness of his views, the impatience of a sectarian—all combined to make him strange and difficult.

"Chertkov has come now," Father wrote in his diary for August 24, 1906. "We rode together to see Masha. Chertkov was very pleasant but I fear it was mostly because he prizes me highly. . . . I was going to say that Masha is very dear to me, but everyone reads my diaries. . . ."

During this summer the strain between Father and Mother grew deeper. The reason was that Mother had had several peasants haled into court for cutting down trees, and they were supposed to be sent to jail. We all implored her to pardon them. Father was in a dreadful state, and once more the question arose as to whether he should

* In 1930 when I was living in Japan before coming to America I made the acquaintance of Tokutomi-San, his widow, and visited their country home where she continued to live near his grave, in very simple surroundings.

leave home. He felt that morally he did not have the right to live in Yasnaya Polyana where such things were done in his name.

"I am much oppressed by the shame of my life. Yet what to do, I cannot tell," was the way he put it.

A young Tolstoyan by the name of Lebrun, whom Father loved very much, lived with us at this time and helped Father. In his memoirs he quotes Father as saying on one occasion: "It's dreadful, intolerable! In times gone by when the people did not notice this one could tolerate it. But now, when it strikes everyone between the eyes, this life is unbearable. I must go away; this is beyond my strength." And later the same evening: "It is quite clear to me that no matter where I went, within two days' time Sophia Andreyevna would appear with all the footmen and the doctors, and everything would fall into the same old pattern!"

It is possible that Father would really have left Yasnaya Polyana then, but toward the end of the summer Mother became seriously ill. She complained of pains and a sense of weight in the lower part of her abdomen. Professor Snegiryov, a specialist in gynecology, found a tumor in her womb and advised an operation. But Mother was afraid, kept putting it off until she began to have really severe pains. Now they could not even consider moving her to a hospital but decided to operate in Yasnaya Polyana. But when Snegiryov arrived with his assistants and paraphernalia, Mother took a turn for the better. There was a further delay. Then her temperature rose sharply and peritonitis set in, making the operation imperative.

What miraculous changes occur in a human being when faced with death! The more severe her suffering, the closer she came to death, the higher Mother rose in spirit. When Father came into the room she made every effort not to groan. She took his hand and kissed it, saying: "Lyovochka, forgive me," and again, "forgive me."

Even I had not realized how fond I was of her. "Sashenka darling, thank you," she said when anything was done for her. I was ready to exert myself to the utmost to help her, to save her. I looked into her beautiful eyes, so helpless and full of suffering, and all the corroding antipathy, even hatred, I had sometimes felt seemed like a faraway nightmare.

On September 2 Father noted in his diary: "Sonya asked to have the priest, and I not only agreed, but was glad to co-operate. There are people who cannot reach an abstract, purely spiritual relationship with the First Principle of Life. They have to have some crude form.

[449]

Yet beyond that form there is also the spiritual content. And it is good that this is so, even in its crude form."

He was growing more and more tolerant in matters of belief. His own needs required different forms, but he did not impose these forms on others. As he explained it: "I sometimes pray . . . at odd hours and in the simplest fashion, I say: 'Lord have mercy,' I cross myself, I pray not so much in thought as in my feeling of recognition that I am dependent on God. I shall not advise anyone else to do this, but it serves my purpose. Just now I heaved a sigh like a prayer."

While the operation was in progress Father went off to Chapyzh —part of the forest near by. When Ilya and I went there to tell him that it was successfully over, he did not express any joy; on the contrary, there was an expression of profound suffering on his face. He did not go back with us, he wanted to be alone.

What were his emotions? In his diary he noted briefly: "Sonya has just been operated on. They say it was successful. But it was grave. This morning she was in a good spiritual state. How death can bring conciliation! . . . In dying Sonya reveals herself. . . ."

It was that revelation which was dearer, far dearer to him than her physical life. Had they done well to allow the physicians to interfere, to obstruct the natural course of her illness, to obstruct the will of God?

Mother began to recover rapidly. Her physical force returned and gradually the light which had so vividly illumined our lives was obscured by worldly things.

Everything returned to normal. We worked on the *Circle of Reading,* and people and letters arrived from all corners of the world: some were interesting, profound, others were stupid as Father called them, still others were begging or angry.

A certain student settled himself on our village, in one of the peasant cottages. He was a vulgar fellow, a drunkard, one of the mean little people who try to scrape together all kinds of horrid gossip. After he left, a revolting lampoon against all the Tolstoys appeared in a Kharkov newspaper.

On rare occasions Father received the visit of a blind peasant, of the sect of Old Believers, a man we nicknamed "the tobacco power." Shaking his goatee, leaning directly over Father and spraying him with his saliva, he would curse him for a liar, a Pharisee, the bloodsucker of the people. Father endured all this as a punishment for his sins.

He wrote: "The last time I made a note I said that I continued to be happy in my acceptance of life, but now I have to write the very opposite: I have weakened spiritually and principally in this, that I desire the love of people—both those near me and far away. Just now I went to Yasenka and brought back the letters, all of them unpleasant. The fact that they could make me feel their unpleasantness shows how far I have sunk. . . . Take the article in the Kharkov paper by that little student who lived here last summer. . . . It is an indubitable sign of deterioration, of the loss of communion with the Eternal via the consciousness, when I feel hurt in reading his malicious and stupid lie in print. . . . Besides, I was physically in a bad, dark mood, and for a long time could not re-establish my communion with God . . . all this comes from the fact that I am rejoiced at love of people and those close to me, and Chertkov, from whom I received a splendid letter about life and God. . . ."

November is the most unpleasant month, especially in the country. It is the time when roads are washed out, there is mud, dampness, and high winds. It is the time of sickness usually. In Russia, everyone waited impatiently for the snow when roads would be passable for sleighs. . . . During the autumn of 1906 the Obolenskis were staying with us. Did Masha catch cold during this weather or was it simply, as the peasants say, "that her time had come"? She fell ill at the end of November, of pneumonia according to the doctor. From the second day it was obvious that her condition was serious. She was housed "in the vaults" where Kolya, Julie and I nursed her.

"I am deeply concerned about Masha," Father wrote to Chertkov. "I love her very, very much."

Within the space of several days Masha changed so that she was unrecognizable. Her thin face became even more hollow, red spots flamed in her cheeks, in her eyes there was a look of concentration, of being separated from us and from life.

"Her death," Father wrote, "for me personally, although she is my best friend of all those close to me, is neither terrible nor piteous— I shall not long outlive her, yet I am simply, without reasoning about it, sorry for her. She should live, and at her age she wants to live, one simply regrets her sufferings and is sorry for her and those closest to her. It is pitiful and unpleasant to see all the vain efforts to lengthen her life by medication. And death, of recent times, has come to be quite close to me, not terrible, but natural, necessary, not at all in contradiction to life, but bound to it, like its continuance, so that to fight it is inherently a trait of the animal and not of reason. And that is why any unreasoned—not reasoned by intelligence—struggle with it, as in medicine—is unpleasant, bad."

Masha died quietly, conscious to the last. Father and Kolya were sitting by her bed. They raised her on her pillow. An hour before she died she opened her eyes wide, saw Father and laid his hand on her breast. Father leaned over her and raised her thin, transparent hand to his lips. "I am dying," she whispered almost inaudibly.

Father went to his room. "It is now one o'clock in the night," he wrote in his diary. "Masha is dead. Strange, I feel neither any horror, nor fear, nor any consciousness that something out of the ordinary has occurred, not even any pity, or pain. I seemed to feel it incumbent on me to call forth in myself some special sentiment of tender grief and I did evoke it, but in the depths of my soul I was calmer than I am in the face of some unknown act that is bad or wrong—and I am not even speaking of my own acts. Yes, this event is on the physical plane and therefore a matter of indifference—I watched her all the while she was dying: it was so amazingly calm. For me she was a being in a state of revelation, preceding my own revelation. I followed her unfolding and was rejoiced by it. But now that unfolding, in so far as it was in a form accessible to me (in this life), has come to an end, i.e., it is no longer visible to me; but what had been revealed still remains. 'Where? When?' Those are questions related to the process of unfolding here and cannot be transferred to the real life outside of space and time."

And after the funeral: "They have just carried her away, taken her to be buried," he wrote. "Thank God, I maintain myself in my earlier good frame of mind."

They carried Masha to the cemetery where Grandfather and Grandmother Tolstoy were buried, our little brothers Nikolenka and Petya, and our sister Varya. They were a long time passing through the village. The peasant women and men all wanted to stop the coffin and say prayers for her. They all knew and loved Masha. Many were the sleepless nights she had spent nursing a child with scarlet fever, or caring for a woman in labor. How much of her strength she had expended, working with the peasants, helping those in need, giving kindness and sympathy to the grieving. There were many who wept for her.

In Father's diary one often comes across this kind of a design:

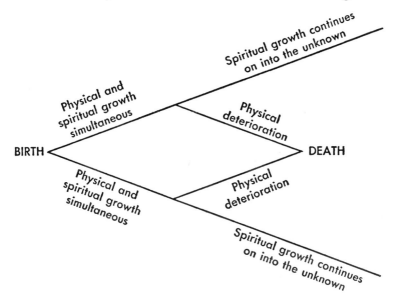

He has put its meaning into these words: "Yes, life is growth, or the unfolding of one's spiritual essence. This unfolding continues up to death itself. In death it is wholly completed for the individual being which I recognize as myself."

We did not talk to Father about Masha, we could not, but she was always in our thoughts.

At the time I found it impossible to understand why the best ones passed away: Vanichka, Masha. They came into the world for a time, to bring light, love and joy. They were both open to all that was good, they had a kind word on their lips for everyone who needed it, they were so like their father, and like each other. . . . Nor did I know how irreparable that loss was to us, how Father would need Masha in the tragedy that was to be played out four years later, when I was destined to take on my young shoulders a responsibility beyond my powers.

❧ 62 ❧

IN APRIL, 1907, Father wrote to Auntie Maria Nikolayevna in her convent:

"Dear Mashenka, I often think of you with great tenderness, and during recent days it seemed as though some voice were speaking to me of you . . . of how good it would be to see you, to hear about you, to commune with you. How is your health? I do not ask about your spiritual state. It must be good with the life you lead. May God help you draw nearer to Him.

". . . To our delight Tanya is living here with her sweet little girl. Her husband is abroad for a while with his son who is ill.

"I feel the loss of Masha very much, but God's will be done, as you say, and I say it over with all my soul. For myself, I have nothing to report except the good I do not deserve. The older I grow, the quieter and more joyous I feel in my heart. Often death seems almost desirable. I am so much at ease in my inner being, and I believe so much in the nearness of Him, in Whom we live both in life and in death.

". . . My respects to the sisters. May God help them find salvation. Life in the world nowadays is so dreadful, so evil, that they have chosen the happier path, and you too along with them. I love you very much. Write me a word about yourself. I kiss you.

"Your brother in the flesh and in the spirit—do not reject me. Lev Tolstoy."

At this moment Auntie was the only person to whom he could, even in a restrained way, express his yearning for simple human affection.

Children, as always, were a great consolation and joy to him, and several boys of a serious turn of mind came to see him every evening. He worked with them downstairs in the library, where his study used to be, leading them in discussions of religious and moral questions. Father was particularly fond of one boy, Nikolka, who had a nice open face with dimpled cheeks, and serious pale-blue eyes which gazed attentively at his teacher to catch every word. His comrades gave him the nickname of "the Tolstoyan."

This summer saw the return of Chertkov and his family from England, his exile ended. After spending a few days at Yasnaya Polyana, he settled his household in an old neglected manor house a little over three miles from us.

There were a great number of people around Chertkov: copyists, secretaries, a photographer brought from England to take pictures of Father from every angle, people with indefinite duties, labeled assistants. They all, except Chertkov's wife, Galya, who was ill and under the care of a nurse, lived on vegetarian food. Galya Chertkov's morbid beauty held a particular fascination for me. Her huge, black, languid eyes, her beautifully wavy black hair, her thin, straight little nose, her bowknot lips, and her unnaturally white skin made her striking. She shared completely the views of my father and of her husband and, to the extent her health permitted, she helped Chertkov in the publication abroad of Father's writings. When I was with her I felt embarrassed by my own physical strength and health. This was especially true when her little face would suddenly turn greenish and transparent, and the tears would come to her eyes: "I feel ill, I am hungry," she would whisper. Then someone would rush to the kitchen and bring back the stalwart cook Annushka, carrying a tray set with all sorts of tiny, toylike cups and bowls filled with some kind of liquid mixtures. When she sang Dukhobor hymns in her low, deep voice, it gave me the shivers.

Many people had come to settle in the district out of a desire to be nearer my father. In Ovsyannikovo, besides Maria Alexandrovna Schmidt, there was the Gorbunov family. The pianist Goldenweiser and his wife lived in my cottage at Telyatinki, and for the use of house and a horse, he gave me music lessons. A painter named Orlov, a small, good-natured man, set up quarters in the village to paint pictures of peasant life. His wife was as small as he, but even so it seemed extraordinary that with their brood of undersized, smiling children they could fit into one peasant cottage and hay shed, with room to spare for visitors. Nikolayev and his family also lived in the village—he was the translator and convinced follower of Henry George—a modest, nice man.

Father was still interested in the single tax theory of Henry George, to such an extent that he wrote Stolypin, the Minister of Internal Affairs, asking him to look into George's theory with the idea of

[455]

introducing land reforms in Russia. His first letter was dated July 26, 1907:

". . . I am writing you, Pyotr Arkadievich, under the impulse of the kindest, most affectionate feelings for one who is on the wrong road.—You have two ways open to you: either you can continue the course of action begun by you, which not only participates in, but also directs [the system of] exile, forced labor, executions, and which, without accomplishing its object will leave behind a bad memory . . . or, by putting yourself in the lead of European nations, you can co-operate in destroying the age-old great and universal injustice of land ownership; you can do a truly good work . . . by satisfying the legitimate desires of the people . . . by putting an end to all the horrible misdeeds which are now being enacted both by the revolutionaries and by the government. . . . Lev Tolstoy."

Under the dates of October 20-23, 1907, Stolypin wrote to Father:

"Do not think I have not paid any attention to your letter. I have been unable to answer it because it cut too deep. You consider evil what I consider good for Russia. It seems to me that the lack of 'property' among the peasants creates all our unbalance—nature implanted certain inborn instincts in man . . . and one of the most powerful . . . is the sense of property. One cannot love what belongs to another as one does one's own, and it is impossible to tend, to improve land, which is only temporarily in one's possession, as one would one's own. The artificial emasculation of our peasantry in this regard, the destruction of his innate sense of property, leads to much that is bad and, above all, to poverty—and poverty, in my opinion, is worse than slavery. . . . It is ridiculous to talk to these people about freedom or about freedoms. First raise the level of his well-being to at least that smallest degree where a minimal prosperity makes a man free. . . . And that can be accomplished only by the free application of labor to the land, that is to say, under the existence of the right of ownership in the land.—I do not reject the teachings of George, and I think that the single tax will in time help in the struggle against very large ownership of property, but now I do not see any purpose here in Russia of driving off the land the more developed class of landholders, but on the contrary I see the undoubted necessity of relieving the peasant by giving him the legitimate opportunity to acquire the piece of land he needs and granting him full ownership of it. . . . Anyhow, it is not for me to convince you. . . . You have always seemed like a great man to me, whereas I am of a modest

[456]

opinion with regard to myself. I have been carried to the top by the tide of events—probably for a single moment! Still I want to use this moment, in so far as it lies in my power, my comprehension, and my feelings, for the good of the people and for my country, which I love as they used to love it in times gone by. How can I do other than that which I feel to be good? Yet you write me that I am proceeding along the path of evil acts, bad repute and above all, sin. Believe me that, feeling as I often do the nearness of death, I cannot but dwell on these questions, and my path seems to me to be the direct one. I realize that I write you all this in vain—this was indeed the reason why I did not reply to you. Forgive me. Yours, P. Stolypin."

To this Father replied:

"Why, for what purpose are you destroying yourself by persevering in your erroneous activities which cannot lead to anything except the worsening of the general situation and yours as well. It is the attribute of a man as courageous, honest and noble as I conceive you to be not to persist in a mistake once made, but to recognize it and bend all your forces to overcome its consequences. You have made two mistakes: the first—you began to use violence to fight violence and you have continued to do this, thereby aggravating and aggravating the situation; the second—you thought to pacify the aroused population . . . which was waiting for and desirous of one thing: the doing away with the right to hold landed property (a right as shocking in our times as the right of serfdom was half a century ago), to pacify the population by destroying the commune in order to form small landed holdings. This mistake was tremendous. Instead of making use of the consciousness still alive among the people of the illegality of individual land ownership, a consciousness which coincides with the teachings of the most forward-looking people in the world on the subject of the relationship between man and land, instead of putting this principle before the people, you thought to pacify them by means of seducing them with the basest, old, outworn concept of the relation of man to land that still exists in Europe, to the great regret of all thinking persons in that Europe. Dear Pyotr Arkadievich . . . life is not a pleasantry. We live it here but once. It is impossible, unreasonable to ruin one's life because of some *parti pris*. . . . Both your mistakes: fighting violence with violence and the confirmation of the oppression of property rather than the dissolution of it—both can be corrected, strange as it may seem, by one and the same clear, easily applied measure: the recognition

[457]

of the fact that all land is equally the property of all the people, and the fixing of a tax which corresponds to the relative advantages of the land, this to replace taxes or a part of them. This measure alone could pacify the people and render powerless the efforts of the revolutionaries, who now draw their support from the people, and it would make unnecessary the dreadful measures of violence which are now being used against the violators. . . . I repeat what I said in the beginning: everything that I write I am writing for you because I wish you well, because I am fond of you. . . ."

Guests and visitors were not unmindful of us this year. During the summer the painter Nesterov came to visit; he made several studies and one large, magnificent portrait of Father; on one occasion 850 school children came over from Tula, to spend a day swimming, hiking, playing games.

Neighbors from among the "dark people" came every evening, to settle themselves in a semicircle around Father, expecting him to say something. Dushan made notes in his pocket. When Father read aloud Dushan would make a rough guess at how long the reading would last, then dash off to his room, set an alarm clock, lie down and promptly go to sleep, worn out from his calls upon the sick and work in the clinic. When the alarm wakened him, he would jump up and return downstairs in time to hear the discussion following the reading.

I must confess that I found all this very boring: the Russian blouses, the boots, the long beards, unkempt hair, the always earnest faces, as if people had vowed not to joke, laugh or be gay. It was only Father and sometimes Chertkov who introduced any liveliness into this group by their jokes, laughter and puns. The fact that all these Tolstoyans were splendid people and Father valued them still could not relieve the overwhelming boredom. My niece Annochka, who was only four years my junior, and I would go off to my corner room and sing gypsy love songs to the accompaniment of a guitar or piano. Sometimes the door would be opened softly and Father would come in: "Go on, go right on," he would say with a smile. "You are doing it very well." And he would stand in the doorway, his hands thrust in his belt, and listen.

Not all the Tolstoyans inspired me with this sense of dreariness. Perhaps it was that I instinctively, as one does sometimes when young, felt an artificial striving in some of them, a striving which

I myself feared. And indeed many of them could not stand the ascetic life. As Father warned them in advance: one cannot undertake a feat unless one is fully prepared for it.

Boulanger gave out—he became involved, gambled away government money at cards and, after leaving a note to the effect that he was taking his life, he vanished. A few Tolstoyans turned into revolutionaries, others entered monasteries, still others became ardent monarchists. Only a few remained, and the majority of them were eventually lost in exile and in prisons during the revolution.

When Father finished his article "Thou Shalt Not Kill," he read it aloud to those who shared his views. He had written a call to love, but around him an atmosphere of evil, hatred and struggle was deepening. My mother was much upset by the death of her brother Vyacheslav, an engineer, who was killed presumably by unemployed workmen while engaged on the excavation of a harbor near St. Petersburg. Yet Uncle Vyacheslav, as it happened, had defended the interests of the workers in the city Duma (Council) just before the incident, and had taken steps to get work given to them.

In Yasnaya Polyana the peasants cut down and carried off 129 oak trees. On Misha's estate they set fire to the sheds which housed all his valuable agricultural equipment. At the Sukhotins' the farm buildings burned down, and arson was suspected. Our neighbor Madame Zvegintseva was also having her troubles. Prowlers in her woods shot down her coachman and a huntsman sent to investigate them.

When someone sneaked in to steal some of our cabbages and shot at the night watchman, my mother and Andrei appealed to the Governor for protection. This brought a sheriff, a police sergeant and several mounted police to the village, with the result that several peasants were arrested for possessing firearms. Father was distressed.

"For the last two or three days I have been in a depressed emotional state which until today I have been unable to throw off," he wrote in his diary for September 7. "Cabbage thieves were shooting at night and Sonya lodged a complaint and the authorities came and now they have grabbed four peasants, and now their wives and fathers come begging to me. They cannot conceive that I—especially since I live here—am not the master, and so they attribute everything to me. This is hard to bear and very bad because it makes it impossible for people to have a good opinion of me, it puts me into the field where the opinion of people has no weight. For the last two days

[459]

I have not been able to get rid of an ugly feeling," Father wrote in
his diary for September 7, 1907.

The Governor himself came to Yasnaya Polyana. "It's revolting
and regrettable," was Father's comment on this visit.

He was so upset that he wanted to go over to Tanya's, but the
life there was not to his taste either—it was a large manorial establishment, a life of idleness.

In our vestibule it smelled of men's sweat and cheap tobacco. The
guards were quartered behind the partitions. Chertkov talked with
them and distributed copies of his *Soldiers' and Officers' Handbook,*
a tract against military service.

I implored Mother to send the guards away, I quarreled with her,
with my brother Andrei, I lost my temper, I wept. It was unbearable to see Father suffering. Finally I went to the Governor with a
letter from Father, begging him to free the peasants who had been
arrested, but his curt reply was: "Your mother, the Countess, requested me to undertake the protection of Yasnaya Polyana and of
your family, and I am merely carrying out her request." There was
nothing more to be said.

I returned home with a heavy heart. On top of that a telegram
was brought from the station which alarmed us all: "Look out for
guest. Goncharov." And several days later: "Look out. Goncharov."
I was nervous, I studied each new visitor: Could he be Goncharov?
I stuck close to Father, who jeered at my fears.

In the autumn Chertkov left to spend several months in England
and put his affairs in order. Before his departure he took pains to
find a real "secretary" for Father, and his choice fell on a Tolstoyan
by the name of Gusev, who established himself in my little house in
Telyatinki when the Goldenweisers returned to Moscow for the
winter. Gusev's main occupation was to take care of Father's correspondence, which he did in great detail. The copying of manuscripts was left to me. But Gusev was scarcely broken in to his work
when he was arrested and put into Krapivna jail.

This was a difficult year. One cause for family distress was
Andrei's divorce and his marriage to Katya Artsimovich. Katya had
been the wife of the Governor on whose staff Andrei served. To
marry Andrei, she abandoned her six children. The situation was
more difficult because all of us were very fond of Olga and her
children, Sonyushka and Ilyushok, and they remained far closer to
our affection although we accepted Katya.

Father tried to take a hopeful view of the matter. He once said jokingly to Maria Alexandrovna Schmidt: "There are two things that I fear above all—that Andrei will divorce his wife again and that Sasha may stop laughing."

Toward the end of December Gusev was released. "How I envy you," Father said to him. "How I wish they would put me in jail, into a real, stinking one. Evidently I have not yet deserved this honor."

❧ 63 ❧

YASNAYA POLYANA was all noise and gaiety. Preparations for the Christmas holidays were afoot. The famous pianist Wanda Landowska and her husband arrived. She played for us endlessly—Rameau, Mozart, Haydn—and we listened enraptured. Father enjoyed himself more than anyone else. His mood in general was gay, buoyant.

Gusev on his release from prison had come to live in Yasnaya Polyana, in the typing room next to Father's bedroom, a study formerly occupied by Jooly-Mooly. My mother now had her own secretary, a city-bred, lively and good-natured woman by the name of V. M. Feokritova. Varya, as we called her, typed and copied Mother's work: *My Life.*

In January Father received a present of a sort we had never seen before—a dictaphone sent him from America by Thomas Edison. When I had set it up, he tried to speak into it, but was so excited that he stuttered and forgot what he intended to say. "Stop the machine, stop it," he cried to me. "It's dreadfully exciting," he added with a sigh. "Probably such a machine is good for well-balanced Americans but it is not for us Russians."

Nevertheless he did, on occasion, make use of it. He wrote a letter of thanks to Edison and they exchanged several letters.

"I respect Edison," he used to say. "He never gave any of his inventions over for military purposes."

Father continued to prepare his *Circle of Reading* for a second

[461]

edition, and Gusev helped him. I copied his essays: "The Law of Force and the Law of Love," and a new one entitled "There Is an End to Everything."

In August of this year (1908) Father would be eighty years old. As early as January there was talk of a jubilee for him and a committee was formed in St. Petersburg to organize for the occasion. Professors, public leaders, writers met to elect officers and set the wheels in motion. There was a warm response from the press, municipal Dumas planned a series of resolutions of a humanitarian and educational character in honor of Tolstoy, from other countries came offers of co-operation and help in raising a Tolstoy Fund, and the Ministry of Internal Affairs—not to be caught napping—sent word to its agencies to exercise "particular vigilance" lest unreliable elements use the occasion for demonstrations against the government. All this furore was distasteful to Father as it interrupted his religious mood of concentration as he prepared for death; but the final push to his decision to do something about it was a letter from a very old acquaintance, Princess Maria Mikhailovna Dondukova-Korsakova, written to my mother. In it she protested that a public celebration honoring a man who had undermined the Orthodox faith was an affront to Orthodox people. Father was touched by this letter, and he dictated a reply to the Princess:

"I am so old, so near to death, I am so desirous to pass on, to go to Him from Whom I came, that all these empty, miserable manifestations are only distressing to me. But all this was personal to me, I had not thought of . . . what impression these eulogies of a man who had destroyed what they believed in would have on other people. I shall attempt to free myself from this evil affair, from any participation on my part in it, from giving offense to people who, like you, are immeasurably closer to me than all those nonbelievers who, God knows why and for what purposes, are going to eulogize me and express themselves in trivial and entirely useless words. Yes, dear Maria Mikhailovna, the older I grow, the more I become convinced that all of us who believe in God, if only we are sincere in our belief, are joined together, for we are all the sons of one God, and brethren among ourselves. . . . Now, farewell. I thank you for your affection and beg you not to deprive me of it." As Father spoke into the Edison machine, his voice trembled with emotion.

Without delay, he then dictated a letter to M. A. Stakhovich, in his capacity as secretary of the committee, which concluded with this request: ". . . do what you can to put an end to this jubilee and to liberate me. I shall be forever very, very grateful to you. Your loving, Lev Tolstoy."

He sent another letter to the press. Although it was not published, his reiterated disapproval of a celebration had its effect and the Jubilee Committee curtailed its activities—to the disappointment of the left elements who hoped to exploit the affair to their own ends.

The Tolstoyans shared Father's views. One of them proposed that the most acceptable way of marking the jubilee would be to put Tolstoy in prison, which would afford him profound moral satisfaction.

"How Bodyanski has delighted me!" Father exclaimed at luncheon, upon hearing the proposal. "That would indeed have been my satisfaction."

Meantime the persecution of those increasing numbers who refused to do military service went on unabated. There were fresh arrests of Tolstoyans for distributing or having in their possession Father's writings.

Before the revolution of 1905 capital punishment in Russia was a rare occurrence; instead, criminals were held in prison or deported to forced labor. But in recent years, since the terrorist acts and agrarian disorders, the number of death sentences had increased. Father suffered acute, almost physical, pain—for those who were executed and for those who pronounced sentence, equally. He felt he must speak out, he could not remain silent. At his request, Davydov and Biryukov obtained material for him on capital punishment.

One morning as he was drinking his coffee and going through his mail, Father opened the newspaper *Rus* and read that in Kherson "because of a predatory attack on the manor of a landowner" twenty peasants had been sentenced to death.

"No, this is impossible! One cannot live like this! . . . It is impossible, absolutely impossible! . . ." There were tears in his voice when he dictated these words into his dictaphone. So he began to write his article "I Cannot Be Silent" on May 11, and finished it on the 31st.

"Nowadays they talk about executions, hangings, murders, bombs the way they used to speak of the weather. Children play at hanging. Those who are scarcely more than children, high school boys, go gladly to kill people in the process of expropriation, as they used to go out hunting," he wrote. And farther on: "It is impossible to live

[463]

like this. I, at least, am unable to live like this, I cannot and I will not do it.—That is why I am writing this and I shall do all in my power to distribute what I write both in Russia and outside it, so that one of two things may happen: either an end will be put to these inhuman practices or else my relationship to these things will be destroyed. . . ."

Several newspapers printed excerpts from "I Cannot Be Silent," and were fined by the government. The article sped all over Russia. It appeared in every country of Europe. It was printed on secret presses, it was mimeographed, copied by hand, and everywhere it caused an extraordinary stir. The revolutionaries did not lose the opportunity of using it for their own purposes after they toned down the author's Christian point of view. Many wrote to thank Father for the article; a few scolded and insulted him.

About this time L. Andreyev's story *The Seven Who Were Hanged* was published. But Father did not like it. "It rings false at every point," he said. "One must write about such things with truth, sincerity and depth, or not at all." Father made diligent efforts to discover some religious outlook on the part of the so-called "forward-looking" people, but such "points of contact," as he called them, were lacking. He received a visit from Father Grigori Petrov, a priest who was playing an important role at the time, but was disappointed. Petrov, as Father said, had not yet begun to understand the essentials of a true life. His assertion that one need not read the Gospels marked him as essentially a revolutionary.

"One must say to the revolutionaries," Tolstoy wrote in his diary for July 28, 1908: "You cannot, my friends, build temples with unskilled hands, much less with unclean ones."

Here is another characteristic entry on the same subject:

"Oh, if only you, the confused, the frivolous people, those who have lost their religion, i.e., the meaning of life, would cease playing this senseless and brutal game of revolution, and the others, the even more stupid and brutal one of upholding the greatness of Russia, and still others the absurdly silly game of a constitution . . . all like children slavishly and smugly imitating their elders; if only all of you . . . would understand that we are a *special* people (not in the sense of being superior, but in the sense of our national life) and that we are living in our own *special* time, and that therefore we should not imitate other peoples or people living in other times, but should live our own lives in the life of our own time, and that what we need . . . the thing after which the whole people thirsts, is the liberation of the land from private ownership; and in the field of international, governmental matters . . . the curtailment of all hostility toward foreign people; and in the field of internal affairs . . . the freedom no one can take away because it is founded on the fulfillment of the highest law for all people . . . religion."

It was this attitude of a "game," a lack of seriousness as to what should constitute the basis of life, that Father could not tolerate. As he said about Bernard Shaw, after reading his *Man and Superman* —"It is terribly witty, and in bad taste. . . . He deals with serious questions and by means of some joke or other he distorts them and you lose all respect for his work."

Father gave us all a fright early in May. He seemed quite well, but suddenly Gusev, who was in the next room, saw him slowly sinking to the floor. Gusev ran in, tried to hold him up but could not. We all hurried to him upon hearing his call—Mother, Jooly-Mooly, Ilya Vasilievich. Father was lifted onto the divan. He spoke, but he had forgotten everything; he did not know his name or where he was.

Next morning, when he had fully recovered, he laughingly said to Chertkov that he thought he had quite "outlived his mind." The doctors explained his condition as being due to a flow of blood away from the brain.

These attacks, provoked by strong emotional upsets, recurred several times, but his forgetfulness lasted only briefly; in a few hours his memory and clarity of thought were entirely restored.

Despite his eighty years Father had not altered his mode of life: he began his day with a walk to Chapyzh, the fir grove, where he rested on a bench and jotted down his thoughts. In the morning he worked largely on his *Circle of Reading*, lunched and then rode out on Delir, his favorite mount. We tried not to let him go alone. Sometimes Dushan would jog along after him at some distance on Katka, a muddy-gray mare of undistinguished strain, and sometimes I rode with him on my bay, whose coat glistened golden in the sunshine.

No one knew the woodsy roads and paths better than Father. At times it seemed to me that we had lost our way in the sleep-bound State Forest. We plunged down deep ravines, the branches struck us in the face, a menace to spectacles; we picked our way across marshes, streams. "Bear to the right, it's narrower here," he would call to me. Delir, with arched hindquarters, would jump lightly and gracefully across a stream, and after him went my bay Orel. "Still alive?"

Father would ask, turning around. Then, regardless of the narrowness of the path, he would race uphill at a gallop. "You see, we got out of it!" he would exclaim as he reined Delir to a trot along a broad forest lane.

Once, as we were riding home along the so-called "swimming" road which led to the Voronka River, we came to the spot where Father and his brother Nikolenka had buried the "green stick." Father drew Delir up for a moment and, turning in his saddle, said to me: "There, among these oaks near the edge of the ravine, I want you to bury me when I die. . . ."

On July 2 of this same year Father started a diary which he would not show to anyone: neither to me, nor to Chertkov, and certainly not to Mother. If I had been older, there were surely many things that Father would have told me. But I understood him even without words. I knew about the diary and I preserved the secret of it from my mother and from Chertkov. Only after his death did I find out what was in it.

Father himself hinted at a knowledge of the special communication between us when he noted in his personal diary: "I had a good talk with Sasha. How strangely things are passed on—to the males the father's mind and the mother's character, and also vice versa."

"If I heard about myself from the outside," Father wrote in this same diary, "as of a person, living in luxury, with police guards, grabbing all he could from the peasants, putting them in the lockup, and professing and preaching Christianity, and handing out small coins, and hiding behind a sweet wife while I did all these base things—I could not but call him a scoundrel! And that is what I have had to submit to, so that I could free myself from human fame and live for the sake of my soul."

These words—the outcry of a soul bared to God—are the best answer to all those who reproached Tolstoy for being inconsistent, pharisaical and even untruthful.

"Help me, O Lord," he wrote another time. "Again I yearn to go away, and I dare not. Nor can I give up. Above all, if I leave, am I doing it for my own sake? I know that I am not acting on my own behalf if I stay. One is bound to think God directs one. That is what I shall do." And again: "I am sorely sad in my soul. I know this is good for my soul, but it is hard. . . . I have a wicked longing for death."

During this period Chertkov was living with Galya, his son Dima, and a numerous circle in one of the cottages in Kozlovka-Zaseka. Knowing how important it was to Father to have Chertkov nearby, I agreed to sell him one half of the small piece of land which I still owned in Telyatinki. Immediately Chertkov began to build a huge two-story house and a series of outbuildings—workshops, stables, sheds.

Although there was no open clash between my mother and Chertkov at this time, still one sensed a covert hostility. My mother was annoyed that Chertkov allowed himself liberties with Father. He sometimes walked into Father's study while he was working, a thing none of us did; he would permit a photographer to take pictures of Father from all possible angles, although it was well known that Father disliked to pose. Yet Father could not say no to Chertkov.

The nearer Father approached his end, the more indifferent he became to worldly fame. Yet he could not elude it. All who surrounded him never forgot it for a moment. They bathed in his fame. Even the saintly Dushan made notes, made pictures, made records for posterity.

"Everyone is writing my biography," Father wrote, "and as in all biographies—there will be nothing about my relation to the Seventh Commandment. There will be none of the dreadful filth. . . . There will be nothing of that in the biographies, they don't put that in. But it is very important, and very important as a vice which I, especially, recognize as one which more than any other imposes self-control."

I confess that posterity did not disturb me greatly. I was preoccupied trying to care for, to preserve, to do what was necessary for the peace and happiness of that person dearer to me than anyone else in the world.

In July Father fell ill again, of an embolism in the veins of his leg—thrombophlebitis. The doctors who came down from Moscow prescribed complete rest. At first he was moved around in his big leather "Crimean" armchair, but in a few days his temperature went up and he was put to bed.

"Although it is only a trifle," he wrote in his diary for August 11, "still I want to say what I'd like done after my death. First, it would be good if my heirs would release all my writings for general use; or if not that, still they absolutely should release all such general writings, as the *Primer*, the *Readers*. Second, although this is the most trifling of trifles, no rites should be performed when my body is put in the ground. A wooden coffin, and let who will carry it, or haul it to the Zakaz, opposite the ravine, to the place of the green stick. At least there is a basis for choosing this or that place."

Toward the middle of August Father's health improved, although he was still not allowed to walk. On August 28 he was eighty years old.

Despite the efforts of Tolstoy, the government and the clergy to stop the celebration, they had not succeeded.

By publishing his article "I Cannot Be Silent," Tolstoy unwittingly added to the already great interest in his jubilee. He was literally overwhelmed with greetings, receiving more than five hundred telegrams, innumerable letters, formal messages and presents.

That day the whole family gathered, except for Lev, who was in Sweden. There were with us also close friends and a Mr. Wright, a friend of Chertkov, who brought a message from England bearing the signatures of hundreds of English admirers.

Father spent the day like any other. He worked in the forenoon, received congratulations at luncheon, then I rolled him into the big reception room to visit for two hours with his guests. In the evening Goldenweiser played Chopin, which Father loved.

Because of his condition, Father was unable even to read all the congratulatory messages, so Mother and our friend Khiriakov sorted out the most interesting and touching ones to show him. He acknowledged them in a letter to the newspapers:

"In the last few days," he wrote, "around August 28, I have received a quantity of all kinds of expressions of sympathy, such as I never could have expected and—I repeat—I am quite sincerely convinced I do not deserve. . . . The letters were most varied, they came from diverse ends of Russia, and all of them, apparently, had but the one purpose: to express agreement—not with me but with the truths which have been noted and expressed by me. This was a great joy to me, for which I express my gratitude—not the kind of gratitude one expresses out of propriety or politeness, but a sincere gratitude I cannot but feel as a result of the unexpected and undeserved joy I have been experiencing in these last days. . . ."

❧ 64 ❧

MUCH as I wrestled with the feeling, I still was jealous of Gusev. I realized that he was able to help Father better than I could. He knew stenography, and I did not. He knew the teachings of Ku Khung Ming and Confucius, and I did not. Gusev could discuss Indian wisdom—I was just making its acquaintance. And so with other things. I loved to sing gypsy love songs with Annochka, to the accompaniment of the guitar, but Gusev, who really liked our singing, forced himself to take "serious note" of the passionate words of the love songs, in order to demonstrate to "posterity" the sinful surroundings in which Tolstoy had to live.

I was very fond of animals. In addition to a large black poodle, Marquis, who was endowed with human intelligence, I had a gray parrot with rose-colored tail and the speech of a human. It was the parrot who got me my revenge on Gusev.

When Gusev, with the eternal smile of *l'homme qui rit*, would sit down to dictate to me I would open the door to the parrot's cage and let the bird out. Gusev, absorbed in something, would not notice how it was stealing closer to him. As it climbed up his leg, higher and higher, he was afraid to touch it, afraid to move. "Take your accursed bird off!" he yelled. But the parrot, perched on his lap, cried: "Ah, ah, ah-ha!" Then with all its might it pecked at his knee. "It hurts!" yelled Gusev. "It hurts! Take it away!"

Having finished its job, the parrot slid down to the floor. "Fool!" it screamed at Gusev, before scrambling up to my shoulder and rubbing its head against my cheek. "Give me your little paw," it chortled caressingly, "Give me your little head, Miss, for a little kiss." "Disgusting bird," muttered Gusev, rubbing his knee.

Everyone loved my poodle Marquis, even my mother, who generally was not fond of dogs. One of our favorite games was hide-and-seek. I would hide the case to my glasses on the book shelf, in the divan, in Father's pocket. Then Marquis would run around sniffing the air, jumping up on the tables, the chairs, nosing into

Father's pocket, until he had located the case. . . . . Probably the Tolstoyans despised me and pitied Tolstoy for having such a foolish daughter. But after all, how did I come by my love of sports, horses, dogs, my buoyancy, even my eagerness? Had the "dark people" never discerned these traits in their teacher, the power of his love and understanding of all life? Father forgave me my youthfulness. He himself was delighted with the intelligence of Marquis, with the ardor and sensitiveness of his faithful Arab horse Delir who carried him cautiously in all kinds of country with a full knowledge of his habits.

Is it possible that life should not be joyous, that one must forever be repenting of something, tormenting oneself? Sometimes I had my dreams: my father and I would have a tiny house in the village. Father would work in the mornings while I would do the housework, clean, wash, cook; we would have a vegetable garden, one cow, several chickens. In the evenings I would copy manuscripts. . . . . But what then would become of Mother? She would not be willing to live that way. She would settle down next door, with physicians, menservants, maids; and Chertkov with his assistants, his photographers, would settle down on the other side. . . . The whole thing would be repeated. Father had imprisoned himself by his fame. These people would never leave him in peace; he was necessary to their existence, without him they would be nothing.

Toward the end of December, 1908, Repin came to Yasnaya Polyana, bringing with him Madame Nordman-Severova. They were both strict vegetarians. For Madame Nordman, vegetarianism was a cult—she knew all kinds of herbs, invented elaborate ways of cooking them; also she ate from a revolving table at home, so that no servant was needed to wait on her. To Father all this seemed too complicated and artificial. He was disturbed, moreover, by Madame Nordman's position. "What am I to call her?" he said. "Is she the wife of Repin? No, he has another wife. His cohabitant? That's rather rude." Then he suddenly beamed. "I know, I know what the peasants would call her: the mistress of Repin's house."

At Christmas I arranged a tree for the peasant children and we all had a jolly time. Father took the children by the hand and made a ring around the tree; we sang, we danced, we distributed presents to everyone. From time to time Father would lean over one of the children. "Whose child are you?" he would ask. "Rezunov's?" "Rezunov's boy Paul," the boy replied. "The grandson of Semyon?" On receiving an affirmative answer Father nodded happily. "How strong the family resemblance is. His grandfather studied under me in school. And that black-eyed little girl with the curling lip is surely one of Makarov's youngsters." Again he had guessed correctly.

Toward the end of January that winter the Bishop of Tula, the Right Reverend Parpheni, came to Yasnaya Polyana, accompanied by two priests and police officers. The Bishop was the first to offer to shake hands, not believing that Father would accept the episcopal blessing. But Father had made up his mind to be extremely amiable.

After some inconsequential conversation, as Father reported later, he invited the Bishop to his room. He was always touched, he said, by visits from members of the clergy, and by letters expressing good wishes; he only regretted that it was as impossible for him to accede to their desires as it would be to fly. One thing was especially unpleasant to him—that was the accusation that he undermined the faith of the people, when all his efforts were directed toward combatting an absence of faith, faith of whatever kind. "Incidentally," Father wrote, "in demonstration of this I read to him the excerpts from my *Circle of Reading* for January 20, the very day when our meeting happened to take place. On that day there were wonderful passages from Channing, Emerson, Thoreau and especially Kant."

After the reading, which had clearly made a good impression on the visitor, the conversation was resumed. To emphasize his point as to the meaning of faith, Father then recounted an incident which had happened long ago:

"I went out for a walk late one evening in winter, and as I was going through the village I looked in a window and saw Matryona, an aged woman, down on her knees praying; I had known her in her youth as one of the most vicious, depraved women in the village. I was much struck by her external appearance in this attitude of prayer. I looked in, then I walked on, but on my return I looked again into the window and found Matryona still in the same position. She was praying, she was bowing down to the floor and then raising her face to the ikons.

"That was—true prayer. God grant that all might pray in the same way, i.e., recognizing our dependency on God—and to destroy the faith that can evoke such prayer I should look upon as the greatest of crimes. . . . In any case it is impossible. No wise man . . . could do it. But the situation with people of our education is not the same—they have *no faith at all*, or else what is even worse—

[471]

they have the pretense of faith, a faith which plays the part only of maintaining a certain decency."

The Bishop made no comment on that, but repeated that it was not good to destroy faith.

The following month Father had another visitor, a Kazan Tatar named Vaisov, who was an adherent of the Bahaist sect. Father was interested in Vaisov's idea of the necessity of *one* religion.

"Actually, when you think of it," Father said, "you are always astonished that such a simple argument does not come to your mind. Take an Orthodox Christian, a Catholic, a Buddhist—all of them believing in what they hold to be the truth. Yet if I cross a certain boundary—I think that the one is a lie, the other the truth. What doubts that arouses, what need to search out the religion which would be common to all!"

Thinking deeply into those words, it is possible to see clearly why Father devoted the last years of his life to bringing together thoughts and precepts which he considered fundamental as a guide for human life: *Thoughts of the Sages,* like a *Circle of Reading for Everyday* grew out of this preoccupation. In choosing what was basic to all the religions, and to the thinking of the wisest men, he was un-doubtedly making an effort to lay the foundation for *one* religion.

Early in March Father again fell ill with an inflammation of the veins in his left leg. Dushan and I implored him to lie still with his leg up and not to move. At times his mood was very depressed, aggravated by the government's persecution of his friends. Again he begged that he be arrested as the author of the banned articles. But the government continued its same tactics: Chertkov was noti-fied that he must leave the province of Tula within three days "be-cause of deleterious activities"; a police search was made at Biryukov's home in the province of Kostroma. He was accused of keeping and distributing banned literature.

Despite the fact that Mother did not like Chertkov, or perhaps because of it, she came forward with the same fire she had evinced during the famine year, and at the time of Father's excommunication, and wrote an article for the press protesting Chertkov's expulsion. This letter was printed in Russian newspapers and also abroad—notably in the London *Times.* Wicked tongues had it that our neigh-bor, Madame Zvegintseva, and my brother Andrei played a decisive part in the affair by requesting the Tula authorities to break up a subversive group of "revolutionaries," as they called the Tolstoyans, living in her vicinity in Telyatinki.

Toward the end of May Father was visited by the celebrated scholar, I. I. Mechnikov and his wife. It goes without saying that the event did not escape the correspondents of the press who followed avidly everything that occurred at Yasnaya Polyana.

"Mechnikov is agreeable and apparently broad-minded," Father noted in his diary for May 30. "I have not yet had a chance to talk with him."

Father was in fine fettle and received his guest with the worldly amiability so characteristic of him, putting Mechnikov immediately at ease. But in the course of their visit together the two men discovered many points of difference in their outlook. Mechnikov was stunned, when he spoke enthusiastically about *War and Peace* and *Anna Karenina*, to have Father show complete indifference to the books; as a matter of fact, he had quite forgotten their contents. They could agree on the bad effects of alcohol and smoking, but their approach to those evils, as well as to vegetarianism, was at variance. Mechnikov took the scientific and hygienic rather than the moral point of view, and his assertion that a man can lengthen his life—that he himself intended to live more than a hundred years—seemed cynical and lacking in seriousness to Father.

On May 31 Father commented in his diary: "Mechnikov has turned out to be a very frivolous person—and nonreligious. . . . As to science he had nothing to offer except his faith in the value of science, for which I asked confirmation. As to religion there was nothing but silence. Evidently he rejects what he considers to be religion . . . he does not choose to understand what religion is."

Shortly after this Father received a telegram from the son of Henry George, asking permission to come to Yasnaya Polyana. "The very thought of meeting the son of one of the most remarkable men of the nineteenth century," as Father wrote, so excited and inspired him that he sat right down and composed a short article on the single tax.

The meeting was touching. Henry George, Jr., was struck, so he told the correspondents, by Father's amazing memory and good spirits, his deep knowledge of George's books, his charm, his love of nature, and his fearlessness with regard to death.

When Father was taking leave of George he said: "I shall die

soon. What do you want me to tell your father in the other world?"
"Tell him," answered George, "that I am carrying on his work."

The presence of my brother Lev in Yasnaya Polyana at this time did not lighten the burden for Father. Lev was nervous, vain, forever throwing himself from one thing to another. At one time he was carried away by music, at another by literature; he even evolved his own theories of hygiene. He would tackle any subject with a categorical self-assurance, without thinking it through. One had to have Father's sweetness and patience to tolerate Lev's pronouncements, such as that the peasants did not need the land at all, or that public order could not be maintained without the death penalty.

Needing a rest, Father went over to the Sukhotins', thereby offending Lev, who was at work modeling a bust of him. Tanya had rented a cottage in a village in the province of Orel, three miles from the Sukhotin estate, and here he could see Chertkov who, despite an appeal to the Emperor, was still forbidden to set foot in Tula. Father's stay with Tanya was briefer than it would have been had not Mother insisted on his return.

The police guards were still keeping order at home. Once when I was passing the big pond I heard cries and saw a group of peasants collected on the shore. When I came closer I saw that a man I recognized was being arrested by the police guard for fishing in the pond with a dragnet. The peasant, wet and blue with cold, was doing his best to explain that he was fishing on the peasants' side and not on the "master's." The guard would not listen but snatched the dragnet out of his hands and struck him several blows with his whip.

I saw red: "You wretch! How dare you!" I yelled. The guard made some brazen retort. When I thrust myself between him and the peasant he was forced to give way, but as soon as I left he arrested the man and held him, wet as he was, for two hours until Mother ordered his release.

Shortly afterward I received a summons; I was charged with insulting an officer while he was performing his official duty. I did not talk with the police captain who came to Yasnaya Polyana, but sent a message to say that if the police considered me guilty, let them have me tried. A charge was drawn up and the next day I went to the Governor's office. The affair was expunged from the record and shortly thereafter the police guards were removed from Yasnaya Polyana.

In the place of the guards there appeared a mounted Circassian, with a fur cap cocked on the back of his head: a Circassian with a whip.

In order to understand what happened in this last year of Father's life, what had been in the making for years, it is useful to recall a letter he wrote to Mother in 1885 when life in our family began to move along two different lines:

"Since it is impossible to tear out of me the thing by which I live, and to return to the past, how can we do away with these sufferings, yours and mine, which derive from my incurable insanity? There is only one solution, whether you look on my point of view as madness or the truth: You must penetrate into this point of view, study, and understand it. And that very thing, unfortunately . . . was not only never done by you nor, following your example, by the children, but it has become something you have even grown to fear. You have elaborated a way of forgetting, not seeing, not understanding, not admitting the existence of this point of view, of looking at it as you would some interesting thought, but not as the key to understanding a human being.

"So it happened that when this spiritual upheaval took place in me, and my inner life was transformed, you did not ascribe any significance or importance to it, you did not even consider what was going on inside me, unfortunately you fell in with the general opinion that a writer and an artist . . . should produce artistically wrought works, and not think about his own life, not better it, that that sort of thing is a kind of folly, or a spiritual malady; and by accepting that state of mind you immediately put yourself in opposition to what for me meant salvation from despair and aversion toward life. . . .

"My writings are all of me. In my own life I could not express my views fully, in my own life I make compromises because of the necessity of living with my family; I live [with them] but in my soul I reject all this life, for what you think my life is, is not my life, and my life, as expressed in my writings, you think is just so many words, lacking all reality. Our whole discord has been caused by the fateful mistake you made eight years ago when you looked upon the overturn which took place in me, an overturn which led me out of the field of dreams and phantoms into real life, when you looked upon that as unnatural, accidental, temporary, fantastic, onesided, something not to be looked into, analyzed, but something you must fight with all your strength. And you have fought it for eight years, the result of that struggle being that I suffer more than ever, but I not only do not abandon my previous attitude, I am going farther in the same direction and I am getting exhausted by this struggle, moreover by my suffering I cause you all to suffer. . . . This is a struggle between us to the death—are we to go God's way or not. . . ."

With the years the breach had widened, the struggle had become acute, mutual understanding more hopelsss. "I find it bad to live because life is bad," Father wrote. "Life is bad because people, because we, live badly." There was no way out.

65

HOW difficult it is to recognize spiritual illness in a person close to you, especially if the habit of years has established that person's power and authority. Had I realized that my mother was ill, my whole attitude toward her would have been different. But people far more experienced than I were equally blind.

With every day Mother grew more nervous. Everything irritated her, made her weep, have hysterics, outbursts of temper. The causes were varied and inexplicable. Her interests shifted constantly, skimming the surface of life: at one time she dried flowers, at another she took to drawing, or, no one knew why, she began to wash and seal up the double window frames for the winter, or she wrote her memoirs. Whenever she entered a roomful of people, they became tense in expectation of some unpleasantness. Her tendency toward self-pity—which her sister Tanya teased her about when young—was now unbearably aggravated.

In early July of 1909 Father received an invitation to the eighteenth Peace Congress in Stockholm. He alone could present the case for universal disarmament, and the outlawing of war so that the world would listen, and he considered it his duty to go. Yet when Father explained his intention, Mother stated firmly that she would not let him. She screamed, she wept, she threatened to kill herself.

"I was unable to sleep until two o'clock and later," he wrote in his diary. "I woke up feeling weak. . . . S. A. did not sleep at all. I went in to see her. It was rather senseless. . . . I am tired and cannot go on, I feel quite ill. I feel it is impossible to maintain an attitude of reason and affection, completely impossible. . . . Now then show your Christianity, *c'est le moment ou jamais*, and I yearn so to go away. It is improbable that there is anyone here that has need of my presence. The sacrifice is difficult and harmful to all. Help me, O Lord and teach me. The one thing I desire is to do—not my will but Thine."

A few days later he made another note: "After dinner I mentioned the journey to Sweden, and it raised a storm of irritation. She wanted to poison herself with morphine; I tore it out of her hands and threw it under the staircase. But when I went to bed and turned things over quietly in my mind I decided to give up the journey. I went in and told her. She is pitiful, I am truly sorry for her. Yet how instructive this is. I did not undertake anything except inner work on my own self; and as soon as I took myself in hand everything cleared up."

Mother's excitement on this occasion was heightened by another problem. She intended starting a lawsuit against the publishers of Father's works, but she was not certain of her rights in the matter.

This summer we had as our guests Lenochka, the youngest daughter of Auntie Maria Nikolayevna, her husband Denisenko who was the presiding judge of the court in Novocherkassk, and their two charming children.

My mother asked Denisenko for legal advice: was her old power of attorney from Father, authorizing her to publish and sell his works, still valid? When Denisenko replied in the negative, Mother again lost her temper. "You don't care if your family has to go begging!" she screamed at Father. "You want to give all rights to Chertkov, and let your grandchildren starve!"

The fact that Andrei and Ilya were in debt and always asking Mother for help also affected her nerves. The only way she could see to help her family was to obtain all the rights to Father's work. She feared especially for the unpublished work written after 1881, as Father regularly gave Chertkov his manuscripts and copies of his diaries. But nothing would move Father to grant her demands, though the tension in the house rose and there was no rest for him either by day or night. In her morbid frenzy, she would even burst into his room in the middle of the night screaming that he was killing her. Not only was she breaking the last strand which bound her to Father, but she was also systematically shortening his life.

On Father's suggestion, Chertkov did not come to Yasnaya Polyana during this period. "You will understand, dear friend," Father wrote him, "the whole burden of the personal sacrifice I am making, I hope only temporarily, in being deprived of intercourse with you, but I know that you love not me, Lev Nikolayevich, but my soul. And my soul is—your soul, and its demands are identical. . . ." And on July 16: "The fact that Sophia Andreyevna did not let me come to you would seem somewhat humiliating, embarrassing if I did not know that it was not Sophia Andreyevna who was preventing my coming to you, but God. . . ."

And again: "If she (my wife) only knew and realized how she is poisoning the last hours, days, months of life. . . ."

But of course she could not know that the end was so near, and that what she feared most was about to happen.

Poor Judge Denisenko, the kindest of men, found himself between two fires. Father now requested him to draw up a formal testament, in which he renounced all property rights in his own works.

I saw the unending struggle taking place in Father; the patience and love he brought to daily trials. He expected the same things of me, saying: "To whom much is given, from him much is expected." When I protested, "It wasn't given to me, Papa, I cannot do it," he would reply, "Well, make an effort beyond your 'I cannot do it.' . . ." Yet even he fell short at times.

"I have been leading a bad life, I have not been kind," he wrote Chertkov on August 2, "and as soon as there is no love—there is no joy, no life, no God. There is only a hole in the bucket—and all the water runs out. . . . Yes, God—is love, and that is to me such a clear indubitable truth, yet . . . to demonstrate love in life is not easy for us wretched people . . . because in fulfilling one demand of love we destroy another. The only salvation lies in living only in the present, in carrying one's cross every day, hour, minute. Yet I am so bad, I yearn more and more for death."

Although Father had deferred to Mother in not going to Stockholm, he still pressed himself to finish his address to the world Congress. But the Congress was postponed because of a workers' strike in Sweden, and when it was eventually held Tolstoy's address was not even mentioned. Father was disillusioned. "There is falseness everywhere," he said. "People fear the truth, they have lost the habit of it. On the one hand they gather together to establish peace . . . but they discuss increased armaments."

Things were much easier when Auntie Maria Nikolayevna came to Yasnaya Polyana. Auntie did not interfere in family matters, but her very presence was sufficient to restrain Mother. We all enjoyed a respite.

One evening Goldenweiser came over and Father sat down with him to play a game of chess. Suddenly my poodle Marquis began to bark angrily, and carriage wheels rattled up to our entrance. It was the district police officer, the police captain, and some guards come to arrest Gusev. In the warrant, which Father demanded to see, it was stated that Gusev was being exiled for two years to Cherdyn in the province of Perm for "revolutionary" activity. Everyone came running in, all the servants, Father went into his study with Gusev. In the half hour allowed him, Gusev quickly turned over his papers and packed. Father was silent, only his face was paler than usual. I stuffed *War and Peace* into Gusev's bag. He had never read it, for it was a literary piece of work which lacked, from his point of view, all religious and philosophical significance. "It will brighten your journey," I whispered. Still in silence, fighting tears, Father embraced and kissed Gusev, then went upstairs. The carriage drove off.

"Phoo!" our nun Auntie spat after the police. "What have they arrested such a kind man for! phoo! phoo!"

Father wrote in his diary: "Yesterday evening the bandits came for Gusev and carried him off. His going off was very nice: the attitude of all of them to him and his to us. Everything was very nice. I have now written a statement about this."

Father was physically more weak than the people who came to see him in a never-ending stream realized. With each one he found some point of contact. With Parkhomenko, who was painting his portrait, he talked about art. With members of the Duma, Vasili Maklakov and others, he developed his ideas for agrarian reform, looking toward the introduction of a bill establishing the single tax of Henry George.

Weary of everything, and longing to see Chertkov, Father decided to go for a visit to the estate of Krekshino near Moscow, where the Chertkovs were living. Dushan, Ilya Vasilievich and I accompanied him. But from the beginning the trip proved to be a mistake.

Despite a refusal of permission, news photographers were on hand to record Tolstoy's departure. They hid in the bushes, then pursued us along the road to the railroad station. In Moscow we had expected to find my brother Sergei and his wife, but they were not there. Instead, the arrival of a correspondent of the newspaper *Russian Word* precipitated an outburst from Father, who was indignant with the publisher of the paper, Sytin, for holding up his last anthology *For Every Day*. . . . Finally, when he arrived at the Chertkovs' among people congenial to him, he still had no opportunity to rest. There was music to listen to from an amazing new invention, the Mignon player-piano, which accurately reproduced the works of Chopin, Strauss and others by master pianists; two violinists and later a quartet came to entertain with his favorite pieces by Haydn, Mozart, Beethoven; a group of teachers from a neighboring school wanted his views on education; peasants from nearby villages visited him, also people from Moscow. . . . All this gave him pleasure, but there was no real rest.

Then a few days later Mother arrived. Nothing was to her taste at the Chertkovs': the "dark people" who surrounded Father, the general dining table where Ilya Vasilievich ate his meals with her. Her nerves were in a dreadful condition. What she did not know was that here in Krekshino Father had decided to write his testament.

In this testament Father waived all rights to his works written after 1881, making them free to anyone who chose to publish them, and he gave editorial authority to Chertkov. I copied the testament, Father and three witnesses signed it. Keeping the original, I gave one copy to Chertkov, who asked me to check on the validity of the document with an attorney in Moscow.

When he left the Chertkovs' Father wished to return directly to Yasnaya Polyana without going through Moscow. But even this drew a protest, tears and reproaches from Mother. For some reason she insisted that Father stop over in Moscow for at least one day.

I was afraid of this stopover, and with reason as it turned out. The news that Tolstoy was to be in the city spread with lightning rapidity. We were met by a crowd at the Bryansk railroad station, and correspondents and photographers literally blocked our way.

The two days in Moscow were spent with my brother Sergei and his wife and several friends. The first evening, at Father's suggestion, we attended the movies, but by a piece of ill luck, the picture was impossibly stupid. As we came out of the theater, Father said: "What a powerful medium this could be in schools, to learn geography, the life of nations, but . . . they make it so trivial, like everything else."

The next day I dashed over to the attorney Muravyov with Father's signed testament. After reading it carefully, he said it had no validity —that it was impossible to will rights to literary works to everyone, but he would think the matter over and prepare a testament having legal power.

Meantime a demonstration in honor of Father was in preparation. People called all day to ask: What train was Tolstoy taking to Yasnaya Polyana? When I refused a definite reply, remembering Kharkov, my mother grew angry, took the telephone herself and announced the exact time of departure.

The next morning we left the house in a landau drawn by a pair of horses—Father, Mother and I. (Chertkov would join us on the train and accompany us as far as Serpukhovo.) But we were unable to drive up to the Kursk station because of thousands of people who crammed the square, waiting for Father. The carriage was stopped, a sea of heads engulfed us, heads were bared. Maklakov met us and we started to walk toward the entrance of the station. The students made a chain but the crowd broke through. At the entrance we were so crushed we could not breathe. Even my broad shoulders were powerless to protect Father. Maklakov and a huge policeman came to our aid. The crowd actually carried us or pushed us out to the platform. Here people were hanging on the posts, scrambling over the tops of the cars. . . .

Father was white as a sheet and his lower jaw was trembling as he stood bowing to the cheering crowd. The train pulled out. Father lay down, intending to nap, but we soon realized that he had fainted in his sleep. His pulse was so weak that we thought he was dying.

Even at home Father was unconscious, but sat in an armchair babbling incomprehensible words.

"Lyovochka," Mother kept badgering him, "Lyovochka, where are the keys?"

"I don't understand. . . . What for?"

"The keys, the keys to the drawer with the manuscripts!"

"Mama," I begged, "please let him be, don't make him force his memory. . . . Please!"

"But I have to have the keys," she said excitedly, "he will die and the manuscripts will be stolen."

"No one will steal them, let him be, I implore you!"

Dushan and I undressed him and practically carried him to bed. We put his head down, got hot water bottles, and Dushan gave him a subcutaneous injection.

Late that night he recovered.

The new testament, drawn up by Muravyov, was signed by Father on November 1, 1909.

At first he had thought to leave the rights to his works to the three of us who were closest to him, Seryozha, Tanya and me, with the understanding that we would in turn give them over for general use. But when I came into his study one morning he said suddenly: "Sasha, I have decided to make my will solely in your favor."

I was silent, thinking of the tremendous responsibility, the attacks to be expected from the family, the offense to my older brothers and sister. At the same time I felt pride, happiness that he wished to confide such a trust to me.

I told him my doubts.

"No, I have decided it that way," he said firmly. "You are the last one now to remain with me, and it is entirely natural that I entrust this matter to you. But in the case of your death," here he smiled gently, "the rights will pass to Tanya."

On July 22, 1910, in the forest several miles away from the house, the will was signed. Sitting on a stump, Father copied it out from beginning to end in his own hand. The witnesses were Radynski, Sergeyenko, junior, and Goldenweiser.

It was not easy for Father to decide on this step, not easy for him to conceal his decision from his family. But he had firmly decided on this way to make amends for the sin, as he called it, of having sold his works.

Once when he was going to bed and I was in his study, he called through the closed door to me.

"Sasha!"

"Yes, Papa."

"I wanted to say this about my testament. . . . If any money is left over from the first edition of my works, it would be good to buy Yasnaya Polyana from Mama and your brothers and turn it over to the peasants. . . ."

He never mentioned this again to me, but I later carried out his wish.

❧ 66 ❧

THE presence of Tanya and her daughter, Tanichka, at Yasnaya Polyana helped to calm Mother down. She adored her grand-daughter, who was an amusing, intelligent, snub-nosed little creature, and she spent days on end taking care of her. To replace Gusev, Chertkov sent Father a new secretary toward the end of January. This was a student by the name of V. F. Bulgakov, a jolly, buoyant youth, a bit in love with himself.

Father continued busy with people and problems of interest to him. Since early fall of 1909 he had been in correspondence with a young Hindu, Mahatma Gandhi, then in London. Explaining the "Black Law" in effect in South Africa, which virtually made slaves of the Hindus, Gandhi wrote:

"I, as well as some of my friends, have for some time firmly believed in the teaching of nonresistance to evil by force, and we still believe in it. Besides, it has fallen to my good luck to study your writings, which have profoundly affected my outlook on life." He went on to say that he was winning British Hindus to his point of view in respect to the situation in the Transvaal, that as a result of the Black Law nearly half of the Hindu population there was emigrating and of the remainder nearly 2,500 proposed to suffer imprisonment rather than submit. At the time of writing there were about 100 passive resisters in the Tranvsaal prisons. In conclusion, Gandhi asked Father to send him his "Letter to a Hindu," with the idea of distributing 20,000 copies of it in India.

"May God help our dear brothers and colleagues in the Transvaal," Father wrote to Gandhi. "This same struggle between the gentle and the brutal, between meekness and love, and pride and violence, is developing here more and more with every day, especially in one of the sharpest encounters between religious and worldly law —in the refusals to do military service. These refusals are becoming more and more frequent. . . ."

Later, Gandhi sent Father his book *Indian Home Rule*. Commenting on it in a letter to Chertkov, Father said: "He [Gandhi] is a man very much akin to us, to me. . . ."

D. P. Makovitski's notes also evidence Father's keen interest in Gandhi and his book: ". . . a profound condemnation, from the point of view of a religious Hindu, of all European civilization."

Who did not come to see Father in this last year! Japanese, Europeans, American journalists, peasants, a colonel from the Black Hundred organization, some kind of crank, a spy who naïvely counted on Tolstoy's approval because he had shot at some revolutionaries, and many others.

During the winter Professor Masaryk visited him again and they talked of religion. "Masaryk is after all a professor," Father commented in his diary, "and he believes in a personal God and the immortality of the personality."

Leonid Andreyev came down from Moscow. Probably the people who had met this much petted and popular writer in the literary and artistic circles of the city would have been astonished to see him in Yasnaya Polyana. Here he was shy, embarrassed. There was not a shade of his usual self-assurance, aplomb, when he was talking with Father; his large, beautiful eyes were fixed in awe-struck attention. Although he was not essentially interested in the questions which preoccupied Tolstoy, he immediately succumbed to Father's charm, sought subjects to his liking, was diffident. In this way he insinuated himself into Father's favor. But though Father found Andreyev agreeable, he immediately sensed that he had "no serious attitude toward life" and that he "touched on this question superficially," questions dealing with religion, with the spiritual life of man.

In January Dorik Sukhotin, Tanya's stepson, came down with measles, which little Tanichka and I caught from him. The children had light cases, but with me the disease developed into a serious form of pneumonia. Physically I was in a bad way, with stabbing pains in my chest and sides and a high fever. Varya nursed me day and night. Sometimes Father would stay alone with me. He would give me water, straighten my pillows.

In flashing moments of consciousness I was aware of his bent figure in the half dark of the room. "Papenka!" Then he would come over. "I want a drink!" His old hand would tremble, the water spill. I would kiss his hand. "Thank you." He would sniffle, take my hand, press it to his lips. "Why are you crying? I am all right, Papa." But he could not restrain his sobs and would move away, loudly clearing his throat.

February 15 he wrote in his diary: "Sasha is touching and disturbing. I am both glad that I love her and angry at myself because my affection is too exclusive. I write and yet I am alarmed. May His will be done."

"February 16. Sasha is no better, I am bracing myself."

Early in March I was on my feet. Bulgakov now was answering letters and helping Father put together the booklets comprising *The Path of Life*, which on Father's insistence were not to be published by "dreadful" Sytin but "kind" Ivan Ivanovich Gorbunov of The Mediator. The booklets contained the treasures of man's spiritual thought: "The concept of God, of the spiritual origin of all things, is such a grand and necessary concept . . ." Father wrote in his diary, "an immense step taken by mankind, yet we imagine that because we have radium, airplanes, electricity, we can manage without it. Yes, we can, but only as animals, not as human beings, as we now live in our cities like New York, London, Paris with their thirty-storied buildings."

He developed this thought in a note later where he speaks of the corruption of peoples—Hindus, Chinese, Negroes—brought about by civilization. "Machines do what? Telegraph and telephone, to transmit what? Schools, universities, academies, to teach what? Meetings, to discuss what? Books, newspapers, to spread information about what? Railroads for whom to travel where? Millions of persons gathered together and subjected to one power, to do what? Hospitals, doctors, pharmacies to prolong life, but prolong it to what purpose?

"Millions are suffering physically and spiritually so that those who have just seized the power may without let or hindrance become corrupted. To this end there are the lie of religion, the lie of science, the stupefying effect of drunkenness and education, and where these do not suffice—there are brute forces, prisons, executions."

In addition to *The Path of Life*, Father tried to write a short play for the young people living in the Chertkovs' house in Telyatinki, *All Qualities Come from It,* and I, just out of bed, took up my customary work of copying. But I had little strength; I was bothered by a cough and weakened by night sweats.

On March 22 Father wrote in his diary: "It is now after nine, I

am a little better. Sasha is still ailing, she is not well. I feel inwardly very much at ease. This clarity of thought is good. I wish
I could express it; but even if I don't—it's good anyhow. Tanya is
sweet and very pleasant to me."

Pleasant as it was to be near Father while ill, I was terrified
when Koch bacilli were found in my sputum. The doctors diagnosed
it as tuberculosis of the upper lobes of both lungs, and prescribed
immediate departure from the springtime dampness of Yasnaya
Polyana, for Crimea. A separation from Father. Would it be for
long? And what if he fell ill without me? How much longer would
he live? On the other hand, what if I did not go, but went on in
this weakened form, half crippled, and not capable of helping him?

It was a difficult parting for both of us.

"It's hard," he wrote in his diary, "and I don't know what to
do. Sasha has gone. I love her, I miss her—not for my work, but
in my heart. The Goldenweisers came to see her off. He played.
Now it's twelve. I am going to bed. My spirits are still low. Look
sharp, keep your chin up, Lev Nikolayevich."

We agreed to write each other every day. Father always wrote
at the end of the day, giving me what news there was, cautioning
me to keep up my courage and report regularly on my state of
health.*

"April 15, 1910. I want to write you, dear friend Sasha, but I
don't know what to write. I know that you would much rather hear
about me and to write about myself is distasteful, nor should I
write about how dear you are to me, thereby committing the sin
of exclusive love, yet I will do it because I am thinking in those
terms now.

"My inner state during these days, and particularly on the day
you went away, has been a struggle against a physically jaundiced
state. This state is good for one because it offers much material for
work, but the bad part of it is that it interferes with clear thinking,
the ability to express one's thoughts, but I am accustomed to that.
Today is the first day that I am better, but I am writing only letters: I haven't yet written to Shaw and some others. G[orbunov]
is busy with the booklets which are already in page proof form and
are a delight to me. Salamakhin has just been, and still is, here
and he also is a delight to me with his serious, religious nature. Why

* The letters which follow have never before appeared in print.

[486]

people are born only to die as children, why the life of some is full of poverty, yet rich in culture, why others live a life luxurious but illiterate, why there are all these seeming inequalities—all that I can explain. Yet why are some people, like Salamakhin, all on fire, i.e., his whole life is guided by religion, while another man or woman, like a spoon has no notion of the food into which it dips.

"Yesterday I went out riding with Bulgakov and today with Dushan. Delir was gentle. The weather is wonderful, Lenka's violets here on my table are enveloping me with their fragrance. And how are things with you? I seem to hear that it's rather cold. You or Varya please write every day.

"I am terribly anxious, more than I have been for a long time, to do something, you know what it is—to picture the senselessness of our lives under the title: 'There Are No Guilty Ones in the World,' and I have an idea for it. I am terribly anxious to do this but I have not yet made a start. I am afraid that this is false appetite. But the mornings are really very distracting. I'd like to make a try. Well, it's not important. Good-by, we have just finished dinner. There is a passing visitor waiting in Dushan's room to talk with me. I am going up to him. I kiss you, and for the sake of brevity, Varya too. Lev."

"April 21, 1910. The letter just come from Varya about you is not good. Don't lose your courage, dearie. All will be well, if you yourself are well, and you can be, you know this, you desire and you know how to be well. Write me more often. Do not believe the doctors. And try to arrange your life more healthfully. . . .

"Sometimes I find it hard, you know why, but I try not to be altogether bad. It is painful to go past your room. It is now nearly midnight, Tuesday, and I am going to bed. I expect a letter from you tomorrow. Greetings to Varya. I love you, as I should not do. Dushan is, as always, a joy. L. T."

"April 22, 1910. I have just received your letter, dear daughter and friend. And I was a little inclined to weep, not out of pity for you or myself, but from emotion because you think so well. Whatever happens, although in all probability things will turn out well, everything will be for the best. Please write more often and without thinking about me, but write as if it were in a diary, about your impressions and thoughts, principally—about the thoughts and feel-

[487]

ings which come to you, or else just about people, about food, about anything that occurs and how it occurred. I am a most condescending judge of your writings. When you are heavyhearted think about using your life to the full, i.e., to be filled with love on what you do and say and think, filled with love toward everyone, and whatever is to happen will happen and all will be well.

"At home we are never without guests. Now the Goldenweisers have come, tomorrow Sibor will arrive. I am well. There is a lot I want to write, but I have quite lost my head with so many things to do. And thank God I am grateful. I love Varya for herself, but even more because she loves you. Good-by, darling. L. T."

"April 23, 1910. We have just received, dear Sasha, your letter to Mother. Please write each day, either you or Varya, the simplest kind of letters about the state of your health, your temperature, cough, etc. But if this is a bore, never mind, Olya probably writes you about the music. Things are all right here. I am not riding, and I have put Delir in with the herd, but I go out walking with your dogs and I am all right. See to it that you are all right, you can do it, my dear. My thanks to Varya. L. T."

"April 24, 1910. You are so close to my heart, Sasha dear, that I cannot write you every day. There is no especial news here; yesterday we had some magnificent music, which I always feel so deeply, and I always reproach myself for the luxury of it. At present I feel unwell physically, as it usually happens from time to time with me: I am drowsy, have heartburn, and no appetite. It is now nearly midnight, I have signed my letters and am going to bed. I am just sending a telegram to The Mediator. It has been in existence twenty-five years. L. T."

"April 25, 1910. No letter from you today, but still I am writing you, dear friend Sasha. I was feeling weak yesterday but today I have recovered, especially my spirits are very good. How I wish that you, although you cannot do so at twenty-five, should feel as well off as I do at eighty-two—it is good to be completely independent of my body and from everything that surrounds me. For two days now I have scarcely been able to do any work, nor have I had any thoughts of value, but in my heart I have felt joyously calm, free.—Although it is awkward to talk by myself—I have no word

[488]

of you—I do what I can. I have the habit in the evening, before I go to bed, of writing in my diary and a little letter to you. I have just had a note from Chertkov who hopes he will be allowed to go to the Sukhotins' and that is very pleasing to me. Good-by until we see each other, not soon, but still until we meet. I kiss you. Greetings to Varya. L. T.

"Now see to it you let us hear from you as often as possible, and as truthfully and with as much detail as possible. I expect only good news, strange as it may seem, above all in the spiritual realm, in the things that lie in our, in your, power. The physical cannot be either good or bad. I kiss you. Thank Varya (for caring) for you. L. T."

No date noted. "I am writing you if only a word or two, Sasha my dear. It is now almost midnight, Friday. I am getting ready for bed. My spirits are not good, yet aside from your illness and your absence there is so much that is good, that even the most jaundiced person could not fail to be gladdened. Bulgakov is a very good helper and is so warmhearted that I am at ease with him and every day there are visits and letters from people who are so close to me even if I do not know them that it is impossible not to be gladdened. How is your life? I'd like to think that even down there you are doing some inner, spiritual work. That is more important than anything else. Although you are young you can and should do it.

"Dear young Dima and old Dima [Chertkov] have just rented a cottage on the other side of Serpukhovo. I hope to visit them. Tanya is, as always, dear and good. I kiss you. Greetings to Varya. L. T."

"May 2nd, 1910. I am writing you, Sasha dearie, from Kochety, in the evening of the 2nd. I came here with Dushan and Bulgakov. The weather is wonderful, the Sukhotins are dears and everything is gladness, I can even think of you without pain, but . . . I am afraid. Here I am writing cheerfully when suddenly there might be bad news of you. Mama was a little displeased that I did not postpone my visit for a day, still she let me leave without any fuss. She will come over on the 4th, the day after tomorrow, if nothing detains her. I confess that for many, many reasons I'd like to leave Yasnaya. There is so much commotion, many visitors, and there are other reasons. Yet just now there was a visitor there whom I re-

[489]

gretted having to leave so soon. I scarcely had time for a quarter of an hour's talk with him. This was Shnyakin, who refused [to do his military service] and spent four years in the penal ranks—such a lover of good, such a serene, steady and happy person. He is powerful, reticent, a worker, does not waste his words, but everything he says is worth while, necessary and kind, and he has such a radiant smile. Along the way here it was unpleasant being gaped at, but here it is wonderful. I am expecting Chertkov. The Tanyas, great and small, are so sweet, and Mikhail Sergeyevich is pleasant, so that one could not ask for more. The bad part of it is that your letters to me and mine to you will now take longer to arrive. *Raison de plus* for writing more often, which is what I am doing. . . ."

"May 7, 1910. I was unwell yesterday, felt weak and that is why I did not write, dear Sasha. Yesterday at last I received your two letters and now another one. Thank you. Now I feel better and I have received the very great pleasure of having Chertkov arrive, he will stay for a week. Also Mama, who intended to come Friday, put off her coming on account of bad weather. Your news is good, but I fear you let yourself be influenced by the doctors and dear Varya. Beware of this, dearie. It's too bad that you have been obliged to eat meat. It's so good to be with C[hertkov]. He is such a friend. His only shortcoming is—the same as yours, both you and he are too fond of me. I cannot reproach you for this because I am guilty of the same thing. L. T."

I was happy that Father was visiting Tanya, where he felt so content. But on May 20, with Tanya and Chertkov, he returned to Yasnaya Polyana, and the annoyances began again. The peasant women complained because the Circassian guard would not let them pass, there were many people with requests which Father found it hard to refuse, in the evenings visitors came just to watch his lips, expecting prophecies to fall. "It is hard to bear," Father wrote in his diary. "It's a strain to speak . . . when one is obliged to do so."

Meanwhile my stay in the Crimea was drawing to a close. I implored our friend Dr. Altschuler to allow me to go home. I had no temperature, my strength had come back, all that remained was a slight cough.

When finally I ran into Father's study we both laughed and cried from joy.

I had brought Father a present: while in the sanatorium Varya had taught me stenography. I could take down eighty-five words a minute.

Only one thing distressed me. I had had to cut off my hair, which fell out in handfuls after the measles, and Father, I knew, did not like women with short hair. Nevertheless, he stroked my head, which was dark and woolly as a sheep.

"Bobbed or shaven—I don't care. I am so, so glad," he said.

67

When we are come to St. Mary of the Angels, wet through with rain, frozen with cold, and foul with mire and tormented with hunger; and when we knock at the door, the doorkeeper cometh in a rage and saith, "Who are ye?" and we say, "We are two of your friars," and he answers, "Ye tell not true; ye are rather two knaves that go deceiving the world and stealing the alms of the poor; begone!" and he openeth not to us, and maketh us stay outside hungry and cold all night in the rain and snow; then if we endure patiently such cruelty, such abuse and such insolent dismissal without complaint or murmuring, and believe humbly and charitably that that doorkeeper truly knows us, and that God maketh him to rail against us; O Friar Leo, write—there is perfect joy.

ST. FRANCIS OF ASSISI

There was no way to protect Father from aggravations and worry. The estate was running along at a loss, the managers were stealing. The Circassian guard continued to hunt down peasants who crossed "the Count's possessions," he got into fights, he caught a former pupil of Father's as the old man was carrying off some poles from the forest and haled him, tied to his whip, all the way to the main house. Father happened in on the scene.

All this had its effect. Father was growing weaker, his fainting spells recurred.

"What's the use of being concerned about external conditions—

[491]

about food, shirts, etc.," my sister Tanya wrote Mother, "if one is not concerned over Father's inner life?"

Tanya advised her to give up the estate, and Sergei's wife Masha suggested turning over all rights in it to the brothers; then Father, Mother and I could move to the Crimea.

As I was leaving Father's study with manuscripts one day, he stopped me.

"Sasha, I have something I want to say to you, but do not be hurt. . . ." He sighed deeply. "I have prepared myself to die. . . ."

But soon he was getting ready to go to Moscow to visit the Chertkovs at their Meshcherski estate. Dushan, Ilya Vasilievich and I went with him.

As always when he found himself in different surroundings Father revived, became gay and began to write. He sketched out a little story entitled "Unawares."

> Writer pacing down the floor
> Unaware of trunk by door
> Carried by his thought along
> Stumbled, fell in it headlong.

Gaily reciting his jingle, he waved the manuscript in the air before handing it to me to copy.

He was interested in everything: in the excellent setup of the rural schools, in the hospitals of the province of Moscow; in the magnificent equipment one hospital had for the care of psychiatric cases. He visited this hospital several times, talked with the patients and the physicians. It was evident that the problem of insanity was on his mind. In his diary and in his article "Insanity" he attempted to find a definition for madness.

"Madness is always the result of irrational and therefore immoral living," he noted in his diary. "This seems to be so, but I must check on it, think about it." And farther on: "Crazed persons are always better able to achieve their purposes than the sane. This derives from the fact that for them there are no moral obstacles; no shame, no veracity, no conscience, nor even any fear."

Our quiet was soon destroyed. I received a telegram from Varya: "Serious nervous upset, insomnia, weeping, pulse 100, requests wire. Varya." After a second telegram Father decided to return to Yasnaya Polyana.

It is difficult to describe the state in which we found Mother. It was the delirium of a psychically ill woman, aggravated now by information just received that the authorities would permit Chertkov to live at Telyatinki as long as his mother was visiting him. There were reproaches, shrieks, sobbing, ignoble insinuations, threats of suicide. No one was able to sleep. I wanted to stay in Father's bedroom to try to protect him in some way. "Go away," he said gently. These scenes went on without let-up day and night.

On the second day after our return Mother ran from the hall down the stairs screaming, "What's there? Who's there?" as if someone were chasing her. Father's desperate cry of "Where has she gone, where?" sent Dushan and me after her. We found her lying on the stone floor in the store room, pressing a vial of opium over her lips. "One little swallow, only one swallow," she was muttering.

Mother wanted Father's promise that he would turn over to her all of his diaries and give up seeing Chertkov. She was provoked by having come across a note in his diary to the effect that "Sonya is again wrought up and hysterical; I decided I must use love in struggling with her."

I was exhausted—by my own helplessness, by the indignation and irritation I felt for Mother, and by the boundless pity I felt for Father.

Mother proposed to take Father to my brother Sergei's in Nikolskoye where he would be farther removed from Chertkov, and Father reluctantly consented. Tanya joined us there. Again we held family councils, sought advice, yet nothing was actually decided. No one paid any attention to my plea that we temporarily separate our parents, or that one of the older children come to live at Yasnaya Polyana.

No sooner did we return home than Mother lapsed again into her hysterical condition. Even the saintly Dushan was indignant: "Sophia Andreyevna does not consider that Lev Nikolayevich is scarcely able to keep going, his heart is giving out." Only dear old Maria Alexandrovna Schmidt looked upon Mother as ill and unhappy, and she felt an entirely unforced sympathy for her. Morally she was on Father's side, but she felt that this ordeal had been sent to him, that he was bearing it with Christian humility and that that was how things should be. In much the same way she had borne the blow when some time before she had learned that her tiny cottage was burned to the ground along with everything she possessed, including Father's manuscripts that she had copied for so many, many years. Even Shavochka (the lame dog she had once taken in when his feet were frozen during a severe cold snap) was burned up.

Tanya immediately gave orders that a new cottage be built for the old lady; she provided her, as Maria Alexandrovna put it, with "a whole new dowry." Yet none could replace her loss. "Dear God! dear God!" she kept whispering. "My little Shavochka . . . the letters of dear Lev Nikolayevich . . . the manuscripts . . ."

Occasionally Father would come to my room and stretch himself out on the sofa while I continued my typing. Neither of us spoke. As he said, "We understand everything without words. If one spoke, it would be superfluous."

My brother Lev arrived but, unfortunately, he did not bring any peace with him.

On July 11 Father wrote in his diary: "Scarcely, scarcely alive. A horrible night. Until four o'clock, and Lev was worst of all. He scolded me as if I were a bad little boy and ordered me to go into the garden after Sophia Andreyevna. . . . I cannot see Lev with equanimity. I am still bad. Sonya, poor thing, has calmed down. It is a cruel and hard sickness. Lord, help me to carry on with love. . . ."

That evening, after the session with Lev, Father said to me: "I even think he called me scum." His eyes were clouded with tears. "I always thought that when a person smites you on one cheek and you offer the other—the one who smites will then recover his senses, stop, and realize the meaning of your act. But no. On the contrary, he will reflect and say: What a good thing I smote him; he feels his guilt and all my superiority over him.—Yet I know that it is better for everyone concerned to offer, if one can, the other cheek when one has been smitten on the first. Herein lies 'the perfect joy.' Do your part, then you can only be grateful for what appears to be sorrow."

It relieved Father to have the older children there, so I again sent for Tanya. We had long talks together. "What Father is achieving now is a feat of love, and better than all the thirty volumes of his writings," she said. "Even if he dies suffering as he is suffering, I would say he could not have acted otherwise."

When I repeated this to Father, he said, "Tanichka is a wise little person," and burst into tears.

Once when Father was sitting in the big Voltaire armchair I went by and he smiled, saying something in a low voice which I did not catch. "What is it, Papa?" I asked. "My lasses are a good lot," he whispered.

But then even Tanya's presence failed to have a pacifying effect. Mother made certain clear-cut demands: either Father would take the diaries away from Chertkov or she would not cease tormenting herself and everyone else with her "illness."

It was with these demands that she came into his room one night. He looked exhausted, emaciated, scarcely able to hold himself upright. He did not sleep the rest of the night, and toward morning he wrote Mother a letter:

"1. My present diaries I shall not give to anyone, I shall keep them myself.

"2. I shall take the old diaries away from Chertkov, but I shall put them in safekeeping myself, probably in a bank.

"3. If you are disturbed by the thought that my diaries . . . where I write, under the impression of the moment, about our discords and clashes . . . may be made use of by future biographers antipathetic to you, then . . . I am glad of an opportunity to express, [either in my diary, or in a sort of letter, my attitude toward you and my estimate of your life. . . . [My opinion] is as follows: as I loved you when young I have, without interruption, and despite the various grounds for the cooling of my affection, always loved and still love you. The reasons for the cooling of my affection were, and I am not speaking of the end of the marital relationship . . . in the first place my own withdrawal farther and farther from worldly interests . . . while you would and could not separate yourself from them . . . all of which was very natural and I do not reproach you for it.

". . . In the second place, your character in recent years has grown more and more irritable, despotic and uncontrolled. The manifestation of these traits of character could not but cool if not the affection itself, at least its expression. . . .

"In the third place . . . everything in our conception of life has been diametrically in opposition: our style of living, our attitude toward people and toward the material means of life, property, which I consider a sin and you consider a necessary condition of life. . . . There were other reasons too for the cooling of my love, for which we were both to blame, but I shall not mention them because they are not pertinent to this. The point is that I, despite all previous misunderstanding, have not ceased to love and value you. My estimate of your life with me is this:

"I, a dissolute, deeply (from the sexual point of view) debauched person, no longer in my first youth, married you, a pure, good, intelligent eighteen-year-old girl, and . . . you lived with me for nearly fifty years, loving me, leading a laborious, hard life, bearing, nursing, training and caring for your children and for me . . . in a way beyond reproach from me. Nor can I reproach you for not following me in exclusively spiritual lines . . . because the spiritual life of each human being is the mystery between that being and God. . . .

"4. As for the fact that at the present moment my relations with Chertkov are hard for you to bear: I am prepared not to see him, although I shall tell you that this is not so much unpleasant for me as for him, because I know how hard it will be on him. But if this is your wish I will carry it out.

"Now, fifthly, unless you accept these conditions for a kindly and peaceful life, I will revoke my promise not to leave you. I will leave and go probably not to Chertkov, indeed I may make it an absolute condition that he would not come and live near me, but I will inevitably go away because it is impossible to continue living this way. I would be able to continue to live this way if I could stand your sufferings with equanimity, but this I cannot do. . . .

"Think things over quietly, dear friend, listen to your heart, give your feelings expression and you will decide everything as you should. As for me, I can say that for my part I have decided that in any case I cannot act otherwise. Do leave off, dear, tormenting not so much others as yourself, because you suffer a hundred times more than others. That is all. Lev Tolstoy. In the morning of July 14."

Tanya and her husband helped to get the diaries from Chertkov and placed them in a bank. Still there was no peace. Needing medical advice, we sent for Rossolimo, a celebrated psychiatrist, as well as our friend and physician Dr. Nikitin.

"It's not Mother who needs medical care," was my brother Lev's comment on this, "but Father who has outlived his mind."

On July 20 Father wrote in his diary: "There is an incessant struggle going on in my soul because of Lev: whether to forgive him or to tell him off with some cruel, biting word. The voice of kindness is beginning to reach me more clearly. One must experience the perfect joy as Francis of Assisi did, by recognizing that the reproaches of the gatekeeper were deserved. Yes, one must do that."

The doctors gave us no help. Rossolimo's diagnosis—"Defects of two aspects of the personality: the paranoiac and the hysterical states, with a preponderance of the former"—was for us just medical jargon. The question remained: What were we to do next? The physicians prescribed the separation of our parents, baths, walks, sedatives for Mother. But how to carry this out? Sophia Andreyevna insisted that she was well and would follow no prescriptions.

Our nice Dr. Nikitin understood everything. In listening to Father's heart he found it seriously distended and weakened. "I'll tell you privately, Alexandra Lvovna," he said to me in warning, "you have much ahead of you that will be hard to bear."

What was there to do? To whom could we turn for advice?

Seated on a birch-log bench in the fir-tree grove, Father tore some pages out of his notebook and wrote to Chertkov:

"I do not cease thinking of you, dear friend. I am grateful that you have helped and are helping to carry me in a better spirit through the ordeal I have deserved and which is necessary to my soul, although this ordeal lies no less heavily on you. And do please help us both to keep from weakening and from doing anything of which we would repent. I am glad that I understand your situation, which may well be more difficult than mine. I am hated because there is, I state it boldly, some good in me which unmasks them, but because of my age and my condition they all—and their name is legion— feel the necessity of maintaining certain *égards* and restraints toward me. Yet they have no qualms because of the elevated and saintly qualities in you—again I state it boldly—and they make no bones about concealing their hatred of what is good, or they hide it under all kinds of different accusations against you which they invent. I realize this and I am deeply sorry for you. But we will stand firm. Please help me and I'll do the same for you. I can't boast about myself. I cannot keep from having unkind feelings. I hope this will pass."

My younger brothers arrived—Andrei, Misha with his wife and children. Lena, Misha's wife, a fine and sensible woman, assured me that Misha understood everything and loved Father, but that he was under the influence of Mother. I had several clashes with Andrei, whom I found incapable of understanding.

On July 27 Father wrote: "Again everything is the same as before. Yet it seems like the lull before a storm. Andrei came and asked: Is there a paper? I said I did not choose to reply. It was all very hard. I do not believe that all they want is money. That is terrible. But for me it can only be good. I am going to bed. Seryozha has arrived. There was a letter from Tanya—an invitation from Mikhail Sergeyevich too. Tomorrow we shall see."

When they could not get any satisfaction out of Father, first Andrei and then Mother began to worry me, questioning me as to whether Father had a will. I refused to answer.

Meantime Biryukov arrived in Yasnaya Polyana and Father told him about his testament. Biryukov gave it as his opinion that Father should have brought the family together and stated his wishes before making his will.

In his private diary Father wrote on August 2, 1910: "If I am spared . . . I have truly, truly realized my mistake. I should have called all the heirs together and announced to them my intentions, and not have done it secretly. I have written to Chertkov. He was much upset."

Chertkov wrote Father a long letter, recalling everything that preceded Father's decision to make his will.

"Pavel Ivanovich [Biryukov] was not right," wrote Father, in answering Chertkov's letter, "nor I in agreeing with him. . . . I entirely approve of your actions, nevertheless I am not at all satisfied with my actions. I feel that I might have acted in some better way, although I do not know how. Now I do not repent of what I did, i.e., of writing the testament which is written, and I can be only grateful to you for the sympathy you have shown in this matter. Now I shall tell Tanya all about it and this will be very pleasant for me."

The atmosphere was somewhat lightened by the arrival of the writer V. G. Korolenko. We all gathered around in the evening while he told us stories about his travels through Russia and his trip to America, where he had heard Henry George speak. Everyone listened with delight, for he was an excellent storyteller with an active interest in and knowledge of simple people wherever he found them.

In the morning I drove Korolenko over to the Chertkovs'. Along the way I realized, from some of his hints, that Mother had talked to him of her troubles and although it was very trying to speak of such things to an outsider, I was compelled to tell him of the true situation. Chertkov later confirmed what I had said. Korolenko's response was: "Well, now I am more convinced than ever that Lev Nikolayevich is an old oak tree which can stand anything without breaking. And here I have been imagining that he lived in such happy surroundings, that everyone was afraid to upset him by expressing even the slightest contradiction. I have always heard that

L. N. did not tolerate contradictions, and I was afraid to express my own views—now I realize what patience he has."

Of Korolenko, Father wrote in his private diary: "Talk with Korolenko, an intelligent and good man, but altogether under the influence of science."

Although I had before me in Father a constant example of gentleness and patience, still I carried the load assigned to me in many ways quite unworthily.

When Tanya again came to get Father, carrying out the doctors' order that our parents be separated, Mother announced that she was going with us. I was indignant. "Mama is sick," Father said to me. "One must have pity on her. I am prepared to do anything she wishes, not go to Tanya's, and to be a nurse to her to the end of her life." I would not listen. I said I did not feel capable of being a nurse and left. "What is the use of doctors, of family councils?" I thought to myself. "Father will be killed by it. . . ." Yet I was so tormented by the thought that my impatience had distressed him that I went to his study in the evening and begged his forgiveness. We both wept and he repeated several times: "How happy I am, how happy I am. I was so downhearted."

It ended up with our all going over to Kochety, to the Sukhotins'.

I loved Kochety. It was a one-story, rambling house, with antique furniture, family portraits on the walls. Surrounding it was an old, shady park—over thirty-five acres in size—in which Father often roamed about. In the park were ponds, fruit trees; beyond them stretched fields of black earth, magnificently cultivated by machine; there were copses, meadows, a herd of Simmental blooded cattle, a drove of trotting mares. Sukhotin was looked upon as a good proprietor.

Life was much easier in Kochety. After dinner we all played *secrétaire* and other games. Tanichka and her contemporary, Lev Sukhotin's little son, were highly amusing as they danced and sang, and Grandfather and Grandmother joined in the fun. Mother was happy in the children and shook with noiseless laughter, as she used to do. It was so easy then to love and pity her.

But then word came that the government had granted Chertkov the right of residence in the province of Tula, and again the calm was broken. There were tears and threats. "I will poison, I will murder Chertkov!" screamed Sophia Andreyevna. And no one, not Sukhotin, not Tanya, could quiet her.

Father stood in need of Tanya's love, and he was worried because he had been concealing something from her. So he decided to tell her about the testament. I was glad, especially when I had a talk with her and learned that she approved Father's action.

Father's private diary records the events of the next few days. "August 16: Again this morning she had not slept. She brought me a note about how Sasha copies my accusations against her out of my diary for Chertkov. Before dinner I tried to calm her by telling the truth, which was that Sasha copies out only individual thoughts and not my impressions of life. She wants to calm herself and she is very pitiful. It is now between three and four, something is bound to happen. I cannot work. Evidently it is not necessary for me to do so anyway. I am not so badly off at heart."

"August 21: Got up late. Feel more refreshed. S. A. is as usual. She told Tanya about how she could not sleep all night because she saw a picture of Chertkov. The situation is threatening. I do so very much wish to say something, i.e., to write."

"August 24: I am slowly reviving. S. A., the poor thing, does not cease to suffer and I feel incapable of helping her. I sense the sin of my exclusive devotion to my daughters."

"August 28: It is getting to be harder than ever to deal with S. A. It is not love but a demand for love, which is close to hatred and turns into hatred. Yes, egoism is madness. She was saved by having children—that love is animal but still it is self-sacrificing. And when that stopped, all that was left was terrible egoism. And egoism is a most abnormal state—it is madness.—I have just been talking to Sasha and Mikhail Sergeyevich, but Dushan and Sasha do not admit it is a sickness. But they are not right."

"August 29: Another empty day. Walks, letters. As for thinking, I can do that well, but I cannot concentrate. S. A. was very wrought up again, she went out into the garden and did not return. She did not come back until afternoon. And she wanted explanations again. This was very difficult for me, but I controlled myself and she calmed down. She has decided now to leave. I am thankful that Sasha decided to go with her. She was very touching when she said good-by, she asked forgiveness of everyone. I am so very, very, affectionately sorry for her. I had some good letters. I am going to bed. I have written her a little note."

Lyova had telegraphed that he was obliged to go to St. Petersburg on some legal errand. As Father was afraid to have Mother go alone to Yasnaya Polyana in her perturbed condition, I went home with her.

After a day or two of rest Father was immediately seized with an impulse to write. "September 3: I began to write with an eagerness I have not experienced for a long time," he wrote. It is possible that this refers to the outline he made in his notebook for "The Tale of the Young Tsar Turned Workman."

Having turned Mother over to Varya's care, I returned to Kochety. A few days later Mother joined us there, giving a series of reasons why we should all go back to Yasnaya Polyana. She wept and threatened. She pointed out that I was under doctor's orders to return to the Crimea in the autumn. Father wrote in his diary: "There has been a depressing conversation about my departure. I have salvaged my freedom, I will go when I choose. It's all very sad, of course, because I am wicked."

"September 9: I am alive, but wicked. Beginning in the morning there have been irritations, morbid ones. I am no longer quite well and I feel weak. I spoke with my whole soul but, evidently, nothing I said was accepted. It's very depressing."

"This is the second day S. A. is not eating," Father wrote on September 10. "They are having dinner now. I am going to ask her to come to dinner. Terrible scenes all evening."

"September 11: Toward evening there were scenes during which she ran out into the garden, wept and screamed. Even earlier, before I went after her into the garden she was crying: He's a beast, a murderer, I can't bear the sight of him, and she ran off to hire a wagon and leave immediately. And so it went on all evening. When I was beside myself and told her what I thought of her she became quite well, and still is so today the 11th. It is impossible to talk with her since in the first place she feels no need of logic, truth or even truthful rendering of words, either those spoken to her or those she speaks. I am very close to the point of fleeing. My heart has deteriorated."

On the 12th of September there is a brief note in his diary: "S. A. drove off in tears. She asked me to come and discuss things but I refused. She did not take anyone with her. I am very, very tired. In the evening I read. I am worried about her."

On September 11 Mother wrote Father a letter:

"I should like, dear Lyovochka, before we part, to say a few words to you. But in your conversations with me you get so irritable that I feel sorry to disturb you.

"I beg you to understand that all my, not *demands*, as you call them, but *wishes* have only one origin and that is: my love for you, my desire to be separated from you as little as possible, and my chagrin at the intrusion of an outside influence, unfavorable with regard to me, on our long, unquestionably loving, intimate married life.

"Once that is removed—although you, I regret to say, repent of this while I am infinitely grateful for this great sacrifice which restores to me my happiness and my life—I swear to you that I will do all that in me lies to surround your spiritual and other life with peace, care and joy.

"There are, after all, hundreds of wives who really do *demand* a great deal from their husbands: 'Let's go to Paris for some beautiful clothes, or let's play roulette, or accept my lovers, don't dare go to your club, buy some diamonds, legitimatize this child, born God knows how,' etc. etc.

"The Lord saved me from all kinds of temptations and *demands*. I was so happy that I did not need anything and I was grateful only to God.

"But for the first time in my life—I made no demands but I suffered dreadfully from your growing coolness and from Chertkov's interference in our life, and for the first time I *longed* with all my suffering soul for what may well be impossible—the return of former conditions.

"The means of accomplishing this were, of course, the worst, the most inept, unkind, upsetting to you and the more so for me and I am very grieved about it. I do not know whether or not I was in control of myself. I think that I was not; everything in me has grown weaker: my will, my soul and heart and even my body. The rare flashes of your former love made me wildly happy in all this time, and my love for you, on which all my acts have been based, even my jealousy and madness, has never weakened, and I shall go to the end of my days with it. Farewell, darling, and do not be angry at this letter. Your wife, yours always and yours alone, Sonya."

On September 24 Father made this entry: "She is ill, and I am sorry for her with all my heart."

How much easier it would have been for Father if we, his nearest ones, could have felt love and pity toward Mother. But I did not pity her. I was angry.

"Then, O Friar Leo, only then shall we see perfect joy."

❧ 68 ❧

SEPTEMBER 23—the wedding anniversary of my parents. Mother wanted snapshots taken. It was cold, a north wind was blowing. Father, with his hands thrust in his belt, stood with uncovered head, looking morosely at the ground in front of him. . . . I was in a bad, ugly mood. Upon returning from Kochety I had noticed that Chertkov's photograph and mine no longer hung on the wall of Father's study. Mother had taken them down. And unable to restrain myself, I had charged him brusquely that he dare not put them back.

In reply Father had nodded, turned around and walked away. "You are acting the way she does," he said.

At dinner we were all silent. Later, I was writing as usual in the office when Father summoned me.

"Sasha, I want to dictate a letter."

"Very well." I picked up a pencil, a sheet of paper, and prepared to write. In my heart I longed to rush over and kiss his hands and beg his forgiveness. But there were tears in my throat and I could not get out a single word.

"I don't need your stenography, I don't need it," Father said suddenly in a low choked voice. Then he threw himself on the arm of his chair and burst into sobs.

"Forgive me, forgive me!" I went to him, kissed him, and for a long time we both wept. After that he began to dictate, but I could scarcely see my symbols.

When we had finished I again asked his forgiveness. "I have already forgotten the whole thing," he said.

The next day the two pictures were back in their places. As Varya and I had gone to Olga's estate, the storm was unleashed in our absence with Maria Alexandrovna Schmidt as witness. Mother, upon seeing the pictures, rushed to her room, fetched a toy pistol and began to shoot at Chertkov's photograph. Then she yanked it off the wall and tore it to shreds.

At Olga's we were preparing for bed after a lovely day, when our coachman suddenly arrived from Yasnaya Polyana with a note from

Maria Alexandrovna Schmidt begging us to return at once. We did so, through a pitch-black night over the roads deep in mud. Three hours later, with a sinking feeling, I entered the house and the terrifying storm of Mother's rage was now turned against Varya and me. She told Varya to clear out, to go to the ends of the earth. As for me—she almost threw me out bodily.

I told Father it would seem best for me to leave. I hoped he would go with me or join me later.

"In general," he replied, "I do not approve of your having been unable to control yourself and your going away. In my opinion, one does not solve problems by altering the external circumstances of life. On the other hand, because of my own weakness, I would be glad if you went away. Things are closer to their solution, they cannot longer go on as they are. Sophia Andreyevna has done away with Chertkov, she has heaped abuse on Maria Alexandrovna, she has chased Varya out of the house. . . . Don't give up, stand firm, everything will turn out for the best."

It was a twenty-minute drive from Telyatinki, where I took refuge, to Yasnaya Polyana. After my departure peace settled on the house; Mother seemed to realize that she had overstepped all boundaries. I went to Yasnaya every day, copied for Father as usual, but at night I had no rest. What if he should fall ill! Perhaps he needed me, right now, this very minute!

After several days I saw that my going away would not, as I had hoped, encourage Father to do likewise. He had decided to stick it out to the end. Mother for her part was not at all pleased by my departure. She wished to become reconciled with me and take Varya back.

"The thing that touched me," Father wrote in his diary for September 29, "was that she thanked me for my tenderness with her. It is terrible, nevertheless one would like to think that she [S. A.] might be won over by kindness."

In his private diary Father wrote on October 2: "The first thing in the morning was an inquiry about my health, then followed endless criticism and talk, and interference in conversations. And I behaved badly. I cannot overcome this feeling of badness, unkindness. Recently I have felt a poignant need to do some literary writing, and yet I see the impossibility of yielding to it because of her [S. A.], because of my inability to extricate myself from my feelings about her, and also from my inner conflict. It goes without saying that this conflict and the possibility of emerging victorious from it is more important than any possible literary productions."

Meanwhile I was beside myself in my little cottage where, in reality, it was extremely cosy. All my thoughts were centered in Yasnaya Polyana.

"What are you moping about, acting quite unlike yourself?" asked Annushka, the broad-faced, snub-nosed, cheerful peasant woman from the village of Yasnaya Polyana, who helped me with the housework. "I never grieve. Even when my Nikita gets drunk, or one of the children is ailing, I just sit down and read Marcus Aurelius. . . ."

"Marcus Aurelius?" I asked, astonished.

"Why yes. That's the little book the Count gave me. As soon as I feel mopey, I immediately call to my oldest boy Petka: 'Petka, read me some Marcus Aurelius!' And I feel easier in my soul right away. . . . And here's another thing," she went on. "I have thought a lot about how it's best to live. Sometimes I look at it one way, and then another, and nothing seems to help. There is only one thing that helps me: to think about death. As quick as you think about death, that you are alive today and tomorrow six feet of earth will be all you'll need and all your troubles will be over, you won't need anything. Then all you think about is how not to sin right now."

I told Father about her. "That's true wisdom for you," he said with a laugh. "There's the person from whom one can learn."

Seryozha and Tanya arrived at Yasnaya Polyana. My removal had had its effect on them and they told Mother roundly that if she did not stop tormenting Father, they would put her in a sanatorium.

Then during the evening of October 3 the coachman from Yasnaya Polyana brought me a note from Bulgakov: "Lev Nikolayevich is in a very bad state, come quickly."

Father was in a deep fainting spell; his whole body twitched from spasms in his legs. Everyone was running about in great agitation. Chertkov was downstairs in Dushan's room. Mother was on her knees, wringing her hands and praying: "Lord, only let it not be this time. . . . Help, O Lord!"

Toward eleven o'clock Father took a turn for the better. Quietly, on tiptoe, I went up to him, kissed his hand. Later in the night he fell asleep and by morning the attack was over. But though he recovered full consciousness, he was greatly weakened.

Tanya and Seryozha talked with Mother, and for the first time I spoke up in their presence and told Mother what Father had gone

[505]

through. I spoke harshly, without extenuation, warning her that if she did not go away or mend her conduct Father would die. And then—who would be to blame?

Seryozha tried to stop me, but I was bound to pour out all that I had suffered. "You cannot stand it even three days," I said, "but I . . ." With this, I burst into tears and ran from the room.

Later in the day I returned to be with Father. Before I left for the night I was told that Mother wished to see me.

She was standing outside the front door with no coat on. Her head trembled helplessly. I was suddenly overcome with a sense of great pity; I had to restrain an impulse to throw myself on her neck. "You wanted to speak to me?" I asked.

"Yes, I want you to forgive me." She began to kiss me, repeating: "Forgive me, forgive me." I kissed her in return, and begged her to calm herself. "Forgive me," she promised, "and I give you my word of honor that I will never again offend you." Then she made the sign of the cross over me.

"Tell Varya that I apologize to her, tell her that we have lived together for four years and, God willing, we shall live together as long again, that I don't know what got into me, what happened to us."

"You must not hurt Father," I said, in tears. "I cannot bear to see him tortured so."

"I shan't, I shan't, I give you my word of honor," she said again, crossing herself. "You will not believe how I have suffered this night, for I know he was made ill because of me and I never would have forgiven myself if he had died. . . . You won't believe how jealous I am. I never in all my life, not even when I was young, felt such violent jealousy as I feel toward Chertkov."

There was now a fresh glimmer of hope. Varya and I immediately returned to Yasnaya Polyana, and for several days things were quieter. I made every effort to maintain the kindly feelings my conversation with Mother had evoked.

"Yesterday, October 6," wrote Father, "I felt weak and morose. Everything was depressing and disagreeable. There was a letter from Chertkov. . . . She is making an effort and she has invited him to come. Tanya went over to the Chertkovs' today. Galya was very upset. Chertkov decided to come over at eight, it is now ten minutes to. S. A. asked me not to kiss him. How disgusting. She had an attack of hysterics. Now it is the 8th [of October]. I said everything I thought necessary to her. She retorted, I became irritable. It was horrid. But perhaps some of it will stick. To be sure the main thing is not to act badly oneself, but I do feel sorry for her, not always, but for the most part. I am going to bed, after having spent the day in a better way."

On October 12 conversation was renewed on the subject of the will. What Mother had told everyone about Father's fainting spell was so dreadful that I do not care to go into the details. She said that if Father had written a will it would be possible to contest it by proving that he was imbecile. Whereupon she rushed into his room, threw herself on her knees, upbraiding him, threatening, imploring him to destroy his will, and meantime kissing his hands.

On October 13 Father wrote: "It seems that she has discovered and carried off my little diary. She knows about some kind of a will, made out to someone, about something—evidently having to do with my writings. What torment, all because of their cash value —and she is afraid that I will interfere with her publishing them. And she is afraid of everything, the unhappy woman."

On October 14 Mother wrote Father a letter, which began:

"Every day you make what would seem to be a sympathetic inquiry concerning my health, you ask how I slept, yet every day there are fresh blows to lacerate my heart, shorten my life, torture me to an intolerable degree and put no end to my sufferings. This fresh blow is this wicked act with regard to depriving your numerous progeny of the royalties; destiny found it proper that this should be revealed to me although the accomplice in this matter *did not order* you to communicate it to the family. He threatened to *make* trouble for me and the family, and brilliantly executed (his design) in trapping you to give him this document of relinquishment. The government, which you and he have spurned and abused in all your pamphlets, will by law take the last crumb of bread from your heirs and give it to Sytin and all their various rich printers and unscrupulous businessmen, while the grandchildren of Tolstoy, in accordance with his wicked and conceited testament, will *die* of starvation. . . ."

The letter concluded: "If you have been made to think that I am motivated by greed, then I am personally prepared, as is Tanya, to renounce my rights in my husband's estate. What would I want with it? I obviously shall soon leave this life, in one way or another, yet I am filled with terror, should I outlive you, by the thought of what evil may spring from your tomb and remain in the memory of your children and grandchildren.

"Do away with it now, Lyovochka, while you are still alive, awaken and soften your proud heart, awaken in it a sense of God, and the love you preach so loudly to other people. S. T."

"Now things are resolving themselves," Father wrote on October 16: "I wanted to go over to Tanya's, but am hesitating. [She had] an attack of hysteria, I am angry. The whole matter is that she suggested my going to the Chertkovs', she begged me to, but now when I told her I am going, she began to storm. It's very, very difficult. Lord help me. I said that I shall not give and am not giving any promises, but that I shall do everything I can not to distress her. I shall probably not go through with the departure planned for tomorrow. Yet I should. Yes, this is an ordeal, and my job is not to be unkind. Lord help me."

Out of deference to Mother's wishes Father did not go to Telyatinki, and he requested Chertkov not to come to our home. But S. A. did not believe him, she went on foot along the road to Telyatinki to watch for him. When she returned she was remorseful, touching.

Father wrote to Chertkov: ". . . I pity, I do pity her and am rejoiced that at times I can, without forcing myself, love her. That is how it was last night when she came in, all repentant. . . . Today I feel physically weak, but I am very much at ease in my soul. And that is why I have the impulse to tell you what I think and, principally—what I feel.

"Until yesterday I had given little thought to my attacks [of illness], in fact I did not think about them at all, but yesterday I had a clear and vivid presentiment of how I might die in one of these attacks. And I realized that although such a death from the physical point of view, without any physical sufferings, would be very good, it would, from the spiritual point of view, deprive me of those precious moments of dying which could be so wonderful. And that led me to the thought that if I am deprived of these last conscious minutes, then, you see, it lies in my power to spread them over all the hours, days, perhaps months, years (this is scarcely likely) which precede my death. I can be as serious, as solemn in my attitude (not outwardly, but in my inner consciousness) toward these days, months, as I would be in my last minutes in the face of consciously impending death. And it is to this thought, even this feeling, which I experienced yesterday and which I am experiencing now, which I shall attempt to sustain until my death, and which is the source of special joy to me, so I want to communicate it to you.—In essence, all this is very old stuff, but it came as a discovery to me from a fresh angle. . . ."

All this time Father was unable to do any writing. He answered letters, he wrote a little about socialism. "I cannot write but, thank God, I can work on myself. I keep moving forward." And the next day, October 18, he explained his words in the following entry: "Thank God, I can feel without regret an excellent *readiness for death*."

October 19. "Last night S. A. came in: 'Again there is a conspiracy against me.'—'What do you mean, what conspiracy?'—'Your diary has been given to Chertkov. It's not there.' 'Sasha has it.' It was very hard on me, for a long time I could not fall asleep because I could not keep down unkind feelings."

On October 21 three peasants came to visit Father. Two were local men. The third was Mikhail Novikov, with whom Father corresponded—an intelligent, cultivated man. It had been a long time since I had seen Father in such a gay mood. On my way to get his letters he beckoned me to follow him. "Come on, come on," he said with a sly smile. "I'll tell you a great secret."

He took me to his study. "Do you know what I have thought up? I told Novikov a bit about our situation here and how hard it is for me. I shall go to him. Nobody would find me there. And Novikov told me about his brother who had an alcoholic wife. When she was kicking up too much of a row, his brother would give her back a good going-over and then she would feel better. It helps." And Father smiled good-naturedly. "See, what contradictions there are in life."

I replied by quoting Ivan, the coachman, who had said in answer to a query from Olga about things being in bad shape in Yasnaya Polyana. "You know what, Excellency," he had added, "we do things the country way. If a woman tries any nonsense, her husband uses the reins on her—and she gets soft as silk."

Father began to laugh. "Yes, yes, just think what kind of people they are. . . ."

"Yes, yes, nevertheless, I shall probably have to go away," he repeated.

In his private diary he made this entry on October 21: "I am taking my ordeal very hard. Novikov's words: 'We used the whip. It made things much better,' and what Ivan said: 'In our life we do it with reins,' keep coming to my mind and I am dissatisfied with myself. In the night I was thinking about going away. Sasha talked a lot with her, but it is with difficulty that I restrain unkind feelings."

On October 24 Father dictated a letter to Mikhail Novikov.

"October 24, 1910. Yasnaya Polyana. Dear Mikhail Petrovich, With regard to what I said to you before you left I now put to you one more request as follows: if it really did happen that I came to you, could you find me in your village even a tiny but separate and warm cottage, so that I would not crowd you and your family except for the shortest time? Furthermore I want to let you know that if I had to telegraph you I would not telegraph you in my own name but in that of T. NIKOLAYEV. I shall wait for your reply. I send my friendly greetings.

"Remember that all this must remain only your private knowledge."

The next day I went in to Father. He was sitting in an armchair by the table, not doing anything. It was a strange and unaccustomed sight to find him without a book or a pen in his hand, not even a game of solitaire which he liked to lay out while he was thinking. "I was sitting and dreaming," he said to me. "I am dreaming of how I shall get away. Do you really insist on going with me?"

I answered him: "I don't want to embarrass you at first. I should not go with you, but I cannot live away from you."

"Yes, yes, but I keep thinking that you are not well enough, you will catch colds and begin to cough."

"No, no," I assured him, "that doesn't matter. I shall be better off in simple surroundings."

"If that is so then the most natural, the most agreeable thing for me would be to have you near me, as an assistant. This is how I plan to act. Buy a ticket to Moscow, send someone, Chertkov, with my belongings to Laptevo, and leave the train there myself. If I am discovered there I'll go elsewhere. . . . Well, these are probably only dreams. I shall be tormented if I abandon her, I'll be tormented by her condition. Yet on the other hand, this situation is painful and is getting more so with every day. I confess to you that I am only waiting for some occasion to go."

Seryozha arrived that day from Tula. He tried to see Father in his study, but Mother was there all the time, interrupting their talk. In the evening the two men discussed literature, played chess, and at Father's request Seryozha played the piano for him. "When I played Grieg's *Ich liebe Dich*," wrote Seryozha, "he burst into tears. On my way to bed I went into his study to say good-by to him. There was no one else in the room. He asked me: 'Why are you going away so soon?' I was planning to leave the next morning. I said that I had to attend to my affairs. That I wanted very much to spend some time in Yasnaya, to find out what was going on there and, perhaps, be of some help, but that I wanted to arrange my personal affairs beforehand. Father's reply to this was: 'You would do better not to leave.' I answered that I would come back soon. Later on I recalled that he said those words with particular expression; he evidently was thinking of his own departure and wanted me to remain with Mother after he had gone: he always thought that I had some slight influence over her. As I said good-by he quickly, and with unusual tenderness, put his arms around me to kiss me. At any other time he would have simply shaken hands with me."

Father wrote to Chertkov, saying how much he missed him and describing several "thought-feelings" as he called them which he could share only with this friend. "If I undertake anything," he promised, "I shall, of course, let you know. I may even ask your help."

The following day, October 26, Father went over to see Maria Alexandrovna Schmidt. Perhaps he went to say farewell.

"I am going to Tanya. I shall write her that I am going to Tanya, and from there I shall go to Optina Pustyn. I shall go to some one of the elders and beg leave to live there. They will surely take me in, they will hope to convert me," he said to Dushan.

That day he wrote: "There has been nothing out of the ordinary. Still my sense of shame and the impulse to act has grown."

✤ 69 ✤

I WAS so sleepy I did not understand anything. Someone was rapping insistently on my door. I jumped up. "Who is there?" Father was standing in the doorway, a candle in his hand, completely dressed in a blouse and boots: "I am leaving immediately. . . . for good. Help me pack."

Dushan, Varya and I moved quietly in the half-dark house, trying not to make any noise, talking in whispers, collecting what was necessary. I gathered up the manuscripts, Dushan the medicines, Varya the linen and clothing. Father put things in boxes, carefully tying them up.

Some of his manuscripts were already tied up. "You can keep these," he said.

"And the diary?" I asked.

"I am taking that with me."

Father's movements were calm and confident, only the break in his voice betrayed his excitement. The door leading across the corridor to Mother's bedroom, which she all these last months kept ajar, was closed.

"You stay here, Sasha," Father said. "I shall send for you in several days, when I decide definitely where I am going. I shall most probably go to Mashenka, to Shamordino."

We hurried. With every minute that passed Father was getting more nervous, restless, and he kept urging us on. Our hands trembled, straps would not pull tight, valises would not close.

"I am going to the stables," he said, "to have the horses harnessed." In five minutes he was back. It was foggy along the road, he had missed his way, stumbled against an acacia branch and fallen, losing his cap, so he had returned to get an electric lantern.

Finally everything was packed. Dushan, Varya and I with difficulty hauled the stuff out to the stable over the slippery mud. When we reached the wing we saw a light. Father was walking toward us. He took one valise from me and went on ahead, lighting the road. Our coachman Adrian was already throwing the reins over the second horse.

When all was ready, the stable boy vaulted onto a horse, holding a brightly burning torch in his hand.

"Drive on!"

The carriage, carrying Father and Dushan, was almost moving when I jumped in and kissed Father.

"Good-by, darling," he said, "we shall see each other soon."

The carriage skirted the house, crossed the apple orchard and went along the park. The flame of the torch was visible through the leafless trees . . . farther, farther away, until it disappeared in a turn toward the village.

A sense of terrible emptiness swept over me as I went back into the house. It was between five and six o'clock. The train left the station at eight. I sat down in an armchair, with a blanket around me; I shook as if I had a fever. I counted the minutes, the hours. At eight o'clock I began to walk from room to room. Ilya Vasilievich already knew what had happened. "Lev Nikolayevich told me he was preparing to go away," he said, "and just now I guessed, by the coats, that he was not here."

Gradually the news spread. The servants whispered together, and drew their own conclusions. Mother, who had not slept for most of the night, awoke late, about eleven o'clock, and with quick steps she came running into the dining room.

"Where's Papa?" she asked me.

"He has gone away."

"Where to?"

"I do not know," I answered, handing her a letter he had left with me.

She ran her eyes quickly through it, her head quivered, her hands trembled, her face was covered with red spots.

"My departure will distress you," Father had written, "and I regret this but you must understand and believe that I could not act otherwise. My situation was getting, did get, intolerable. In addition to everything else I cannot live any longer in such circumstances of luxury as those in which I have been living, and I am doing what old men of my years do—they withdraw from worldly life to live in solitude and quiet for the last days of their lives.

"Please understand this and do not come after me if you discover

[513]

where I am. Your coming would only worsen my and your situation, it cannot alter my decision.

"I thank you for your faithful forty-eight years of life with me and I beg you to forgive me for everything of which I have been guilty with regard to you, just as I, with all my soul, forgive you for everything in which you may have been guilty toward me. I advise you to reconcile yourself to this new situation in which my departure will put you, and not to harbor unkind feelings toward me. If you wish to communicate with me, give the message to Sasha, she will know where I am, and she will forward whatever is necessary. But she cannot say where I am because I made her promise not to tell anyone. Lev Tolstoy.

"I commissioned Sasha to collect my belongings and manuscripts and send them to me."

Mother did not read the letter to the end, but threw it on the floor crying out: "He's gone, gone for good! Good-by, Sasha, I am going to drown myself." And she rushed from the house without taking a wrap.

I called to Bulgakov to follow her as she ran through the park in the direction of the middle pond. Then I went after them as fast as I could, trying to head her off. I reached the planked platform, where the peasant women usually did their washing, at the moment when Mother slid and fell on the slippery boards and rolled into the water, fortunately on the side where it was not deep. An instant later I was in the water and had hold of her by her dress. Bulgakov threw himself after me and together we lifted her out and handed her over to our fat, puffing cook, Semyon, and the footman Vanya, who had followed us.

For the rest of the day we never left Mother's side. Several times she tried to tear herself away from us and run out of doors. She threatened to throw herself out of the window, to drown herself in the well in the courtyard.

I sent a telegram to Tanya and to my brothers, telling them what had happened and asking them to come at once. I also sent to Tula for a psychiatric physician. All day and all night I kept a constant watch.

But even while I was changing my wet clothing she succeeded in sending Vanya to the railway station to find out what train Father had taken and dispatching this wire: "Return at once—Sasha." On the heels of that telegram I sent a second one: "Do not worry, real telegrams will be signed only Alexandra." Fortunately Father did not receive either telegram.

The Tula doctor, when he came, gave me small comfort. He did not exclude the possibility that Mother, in an attack of nervous excitement, would commit suicide. It was a tremendous relief when later in the day first Andrei and then the rest of the family arrived.

All, including Tanya, were of the opinion that Father as a Christian should have borne his cross to the end. They said that he must come back to Mother. Only Sergei understood Father's point of view. "Dear Papa," he wrote, "I am writing to you only because Sasha says that you would like to know our (your children's) opinion. I believe that Mother is nervously affected and in many ways irresponsible, and that you should have separated from her (perhaps long ago), no matter how hard this was on you both. I even think that if anything should happen to Mama, which I do not expect, you would not have any grounds for self-reproach. There was no solution to the situation and I think you chose the only real way out of it. Forgive me for writing so frankly. Seryozha."

The others, except Misha, sent Father letters urging him to return. "Lyovochka darling," wrote my mother, "come home, dear, save me from a second suicide. Lyovochka, friend of my whole life, I will do everything, everything, that you wish, I will give up entirely every kind of luxury; I will be friends with your friends, I will put myself in the care of doctors, I will be submissive. . . ."

The family guessed that Father had gone to Auntie Maria Nikolayevna's and Mother asked Andrei to follow him to Shamordino and persuade him to return.

While in Optina Pustyn, Father made a diary entry dated October 28 describing how he left home: "I went to bed at half past eleven. I slept until after two. I awoke and again, as in preceding nights, I heard my door opened and footsteps. On the preceding nights I did not look at my door, but now I did and saw a bright light through the crack of the door in my study and heard some rustling. It was S. A., evidently searching for something, and probably reading. The evening before she asked, she demanded, that I would not lock the door. Her two doors were open so that my slightest movement was audible to her. So day and night all my movements, my words, were of necessity known to her and under her surveillance. Again there were steps, the careful closing of a door and she went away. I do not know why, but this aroused in me a feeling of uncontrollable aversion, resentment. I wanted to go back to sleep but could not. I kept turning over for about an hour, then I lit a candle and sat up. The door opened and S. A. came in, inquiring about my 'health,' astonished to see the light in my room. . . . My aversion and resentment kept rising, it was hard for me to breathe, I took my pulse—it was ninety-seven. I could not lie down, and suddenly I made my final decision to leave. I wrote her a letter, began to pack the bare necessities, only to get away. I wakened Dushan, then Sasha. They helped me to pack. I trembled at the thought that she would hear, that there would be a scene, hysterics, that after all I could not get away without a scene. . . ." And further on: ". . . Then we took our seats in the train, it pulled out and the fear subsided, and pity for her increased, but not doubt as to my having done what was right. Perhaps I am mistaken, but it seems to me that I was saving myself, not Lev Nikolayevich, but that thing which, sometimes and perhaps only in small degree, is inside of me. . . ."

It was this that people around him did not understand—the need of inward and outward quiet which would allow him to concentrate on the one significant thing, on death and its spiritual meaning.

On October 29, Chertkov sent Alyosha Sergeyenko to Father with a letter expressing wholehearted approval of his action.

"I cannot put into words the joy it was to me that you went away. With all my being I feel that you were compelled to act as you did, and that the continuation of your life in Yasnaya, in view of the way circumstances developed there, would have been bad for you. And I believe that you have postponed long enough, fearing to take this step 'for yourself,' so that this time there is nothing of personal egoism in your basic motivation. . . . I am sure that as a result of your act things will be easier for everyone, and above all for poor Sophia Andreyevna, no matter what its external effect may be on her. . . ."

Now that the family could look after Mother, I went to Father in Shamordino, taking Varya with me. I found him saddened by the letters from his children, with the exception of Seryozha's which touched him deeply. He had written me two letters which I failed to receive before leaving home. The first one, dated October 28, read in part:

"We have arrived in good shape, Sasha dear. Oh, if only things aren't in too bad shape with you. . . .

"I try to be calm and I must confess that I am experiencing the same restlessness that I always have felt when facing the most difficult

[516]

things; but I am not experiencing the shame, the embarrassment, the lack of freedom which I always experienced at home. . . . Tell V. G. [Chertkov] that I am very happy and very fearful of what I have done. I shall try to write down the themes of my dreams and various literary pieces which are crying to be written. I think it best to refrain from meeting him for the time being. He, as always, will understand me. Good-by, darling, I kiss you, L. T."

The second letter was dated October 29:

"Sergeyenko will tell you all about me, dear friend Sasha. Things are difficult. I cannot but feel a great weight. The main thing is not to commit a sin, and therein lies the difficulty. Of course I have sinned and I shall sin, but at least less. That is what, principally, I wish for you above all else, especially as I know that a terrible problem, one beyond your strength because of your years, has fallen to your lot.

"I have decided nothing and do not care to decide anything. I am trying to do only what I cannot but do, and not to do that which I might leave undone. From my letter to Chertkov you will find that it is not how I look at, but what I feel about it. . . . I am not sending for you yet but I shall, as soon as it is possible, indeed, very soon. Write me about your health. I kiss you. L. Tolstoy."

In reply to my question as to whether he regretted what he had done, Father asked me a question: "Can a man have regrets if he was *unable* to act differently?"

It was not accidental that in this perhaps most difficult crisis of his life, he had chosen to be with a person to whom he was most akin. Auntie and her daughter Lisa, who was visiting her, did everything to comfort him. He felt in them no tinge of condemnation or criticism. They put him wholly at ease.

"I have received the most comforting, joyous impression from Mashenka," he wrote in his diary for October 29, "and also dear Lizanka. . . . On my way here I kept thinking about a way out of my and her situation, and I could not think of anything, yet it will come, whether one likes it or not, and it will not be what you foresee. Yes, all one must think about is not to commit sins. What will be, will be. It is not my affair. . . ."

The tranquil, well-ordered life of monasteries always attracted Father. He talked with the nuns, with the monks of Optina Pustyn. Several times he walked up to the sacred gates of the hermitage, evidently wishing to talk with some of the elders.

[517]

Father would have stayed on in Shamordino. He had already looked up a place in which to live in the village—a cottage for three rubles (about $1.50) a month. But the news I brought upset him. He realized that the family had guessed his whereabouts and that Mother would come to him—if not immediately, eventually.

We were sitting in Aunt Masha's warm, cozy cell and chatting. Father was listening in silence. Suddenly he grasped the arms of his chair and, rising quickly, went into the next room. It was obvious that he had arrived at a decision. After a while he called me. "Send this letter to Mother," he said. He had written:

"Any meeting between us and more than that, my return *now*, is completely impossible. For this would be, as everyone says, highly harmful, for me it would be dreadful. . . . I advise you to reconcile yourself to what has happened, to adjust yourself to it . . . to have yourself taken care of.

"If you do not actually love me, but only do not hate me, you should enter at least slightly into my situation too. And if you will do that you not only will not condemn me, but you will try to help me find peace, the possibility of having some kind of a human life. . . . No one but yourself can deliver those closest to you, me, and above all you yourself, from the sufferings they are experiencing. Try to direct your energy, not toward having all you desire—at present it is my return—but toward the pacification of yourself, your soul—and you will receive what you desire.

"I have spent two days at Shamordino and Optina and am leaving. . . . I am not saying where I am going because I consider it necessary for you and me to be separated. Do not think I went away because I do not love you. I love you and am sorry for you with all my soul, but I cannot act otherwise than I am acting. . . .

"Farewell, dear Sonya. May God help you. Life is not a toy, we have no right to throw it aside on a whim. And to measure it by length of time is not sensible either. Perhaps the months which are still left to us to live may be more important than all the years already lived, and we must live them well. L. T."

The next day we started off again to make an eight o'clock train. Father did not say good-by to Aunt Maria, but left a note for her written at four o'clock in the morning. He did not even wait for our second carriage but rushed off to the station in Kozelsk, leaving Varya and me to follow. Aunt Maria found me still at the hostel when she arrived hoping to have a last word with Father.

"My Lord, my Lord," she said with a deep sigh, "we did not even say good-by to each other, who knows if we shall meet again? Well, what can one do, if only he is all right."

We were excited, there was so little time left before the departure of the train. Finally the postilion drove up. "If Mama comes I'll meet her," Aunt Maria called out after us. "Take care of Father!"

At the station Varya and I had just time to buy our tickets and board the train. Where were we going? Dushan said: "To Novocherkassk, to the Denisenkos, from there, if we get passports, we'll go to the Tolstoy colony in Bulgaria, if not—to the Caucasus."

In the railroad carriage people recognized Father, and before we knew it the news had spread through the whole train. Curious onlookers began to appear. The conductors were very amiable, arranging a separate compartment, helping me to make oatmeal gruel, and chasing away the intruders.

Between three and four o'clock Father called me. He was having a chill. I covered him more warmly and took his temperature. He had fever. Suddenly I felt so weak I had to sit down. I was close to despair.

The stuffy, smoke-filled second-class carriage, with strangers all around, the measured rhythm of the train as it carried us farther and farther into the unknown—and under the blankets a helpless old man who should be undressed, put to bed, given hot liquids. . . . Where was our destination? Where our home?

Father understood. Stretching out his hand, he squeezed mine firmly.

"Don't lose your courage, Sasha. Everything is all right, very much all right."

At the next stop I ran out to get boiling water. Dushan said we must give Father tea with wine, perhaps that would help. But the chill persisted, his temperature rose.

At the station I noticed two people following us, and when the train pulled out they jumped into our car. As I suspected, the police department had ordered a police sergeant "to inquire immediately whether the writer Lev Tolstoy was traveling with this train."

It was impossible to continue, so when toward eight in the evening the train came to the large, brightly lighted station Astapovo, we got off there. Dushan asked the station master about a place to stay, but there was no hotel in the town. The station master offered to put us up in his own house.

Holding Father up under his arms, we took him through the station waiting room, where a crowd of people gathered, baring their heads and bowing. Father was scarcely able to walk, but he returned the greetings, raising his hand with difficulty to his hat.

We had hardly undressed him and put him to bed when he went into a deep faint, spasms convulsed the left side of his face, his arm and leg. Dushan and I thought the end had come. But when the station doctor had injected some stimulant, Father dropped off to sleep. He slept for two hours, then wakened and called for me.

"What's the matter, Sasha?" he asked.

"The matter? Things aren't going well."

"Don't lose heart. What more do you want? After all, we are together."

Toward nightfall we were relieved. His temperature dropped and he slept well.

Despite his weakness, Father wanted to go on, but Dushan and I said no. He was much chagrined. "If I am better, we shall go on tomorrow," he said, and sent Chertkov a telegram: "I fell ill yesterday, passengers saw me, left train in weakened condition, fear publicity, better now, am continuing journey, take steps, advise."

He did not guess that everyone already knew where he was, that the newspaper *Russian Word* had begun to bombard the station master with inquiries about his health, that telegrams were being rushed to provincial Governors, to intelligence and police departments.

In the morning Father had me wire Chertkov, asking him to come, and he dictated some items for his Notebook:

"God is the infinite All: man is only His finite manifestation. God is that infinite All of which man recognizes himself to be a finite part. Only God truly exists. Man is His manifestation in matter, time and space. The more the manifestation of God in man (life) unites itself with the manifestations (the lives) of other beings, the more he himself exists. The union of his life with the lives of other beings is accomplished through love.

"God is not love, but the more love man has, the more he manifests God, the more he truly exists."

Some time later Father again called for me to take a letter to Tanya and Seryozha.

"November 1, 1910. Astapovo. My dear children, Tanya and Seryozha. I hope and I am sure that you will not reproach me for not having sent for you. To send for only you and not Mama would constitute a great grievance for her and also for your other brothers.

[520]

Both of you will understand that Chertkov, for whom I have sent, is in a unique position with regard to me. He has devoted his entire life to the service of the undertaking which I have served for the last forty years of my life. This work is not as dear to me as the recognition I have—rightly or wrongly—of its importance to others, including you.

"I thank you for your kind attitude toward me. I do not know whether or not this is farewell, but I felt impelled to say what I have said. . . .

"Farewell, try to calm your mother toward whom I have sincere feelings of compassion and love. Your loving father, Lev Tolstoy."

"Give them this letter after my death," he said, and began to weep.

On November 2 his temperature rose in the forenoon, he started to cough, there was blood in his sputum. He had pneumonia. I telegraphed my brother Sergei to send Nitikin at once.

Chertkov arrived, and Father questioned him in detail about Mother—whether she knew where he was and were the older children with her?

On the same day Dushan received a telegram informing him that the Countess had ordered a special train and was leaving for Astapovo with Andrei, Mikhail, Tatiana, Vladimir Filosophov, a doctor and nurse.

The situation was terrifying. Could it be that the family even now did not realize how things stood? But Seryozha fortunately reached us ahead of the others. For a long time he hesitated about going in to see Father, fearing his presence would be too disturbing. When he did approach the bed finally, Father was indeed extremely excited. He wanted to know how my brother had discovered his whereabouts, heard of his illness, what he knew about Mother. Seryozha replied that he had come from Moscow, that Mother was in Yasnaya with a doctor and nurse and his younger brothers.

"Mama must not be allowed to see Father," he said when he emerged from the sickroom. "It would excite him too much."

When Seryozha had gone Father called me in.

"What a fellow Seryozha is!"

"In what way, Papa?"

"How did he find me? I am very glad to see him, he is very agreeable to me. . . . He kissed my hand. . . ."

By chance Father found out that Tanya also was in Astapovo. Dushan brought a small, soft pillow to put under his head.

"Where did this come from?" Father asked.

"Without thinking, Dushan replied, "Tatiana Lvovna brought it."

When Tanya, with the doctor's permission, went in to Father, he cross-questioned her in the same way he had Seryozha. Not wanting to lie, Tanya became confused, did not know how to answer and quickly left the room.

On November 3 Dr. Nikitin arrived. Gorbunov and Goldenweiser also came, and by Father's wish were allowed to see him. With Gorbunov he discussed at length the publication of his little books *The Path of Life*. Upon leaving, Gorbunov said: "What are you thinking of, Lev Nikolayevich? We shall still carry on the fight!"

Father looked sternly at him: "You will, but not I," he said.

That evening Father dictated a telegram to my brothers, roughly to the effect that his condition was better but his heart so weak that a meeting with Mama would be devastating.

It had not remotely occurred to him that news of his illness had circled the globe, and that his entire family was in Astapovo. An army of photographers lived in the station, trying to catch every word that came out of the house of the station master. The doctors gave out daily bulletins. The telegraph wires were constantly busy. The sleepy little town of Astapovo, buried in the province of Ryazan, was suddenly the focus of world attention.

All this passed unnoticed by those of us who, day and night, were at Father's side.

"It was a hard night," was the last entry in his diary, "I have lain in a fever for two days. Chertkov came on the 2nd. On the 3rd, Tanya. That night Seryozha arrived, this touched me very much. Now, the 3rd, Nitikin, then Goldenweiser and Ivan Ivanovich. So this is my plan. . . . *Fais ce que dois, adv* . . .

"And everything is for the good of others also, and above all of me."

Despair alternated with hope as his temperature rose and dropped. From one lung the pneumonia spread to the other. They sent for oxygen. Seryozha wired to Moscow for a comfortable bed. One of us and a doctor were always by his side.

"But the peasants, you know how they die," said Father with a sigh when his pillows were straightened.

On November 4 he was almost unconscious. Part of the time he was delirious, trying to explain something, part of the time he lay silent, his emaciated hands fingering the sheet. His stern, piercing eyes seemed withdrawn, as if fixed on the unattainable distance.

One sentence could be made out of his delirious ramblings: "Search, always keep searching."

That evening when Varya came into the room Father raised himself on his pillow, stretched out his arms, and in a loud, happy voice exclaimed: "Masha! Masha!"

Doctors arrived from Moscow: Berkenheim, Usov, the celebrated Shchurovski. But the last hope had flickered out.

On November 6 Father was especially affectionate with everyone. "Dear Dushan, dear Dushan!" he would say for any little service. While we were changing his sheets and supporting his back, I felt his hand trying to grasp mine. I thought he wanted to lean against me but instead he pressed my hand firmly once, and then again.

That day Tanya and I sat on either side of his bed. Suddenly he made a strong movement and sat upright. I leaned over him. "Shall I fix your pillows?"

"No," he said, and his voice was firm and clear. "No, I just wanted to advise you to remember that there are in the world many people besides Lev Tolstoy, and you are looking only at this one Lev."

Those were his last words to Tanya and me.

Toward evening he was much worse. They gave him oxygen, made injections of camphor. He was calm. "Seryozha!" he called. "The truth . . . I love many. . . . How are they . . ." He then drowsed off quietly, his breathing was more regular. As it seemed the immediate danger was past, everyone except those on watch went to bed. But we were all roused about midnight. He had had a relapse and was dying. They called in my mother and my brothers. . . .

I sat alone in his study in Yasnaya Polyana. It seemed as though life had come to an end. There was nothing, no one for whom to live, only emptiness, despair. . . . Old Maria Alexandrovna Schmidt slipped noiselessly into the room. "Don't cry," she said to me. "Don't cry. . . . Let's look at the *Circle of Reading* for November 7, the day of his death."

She took the book from his writing table, found the date and began to read: "Life is a dream, death—the awakening."

November 9. The funeral train reached the Zaseka station early in the morning. All the trains from Moscow were crammed. An immense crowd gathered, thousands, perhaps tens of thousands. The procession was miles long. Tolstoy's coffin was carried by his sons and by Yasnaya Polyana peasants. At the head of the procession was a placard which read: "Lev Nikolayevich, the memory of your good-ness will not die among us, the bereft peasants of Yasnaya Polyana." Through the frosty quiet of early morning rang the voices of thou-sands singing the familiar hymn "Eternal Memory."

The coffin was set up in the library—Father's first study. A seem-ingly unending line of people passed through the door from the vestibule to bow to Tolstoy for the last time, then leave via the terrace.

A grave was dug in the Zakaz, among the oaks near the ravine—the site of the green stick. It was dug by one of Father's former pupils, Mikhail Zorin.

There were mounted police in the forest, some distance away.

The coffin was slowly lowered into the grave—while the crowd, on their knees, sang "Eternal Memory."

One irate voice produced a harsh discord: "Policemen, on your knees!" The men obediently knelt down.

The grave was covered over. There were speeches. We went home. People . . . people—yet emptiness yawned.

"There are many people in the world. . . ." These words did not at the time penetrate my consciousness. One had to go on living.

1911-1913. There was the carrying out of Father's will: the pub-lication of his unpublished works, the purchase of the land from my brothers and its distribution to the peasants, the transfer of the rights to Father's works to the public domain for general use.

1914. I was leaving for the Turkish front as a nurse, and went down to Yasnaya to say good-by to Mother.

Grief had aged her. She said little, mostly she drowsed, sitting in the Voltaire armchair where Father so loved to sit. Apparently noth-ing interested her. Her head shook more than formerly, she was all bent over, she seemed wizened, her large black eyes, which used to be so brilliant and snapping, were dull, she saw very badly.

"Why are you going to the war?" she asked. "Father would not have approved."

1917. Mother, Tanya—her husband had died—Tanichka were in Yasnaya Polyana.

All around there was destruction, the landed proprietors were being burned out. Vicious rumors were spread, causing terror to the inhabitants of Yasnaya Polyana. They said the peasants from neighboring villages were coming to destroy Yasnaya Polyana. The rumors proved true. The mobs came nearer and nearer. Horses were harnessed; Mother, Tanya and her daughter were sitting on their packed trunks, ready to flee. . . .

But suddenly news came—the Yasnaya Polyana peasants had met the mutineers with spades, scythes, pitchforks, and chased them away. The Yasnaya Polyana estate was one of the few in that area to remain intact.

1918. I went to Yasnaya Polyana. There was a famine. Yet Ilya Vasilievich was noiselessly serving dinner in his white, if patched, gloves. The table was covered with a snowy white cloth, silver, but on the plates . . . there were boiled winter beets, no meat, some little, very little, pieces of black bread made of flour mixed with chaff.

1920. I had gone down to spend several days in Yasnaya Polyana with Mother, Auntie Tatiana Andreyevna, Tanya and her daughter. But on the very day I planned to leave Mother fell ill with pneumonia and I stayed to nurse her. She was gentle, bore her sufferings with extraordinary fortitude.

"Sasha dear, forgive me. I do not know what came over me. . . . I always loved him. We both, all our lives, were faithful to each other."

"Forgive me too—I am much to blame with regard to you," I said through my tears.

She developed emphysema, and was unable to breathe. She died peacefully after confession and communion. I was the one to close her eyes.

War, revolution, the death of closest relatives and friends, prison, famine . . . the loss of my own country.

My own life is on the decline, but there is no loneliness in it, because now I know that there are many people in the world besides Lev Tolstoy. . . .

INDEX

Note: ("q."=quoted)

Marx, Karl, *Das Kapital*, 237
Marxists, 289
Masaryk, Professor, 287, 484
Maslovs, 369, 384
Maude, Aylmer, 377, 400
Maupassant, 329, 418; "Françoise," 307; "Loneliness," 430
Mazzini, Pietro, 413
McGahan, 338
Mechnikov, I. I., 473
Mediator, The, 272, 273, 276, 277, 284, 292, 295, 298, 341, 343, 371, 390, 405, 429, 485, 488
Memoirs, Golovachova-Panayeva, 75 q.
Memoirs of Fet, N. Tolstoy, 95 q.
Mendelssohn, "Songs Without Words," 384
Merezhkovski, 401
Meschcherski, 492
"Message to Mischief Makers, A," 317
Meyer, Professor, 33
Military Academy, 67
Military Council, 72
Milyutin, 188
Minor, Rabbi, 250
Mironych, 389
Mohammedans, 211
Molière, 22, 191
Molokans, 243, 250, 254, 377, 378, 379, 390
Molostvova, Zinaïda, 30, 46
Mongolian, 28
Mongols, 211
Montaigne, 264
Montesquieu, *The Spirit of Laws*, 33
Morning, 404
Morozov, Vasili, 110, 111, 112, 117, 142, 202
Mortier, 82, 99
Moscow, passim; Archives, 226; Assembly of the Nobility, 78; Art Theater, 401, 403, 404, 418; Committee for Literacy, 202; Conservatory, 99, 215, 300, 350; Governor General of, 143; Historical Museum, 432; Psychology Society, 330; River, 343; School of Painting and Sculpture, 243; University 243, 287
Moscow Journal, 184 q.
Moscow News, 207, 210, 317, 318, 320, 407
Moscow-Kursk railway, 195, 414, 420, 423

Mother of God, 158
Mozart, 40, 97, 99, 358, 366, 373, 461, 480
Mueller, Max, 222
Muravian Brethren, 17
Muravyov, 97, 480, 482
Muromtsov, S. A., 444
Mussin-Puchkin, Sasha, 22
My Life, Sophia Andreyevna Tolstoy, 461

"Nach Frankreich Zogen Zwei Grenadiere," 402
Nagornov, 363
Nakashidze, 391
Nakhimov, Admiral, 60
Naples, 124
Napoleon, 86, 181, 182, 183, 333, 400
Narodny Dom, 414
Naryshkin, 182
Nation, The, 197
National Assembly, 440
Naval Academy, 149, 273
Naval College, 155
Navy, 356
Nazaryev, V. N., "Life and People of Other Days," 71 q.
Negroes, 279, 485
Nekhlyudov, 27, 338
Nekrasov, 56, 57, 58, 61, 64, 75, 76, 77, 125, 175; *The Press and the Revolution*, 73 q.
Nemirovich-Danchenko, 401, 404
Neo-Stundist movement, 332
Nest of Gentlefolk, 130
Nesterov, 458
Neva, 225
Nevski Prospect, 57, 376
New Life, A., Auerbach, 125 q.
New Testament, 96, 135, 199, 220, 230, 234
New Year's, 16, 141
New York, 485; *Tribune*, 237; *World*, 396 q.
Nice, 124
Nicholas I, 23, 68, 224, 259, 298, 424
Nicholas II, 285, 339, 356, 368, 417
Nicholas Institute for Wellborn Young Ladies, 261
Nietzscheans, 428
Nikander, Archbishop, 230
Nikisch, 428
Nikita, 505

[535]

"Pobedonostsev," 408
Pobedonostsev, K., 239, 285, 317, 354, 379, 380, 405, 412
Pokrovskoye, 56, 61, 172, 173
Polentz, *The Peasant*, 413
Polivanov, 149, 155, 158, 243, 334
Polonski, 84, 217
Poltava, 422
Popov, E. I., 305, 308, 321, 325, 331, 340, 382
Port Arthur, 438
"Post Box," 254, 256
Potapenko, 329
Potapovs, 145
Potemkin, 2
Povarskaya Street, 184
Poverty Is Not a Vice, 283
Pozdnishev, 301
Press and the Revolution, The, Nekrasov, 73 q.
Pressburg, Peace of, 181
Procession of the Cross, 439
Progress and Poverty, George, 278
"Prostov," 183
Protestant school, 122
Proudhon, Pierre Joseph, 125, 222
Provincial and County Marshals of the Nobility, 127
Prugavin, A. S., 278; *Leo Tolstoy and the Tolstoyans*, 244 q.
Psalms, 353
Public Education, Minister of, 114, 123, 202
Public Library Art Department, 375
Publications, Committee on, 297
Pushkin, A. S., 1, 22, 43, 44, 52, 59, 75, 132, 191, 204, 205, 217, 234, 235, 418; *Count Nulin*, 6; *Eugene Onegin*, 29; *Tales of Belkin*, 205

Quakers, 322, 354, 391

Rabinowitz, *see* Aleichem, Sholem
Rachinski, Manya, 359
Rachinski, S. A., 242, 405
Rachmaninov, 401
Racine, 411
Radstock, Lord, 260
Radynski, 482
Rameau, 461
Rayevski, Ivan Ivanovich, 314, 315, 317, 322
Rayevski, Petya, 321
Red Cross, 399

Redlich, 176
Renan, 222
Repin, I. E., 273, 277, 294, 300, 312, 313, 335, 375, 386, 408, 413, 470
Ressel, Fyodor Ivanovich, 12, 13, 15, 20, 21, 49
Revolution, 374
Rezunov, Paul, 470
Ris, 201
Rivoli, 181
Robbers, Schiller, 29
Robinson Crusoe, 345
Rodionov Institute, 28
Rolland, Romain, 296
Rome, 124, 326
Rossolimo, 496
Rostopchin, 184
Rostov, Natasha, 170, 171, 174, 183
Rostov, Nikolai, 170, 339
Rostovs, 149, 184
Rousseau, 29, 35, 59; *Confessions*, 32, 56; *Discours*, 35
Rousseau Society, 35
Rubinstein, Anton, 335
Rubinstein, Nikolai, 215, 216
Rudnev, 327
Rumania, 413
Rumyantsev Museum, 167, 186
Rus, 391, 442, 463
Rusanov, Gavril Andreyevich, 293, 302, 307, 318, 337
Ruskin, John, 401
Russia, 19, 44, 58, 59, 61, 66, 67, 68, 70, 71, 94, 109, 114, 119, 120, 124, 125, 126, 132, 134, 146, 168, 179, 182, 187, 198, 221, 230, 237, 239, 252, 261, 271, 273, 278, 279, 285, 296, 297, 311, 316, 317, 319, 321, 341, 354, 386, 391, 395 n., 399, 401, 406, 408, 414, 429, 433, 434, 438, 439, 440, 441, 444, 445, 448, 451, 456, 463, 464, 468, 498
Russian army, 62; culture, 75; Empire, 307; Government, 49; law, 33; literature, 75, 401; navy, 438; soldiers, 66, 69
Russian Herald, 137 q., 177, 210, 213, 216, 272
Russian News, 316, 329, 391
Russian Thought, 250
Russian Word, 273, 480, 520
Russian Worker, The, 276
Russkoye Slovo, 273
Ryazan, 314, 323, 522

Father Sergius, 305, 306, 348; "Felling of the Forest, The," 59, 64; "First Distiller, The," 276, 298; *For Every Day*, 480; "Freedom Is Stronger Than Violence," 105 q.; *Fruits of Enlightenment, The*, 306, 307, 310; "Fundamentals of Music and Rules for Its Study, The," 40; "God Sees the Truth but Waits," 199, 272, 298; "Government, the Revolutionaries and the People, The," 444; "Great Sin, The," 442; *Hadji Murat*, 371, 373, 403, 424; "Handbook for Soldiers and Officers, A," 413; "History of Yesterday, The," 43 q.; "How Hell Was Destroyed and Resurrected," 424; "How Much Land Does a Man Need?" 276; "How to Read the Gospels," 371, 373; "I Cannot Be Silent," 463, 464, 468; "In What Does My Faith Consist?" 256 q., 257, 260, 261; *Infected Family*, 175; "Insanity," 492 q.; "Karma," 342; "Kholstomer," 165; "Kingdom of God Is Within You, The," 306, 307, 321, 326 q., 329; "Korney Vasiliev," 445; *Kreutzer Sonata, The*, 300 q., 301, 302, 303, 304, 306, 310, 394; "Law of Force and the Law of Love, The," 462; "Letter from the Caucasus," 56; "Letter to a Hindu," 483; "Letter to Liberals, A," 371; *Light That Shines in the Darkness, The*, 348; "Living Corpse, The," 403, 404; "Lost One, The," 97; "Lucerne," 92 q., 97; "Master and Workman," 339, 340, 341, 342, 343; "Meeting While on Duty, A," 59; *Memoirs*, 40 q.; *Memories of Childhood*, 432; *Migrants and the Bashkirs, The*, 348; "Morning of a Landowner, The," 37 q., 39 q., 56, 78; *Murderer of His Wife, The*, 300; "Musician, The," 97; *New Primer*, 202; "Nicholas Stick," 298; *Nihilist, The*, 186; "Notes of a Billiard Marker," 56, 59, 68; "Notes of a Madman," 192 q., 275; *Notes of a Mother, The*, 348; "Notes of a Noncommissioned Officer," 64; "On Life," 288 q., 296; "On Life and Death," 288 q.; "Only Means, The," 400, 413; "Outline of a General Plan for the Institution of Public Schools," 123 q.; *Path of Life, The*, 485, 522;

"Patriotism and Government," 400; "Polikushka," 126, 165; *Power of Darkness, The*, 283, 284, 285, 297, 303, 356, 357; *Primer*, 195, 198, 201, 202, 203, 204, 467; *Primers*, 349; "Prisoner in the Caucasus, A," 54, 199, 272, 274; "Progress and a Definition of Education," 137 q.; "Raid, The," 56, 59; *Reader*, 195, 198; *Readers*, 202, 467; "Register of the Psychopathic Ward . . ., The," 255 q.; "Religion and Morality," 329; *Resurgence of Hell, The*, 348; *Resurrection*, 295, 306, 338, 348, 392, 394; *Russian Landowner, The*, 67; "School Holiday," 289 q.; "Seed, The," 298; "Serfdom of Our Times, The," 400; *Sevastopol in August, 1855*, 66 q.; *Sevastopol by Day and by Night*, 69; *Sevastopol in December, 1854*, 69 q., 70; *Sevastopol Stories*, 129, 188; *Story of Fredericks, The*, 304; *Story of My Childhood, The*, 49, 55; *Study and Translation of the Four Gospels*, 249, 261, 267; "Tale of Ivan-the-Fool, The," 276 q.; "Tale of the Young Tsar Turned Workman, The," 501; "Terrible Question, The," 318; *Themselves Outwited*, 306; "There Are No Guilty Ones in the World," 487; "There Is an End to Everything," 462; "Thou Shalt Not Kill," 400, 459; "Thoughts on the Relations of the Sexes," 303 q.; *Thoughts of the Sages*, 472; *Thoughts of Wise People*, 429, 431; "Three Deaths," 98, 99; "Three Elders," 276, 298; "Three Hermits," 276; "Three Questions," 428; "Tikhon and Melania," 165; "Tsar Asarkhadon," 428; "Two Hussars," 77, 79; "Two Old Men," 276, 277, 298; "Unawares," 492 q.; "Walk in the Light While Light Remains," 306; *War and Peace*, 2, 7 q., 149, 167, 168, 170, 173, 174, 178, 179, 181, 182, 186, 187, 188, 189, 191, 193, 195, 214, 215, 226, 227, 232, 235, 282, 333, 339, 364, 400, 473, 479; "Watch, The," 214; "What Are We to Do?" 85 q.; "What For?" 445; "What Is Art?" 290, 303, 373, 377, 386 q.; "What Is Religion . . . ?" 416; "What Then Must We Do?" 245, 246, 250, 275; "What the Ma-